INVISIBLE WOMEN, VISIBLE HISTORIES

INVISIBLE WOMEN, VISIBLE HISTORIES

Gender, Society and Polity in North India
(Seventh to Twelfth Century AD)

DEVIKA RANGACHARI

MANOHAR
2009

First published 2009

ISBN 978-81-7304-808-1

Published by
Ajay Kumar Jain *for*
Manohar Publishers & Distributors
4753/23 Ansari Road, Daryaganj
New Delhi 110 002

Printed at
Salasar Imaging Systems
Delhi 110 035

Contents

Acknowledgements

For a decade and more, Professor Nayanjot Lahiri has shown me how many aspects the word 'guide' encompasses—from supervising my work to providing encouragement, advice and support, and, most importantly, for having such abiding faith in my abilities. I am deeply grateful to her for all this and much more besides. I would also like to thank Professor B.P. Sahu for all the help and suggestions he gave me through the years of my research. The book owes everything to both of them.

My family, who has always given me unflinching support, deserves all my gratitude. I am particularly obliged to Gautam and Uttara for their cheerful presence through the years of my study and writing of this book. As for Alka, Deeksha and all my other friends who propped me up and cheered me on when I needed it the most, I'm not sure that mere words could convey the debt I owe them.

I would also like to thank the library staff of the Indian Council of Historical Research, particularly Nardevji who supplied all the books I needed so promptly and uncomplainingly, and the staff of the Sahitya Akademi library, particularly Mr. Padmanabhan for his ready assistance. I am also very grateful to Siddharth Chowdhury of Manohar for cheefully plodding through interminable lists of errors and patiently resolving all my doubts.

Last, but not the least, I am grateful to all those historians who have seen women as relevant historical figures and made them the focus of analytical research. This book is an attempt to add to their work and to reiterate that gender is a legitimate subject of historical research and investigaton.

DEVIKA RANGACHARI

Abbreviations

GV	*Gauḍavaho*
HC	*Harṣacarita*
KM	*Kuṭṭanīmatam*
KPM	*Karpūramañjarī*
NN	*Nāgānandam*
NP	*Nīlamatapurāṇa*
PD	*Priyadarśikā*
RC	*Rāmacarita*
RT	*Rājataraṅgiṇī*
RV	*Ratnāvalī*
SM	*Samayamātṛkā*
MM	*Mālatīmādhava*
UR	*Uttara-Rāmacarita*

CHAPTER I

Introduction

This book aims to examine some important aspects of the society and polity of early medieval north India between the seventh and the twelfth century AD from a gender perspective. It aims to do so through an examination of the available epigraphic and literary sources of important kingdoms located in Kashmir, Kanauj, and across Bengal and Bihar. The selection of the three case studies is impelled not just by their position as major regional polities in the early medieval context, but also because of an element of mutuality in their histories.[1]

As its underlying essence, this work accepts the contention of Uma Chakravarti and Kumkum Roy that there has been a consistent attempt to 'invisibilize' women in history, so that their contribution is met by a vast silence.[2] This invisibility varies over time and space, social and cultural practices, and even if space is conceded to women, it exists only 'within clearly defined parameters'. Thus, the depiction of women as passive beings or as playing insignificant roles, an overemphasis on the management of their sexuality and on their roles as mothers/wives, and an underestimation of their contribution as decision makers are all aspects of this 'distorted visibility'.[3] This, in turn, makes their visibility as 'problematic' as their invisibility.[4]

How, then, can a more meaningful and inclusive socio-political history be evolved? Roy observes that there are two ways of situating women *vis-à-vis* major historical processes.[5] The first—which seems to be the focus of most secondary works—envisages historical developments as autonomous and focuses on their impact on women. Thus, women are viewed as passive receptacles with their 'status' or 'position' changing to reflect the state of the world around them. The second, articulated less frequently and systematically, envisages a certain degree of agency for women *vis-à-vis* historical processes. The focus of my study is largely this aspect.

The scope of any historical context widens considerably with the inclusion of gender as an analytical category.[6] Gender largely relates to the social and cultural distinctions that being a man or woman entail in a given society at a given time.[7] To refer to gender instead of sex indicates that women's position is not dictated by nature, by biology or sex, but is a matter of social and political contrivance. It also stresses the limitations of terms like the 'status of women' that obscure the fact that the attributes and activities of women vary in relation to the diverse intersections of caste, class, age, kinship, religion, region and so on.[8]

The varying extent of women's subordination in society over time, the need for control over women to safeguard the purity of the Brahmanical structure, and the association of kingship/state in this subjugation are aspects that have a direct bearing on a gender analysis. Chakravarti, for instance, notes that caste, class, and state connections provide the structural framework within which gender relations operated.[9] Thus, gender concepts and constructs should be contextualized or viewed with reference to their particular cultural, political, social, religious, and historical contexts. The intention, however, is not merely to locate important women figures in Indian history but to acknowledge the agency of women in any context.

SOURCES

I have selected for my study only the most important texts and inscriptions amenable to a gender analysis. While the aim is to integrate the evidence of epigraphic and literary sources, the manner in which these can be used varies from region to region. Thus, while literary texts are crucial in a gendered reconstruction of early medieval Kashmir, epigraphic evidence is more useful in the case of the kingdoms located across Bengal and Bihar. In the case of Kanauj, though, there is a largely fruitful conjunction of literary and epigraphic evidence.

Our literary sources span different genres such as historical chronicles, biographies, and plays. These are generally in Sanskrit, with the exception of two Prakrit texts specified below. The inscriptions are also in Sanskrit. Additionally, a certain commonality of sources exists for the period in all three regions.

In the case of Kashmir, much of the reconstruction attempted here is based on the *Rājataraṅgiṇī*, a chronicle of the rulers of Kashmir from the earliest times to AD 1149/50, written by the brāhmaṇa poet, Kalhaṇa.[10] The *Rājataraṅgiṇī* deals with six major dynasties and 107 rulers, among whom three women—Yaśovatī (*circa* date unknown), Sugandhā (AD 904–6) and Diddā (AD 980/1–1003)—are prominent. The sequential narrative is painstakingly exacting in detail and also lucid, coherent, and relatively objective. Most importantly, Kalhaṇa makes women a crucial feature of his narrative, pointing to their power and presence in Kashmir, thereby ensuring the immense potential of his text for a gender analysis.

The *Nīlamatapurāṇa* (seventh/eighth century AD), an account of the customs and traditions of early Kashmir, is another important literary source. I also examine the *Kuṭṭanīmatam* of Dāmodaragupta (eighth century AD) and the *Samayamātṛkā* of Kṣemendra (eleventh century AD), both dealing with prostitutes in early medieval Kashmir.[11] The information yielded by these works is integrated with that of the *Rājataraṅgiṇī* to provide a cohesive and corroborative picture of the role of women in this period.

Inscriptions for this period are, however, meagre and provide very sketchy historical information. They are generally brief and not very well preserved. There are, however, a couple of inscriptions belonging to Queen Diddā's reign. In addition, a few inscriptions document the erection of temples or buildings but, for even this kind of information, it is the *Rājataraṅgiṇī* that provides a more detailed and accurate picture.

As regards Kanauj, over 111 inscriptions constitute the epigraphic sources, and these span the rule of four major dynasties. The first inscription can be dated to the time when Śaśāṅka was a feudatory (*c.* seventh century AD) and the last to the end of the reign of Govindacandra, the Gāhaḍavāla king (*c.* AD 1114–54). A range of information can be extracted out of these charters, largely donative in nature, about several women and their involvement in politics, endowments, and building activities. Interestingly, the inscriptions document details of both the royal and non-royal sections of society throughout the stipulated time span. Thus, their information can be integrated very usefully with the literary evidence.

The literary sources of this period are of varied genres. The *Harṣacarita* (seventh century AD) is an important text for the reconstruction of certain aspects of the life of Harṣavardhana of Kanauj (AD 606–48), written by his own court poet, Bāṇabhaṭṭa. I also examine Bāṇa's prose romance, *Kādambarī*, and the three plays of Harṣa—the *Priyadarśikā*, the *Ratnāvalī* and the *Nāgānandam*—the first two dealing with harem intrigues, and the third, the theme of self-sacrifice. The Prakrit chronicle, Vākpati's *Gauḍavaho*, provides information on the reign of Yaśovarman (*c.* eighth century AD), while Bhavabhūti's *Mālatīmādhava* and *Uttara-Rāmacarita* also pertain to this time. Last, there is the Prakrit play, *Karpūramañjarī*, of Rājaśekhara (tenth century AD), the court poet of the Pratihāra king, Mahendrapāla, which is another harem intrigue in the fashion of Harṣa's plays.

In the case of early medieval Bengal–Bihar, the analysis almost entirely depends on inscriptions. Over 100 inscriptions provide information on the major and minor dynasties that ruled the area in this period. Their value as sources is particularly crucial as there is no comprehensive written account of the region for this time span. The gendered information yielded by the inscriptions covers a wide range of aspects. Thus, for instance, the inscriptions of the Later Guptas (*c.* seventh–early eighth century AD) and the Khaḍgas (*c.* AD 650–700) document important donative activities of the royal women of these dynasties, while those of the Sena dynasty (*c.* AD 1050–1280) point to their public presence. On the other hand, the epigraphs of the Pāla dynasty (*c.* AD 765–1162) maintain a near total silence on the royal women, while simultaneously documenting the vibrant presence and the donation activities of non-royal women.

The literary sources of this period being meagre and inadequate for a comprehensive gendered reconstruction, the *Harṣacarita* can be used as a corroborative text for some phases of pre-Pāla history. In addition, the historical chronicle, *Rāmacarita*, by Sandhyākara Nandi (*c.* eleventh century AD), the court poet of Rāmapāla of the Pāla dynasty, can be used as a source for Rāmapāla's reign, although its difficult prose with double meanings pose a major obstacle to analysis. What is relevant, though, is that it provides information on the influence of Rāmapāla's maternal uncle, Mathaṇa, on him and his rule, which has significant implications for us. A large body of religious texts, the Upapurāṇas (*c.* eighth-thirteenth century AD), also exist but these are more amenable to orthodox religious investigation rather than a study of this kind.

At this juncture it is perhaps necessary to make a few observations on the potential of the two types of sources. The epigraphic sources document a range of political, social, religious and economic relations and realities,[12] within which women's participation in society, and their activities and arrangements, get recorded. This offers a qualitatively different perspective from the idealized images of women in religious and prescriptive texts.

Genealogical data recorded in land grants are another source that help in locating women in a specific and historical context. On the one hand, such data plot the settling of lineages in various areas, recording the system of succession of groups who had access to socio-political status and also providing information on kinship patterns, geographical settlements, and migration.[13] On the other hand, they also indicate the importance of politically crucial marriage alliances and power equations between men and women as aspects of the process of state formation. Inscriptions of the Sena dynasty of Bengal, for instance, exemplify this aspect where women involved in politically strategic alliances are accorded prominence.

As regards literary sources, although the texts were composed by a literate male elite largely associated with the court and frequently reflect the premises and practices of the elite sections of society,[14] it is possible to situate them in a wider socio-cultural context. In such situations, though, the pertinent gendered information is not necessarily gleaned in a straightforward fashion and requires an ability to read between the lines, to analyse 'the implicit structures and unarticulated tensions' of the text.[15] Bhavabhūti's *Uttara-Rāmacarita* is a case in point, a reworking of Vālmīki's text that has the epic hero, Rāma, questioning his abandonment of Sītā on the issue of her purity. This departure from the original text has important implications *vis-à-vis* contemporary social thought regarding women.[16]

On the other hand, the tension that is reflected in the literary sources of Kashmir and Kanauj, in particular, at the interface between textual stipulations and actual practice can throw light on the socially prescribed roles for women and changing social attitudes. Contradictions between the narrative and didactic sections of a text can also reflect a narrative strategy, as in the case of Kalhaṇa's *Rājataraṅgiṇī.*[17] Here the dichotomy appears to be the result of the author's desire to show the exercise of power and influence by women that directly contravene norms requiring their supervision and control. Thus, the specific intersection between narrative and normative provides pointers to women's agency.[18]

The close link between gender and literature, therefore, is vitally important, involving the ability to critically reinterpret the 'constructions of women, positive and negative' from texts composed by a male elite.[19] By understanding the role gender plays in any socio-political context, one can better appreciate the context of literary works and the presentation of women in them. This does not imply that women had a radically different perspective about their roles or status than that allocated to them in male-authored texts. However, it is the 'small deviations from the norm which may be crucial . . . the way the apparently negative is transformed into something positive and powerful'.[20]

EARLY MEDIEVAL NORTH INDIA: SOME REFLECTIONS

In enumerating the 'vast chronological expanses' that remain 'unexplored' from the perspective of women's history, Roy points to the early medieval period of Indian history as requiring investigation.[21] Writings on this period are characterized by the same sort of 'sweeping generalizations' about the position of women that mark writings on women in early India. They are usually seen as a practically undifferentiated group, with a fixed set of norms and duties. Additionally, there is an 'almost uncanny consensus' in the focus on women in terms of certain chosen themes in various publications.[22] Both these aspects, therefore, effectively obscure the need for a rigorous gender analysis.

Thus, for instance, gross inattention to gender issues is most evident in writings that profess to detail the social, political and other aspects of this period. While painstaking analysis is applied to characterizing the type of polity and society—largely in terms of feudalism or its absence—women are treated as a large, undifferentiated group whose existence is inferred rather than detailed, and who are mostly peripheral to the central debates. In this regard, a brief outline of the main debates concerning this period is a worthwhile exercise. Among other things, it serves the dual purpose of providing a framework to the period and highlighting existing gender bias.

The term 'early medieval' India refers to a period of significant changes in production relations, state structure and ideological forms. Thus, whether these changes are spoken of in terms of feudalism, the 'vertical' expansion of the state, or an increasingly 'integrated' urbanism, one is faced with a radical transformation of society at large.[23] The emergence of new social contexts that demanded different categories, and the transformation and spread of urban and courtly ideologies to the countryside are seen as some manifestations of this change.

There are, typically, two main ways of viewing this period. The first sees the post-Gupta period as a catastrophic break and relapse to a subsistence economy of agriculture.[24] The 'feudal polity' is seen as a stage which represents a structural change in the social and economic order, and the emergence of a hierarchical structure of society with different tiers of intermediaries. The *sāmanta*-feudatory system is viewed as its hallmark. There is mention of a 'fast-changing political kaleidoscope, characterized by strong centrifugal tendencies, Muslim invasions, recurrent periods of political confusion and chaos and chronic warfare' that provided the soil for the development of a feudal structure.[25]

That land was the main source of wealth and power is evident from the sources. B.N.S. Yadava, for instance, talks of economic factors determining social status, thereby cutting across the hierarchy of caste status based on birth.[26] Thus landed property emerged as the most tangible basis for social and political differentiation. The emphasis on territory is connected with the jostling of new states, and with legitimizing economic and administrative changes introduced by the system of land grants into the kingdoms.[27] In the eleventh and twelfth centuries, there is evidence of the emergence of a small section of rich traders, merchants, and usurers, progress in trade and commerce, and the growth of a money economy, as also a comparatively developed agrarian economy. Yadava points out that with the development of urban life in this phase, merchants, artisans, and craftsmen began to play a significant role in society.[28]

The second way of viewing this period is to see it as one of agrarian expansion leading to the emergence of regional agrarian structures, the horizontal spread of state societies through the process of local state formation, the 'peasantisation' of tribes, and their positioning in the caste hierarchy.[29] The transition is seen as deriving from an acceleration and expansion of early historical processes of change. Thus, land grants and religious beneficiaries are seen as instruments of state formation rather than agents of dismemberment, facilitating extension and consolidation of state power through the integration of rural economy and society.

Thus, the post-Gupta centuries are characterized by the formation and consolidation of an agrarian base in many areas, manifested in the rise of several new ruling lineages across the country.[30] The formation of these lineages can also be viewed from the perspective of the social mobility of the period that was generally upwards from an agrarian base. The constant validation of power is seen as another dimension of this period.[31] The practice of making land grants to religious beneficiaries, a method of acquiring social prestige and religious validation for newly-won political power by royal donors and ruling chiefs who lacked an illustrious ancestry, can be seen as aspects of legitimation of the state structure. Urbanization was another aspect of this social change that was geographically widely distributed in the early medieval period, urban centres of various dimensions finding mention in the records.[32]

The historiography of this period, however, is marked by an inexplicable indifference to the actual role of women. On the whole, the perspective on women is confined to the context of the household, building on assumptions of their insignificance/passivity. Their social position is usually seen in terms of their inclusion/exclusion from public processes and spaces.[33] Token information is provided on the 'position' or 'status' of women as an integral part of 'social life' and usually juxtaposed with comments on the food, amusements and pastimes of the people.

The entire course of the feudalism debate, for instance, is a classic example of making 'man' stand for humanity and subsuming women under this generalized term. And yet, it has been demonstrated, in other contexts, that historical changes affect the lives of women in often very different ways than the life of men of the same class or social group.[34]

There is sufficient evidence of women's agency and power in the sources on early medieval India, to propose an alternative perspective. Women appear as rulers, advisers, court participants, donors, builders, and in a range of other prominent roles in Kashmir, Kanauj, and Bengal–Bihar, and, significantly, this spans the royal *and* non-royal segments of society in most cases. On the one hand, this indicates the wielding of power and influence by women, in formal and informal ways, as also their access to wealth. On the other hand, it also points to a discrepancy between the image of women largely derived from Brahmanical normative works that perceive an abject dependence of women on men,[35] on the one hand, and their actual role in the socio-political milieu, on the other.

Although the subsequent section on the scope of the book will enumerate these aspects in some detail, it is pertinent to note here that these pointers to female agency are usually ignored or trivialized in accounts of the period. This supports the contention that modern texts often carry a heavier load of gender blindness than the primary sources.[36] A few illustrative examples may be cited.

Society and Culture in Northern India in the Twelfth Century by Yadava is considered a standard work on the period, aiming to study 'the main aspects of the society and culture of northern India in the twelfth century in the background of the development and change brought about by the operation of social forces' during late ancient and early medieval times.[37] It attempts to 'assess the nature and significance of the conflict of these social forces', of the tension which gripped the age, and of the interaction and interconnection of the major spheres of life—social, political, economic and religious.

Significantly, however, in such a purportedly comprehensive study, there is no room for a gender analysis or the recognition that it was, in all probability, one of the primary sources of social and political tension and conflict. Ironically, Yadava covers almost all the sources that I use. All through his book, the treatment has a predominant male focus in the standards of reference and in the delineation of historical developments, women merely being fitted into occasional gaps. Thus, for instance, the 'Position of Women' that features at the end of the chapter on 'Castes, Classes and the Family' does not take note of their role so much as 'the general attitude of society towards them'.[38]

Yadava treats each varṇa as an exclusive male category, his description of its duties and privileges clearly pertaining to the men—as in the remark that 'the *upanayana* was meant only for the three higher varṇas'.[39] References to the composition of villages have a male focus as well in that Yadava ignores the presence of women and talks only of the artisans, craftsmen and other occupational groups who lived there. Likewise, when he talks of a 'marked difference' between the 'liberal atmosphere' of urban areas and the low position of rural women *vis-à-vis* their husbands, he does not speculate on the otherwise palpable presence of non-royal women in the contemporary milieu.[40] Similarly, he does not analyse the implications of women rulers and women as political participants, preferring, instead, to stress the 'nefarious harem intrigues and fatal harem influences' that indicate a 'decadence' in political life.[41] In addition, the names of many prominent royal and non-royal women are, inexplicably, not mentioned by Yadava.[42]

Although Yadava notes the 'mass of epigraphic and literary evidence' of villages and lands given to brāhmaṇas and religious institutions, there is no mention of the considerable body of women donors—royal and non-royal—involved in this activity.[43] If, as he says, the practice of making land grants *by kings and vassals* (italics mine) coupled with the weakness of central authority and rise of local chiefs contributed to the rise of the hierarchical system of vassalage, what is the role of women donors in this change? Likewise, temple-building is repeatedly talked of as a male-centred activity indulged in by kings, merchants, *sāmantas* and so on but, apparently, not by women, despite evidence to the contrary.[44]

Finally, Yadava talks of courtesans as 'public women' who 'constituted a separate section' of society.[45] He talks of prostitution being concomitant with court culture and increasing to objectionable limits by the eleventh century. However, he fails to mention the very powerful and pivotal role of prostitutes in the dynastic politics of Kashmir. Instead, he confines them to a brief discussion in the chapter on 'Pursuit of Kāma', which is followed by a section on 'Drinking' and 'Games and Pastimes'. While his work may profess to take up the question of society in northern India, it ignores women who are an integral part of that world.

Social Life in Northern India (AD 600–1000), published in 1966, is also marked by gender blindness. Its author, B.N. Sharma, states in the Preface that Chapters II to XI 'deal with the main aspects of Indian society, viz., marriage and the position of women, caste system, education and literary activities, religions, pilgrimage, . . . dress and ornaments, food and drink. . . .'[46] Thus women are incidental to social life as well. According to Sharma, this was a 'period of transition' in many respects, but the 'position of women was perhaps neither worse nor better than before'.[47]

As will be evident in the next section of the book, this flies in the face of what we know about regions like Kashmir, where we encounter the actualization of women's power in many important social and political spheres. Oblivious of this, Sharma relegates Sugandhā and Diddā, the women rulers of Kashmir, to a chapter on 'Marriage and the Position of Women'.[48]

Savita Vishnoi's 'historico-analytical account' of women's economic rights in ancient India is an even more notable example of this trend in that she completely omits to mention the Kashmir queens in her detailing of women's political rights as rulers.[49]

Secondary sources pertaining to the kingdoms of Kashmir, Kanauj, and Bengal–Bihar are also marked by a general inattention to gender issues. For instance, there is M.A. Stein's omission of the names of Yaśovatī, Sugandhā and Diddā as formal rulers of Kanauj in the introductory preface to an otherwise excellent translation of the *Rājataraṅgiṇī*—a classic case of pushing women out of sight.[50] As regards the kingdom of Kanauj, there are numerous secondary sources that do not consider the importance of Rājyaśrī, Harṣa's sister, through whom, in fact, he acquired the throne of Kanauj.[51] In the case of Bengal–Bihar, N. Ray's *History of the Bengali People* may have a critically clear approach to most facets of the area's history but this is not applied to its gendered aspects. He claims that the inscriptions of the Pāla–Sena period show that the aim of women was to be faithful and productive and to bear comparison with the female characters of the epics.[52] As no inscription makes any claim to this effect, Ray cannot cite specific evidence on this.

It would be worthwhile, at this juncture, to point out that some studies on early medieval north India are notable exceptions. R.S. Sharma, for instance, attempts to integrate women into his analyses by linking their position with changing socio-economic trends.[53] To Sharma, the background to the social changes in early medieval India is provided by certain economic developments that had a clear impact on women. He talks of the growing importance of patriarchy as a result of increasing Brahmanical influence and property rights in the hands of men, and the non-participation of women in agriculture.

Sharma notes that land grants to brāhmaṇas in tribal or peripheral areas and the resultant amalgamation of tribal people with the Brahmanical sector had implications for the position of women.[54] He speculates on the 'strong male domination' of the 'feudal phase'.[55] Sharma feels that the age was marked by military activity that became an exclusive male preserve. Hence, there was an increasing tendency to degrade women and equate them with property.

Daud Ali's observations are also noteworthy.[56] He wonders why it is so difficult to recover unmediated female voices from medieval Indian texts even when the images and voices of the feminine appear throughout the corpus. He suggests there is a way to tease out the subjective experiences of women through these Sanskrit texts rather than concentrating on śāstric injunctions that only provide a partial picture of the feminine. Additionally,

Ali feels that it is only an understanding of texts composed around the court that can highlight the 'genealogy' of this 'female subjectivity', which became extremely important for consolidating masculine sovereignty, both within the early medieval household and beyond.

There are a handful of other insightful observations of this kind as, for instance, Shalini Shah's work on prostitution.[57] The limited number of such studies underscores, more than ever, the importance of exploring gender in early medieval north India, and there is a range of sources that enables us to do so.

SCOPE OF THE PRESENT STUDY

The attempt, in this book, is to provide a two-pronged gender analysis of the early medieval period in north India. On the one hand, there is the issue of situating women in the socio-political milieu of the period, and the problems and possibilities inherent in such an exercise. On the other hand, the insensitivity to gender issues in a majority of secondary sources on the period is highlighted, to show the manner in which the presence and agency of women has been trivialized, ignored, or 'explained away'.[58]

This book is divided into three main sections dealing with the early medieval kingdoms of Kashmir, Kanauj, and those located in Bengal–Bihar, respectively. Each section has chapters on the sources and historical background; a detailed gender analysis; and a concluding summary. The study concludes with a comprehensive summation of the evidence and analysis, the overall aim being to stop the perpetration of a gender-blind '(non) understanding of the past' and to 'engender history in as many directions as possible'.[59]

There is a palpable difference between the role and presence of women in Kashmir, Kanauj, and Bengal–Bihar. The literary sources for Kashmir, specifically Kalhaṇa's *Rājataraṅgiṇī*, show the existence of formidable female power, ranging from formal political authority to informal influence behind the throne to active participation in socio-political life, and spanning the four major dynasties of this period. Stellar examples are the rulers, Sugandhā and Diddā, the powerful queen, Sūryamatī, and a range of female donors and influential courtesans, from both the royal and non-royal sections of society.

Thus, the section on Kashmir examines the extent of female power in the kingdom and the factors that enabled women to wield authority and register their active presence. In addition, some other issues are raised and explored. For instance, are the sources for this period—primary and secondary—equally objective in recording the power and presence of women? What, if any, are the distortions in the history of the women of Kashmir? What impelled Kalhaṇa to make women a crucial feature of his text and render details of their masterful presence? We need to ask what other sources are conducive to a gender study of Kashmir and why there is a palpable presence of prostitutes in Kashmir that does not find a parallel in the other two regional entities.

As regards the kingdom of early medieval Kanauj, the public presence of women can be gleaned but only in specific phases of its history. Thus, the pivotal role of Rājyaśrī, Harṣa's sister, is palpable in Bāṇa's *Harṣacarita*, while Harṣa's plays deal with harem intrigues and forceful wives. Genealogical information also assumes great importance in Kanauj's history, as in the presence of the Pratihāra royal women in inscriptions that indicate their family connections and their participation in wrangles for the throne. Non-royal women assert their presence as donors in an intermittent fashion throughout the period. However, the power and presence of royal and non-royal women in Kanauj presents only a faint parallel to the situation in Kashmir.

We can pose questions on the relative potential of the sources for a gender study and on the role of women itself. Thus, for instance, is Rājyaśrī's role greater than is presumed in most secondary sources on the period? What was the power equation, if any, between Harṣa and Rājyaśrī? What was the actual role of royal women of the Pratihāra and Gāhaḍavāla dynasties in the socio-political milieu? When and in what cases was the role of non-royal women apparent? Is the usual reliance on epigraphic rather than literary sources justified for a particular period?

As regards the third and final case study on the early medieval kingdoms located across Bengal and Bihar, one finds a sharp contrast with Kashmir and Kanauj. The time-span largely relates to the Pāla rule of 400 years, along with that of the Senas and some minor dynasties. Royal women, curiously, are largely absent in the inscriptions of the Pāla dynasty—the main source for the period—making the task of reconstruction a difficult one. Conversely, some non-royal women of the time seem to have been active as donors and builders. Interestingly, while the presence and influence of royal women is recorded for the Sena period, their non-royal counterparts do not find mention in the sources. The female presence in the minor dynasties, meanwhile, fluctuates.

Thus, the questions inevitably pertain to the relative invisibility of women in the sources. Why are royal women largely absent from the Pāla inscriptions and is their role as insignificant as the sources seem to suggest? Why is the presence of non-royal women so vibrant in the same period? Is it possible to postulate a linear progression in the role of women in the kingdom? Why does the role of women seem to fluctuate from one dynasty to another? Are the literary sources useful in any way in a gendered reconstruction?

My study examines issues that pertain to the role and perception of women in the early medieval age as a whole. A question that derives from the entire body of sources is the relationship between prescriptive literature composed by a brāhmaṇa male elite and the actual experience of women. The basic assumption of Sanskrit religious law (*Dharmaśāstra*) is that if every individual performs his/her allotted role, universal harmony will prevail.[60] When women are shown to exercise formal or informal power and have a palpable presence in complete contravention to śāstric norms that require their submission and silence, are these deviations from the norm condoned or are they regarded as transgressions?

That such deviations have a bearing on the entire issue of patriarchy—a system of social organization that accords privileges to men and denies them to women[61]—is obvious. The Sanskritic tradition displays a preoccupation with the problematic nature of women (*strīsvabhāva*)[62] and an insistence on women's duty (*strīdharma*). Chakravarti, for instance, discusses the notion that the essential nature of women is vested in their sexuality.[63] As uncontrolled sexuality is seen as a threat, women's essential natures had to be organized or ordered by paternal power in emerging class-based societies to serve the new socio-political arrangements made by men of the dominant classes—for which women's general subordination was essential. This 'obsessive need for control over women' in the patriarchal network was backed by physical coercion, by the king, and by the ideology of *strīdharma*.

Clearly it was possible for women not to conform: they were able to contest or even subvert desired norms. Roy, for instance, observes that the preoccupation with reiterating both problem and situation implies either the intractable nature of women, or difficulties in enforcing specific constructs of womanhood in a range of historical situations.[64]

Thus, evidently, patriarchal norms were not always hegemonic in practice and the system itself had 'permeable boundaries'.[65] Women, therefore, should be seen as 'evaluative agents', not merely 'passive bearers of prescribed norms'.[66] However, instances of female assertion within patriarchy are still governed by a cultural and material context that requires investigation.[67] In the course of my discussion, I will analyse the contention that women's power is a contextual question, and that the role and status of women varied between groups, within groups, and across time spans. Women enjoyed spheres of influence and power at different times and in different ways.

By extension, there is a need to consider the differential structure of power and authority for different categories of women—royal and non-royal—in the early medieval milieu. The fact of women's 'multiple identities', therefore, questions the attempt to treat them as a single, amorphous, undifferentiated entity.[68] The complex and dynamic character of their identity precludes the possibility of regarding them along a single, unified axis.

The role of women in the political networks of the early medieval period is a crucial issue. Political bonds, including marital alliances and interests, invested women with great importance. Genealogical links recorded in the land grant charters stress the attempt among new ruling families to enhance their status through matrimonial connections and thereby establish supremacy over competing claims to power.[69] Interestingly, the attempt to extract mileage from marital bonds seems to have been emulated by non-royal sections of society in several cases as well.

Thus, women played a significant role in the creation of alliance structures that forged links between kin groups. These marriage alliances can be seen as techniques for 'legitimisation' and conflict reduction, and as pointers to the involvement of women in political bonds.[70] Elise Boulding, for instance, notes that the 'conflict specialization' role for women as a consideration in marriage alliances is particularly important. Additionally, the real significance of royal marriages lay in the large band of secondary wives, each brought to court in relation to a specific diplomatic need.[71] The social mobility in the system as seen in their diverse backgrounds and the constant fluctuation in their relational status are other notable factors.

By extension, the role of women in fostering rivalries among sibling claimants to the throne can be discerned largely through genealogical records of succession. The śāstric assumption that the rule of primogeniture is normal, desirable, and superior to other modes of succession[72] is challenged most noticeably in Kaṣhmir, where women rule and dynasties are created through associations with them. The 'lines of cleavage' that appear between rival siblings can often, in such a scenario, be reflections of harem rivalries at the court, whereby a more powerful queen could foster and accomplish the ambition of her son against the natural heir.[73]

As regards the aspect of royal and non-royal female donations, of which a considerable body of evidence exists, the diverse forms of patronage and their implications can be examined in each of my three case studies. There are records of women's gifts, indicating their role as agents, capable of possessing and alienating property.[74] The motives impelling such donations, the implied access to resources thereby, and the factors enabling non-royal women to donate in near-parallel profusion with their royal counterparts, are some of the issues that will be analysed. How did women donors involve themselves in this activity in view of their circumscribed property rights as sanctioned by religious law?[75] Could female donations have been for motives apart from the usual religious ones? Were they prompted by the desire for social recognition and political advantage, as in the 'implicit deification' of some donors and the opportunity to become implicated in the network of politico-economic transactions?[76]

At this juncture, it is important to note that *both* men and women were involved in making land grants in different parts of early medieval north India. Most scholars have seen such a practice as being crucial in regard to the process of legitimizing newly established power.[77] Practically speaking, this clearly means that women donors were obvious contributors to and participants in the resultant changes. By extension, the control of significant economic resources by women donors and the consequent social prestige could have led to their involvement in shaping political decisions and policies.[78]

Non-royal women played varied roles—ranging from political participation and influence in Kashmir, to being donors and builders in the kingdoms of Kanauj and those of Bengal–Bihar. It is possible to link their emergence and position with the rise of a rural aristocracy. Yadava talks of the development of landed property by indigenous merchants and traders due to the agrarian character of society and the emergence of land as the basis of socio-political status.[79] The wives of local chiefs, merchants and landowners could have donated as a reflection of their husbands' rising prominence, thereby providing an index of the prevailing socio-economic situation.

Although religious aspects are 'interwoven with social and political concerns',[80] the issue of religion *per se* is not the focus of this book. Religion in the early medieval period and its complex relationship with gender is a vast canvas by itself, the extent of whose effect on the socio-political scenario would constitute a separate topic for research. However, certain issues like the religious freedom enjoyed by some royal women and the implications of certain types of worship are integrated into the present study.

This study does not focus exclusively on women, but on the power equations and relations between men and women, as also the imaging of the latter in relation to the former. The perception of women's position in a society and an understanding of their lives and concerns is often seen as hinging on the issue of how much power they have *vis-à-vis* men.[81] This necessitates the rejection of the narrow definition of power as manifest exclusively in the public, political arena of men while women, confined to the domestic realm, were seemingly excluded from these kinds of larger societal concerns.[82] The attempt in this book, therefore, is of 'decentering' men and 'recentering' the women, to penetrate the obscurity pervading their history, viewing them from a sharper and more meaningful perspective.[83]

NOTES

1. For instance B.D. Chattopadhyaya, *The Making of Early Medieval India*, Delhi, Oxford University Press: 1994, pp. 18, 28, says that not only is the time span of sixth–seventh century to twelfth–thirteenth century AD crucial for the evolution of regional agrarian structures, it is very significant in the history of regional political structures. The selected regional entities are exemplars not only of their time, but also of the 'interactive' and 'interlocking' polities that characterized this period. See also B.D. Chattopadhyaya, 'Political Processes and Structure of Polity in Early Medieval India: Problems of Perspective', Presidential Address, *Indian History Congress Proceedings*, 44th Session, Burdwan, 1983, p. 39.
2. Uma Chakravarti and Kumkum Roy, 'In Search of Our Past: A Review of the Limitations and Possibilities of the Historiography of Women in Early India', *Economic and Political Weekly*, vol. 23, no. 18, 30 April 1988, p. 2. Women have been excluded both as actors and as authors from featuring in history as they should, and remain one of its most neglected subjects. Note that the article reviews and analyses writings on women and finds them to be limited in many respects. Kumkum Roy, 'Introduction', in *Women in Early Indian Societies*, ed. Kumkum Roy, Delhi, Manohar: 1999, p. 4 talks of certain spheres/institutions like the family being isolated as particularly relevant to women. Leslie C. Orr, *Donors, Devotees, and Daughters of God: Temple Women in Medieval Tamilnadu*, New York, Oxford University Press: 2000, p. 10, stresses that ideas on women's roles in Indian society are derived from religious texts, myths, symbols, and rituals rather than the behaviour or experience of individuals.
3. B.D. Chattopadhyaya points out that the dominant discourse of women in early Indian society, derived mostly from Brahmanical normative texts, has remained confined to women within the household. Gender relations in past societies within the overarching frame of patriarchy are inevitably becoming a major focus of the social history of such societies. See B.D. Chattopadhyaya, 'General Editor's Preface', in *Women in Early Indian Societies*, ed. Roy, pp. ix–x. See also Leela Dube, 'Introduction', in *Visibility and Power: Essays on Women in Society and Development*, ed. Leela Dube, Eleanor Leacock and Shirley Ardener, Delhi, Oxford University Press: 1986, p. xxiii. Also Uma Chakravarti, 'Beyond the Altekarian

Paradigm: Towards a New Understanding of Gender Relations in Early Indian History', in *Women in Early Indian Societies*, ed. Roy, pp. 72–3; Mandakranta Bose, ed., *Faces of the Feminine in Ancient, Medieval and Modern India*, Delhi, Oxford University Press: 2000, p. 4; Wendy Doniger, *Splitting the Difference: Gender and Myth in Ancient Greece and India*, Chicago, University of Chicago Press: 1999, pp. 303–4; M.K. Raj, 'Permeable Boundaries', in *Ideas, Images and Real Lives: Women in Literature and History*, ed. Alice Thorner and M.K. Raj, Mumbai, Orient Longman: 2000, pp. 1–2; Shirley Ardener, 'The Representation of Women in Academic Models', in *Visibility and Power*, ed. Dube, Leacock and Ardener, p. 6; and Doris R. Jakobsh, 'The Construction of Gender in History and Religion: The Sikh Case', in *Faces of the Feminine*, ed. Bose, pp. 271, 279.

4. Patricia Uberoi, 'Feminine Identity and National Ethos in Indian Calendar Art', in *Ideas, Images and Real Lives*, ed. Thorner and Raj, p. 342; Ardener, 'The Representation of Women', in *Visibility and Power*, ed. Dube, Leacock and Ardener, p. 3 says that visibility alone does not give women a voice. Kumkum Sangari, *Politics of the Possible: Essays on Gender, History, Narrative and Colonial English*, Delhi, Tulika: 1999, p. 369; Ursula King, ed., *Religion and Gender*, Oxford, Blackwell Publishers: 1995, p. 1; Gerda Lerner, *The Creation of Patriarchy*, New York, Oxford University Press: 1986, p. 4; Leela Dube, 'Gender Bias and Social Sciences', in *Women in Indian History: Social, Economic, Political and Cultural Perspectives*, ed. Kiran Pawar, Delhi, Vision & Venture: 1996, p. 3; Rosalind I.J. Hackett, 'Women and New Religious Movements in Africa', in *Religion and Gender*, ed. King, p. 260; and Sally J.M. Sutherland, ed., *Bridging Worlds: Studies on Women in South Asia*, Delhi, Oxford University Press: 1992, p. 6.
5. Kumkum Roy, 'Introduction', in *Women in Early Indian Societies*, p. 3.
6. Kumkum Sangari and Sudesh Vaid, 'Recasting Women: An Introduction', in *Recasting Women: Essays in Colonial History*, ed. Kumkum Sangari and Sudesh Vaid, rpt., Delhi, Kali for Women: 1993, p. 2; Chattopadhyaya, 'General Editor's Preface', in *Women in Early Indian Societies*, ed. Roy, p. ix; June O'Connor, 'The Epistemological Significance of Feminist Research in Religion', in *Religion and Gender*, ed. King, p. 57; Elise Boulding, *The Underside of History*, revd edn, Thousand Oaks, Sage Publications: 1992, vol. 1, p. 8.
7. Roberta Gilchrist, *Gender and Material Culture: The Archaeology of Religious Women*, London and New York, Routledge: 1994, p. 1 defines gender as an aspect of social structure which is socially created and historically specific, in contrast with the categories of male and female sex which are fixed and biologically determined. Chakravarti and Roy, 'In Search of Our Past', *Economic and Political Weekly*, p. 9, note that specific elements regarded as crucial to definitions of masculinity and femininity vary considerably over space and time. Also Peter N. Stearns, *Gender*

in World History, London and New York, Routledge: 2000, p. 1; Merry E. Wiesner, *Women and Gender in Early Modern Europe*, Cambridge, Cambridge University Press: 1993, p. 5; Julia Leslie and Mary McGee, ed., *Invented Identities*, Delhi, Oxford University Press: 2000, pp. 34, 44.

8. Seemanthini Niranjana, 'On Gender and Difference: Towards a Re-Articulation', *Social Scientist*, vol. 22, nos. 7–8, July–August 1994, p. 29; Carole Pateman, 'The Sexual Contract: The End of the Story?', in *The Woman Question*, ed. Mary Evans, London, Sage Publications: 1994, p. 238; Elaine Showalter, ed., *Speaking of Gender*, London, Routledge: 1994, p. 3, states that as gender is always shaped within an ideological framework, it should be seen as a part of the process of social construction.
9. Uma Chakravarti, 'Conceptualising Brahmanical Patriarchy in Early India: Gender, Caste, Class and State', *Economic and Political Weekly*, vol. XXVIII, no. 14, 3 April 1993, pp. 579, 584–9. Chakravarti notes that the purity of caste was contingent on the purity of women. Hence, the safeguarding of the caste structure was achieved through the highly restricted movement of women. The purity of women ensured the purity of the social order itself. Moreover, the control of women of ruling clans and landholding groups ensured legitimacy in terms of succession.
10. The *Rājataraṅgiṇī* is the single most important source for the period.
11. Note here that although 'sex workers' is the more appropriate term, the word 'prostitute' is being used for purposes of convenience.
12. Orr, *Donors, Devotees, and Daughters of God*, pp. vi, 28, 30.
13. Romila Thapar, 'Genealogy as a Source of Social History', *Indian Historical Review*, vol. II, no. 2, Delhi, 1976, pp. 260, 279. Also Romila Thapar, 'Society and Historical Consciousness: The Itihāsa-Purāṇa Tradition', in *Situating Indian History*, ed. S. Bhattacharya and Romila Thapar, Delhi, Oxford University Press: 1986, p. 370.
14. For instance B.D. Chattopadhyaya, *Representing the Other?: Sanskrit Sources and the Muslims (Eighth to Fourteenth Century)*, Delhi, Manohar: 1998, p. 21.
15. Julia Leslie, *The Perfect Wife*, Delhi, Oxford University Press: 1989, p. 329. Daud Ali, 'From *Nāyikā* to *Bhakta*: A Genealogy of Female Subjectivity in Early Medieval India', in *Invented Identities*, ed. Leslie and McGee, p. 160, says that one of the most intractable problems in approaching poetic or dramatic texts from a gender perspective lies in the fracture of the authorial, narrative and dramatic voices within them.
16. Romila Thapar opines that changes in the theme of a text in accordance with its location at one point can highlight that particular moment and provide pointers to its influence, in turn, on the text. A focus on different versions of the same narrative can, therefore, be viewed in terms of historical change, showing the historical interface between gender and

culture. Romila Thapar, *Śakuntalā: Texts, Readings, Histories*, Delhi, Kali for Women: 1999, pp. vii–ix, 1.

17. Jasbir Jain, 'Gender and Narrative Strategy', in *Gender and Literature*, ed. Iqbal Kaur, Delhi, B.R. Publishing Corporation: 1992, p. 48. She states that when gender is seen in relation to narrative strategy, it unveils additional meanings. Thus, 'when the experience which is being narrated moves against the current, is unconventional or unusual, is radical in its standpoint . . . strategy is resorted to'. This is fully borne out in the case of Kalhaṇa's *Rājataraṅgiṇī*. See also Leonie J. Archer, Susan Fischler and Maria Wyke, eds., *Women in Ancient Societies*, London, Macmillan: 1994, p. xvii.
18. Sangari, *Politics of the Possible*, p. 380 says prescriptive and narrative forms bear not only the histories of patriarchies but of many different social tensions. Reading these forms through each other or making them collide may be a way of locating social tension or contradiction. Kumkum Roy, 'Defining the Household: Some Aspects of Prescription and Practice in Early India', *Social Scientist*, vol. 22, nos. 1–2, January–February 1994, p. 3, notes that indications of social change are provided by prescriptive literature as prescriptions were modified, abandoned, or even tacitly reversed on occasion.
19. Sutherland, *Bridging Worlds*, p. 13. Madhusraba Dasgupta, 'Usable Women: The Tales of Ambā and Mādhabī', in *Faces of the Feminine*, ed. Bose, p. 49 talks of close studies of textual narratives providing meanings 'contrary to the surface meanings'. Ali, 'From *Nāyikā* to *Bhakta*', in *Invented Identities*, ed. Leslie and McGee, pp. 161, 178, says that female voices are not available in an unmediated form but can only be recovered though their patriarchal structuring. He adds that women's voices in early India are less audible but more autonomous than in later times, and must be seen in the context of an exclusive and rarefied courtly culture, forming an important link in the ideological complex of sovereignty than in earlier times. Iqbal Kaur, 'Introduction', in *Gender and Literature*, ed. Kaur, p. xi, talks of the close relation between gender and literature in that neither can be conceived apart from society and culture. She says that literature, therefore, offers the best view of the politics of gender.
20. Julia Leslie, 'Introduction', in *Roles and Rituals for Hindu Women*, ed. Julia Leslie, London, Pinter Publishers: 1991, p. 3; Leslie, *The Perfect Wife*, p. 328. Although the entire religious and ideological edifice of Hindu orthodoxy constructed in Sanskrit texts is almost entirely written or recorded by men, the traditional male perception of a woman's role must be seen in relation to what is found in real life. See also Chakravarti and Roy, 'In Search of Our Past', *Economic and Political Weekly*, p. 9. As women have had little to do with the composition of the texts at our

disposal, we need to be sensitive to the ways in which women's collective consciousness may be reflected/refracted in these texts.

21. Kumkum Roy, 'Introduction', in *Women in Early Indian Societies*, ed. Roy, p. 11.
22. Chattopadhyaya, 'General Editor's Preface', in *Women in Early Indian Societies*, ed. Roy, pp. ix–x, says that we can detect a rationalization of 'particularly vicious modes of women's subordination in ancient texts'.
23. Ali, 'From *Nāyikā* to *Bhakta*', in *Invented Identities*, ed. Leslie and McGee, p. 168. Vaiṣṇavism and Śaivism, which dominated the imperial court of early medieval India, were integral to this transformation, as they articulated new conceptions of power or lordship through the temple, one of the key 'integrative' links in medieval society. R.S. Sharma, *Perspectives in Social and Economic History of Early India*, Delhi, Munshiram Manoharlal: 1983, p. 236, notes that the social structure of India from the sixth century AD onwards underwent a significant change and that, in many ways, the medieval period was an age of elaboration and proliferation.
24. B.P. Sahu, 'Introduction', in *Land System and Rural Society in Early India*, ed. B.P. Sahu, Delhi, Manohar: 1997, p. 6, contests this framework. Chattopadhyaya, 'Political Processes and Structure of Polity', *Indian History Congress Proceedings*, pp. 28–31, 43, says the hierarchical social structure explains the mechanism of exploitation and coercion in the early medieval state. Chattopadhyaya, acknowledging the differential distribution of power represented by this structure, questions this view on several counts. See also Chattopadhyaya, *The Making of Early Medieval India*, p. 190. Note that *sāmanta* broadly pertains to the 'landed aristocracy' of the period. See B.N.S. Yadava, 'Problem of the Interaction Between Socio-Economic Classes in the Early Medieval Complex', *Indian Historical Review*, vol. III, no. 1, July 1976, p. 43.
25. B.N.S. Yadava, *Society and Culture in Northern India in the Twelfth Century*, Allahabad, Central Book Depot: 1973, p. 139, talks of feudal elements appearing in a developed form in the empire of the Vardhanas of Thānesar, and includes the Pālas and Gurjara–Pratihāras within this feudal bracket.
26. Yadava, *Society and Culture in Northern India*, pp. 54–5; Yadava, 'Problem of the Interaction Between Socio-Economic Classes', *Indian Historical Review*, p. 45. See also, for instance, Saroj Gulati, *Women and Society: Northern India in the 11th and 12th Centuries*, Delhi, Chanakya Publications: 1985, pp. 144–5. She notes that large-scale migration in the post-Gupta period and frequent wars led to land becoming the dominant form of wealth.
27. Thapar, 'Society and Historical Consciousness', in *Situating Indian History*, ed. Bhattacharya and Thapar, p. 379; R.S. Sharma, *Early Medieval*

Indian Society: A Study in Feudalisation, Kolkata, Orient Longman: 2001, pp. 7, 186, talks of land grants playing a crucial role in the transition from ancient to medieval society. Thus, the most significant change in the economy of the period was the large-scale transfer of land revenues and land to secular and religious elements by princes or their vassals. Sharma says that land grants and sub-infeudation led to unequal distribution of land and power, and created new social groups that did not fit into the existing fourfold varṇa system. Existing varṇas broke up into many castes and numerous new tribes/castes were formed. Sharma says that as women were bracketed with śūdras in the Brahmanical system, a change in the ritual status of the latter had to be accompanied by changes in that of the former. See pp. 191, 197, 204, 244. Also Devangana Desai, 'Art Under Feudalism in India (*c.* A.D. 500–1300)', in *The Feudal Order: State Society and Ideology in Early Medieval India*, ed. D.N. Jha, Delhi, Manohar: 2000, p. 487.

28. Yadava, *Society and Culture in Northern India*, pp. 171–2, 284, talks of the growth of trade that raised the material standard of life, leading to the emergence of a rich class of merchants and the growing prosperity of cities by the twelfth century. B.D. Chattopadhyaya, 'State and Economy in North India: 4th century–12th century', in *Recent Perspectives of Early Indian History*, ed. Romila Thapar, Bombay, Popular Prakashan: 1995, p. 325; Sharma, *Early Medieval Indian Society*, p. 194, says that artisans and merchants were given feudal titles indicating military and administrative ranks such as *rāṇaka*.
29. Sahu, 'Introduction', in *Land System and Rural Society*, ed. Sahu, p. 6. Chattopadhyaya, *The Making of Early Medieval India*, pp. 34–5, talks of the shaping of regional societies as the dominant pattern of the period—a movement from within as a result of several major historical processes in regional contexts. See also B.D. Chattopadhyaya, 'Historiography, History, and Religious Centers: Early Medieval North India, *circa* AD 700–1200', in *Gods, Guardians, and Lovers: Temple Sculptures from North India A.D. 700-1200*, ed. Vishakha N. Desai and Darielle Mason, New York, The Asia Society: 1993, p. 37.
30. Sahu, 'Introduction', in *Land System and Rural Society*, ed. Sahu, p. 20, says this led to the emergence of regional agrarian and state structures from the ninth/tenth centuries onwards, as in Orissa under the Somavaṁśīs and Later Gaṅgās, Tamil Nadu under the Pallavas and Coḷas, and Bengal under the Pālas and Senas. Chattopadhyaya, 'Political Processes and Structure of Polity', *Indian History Congress Proceedings*, p. 39; B.P. Mazumdar, 'Merchants and Landed Aristocracy in the Feudal Economy of Northern India: Eighth to Twelfth Century', in *Land System and Rural Society*, ed. Sahu, pp. 142–3, says that the medieval period saw the mobility of intellectual people on a large scale, Bengal and Bihar being possibly the most favoured area for adventurers.

31. This was a factor not only in areas where a community was passing from a pre-state to a state society but even in established state societies. This is broadly labelled the 'legitimisation' process in the early medieval context: Chattopadhyaya, 'Political Processes and Structure of Polity', *Indian History Congress Proceedings*, p. 32. Vijay Nath, '*Mahādāna*: The Dynamics of Gift-economy and the Feudal Milieu', in *The Feudal Order*, ed. Jha, p. 416, notes that *dāna* was a major means of gaining prestige and imparting ritual purity and status in widely different social and religious contexts. Although Nath says this with reference to post-Mauryan western Deccan, it can be applied to the three case studies of this book too. Nath herself applies this in the context of a state system with a prominently feudal and regional base. See pp. 411, 419.
32. B.D. Chattopadhyaya, 'Urban Centres in Early Medieval India: An Overview', in *Situating Indian History*, ed. Bhattacharya and Thapar, pp. 10, 19.
33. Chakravarti, 'Beyond the Altekarian Paradigm', in *Women in Early Indian Societies*, ed. Roy, pp. 73–4; Chakravarti and Roy, 'In Search of Our Past', *Economic and Political Weekly*, p. 3.
34. Wiesner, *Women and Gender in Early Modern Europe*, pp. 2, 4, stresses the limitations of simply trying to fit women into historical developments largely derived from the male experience; Joan Kelly, *Women, History and Theory*, Chicago, University of Chicago Press: 1984, pp. 19–50; Dube, 'Introduction', in *Visibility and Power*, ed. Dube, Leacock and Ardener, pp. xi, xxiii–xxiv.
35. For instance, Gulati, *Women and Society*, p. 112. She notes that this was the general attitude of the lawgivers between the seventh and twelfth centuries AD (the later Purāṇic and Dharmaśāstra period). Thus, women's rights were identified with those of śūdras, slaves and children. Kumkum Roy, 'Where Women are Worshipped, there the Gods Rejoice', in *Women and the Hindu Right*, ed. Tanika Sarkar and Urvashi Butalia, Delhi, Kali for Women: 1995, pp. 11, 18, says the *Manusmṛti*, along with Vedic traditions, structures the relationship between men and women in terms of inequality, but that specific elements of the relationship were emphasized to a greater or lesser degree in different contexts.
36. Leonie J. Archer, 'Notions of Community and the Exclusion of the Female', in *Women in Ancient Societies*, ed. Archer, Fischler and Wyke, p. 55; Werner F. Menski, 'Marital Expectations as Dramatized in Hindu Marriage Rituals', in *Roles and Rituals*, ed. Leslie, p. 51, talks of the 'surprisingly lax' approach that leading researchers in the field of ancient India adopt towards textual analysis.
37. Yadava, *Society and Culture in Northern India*, p. ix.
38. Ibid., p. 71. For the entire chapter, see pp. 1–111.
39. Ibid., p. 17. In this, the śūdra men share an ironic commonality with their higher varṇa counterparts, while the brāhmaṇa women are linked with

the śūdra women. See pp. 18–32 for the detailing of the sects, duties and privileges of the varṇas that has an exclusive male focus. See also p. 236.

40. Ibid., p. 71. Yadava talks of the cultural level and role of women among the ruling aristocracy appearing to have been significant, but does not speculate on the contribution of other women. While he talks of the education of aristocratic women being in vogue, he does not detail the curriculum as he does for male education. See pp. 402–3.
41. Ibid., p. 125. The chapter following the one on 'Castes, Classes and the Family' is on 'Kings and Courts'; women rulers are clearly peripheral to Yadava's discussion.
42. For instance, he talks of the prominent practice of temple dancers in the early medieval period but fails to name an important temple dancer of Bengal, Kamalā, who plays a very significant role in the *Rājataraṅgiṇī*, merely referring to her as 'a very accomplished courtesan' (p. 330).
43. Ibid., pp. 147, 149.
44. Ibid., p. 375.
45. Ibid., pp. 331, 332.
46. B.N. Sharma, *Social Life in Northern India (A.D. 600–1000)*, Delhi, Munshiram Manoharlal: 1966, p. ix.
47. Ibid., p. 337. He specifies that northern India was split into several independent warring states, facing eruptions of the Hūṇas, Gurjaras and Arabs. As a result, the caste system and marriage rules were tightened, and the doctrine of impurity extended to contact with foreigners, the king's duty being to keep the castes confined to their respective duties. However, there was an attempt to assimilate and convert foreign elements as well. Women, it would seem, were apparently not affected by these socio-religious changes—a surprising and untenable assumption in itself.
48. Ibid., pp. 10–35. There is no specific analysis of their power but only a discussion on peripheral issues like their general visibility.
49. Savita Vishnoi, *Economic Status of Women in Ancient India*, Meerut, Kusumanjali Prakashan: 1987, pp. vii, 9–11. In addition, although she provides information on the 'proprietory rights' of women from the earliest times to AD 1200, she makes several sweeping statements: for instance, given the political order and the fragmentation of power, not much attention could be paid to women's property rights (p. 119).
50. M.A. Stein, tr., *Kalhaṇa's Rājataraṅgiṇī*, 3rd rpt., Delhi, Motilal Banarsidass: 1989, 'Introduction', vol. I, Appendix II, pp. 139–44 for the genealogical tables of Ḳashmir's rulers that contains the omission.
51. The works of Shankar Goyal and R.S. Tripathi are two such examples.
52. Niharranjan Ray, *History of the Bengali People (Ancient Period)*, tr. J.W. Hood, Calcutta, Orient Longman: 1994, pp. 380–1.

53. For instance, Sharma, *Early Medieval Indian Society*, pp. 12, 41, talks of the continuous interplay between the mode of production and social, political and cultural trends, and the 'superior historical perspective' achieved by considering both. He also notes that the new system required women's alienation from iron plough agriculture, gradually elevating patriarchy over matriarchy. Note that Sharma's work is hardly ever judged by his contribution to gender issues. Lone acknowledgement of the 'somewhat exceptional' nature of Sharma's studies has been extended by Chakravarti and Roy (p. 6). They point to his systematic information on women and his analyses on crucial linkages such as the equation of women with property and śūdras, promiscuity in early literature and the economic dimensions of marriage. (The reference here is to Sharma, *Perspectives in Social and Economic History*, pp. 43, 45.) However, they note the limitations of his work in that women are relegated to the background in his analysis of material culture and social formations.
54. Sharma, *Early Medieval Indian Society*, pp. 41–2. Sharma says that in order to assimilate tribal people into the feudal Brahmanical society, the mother goddess was given an honourable place in Brahmanical texts and iconography. However, tribal women suffered in importance as a result of interaction with the Brahmanical feudal order. Sharma adds, at a later juncture, that the large-scale accession of tribal people led to the insertion of new provisions in the marriage laws of the Dharmaśāstras, incorporating matrilineal customs. Early medieval lawbooks enlarge the scope of *strīdhana* (women's property/wealth) and permit widow marriage under certain conditions. All these seem to have been the result of the incorporation of tribal people into the Brahmanical system (pp. 242–3).
55. Ibid., pp. 271–2. Sharma says this was accompanied by the imposition of disabilities on women. See also R.S. Sharma, 'The Feudal Mind', in *The Feudal Order*, ed. Jha, p. 459.
56. Ali, 'From *Nāyikā* to *Bhakta*', in *Invented Identities*, ed. Leslie and McGee, pp. 157, 160–2, 19–20.
57. She talks of prostitutes as social agents with relative autonomy within the parameters of patriarchy. See Shalini Shah, 'In the Business of *Kāma*: Prostitution in Classical Sanskrit Literature from the Seventh to the Thirteenth Centuries', *The Medieval History Journal*, vol. 5, no. 1, January–June 2002, pp. 121–56. B.D. Chattopadhyaya, *Studying Early India: Archaeology, Texts, and Historical Issues*, Delhi, Permanent Black: 2003, pp. 7, 13, talks of 'new angles' to view familiar sources, of the opening up of 'crevices of history' that reorient our ways of thinking about what was visible so far—and includes gender histories in this. See pp. 15, 24.
58. Chakravarti and Roy, 'In Search of Our Past', *Economic and Political Weekly*, p. 9, talk of the need 'to explain rather than explain away' in

view of the occasional tendency to treat women's history as a soft option. Dube, 'Introduction', in *Visibility and Power*, ed. Dube, Leacock and Ardener, p. xxiii, notes that male-centred investigations may have ignored the role of women but there is also a bias in the degree of significance accorded to them in various avenues of activity in a society.

59. Archer, 'Notions of Community', in *Women in Ancient Societies*, ed. Archer, Fischler and Wyke, p. 66; Uma Chakravarti, *Everyday Lives, Everyday Histories: Beyond the Kings and Brahmanas of 'Ancient' India*, Delhi, Tulika Books: 2006, p. xxviii.
60. Julia Leslie, 'Suttee or *Satī*: Victim or Victor?', in *Roles and Rituals*, ed. Leslie, pp. 183–4. These roles were allotted by the precepts of religious law relating to men (individual or *svadharma*) and to women (*strīdharma*). Reinforcing the proper role of women in society was, thus, the surest way to uphold the orthodox Hindu code and, by extension, the perfect world.
61. Sangari, *Politics of the Possible*, p. 371 where patriarchies are broadly defined as systems of subordinating women. Sangari argues that they function through coercion, through making a wide social consensus, and obtaining different degrees of consent from women. See also Iqbal Kaur, 'Introduction', in *Gender and Literature*, ed. Kaur, p. xi, who states that a patriarchal social set-up is based not on mutuality but on oppression. Masculinity implies strength, action, and self-assertion, whereas being feminine implies weakness, passivity, and self-negation. Also Lerner, *The Creation of Patriarchy*, p. 239; Raj, 'Permeable Boundaries', in *Ideas, Images and Real Lives*, ed. Thorner and Raj, p. 10.
62. Leslie, 'Suttee or *Satī*', in *Roles and Rituals*, ed. Leslie, p. 189.
63. Chakravarti, 'Conceptualising Brahmanical Patriarchy', *Economic and Political Weekly*, pp. 581–4. Thus, the narrative and normative literature of ancient India is full of references to the wickedness of women and their 'insatiable' lust.
64. Kumkum Roy, 'Introduction', in *Women in Early Indian Societies*, ed. Roy, p. 30. Suvira Jaiswal observes that though Kauṭilya's *Arthaśāstra* deals with practical concerns in a patriarchal and Brahmanical framework, it gives a better idea of the visibility of women in public spaces than the *Dharmaśāstra* literature. Suvira Jaiswal, 'Female Images in the Arthaśāstra of Kauṭilya', *Social Scientist*, vol. 29, nos. 3–4, March–April 2001, p. 51.
65. Raj, 'Permeable Boundaries', in *Ideas, Images and Real Lives*, ed. Thorner and Raj, pp. 15–16, says these boundaries can be enlarged or narrowed at different times by different agents. There are many instances of female assertion within patriarchy and autonomous space for them within it. Feminist historiography seeks to uncover such contestation (p. 27).
66. Sangari, *Politics of the Possible*, p. 379; Leslie, 'Introduction', in *Roles and Rituals*, ed. Leslie, p. 1.

67. Kumkum Sangari and Uma Chakravarti, 'Disparate Women: Transitory Contexts, Persistent Structures', in *From Myths to Markets: Essays on Gender*, ed. Kumkum Sangari and Uma Chakravarti, Delhi, Manohar: 1999, p. xv. They say that celebrations of women's 'space' and 'resistance' should be accompanied by questions on how the structures are subsumed in the first place and how much of a dent is made in practice.
68. Sangari, *Politics of the Possible*, p. 378.
69. Thapar, 'Society and Historical Consciousness', in *Situating Indian History*, ed. Bhattacharya and Thapar, pp. 368, 370, 379, says the reliance on genealogical links stemmed from the kaleidoscopic formation of states in the post-Gupta period. Political decentralization in the post-Gupta period, inherent in the granting of land on a large scale, encouraged competition among families aspiring to dynastic status.
70. Boulding, *The Underside of History*, I, pp. 46–8; Leela Dube, 'On the Construction of Gender—Hindu Girls in Patrilineal India', *Economic and Political Weekly*, 30 April 1988, p. 11; Chattopadhyaya, 'Political Processes and Structure of Polity', *Indian History Congress Proceedings*, p. 32.
71. Boulding, *Underside*, I, p. 193, says this is more important than distinguishing between queens and concubines, as historians are wont to do.
72. Thomas R. Trautmann, *Dravidian Kinship*, Cambridge, Cambridge University Press: 1981, p. 425.
73. Ibid., p. 451. Trautmann says that when the main line is prolific in sons, there are multiple threats to an orderly succession. Note here that mothers are expected to support and further the interests of their sons, according to the *Arthaśāstra* (1.18.13): Kumkum Roy, 'The King's Household: Structure and Space in the Śāstric Tradition', in *From Myths to Markets*, ed. Sangari and Chakravarti, pp. 25, 35.
74. K.K. Shah, 'Legal Rights of Women to Landed Wealth: A Case-Study of Candella Queens', in *Women in Indian History*, ed. Pawar, p. 76, notes that queens who donated obviously had specific personal rights over movable and immovable forms of property.
75. Prabhati Mukherjee, *Hindu Women*, revd edn, Calcutta, Orient Longman. 1994, pp. 78–9 on Kauṭilya respecting the separate economic entity of a woman, but Manu being opposed to women's claims to property. Also Vishnoi, *Economic Status of Women*, p. 102 on Medhātithi, the lawgiver, indicating that the wife, son, and slave may have property but not ownership. Hence, the wife cannot use her property without the husband's sanction. Yet there are several cases of independent female donations in this period from all three areas under consideration.
76. Kumkum Roy, 'Introduction', in *Women in Early Indian Societies*, ed. Roy, pp. 41–2, talks of the principal deity of a new shrine often being

named after the donor or her spouse. She says the extent to which this practice of implicit deification prevailed, as also its context, can be fruitfully investigated. Roy rightly questions blanket assumptions of the donors' generosity in all cases and stresses the need to explore other interpretations behind donations: the desire for fame, for instance. Other kinds of religious endowments include wells and tanks, donated to acquire religious merit but also for more mundane purposes. See also Orr, *Donors, Devotees, and Daughters of God*, p. 26.

77. State formation was invariably linked to the practice of grants to brāhmaṇas, temples, Buddhist monasteries and so on, thereby reinforcing the nexus between royal power—usually from obscure origins—and the sacred authority that legitimized it. Chattopadhyaya, 'Historiography, History, and Religious Centers', in *Gods, Guardians, and Lovers*, ed. Desai and Menon, p. 39; Roy, 'Introduction', in *Women in Early Indian Societies*, p. 42; Nath, '*Mahādāna*', in *The Feudal Order*, ed. Jha, pp. 418–19.

78. For instance, Cynthia Talbot, 'Rudrama-devī, the Female King: Gender and Political Authority in Medieval India', in *Syllables of Sky: Studies in South Indian Civilization in Honour of Velcheru Narayana Rao*, ed. David Shulman, Delhi, Oxford University Press: 1995, p. 392, specifies that these resources could have been held by royal women either in their own right or as agents for their children.

79. Yadava, *Society and Culture in Northern India*, pp. 15, 271: merchants joined the ranks of the ruling aristocracy between *c.* 800 and 1200. The often-unprofitable nature of trade and the development of the *sāmanta* system were other contributory factors. He believes that with the decline of trade and commerce, the economy tended to become increasingly agrarian during the early medieval period (p. 260). Also Desai, 'Art Under Feudalism in India', in *The Feudal Order*, ed. Jha, p. 487, says that the decline of trade and urban centres undermined the socio-economic status of the mercantile class and enhanced that of feudal chiefs like the *sāmantas*, *rāṇakas* and others.

80. Kumkum Roy, 'Investigating Gendered Religious Traditions: A Review', in *Breaking Out of Invisibility: Women in Indian History*, ed. Aparna Basu and Anup Taneja, Delhi, ICHR/Northern Book Centre: 2002, p. 13.

81. For instance, Wiesner, *Women and Gender in Early Modern Europe*, pp. 240–1. It is now acknowledged that the forms of power are manifold, ranging from formal sanctioned authority, and autonomous influence to other forms of informal influence. Talbot, too, distinguishes between power, defined as informal influence, and the socially sanctioned and legitimized authority to make decisions ('Rudrama-devī', in *Syllables of Sky*, ed. Shulman, p. 393).

82. Talbot, 'Rudrama-devī', in *Syllables of Sky*, ed. Shulman, pp. 391–3. This explanation for the widespread restrictions on women's political activity on the basis of gendered public and private domains was rejected by feminist scholars as leading to the devaluation of women. Power is not only manifest in the public and political but also in multiple forms besides the possession of formal political office. The perception of women as largely powerless has to be revised in the light of such evidence.
83. Pankaj K. Singh and Jaidev, 'Decentering a Patriarchal Myth: Bhisham Sahni's *Mādhavī*', in *From Myths to Markets*, ed. Sangari and Chakravarti, p. 13.

PART I

KASHMIR

CHAPTER II

Kashmir: A Political Framework

(Seventh–Twelfth Century AD)

This chapter provides a brief historical outline of Kashmir between the seventh and the twelfth century AD, as a precursor to a gender study of the polity and society of the time. While providing the framework, some of the sources that can be used for a gender study of Kashmir in this time span are identified. At the outset, it is necessary to note that a single text, the *Rājataraṅgiṇī*, written by the Kashmiri brāhmaṇa poet, Kalhaṇa (*c.* 1149/50), a contemporary of King Jayasiṁha (AD 1128–54/5), provides nearly all the material required for a reconstruction of various aspects of the political history of early Kashmir. The epigraphic evidence, in contrast, is inadequate and cannot be relied upon to provide a comprehensive picture.[1]

SOURCES

Epigraphic sources on early medieval Kashmir are meagre, there being practically no inscriptions either on metal or stone.[2] The few inscriptions that have come to light are mostly brief and generally only partly preserved. They provide no detailed information on the history or culture of Kashmir. Hence, there is generally an overwhelming reliance on literary sources for reconstructing Kashmir's history. However, a few inscriptions have been used in the course of this analysis to corroborate the literary data.

There are some inscriptions that cannot be ascribed to any period with certainty. A notable example is the Mārtaṇḍ stone inscription that is partially effaced. As the king's name is lost, it is difficult to identify either him or the donor.[3] Similarly, the date of the Buddhist image inscription of Śaṅkarasena and Devaśrīyā, which records the gift of the image by the former, is not very clear.[4] The identity of the couple is doubtful too. It is presumed that Śaṅkarasena, who is called the *mahāgajapati*/the chief of the elephant corps, may have been a śāhī noble from Kabul in the employ of some Kashmiri king. Another stellar example is the undated Wularhama Bath inscription that records the construction of a sacrificial altar by a lady, the wife or beloved of Ritibha, described as a king.[5] As there is no Kashmiri ruler by this name, the reference may be to a local chief/outsider.

Some inscriptions, however, provide more accurate information and can be used to supplement the information from literary sources. Thus, for instance, the Avantipur Ghaṭa inscription of the reign of 'A(va)ntivarman', inscribed on a storage vessel and purporting to belong to him, is believed to pertain to the ruler Avantivarman (855–83).[6] Similarly, inscriptions belonging to the reign of Diddā (980/1–1003), the most notable female ruler of early medieval Kashmir, are important historical sources. Thus, the Buddhist image inscription of the reign of Queen Diddā (*laukika* year 65/AD 989) records a religious gift by Rājānaka Bhīmaṭa, a Buddhist devotee, and is a vital corroborative source for her rule.[7] The inscription is incised on three sides of the pedestal of a bronze statue of the *bodhisattva* Padmapāṇi but is partly lost, as part of the pedestal is broken. It indicates the continued popularity of Buddhism in the contemporary religious milieu,[8] as also the use of masculine epithets by Diddā.

The Srinagar inscription of the reign of Diddā (*laukika* year 68/AD 992) is the second notable record of Diddā's rule.[9] It is inscribed on a stone slab and appears to be dedicatory in nature, although the donor's genealogy and the dedicatory portion are lost. The inscription mentions a certain Dharmāṇika who made a dedication in his mother's honour. It refers to Diddā by a masculine epithet and mentions various Brahmanical deities like Gaurī, Gaṇapati, Kārttikeya, and so on. Hence, taken in conjunction with the first record, it is seen to present a picture of religious coexistence at the time.[10]

One can also note the Dacchan stone inscription of the reign of '(A)nantadeva' that records the construction of a bridge/embankment by a certain Mahimgupta in the *laukika* year 12.[11]

As its date corresponds to AD 1036, it is seen as a reference to Anantavarman (1028–63). It is important evidence of the participation of commoners in works of public utility, even in remote corners of Kashmir.

Finally, as corroborative sources for Jayasiṁha's reign, one can mention the Srinagar stone slab inscription of *laukika* year 25/AD 1149 that records a consecration by a *bhaṭṭa* Govinda in 'Jayasiṁhadeva's' reign, and the fragmentary inscription of *laukika* year 21/AD 1145, which mentions the construction of a house and the installation of images inside an unnamed deity's temple by an ascetic, Gagga.[12]

The crucial importance of Kalhaṇa's *Rājataraṅgiṇī* in reconstructing the history of early Kashmir necessitates a brief survey of its salient features.[13] This historical chronicle provides a sequential narrative of the rulers of Kashmir from the earliest times until Kalhaṇa's own (*c.* 1149) and is the fullest and most authentic of the various extant accounts of the early history of Kashmir. The text is in the form of a *kāvya* (poem) of 7,826 verses divided into eight books or *taraṅgas* (waves) of differing length. Thus, details are provided of six dynasties and 107 rulers.

Books I–III deal with the largely legendary history of Kashmir, while Books IV–VI, based on older written records, gain steadily in historical veracity and lucidity. Books VII–VIII, being largely eyewitness accounts, are painstakingly exacting in detail. For my analysis, I use M.A. Stein's edition and translation of the text, since he subjects the work to a thorough scrutiny and provides useful related information.[14]

The significance of the *Rājataraṅgiṇī* spans several aspects. First, it is a unique example of the genre of Indian historical narratives and an invaluable source for Kashmir's history.[15] In terms of narrative style and authenticity, it is demonstrably superior to almost all other works of the early Indian historical tradition that deal with particular rulers. One can, for instance, contrast the *Rājataraṅgiṇī* with Bāṇabhaṭṭa's *Harṣacarita* (seventh century) and Bilhaṇa's *Vikramāṅkadevacaritam* (twelfth century) in this regard.[16]

In neither of these works is there a precise chronology or presentation of facts as in the *Rājataraṅgiṇī*.[17] Fact, legend, and mythology are interwoven into the *Harṣacarita* and the *Vikramāṅkadevacaritam* in such a way as to make them indistinguishable from the actual course of events. More significantly, Kalhaṇa's objective treatment of women and gender relations can be contrasted with the limited, prejudicial view of women articulated by Bilhaṇa and, to a lesser extent, in the *Harṣacarita*, where they are either supernatural figures or dutiful, diffident characters.[18] Thus, the role of the princess Candralekhā, in the *Vikramāṅkadevacaritam*, is merely to symbolize Vikramāditya's sovereignty by her association with him.[19] So, too, Rājyaśrī and Harṣa in the *Harṣacarita*.

The *Rājataraṅgiṇī* can also be contrasted with chronicles such as Sandhyākara Nandi's *Rāmacarita* (eleventh–twelfth century),[20] and the works of the four Kashmiri poets, Jonarāja, Śrīvara, Prājñabhaṭṭa and Śuka—who sought to continue the tradition of the *Rājataraṅgiṇī*[21]—on similar grounds of factual presentation and visibility of women.

Kalhaṇa provides so much information on the politics, society, culture, topography and religion of Kashmir that it is virtually impossible to attempt a history of this area without recourse to his text.[22] Kashmir's rulers are often shown intervening in the destinies of distant lands. At the same time, there is a recognition that 'Sanskritic and Brahmanical traditions' were derived from the 'world beyond the mountains', and that the struggle for power within the realm and with neighbouring kingdoms was constant. This is thus an instance of the complex process by which regional identities were constituted in the early medieval period.[23]

Despite Kalhaṇa's often-inaccurate chronology (particularly in Books I–III of the *Rājataraṅgiṇī* that deal with the legendary and mythical history of Kashmir, his credulous belief in the implausible and the irritating ambiguities in the later portions, the account is largely objective and historically evocative. His non-panegyric style implies that this task was an independent endeavour and not a royally commissioned one.[24]

Besides, Kalhaṇa displays admirable lucidity and coherence and, as noted by R.C. Majumdar, also anticipates the modern critical method of historical research.[25] Thus, not only does he glean his information by a systematic study of existing chronicles and other sources like inscriptions, coins, architectural remains, and literary compositions, but he also outlines the need for impartiality and objectivity as a precursor to writing about the past.[26] He also endeavours to conform to a strict notion of chronology in his work, using the *laukika* or *saptarṣi* era.[27] Interestingly, he adopts a self-imposed moderation as also a 'studied reticence' about himself in that the fact of his father, Caṇpaka, being a minister is only known through the colophon at the end of the text.[28]

Third, and most significant, the *Rājataraṅgiṇī* has immense potential for a gender analysis since it deals with a profusion of male and female rulers over a huge span of time, and shows the women to have remarkable formal and unstated status.[29] The text does not simply provide a roster of powerful women; more importantly, it conveys a sense of the struggle and tension between the sexes, and of existing potentials and constraints to their relations.[30] Kalhaṇa lends a purposeful ambiguity to the *Rāja-taraṅgiṇī* by juxtaposing statements on women's power with stereotyped comments on them, thereby stressing their presence. This narrative style of Kalhaṇa's whereby he portrays women as historically relevant rather than minimizing their agency, is noteworthy.[31]

The political outline provided in this chapter is almost wholly based on the *Rājataraṅgiṇī*. However, there are a few other texts that provide significant information on early medieval Kashmir. The *Nīlamatapurāṇa* (seventh/eighth century AD), for instance, is an important source that provides information on the legendary lore, topography, and customs of Kashmir, thereby apparently providing 'the social background' to Kalhaṇa's 'dynastic and political history.'[32]

Dāmodaragupta's *Kuṭṭanīmatakāvya* (eighth century) is another important text that deals with prostitution and its repercussions on society. This theme is developed to its full potential in Kṣemendra's *Samayamātṛkā* (eleventh century), which provides invaluable evidence of the power of prostitutes in the society of early medieval Kashmir. Somadeva's *Kathāsaritsāgara* (eleventh century) and Bilhaṇa's *Vikramāṅkadevacaritam* provide information of a corroborative nature.

EARLY HISTORY OF KASHMIR

The ancient kingdom of Kashmir was confined to the valley of the Vitastā (Jhelum) and the inner slopes of the ring of mountains that surround it, except for occasional suzerainty over neighbouring hill-states. S.C. Ray, for instance, talks of the surrounding mountain ranges of the Kashmir Valley having largely determined its political destiny, making it impregnable/inaccessible.[33] Hence, Kashmir was able to preserve its ancient culture for a long time and develop its own social and economic system.

In Sanskrit literature, the earliest references to Kashmir are to be found in Pāṇini's grammar and in Patañjali's commentary on it.[34] The *Mahābhārata* also refers to the 'Kāśmīras' and their king but merely indicates that the valley is situated in the hill regions to the north of India. Varāhamihira, in his *Bṛhatsaṁhitā* (AD 500), includes 'Kāśmīras' in the north-eastern division, while Harṣavardhana, in his *Ratnāvalī* (seventh century), refers to Kashmiri saffron as the best in colour and in scent.[35]

A very significant corroborative account is that of Yuan Chwang, the Chinese pilgrim, who visited Kashmir in 631 and stayed there for two years. He gives the geographical profile of the kingdom of 'Kia-shi-mi-lo' and talks of Buddhism's entrance into the valley. Some of the *vihāras* noticed by him have, in fact, been identified with the help of Kalhaṇa's details.[36]

The earliest indigenous Sanskrit text for the history of Kashmir is the *Nīlamatapurāṇa* that George Bühler labels 'a real mine of information regarding the sacred places of Kashmir and their legends'.[37] The text talks of the legendary origin of the country, the rites prescribed for the people by Nīlanāga, the tutelary deity of Kashmir, the principal *nāgas* or sacred springs, the places dedicated to Viṣṇu and Śiva, the sacred river confluences, and the sanctity of the river Vitastā. Written in the characteristic purāṇic style of interwoven dialogues, it is ascribed to the seventh/eighth century AD, as it refers to the Buddha as Viṣṇu's incarnation.[38] Besides, a regular tradition of historical writing also seems to have started around this period.[39]

The *Nīlamatapurāṇa* is of great significance for several reasons. First, it is the only source that provides an account of the emergence of the landscape, which Kalhaṇa borrows in his work. Viṣṇu, with the aid of Ananta and the support of all the gods and goddesses, drained the lake of Satī to destroy the demon Jalodbhava, who dwelt in it and, thereafter, consecrated this new land of Kaśmīra with various shrines.[40] Interestingly, geological observations tend to support the theory that the land of Kashmir was originally under water.

The subsequent account, in the *Nīlamatapurāṇa*, of the occupation of the land by *nāgas*, *piśācas*, and then men, could indicate language groups or ethnic communities supplanting each other. P.N.K. Bamzai, for instance, says that the *Nīlamatapurāṇa* and the *Rājataraṅgiṇī* indicate that there were tribes in the valley called *nāgas*, *piśācas*, and *yakṣas* who went to Central Asia and Tibet in the summer, returning to Kashmir in the winter.[41] These tribes harassed immigrants from the south who were brought to Kashmir by Kaśyapa.

However, eventually, at Nīla's suggestion, food and other items were given to the tribes on specific occasions to gain their goodwill. Thus the prosperity of the inhabitants apparently depended on the observance of the sixty-five rites, ceremonies, and festivals described in the text, imparted to a brāhmaṇa, Candradeva, by Nīlanāga. This has also been seen as an attempt to combat Buddhism and restore Brahmanical practices in the land.[42]

Moreover, the *Nīlamatapurāṇa* identifies the land of Kashmir and its sovereign with goddess Pārvatī (Umā), as part of Lord Krishna's justification for crowning its first woman ruler, Yaśovatī, on the throne. In addition, the text seems to allow a lot of space to women in the performance of, and participation in, rites and festivals, and even prostitutes seem to hold an important social position. The implications of this unconventional picture of women have been analysed in a subsequent chapter.

Significant light is thrown on the contemporary religious milieu. Prominence is accorded to goddesses and their worship, especially Pārvatī and her incarnations. In fact, Pārvatī is accorded a higher position than her consort, Śiva, and it is even speculated that Kashmir is named after goddess Kaśmīrā, one of her incarnations.[43] In addition, the text, though largely Vaiṣṇavite in tone, records the names of 527 principal *nāgas* worshipped in Kashmir, the popularity of this cult being confirmed by Kalhaṇa.[44] The text reveals the coexistence of the cults of Viṣṇu, Śiva, Buddha, other brahmanic and folk deities, and the *nāgas.*

Before considering the dynasties from the seventh century onwards in Kashmir, it is necessary to have some idea of the political background, the details of which are provided by the first three books of the *Rājataraṅgiṇī.* Kalhaṇa's account of the first dynasty, the Gonanda dynasty (Book I), is full of gaps created by 'lost kings', legendary suppositions, improbable chronology, and incomplete details cited from earlier historians such as Helārāja and Chavillākara.[45] He borrows the names of the first four rulers of Kashmir from the *Nīlamatapurāṇa.* These are Gonanda I, Dāmodara I, Yaśovatī (the first woman ruler of Kashmir) and Gonanda II. Their dates are not known but the *Nīlamata* talks of Gonanda II being an infant at the time of the Mahābhārata war.[46]

Interestingly, Kalhaṇa talks of the Mauryan king, Aśoka's rule in Kashmir, a fact attested by the Buddhist tradition and recorded by the Chinese pilgrims.[47] His account of the Kuṣāṇa kings, Huṣka, Juṣka and Kaniṣka, also preserves genuine historical data.[48] In fact, Kaniṣka is said to have held the third Buddhist council in Kashmir. Kalhaṇa also talks of Mihirakula, the Hūṇa ruler, whose presence is attested by epigraphic sources and local tradition.[49]

The six kings mentioned in Book II of Kalhaṇa's text apparently have no connection with the Gonanda dynasty, being of different lines of descent.[50] Kalhaṇa's indications of a period of foreign dominion over Kashmir could explain this break. There is an interesting and appreciative account of the power and saintly qualities of Vākpuṣṭā, the queen of Tuñjīna I, who saved the people from a famine. Although Kalhaṇa's account of King Saṁdhimati-Āryarāja, the sixth king, is full of legendary details, local traditions extant in his time seem to have connected Āryarāja's memory with some shrines and religious endowments.

Book III begins with the restoration of the Gonanda family to power after Āryarāja's abdication.[51] The Amṛtabhavana *vihāra* that was apparently built by Amṛtaprabhā, the queen of the first king, Meghavāhana, was known to the Chinese pilgrim, Ou-kong. Kalhaṇa also talks of the reign of the poet, Mātṛgupta, whose existence, though confirmed by Kashmiri poets like Kṣemendra who quote him, cannot be established by independent evidence.[52] Kalhaṇa's account of the reign of Pravarasena, who was apparently raised by a female potter, can, however, be historically verified to some extent. Gold and silver coins bearing Pravarasena's name, along with Kalhaṇa's accurate description of the capital, Pravarapura (modern Srinagar), built by him, confirm this king's presence and show the reliability of traditions available to the poet here.[53]

Kalhaṇa's account of the last king of this dynasty, Bālāditya, is significant in that his humble son-in-law, Durlabhavardhana, is shown to succeed him, against his wishes, as the founder of a new dynasty, thereby winning over the loyalties of his adulterous wife (and Bālāditya's daughter), Anaṅgalekhā. This is discussed in a subsequent chapter.

THE DYNASTIC FRAMEWORK

The Kārkoṭa Dynasty (Seventh Century AD*–*AD *855)*

With the Kārkoṭa dynasty, the focus of Book IV of Kalhaṇa's *Rājataraṅgiṇī*,[54] we are on surer historical ground. It is now possible to corroborate Kalhaṇa's account with other literary, epigraphic and numismatic evidence. The *Nīlamatapurāṇa*, for instance, has been generally ascribed to the Kārkoṭa period and, as has been mentioned, is important for purposes of historical reconstruction.

It is crucial to note here that the accession of the Kārkoṭa dynasty was the first of the four dynastic changes in Kashmir that could be associated with a woman. Thus, Durlabhavardhana, the founder of the Kārkoṭa dynasty, obtained the throne on account of being married to Anaṅgalekhā, daughter of the preceding king, Bālāditya. The first regular series of Kashmiri coins is said to begin with Durlabhavardhana's reign.[55]

An important corroborative source for Durlabhavardhana's reign is Yuan Chwang's account of his stay in Kashmir between 631 and 633. The *Life* records the hospitable reception accorded to the pilgrim by a king who gave him twenty clerks and five attendants.[56] This king has been identified as Durlabhavardhana on the basis of dates. Although Yuan Chwang's account of the sacred sites and traditions of Kashmir contains no reference to the political situation, it is possible to speculate that the country was prosperous and peaceful. The extent of Kashmir's political power at this time is attested by the fact that the pilgrim found all adjacent territories on the west and the south subject to Kashmir's sway.[57]

It is pertinent to mention the names of Durlabhavardhana's son and successor, Durlabhaka Pratāpāditya II, and his son, Candrāpīḍa, since Kalhaṇa associates both with women in significant ways. Durlabhaka, whose rule extends over fifty years, was involved with Narendraprabhā, the wife of a foreign merchant settled in Kashmir, and eventually married her. They had three sons, Candrāpīḍa, Tārāpīḍa and Lalitāditya, the last being militarily the most successful ruler of Kashmir. Durlabhaka was supposed to have built the town of Pratāpapura and to have struck coins with the title *śrīpratāpa*.[58]

Candrāpīḍa, Durlabhaka's successor, has been identified with 'King Tchen t'o-lo-pi-li' mentioned in the Chinese *Annals* as ruling over Kashmir in 713 and again in 720. Apart from the foundation of some minor shrines, Candrāpīḍa's association with a brāhmaṇa widow in her quest for justice is significant and will be discussed in detail subsequently. He was eventually murdered by his brother, Tārāpīḍa, who in his turn was succeeded by Durlabhaka's youngest son, Lalitāditya.

Kalhaṇa's account of Lalitāditya-Muktāpīḍa's reign is detailed and of considerable interest. He appears as a very strong ruler, asserting his power far beyond Kashmir and its adjacent territories. Though no coins of Lalitāditya have come to light, foreign notices and monumental remains provide corroborative sources to Kalhaṇa's data.

Kalhaṇa's description of Lalitāditya's warlike expeditions abroad is a curious mixture of historical and legendary details. His enterprise against Yaśovarman, the ruler of Kanauj, will be discussed in Chapter VIII. Yaśovarman apparently first made a peaceful submission but angered Lalitāditya during the treaty negotiations, and lost his throne.[59] The claim of Lalitāditya's ambassador, in the T'ang *Annals*, that a king of central India (identified with Yaśovarman) was his king's ally against the Tibetans, fits in with Kalhaṇa's account.[60]

After defeating Yaśovarman, Lalitāditya apparently commenced a march of triumphal conquest around the whole of India that, as Stein points out, is manifestly legendary, with a few historical details provided by Kalhaṇa, such as the obtaining of the minister, Caṅkuṇa, from the *tuḥkhāra* country.[61]

Kalhaṇa's detailed description of Lalitāditya's buildings and foundations stresses the extent of his resources and magnificence, and is significant because of the involvement of women. He also mentions that numerous shrines and sacred images were erected during Lalitāditya's reign. Ou-k'ong attests that the Buddhist cult was in a flourishing condition on the basis of the numerous *stūpas* and *vihāras*. This accords with Kalhaṇa's record of their construction alongside numerous Viṣṇu shrines as among Lalitāditya's pious acts. Lalitāditya's end is shrouded in mystery but seems to be linked with an expedition in the north.[62]

The next ruler of note in the Kārkoṭa dynasty is Lalitāditya's grandson, Jayāpīḍa-Vinayāditya, who, as per Kalhaṇa's account, seems to have been as much of a hero as his grandfather. Mixed-metal coins of the Kārkoṭa type bearing the name Vinayāditya attest to this king's existence.[63]

Jayāpīḍa seems to have undertaken several successful campaigns in a fashion reminiscent of Lalitāditya, which are recounted in a similarly exaggerated manner. It appears that he initially lost his throne to a usurper, Jajja, while engaged in a foreign expedition.[64] Stein suspects that Kalhaṇa's details of Jayāpīḍa's adventures, prior to regaining the throne, have been embellished by popular imagination. In addition, the accounts of Jayāpīḍa's victory over Bhīmasena, 'king of the eastern region', and Aramuḍi, the ruler of Nepal, are somewhat problematic as neither of these adversaries can be traced as historical persons.

A significant aspect of Jayāpīḍa's reign is his association with two women, Kalyāṇadevī (a princess) and Kamalā (a temple dancer), in the course of his travels in Puṇḍravardhana (Bengal). Kamalā penetrated Jayāpīḍa's disguise and indirectly enabled his restoration to power, while Kalyāṇadevī functioned as the chief chamberlain in his court. Moreover, both women established towns in their names. This will be discussed in detail in the course of this analysis.

Another notable source for Jayāpīḍa's reign is the *Kuṭṭanīmata-kāvya* (*Teachings of the Procuress*), written by Dāmodaragupta, his chief minister, and referred to by Kalhaṇa.[65] In this poem, a prostitute is instructed by a procuress on the art of feigning love for a rich man to extract his money. This 'exclusively erotic' work can be seen as a satire on the moral depravity of certain social classes.[66] Thus, although the locale is Varanasi, a somewhat fragmentary picture of contemporary Kashmiri life, especially the corruption and depravity of the higher classes, is provided. The reference to kings neglecting their duties could be a reflection of Jayāpīḍa's alleged greed and arrogance in the later stages of his reign.[67]

The reign of Jayāpīḍa's son and successor, Lalitāpīḍa, is known only from the *Rājataraṅgiṇī*, with no coins or other corroborative sources. However, his reign and that of his son, Cippaṭajayāpīḍa, are relevant in marking the continuation and elaboration of female associations in politics. Lalitāpīḍa's concubine, Jayādevī, was instrumental in the rise to power of her five brothers, who wielded total power in Cippaṭajayāpīḍa's reign and eventually murdered him in 813/14. It is important to note here that the date of Cippaṭajayāpīḍa's murder is the first one provided by Kalhaṇa in the *laukika* era and is, therefore, of great chronological and historical value.[68]

Perhaps the most significant aspect of the brothers' rise to power was that the Kārkoṭa dynasty was replaced by that of the successors of Utpala, the second of Jayādevī's brothers. Kalhaṇa shows the rivalry between the five brothers to have spanned the reigns of a series of puppet-kings, crystallizing around the efforts of Utpala's son, Sukhavarman, to singlehandedly assume royal power.[69] Although Sukhavarman was murdered at this juncture (855/6), the throne was secured for his family. His son, Avantivarman, assumed power with the help of his minister, Śūravarman, and started a new dynasty.

The Utpala Dynasty (AD 855/856–939)

The Utpala dynasty forms the focus of Book V of Kalhaṇa's *Rājataraṅgiṇī* and was the second dynastic change in Kashmir caused by association with a woman. With the accession of

Avantivarman (AD 855/6–83), Kalhaṇa's work resembles a truly historical record in the use of contemporary accounts, exact dates (by stating the *laukika* year, the month and day of the closing and commencing of reigns) and the generally straightforward rendering of facts.

Avantivarman's reign was significant in several ways. It apparently brought a period of consolidation for the country after the internal troubles of the preceding reigns, which is plainly indicated by the large number of temples and endowments made by the king and his court that Kalhaṇa records in great detail. The town of Avantipura with its imposing temples, for instance, attests to the resources of Avantivarman.[70] It is interesting to note here that an inscription on an earthen vessel, among the antiquities found at the excavation of the Avantiswāmi temple, states that it belongs to 'the great and illustrious A(va)ntivarma' (*mahā śrī a(va)ntivarma ghaṭa*), obviously a reference to Avantivarman.[71]

The powerful minister Śūravarman, to whom the king owed his throne, seemed to have vied with the latter in exemplifying his piety through great foundations like his town, Śūrapura (modern Hurpor). The anecdote that Kalhaṇa relates of Śūravarman's draconian judgement at the Bhūteśvara *tīrtha*, involving the killing of a ḍāmara, Dhanva, to please the king, is evidently based on a real incident and is of historical interest. Not only does it indicate Śūravarman's power and influence but also introduces, into the narrative, the class of ḍāmaras or feudal landholders who played an important part in the politics of subsequent times.[72]

Avantivarman's preoccupation with the kingdom's internal recovery is also seen from the fact that there is no information of his having reasserted Kashmir's power abroad. A logical extension of this period of peace are Kalhaṇa's references to poets like Ratnākara (cited earlier) and Ānandavardhana, proving the liberal patronage that they enjoyed at the court.[73]

The reign of Avantivarman's son and successor, Śaṁkaravarman (883–902), is important in several ways. Stein points out that his copper coins are common enough and that from him onwards, Kalhaṇa's list of kings is illustrated by the evidence of an unbroken series of coins.

Kalhaṇa attributes a series of foreign campaigns to Śaṁkaravarman that apparently revived 'the tradition of the conquest of the world'.[74] However, his subsequent references to the territories invaded show that the king's operations were actually restricted to the narrow limits of the regions adjoining Kashmir on the south. Kalhaṇa mentions Dārvābhisāra as Śaṁkaravarman's first conquest, but his main force seems to have been directed towards achieving a victory over Alakhāna, the ruler of Gurjara. Śaṁkaravarman is also supposed to have curbed the power of 'the superior king' Bhoja, whose identity with King Bhoja of Kanauj (862–83) has often been assumed but cannot be proved.

The details that Kalhaṇa provides of Śaṁkaravarman's efforts to raise revenues are also of great interest in showing that the elaborate system of taxation maintained in Kashmir 'until quite recently' had been already fully developed in ancient times.[75] However, his rule seems to have been characterized by excessive fiscal exactions and consequent oppression. Kalhaṇa talks with bitterness of the baneful effects of this regime that favoured only unscrupulous officials (kāyastha) and left men of learning without emoluments. Stein believes that the stress laid on this latter grievance may indicate the source from which Kalhaṇa gathered his information.

A very significant aspect of Śaṁkaravarman's reign was his marriage to Sugandhā, the daughter of King Svāmirāja of the northern region (either the Dard territory or a nearby tract). She appeared as a prominent figure in the last stages of his reign, accepted guardianship of their minor son, Gopālavarman, on Śaṁkaravarman being mortally wounded in a Uraśā campaign,[76] and ascended the throne of Kashmir at a subsequent stage, thereby becoming the second woman ruler of Kashmir. Kalhaṇa shows her career to span Gopālavarman's reign (902–4) and her own (904–6). Sugandhā emerges, in Kalhaṇa's narrative, as a determined individual not averse to participating in politics.

Sugandhā's paramour, the minister Prabhākaradeva, apparently exercised a lot of influence. Kalhaṇa records that he led a victorious expedition against the śāhī power at Udabhāṇḍa and bestowed the kingdom upon one Toramāṇa, giving him the new name of Kamaluka. (This reference is of historical value in that this

Toramāṇa–Kamaluka is clearly the same ruler as the 'Kamalu' of Alberuni's list of Hindu śāhīyas.) Prabhākara apparently killed Gopālavarman through witchcraft, at a subsequent stage, and Sugandhā's connivance in this is hinted at by Kalhaṇa.

Sugandhā assumed power shortly after at, significantly, the bidding of the subjects.[77] Interestingly, her coins bore the masculine epithet *śrī sugandhā deva*. Kalhaṇa shows her rule to be marked by conflict between two rival military bodies. She was eventually ousted in an open rebellion by the tantrins who placed Nirjitavarman's minor son, Pārtha (906–21), on the throne. Sugandhā's abortive bid to regain power in 914 resulted in her imprisonment and eventual execution, the first of any ruler in Kashmir.

An analysis of Sugandhā's rule is relevant not merely on account of her exercise of power, but also because of the efforts of certain writers to conventionalize her role, thereby contradicting the details of Kalhaṇa's narrative. Thus, while Kalhaṇa clearly indicates her desire for and exercise of power, their aim is to stress her piety and helplessness in conformity with female stereotypes, thereby minimalizing Sugandhā's role.

In 921, Pārtha was deposed by the tantrins in favour of his father, Nirjitavarman, Sugandhā's initial nominee. On Nirjitavarman's death two years later, his minor son, Cakravarman, was put on the throne (923–33, 936–7). Cakravarman's reign is significant in two ways.[78] First, his initial rule was marked by the guardianship of his mother, Bappaṭadevī, and that of his grandmother, Kṣillikā, further instances of women in positions of power. He was eventually ousted by the tantrins who acted as king-makers for a succession of rulers in return for bribes. Kalhaṇa does not provide information on the fate of Cakravarman's mother and grandmother at this juncture. However, Cakravarman eventually regained power with the help of the powerful ḍāmara, Saṁgrāma, who defeats the tantrins in 936.

Second, Cakravarman's later phase of power was marked by his association with ḍomba women and the consequent rise of this 'lowly' caste to prominence. Kalhaṇa recounts Cakravarman's excesses in this regard with great distaste. The king's behaviour apparently prompted a ḍāmara conspiracy, resulting in his murder in 937 and the ineffectual rule of Unmattāvanti (937–9) and Śūravarman II (939), the last two rulers of the Utpala dynasty.[79]

The Dynasty of Yaśaskara and His Descendants (AD 939 to 1003)

The dynasty of Yaśaskara and his descendants forms the focus of Book VI of the *Rājataraṅgiṇī*.[80] It is important to note here that this dynastic change is also caused by association with a woman in that the founder, Yaśaskara (AD 939–48), was the son of Prabhākara, Sugandhā's lover, and probably owed his prominence to this connection.

Kalhaṇa provides a very favourable account of Yaśaskara's administration and judicial wisdom. He was also supposed to have built a *maṭha* for students of the country and made various other endowments. Yaśaskara was succeeded by his son, Saṁgrāmadeva (948–9), who, however, was killed by the powerful minister, Parvagupta (949–50). Parvagupta's sudden death by dropsy resulted in the rule of his son, Kṣemagupta (950–8).

The one enormously significant aspect of Kṣemagupta's reign was his marriage to Diddā, the daughter of Siṁharāja, the ruler of Lohara, a territory comprising the mountain districts immediately adjoining Kashmir on the south-west.[81] Diddā's exercise of power spanned the reign of Kṣemagupta and that of his son and grandsons, until she herself ascended the throne in AD 980 or 981. She was also instrumental in bringing Kashmir under the rule of the Lohara family, which continued until Kalhaṇa's time and later.

Diddā's influence on Kṣemagupta is amply proved by his coins where the *di* prefixed to his name was intended as an abbreviation of hers, a completely unusual procedure.[82] Kalhaṇa, too, reveals the king's nickname to be *diddākṣema* as added proof of their relations.[83] Kṣemagupta died in 958 of a fever contracted during a jackal-hunt and was succeeded by his son, Abhimanyu II (958–72).

Diddā exercised total power during Abhimanyu's reign as his guardian, displaying political sagacity and fortitude.[84] She was able to withstand the troubles of the early years of her regency by bribing some opponents and killing the rest. Her growth in confidence, as a result, enabled her to dismiss the help of male councillors like Naravāhana and pursue power on her own.

Abhimanyu's death in 972 apparently prompted Diddā to divert her energies to building activities. Kalhaṇa dates from this period the foundation of various temples and buildings intended to perpetuate her memory and that of her family. One of these structures, the Diddāmaṭha, has given its name to the Didmar quarter of modern Srinagar.

Subsequently, Diddā raised her grandsons to the throne, but disposed them off in quick succession. Nandigupta (972–3) and Tribhuvana (973–5) were apparently destroyed by witchcraft, and Bhīmagupta (975–80/1) was tortured to death. Diddā assumed formal power in 980/1 and remained in peaceful possession of the throne for twenty-three years. The two available inscriptions of her reign in the Sri Pratap Museum, Srinagar (cited earlier), refer to her by the masculine epithets of *rājan* and *deva* rather than *rājñī* and *devī*, an interesting reversion in terms of gender.

Kalhaṇa also talks of Diddā's affair with Tuṅga, a khaśa letter-carrier whom she raised to the rank of prime minister.[85] Her diplomacy is, once again, in evidence in preventing discontented factions from ousting Tuṅga. However, Kalhaṇa also stresses Tuṅga's valour in a successful expedition against Pṛthvīpāla of Rājapurī (modern Rajauri), whereby the latter was compelled to pay tribute.

Diddā's shrewdness was evident yet again in her selection of her nephew, Saṁgrāmarāja—the son of her brother Udayarāja, the ruler of Lohara—as her successor, on the basis of a test assigned to her various nephews. She took the extremely wise and far-sighted step of making Saṁgrāmarāja and Tuṅga vow not to harm each other. As a result, the rule of Kashmir passed to the house of Lohara on her death in 1003 in a peaceful and undisputed manner.

Diddā's rule is extremely significant not just because she was the third woman ruler of Kashmir, but also because of her forceful pursuit of power and her palpable diplomatic talents. Moreover, as with Sugandhā, the attempt of various writers to conventionalize Diddā's personality or, alternatively, to concentrate on the ruthless or sensual aspects of her nature contrasts forcibly with Kalhaṇa's appreciation of her and would bear analysis.

The Lohara Dynasty (AD 1003–1171)

The Lohara dynasty forms the focus of Books VII and VIII of the *Rājataraṅgiṇī* and was the third dynastic change in Kashmir caused by association with a woman. These books constitute the most detailed and involved parts of the chronicle, being a largely eyewitness account. For purposes of convenience, therefore, the account of this dynasty has been divided into two sub-sections, dealing with Books VII and VIII, respectively.

One should note, at the outset, that there are no women rulers in this section but, instead, several prominent women who act as powers behind the throne. Women appear as powerful wives and concubines who influence the polity in various ways. Moreover, instances of marriage alliances to secure power and the role of non-royal women, especially of ḍāmara families, are more palpable here.

THE FIRST LOHARA DYNASTY (AD 1003–1101)

This sub-section deals with the narrative of Book VII of the *Rājataraṅgiṇī*. The period covered by Saṁgrāmarāja's reign (1003–28) witnessed an upheaval: the conquest of Mahmud of Ghazni. This invasion across the Indus Valley and Punjab plains stopped short of Kashmir's mountain barrier, but Saṁgrāmarāja apparently dispatched an expedition under Tuṅga to assist śāhi Trilocanapāla, the last independent prince of the Hindu śāhīya dynasty, against 'Hammīra', king of the 'Turuṣkas'.

This has been recognized as Kalhaṇa's reference to Mahmud, the designation 'Hammīra' being an adaptation of the title *Amir-ul-Mu'minin* of the Ghaznavid Sultans. Kalhaṇa also notes Trilocanapāla's valiant but unsuccessful efforts to save his kingdom. The description of Tuṅga's overbearing assurance during the campaign is indicative of his growing predominance and influence in the largely ineffectual court of Saṁgrāmarāja.

When one considers the narrow territorial limits to which his narrative is confined, Kalhaṇa's record of these events is appreciable. However, as Stein points out, Kalhaṇa makes no reference to a subsequent expedition of Mahmud that brought him to the very gate of Kashmir, to the fort of 'Loh-kot' or Lohara, which barred the way into the valley.[86] The siege of this stronghold (to which dates of 1015 and 1021 have been provided by Muslim historians) had to be abandoned due to excessive snow and other reasons. Kalhaṇa's silence on this most serious threat to Kashmir is surprising and, more so, in view of the fact that Lohara otherwise plays an important part in his record.

Kalhaṇa, thereafter, records Tuṅga's murder at the hands of his enemies and Saṁgrāmarāja's death, thereby bringing the latter's son, Harirāja, to the throne (1028). Interestingly, Śrīlekhā, Saṁgrāmarāja's wife, made an attempt to secure the throne after allegedly killing Harirāja by witchcraft. Her design was frustrated by the installation of her other son, Ananta, on the throne by the royal bodyguards. Interestingly, there is some epigraphic corroboration for Ananta's reign (1028–63) in that the Dacchan stone inscription of one '(A)nantadeva's' reign is held to be a reference to Ananta on the basis of its date—AD 1036, which fits in with Kalhaṇa's information.[87]

The works of the prolific poet, Kṣemendra, that can be dated between 1037 and 1066, fall within Ananta's reign and include narratives, satiric sketches, and treatises on rhetoric and prosody.[88] Kṣemendra attacks prostitution in almost all his writing and does not talk of the positive aspects of society at all.[89] His pornographic *Samayamātṛkā* describes the arts and trickeries of the harlot, Kaṅkālī,[90] in imitation of the *Kuṭṭanīmata*. It also furnishes topographical details as Kaṅkālī travels extensively through Kashmir. Kṣemendra's *Deśopadeśa* deals with the daily life of 'depraved' sections of society like cheats, misers and prostitutes, his *Kalāvilāsa* talks of rapacious kāyasthas, and his *Narmamālā* is a satire on the misrule of officials before Ananta's time and, therefore, highly reminiscent of portions of the *Rājataraṅgiṇī*.[91]

The *Rājataraṅgiṇī* records that Ananta was able to quell a dangerous rising of the ḍāmaras under their chief, Tribhuvana.[92] Subsequently, he succeeded in repelling an invasion of the Dard ruler, Acalamaṅgala, and certain *mleccha* chiefs allied with him, with the help of Rudrapāla śāhī. This victory is referred to by the poet

Bilhaṇa, Ananta's contemporary, in his *Vikramāṅkadevacaritam*. He calls the *mlecchas*, who were probably Muslim tribesmen from the Indus region, Śakas.

Subsequently, Ananta apparently tried to assert Kashmir's authority in the neighbouring hill tracts. Although Kalhaṇa states that his expeditions against the hill-states of Uraśā and Vallāpura ended in failure, Bilhaṇa's *Vikramāṅkadevacaritam* talks of Ananta's supremacy being acknowledged in Dārvābhisāra and adjacent territories.

Perhaps the most significant aspect of Ananta's reign was the power and influence exerted by his wife, Sūryamatī or Subhaṭā, the daughter of Inducandra, 'lord of Jālaṁdhara'.[93] The reversion of traditional gender equations in their relationship, and Kalhaṇa's apparent approval of the same, provides ample scope for analysis. Thus, Sūryamatī rescued Ananta and the throne from a severe financial crisis by taking complete charge of royal affairs. In addition, her bestowal of the prime ministerial rank on an able individual, Haladhara, paid rich dividends in the form of a strong administration and prosperous conditions in Kashmir.

Not only did Sūryamatī obtain Ananta's compliance to her general will, but his abdication in favour of their son, Kalaśa, in 1063, an act that had momentous repercussions. Kalaśa (1063–89) was worthless and dissolute, causing his parents to regret their decision and prompting Ananta to resume charge of regal functions. At the same time, Ananta's cousin, Kṣitirāja of Lohara, bestowed his throne upon Utkarṣa, Kalaśa's second son, because of his enmity with his own son. This arrangement was destined to lead, on Utkarṣa's eventual succession in Kashmir, to the political union of the two territories.

Sūryamatī continued to dictate the relations between Ananta and Kalaśa in that after a subsequent rupture with Kalaśa in 1076, she induced Ananta to retire to Vijayeśvara (modern Vijbror) with the royal treasure, nobles, and troops, instead of imprisoning Kalaśa, his original intention. Thereafter, she prevented the outbreak of open hostilities between father and son but kept Ananta from forcibly deposing Kalaśa. On Kalaśa's subsequent burning of Vijayeśvara, Ananta committed suicide after an altercation with Sūryamatī (1081) who, in turn, burnt herself on his funeral pyre.

Interestingly, Somadeva's *Kathāsaritsāgara* (*The Ocean of Streams of Stories*), another abstraction of Guṇādhya's *Bṛhatkathā*, was supposed to have been composed between 1063 and 1089 while Kalaśa was on the throne, for the amusement and diversion of Sūryamatī from her various problems.[94] Its main theme, like that of the *Bṛhatkathāmañjarī*, is the story of Naravāhanadatta, the son of Udayana of Kauśāmbī, which forms a framework for more than 350 stories, most of which portray women in a derogatory light.[95] This voluminous text comprises eighteen books of 124 chapters and over 21,000 verses. Somadeva seems to have been inspired by an old Kashmiri version of the *Bṛhatkathā*,[96] but the numerous locales and characters in the *Kathāsaritsāgara* make the task of sifting the information a difficult one. However, he describes the location of Kashmir and its holy sites like Vijayakṣetra, Nandikṣetra and so on.

Bilhaṇa's *Vikramāṅkadevacaritam* praises Sūryamatī at some length, and refers to the king's submission to her and the co-wives' worry on this account. This is extremely significant in view of the fact that Bilhaṇa's other references to Kashmir—the beauty of his home-town, Khonamuṣa (near Pravarapura), the learned women, their excellence in dramatics and so on—are often quoted but *never* his account of Sūryamatī, thereby pointing to a bias on the part of those who use this work.[97]

Kalhaṇa indicates a change in Kalaśa's attitude on his parents' death, evident in his reconciliation with his eldest son, Harṣa, whom Ananta and Sūryamatī had desired to place on the throne. He apparently tried to relieve financial conditions by careful administration and even sent an expedition in support of Saṁgrāmapāla of Rājapurī, enabling the reassertion of Kashmir's suzerainty over that area. Kalaśa's influence was gradually felt among the surrounding hill-states. The success of his foreign policy was proved in 1087/8 when the rulers of eight hill territories around Kashmir assembled at his capital. Among them was Āsaṭa, the chief of Cambā, whose name is found in epigraphic records and the genealogical list of the Cambā *rājās*.

Kalhaṇa, however, indicates a resumption of Kalaśa's wild ways on his subsequent split with Harṣa. Prior to his death in 1089, Kalaśa imprisoned Harṣa and installed his younger son, Utkarṣa, as ruler of Kashmir. Utkarṣa, however, ruled only for twenty-two days before the resourceful Harṣa, with his younger half-brother Vijayamalla's support, managed to evade death in prison and seize the throne, prompting Utkarṣa to kill himself.[98]

Kalhaṇa's account of Harṣa's reign (1089–1101) is significant in that it is based on first-hand information provided by Caṇpaka, Kalhaṇa's father and a minister in Harṣa's court. Kalhaṇa stresses his strongly contrasting qualities of bravery and perversity. What emerges is the picture of a striking and forceful personality of, however, a somewhat unsound mind.

The *Rājataraṅgiṇī* provides a glowing account of the splendour of the Kashmir court in the early part of Harṣa's reign. Although the description of courtly magnificence is somewhat conventional, there are indications—like the issue of gold and silver coins—that Kashmir did enjoy a period of affluence and prosperity at the time. Besides, Harṣa's munificence towards poets and scholars is said to have made even Bilhaṇa regret that he had left Kashmir during Kalaśa's reign.

Interestingly, Kalhaṇa talks of Harṣa's introduction of elaborate fashions in dress and ornaments into the court, of possibly Muslim influence. He also refers to the *dekhan* fashions that Harṣa copied in his amusements and in his coinage. This is corroborated, to some extent, by some extant gold coins of Harṣa that imitated the contemporary coinage of *karṇāṭa* in type.

Harṣa seems to have asserted his authority outside Kashmir by sending a successful expedition against Saṁgrāmapāla of Rājapurī, compelling the latter to pay tribute. However, extravagant expenditure on troops and senseless indulgence in costly pleasures soon involved Harṣa in financial troubles. He apparently engaged in the ruthless plunder of sacred shrines to extricate himself from this crisis. Kalhaṇa talks in a humorous vein of the incidental discovery of the treasures hoarded at the temple of Diddā's grandfather, King Bhīma Śāhī, which showed Harṣa a way of replenishing his finances.

After exhausting the temple treasuries, Harṣa apparently used the valuable metal of confiscated divine images. Kalhaṇa's specification of the few metal statues of gods in Kashmir that escaped this fate indicates the extent and thoroughness of Harṣa's iconoclasm.[99] In fact, Kalhaṇa gives Harṣa the epithet 'Turuṣka' or Muslim and even refers to 'Turuṣka' captains being employed in his army and enjoying his favour. Kalhaṇa provides exhaustive details of Harṣa's misgovernment and other excesses. These include the imposition of oppressive taxes, the failure of two successive campaigns, the relentless and cruel persecution of the ḍāmaras, the favouring of parasites at court and, significantly, acts of rape and incest committed by him on his sisters and Kalaśa's widows. Harṣa's fiscal exactions continued even during a plague, flood and famine in 1099.

Significantly, this was also the stage when Uccala—the fourth direct descendant of Kāntirāja, Diddā's brother—and his brother, Sussala, appeared as potential claimants to the throne.[100] A courtesan saved them from death at Harṣa's hands and enabled them to escape. Uccala's subsequent abortive attack on the capital with the help of rebel ḍāmaras was followed by Sussala's diversionary incursion, enabling the former to regroup his forces and launch a second decisive offensive. Harṣa, plagued by desertions and treason, made the blunder of killing Malla, the father of the claimant brothers, thereby invoking the latters' wrath and resulting in his complete defeat.

The account of Harṣa's flight from the capital, accompanied by a cook of Caṇpaka's household and an attendant,[101] and his eventual death at the hands of Uccala's soldiers is of significance in that Kalhaṇa must have derived it from the only surviving witness, the cook. One should note here that Kalhaṇa stresses his father, Caṇpaka's loyalty to Harṣa and takes special care to explain his absence from the king's side at this juncture.[102]

THE SECOND LOHARA DYNASTY (AD 1101–1171)

I now deal with Book VIII of the *Rājataraṅgiṇī*, which comprises 3,449 verses or nearly one-half of the entire text. The advantages of this lengthy treatment, as Stein points out, lies in the authenticity and ample detail of the picture that Kalhaṇa provides of contemporary Kashmir in its political and social aspects.[103]

Kalhaṇa portrays Uccala's reign (1101–11) as beset with problems posed by rebellious ḍāmaras, to whose support he owed his throne, and his ambitious brother, Sussala, who sought the throne. Uccala tackled the first danger by fomenting discord amongst the ḍāmaras, and the second by ceding Lohara to Sussala as an independent chiefship. Kalhaṇa also describes, with humour and relish, Uccala's systematic persecution of kāyasthas (officials). This might have been done to secure the attachment of the lower classes, as a safeguard against feudal turbulence.

A significant aspect of Uccala's reign was the role played by his queen, Jayamatī, originally a concubine of low origin. She apparently saved the life of Bhikṣācara, the grandson of King Harṣa and a future claimant to the throne, from the vengeful Uccala. By secretly sending him to the court of Naravarman of Mālava, she enabled Bhikṣācara to claim the throne at a later stage. Naravarman, one of the later Paramāra princes, is shown by epigraphic record to have ruled Mālava in about 1105.[104] Kalhaṇa places Bhikṣācara's escape at about the same time, as also the birth of Sussala's son, Jayasiṁha.

Jayasiṁha's birth is shown to effect a reconciliation between Uccala and Sussala. However, a conspiracy engendered by the city-prefect, Chuḍḍa, and his brothers led to Uccala's murder in 1111 and the installation of Chuḍḍa's brother, Raḍḍa-Śaṅkharāja, on the throne for a few hours. Raḍḍa's claim to rule was based, significantly, on his alleged descent from Kāmadeva, the grandfather of King Yaśaskara, thereby again recalling Sugandhā's indirect hand in Yaśaskara's rise to power. However, Raḍḍa was overthrown by Gargacandra, a leading ḍāmara of the Lahara district who had gained power under Uccala.

Kalhaṇa talks, thereafter, of the brief rule of Salhaṇa (1111–12), Uccala's half-brother, who was placed on the throne by Gargacandra.[105] Though an indolent and helpless figure, Salhaṇa's rule is notable for showing the existence of rival claimants to the throne in the same family, owing to the different spouses/concubines of kings.

Sussala eventually occupied the throne (1112–20) after ousting Salhaṇa with Gargacandra's support.[106] Interestingly, this mutual support was underlined by Sussala's acceptance of Garga's two daughters as brides for himself and his son, Jayasiṁha. This double matrimonial alliance did not, however, deter Garga from rebellion, or Sussala from destroying him at a later stage. At this juncture, it is important to note the stellar role played by Garga's wife, Chuḍḍā, in anticipating Sussala's moves and endeavouring to circumvent them. This has been discussed in a subsequent chapter.

Kalhaṇa shows Sussala's reign to be marked by crippling rebellions of powerful ḍāmaras that the king was unable to quell, and by the emergence of Bhikṣācara as a dangerous claimant to power. However, Sussala was able to crush Garga by raising a rival ḍāmara, Mallakoṣṭha and, subsequently, destroyed Garga's entire family, including his own brothers-in-law, in 1118. After this, Sussala renewed his alliance with the chiefs of the neighbouring hill tracts.

Sussala seems also to have increased his resources by a more exacting revenue administration. For this purpose, the kāyastha Gauraka was made the prime minister, thereby allowing a free hand to the officials whose oppression benefited the treasury but also fostered discontent. This was aggravated by a failed expedition to Rājapurī, the life of whose ruler, Somapāla, is, incidentally, described in the poet Jalhaṇa's *Somapālavilāsa* (early twelfth century).[107]

Kalhaṇa describes, thereafter, the uprisings of several ḍāmaras and Sussala's cruel reprisals, the fickleness of the populace, the protest fasts of the brāhmaṇas, desertions by troops, and the siege of Śrīnagara by Mallakoṣṭha and Bhikṣācara.[108] As Kalhaṇa describes the loss of 250 rebels in one engagement, the fighting was obviously serious. Sussala was eventually forced to flee with his family to Lohara for safety and Bhikṣācara was installed as king.

Bhikṣācara's rule (1120–1) was of significance since it marked the brief restoration of Harṣa's lineage and also underlined Queen Jayamatī's alleged hand in his rise to prominence.[109] However, problems posed by rival ḍāmaras and ministers, as also the scarcity of money and the decline of trade, threatened the inexperienced Bhikṣācara. In addition, Bimba, Bhikṣācara's prime minister, led an expedition against Lohara, securing the alliance of Somapāla of Rājapurī and a force of 'Turuṣkas'.[110] Sussala routed them completely and was able to re-conquer Kashmir in 1121, supported by the populace.

The second phase of Sussala's rule (1121–8) was marked by

clashes with Bhikṣācara, a famine caused by a raging fire and threats from the ḍāmaras.[111] He eventually paved the way for his own murder by conniving with a treacherous agent, Utpala, to kill Bhikṣācara, little realizing that Utpala would murder him instead. Sussala's son, Jayasiṁha, succeeded him to the throne in 1128.[112] One should note here the role played by Sussala's chief queen, Meghamañjarī. Sussala's deep reliance on her support and advice led to him being completely traumatized on her untimely death, even to the extent of considering abdication of the throne.

Kalhaṇa prefaces the description of Jayasiṁha's character and reign (1128–49) with the need to take into consideration the state of affairs at the commencement of his rule. He had succeeded to the throne in the midst of an open rebellion while the land had been suffering from struggles. Thus, the fact that he was able to secure and maintain his footing for twenty-seven years reflects on his personality. Jayasiṁha apparently displayed cunning diplomacy and unscrupulous intrigue in his struggles and political relations.[113]

A significant aspect of Jayasiṁha's reign was the death of Bhikṣācara in 1130, after a clash with the king's troops, and the consequent removal of a looming threat. However, threats were also posed by Loṭhana, Salhaṇa's brother, and Mallārjuna, Jayasiṁha's half-brother. Jayasiṁha was able to win over Loṭhana's ally, the powerful ḍāmara Koṣṭheśvara, which had the indirect result of prompting Mallārjuna to flee. Kalhaṇa's description of the precautions taken by Jayasiṁha's envoy *en route* to imprison Mallārjuna, at a later stage, shows that the mountain routes through the southern border of Kashmir were entirely at the mercy of marauding khaśa hill-men.[114] Loṭhana was eventually captured in 1144.

Perhaps the most significant event of Jayasiṁha's reign was his reconciliation with Bhoja, the rebel son of Salhaṇa, through the mediation of his queen, Kalhaṇikā. This was an enterprise fraught with danger in that rival ḍāmaras were interested in perpetuating the feud.[115] However, Kalhaṇikā's role, at this juncture, had the crucial result of crushing an incipient ḍāmara rising. This has been discussed in detail in a subsequent chapter.

One should also note here the significant presence of Jayasiṁha's chief queen, Raḍḍādevī. Kalhaṇa shows she was a strong support, conversant with state policy: for instance, she independently fixed a marriage alliance between her daughter, Menilā, and Bhūpāla of Rājapurī. Interestingly, the concluding verses of Kalhaṇa's text are in praise of Raḍḍādevī.

Jayasiṁha apparently maintained friendly relations with distant kingdoms. This is attested by the poet, Maṅkha's account of the assembly held by his brother, Alaṁkāra, one of Jayasiṁha's ministers, to commemorate the completion of his poem, *Śrīkaṇṭhacarita*, written between 1135 and 1145.[116] The twenty-fifth or last canto is the most significant in that Maṅkha gives the names of thirty contemporary scholars, poets and officials assembled at Alaṁkāra's house, and the sciences in which they specialized, presenting a very lively picture of a *sabhā*. Among the persons present were the ambassadors of Govindacandra of Kanauj and of Aparāditya, the Śīlahara prince of the Koṅkaṇ, both of whom are known from their inscriptions.[117] Incidentally, the poem also serves the purpose of confirming Kalhaṇa's presence and prominence.[118] Maṅkha mentions Kalyāṇa (seen as a reference to Kalhaṇa), the poet Jalhaṇa, and some of Jayasiṁha's ministers mentioned in the *Rājataraṅgiṇī*, including his own brothers, Alaṁkāra and Śṛṇgāra, thereby corroborating Kalhaṇa's details.

The Srinagar stone slab inscription of Jayasiṁha's reign (1149) has already been cited as a corroborative source for his rule, as also the fragmentary inscription of the ascetic donor, Gagga, which corresponds to 1145. In addition, Kalhaṇa's references to Jayasiṁha's numerous pious endowments and the religious foundations made by his wives, members of his court and their families serve the same purpose and are significant in several ways. First, they provide indications of Kalhaṇa's personal connections and, by mentioning one of Maṅkha's donations, corroborate the latter's existence as Kalhaṇa's fellow-poet. Second, Kalhaṇa's appreciation of Jayasiṁha's restoration of ruined temples, *maṭhas* and so on indicates the damage caused by the long civil wars and consequent neglect of these shrines as the resources of the land were depleted.[119] Third, and most significant, they provide material for the analysis of the gendered aspect of building activities in Kashmir, undertaken in a subsequent chapter.

The *Rājataraṅgiṇī* closes in around 1150 with a brief account of Raḍḍādevī's children and a reiterative survey of the prominent rulers of Kashmir.[120] From a subsequent work, it is apparent that Jayasiṁha ruled for five more years during which he undertook a successful expedition against the *yavanas*.[121] He was succeeded by his eldest son, Gulhaṇa (Paramānuka?), who had already been crowned king of Lohara in Jayasiṁha's time, probably to secure his succession against future risks. This concludes the brief survey of early medieval Kashmir's political framework, as a precursor to a gendered reconstruction of its society and polity.

NOTES

1. Numismatic material is also comparatively scanty. For the coinage of early medieval Kashmir, S.C. Ray, *Early History and Culture of Kashmir*, 2nd revd edn, Delhi, Munshiram Manoharlal: 1970, p. 232.
2. H.C. Ray, *The Dynastic History of Northern India*, 2nd edn, Delhi, Munshiram Manoharlal: 1973, vol.1, p. 111. B.K. Kaul Deambi, *Corpus of Śāradā Inscriptions of Kashmir*, Delhi, Agam Kala Prakashan: 1982, p. 95 says that it is surprising that not a single copper-plate inscription recording a grant of land has come to light. Krishna Mohan, *Early Medieval History of Kashmir*, Delhi, Meherchand Lachhmandas: 1981, p. 11 points out that the stone inscriptions and copper-plate title deeds consulted by Kalhaṇa have almost all perished.
3. Deambi, *Corpus of Śāradā Inscriptions*, pp. 136–7. For an account of unedited Śāradā inscriptions that are lost, defaced or inaccessible, Appendix I, pp. 157–60.
4. Ibid., pp. 140–1. Deambi, however, says that the Śāradā script represents the earliest phase of its development.
5. Ibid., pp. 145–7.
6. Ibid., pp. 133–5.
7. Ibid., p. 97. The inscription is in Sanskrit and in the Śāradā script.
8. Ibid., p. 98. However, Deambi says that the influence of Brahmanism is seen in the sacred thread on the statue.
9. Ibid., p. 100. This slab was discovered in a private house in Srinagar.
10. Ibid., pp. 100–1, 303. Deambi talks of the 'idealistic monism' in Kashmir, along with the existence of Buddhist, Vaiṣṇava and tāntric sects, indicating a situation of 'perfect toleration' and 'marvellous religious harmony' in Kashmir.
11. Ibid., pp. 149–50.
12. Ibid., pp. 102, 143–4.
13. For a history of the text and its various translations, P.N.K. Bamzai,

Culture and Political History of Kashmir, 1: *Ancient Kashmir*, Delhi, MD Publications: 1994, p. 32; R.S. Pandit, tr., *Rājataraṅgiṇī*, Delhi, Sahitya Akademi: 1935, pp. xiii, xiv. For a discussion on the growth of the Indian historical tradition, Romila Thapar, *Ancient Indian Social History*, Delhi, Orient Longman: 1978, pp. 242, 268, 273–5, 355–6, Dilip K. Chakrabarti, *Colonial Indology: Sociopolitics of the Ancient Indian Past*, Delhi, Munshiram Manoharlal: 1997, pp. 152, 154–6; R.S. Tripathi, *History of Ancient India*, 3rd rpt., Delhi, Motilal Banarsidass: 1967, p. 3. R.C. Majumdar, 'Ideas of History in Sanskrit Literature', in *Historians of India, Pakistan and Ceylon*, ed. C.H. Philips, 2nd rpt., London, Oxford University Press: 1967, pp. 24–5 praises the text for disproving the notion that the ancient Indians had no real historical sense.

14. M.A. Stein, tr., *Kalhaṇa's Rājataraṅgiṇī*, 3rd rpt., Delhi, Motilal Banarsidass: 1989, vols. I, II and III, rpt., Bombay, Motilal Banarsidass: 1988). Stein's translation was chosen over others due to his extremely lucid style and exhaustive analysis of the topography, chronology, historicity and other aspects of Kalhaṇa's work. He also examines Kalhaṇa's descent, skills, motives, style, affiliations and other factors that are conducive to a better understanding of the text. G.M.D. Sufi, *Kashir: A History of Kashmir*, Delhi, Light & Life Publishers: 1974, vol. I, p. 13, mentions Stein's 'exhaustive exposition' of the period that he uses as his framework. Note that R.S. Pandit's translation of the text translates some eighty odd verses that Stein ignores in the *Rājataraṅgiṇī* and focuses on the poetic qualities of the work (Pandit, tr., *Rājataraṅgiṇī*, p. xv). However, problems are posed by his extremely (and self-confessedly) literal translation and his usage of French terms for words that cannot be conveyed in English. Besides, his analysis is sketchy in comparison with Stein's well-structured and comprehensive study of the text.
15. Maurice Winternitz, *History of Indian Literature*, rpt., Delhi, Motilal Banarsidass: 1985, vol. III, pts I and II, p. 101 says that the *Rājataraṅgiṇī* permits us 'to get an insight into Indian cultural traditions of the 11th century and 12th century as few works of the Indian literature do'. Stein, *Rājataraṅgiṇī*, I, 'Introduction', p. 4, says the text represents 'a class of Sanskrit composition which comes nearest in character to the Chronicles of Medieval Europe and of the Muhammadan East'. B.N.S. Yadava, *Society and Culture in Northern India in the Twelfth Century*, Allahabad, Central Book Depot: 1973, p. xi talks of the 'exceptional importance' of the text and its significant references to the social, political, economic and religious life of the age.
16. E.B. Cowell and F.W. Thomas, tr., *The Harṣacarita of Bāṇa*, 2nd rpt., Delhi, Motilal Banarsidass: 1993. It is a historical romance that presents actual events in the life of Bāṇa's sovereign, Harṣa of Thānesar and Kanauj (606–48). S.C. Banerji and A.K. Gupta, tr., *Bilhaṇa's Vikramāṅkadevacaritam*, Calcutta, Sambodhi Publications: 1965. This

poem of eighteen cantos details the life of Bilhaṇa's patron, the Cālukyan king, Vikramāditya Tribhuvanamalla VI of Kalyāṇa (1076–1126). Thapar, *Ancient Indian Social History*, pp. 270, 274–5, says that from the seventh century AD onwards, the historical tradition as expressed in the idea of *itihāsa* and *purāṇa* enlarged to form the various *vaṁśāvalī* in many kingdoms, giving rise to a new genre of historical writing, the historical biography or *carita*, like these two texts. The *Rājataraṅgiṇī* owes a lot to the *itihāsa-purāṇa* tradition but, in attempting to provide a connected narrative of Kashmir's ruling dynasties, it sets itself consciously within the genre of royal historical accounts. Thus, it is essentially a *vaṁśāvalī* and more akin to the Persian chronicles, whereas the other two texts are *caritas* of a typically eulogistic nature and, therefore, of a different genre and style.

17. For instance, time is referred to in phrases like 'after many days', 'with time', etc., in the *Harṣacarita*, and the identity of important personages is left unclear. Similarly, Bilhaṇa is inconsistent in providing place-names and dates, and clutters the narrative with irrelevant details. See, for instance, canto VII, verses 34–54. Majumdar, 'Ideas of History', in *Historians of India*, ed. Philips, p. 23 mentions Kalhaṇa's 'wonderful moderation' in contrast to Bāṇa and Bilhaṇa.
18. Although women in the *Harṣacarita* form part of the general descriptions and are variously introduced as goddesses or mothers, it is possible to discern, at points, a more substantial role for them. See the section on Kanauj for more details. Bilhaṇa, on the other hand, marginalizes his female characters completely.
19. V.S. Pathak, *Ancient Historians of India*, 2nd impression, Gorakhpur, Purva Samsthana: 1984, p. 76. See also p. 49. Pathak views this equation of women with fortune as a convention of *itihāsa* works.
20. Haraprasad Sastri, ed., *Rāmacarita: A Historical Record of the Pāl Dynasty*, Varanasi, Bhartiya Publishing House: 1973. It deals with Rāmapāla (1084–1126) of Bengal's Pāla dynasty and the *double entendre* used effectively obscures much of its meaning. Contrast this with Kalhaṇa's largely clear and lucid presentation.
21. Devika Rangachari, 'Gender and the Historical Chronicle: A Study of Kalhaṇa's *Rājataraṅgiṇī*', unpublished M.Phil. dissertation, Department of History, University of Delhi, 1997, pp. 17–18 for more details.
22. The histories of Assam, Nepal, Bengal, Bihar, Orissa, the Rāṣṭrakūṭas, the Gāhaḍavālas and the Gurjara Pratihāras of Kanauj are all reconstructed by H.C. Ray, *Dynastic History of Northern India*, pp. 111–73 on the basis of land grant inscriptions, whereas he only uses the *Rājataraṅgiṇī* for Kashmir's history. S.C. Ray, *Early History and Culture*, pp. 11–12 talks of the 'marvellous accuracy of Kalhaṇa's topographical knowledge', showing his personal knowledge of various places cited. For instance, the identity of the capital, Pravarasenapura (modern Śrīnagara, built in

the sixth century AD), was largely based on Kalhaṇa's exact description of it being situated at the confluence of two rivers with a hill in its centre (p. 21).

23. Kumkum Roy, 'The Making of a *Maṇḍala*: Fuzzy Frontiers of Kalhaṇa's Kashmir', in *Negotiating India's Past: Essays in Memory of Partha Sarathi Gupta*, ed. Biswamoy Pati, B.P. Sahu and T.K. Venkatasubramanian, Delhi, Tulika Books: 2003, pp. 52–66.
24. Stein, *Rājataraṅgiṇī*, 'Introduction', I, pp. 17–18. The fact of his father, Caṇpaka, having served King Harṣa (1089–1101), who was deposed by Jayasiṁha's father and uncle, may have influenced Kalhaṇa's decision to shun court appointments and turn to poetry instead. Note that Kalhaṇa apparently wrote the *Jayasiṁhābhyudaya*, which is lost: S.C. Banerji, *Cultural Heritage of Kashmir*, Calcutta, Sanskrit Pustak Bhandar: 1965, p. 56.
25. R.C. Majumdar, 'Sources of Indian History', in *The Vedic Age*, ed. R.C. Majumdar, 4th edn, Bombay, Motilal Banarsidass: 1965, p. 50.
26. *RT*, I.9–10, 15. Also *RT*, I.11–20 for an account of the sources consulted by Kalhaṇa prior to embarking on his work and their shortcomings. George Bühler distinguished these into four kinds of records: Stein, *Rājataraṅgiṇī*, I, p. 3, fn. 15. The first are the *pratiṣṭhaśāsana* edicts or inscriptions recording the erection or consecration of temples and buildings. Of these, only a few specimens have been found in Kashmir and only few can be ascribed with certainty to a period earlier than Kalhaṇa. The second type are the *vastuśāsana* edicts or inscriptions recording grants of land/allowances and engraved on copper plates. No inscriptions of this kind have been unearthed, although Kalhaṇa's work indicates that inscriptions, probably on copper plates, were used for the record of land grants in Kashmir. The third type are the *praśastipaṭṭas*, or tables of laudatory inscriptions of persons or places to be found in temples or public buildings. There are no specimens of this kind so far. The fourth type are the *śāstras* or works on the various sciences and manuscripts of Sanskrit books that provide information on authors, kings, and dates.
27. This era was used in Kashmir from early times. Stein, *Rājataraṅgiṇī*, 'Introduction', I, pp. 56–70, talks of it being in use among the brāhmaṇa population of Kashmir and the hill territories to the south–east such as Cambā, Kāngrā, and Maṇḍī.
28. Their relationship can also be discerned from Kalhaṇa's affectionate handling of Caṇpaka's history (ibid., p. 6). Contrast this with Bāṇa and Bilhaṇa who trace their antecedents in great detail and the latter with much self-praise. See G.L. Kaul, *Kashmir (Through the Ages) (5000 B.C. to 1900 A.D.)*, Srinagar, Chronicle Publishing House: 1960, p. 6.
29. For a detailed examination of this theme, Rangachari, 'Gender and the Historical Chronicle', unpub. M.Phil. dissertation, University of Delhi;

Devika Rangachari, 'Kalhaṇa's *Rājataraṅgiṇī*: A Gender Perspective', *The Medieval History Journal*, vol. 5, no. 1, 2002, pp. 37–75. Although less than a fifth of the verses in the *Rājataraṅgiṇī* deal with women, Kalhaṇa permeates the text with their power and presence.

30. Kumkum Sangari, 'Consent and Agency: Aspects of Feminist Historiography', in *Women in Indian History: Social, Economic, Political and Cultural Perspectives*, ed. Kiran Pawar, Delhi, Vision & Venture: 1996, p. 25; Ania Loomba, *Gender, Race, Renaissance Drama*, Manchester, Manchester University Press: 1989, p. 116.
31. Kalhaṇa's narrative strategy has often been ignored or misconstrued, as will be analysed in the following chapters. Somnath Dhar, *Kalhaṇa: The Poet Historian*, Delhi, Sahitya Akademi: 1978, p. 45 says Kalhaṇa provided information on the solution of his contemporary men and women to 'the eternal problem of the relation between the sexes', yet neglects to discuss this further. Roy, 'Making of a *Maṇḍala*', in *Negotiating India's Past*, ed. Pati, Sahu and Venkatasubramanian, p. 60, notes that Kalhaṇa records the 'active and independent' political roles played by the women rulers of Kashmir, 'in spite of his obvious disapproval'.
32. Ved Kumari, *The Nīlamata Purāṇa*, Srinagar-Jammu, J&K Academy of Art, Culture and Languages: 1968, vol. I, p. v: the text 'throws much light on the social conditions of ancient Kashmir'. Note that Kalhaṇa also calls it the *Nīlapurāṇa* (*RT*, I.14).
33. S.C. Ray, *Early History and Culture*, p. 2. See also p. vii where he notes that the kingdom of ancient Kashmir was a much smaller territory than the modern state of Jammu & Kashmir. H.C. Ray, *Dynastic History of Northern India*, pp. 107–11 for other geographical and topographical details.
34. S.C. Ray, *Early History and Culture*, pp. 4–5. Kashmir was seldom dominated by the plains or tried to penetrate into it, but its cultural, religious, and literary life seems to have been closely integrated with that of the Punjab and the Gangetic valley. Banerji, *Cultural Heritage of Kashmir*, p. 3.
35. S.C. Ray, *Early History and Culture*, p. 7, notes that the information of Muslim writers is rather scanty, except for the detailed and accurate account provided by Alberuni's *Kitab-ul Hind* (eleventh century). Alberuni says that Kashmir was the seat of Hindu sciences at the time and that many Kashmiri scholars were among his informants. He adds that the people were aware of the natural strengths of the valley and guarded all frontier routes closely (p. 8).
36 The *vihāras* were identified by Stein on the basis of the geographical details provided. Stein also identified the *vihāras* noticed by the Chinese pilgrim, Ou-kong, who visited Kashmir in around 750 and spent four years there studying Sanskrit. S.C. Ray, *Early History and Culture*, p. 7.

37. Ibid., pp. 9–10. Bühler says that the *Nīlamatapurāṇa* is necessary to explain the *Rājataraṅgiṇī* and also to show how Kalhaṇa used his sources. Ved Kumari, tr., *The Nīlamata Purāṇa*, Srinagar, J&K Academy of Art, Culture and Languages: 1973, vol. II, p. vii; for details of the manuscripts of the text and related matters, pp. vii–xi, *NP*, 1326–1408 for the prominent *tīrthas* in Kashmir sacred to Viṣṇu, Śiva, and other deities and the merit accruing from them, as also *NP*, 1275–1324 for details of the sacred places near Kashmir and their merit. The chief holy places are described in topographical order. S.C. Ray, *Early History and Culture*, pp. 32, 191, calls the text a 'handbook of rites and ceremonies' observed by the people of ancient Kashmir.
38. This statement could not have been made later than the eighth century AD: after that, Buddhism was not so strong as to induce the Vaiṣṇavas to identify the Buddha with Viṣṇu. The lower limit for the text thus being the eighth century, it can be assigned to the sixth/seventh century. Kumari, *Nīlamata Purāṇa*, I, pp. 10, 14–15 notes that the text's favourable attitude towards Buddhism is not shared by the later writers of Kashmir (p. 177). For the equation between the Buddha and Viṣṇu, see *NP*, 709–10a.
39. Of the earliest Sanskrit compositions of Kashmir, none have survived that can be dated with certainty to the period prior to the sixth century AD. S.C. Ray, *Early History and Culture*, p. 185.
40. Note that Yuan Chwang cites native records as indicating that Kashmir was originally a dragon lake: ibid., p. 156. Deambi, *Corpus of Śāradā Inscriptions*, p. 264, says Yuan Chwang calls the *nāgas* 'dragons' because they are represented in the form of serpents living, like Chinese dragons, in the water of the springs they are to protect. However, Thomas Watters, *On Yuan Chwang's Travels in India*, 2nd Indian edn, Delhi, Munshiram Manoharlal: 1973, pp. 264–5, finds that the legend of dessication is ascribed to a Buddhist *arhat*, Madhyāntika. M.L. Kapur, *The History and Culture of Kashmir*, 2nd revd edn, Delhi, Anmol Publications: 1992, pp. 10–11; S.L. Shali, *Kashmir: History and Archaeology Through the Ages*, Delhi, Indus Publishing Company: 1993, pp. 37–44 for a discussion of the scientific observations supporting the theory that Kashmir was originally a lake.
41. P.N.K. Bamzai, *Kashmir and Central Asia*, Delhi, Light & Life Publishers: 1980, pp. 5–6.
42. Deambi, *Corpus of Śāradā Inscriptions*, p. 263.
43. Kumari, *Nīlamata Purāṇa*, I, p. 23.
44. S.C. Ray, *Early History and Culture*, pp. 157–8. The existence of the *nāga* cult is corroborated by Abul Fazl who observes that, in the period 1556–1605, 45 places in Kashmir were dedicated to Śiva, 64 to Viṣṇu, 3 to Brahmā, 22 to Durgā and 700 to carved images of snakes. Bamzai, *Kashmir and Central Asia*, p. 146, suggests *nāga* worship was the earliest form of symbolic deification. It apparently flourished in Kashmir during prehistoric times, long before Aryan and Brahmanical influences

penetrated the valley. See also Kumari, *Nīlamata Purāṇa*, I, p. 139.

45. Stein, *Rājataraṅgiṇī*, 'Introduction', I, p. 72 for more details. Kalhaṇa begins his account by stating that the names of the fifty-two earliest rulers of the land have not been recorded by early chroniclers.
46. Ibid., pp. 72–3. This apparently explained the non-participation of Kashmir in the 'Great War' of the *Mahābhārata*. Stein also cites Bühler's view that this contention is part of an attempt to link the legends of Kashmir with those of the *Mahābhārata* and the rest of India. According to Roy, 'Making of a *Maṇḍala*', in *Negotiating India's Past*, ed. Pati, Sahu and Venkatasubramanian, p. 56, such stories were a part of constructed traditions that attempted to claim a space for Kashmir 'within dominant supra-regional narratives'.
47. Stein, *Rājataraṅgiṇī*, 'Introduction', I, pp. 74–5. Kalhaṇa portrays Aśoka as a pious follower of Buddhism and mentions Suṣkaletra and Vitastātra as places where he erected *vihāras* and *stūpas*. He also attributes the foundation of Śrīnagarī, the old capital, to Aśoka.
48. Ibid., p. 76. Kalhaṇa describes the three kings as princes of Turkish nationality and patrons of Buddhism which is corroborated by other records. The existence of their foundations— Kaniṣkapura, Huṣkapura and Juṣkapura—is other significant evidence.
49. Ibid., p. 78. Stein calls this a record 'of truly historical interest'. Mihirakula seems to have been ousted from the greatest part of his territories by a hostile alliance and forced to retreat northwards towards Kashmir about AD 530. Kalhaṇa recounts several legendary anecdotes about Mihirakula. These accounts of his apparent cruelty and vindictiveness find corroboration in the accounts of Yuan Chwang and an earlier Chinese pilgrim, Sung-yun. For details on the period between the Kuṣāṇas and Mihirakula, see pp. 76–8.
50. Ibid., p. 80. For the period between Mihirakula and the kings of Book II, pp. 78–80.
51. For details on the kings of Book III, ibid., pp. 81–8.
52. Ibid., pp. 83–4. Mātṛgupta's rule is placed between that of Meghavāhana's elder grandson, Hiraṇya, and the advent of Pravarasena II, the son of Toramāṇa, Meghavāhana's grandson. See pp. 82–3 for more details.
53. Ibid., pp. 84–5. The records of the Chinese T'ang dynasty prove that Pravarapura was the official designation of the city in the early part of the eighth century AD. Pravarasena is also supposed to have built the temple of Śiva Pravareśvara as the chief shrine of this city. This temple was still extant in Kalhaṇa's time. See pp. 84–6 for details on Pravarasena's coins, his conquests and his successors.
54. Sufi (*Kashir*, p. 49) speculates that the word 'Kārkoṭa' might have some connection with the word 'Cārkoṭa' which, in the *Atharvaveda*, indicates some kind of poisonous snake. In the list of principal *nāgas* in epic literature, Nāgarāja Kārkoṭa has an honourable place.

55. Certain coins bearing the name Durlabhadeva have been attributed to him. Their bold but rude execution apparently characterizes all the known issues of rulers of this dynasty. Stein, *Rājataraṅgiṇī*, 'Introduction', I, p. 87; A. Cunningham, *Coins of Medieval India: From the Seventh Century Down to the Muhammadan Conquests*, Varanasi, Oriental Books: 1967, p. 26.
56. Watters, *On Yuan Chwang's Travels*, p. 259 points out that neither the pilgrim's memoirs nor the *Life of Hiuen-Tsiang* (a biography of Yuan Chwang by his disciple, Shaman Hwui-Li) mention the Kashmiri king's name. Yuan Chwang apparently spent his two years studying the *sūtras* and *śāstras* and worshipping at sacred sites. Deambi, *Corpus of Śāradā Inscriptions*, pp. 272–3, says that although Yuan Chwang does not provide a very favourable picture of Buddhism, the fact that the ruling king came to see him and pay his respects shows some regard for the faith.
57. Stein, *Rājataraṅgiṇī*, 'Introduction', I, p. 87. Yuan Chwang specifically mentions Uraśā, Siṁhapura, Rājapurī and Parṇotsa among other tributary kingdoms.
58. For this and details of Candrāpīḍa and Lalitāditya Muktāpīḍa, ibid., p. 88. The *Annals* of the T'ang dynasty in China refer to Lalitāditya-Muktāpīḍa by the name 'Mu-to-pi' as the king of Kashmir who sent an embassy to the Chinese court during the reign of Emperor Hiuen-tsung (713–55), after the first Chinese expedition against Baltistan (*c.* 736–47). As the exact date of the embassy is not given, Kalhaṇa's chronology for Lalitāditya (699–736) cannot be ascertained with accuracy. However, the details recorded of the embassy reveal much about the king's foreign relations.
59. Ibid., pp. 88–9 for more details. Note Kalhaṇa's incidental mention of Bhavabhūti and Vākpati as notable poets in Yaśovarman's court. Roy, 'Making of a *Maṇḍala*', pp. 59, 61 observes that the attitude towards the Gaṅgā Valley is ambivalent.
60. Yaśovarman is also identified with the king of central India, I-cha-fon-mo, who sent an embassy to the Chinese court in 731. See Stein, *Rājataraṅgiṇī*, 'Introduction', I, p. 89. Stein believes that Lalitāditya's attack on Kanauj presupposes his having been in possession of territories outside Kashmir, particularly to the south and south-east. Kalhaṇa particularly mentions Jālaṁdhara and Lohara as held by Lalitāditya's feudatories. Thus, an extension of Kashmir's dominion to the east towards the Yamunā would have brought Lalitāditya into collision with Yaśovarman. Stein says that Lalitāditya seems to have asserted his authority over the region of the lower hills to the north of Punjab.
61. Ibid., p. 90. Stein identifies the country of the Tuḥkhāras as the region comprising Badakshan and adjoining tracts, inhabited by Turkish tribes.
62. Kalhaṇa offers several legendary versions of his death (ibid., p. 93).

What is of note here, however, is that Kalhaṇa makes Lalitāditya provide detailed maxims of policy that seem to have influenced Kashmiri administration thereafter.

63. Ibid., p. 94.
64. Ibid. for details of this expedition and of Jayāpīḍa's adventurous sojourn in Bengal.
65. A.M. Shastri, *India as Seen in the Kuṭṭanīmata of Dāmodaragupta*, Delhi, Motilal Banarsidass: 1975, pp. 1-2, talks of the great respect accorded to this poem: many of its stanzas are cited in standard works on literary criticism, grammar, and anthologies, as in the *Alaṅkārasarvasva* of Maṅkha (1150).
66. Winternitz, *History of Indian Literature*, III, p. 169. S.C. Ray, *Early History and Culture*, p. 192, calls it a 'practical treatise on erotics'.
67. Interestingly, a prostitute's acting skills, in this work, are shown while staging Harṣa's *Ratnāvalī*. Shastri, *India as Seen in the Kuṭṭanīmata*, p. 8, says it is the earliest known reference to the *Ratnāvalī*, the elaborate account of its enactment showing its great popularity in Dāmodaragupta's time. Kṣemendra, whose *Samayamātṛkā* was probably a close imitation of Dāmodara's work (Winternitz, *History of Indian Literature*, III, p. 169), indicates that Dāmodara belonged to a high Brahmanical social order. While quoting a stanza in his *Kavikaṇṭhābharaṇa* (5.39), he prefixes the title *bhaṭṭa* to Dāmodara's name. In epigraphic records, the title is attached as a mark of reverence to learned brāhmaṇas (p. 18).
68. It was Bühler who first drew attention to the chronological value of this notice (Stein, *Rājataraṅgiṇī*, 'Introduction', I, pp. 95–6). Corroboration of this date is provided by the colophon that the Kashmiri poet, Rājānaka Ratnākara, has attached to his work, the *Haravijaya*, wherein he states that he wrote it under the patronage of 'the young Bṛhaspati', another name for Cippaṭajayāpīḍa. Ratnākara is distinctly mentioned by Kalhaṇa as among the poets who obtained fame under a subsequent king, Avantivarman (855–83), it is clear that the king meant in the colophon of the *Haravijaya* is Cippaṭajayāpīḍa.
69. Ibid., pp. 96–7 for details of this succession wrangle.
70. Ibid. This corresponds to the town of Vantpor, the ruins ranking among the most imposing monuments of ancient Kashmiri architecture, according to Stein.
71. Deambi, *Corpus of Śāradā Inscriptions*, pp. 133-5.
72. Stein, *Rājataraṅgiṇī*, 'Introduction', I, pp. 97–8; B.D. Chattopadhyaya, 'Political Processes and Structures of Polity in Early Medieval India: Problems of Perspective', Presidential Address, *Indian History Congress Proceedings*, 44th Session, Burdwan, 1983, p. 40, says the rise of the ḍāmaras in Kashmir between 1000 and 1170 suggests the emergence of potentially dominant elements from within the local agrarian base.
73. Stein, *Rājataraṅgiṇī*, 'Introduction', I, p. 98. Avantivarman's reign

was also marked by important engineering operations undertaken by an individual, Suyya, whose memory was preserved by his town of Suyyapura (modern Sopore).

74. Ibid., p. 99. Mohan, *Early Medieval History*, p. 22, talks of Śaṁkaravarman extending Kashmir's sovereign power to all of Punjab from the Indus to the Sutlej.
75. See ibid., p. 100, for this observation and the details in this paragraph.
76. See ibid., pp. 99–100, for details of Śaṁkaravarman's 'violent end' in his attempt to avenge the death of his *dvārapati* in a frontier-affray and his consequent fatal skirmish with the inhabitants of Uraśā (modern Hazara district).
77. After Gopālavarman's death, Saṁkaṭa, 'a suppositious son of Śaṁkaravarman', was put on the throne but died after ten days. Ibid., p. 101. Kalhaṇa says this brother of Gopālavarman had been 'picked up from the highway' (*RT*, V.242).
78. Ibid., p. 102.
79. Ibid., p. 103.
80. Ibid., pp. 103–4.
81. Lohara, or the modern Lohrin valley, is now included in the Punch district. Diddā was the maternal granddaughter of Bhīma Śāhī of Udabhāṇḍa, who is mentioned in Alberuni's list of the 'Hindu Shahiyas of Kabul' as the successor of Kamalu and who is also known from his coins. Stein mentions having identified the remains of Bhīma Śāhī's temple, Bhīmakeśava, 'in a Muhammadan Ziarat' near Mārtaṇḍa (ibid., p. 105).
82. Ibid.; S.C. Ray, *Early History and Culture*, pp. 242–3.
83. The only 'signal act' of the ineffectual Kṣemagupta seems to have been the building of the temple of Kṣemagaurīśvara in Srinagar, for which he apparently plundered the ancient Jayendravihāra. Stein, *Rājataraṅgiṇī*, 'Introduction', I, p. 104.
84. For details of Diddā's regency, ibid., p. 105.
85. He came from the hills of Parṇotsa or Prunts and was formerly a buffalo herdsman.
86. Stein, *Rājataraṅgiṇī*, 'Introduction', I, p. 108 for details of this expedition. Alberuni was present at the siege of the Lohara stronghold, and records Mahmud's failure to withstand its strength and the cold weather.
87. Deambi, *Corpus of Śāradā Inscriptions*, pp. 49-50.
88. S.C. Ray, *Early History and Culture*, p. 201; Winternitz, *History of Indian Literature*, III, pp. 23–34, 55. Kṣemendra also wrote epics and dramas, abridged the *Rāmāyaṇa* and the *Mahābhārata*, rendered the *Kādambarī* into verse, and composed religious poems and didactic stanzas. Uma Chakraborty, *Kṣemendra: The Eleventh Century Kashmiri Poet*, Delhi, Sri Satguru Publications: 1991, pp. 11–12..
89. N.S. Shukla, *Cultural Trends in Kashmir and Kṣemendra*, Delhi, Nirman

Prakashan: 1990, pp. 140, 171, finds that Kṣemendra's opinion of women was poor (pp. 216–17). In addition, he portrays widows as leading an immoral life and even describes the wives and sisters of kāyasthas in terms likening them to prostitutes (pp. 161, 154–5). Deambi, *Corpus of Śāradā Inscriptions*, p. 236.

90. R.S. Tripathi, ed. and tr., *Samayamātṛkā of Mahākavi Kṣemendra*, Varanasi, Chowkhambha Vidyabhavan: 1967; Winternitz, *History of Indian Literature*, III, pp. 169–70.
91. S.C. Ray, *Early History and Culture*, p. 202; Mohan, *Early Medieval History*, p. 7; Shukla, *Cultural Trends in Kashmir*, p. 52, says it was Kṣemendra's attitude of a reformist that prompted him to write these texts. See also Chakraborty, *Kṣemendra*, p. 60. The *Samayamātṛkā* is clubbed along with the *Narmamālā*, the *Deśopadeśa* and the *Kalāvilāsa* as his 'satirical compositions'. Note that Kṣemendra came from a wealthy and well-connected family and so, was obviously in a position to review administrative, courtly and social foibles. His father, Prakāśendra, was a 'well-established citizen of Kashmir' and his great-grandfather, Narendra, was a minister. Kṣemendra's son, Somendra, was also a poet and added to some of his works.
92. Stein, *Rājataraṅgiṇī*, 'Introduction', I, pp. 109–10.
93. Ibid., p. 109. Stein identifies Inducandra with the Indracandra named in the genealogical list of the Katoch Rājās of Kāngrā. Inducandra's elder daughter, Āsamatī, had married Rudrapāla Śāhī. For details of Ananta and Kalaśa, see pp. 110–11.
94. C.H. Tawney, tr., *The Kathā Sarit Sāgara*, 3rd edn, Delhi, Munshiram Manoharlal: 1992, vols. I, II; S.C. Ray, *Early History and Culture*, p. 204; Winternitz, *History of Indian Literature*, III, pp. 352–4, says that Somadeva lays no claim to originality but has merely abridged Guṇādhya's original *Bṛhatkathā* and changed the language. However, the main story is overrun by the rest of the narrative, and the stories are misplaced and often repeated. Winternitz observes that the importance of the text lies in the fact that several stories have been worked on by several poets (pp. 354–5, 364). Kṣemendra also wrote the *Bṛhatkathāmañjarī* (*Bud of the Tree*), a versified version of the *Bṛhatkathā*. However, the stories, that are often so factually short as to be unintelligible, tend to focus on erotic and religious scenes alone (Winternitz, p. 352).
95. Winternitz, *History of Indian Literature*, III, pp. 358–9, says that stories of faithless or wicked wives prevail, as compared to the few on honest and faithful ones. A.B. Keith, *A History of Sanskrit Literature*, London, Oxford University Press: 1920, p. 284 refers to tales on women in the Kashmir recension of the *Bṛhatkathā* that seem to have been used to their disadvantage—as in the focus on murderous and unchaste women, for instance.

96. S.C. Ray, *Early History and Culture*, p. 204.
97. Bilhaṇa lived in the reigns of Kalaśa and Harṣa. He received his early education in Kashmir but left to seek fame and fortune at the time of Kalaśa's nominal accession.
98. Stein, *Rājataraṅgiṇī*, 'Introduction', I, pp. 111–13 for details of this succession wrangle and Harṣa's reign.
99. Stein wonders whether Harṣa was influenced, in this regard, by the spread of 'Muhammadanism' in the neighbouring territories (ibid., p. 113).
100. Ibid., pp. 114–16 for the tussle between Harṣa and the brothers, Uccala and Sussala, as also the role of the ḍāmaras in ousting Harṣa. Note that the emergence of the brothers as rival claimants to the throne underlines the importance of Diddā in Kashmir's politics.
101. Their names were Mukta and Prayāga, respectively. Ibid., pp. 116–17.
102. Harṣa apparently sent Caṇpaka to follow his son, Bhoja, who had previously fled with a few attendants (ibid., p. 116).
103. Ibid., p. 117.
104. Ibid.
105. For details of Salhaṇa's rule and another abortive attempt by Sussala to gain the throne, ibid. Gargacandra, at this point, is 'the king-maker' of the land.
106. This is a direct consequence of Salhaṇa's incompetence and of his encouraging attacks on Gargacandra by rival chiefs.
107. Winternitz, *History of Indian Literature*, III, p. 102. Stein, *Rājataraṅgiṇī*, 'Introduction', I, p. 120.
108. Stein, *Rājataraṅgiṇī*, 'Introduction', I, pp. 120–1.
109. Ibid., p. 121.
110. Stein indicates they were Muslims under Sallāra Vismaya. Sussala defeated them at Parṇotsa (or Punch), south of Lohara.
111. Ibid., pp. 122–3. Note that the ḍāmaras were used alternately by Sussala and Bhikṣācara to gain leverage over each other.
112. Sussala had Jayasiṁha crowned as king in 1123 but subsequently changed his mind and retained the government in his hands. At the time of Sussala's murder, Jayasiṁha was not in the royal palace (ibid., p. 123).
113. Note, for instance, that, at the outset, he proclaimed a general amnesty to ensure his safety and sought the help of Pañcacandra, the son of the ḍāmara Gargacandra. This was an important move considering that Gargacandra had been destroyed by Sussala, Jayasiṁha's father. However, Kalhaṇa indicates that the power of the ḍāmaras remained uncurbed, thereby causing unrest and wastage of resources in clashes between them and the king (ibid.).
114. Ibid., p. 126.

115. Bhoja initially allied with Loṭhana, Vigraharāja (Jayasiṁha's half-brother) and Alaṁkāracakra, a powerful ḍāmara in the district of Karṇāha on the Upper Kiṣangaṅgā (ibid., p. 127). He subsequently joined forces with Rājavadana, an influential and discontented officer of Jayasiṁha. Rājavadana later captured Bhoja in order to blackmail Jayasiṁha, thereby prompting Bhoja to secretly negotiate with the king for his surrender (ibid., pp. 127–8). Stein stresses Kalhaṇa's sympathetic treatment of Bhoja (p. 129).
116. S.C. Ray, *Early History and Culture*, p. 207; Winternitz, *History of Indian Literature*, III, p. 86. The theme of this work is the legend of Śiva's overthrow of the demon, Tripura, in the course of which court scenes, changing seasons, and so on are described. See B.C. Mandal, tr., *Śrīkaṇṭhacarita—A Mahākāvya of Maṅkhaka*, Calcutta, Sanskrit Pustak Bhandar: 1991, p. 44. Alaṁkāra was an officer in the affairs of peace and war in the courts of Sussala and Jayasiṁha. Kalhaṇa, however, refers to him as the chief of the high treasury (*RT*, VII.2423).
117. Mandal, *Śrīkaṇṭhacarita*, pp. 46-7 for details.
118. Stein, *Rājataraṅgiṇī*, 'Introduction', I, p. 13. See, however, Mandal, *Śrīkaṇṭhacarita*, pp. 180–3 where this contention is refuted.
119. Stein, *Rājataraṅgiṇī*, 'Introduction', I, p. 126 points out that none of the structures ascribed to the various ministers and members of Jayasiṁha's court can be traced in ruins or in other records. Hence, he infers that 'notwithstanding Kalhaṇa's fulsome praise', these were of 'a modest description'.
120. Kalhaṇa mentions the names of four of Raḍḍādevī's five sons, Gulhaṇa, Jayāpīḍa, Lalitāditya and Yaśaskara, and her two daughters, Menilā and Rājyaśrī (ibid., p. 129).
121. The reference is to Jonarāja's *Dvitīya Rājataraṅgiṇī*, a pale imitation of Kalhaṇa's work that covers the history of Kashmir from Jayasiṁha's reign to 1459. As Stein observes, Jonarāja's record is very brief and does not supplement the picture that Kalhaṇa has drawn of Jayasiṁha and contemporary Kashmir.

CHAPTER III

Kashmir: A Gendered Perspective (The Pre-Diddā Period c. AD 600–958)

This chapter pertains to the period from the Kārkoṭa dynasty (c. seventh century AD) until the year of Queen Diddā's regency, AD 958, which represents the pinnacle of power held by women in Kashmir. It will attempt to analyse the power and involvement of various categories of women—royal and non-royal—in the political and social domain in this time span, just as the next chapter will execute the same analysis from 958–1150, or the Diddā and post-Diddā periods. As a logical consequence of this bifurcation, the broad themes of analysis will remain largely the same for both chapters.

As stated in the previous chapter, the *Rājataraṅgiṇī* is our crucial source, with some amount of corroboration from the *Nīlamatapurāṇa* and Dāmodaragupta's *Kuṭṭanīmatam*. Kalhaṇa's text highlights the power and agency of women in the royal court culture in two essential ways—as sovereign rulers in their own right and as powers behind the throne. Power is wrested and exercised by them in what is essentially a patriarchal edifice, thus causing a certain amount of tension and ambiguity, not only in specific phases of history, but also in Kalhaṇa's portrayal of them. Thus, as stated before, Kalhaṇa's deliberate narrative style of alternately glorifying and denigrating the role of women not only stresses their instrumentality but also reflects the complex and ambiguous power equations involved in the construction of the institution of kingship in Kashmir.[1]

As a corollary to this, the *Nīlamatapurāṇa*, the treatise on the traditions of early Kashmir, provides, among other things, indications of the palpable presence of non-royal women.

Meanwhile, Dāmodaragupta's 'erotico-comic' *Kuṭṭanīmatam*[2] highlights the position and influence of prostitutes in the socio-political milieu of early Kashmir.

One should note here that an attempt will be made, wherever possible, to provide an idea of the many divergences made from the notions of kingly authority and other aspects in the Dharmaśāstras and similar texts.[3] Not only would this provide insights on the extent of subversion of supposedly hidebound norms, but would also show the benefit of studying royal power from texts other than prescriptive and didactic ones that has usually been the pattern.

THE DOMAIN OF WOMEN RULERS

At the outset, we should consider the title of Kalhaṇa's text, noting that the identity of the three women rulers of Kashmir discussed by him is subsumed within an aura of male dominance. The author explicitly states his work to be a *Rājataraṅgiṇī* or *River of Kings*. As he puts it:

> Imbibe, therefore, straight with the folds of your ear-shells, this 'River of Kings', which is rendered pleasant by under-currents of powerful sentiments (*RT*, I.24—*tad-mandara-sasyanda-sundareyaṁ nipīyatāṁ, śrotra-śuktipuṭaiha spaśta-maṅga rājataraṅgiṇī*).

Yet Kalhaṇa does not confine himself to the dictates of his title and provides crucial details on Yaśovatī (Gonanda dynasty), Sugandhā (Utpala dynasty, AD 904–6) and Diddā (Yaśaskara dynasty, 980/1–1003). The pivotal relevance of Kalhaṇa's details on them, and of this overall analysis, is highlighted by the dearth of meaningful information on female rulers and rulership in several primary and secondary works pertaining to early India.

It is important to note here that the three female rulers of Kashmir constitute a point of divergence from stipulated norms. A general survey of the Dharmaśāstra and epic literature shows a blatant hostility to the idea of female royal authority. Consequently, it merits only fleeting mentions in both these types of literature, in contrast with the extensive material on male rulership. The *Mahābhārata*, for instance, dismisses the possibility of female rulership in the following hard-hitting words—'The country where a woman, a child, or a gambler rules sinks helplessly as a stone raft in a river.'[4]

The *Majjhima Nikāya*, the *Arthaśāstra*, and the *Jātakas* detail the inherent limitations of a woman, so as to demonstrate her complete unsuitability for rulership and administration.[5] Somadeva's *Nītivākyāmṛtā* stipulates the order of royal succession: the son, full-brother, half-brother, uncle, a male of the same family, daughter's son or a stranger (who is elected or assumes the throne).[6] That women are excluded from the exercise of power is all too obvious. Although a tone of lukewarm dissent is provided by the Śāntiparva that authorizes the coronation of a vanquished ruler's daughter in the absence of suitable male candidates, this was rarely executed in practice.[7]

Significantly, the norms of the prescriptive literature are echoed in secondary books on Kashmir as well: most scholars have tended to gloss over the immense potential of the *Rājataraṅgiṇī's* details for a meaningful analysis of the exercise of royal power by women.[8] Alternatively, they attempt to mould these women into typical feminine stereotypes, thereby diluting their actual role and aspirations. Evidence of this will be integrated into the analysis and highlighted, wherever possible.

Yaśovatī

Prior to a discussion on Yaśovatī's reign, it may be relevant to note that the origin myths of Kashmir identify the land as Pārvatī's material manifestation and reiterate this in the context of the definition of its rulership. Great importance is attached not only to her and her manifestation, the river Vitasta, but also to the other goddesses who seem to have helped form the land of Kashmir on an equal, if not superior, plane to their male counterparts.[9] This has a dual significance. On the one hand, it brings the land, people and ruler into one organic whole.[10] On the other hand, it warrants an analysis of the link between goddesses and the position of women.[11] In some ways, the prominence accorded to the former in the legends of origin seems to be a precedent for, and reflector of, the gender relations in early Kashmir, and seems to set the tone for the acceptance of women rulers here.[12]

Yaśovatī's reign belongs to a very early period of Kashmir's history and is technically not within the stated time-span of this study. However, the definition and content of rulership in Kashmir is specified, both in the *Nīlamatapurāṇa* and the *Rājataraṅgiṇī*, as a part of a justification for her rule, thereby investing it with much significance. Hence it is necessary to make a brief survey of her reign.

Although Kalhaṇa deals with Yaśovatī in five verses alone, his account is more comprehensive than that of the *Nīlamatapurāṇa* from where he derives his information. Thus, this pregnant widow of Dāmodara I (of the Gonanda dynasty) is the third among the first four rulers of Kashmir. Krishna apparently justifies his crowning of Yaśovatī by underlining Kashmir's spiritual importance as Pārvatī's incarnation, and declaring its king to be a portion of Śiva, to be respected by all who desire prosperity.[13] Thus:

> Kaśmīr-land is Pārvatī: know that its king is a portion of Śiva. Though he be wicked, a wise man who desires (his own) prosperity, will not despise him (*RT*, I.72—*kaśmīrāha pārvatī tatra rājā gyeyo haran-śajaha, nāvagyeyaha sa duśtopi viduśā bhūtimicchtā*).

There are several important implications of this statement. Here a ruling queen, like a king, is considered to be a portion of Śiva and the entire land apparently represents his *śakti*, an exemplification of Pārvatī.[14] Thus, the rule of a woman is justified by the need to obey even a wicked king, or *any* other occupant of the throne.

The original verse from the *Nīlamatapurāṇa*, which forms part of Sage Bṛhadaśva's advice to King Gonanda (as retold by Sage Vaiśampāyana), reads,

> Desiring continuous welfare, you should regard the king of Kaśmīrā as born of a portion of Hara (Śiva) and never disobey him (*NP*, 246—*kaśmīrāyāṁ tayā rājā tvayā gyeyo harānśajaha, tasyāvagyā na kartavyā satataṁ bhūtimichhatā*).

Thus, Kalhaṇa's added stipulation of the need to obey even a wicked ruler is seen as a development of the theory of absolute monarchy.[15] This has obvious implications for the women rulers of Kashmir as well, in that their rule is justified under this comprehensive injunction that, additionally, bears a strong divine sanction. One can note an interesting parallel here with Rudramadevī, the fourth independent ruler of the Kākatīya dynasty of thirteenth-century Andhra, whose rule is sought to be justified by divine sanction in a contemporary text, the *Pratāparudrīya.* How else, says the text, could independent rulership reside in a feminine form unless with divine sanction?[16]

At the same time, a detailed description of Yaśovatī's reign is not forthcoming in either text. The paucity of details on her persona could be linked to the fact that her significance seems to lie in giving birth to the future heir, Gonanda II. Thus, the *Nīlamatapurāṇa* states:

> Out of respect for that country, Vāsudeva coronated his pregnant queen, so that the posthumous son might rule (*NP*, 8–9—*tataha sa vāsudevena suyuddhe vinipātitaha; antarvatnīṁ tasya patnīṁ vāsudevo bhyaśecayat, bhaviśyatputrarājyārtha tasya deśasya gauravāt*).

The *Rājataraṅgiṇī* echoes the same sentiment (*RT*, I.74), but states that Yaśovatī's coronation wrought a change in the male perception of women from a disrespectful equation of them with 'objects of enjoyment' to reverence for Yaśovatī as their 'mother' and a 'goddess' (*RT*, I.73). This precedent seems to set the tone for the acceptance of the other two women rulers of Kashmir.

Sugandhā

Sugandhā's rule is based on much firmer historical ground than that of Yaśovatī. The wife of Śaṁkaravarman (883–902), who accompanied him on a fatal military expedition near Uraśā, she is spared from becoming a *satī* on her husband's death, owing to the task of guardianship of the heir, Gopālavarman, that is thrust upon her (*RT*, V.220–2). After a brief period of regency, she ascended the throne and ruled for two years before her execution.

At the outset, after stressing her natal connections and Śaṁkaravarman's fascination for her (*RT*, V.157), Kalhaṇa hints at Sugandhā's importance in participating, passively or otherwise, in a dangerous military expedition and acquiescing in a bid to temporarily conceal the fact of Śaṁkaravarman's death for political reasons (*RT*, V.223–5). Subsequently, her affair with the minister

Prabhākaradeva apparently led her to bestow 'fortune, rank and love' upon him like a trio of adornments (*RT*, V.231). He is shown to deplete her treasury, to increase in arrogance after his victorious śāhī campaign, and to cause Gopālavarman's death by his malignant influence, thereby paving the way for Sugandhā's accession (*RT*, V.239–40).

Significantly, Sugandhā is shown to assume power at the behest of her subjects, thereby testifying to her popularity. As Kalhaṇa puts it:

> Thereupon, when King Śaṁkaravarman's lineage had died out, Sugandhā herself assumed the royal power at the bidding of the subjects (*RT*, V.243—*atha vaṅśakṣaye vṛtte rāgyaha śaṁkara-varmanaha, prajā-prārthanayā rājyaṁ sugandhā vidadhe svayaṁ*).

She maintained herself with the help of the ekāṅgas and tantrins for two years but her desire to crown her relative Nirjitavarman (a descendant of Śūravarman, Avantivarman's half-brother) on the throne is an ongoing quest, evidenced by her confabulations with various court factions to this end.[17] However, her preference was overruled by the courtiers who made Nirjitavarman's ten-year-old son, Pārtha (906–21), the new child-king. This apparently stemmed from their desire to spite Sugandhā and Prabhākara.

On this betrayal by her servants (*RT*, V.257), the grief-stricken Sugandhā left the palace. Her subsequent comeback bid (*RT*, V.259) was short-lived and resulted in her execution, prompting a speculation on the vagaries of fate by Kalhaṇa. 'After imprisoning her, they put her to death in the Niśpālaka vihāra. Strange are the ways of fate, ever falling and rising' (*RT*, V.262).

Kalhaṇa's portrayal of Sugandhā's rule is deliberately ambivalent, in keeping with his narrative style. On the one hand, he portrays her as a puppet used by various court factions to further their interests. Thus, not only did they combat her proposals for a new ruler and appoint one of their own choice, but the ekāṅgas also prevailed upon her to return as the ruler in their battle against the tantrins. On the other hand, Kalhaṇa provides unmistakable signs of her ambition and shrewdness, thereby stressing the need to consider carefully the implications of the narrative.

This ambiguous portrayal of Sugandhā, however, has been

misconstrued by most writers on Kashmir. This is nowhere more evident than in M.L. Kapur's endeavour to mould Sugandhā into a feminine stereotype of political ignorance, helplessness, and passivity. At the outset, he exonerates Sugandhā of any real desire for the throne, based on her seeming lack of political and administrative experience, and the rare mentions of her in Śaṁkaravarman's lifetime.[18]

The fact of Sugandhā accompanying her husband on the expedition, being privy to the concealment of his death and assuming power herself with the subjects' approval, militates against this notion. After all, there is no indication of her having been forced to assume power at any stage, even as a 'stop-gap arrangement'.[19] Besides, the fact that she maintained herself with the support of the ekāṅgas and the tantrins for a span of time indicates clear survival instincts, however transitory or unsuccessful.

Kapur himself talks of the quelling of the śāhī rebellion in Sugandhā's time and the cooperation of rival groups, thereby showing her to be a 'successful ruler' and a 'good diplomat'.[20] Besides, Kalhaṇa clearly states that she supported Nirjitavarman's candidature 'as he would follow her will' (*RT*, V.251–2—*anuvrato me saṁbhandi-snehā-devaṁ bhavediti, rājye nirjita-varmākhyaṁ kartuṁ tasyā manobhavat*). Kapur may insist that such a statement is not in consonance with her career and character as portrayed by Kalhaṇa himself, but the evidence points to Sugandhā's ambition to be a power.[21] Thus, she may have been 'simple, sincere and . . . of religious bent of mind . . .', but that she had 'no hunger for power' is open to doubt.[22]

In a similar vein, Kapur explains Prabhākara's presence as arising from the necessity of a strong male helping hand in the administration, in view of the new child-king and the untrained female regent. This necessity apparently brought Sugandhā and Prabhākara together, resulting in an 'unfortunate intimacy' that proved to be her 'Achilles' heel'.[23] However, Kalhaṇa categorically stresses Sugandhā's amorous feelings for Prabhākara and her being instrumental in his rising power (*RT*, V.230–2).

In addition, Kapur accuses Prabhākara of solely masterminding the murder of Gopālavarman. He precipitately concludes that since

Prabhākara is not heard of after Gopālavarman's death, he had probably fled to 'escape punishment for his treacherous conduct and faithlessness to his beloved'.[24] Yet the wording of the text does not allow one to wholly exonerate Sugandhā of complicity in the murder. The court's perception of them as a complicit duo is indicated in their crowning Pārtha to spite Sugandhā and Prabhākara.[25] Thus:

> They thought by the ousting of Sugandhā that they obtained revenge for the sayings of the treasurer injurious to their honour (*RT*, V.256—*te ganjā-dhipa-vākyānāṁ sugandhotpātanātkṛtaṁ, prāyaścittaṁ-manyanta mānakṣti-vidhāyinām*).

Moreover, Kalhaṇa's silence on Sugandhā's reaction to Gopāla-varman's death is pregnant with unspoken possibilities. By extension, if she were shattered by his death as Kapur seems to think, why would she have assumed power at all, the subjects' wishes notwithstanding?

Finally, Kapur attributes Sugandhā's comeback bid to her love for the people and invests her 'with a halo of martrydom'.[26] Thus, though she had 'retired from politics and loved peace', she apparently 'loved the people's welfare even more' and sought to free them from the tantrin misrule. However, Kalhaṇa nowhere indicates such a motive, thereby rendering Kapur's explanation an unconvincing one.

Besides, there is a contradiction in terms here. Kapur claims that Sugandhā did not oppose the rebellious tantrins during her reign, despite having the means to do so, thereby making her a 'democratic-minded queen' and showing that she was 'least interested in power'. If this were so, why would she feel an urge to quell the same tantrins at a later stage? It is more likely that her decision in this regard was based on a practical appraisal of the situation. By extension, if she was so burdened by royal power and politics as Kapur believes, why did she wish to assume power again? Her obvious reluctance to leave the palace the first time around is relevant in this context as implying a reluctance to abandon power.

Three factors highlight the overall importance of Sugandhā's reign. First, since Yaśovatī's reign and persona are not clearly fleshed out, Sugandhā's rule is the first concrete and historically verifiable one of a woman ruler in Kashmir's history. Second, her reign witnessed important landmarks such as the first royal execution,[27] and the arrival of the ekāṅgas and tantrins as a formidable force in politics. Finally, Sugandhā was indirectly responsible for an important dynastic change in subsequent years whereby Yaśaskara, the son of Prabhākara, who owed his prominence to association with Sugandhā, became the founder of a new dynasty in AD 948.[28]

It is interesting to note here that as popular ideology associated political authority with maleness, several women rulers often felt the need to adopt certain external attributes of male rulers to seek acceptance. For instance, rulers like Rudrama-devī adopted male attire and the title of 'king'.[29] Although Kalhaṇa does not indicate any deliberate effort at this sort of conformity on Sugandhā's part, it is interesting to note that her coins have the male appellation of *deva* rather than *devī* inscribed on them, i.e. *śrī sugandhā deva.*[30] Whether these reflected her orders or not is a matter for conjecture.

In conclusion, one should note the attitude of M.A. Stein (on whose edition and translation of the *Rājataraṅgiṇī* this work is based) towards the women rulers of early Kashmir. One cannot fail to notice the manner in which he has ignored the presence of these rulers in his 'Genealogical Tables of Kaśmīr Dynasties According to Kalhaṇa', which forms the concluding part of his lengthy 'Introduction'.[31] In the list of kings taken from the *Nīlamatapurāṇa* in Book I, Yaśovatī features only as the wife of Dāmodara I and not as an independent ruler. The table makes Gonanda II the successor of Dāmodara, which is incorrect. Similarly, Sugandhā features in the Tables of the Utpala dynasty (Book V) only as Śaṁkaravarman's wife and not as an independent ruler. The only two rulers mentioned after Śaṁkaravarman are Gopālavarman and Saṁkaṭa. Stein follows the same procedure in Diddā's case as well.

These glaring omissions are inexplicable in that Stein evaluates all three reigns in his exhaustive and well-researched 'Introduction'. His lapse brings alive the dangers of misinterpretation more clearly than ever. Thus, for instance, to a casual browser through the genealogical tables, who does not tackle the actual text of the *Rājataraṅgiṇī*, the female sovereigns would remain non-existent. This could lead to a very different and incorrect evaluation of the political milieu and of Kalhaṇa himself.

FEMALE AGENCY IN THE DOMAIN OF MALE RULERS

The power of women in the court culture can be examined under several categories. Although the power of queens was more palpable in the Diddā and post-Diddā period, the pre-Diddā period too was marked by the strong influence of courtesans and prostitutes on kings and thereby on politics.

Dynastic Foundation and Women

It is highly significant that four of the six dynastic founders, in early Kashmir, owed their prominence to their association with a woman or her family. These dynastic groups are the Kārkoṭa, the successors of Utpala, and of Yaśaskara, and the Lohara. This was an important deviation from norms established in the ancient Indian prescriptive and normative literature, such as the *Mahābhārata*,[32] Kauṭilya's *Arthaśāstra*[33] and the *Smṛtis* (of Manu, Nārada, and Yājñavalkya), regarding kingship and succession. As per the tenets, monarchy was divinely ordained, and hereditary rights acquired by birth and the law of primogeniture were paramount.[34] Yet there is a degree of contradiction within the tenets itself. Medhātithi, for instance, says that individuals who had the 'attributes of coronation, lordship and similar qualities' could also be considered for the royal title.[35] However, for Manu, the *rājā* was ideally to be a kṣatriya, versed in the Vedas.[36]

The seventh-century founder of the Kārkoṭa dynasty, Durlabhavardhana, was a lowly official in charge of horse fodder (*aśvaghaśakāyastha*) and son-in-law of King Bālāditya, the last scion of the Gonandiya dynasty. Bālāditya had no male heirs and, in fact, had chosen Durlabhavardhana for his daughter, Anaṅgalekhā, because of his low status, as he did not want the descendants of his daughter to acquire power. Thus:

. . . the king, who did not wish the sovereign power (to go) to the descendants of his daughter, endeavoured to defeat fate by human effort. Thinking that if she were given to someone not of royal blood, she would not carry away the sovereignty, he did not give the maid (in marriage) to any prince (*RT*, III.487–8—*sutā-santāna-sāmrājyamanichhannatha pārthivaha, daivaṁ puruṣakāreṇa jetumāsītkṛtodyamaha; arājānvayine dattā neyaṁ sāmrājya-hāriṇī, matveti pradadau kanyāṁ na kasmaicana bhūbhuje*).

Contrary to Bālāditya's scheme, however, Durlabhavardhana did succeed him and, interestingly, the *abhiṣeka* ceremony was performed by a minister, Khaṅkha, the former lover of Anaṅgalekhā! Thus, a lowly official became king by virtue of being married to a king's daughter.[37] Interestingly, Kalhaṇa regards this change, wrought by a commoner, as quite commonplace and talks in terms of one 'pure' family replacing another (*RT*, III.530).

The Utpala dynasty was founded in 853 by the descendants of Utpala, the brother of King Lalitāpīḍa's concubine, Jayādevī. Utpala and his four brothers, who were descendants of a spirit-distiller, used their sister's beauty to acquire power in the court of Kashmir by murdering the rightful heir, Cippaṭajayāpīḍa, around 813 or 814, and crowning a series of puppet rulers like Ajitāpīḍa and Anaṅgāpīḍa. Finally, Utpala's grandson, Avantivarman, with the help of the powerful minister, Śūravarman, took the throne.

The succeeding dynasty of Yaśaskara and his descendants was founded by Yaśaskara, the son of Prabhākaradeva (Queen Sugandhā's lover), in 948. Although he was an elected king, he clearly owed his prominence to this liaison. Obviously, a man of tribal origin (Kārkoṭa), a descendant of a spirit-distiller, a royal concubine's brother (Utpala), or a queen's lover's son (Yaśaskara) do not fit in with prescriptive eligibility considerations for kingship. There was a notable gap between theory and practice.

The final and, perhaps, most significant dynastic change was the handing over of the throne by the powerful Queen Diddā to her own family from Lohara, by her selection of her nephew, Saṁgrāmarāja (1003–28), as her heir, thereby leading to the foundation of the Lohara dynasty. This will be discussed in detail in the next chapter; here we may note that the Lohara dynasty ruled Kashmir until and beyond the date of the *Rājataraṅgiṇī's* completion, 1150. Interestingly, Kalhaṇa makes a statement of appreciation here that seems to encapsulate his attitude towards female associations in royal politics. As he puts it:

By association with women, this is the third wonderful change witnessed in the royal dynasties of this realm (*RT*, VI.366—*strī-saṁbandhena bhūpāla-vaṁśyānāṁ bhuvanādbhutaha, tṛtīyaha parivartoyaṁ vartatemutra maṇḍale*).

This is an obvious reference to the marriage of Durlabhavardhana and Anaṅgalekhā, the relation of Sugandhā with Prabhākara, and the association of the Lohara family with Diddā.

Here the word *strī-saṁbandhena* indicates an 'association or relationship with women' rather than 'relationship by marriage', which is how Stein translates it.[38] This affords a deeper meaning. Therefore, the second dynastic change could either pertain to Yaśaskara obtaining the throne due to his relation with Prabhākara, or to Utpala and his descendants assuming power on account of their association with Jayādevī. Note that Stein enumerates these changes as the marriage of Durlabhavardhana and Anaṅgalekhā, the relation of Nirjitavarman with Sugandhā that enabled the former's accession (and, therefore, an implied reference to the marriage of Sugandhā and Śaṁkaravarman) and the accession of Diddā's nephew, Saṁgrāmarāja of Lohara to the throne—and, therefore, an allusion to the marriage of King Kṣemagupta and Diddā. Thus, he sees Kalhaṇa's remark from the more conventional standpoint of marriage.

Interestingly, women are also shown to be agents of dynastic extinction—either directly or indirectly—in Kalhaṇa's text, in the pre-Diddā and Diddā/post-Diddā periods. This recalls the ancient orthodox literary strictures about women's potential for destruction. Thus, Kauṭilya's *Arthaśāstra* and Vaiśampāyana's *Kāmandakīya-nītisāra*, for instance, advise the king against fondness for women or reposing trust in them, if he wishes to retain his life and kingdom.[39] Both mention seven kings who died in their queen's chambers by the strategies of the latter. One can also note an interesting parallel with Bāṇa's *Harṣacarita* where women are portrayed as destroyers of men or lineage.[40]

Evidence of the latter comes in sequentially in Book IV of the *Rājataraṅgiṇī*. In the pre-Diddā period, King Candrāpīḍa (*c.* 712–20) was killed for his involvement in a brāhmaṇa woman's search for justice against her husband's murderer (*RT*, IV.112); and Cippaṭajayāpīḍa (813/14) was murdered by his ambitious maternal uncles (*RT*, IV.685–6). Gopālavarman (902–4) was murdered by his mother, Sugandhā's lover, Prabhākaradeva (*RT*, V.239–40). Cakravarman was murdered for his involvement with a low-caste śvapāka woman (*RT*, V.407–13). Yaśaskara's association with a courtesan, Lallā, eventually forced him to abdicate (*RT*, VI.84). Lastly, King Parvagupta's (949–50) death by dropsy was apparently prompted by the death of one of Yaśaskara's queens, whom he had desired (*RT*, VI.143).

Evidence of this theme in the later period will be examined in the next chapter, along with its overall implications. One should also note here that Kalhaṇa, in keeping with his usual ambivalence, heavily underscores the role of women as protectors and saviours as well. However, this is more apparent in the post-Diddā period, particularly in Books VII and VIII of the *Rājataraṅgiṇī*.

Courtesans, Prostitutes, and Women of Low Birth

The palpable presence of courtesans in the socio-political milieu is attested in Kalhaṇa's *Rājataraṅgiṇī*, in the *Nīlamatapurāṇa*, and in Ḍāmodaragupta's *Kuṭṭanīmatam*. It is important to note here that 'low' origin does not seem to stand in the way of such women becoming queens or exercising power. Kalhaṇa's hostility towards them is evident from his accounts of their actions and from other disapproving comments, but he charts their rise to power in minute detail. He thereby clearly indicates a discordance between the prescriptive sections of the *Rājataraṅgiṇī* and the possibilities of actual practice. It would be worthwhile to examine the evidence of each of these texts to identify points of corroboration, if any.

THE EVIDENCE OF THE *RĀJATARAṄGIṆĪ*

Kalhaṇa provides numerous instances of courtesans and low-caste women forming alliances with kings and asserting an influence on their royal lovers in various ways. However, his attitude towards them is marked by his characteristic ambiguity. Thus, on the one hand, he uses courtesans as a standard of unfavourable comparison, since he invariably demands a high standard of morality from rulers. He seems to indicate that when a king—who should ideally exercise control on all aspects of his life—surrenders to these women, destruction is imminent.

A striking example in this regard was King Lalitāpīḍa's palace, which came under the influence of courtesans and was avowedly defiled by immorality (*RT*, IV.661). Kalhaṇa uses the antecedents of Lalitāpīḍa's concubine, Jayādevī (of a spirit-distiller family), as an indictment of her and her kin (*RT*, IV.677–8). In fact, he feels that the limitations of a later king, Śaṁkaravarman (Sugandhā's husband), are due to his descent from this family. As he puts it:

Thus this (king), who did not speak the language of the Gods, but used vulgar speech fit for drunkards, showed that he was descended from a family of spirit-distillers (*RT*, V.206—*kalyapāla-kule janma tattenaiva pramāṇitaṁ, kṣīvocitāpabhraṁśokter-daivī vāgyasya nābhavat*).

Kalhaṇa shows that Jayādevī's beauty is used by her five brothers, Padma, Utpalaka, Kalyāṇa, Mamma and Dharma, to capture power and wield control over the infant-king, Cippaṭajayāpīḍa (*RT*, IV.680). Eventually, Utpala and his descendants established a new dynasty.

Kalhaṇa deals in a similar fashion with King Cakravarman whose 'wicked character' was brought to its zenith by his association with two girls of the 'lowly' ḍomba caste, Haṁsī and Nāgalatā (*RT*, V.360–86). Concerning her newly exalted status and that of her family, Kalhaṇa makes sarcastic remarks on 'this royal lover of a śvapāka woman' (*RT*, V.405) and gives exaggerated accounts of Haṁsī's degenerate habits. In fact, Cakravarman was eventually murdered by the ḍāmaras to curb the rising power of Haṁsī's relatives. Cakravarman was supposed to have raped a brāhmaṇa woman in order to purify himself of his association with Haṁsī (*RT*, V.400–2), which Kalhaṇa cites as further evidence of his depravity.

Similarly, in the beginning, Yaśaskara (939–48), Prabhākara's son, was apparently indifferent to women, but eventually came under the control of a courtesan, Lallā (*RT*, VI.73–4), who simultaneously had an affair with a cāṇḍāla watchman. Interestingly, knowledge of this affair prompted Yaśaskara to perform expiatory rites (*RT*, VI.82). Kalhaṇa is, once again, afforded an occasion to indulge in his contempt for such liaisons and their effects.

On the other hand, Kalhaṇa occasionally softens his stand towards such lowborn women. This is evident in his description of the alliance between King Jayāpīḍa (about AD 800) and a temple-dancer, Kamalā (*RT*, IV.424–70). Kamalā penetrated the exiled Jayāpīḍa's disguise, offered him shelter and was indirectly instrumental in his recovery of power. She later accompanied him as part of his harem. However, the political connections of the princess, Kalyāṇadevī, whom Jayāpīḍa subsequently married, were equally vital. Although Jayāpīḍa definitely shared a closer rapport with Kamalā, he made Kalyāṇadevī the chief chamberlain (*mahāpratihārapīḍa*) as part of his 'polite' kindness to her (*RT*, IV.485).[41]

Another significant alliance is that between King Durlabhaka-Pratāpāditya II (*c.* 650) and Narendraprabhā, a merchant's wife (*RT*, IV.17–30). There is much agonized speculation on the rightful conduct of a king, wherein Durlabhaka shows his awareness of the transgression of ethics involved in his coveting another's wife while he himself was the guardian of morality/ law (*RT*, IV.28–30). One should note here that Kalhaṇa points to Narendraprabhā's attraction for Durlabhaka but not in a condemnatory vein. Interestingly, the merchant, Noṇa, blatantly encouraged Durlabhaka, cited abandonment of restraint as a precedent, and eventually gave his wife to the 'reluctant' king (*RT*, IV.33, 37). This violates, for instance, the *Arthaśāstra's* norms for a *rājarṣi* (a wise king),[42] but Durlabhaka is projected in the same mould—as a just and model king, thereby indicating another point of divergence from stipulated norms.

Further evidence of this theme in the Diddā and post-Diddā period will be examined in the next chapter. However, an interesting observation can be cited at this juncture. Krishna Mohan talks of the Kashmiri kings marrying into lower castes for the purpose of encouraging a liberal policy in the administration.[43] This is open to debate, but the diverse origins of the queens, as revealed by Kalhaṇa, clearly indicate the various opportunities open to women in the hitherto male-defined realm of politics. Thus, dancing-girls like Kamalā or commoners like Narendraprabhā could aspire to become queens and then influence policy decisions.

THE EVIDENCE OF THE *NĪLAMATAPURĀNA*

Significantly, the *Nīlamatapurāṇa* corroborates Kalhaṇa's picture of the power wielded by courtesans, but does not decry or condemn this in any way. They are dealt with as an integral part of the composite society and are mentioned in connection with royal ceremonies, as well as with ordinary festivals. The *Kāmasūtra* says that a prostitute (*veśyā*) 'possessed of the requisite virtues, looks and qualities' obtains the title of *gaṇikā* (courtesan) in the assembly of the people (*janasaṁsad*), and is apparently 'worshipped and praised by the ruler and those who are qualified'.[44] The tone of the *Nīlamatapurāṇa* bears this out.

An important indicator of the socio-political status of courtesans is their participation in the king's coronation bath, as well as in annual anniversaries of this event 'in the same manner as in the beginning'.[45] Thus, 'the prominent courtesans, the prominent citizens, the outsiders and the chief of the gaṇas' are enjoined to go to the king's palace for the ceremony (*NP*, 845—*gantavyaṁ vāra-mukhyā-bhistathā rāja-niveśanaṁ, paura-mukhyaistathā brāhmairgaṇa-mukhyaistathaiva ca*). After his bath, the king was to be anointed with sacred water by 'the well-dressed people'—the brāhmaṇas, kṣatriyas, vaiśyas, chiefs of the śūdras, 'the leading courtesans and the merchants' (*NP*, 856–8).

The very equation of courtesans with prominent citizens and other pre-eminent categories speaks volumes for their influence/position and public acceptance of the same. By extension, they were, in all probability, recipients of royal largesse as enjoined in the text: the king was required to honour the subordinate kings 'and the leading citizens with wealth' (*NP*, 863–5).

The participation of courtesans in ordinary festivals as well is another significant feature. Thus, during the Śiva festival, for instance, 'sportive men' are instructed to spend the night with courtesans with, interestingly, 'the observance of the vow of celibacy' and with singing, dancing and music (*NP*, 581). Similarly, the celebration of the first snow includes the eating of special food, listening to music, and watching the dance of harlots (*NP*, 483-4). Ved Kumari feels that the stress laid on the singing and dancing of courtesans rather than on intercourse with them 'shows less moral laxity' among the people than shown in the works of Kalhaṇa, Kṣemendra and Somadeva.[46] This, however, is highly debatable.

Hence, obviously, the role of prostitutes in the socio-political milieu, as per the *Nīlamatapurāṇa*, was substantially contradictory to the stance of the Smṛtis and certain Purāṇas that forbid interaction with them and condemn them.[47] Although the author/s of this text is unknown, the depiction of prostitutes as an important component of society and the tone of acceptance thereof are highly significant.[48] Was this an accurate reflection of its milieu? If so, what were the factors that enabled the acceptance and inclusion of prostitutes in social and political activity on such a scale? By extension, if the *Nīlamatapurāṇa* reflects the attempt to combat Buddhism and restore Brahmanical practices in Kashmir, how does one reconcile the space accorded to prostitutes who are otherwise condemned in Brahmanical prescriptive works?[49] There is no definite answer but that this question can be posed is a noteworthy fact in itself.

THE EVIDENCE OF THE *KUṬṬANĪMATAM*[50]

Dāmodaragupta's *Kuṭṭanīmatam* reveals the status of prostitutes in an unwitting manner, as the author's intention is to stress their vices rather than their power.[51] At the outset, one should note the consistently condemnatory tone of the *Kuṭṭanīmatam* that distinguishes it from both the *Rājataraṅgiṇī* and the *Nīlamatapurāṇa*. Dāmodaragupta's object is to stress 'the vices of prostitution' by citing instances of persons, under fictitious names, who were ruined due to addiction to whores. Hence, his poem apparently serves the purpose of preventing people from being duped by parasites, courtesans, rogues, and procuresses (*KM*, 1059—*kāvyamidaṁ yaha sṛṇute samyak kāvyārtha-pālane-nāsau, no vañcayate kadācidvita-veśyā-dhūrta-kuṭṭanī-bhiriti*).[52]

Significantly, while A.M. Shastri acknowledges that 'the destinies of the people of Kashmir . . . lay with courtesans and concubines' to a large extent after Jayāpīḍa's reign,[53] he also discerns a parallel between one of the two main stories of the *Kuṭṭanīmatam* (that form the bulk of the text, 642 of the 1,059 verses) and the lives of Kings Jayāpīḍa and Lalitāpīḍa. These stories, that demonstrate the treacherous character and selfless love of a prostitute, respectively, are quoted by the procuress, Vikarālā, to illustrate her advice to the prostitute, Mālatī, on the process of ensnaring rich clients and usurping their wealth, which forms the core theme of the text.

Although these disconnected episodes are set in diverse locales without any specific reference to Kashmir and diverge considerably from the main narrative, it is possible to glean some relevant information on the general role of prostitutes.[54] Interestingly, Shastri points out that several personages are mentioned by name (albeit fictitious ones) in the text, to give a semblance of reality.

Vikarālā's aim is to convince Mālatī, through these stories, to view a client as a person to be stripped of wealth and then discarded. She draws interesting parallels with a fully-chewed mango that is then thrown out (*KM*, 733), or a fish whose flesh is eaten and its skin and bones cast away (*KM*, 735). Mālatī's target was Ciṅtāmaṇi, the son of an influential government officer, who was to be 'entangled' and pleased in every way.[55]

Thereafter, the story of the prostitute, Hāralatā, and the brāhmaṇa, Sundarasena, set in Pataliputra, was to be related by Mālatī to convince Ciṅtāmaṇi that her love was selfless and above pecuniary considerations (*KM*, 164–497), thereby lulling his suspicions. The story dealt with the intense love of the couple that was, however, thwarted by Sundarasena's father who recalls his son home. This resulted in the faithful Hāralatā's suicide and Sundarasena's transformation into an ascetic. It is interesting to note here that although Sundarasena wanted to burn himself on Hāralatā's funeral pyre, he overheard a verse 'dissuading him from such a cowardly act' (*KM*, 492) and became an ascetic instead. This highlights the different social standards for men and women.

Mālatī was then to capitalize on the effect of this story and completely strip Ciṅtāmaṇi of his wealth by various devious means (*KM*, 528–614). She was then to discard him by degrees—by ignoring him, praising his rivals, condemning him and so on.

(*KM*, 615–63). Thereafter, she was to woo another man, preferably an earlier conquest who had regained his wealth, and blame their separation on a villain's misunderstanding. This man was, inevitably, to be discarded again after *his* riches were exhausted.

The parallel drawn between the story of the dancing-girl, Mañjarī, and prince Samarabhaṭa (*KM*, 736–1056), and King Jayāpīḍa's alliance with the temple-dancer, Kamalā (cited earlier), is interesting.[56] Set in Varanasi, it revolves round the prince's meeting with Mañjarī through a dance-master who, incidentally, laments the deplorable condition of the fine arts of music/dance, as a result of the courtesans' greater interest in clients.

Thereafter, Mañjarī's initiative is reminiscent of Kamalā's act of boldly confronting King Jayāpīḍa, after an intelligent assessment of his royal blood, and offering him shelter and support. However, the fact that Kamalā's love was apparently genuine, whereas Mañjarī's was faked to appropriate the prince's wealth, constitutes the one major difference between these parallel stories. Vikarālā views Mañjarī's behaviour of using and deserting the prince as a worthy precedent for Mālatī, who, in turn, is convinced of the sense in the advice of the procuress.

Additionally, Shastri feels that the story of Samarabhaṭa is a veiled reference to King Lalitāpīḍa's debauchery (cited earlier).[57] He cites, as proof, Samarabhaṭa's view that the pleasure of Mañjarī's embrace makes a person forget his duties towards his subjects (*KM*, 1039). As Dāmodaragupta was in a position to appraise Lalitāpīḍa's functioning as well, this is quite a feasible theory and is, perhaps, an allusion to Jayādevī's influence on her royal lover, and the neglect of the administration. Additionally, there is the interesting fact of Samarabhaṭa's minister attempting to wean him away from Mañjarī by attracting him to the possibility of involvement with other people's wives.[58] The contradictory moral stance revealed here is noteworthy.

It is, perhaps, this portrayal of the supposedly cold-blooded reasoning of prostitutes that prompts Shastri to talk of the 'gravity of havoc that prostitution wrought in the history of Kashmir'.[59] He writes about Dāmodaragupta's disgust with the 'moral degradation' in Kashmir after Jayāpīḍa's demise and his desire to highlight it. Shastri also points to the condemnatory verses on prostitutes in the text (*KM*, 301–24, 411–24) and the claim that they were looked down upon by society (*KM*, 546), thereby providing a wholly divergent view from the *Nīlamatapurāṇa*, for instance.

However, Shastri's view does not take into consideration the actual potential of the *Kuṭṭanīmatam* (and the other two texts) in discerning the role of prostitutes in the contemporary milieu. He does not mention their extraordinary influence on politics revealed by Kalhaṇa or the *Nīlamatapurāṇa*, ignoring women except for the lament that public money was wasted on prostitutes.[60]

My intention is not to contest this fact but to draw attention to some singular evidence, in the *Kuṭṭanīmatam* itself, of the powerful position of prostitutes. Kumkum Roy asserts that the *Kāmasūtra* views the prostitute as being similar to the ruler, 'in that wealth was important for both'.[61] Although the *Arthaśāstra*, for instance, classifies the prostitute as a source of income, she was more probably a 'contender for resources'.[62] Roy also points out that while the *Kāmasūtra* prescribes what the prostitute ought to do with her wealth, such as funding 'good works', there is no reference to the payment of taxes or any state intervention in this respect.[63]

Thus, if one applies this reasoning in the *Kuṭṭanīmatam's* context, the very fact that prostitutes are shown making inroads into the wealth of royal and other influential ministerial clients is significant. The consequent repercussions on the administration and state finances are obvious.[64] It is interesting to note, in this regard, a verse that talks of the payment of the entire revenue of a village to a prostitute by a village chief (*KM*, 537).

The fact that prostitutes were often very cultured, articulate, and witty members of society indicates their training, education, and latent potential.[65] Thus, the fictitious Mañjarī's comprehensive curriculum included Vātsyāyana's *Kāmasūtra*, Bharata's *Nāṭya-śāstra*, Viśākhila's treatise on art, Dantila's writing, practical arts like woodwork, needlework, metalwork, and painting, music and dance (*KM*, 123–5). An accomplished prostitute, therefore, was a clearly attractive figure. Incidentally, the 'intellectual context' to a prostitute's formal training[66]—documented in a range of sources—contrasts with the limited knowledge available on education for other women. Was the prostitute more 'cultured' than royal women, for instance?

In conclusion, one can note an interesting imagery in the *Kuṭṭanīmatam* that indicates the potential power of a beautiful courtesan in that she could wipe out Śiva's existence, if she chose, by appearing before him and, thereafter, occupying his right half, the left already being reserved for Pārvatī (*KM*, 119).

NON-ROYAL WOMEN

Although the *Rājataraṅgiṇī* deals almost exclusively with royalty and court machinations, it provides significant instances of non-royal women exercising power and influence on courtly happenings, in a direct or indirect fashion, especially in the Diddā and post-Diddā period.[67] Nevertheless, the information of the *Nīlamatapurāṇa* proves particularly useful here as a corroborative source.

One of the most significant cases, in Kalhaṇa's text, of ordinary women influencing the court is that of the brāhmaṇa woman who sought justice from King Candrāpīḍa. In her quest for vengeance for her husband's murder by a sorcerer, this tough and determined individual admonished the vacillating king to confront the murderer, almost compelling him to propitiate the gods for a solution (*RT*, IV.83–5, 95–6). Her decision to undertake the *prāyopaveśa* (fast unto death) as her means of protest (*RT*, IV.82) is remarkable.[68]

Importantly, although Candrāpīḍa is later praised for rectifying this miscarriage of justice, it is actually the brāhmaṇa woman who conferred and confirmed the attributes of fairness associated with the king. This is another example of Kalhaṇa's usage of women as a standard for measuring the character of certain rulers. One can also note the irony inherent in Candrāpīḍa's involvement in this quest for justice in that he met his death at the hands of the same sorcerer at a later stage.

One can also consider the interesting case of the servant girls of King Unmattāvanti's harem (937–9) who procured a young boy from somewhere and falsely declared him to be the king's son.

Accordingly, the child, Śūravarman, was actually crowned the next king on Unmattāvanti's death (939), thereby affecting the course of royal politics (*RT*, V.445–8).

Kalhaṇa's indications of the potential power of non-royal women in the political sphere are corroborated, on a social level, by the *Nīlamatapurāṇa*. Ved Kumari states that the position of women as revealed by the *Nīlamatapurāṇa* is the 'most relieving feature of the family-life' of Kashmir.[69] She bases her claim on the absence of deprecatory stanzas on women, and the free movement they seem to have enjoyed, participating in almost all festivals and religious ceremonies along with men.

True, there are notable indications of the participation of both sexes, on an equal plane, in socio-political functions. For instance, the 'citizens' (*pauraiha*) are enjoined to participate in the king's coronation-bath ceremony (and its anniversaries) by being well-dressed and carrying auspicious things (*NP*, 854–5). In addition, 'all the subjects' are enjoined to see the king after he is bathed and decorated, with auspicious things in their hands (*NP*, 863–5). There is no specific gender connotation indicated here. Likewise, in the description of the annual pilgrimage to various temples, wherein the images are to be bathed amid sounds of song and dance 'of fortunate ladies' (*NP*, 886–7), reference is made to the active participation of 'citizens'. Thus:

> Thereafter, the citizens, with dances leading their procession, should bring the holy water for bathing the image, with great pomp and show (*NP*, 888—*tatorcā-snāpanasyārthaṁ paurairnṛtta-puraha-saraiha, ānītvyaṁ ca mahatā vibhavenodakaṁ śubhaṁ*).

Similarly, the festival to mark Kaśyapa's construction of Kashmir (*NP*, 465–6) is to be celebrated 'by all human beings' (*sarvamānavaiha*) and in the absence of any specifically contrary evidence, it would be reasonable to presume these terms/phrases to include both sexes.

As a corollary to this, there are interesting indications of the intermingling of both sexes at various levels. Thus, for instance, the worship of Nikumbha, the head of the *piśācas* (*NP*, 389–410), involves the eating of food 'in the company of friends, servants, wife, children' (*NP*, 407),[70] as does the worship of Kaśmīrā that involves eating with 'friends, wife and dependants' (*NP*, 567-8). The prescribed worship of goddess Śyāmā involves the wife, servants, and friends, to be followed by a festival of singing and dancing. Additionally, the full-moon night of *Mārgaśīrṣa* involves the presentation of a set of red clothes to 'the wife of a friend' among others (*NP*, 471–4).

That women could accept gifts from their husbands' friends, and dine and celebrate with them, argues a degree of freedom and liberality in society at obvious divergence from prescribed norms that dictated regulation of contact between the sexes. Not only are women shown enjoying themselves in indoor and outdoor festivals along with men, but they also participate in and perform certain rites. In the worship of Kaśmīrā, in fact, the preliminary rites are to be performed by women, 'by no means by men' (*NP*, 552). One can also consider the exclusive worship of the god Chandah by women, as per the stipulations of a boon apparently obtained by the former (*NP*, 569–70).

Significantly, stress is also laid on honouring maternal relatives and relatives by marriage. Thus, the celebration of *śukha suptika*, for instance, includes the stipulation to honour friends, 'relatives made by marriage' and 'the maternal relatives' with new clothes (*NP*, 420—*navaiśca vastrāiha pūjyāśca suhṛt-saṁbandhi-bāndhvāha* . . .). Another three-day festival enjoins the worship of a triad of brāhmaṇas, relatives by marriage, and maternal relatives (*NP*, 520).

The worship of women on various occasions is a notable refrain of the *Nīlamatapurāṇa* as, for instance, the injunction to worship the 'lucky ladies whose husbands are alive and who are devoted to their husbands', along with sisters and others (*NP*, 807–8). Similarly, on the full-moon night of *Mārgaśīrṣa*, women whose husbands and sons are alive are to be worshipped, along with the moon and the brāhmaṇas. In addition, a pair of red clothes is to be presented to a brāhmaṇa woman whose husband and sons are alive, as also to the father's sister (*NP*, 471–4). Once again, verses 511 to 514 enjoin the worship of women devoted to their husbands and those whose husbands are alive. One can also consider the *Irāmañjarī* festival that draws an interesting parallel between the worship of women and goddesses, and talks of women being honoured with gifts of *irā* flowers on the same plane as goddesses Durgā and Kārīṣiṇī (*NP*, 695–6, 699, 702).

The worship of women does not, however, necessarily indicate an exalted position for them. Roy notes that what is often overlooked is the context within which the statement is located and the forms of worship enjoined, 'the former explicitly domestic, a domesticity overlaid with patriarchal values'. The forms of worship include giving women ornaments, clothes, and food on festive occasions. Roy stresses that any claim to similarity with the worship of gods is superficial, if not fraudulent. Hence, the worship of women is not really an acknowledgement of their power.[71]

Equating women with goddesses is tantamount to denying them a status of normality of existence. This symbol of transcendence detracts from women's actual position in society. On the other hand, the stipulated precondition is that only married mothers of sons are to be worshipped: widows or single women are clearly proscribed categories—hardly an indication of the independent value of womanhood! Hence, female worship does not automatically imply an exalted social status for women.

The linkage of female worship with fertility is another related aspect, amply exemplified by the worship of goddess Kaśmīrā. Rites performed by women for the 'menstruating' Kaśmīrā are followed by the planting of the seed in the field, thereby drawing a connection between the pregnant Kaśmīrā and cultivation (*NP*, 549–68). In a similar vein are injunctions to unmarried girls to indulge in water sports on *śrāvaṇī* (*NP*, 741), the bathing of virgins and their decoration (*NP*, 785), and the worship of 'the ladies of the house' as part of the worship of Kāmadeva (the god of love), which involved the bathing of the wife by the husband (*NP*, 679–82).

Significant to gender parity, however, is the specific prescription of *śrāddha* days for men and women (*NP*, 485–6): equal weight accorded to each sex.[72] Likewise, there are repeated references to 'happy women—well-fed, well-dressed, well-scented, well-anointed and decorated with ornaments' (*NP*, 548) to be 'pleased' on particular days (*NP*, 557), playing in the company of men (*NP*, 402–6), or being honoured on the day of the first snow (*NP*, 483–4). These injunctions form part of the 'good customs' laid down by Nīla, the head of the *nāgas*, for the acquisition of prosperity and peace by the people of Kashmir (*NP*, 225, 900–1). Hence, the enjoining of respect to women and their participation in contemporary affairs here is highly significant.

Clearly, ambiguous signals of the agency of non-royal women can be recovered from the *Nīlamatapurāṇa*. On the one hand, there are indications that their position may not have been so remarkably exalted, as Ved Kumari, for instance, seems to think. And yet, on the other hand, the perception of women as participants stresses their importance to the contemporary socio-political milieu, thereby corroborating the *Rājataraṅgiṇī's* evidence.

Was the space accorded to women a reflection of reality, or was it merely a desired state of affairs? By extension, could this be a reflection of the unknown author's liberality, or was the palpable presence of women an integral aspect of early Kashmir? If the latter, then could this have laid the ground for the assumption of formal and informal power by various categories of women during subsequent ages in Kashmir? There are no clear answers.

BUILDING ACTIVITIES AND PATTERNS OF DONATION

The *Rājataraṅgiṇī* makes profuse references to building activities and to donations. They have two broad implications. On the one hand, they bear testimony to a well-documented sphere of female participation in public life. On the other hand, building activities have differential implications for both men and women. The information in this regard is spread evenly over the pre-Diddā and Diddā/post-Diddā sections, and needs to be considered in conjunction for a fuller understanding. However, before embarking on an analysis of the pre-Diddā period which is the ambit of this chapter, it would be worthwhile to outline some of the common features of this theme that can be discerned in both phases.

First, building activity, in the text, seems to reflect the traditionally idealized image of both sexes: men being largely associated with power, aggression, and glory, and women with piety, purity, and nobility. However, although Kalhaṇa imputes differential motives and associations to the buildings of both sexes, there is a great deal of ambiguity in his treatment. He avoids compartmentalization. Second, royal and non-royal people of both sexes erect the same kind of structures: towns, *maṭhas*, *vihāras*, *agrahāras*, and public welfare works like tanks, canals, and gardens. Thus, though the Anuśāsanaparva of the *Mahābhārata*, for instance, limits the construction of meeting-halls, tanks, temples, and lodging places (for brāhmaṇas) to good kings, this does not seem to have remained an exclusive royal or male prerogative in practice.[73]

Third, the patterns of donation of both sexes—of the royal and non-royal strata—are aligned along broadly similar lines, mostly, in the *Rājataraṅgiṇī*, in the purview of *dāna*, or the act of giving, bestowing or granting—irrespective of the nature of the gift—as a means of atonement and for the acquisition of spiritual merit or personal welfare.[74] However, there are many buildings that are prompted by other motives as well and thereby fall outside this category.

Obviously, the buildings reflect the religious and personal proclivities of the donor in question. The importance attached to religious merit finds expression in a superabundance of temples, shrines, and godly images, with a clear bias towards Śiva rather than Viṣṇu.[75] The profusion of *vihāras*, on the other hand, bears testimony to the undoubted significance of Buddhist donations. In this context, Romila Thapar's view that more women seem to donate in the Buddhist cause than any other is borne out by the fact that *vihāras* are erected by thirteen of the thirty-four women builders in the text.[76]

Building Activities of Kings

Despite the varying percentage of royal attention to building activities, there is a common pattern of motives and associations governing this endeavour. Kalhaṇa shows most male rulers building to concretize and affirm their power and glory, to assert their munificence, and to validate their political power.[77] To this end, he invariably describes their building activities on the heels of victorious battles.

The most illustrious example is that of Lalitāditya Muktāpīḍa whose 'flaming glory' (*RT*, IV.132) and 'shining majesty' (*RT*, IV.159) evoked his wide-ranging conquests, and were concretized immediately in his efforts to make 'the earth golden' by his buildings (*RT*, IV.217).[78] Thus:

There is no town, no village, no river, no sea and no island where he did not consecrate a shrine (*RT*, IV.181—*na tat-puraṁ na sa grāmo na sā sindhurna sorṇavaha, na sa dvīposti yatrāsau pratiṣṭāṁ na vinirmame*).

Some of his creations clearly symbolized military success and political power, as in his building the town of Suniścitapura when he 'had resolved upon the conquest of the world' (*RT*, IV.183), or the building of a town at Lokapuṇya after a victory. As Kalhaṇa puts it:

After constructing at Lokapuṇya a town, which was provided with the requisite accessories, the victorious (king) made it, together with villages, an offering to Viṣṇu (*RT*, IV.193—*loka-puṇye puraṁ kṛtvā nānopakaraṇāvalīṁ, pratipāditavānjiṣṇur-grāmaiha sākaṁ sa viṣṇave*).

However, Lalitāditya was equally prompted by whimsical reasons: he built Darpitapura while 'feeling proud', the Krīḍārāma *vihāra* while at play, and Phalapura while receiving fruit (*RT*, IV.183–4).

In addition, the colossal grandeur of Lalitāditya's buildings is often stressed to magnify his might.[79] This is clear, for instance, in the town of Parihāsapura that he built in a light mood:

Then again that Indra of the earth, when given to merry jesting (parihāsa), built the town of Parihāsapura, which mocked the residence of Indra (*RT*, IV.194—*tataha paraṁ parīhāsa-śīlo bhūloka-vāsavaha, vihasa-dvāsavāvāsaṁ parihāsa-puraṁ vyadhāt*).

One can also consider the following evocative verse:

That liberal (king) built the wonderful (shrine) of Mārtaṇḍa, with its massive walls of stone within a lofty enclosure, and its town swelling with grapes (*RT*, IV.192—*sokhaṇḍitāśma-prākāraṁ prāsādāntara-vyadhatta ca, mārtaṇḍasyādbhutaṁ dātā drākṣā-sphītaṁ ca pattanaṁ*).

Likewise:

With just as many thousands of Prasthas of copper he made the glorious (statue of) the 'Great Buddha' which reached up to the sky (*RT*, IV.203—*rīti-prastha-sahastraistu tena tāvadbhireva saḥ, vyoma-vyāpi-vapuḥ śrīman-bṛhaddha-buddho vyadhīyata*).

In a similar vein, King Śaṁkaravarman, Sugandhā's husband, built the town of Śaṁkarapura after victory in war:

When, after thus effecting the conquest of (all) regions, he returned to his own land, he built in a locality called Pañcasatra a town (called Śaṁkarapura) after his own name (*RT*, V.156—*evaṁ dig-vijayaṁ kṛtvā prāptaha sa nija-maṇḍalaṁ, pradeśe pañca-satrākhye svanāmnā vidadhe puraṁ*).

At this juncture, one can cite an interesting parallel with the *Nīlamatapurāṇa*. During the formation of Kashmir, Brahmā, Viṣṇu and Śiva gave their names to various mountain peaks and, along with 'other gods', built hermitages to exemplify their victory over the demon, Jalodbhava. Subsequently, Viṣṇu made a statue of Śiva as a 'gift' in return for the *sudarśana cakra* that Śiva had seized as a prank, and to exemplify the fact that they had joked about it (*NP*, 199–200).[80] This is reminiscent of Lalitāditya's buildings that reflected his various moods and fancies.

Although Kalhaṇa glorifies these male builders for their aggression, he also provides instances of royalty enshrining their piety and charity in buildings. The buildings of King Avantivarman's stepbrother, Śūravarman, for instance, fell into this category. As Kalhaṇa puts it:

He (Śūravarman), who was accomplished, full of (spiritual) greatness and devoted to pious works, granted the (Agrahāra) of Pañcahasta and built a Maṭha, which was an abode of divine greatness (*RT*, V.24—*sampūrṇaha pūrṇa-mahimā-martya-māhātmya-mandiraṁ, pañca-hastā-pradasracakre maṭaṁ sukṛta-karmaṭaha*).

However, these cases were fewer in number and, even here, the aura of power predominated in the frequent donations of *agrahāras* and *maṭhas* to the brāhmaṇas and the people, as an exemplification of the king scattering his largesse among them.

Building Activities of Female Rulers and Queens

This topic has not always received due recognition. For instance, M.L. Kapur dismisses the buildings of Lalitāditya's wives in one sentence, and his reference to the 'magnitude and grandeur' of the building activity in Lalitāditya's reign obviously pertains to the king's buildings, which he praises expansively, and not that of his queens.[81]

In complete contrast to the motives governing the building activities of kings, women rulers and queens apparently built largely to symbolize their piety and nobility, or as an act of atonement. Of the female rulers in the pre-Diddā period, only Sugandhā is shown to build on any scale. It is interesting to note here that Kalhaṇa deliberately attributes religious overtones to her buildings. For instance, the town she built in her name after assuming power was apparently prompted by a religious motive and not by a desire to assert her strength. Thus:

> She built (the town of) Gopālapura, the Gopālamaṭha, the (temple of Viṣṇu) Gopālakeśava, and also a town called after her own name, for the increase of religion (*RT*, V.244—*gopāla-pura-gopāla-maṭa-gopāla-keśavān, sā puraṁ ca svanāmāṅkaṁ vidadhe dharma-vṛddhye*).

In a similar vein, Kapur invests Sugandhā's buildings with an aura of grief and remorse, whereby she apparently 'tried to console herself' after her son, Gopālavarman's death, by 'laying out some foundations'.[82] However, she might have been attempting to make a political statement, in the manner of new rulers.

In the case of queens, Kalhaṇa talks of sin-atonement, piety, and charity as the motives that governed their building activities. In this context, one could cite George W. Spencer's view that the 'pious philanthropy' of queens was intended to project them as dhārmic figures. In this way, they apparently reinforced the image of the kingdom as a moral order.[83]

Thus, for instance, Queen Anaṅgalekhā (Durlabhavardhana's wife) built the Anaṅgabhavana *vihāra* to show her redeemed character and to indicate that her adulterous ways were now behind her (*RT*, IV.3). Similarly, Narendraprabhā atoned for her conduct in luring and marrying Durlabhaka Pratāpāditya II (cited earlier) by building a shrine. As Kalhaṇa puts it:

Removing the levity of such conduct by noble works, Queen Narendra-(prabhā) built the illustrious (shrine of) Nareṇdreśvara (*RT*, IV.38—*kṛtyai-rūdāttaiha sāpāstatādṛk-cāritra-lāghavā, narendra-mahiṣī cakre śrī-narendreśvaraṁ haraṁ*).

Charity was another strong motive underlying the building activities of queens. For instance, Īśānadevī (Lalitāditya's wife) constructed a well:

His wife Īśānadevī constructed a well, the water of which was pure as nectar and gave health to the ailing (*RT*, IV.212—*īśāna-devyā tat-patnyā khātāmbu pratipāditaṁ, sudhāra-samiva svachham-ārogyā-ḍhāyi rogiṇāṁ*).

By extension, one should note the automatic attribution of nobility to the buildings of queens in the text, an example being the Prakāśavihāra of Prakāśadevī (Candrāpīḍa's wife) which symbolized her nobility and brightness (*RT*, IV.79).

In addition, Kalhaṇa gives interesting instances of royal women enabling their male associates to valorize their strength and influence through their buildings. Jayādevī's five brothers (Utpala and others) built to monumentalize the power they had gained through their sister's influence on Lalitāpīḍa. Incidentally, Kalhaṇa is quite generous with his praise here despite his dislike of this family.[84] He says:

By the side of the temples which they built, the other shrines appeared (small), like young elephants by the side of the elephants of the quarters (*RT*, IV.702—*kṛtā deva-gṛhāstairye tat-pārsvenya-surāspadaiha, diṅgā-taṅga-samīpastha-kalabhopamyamāsritaṁ*).

Yet Kalhaṇa is ambiguous. Although he largely associates piety and humility with female builders, either as a deliberate stereotypical stance or as a portrayal of public perception, he hints at several other motives besides these. For instance, he shows the attempt of certain queens to perpetuate their own names through their foundations, in a manner reminiscent of most male rulers. A stellar example is that of Cakramardikā (Lalitāditya's wife) who built the town of Cakrapura with 7,000 dwellings (*RT*, IV.213). Similarly, Kalyāṇadevī and Kamalā (Jayāpīḍa's wives) eṣtablished towns in their names—Kalyāṇapura (*RT*, IV.483) and Kamalāpura (*RT*, IV.484), respectively.[85] Likewise, Kamalavatī, another wife of Lalitāditya, built the Kamalāhaṭṭa (IV.208).

Even in the case of Sugandhā, Kalhaṇa does not clarify that her motive in building the Gopālapura town, the Gopālamaṭha and the Gopālakeśava temple was to enhance the glory of her dead son, Gopālavarman. By extension, the extremely contrived attribution of a religious motive to her buildings again recalls Kalhaṇa's ambiguity and raises the possibility of her having built on this scale to establish her power and presence.

Building Activities of Non-Royal Men and Women

There are numerous examples, in the *Rājataraṅgiṇī*, of ministers, merchants, and engineers engaged in building activities and making foundations in their own right. In a fashion reminiscent of their royal employers, and perhaps as a reflection of the formers' glory, ministers also built to monumentalize their power and influence. An illustrative example was that of Ratna (Utpalāpīḍa's minister), who built the Ratnasvāmin temple as a symbol of his power. Thus:

> Ratna, the king's minister of foreign affairs, possessed power (and was able), to erect even at that time the temple of (Viṣṇu) Ratnasvāmin (*RT*, IV.711—*sāṁdhi-vigrahikas-tasya ratno nāma vibhūtibhāk, tasmin-kālepi yaścakre ratna-svāmi-surāspadaṁ*).

Likewise, Śaṁkaravarman's minister, Ratnavardhana, built the Ratnavardhaneśa temple:

> The minister Ratnavardhana, who had secured the crown for the king, built the glorious (temple of) Sadāśiva, called Ratnavardhaneśa (*RT*, V.163—*rājya-pradena nṛpate ratna-vardhana-mantṛṇā. śrīratna-vardhane-śākhyo vyadhīyata sadā-śivaha*).

By extension, the buildings of non-royal men are described in an almost parallel fashion with those of kings. An example of this in the pre-Diddā phase was the engineer, Suyya's town. Kalhaṇa says:

On the bank of the Vitastā, where she leaves the waters of the Mahāpadmā (lake), he built a town resembling heaven, which bore his own name (*RT*, V.118—*nirgatāyā mahā-padma-salilāt-svarga-samnibhaṁ, vitastāyāstate cakre svanāmāṅkaṁ sa pattanaṁ*).

However, as in the other cases, Kalhaṇa's ambiguity is displayed here, too. For instance, piety is shown as motivating the building of the Noṇamaṭha by the merchant, Noṇa (Narendraprabhā's first husband). Thus:

That virtuous man built the Noṇamaṭha, most eminent for its religious merit, for the accommodation of Brāhmaṇs born in the Rauhīta land (*RT*, IV.12—*rauhīta-deśe jātānāṁ niveśāya dvijanmanāṁ, maha-guṇo noṇa-maṭaṁ puṇya-jyeṣṭam cakāra saha*).

Furthermore, significantly, Suyya named a stone dyke Suyyāsetu, after his mother, Suyyā, thereby displaying the trend of building in a woman's name (more frequent in the post-Diddā phase). Thus:

After bestowing on Brāhmaṇs the village called Suyyākuṇḍala, in honour of (his mother) Suyyā, he constructed the (dyke called) after her name, Suyyāsetu (*RT*, V.120—*suyyā-kuṇḍala-nāmānaṁ grāmaṁ kṛtvā dvijātisāt, suyyāmuddiśya tannāmnā suyyā-setuṁ sa nirmame*).[86]

However, one should note that such trends did not always conform to particular patterns, unlike the definitive patterns of royal male endowments.

Similar evidence for non-royal women was largely concentrated in the Diddā and post-Diddā phase and will, therefore, be considered in the next chapter, but there is one instance belonging to the pre-Diddā phase. The courtesan, Sāmbavatī (King Pārtha's mistress), built the Sāmbeśvara shrine.

The courtesan Sāmbavatī, a mistress of Pārtha, who was known for the skilful plotting by which she conciliated the bands of Tantrins, founded the (shrine of Śiva) Sāmbeśvara (*RT*, V.296—*abhūt-sāmbavatī veśyā sāmbeśvara-vidhāyinī, pārtha-priyā tantri-cakra-saṁgrahe gyāta-cakrikā*).

The indication of Sāmbavatī's power and prowess in the political scenario that obviously translated into her desire to concretize it is very significant.

As stated at the outset, the potential relevance of the details of the building activities in the *Rājataraṅgiṇī* can be fully appreciated only by a comprehensive analysis of both pre-Diddā and Diddā/post-Diddā phases. However, irrespective of whether the differential implications are real or constructed, one can note the crucial importance of this activity in depicting women's active involvement in religious and secular activity. The final implications of this theme will be considered in detail in the next chapter.

As a concluding reiteration, the presence and agency of women—encompassing royal and non-royal spheres—was forceful in the society and polity of early medieval Kashmir. All the three texts that have been used for this analysis corroborate each other in this regard. Thus, women are shown to exercise much influence and pressure not only in a formal sense but also by association, thus stressing a divergence from traditional gender equations.

As stated earlier, one needs to appreciate the authorial stance behind these literary sources. Whether it is Kalhaṇa who chooses to reveal the public and unspoken agency of women, or the unknown author/s of the *Nīlamatapurāṇa* who stresses the role and status of non-royal women, or Dāmodaragupta who unintentionally highlights the prostitute's power—all work towards the same end of providing a significant gendered perspective on the society and polity of early medieval Kashmir.[87]

However, the need for appreciating the potential of these sources is a crucial one. Ved Kumari's views are illustrative. She contrasts the 'pleasant picture' of the women of Kashmir in the *Nīlamatapurāṇa* with the accounts of other Purāṇas where they are generally despised and deprecated 'as seducers of men'. She thereby points to the 'somewhat different and unconventional picture' of female life in this text, which is corroborated by other Kashmiri writers such as Kalhaṇa, Bilhaṇa, and Dāmodaragupta.[88]

At the same time, to cite one instance, Ved Kumari does not subject Yaśovatī's rule to the analysis it deserves.[89] Her role is mentioned in passing at the conclusion of a discussion on 'Women in the Family', as a part of the 'Position of Women' in the chapter on 'Social and Economic Organization'. Yaśovatī does not merit mention in Kumarī's discussion of the 'King and his Functions', despite the fact of her being the first woman ruler in Kashmir. She is mentioned, inexplicably, in the 'Army and War' section as showing that a 'childless pregnant widow-queen' was allowed to occupy the throne.

In addition, Ved Kumari does not refer to Yaśovatī by name, preferring to use appellations like the above instead. She is as guilty of minimizing the potential of the *Nīlamatapurāṇa* for a gender analysis as Stein is for ignoring the presence of the women rulers of early Kashmir in his genealogical tables. The analysis of the Diddā and post-Diddā phase, in the next chapter, will highlight similar lapses that minimize the actual contribution of women evident in the relevant sources.

NOTES

1. Thus, the same women who handle the kingdom, advise the king, deal with rebels and formalize their rule are compared to the wind, to items of possession and to creepers that evoke, in turn, a strong aura of dependence and weakness. In addition, their emotional outbursts and actions belie much of their idealized descriptions and intentionally so. For instance, Sally J.M. Sutherland, 'Sītā and Draupadī: Aggressive Behaviour and Female Role-Models in the Sanskrit Epics', *Journal of the American Oriental Society*, 109.1, 1989, p. 71, talks of the epic poet's attempt to render the multivalence of characters more dramatic by repeated juxtaposition of Sītā's emotional outbursts against stereotyped descriptions of her as an ideal woman and queen. Note that Kalhaṇa uses dichotomous images of women very effectively. They are alternately malevolent and benevolent, powerful and weak.
2. A.M. Shastri, *India as Seen in the Kuṭṭanīmata of Dāmodaragupta*, Delhi, Motilal Banarsidass: 1975, p. 35, cites this view of S.K. De, *A History of Sanskrit Literature*, p. 197.
3. Some of the texts cited in the course of this thesis include Kauṭilya's *Arthaśāstra* (fourth/third century BC-second century AD), the *Manusmṛti* (second century BC-second/ fourth century AD), Vātsyāyana's *Kāmasūtra* (second–fourth century AD), the *Rāmāyaṇa* and the *Mahābhārata*. Although the epics are not strictly prescriptive in nature, their norms represented social ideals. Tuvia Gelblum, 'Classical Hindu Scriptures', in *Institutions and Idealogies*, ed. David Arnold and Peter Robb, Richmond, Curzon Press: 1993, pp. 38–9 for a discussion on the content of the Dharmaśāstra and *Smṛti*, as also the ethico-religious status of certain texts.

4. Cynthia Talbot, 'Rudrama-devī, the Female King: Gender and Political Authority in Medieval India', in *Syllables of Sky: Studies in South Indian Civilization in Honour of Velcheru Narayana Rao*, ed. David Shulman, Delhi, Oxford University Press: 1995, p. 391. The line is from the *Mahābhārata*—5.40. It reads, *yatra strī yatra kitvo bālo yatrānuśāsitā, majjanti tevaśā rājānnadyāmaśmaplava iva* (J.A.B. van Buitenen, tr., *The Mahābhārata: IV* and *V*, Chicago, University of Chicago Press: 1978).
5. A.S. Altekar, *State and Government in Ancient India*, 3rd edn, Delhi, Motilal Banarsidass: 1958, p. 87; A.K. Majumdar, *Concise History of Ancient India*, Delhi, Munshiram Manoharlal: 1980, 2, p. 55. The *Majjhima Nikāya* says, *duṭṭaṁ taṁ janapadaṁ yathā ithi parināyikā, anāvakāśaṁ yamithī rājā asma cakkavartī* (III, 65–6). A.S. Altekar, *The Position of Women in Hindu Civilization*, 2nd edn, Delhi, Motilal Banarsidass: 1959, pp. 185–6 talks of a proposal, in the *Rāmāyaṇa*, to offer the crown to Sītā consequent on Rāma's exile that, however, did not materialize owing to her decision to accompany Rāma. Altekar clarifies that the school opposing this represented the general opinion of society.
6. P.V. Kane, *History of Dharmaśāstra*, Poona, Bhandarkar Oriental Research Institute: 1946, vol. III, p. 249 for details.
7. Ibid., p. 40, Śāntiparva 33.43–6.
8. P.N.K. Bamzai and S.C. Ray are some of these scholars whose works will be discussed in the course of this section. P.N.K. Bamzai, *Culture and Political History of Kashmir, 1—Ancient Kashmir*, Delhi, MD Publications: 1994; S.C. Ray, *Early History and Culture of Kashmir*, 2nd revd edn, Delhi, Munshiram Manoharlal: 1970.
9. In fact, the text has the additional title of *Vitastā Māhātmya* (*NP*, 1453). See *NP*, 12 where Krishna claims that 'the goddess Umā is the same as Kaśmīrā' (*yaiva devī umā saiva kaśmīrā*). For the Vitastā's importance, *NP*, 26, 237–8, 1423–53. The text also provides instances of Pārvatī's importance, her arrogance, her rivalry with Lakṣmī and the formation of other rivers by the goddesses. Information is also provided on the mounts used by various goddesses and, interestingly, Mandākinī's use of man for this purpose (*NP*, 161). Could this imply the superiority of females over males and, by extension, the possibility of reversing traditional gender equations in actual life?
10. B.K. Kaul Deambi, *Corpus of Śāradā Inscriptions of Kashmir*, Delhi, Agam Kala Prakashan: 1982, p. 302. Note that the Brahmanic section of Kashmiri society worshipped *Ardhanārīśvara*, representing Śiva in union with Pārvatī (*Śakti*) (p. 294). In fact, Kalhaṇa invokes this deity at the beginning of each of his eight books, seemingly an indication of the weight accorded to both sexes in his work. J.N. Banerjea, *The Development of Hindu Iconography*, Calcutta, University of Calcutta:

1956, pp. 181, 465 for a description of this form. Samjukta Gombrich Gupta, 'The Goddess, Women, and Their Rituals in Hinduism', in *Faces of the Feminine in Ancient, Medieval, and Modern India*, ed. Mandakranta Bose, New Delhi, Oxford University Press: 2000, pp. 93, 95, says that *śakti*, the feminine principle, represents sovereign divine authority and the concepts of 'power, potency and potentiality' are all present in it.

11. Ved Kumari, *The Nīlamata Purāṇa*, Srinagar, J&K Academy of Art, Culture and Languages: 1968, vol. I, p. 93 points to the prominence of goddesses in the religion depicted in the text as yet another indicator of the high position of women in early Kashmir. Kathryn Hansen, 'The *Vīrāṅganā* in North Indian History—Myth and Popular Culture', in *Ideas, Images, and Real Lives: Women in Literature and History*, ed. Alice Thorner and M.K. Raj, Mumbai, Orient Longman: 2000, p. 260, quotes Joanna Liddle and Rama Joshi as connecting goddess worship with a strong self-image of women. It apparently represents 'the acknowledgement of women's power by women and men in the culture', empowering women to act in a strong and assertive manner (*Daughters of Independence: Gender, Caste and Class in India*, London, 1986, pp. 55–6). Hansen also raises questions on whether the goddess served to enhance women's status, or whether these goddess cults reflected women's experience and self-perceptions. However, she notes that the power of the goddess is 'often subverted or leashed' by subordination to a male deity (p. 259).
12. Gerda Lerner, *The Creation of Patriarchy*, New York, Oxford University Press: 1986, p. 145 cites anthropologist Peggy Reeves Sanday that gender symbolism in creation stories proves a valuable guide to sex roles and sexual identities in a given society. This is clearly applicable in the case of Kashmir.
13. M.A. Stein, tr., *Kalhaṇa's Rājataraṅgiṇī*, 3rd rpt., Delhi, Motilal Banarsidass: 1989, vol. I, p. 14. The verse is not found in this form in the present text of the *Nīlamata*. It can, however, be seen as a reference to *NP*, 246. See also *NP*, 12–13 where it is indicated that Umā is the same as Kaśmīrā.
14. Krishna Mohan, *Early Medieval History of Kashmir*, Delhi, Meherchand Lachhmandas: 1981, p. 73—the word *duśtopi* seemingly refers to 'the irregularity of succession' and the attempt to justify a woman's accession. Kingship is not divinely ordained but the divinity (*Ardhanārīśvara*) is personified in the form of the king (p. 296). She also talks of the kings of Kashmir wearing crowns with three circles (*cakra-traya*) and a seventh-century sculpture of Pārvatī with a crown of three 'crescents'. Images of Viṣṇu wear the crown but there are no such images of Śiva. She recalls the importance of Viṣṇu as a form of the *śakti* of Śiva, as per Kashmir Śaivite theology, and says that the crowns are to be regarded as implying that the ruler is a manifestation of Śiva (pp. 85–6).
15. Kumari, *Nīlamata Purāṇa*, I, p. 132.

16. Talbot, 'Rudrama-devī', in *Syllables of Sky*, ed. Shulman, p. 401.
17. Stein, *Rājataraṅgiṇī*, 'Introduction', I, pp. 219–20, nn. 248, 249. The ekāṅgas were royal bodyguards or a body organized in military fashion and employed for police duties. The tantrins were a military caste of unknown origin and strong organization, serving mainly as foot soldiers. Note that Nirjitavarman ruled between 921 and 923.
18. M.L. Kapur, *Eminent Rulers of Ancient Kashmir*, Delhi, Oriental Publishers: 1975, p. 62.
19. M.L. Kapur, *The History and Culture of Kashmir*, 2nd edn, Delhi, Anmol Publications: 1992, p. 43. He says Sugandhā 'did not aspire to rule'. Her 'stop-gap' assumption of power was apparently because she wanted to crown Gopālavarman's child whom his wife, Jayalakṣmī, was expected to deliver. The child, however, died soon after birth. See Kapur, *Eminent Rulers*, pp. 64-5.
20. Kapur, *History and Culture*, p. 46.
21. Kapur, *Eminent Rulers*, p. 66.
22. Ibid., p. 67. See also Ashvini Agrawal, 'Women in the Political Life of Kashmir (*c.* A.D. 650–1150)', in *Dimensions of Indian Womanhood*, ed. C.M. Agrawal, Almora, Shri Almora Book Depot: 1993, vol. I, pp. 91, 93 where similar views are stated. Thus, Agrawal notes Sugandhā's role in 'guiding' her husband in important matters and in ruling capably but talks, at the same time, of her being a 'wise lady of religious disposition'.
23. Kapur, *Eminent Rulers*, pp. 62–3; Kapur, *History and Culture*, p. 46.
24. Kapur, *Eminent Rulers*, p. 63.
25. Although Prabhākara is not heard of after Gopālavarman's death, if he had truly disappeared by then, why would the courtiers want to spite his memory by contravening Sugandhā's decision, when she was apparently so popular?
26. Kapur, *History and Culture*, p. 46.
27. Her execution seems to set a precedent in that several rulers like Harṣa, Uccala and Raḍḍa are all executed during their reigns.
28. This is appreciated by Kalhaṇa as the second marvellous change in royal dynasties by association with a woman (*RT*, VI.366).
29. Talbot, 'Rudrama-devī', in *Syllables of Sky*, ed. Shulman, pp. 397–9.
30. This is a fact that is usually ignored in most writings on Kashmir. A. Cunningham, *Coins of Medieval India: From The Seventh Century Down to the Muhammadan Conquests*, Varanasi, Oriental Books: 1967, p. 45, incorrectly notes the word as 'devya' whereas it should be 'deva'. See also Devika Rangachari, 'Coinage and Gender: Early Medieval Kashmir', in *Coins in India: Power and Communication*, ed. H.P. Ray, Mumbai, Marg Publications: 2006, pp. 46–55.
31. Stein, *Rājataraṅgiṇī*, I, Appendix II, pp. 139–44.
32. This is taken from the *Rājyadharma* section of the Śāntiparva—I.85, 22.

Note that this part of the *Mahābhārata* is considered by R.C. Majumdar and Beni Prasad to be an important source of political theory, along with the *Arthaśāstra* and certain *Smṛtis*. Beni Prasad and R.C. Majumdar, 'Political Theory and Administrative System', in *The Age of Imperial Unity*, ed. R.C. Majumdar, 4th edn, Bombay, Bharatiya Vidya Bhavan: 1968, p. 303.

33. L.N. Rangarajan, ed. and tr., *Kauṭilya: The Arthaśāstra*, Delhi, Penguin Books: 1987, p. 169.
34. Altekar, *State and Government in Ancient India*, p. 84, quotes from the *Śukranītīsāra* (I.346–8) to reiterate this right of the eldest son to the throne. V.S. Pathak, *Ancient Historians of India*, 2nd impression, Gorakhpur, Purva Samsthana: 1984, pp. 70–1 cites the *Rāmāyaṇa* (II.110, 36), the *Mahābhārata* (I.85, 72), the *Nirukta* (II.10) and the *Arthaśāstra* (XII.1, 17) to show that, except in a crisis, the law of primogeniture was inviolable. In the *Rāmāyaṇa*, Vasiṣṭha tells Rāma that the law of primogeniture is a prescriptive law among the descendants of the Ikṣvākus and he is asked not to violate it. R.S. Pandit, tr., *Rājataraṅgiṇī*, Delhi, Sahitya Akademi: 1935, p. 150.
35. Medhātithi was an early lawgiver. This is cited in Mohan, *Early Medieval History*, p. 84. Robert Lingat, *The Classical Law of India*, tr. J.D.M. Derrett, Delhi, Munshiram Manoharlal: 1973, pp. 209–10, stresses the lack of unanimity among lawgivers on the qualifications of a king. Manu (VII:2) does not allow him to be other than a kṣatriya, while Yājñavalkya (1.119) says that he should be 'of good family, of high birth'. Yet Medhātithi says that in default of a kṣatriya, a man of another varṇa can be substituted. Lingat says that a large number of interpreters talk of 'the power to command' as desirable.
36. Kumkum Roy, 'The King's Household: Structure/Space in the Śāstric Tradition', *Economic and Political Weekly*, vol. 27, 24–31 October 1992, pp. 55–60, citing the *Manusmṛti*—VII.2; Wendy Doniger and Brian K. Smith, tr., *The Laws of Manu*, London/New York, Penguin Books: 1991, p. 128.
37. The eventual accession of his son, Durlabhaka-Pratāpāditya II, is 'an interesting point of the law of succession to the crown in favour of a daughter's son', according to Pandit, *Rājataraṅgiṇī*, p. 118.
38. Stein, *Rājataraṅgiṇī*, I, p. 266.
39. This idea finds expression in the epics as well. Kane, *History of Dharmaśāstra*, III, pp. 231-2, cites the *Arthaśāstra*—1.20, and the *Kāmandakīya Nītisāra*—XIV.57–8 and VII.44, 50; R.C. Majumdar, *Classical Age*, Bombay, Bharatiya Vidya Bhavan: 1954, p. 341; Rangarajan, *Kauṭilya*, p. 154. Kauṭilya (1.17.1) says that 'a king can protect himself only when he himself is protected from persons near him, particularly his wife and children'—see R.S. Sharma, *Aspects of Political Ideas and*

Institutions, 2nd edn, Delhi, Motilal Banarsidass: 1968, pp. 134-5 on the *parivṛkṛti*, or soulless discarded wife, who appears after the enumeration of the *ratnins* (high state functionaries) as someone who was capable of causing harm to the king. Kumkum Roy, 'The King's Household: Structure and Space in the Śāstric Tradition', in *From Myths to Markets: Essays on Gender*, ed. Kumkum Sangari and Uma Chakravarti, Delhi, Manohar: 1999, pp. 23–4, portrays the relationship between the king and queen as 'fraught with danger': the *subhagā*, or king's favourite wife, was regarded as even more dangerous than the *kumāra*, or prince, as the latter could be controlled by ministers and priests, but not the wife. The dangerous queen, therefore, was more central to popular perceptions than the rebellious prince.

40. E.B. Cowell and F.W. Thomas, tr., *The Harṣacarita of Bāṇa*, 2nd rpt., Delhi, Motilal Banarsidass: 1993, p. 224.
41. Interestingly, while talking about different categories of officers in Kashmir, S.C. Ray omits to mention Kalyāṇadevī—the only woman to have clearly held an administrative post. See S.C. Ray, 'Administrative System in Early Kaśmīrā', *Annals of the Bhandarkar Oriental Research Institute*, vol. XXXVIII, pts III–IV, 1957, p. 177.
42. Rangarajan, *Kauṭilya*, p. 145. The norms laid down by Kauṭilya for a *rājarṣi* is that, being disciplined, he should keep away from another's wife (1.7.1–8).
43. Mohan, *Early Medieval History*, p. 79.
44. Roy, 'The King's Household', in *From Myths to Markets*, ed. Sangari and Chakravarti, p. 28. The reference is to the *Kāmasūtra*—I.3.17–18. Suvira Jaiswal, 'Female Images in the Arthaśāstra of Kauṭilya', *Social Scientist*, vol. 29, nos. 3–4, March–April 2001, p. 53, notes that the *gaṇikā* was a state-appointed institutionalized position for the purpose of serving the king, fanning him, holding the umbrella over his head, and accompanying him on processions.
45. Kumari, *Nīlamata Purāṇa*, I, p. 95. She also cites the examples of Kayyā, Jayamatī, and Sahajā from the *Rājataraṅgiṇī*.
46. Ibid.
47. Moti Chandra, *The World of Courtesans*, Delhi, Vikas Publishing House: 1973, p. 11, cites the *Agnipurāṇa* (168.3), which holds the eating of their food a moral lapse, and the *Garuḍapurāṇa* which condemns them.
48. One can contrast this, for instance, with *The World of Courtesans*. See Uma Chakravarti and Kumkum Roy, 'In Search of Our Past: A Review of the Limitations and Possibilities of the Historiography of Women in Early India', *Economic and Political Weekly*, 30 April 1988, p. 5. They find that Moti Chandra has only culled references from various sources, and not related the institution of prostitution to the wider social context or examined its integration into the patriarchal system.

49. Kumkum Roy, 'Introduction', in *Women in Early Indian Societies*, ed. Kumkum Roy, Delhi, Manohar: 1999, p. 29 points out that despite the marginality of prostitutes in the dominant Sanskritic tradition, they were also viewed as symbolic of fertility and incorporated in diverse ritual contexts.
50. T.M. Tripathi, tr., *Kuṭṭanīmatam, or Shambhalimatam by Dāmodaragupta*, Varanasi, Krishnadas Academy: 1991.
51. Shalini Shah, 'In the Business of *Kāma*: Prostitution in Classical Sanskrit Literature from the Seventh to the Thirteenth Centuries', *The Medieval History Journal*, vol. 5, no. 1, January–June 2002, p. 124, says that the *Kuṭṭanīmatam* indicates the prostitute's sexuality to be non-marital and non-procreative, therefore dangerous.
52. Shastri, *India as Seen in the Kuṭṭanīmata*, pp. 37–8.
53. Ibid., p. 3.
54. Ibid., p. 41.
55. Interestingly, Vikarālā advises Mālatī to first dispatch a shrewd female messenger (*dūtī*) to Cintāmaṇi to try and win him over. The *dūtī* is described as endowed with sarcastic speech (*KM*, 89).
56. Shastri, *India as Seen in the Kuṭṭanīmata*, p. 28. The play occupies verses 881–928. Interestingly, Mañjarī enacts the role of Sāgarikā in Harṣa's *Ratnāvalī* to demonstrate her acting prowess.
57. Ibid., p. 30.
58. *KM*, 811–61. Note that Hindu mythology is quoted in defence of this procedure.
59. Shastri, *India as Seen in the Kuṭṭanīmata*, pp. 28, 16, 111.
60. Ibid., p. 53. See also pp. 43-56. Shastri cites *KM*, 889 and 894 that deal with the freedom of movement for women, their participation in festivities and their use of obscene words in public during these, but fails to consider their implications on the role of (non-royal) women in the contemporary milieu (p. 108).
61. Roy, 'The King's Household', in *From Myths to Markets*, ed. Sangari and Chakravarti, p. 29. The reference is to the *Kāmasūtra* 1.2.15. In the location of common features between the king and the courtesan, there is an underlying parallel with the *digvijaya*.
62. Ibid. *Arthaśāstra* II.6.2. The *gaṇikādhyakṣa*, or the official in charge of courtesans or prostitutes, was expected to keep an eye on their fees, property, income and expenditure (*Arthaśāstra* II.27.10).
63. Ibid. *Kāmasūtra* VI.2.28–30.
64. Sukumari Bhattacharji, 'Prostitution in Ancient India', in *Women in Early Indian Societies*, ed. Roy, pp. 206–7. She says prostitutes became a symbol of the prosperity concomitant with urban civilization and were an indispensable part of city life. She also talks of the 'evident ambivalence' regarding the profession. See p. 219.
65. The text reveals them to be witty and expert talkers (*KM*, 143–8),

repositories of fine arts like music (*KM*, 357), dance (*KM*, 346, 355) and drama (*KM*, 794), and trained in the literary/practical lore of their profession. See Shastri, *India as Seen in the Kuṭṭanīmata*, pp. 111–12.

66. Shah, 'In the Business of *Kāma*', *Medieval History Journal*, p. 144.
67. Although almost all of them function as wives or mothers, there is great scope for power and flexibility even within such restricted categories.
68. This form of protest was usually adopted by brāhmaṇa men. There is no other instance of a woman undertaking it.
69. Kumari, *Nīlamata Purāṇa*, I, p. 90.
70. *NP*, 402–6 contain a curious injunction for women and men to play together for sexual arousal, to indicate a total lack of control—as exemplifying *piśāca* behaviour.
71. Kumkum Roy, 'Where Women are Worshipped, there the Gods Rejoice', in *Women and the Hindu Right*, ed. Tanika Sarkar and Urvashi Butalia, Delhi, Kali for Women: 1995, p. 21. Also Madhu Khanna, 'The Goddess—Women Equation in Śākta Tantras', in *Faces of the Feminine*, ed. Bose, p. 119. Roy, 'Introduction', in *Women in Early Indian Societies*, ed. Roy, p. 40, notes that goddesses are obviously gendered symbols but cannot all be incorporated in a single explanatory framework. Women's relationships with the goddess constitute one example of the complex connections between gender and religion.
72. The *Manusmṛti* does not clearly single out women and men in its discussion of death ceremonies. Its focus seems largely on ceremonies for men and their salvation rather than on women. Doniger and Smith, *The Laws of Manu*, pp. 55–73; in P.V. Kane, *History of Dharmaśāstra*, Poona, Bhandarkar Oriental Research Institute: 1953, vol. IV, pp. 334–515, laws regarding *śrāddha* are seen to have an implicit male focus.
73. Kane, *History of Dharmaśāstra*, III, p. 60 where he cites this; Pandit, *Rājataraṅgiṇī*, Appendix A, pp. 708-16 for a detailed reign-wise progression of the building activities in Kalhaṇa's work.
74. Romila Thapar, *Ancient Indian Social History*, Delhi, Orient Longman: 1978, pp. 105–7; Vijay Nath, *Dāna: Gift System in Ancient India: A Socio-Economic Perspective*, Delhi, Munshiram Manoharlal: 1987, pp. 17, 70; Cynthia Talbot, 'Temples, Donors, and Gifts: Patterns of Patronage in Thirteenth-century South India', *Journal of Asian Studies*, 50, 2 May 1991, p. 335.
75. Mohan, *Early Medieval History*, pp. 240–1. P.V. Kane, *History of Dharmaśāstra*, Poona, Bhandarkar Oriental Research Institute: 1941, vol. II, pt 2, pp. 906–7.
76. Romila Thapar, *Cultural Transaction and Early India: Tradition and Patronage*, Delhi, Oxford University Press: 1987, p. 31. In her view, this is also applicable to the Jain cause.
77. Nath, *Dāna*, p. 44 where she notes this common aspect of royal donation/construction. She says that royal gifts by kings would seem to be inspired

by a royal ambition to assert their superior wealth and power. A spirit of competition existed between kings and others who vied with them in this sphere.

78. Kapur, *History and Culture*, p. 29.
79. Modern scholars view building activities in the same mould. Kapur (ibid., p. 30) calls the Mārtaṇḍa temple the 'standing memorial of Lalitāditya's greatness'.
80. Interestingly, the statue is not of Śiva alone but of him and Pārvatī (*NP*, 201–4).
81. Kapur, *History and Culture*, pp. 30–1.
82. Ibid., p. 43.
83. George W. Spencer, 'When Queens Bore Gifts: Women as Temple Donors in the Chola Period', in *Śrīnidhīh: Perspectives in Indian Archaeology, Art and Culture* (K.R. Srinivasan Festschrift), ed. K.V. Raman et al., Madras, New Era Publications: 1983, p. 362.
84. The dislike stems from their origin from the spirit-distiller, Uppa's family. This is, therefore, another tribute to Kalhaṇa's objectivity.
85. Note that Kalhaṇa mentions their buildings almost in the same breath, despite their totally diverse backgrounds—Kalyāṇadevī being a princess and Kamalā a temple dancer. The buildings act as a levelling factor here.
86. The case of Suyya is interesting in that he is found as an abandoned child by a cāṇḍāla woman, Suyyā, who adopts him, yet is careful not to defile him by her touch. Suyya's gratitude to his foster-mother is evidenced by the naming of buildings after her.
87. Note that the *Rājataraṅgiṇī* nowhere categorically states that the women of ancient Kashmir enjoyed considerable freedom, as D.C. Sircar seems to think: D.C. Sircar, 'Great Women in North India: *c*. 400 BC to 1200 AD', in *Great Women of India*, ed. Swami Madhavananda and R.C. Majumdar, Almora, Advaita Ashrama: 1953, p. 290.
88. Kumari, *Nīlamata Purāṇa*, I, pp. 94–5, cites Bilhaṇa's description of the 'literary efficiency' of Kashmiri women, Dāmodaragupta's provision of the list of subjects they learnt, and Kalhaṇa's depiction of their high status 'in religion and politics'.
89. Ibid., pp. 94, 131–6.

CHAPTER IV

Kashmir: A Gendered Perspective

(Diddā's Reign and the Post-Diddā Period AD 980/1–1149/50)

This chapter pertains to the Diddā and post-Diddā phase of Kashmir, or the period from Queen Diddā's accession, AD 980/1, to 1149/50—the date of the completion of the *Rājataraṅgiṇī*. In continuation of the previous chapter, it attempts to examine the place of royal and non-royal women in the political and social domain. While the themes of analysis remain largely the same, there are several points of divergence from the pre-Diddā period that necessitate the inclusion of some new themes.

Kalhaṇa's *Rājataraṅgiṇī* remains the crucial source for the Diddā and post-Diddā period. In addition, Kṣemendra's *Samayamātṛkā* (tenth century) also offers great potential in its focus on prostitutes and their power, and as an important corroborative source. As in the previous chapter, the attempts of various historians to minimize the place of women—as revealed by the sources—have been highlighted, wherever possible, to reiterate the necessity for a careful interpretative analysis of the relevant texts.

THE DOMAIN OF WOMEN RULERS

As mentioned in the previous chapter, in the *Rājataraṅgiṇī*, Diddā represents female power at its vibrant peak in early medieval Kashmir. Her rule of nearly fifty years spanned the life of her husband Kṣemagupta, her regency, and her actual accession to the throne as the formal ruler of Kashmir in about 980. The tenacity of Diddā's rule, witnessing a consistent overcoming of obstacles (including those stemming from her lameness and her sex), is a striking feature of Kalhaṇa's account, stressing her toughness and shrewdness.

At the outset, Kalhaṇa gives Diddā's powerful family connections: her being the daughter of the Lohara ruler, Siṁharāja, and the granddaughter of the mighty Bhīma Śāhī (*RT*, VI.176, 178).[1] Thereafter, he comments on Kṣemagupta's fascination for her, concretized by his nickname *diddākṣema* on his coins (*RT*, VI.177—*sa tasyāṁ śāhī-dauhitrayāṁ diddāyāṁ sakta-mānasaha, diddākṣema iti khyātiṁ yayo lajjā-vahāṁ nṛpaḥ*).[2] This fact, taken in conjunction with Diddā's apparent hostility to the prime minister, Phalguṇa (on account of his daughter's marriage to Kṣemagupta), conveys an impression of her having exerted much influence in the court.

Subsequently, Diddā assumed guardianship of her son, Abhimanyu, on Kṣemagupta's death, having been spared from burning herself by the minister Naravāhana's intervention (*RT*, VI.196). It is at this juncture that Kalhaṇa's familiar ambivalence comes into play. On the one hand, Diddā is portrayed as being the stereotypical woman, indecisive and unable to reason for herself; on the other hand, Kalhaṇa traces the establishment of her undisputed rule in the land in painstaking detail, constantly stressing her abilities and determination. As a result, Diddā's growth towards power and political maturity is clearly underlined. It would be worthwhile to examine this aspect in some detail.

Initially, Kalhaṇa provides an account of the ministerial rivalries that faced the regent Diddā, prompting her to take unsound and impulsive decisions. Thus:

> The king's mother and guardian, confused in her mind and listening to everybody, after women's wont, did not reflect what was true and what not (*RT*, VI.193—*rakṣitrī kṣmā-patermātā strī-svabhāvā-dimūḍadhīha, sārā-sāra-vicāreṇa lola-karṇī na paspṛśe*).

Diddā was privy to wrong counsel emanating from rival courtiers like Rakka and his cronies, thereby antagonizing loyal ministers like Yaśodhara (the commander-in-chief). Kalhaṇa seems to be torn between recognition of her potential to rule well and impatience with her for heeding the advice of unworthy councillors, and this is clearly exemplified in his despairing lament on those 'in which cleverness and stupidity are blended' (*RT*, VI.274–5)—an obvious allusion to Diddā.

However, importantly, the shrewdness of Diddā's schemes for safeguarding her power, as in her alternate bribe-and-placation policy, is equally stressed. On the one hand, she bribed the brāhmaṇas to rectify the impasse between herself and the rebel grandsons of Parvagupta (Kṣemagupta's father), and bestowed offices on other malcontents. On the other hand, she had no qualms in destroying the more intractable rebels by 'witchcraft', thereby exhibiting a ruthless streak that subsequently came to the fore. Interestingly, while Diddā's deeds were usually in conformity with some minister's advice, she seemed to keep her own counsel in wriggling out of potentially dangerous situations. Kalhaṇa pays a significant and flattering tribute to her growing political maturity in the following words:

> The lame (queen) whom no one had thought capable of stepping over a cow's footprint got over the ocean-like host (of her enemies), just as Hanuman (got over the ocean) (*RT*, VI.226—*gośpadollaṅkane yasyāha śaktirnāgyāyi kenacit, vāyu-putrā-yitaṁ-paṅga tayā sanghābdhi-laṅkane*).

Comparisons are also drawn between Diddā and goddess Durgā in the quelling of enemies by the 'angry' and morally indignant queen (*RT*, VI.254–8).

Interestingly, Diddā was helped in this endeavour by the minister, Naravāhana, who counselled her against wrong advice and defended her against rebel forces. As part of the exceptionally strong, yet apparently platonic understanding between them, the queen even attuned her moods and habits to his (*RT*, VI.260–3). However, Diddā's dependence on Naravāhana was stemmed by a court intrigue that precipitated his suicide. Diddā then becomes 'an object of reproach' for Kalhaṇa (*RT*, VI.276) and he euphemistically alludes to her—in Naravāhana's absence—as a reduced royal dignity, akin to a moonless night or an untruthful speech (*RT*, VI.279).

Kalhaṇa now concentrates on the ruthless aspect of Diddā's character and talks of her, 'hardened by continued cruelty', scheming to kill her enemies (*RT*, VI.280), as also her astute placation of the old prime minister, Phalguṇa. At this point, significantly, the 'evil' emanating from her and her companions is held responsible for the death of her son, Abhimanyu (958–72), whereby he apparently 'withered' away like a flower (*RT*, VI.289–291—. . . . *tathā viśrudha-prakṛtestasya duṣkṛta-saṅgamaha, śośādhāyī śirīśasya ravi-tāpa ivā-bhavat*). This is an ironic perspective in view of Diddā's genuine concern for Abhimanyu's safety at several stages during her regency, especially in the wake of the rebel onslaughts, and her exertions to maintain the throne under his (nominal) rule.

At this juncture, Diddā apparently embraced a newfound piety; her 'evil' designs on hold, she began building activities as proof of her reformed nature. This change, however, proved to be short-lived and she speedily destroyed her two grandsons, Nandigupta (972–3) and Tribhuvana (973–5), by 'witchcraft' (*RT*, VI.310–12), causing Kalhaṇa to compare her with a rampaging 'female elephant in rut' (*RT*, VI.315).

The pronounced aura of death surrounding Diddā forms part of the narrative's attempt to portray women as possessing the potential to destroy, as stressed in the previous chapter. Thus, significantly, even the throne is said to take on the aspect of death in her presence. As Kalhaṇa puts it:

> Then the cruel (queen) put without hesitation her last grandson, Bhīmagupta, on that path of death which bore the name 'throne' (*RT*, VI.313—*atha mṛtyu-pathe rājyanāmni svairaṁ niveśitaha, krūrayā caramaha pautro bhīma-guptā-bhidhastayā*).

Diddā subsequently ascended the throne after torturing Bhīmagupta (975–980/1) to death (*RT*, VI.332).

The epigraphic evidence for Diddā's reign consists of the Sri Pratap Singh Museum, Srinagar, Buddhist image inscription of (*laukika*) year 65, or AD 989 of her reign and the Srinagar inscription of (*laukika*) year 68 (992). The first records the consecration of a religious gift (*deya dharma*) of a bronze statuette of Bodhisattva Padmapāṇi by Rājānaka Bhīmaṭa, a Buddhist devotee and son of Cāvata, and by the four brothers (*bhrātṛ-catuṣṭana*) of Gaṅgā Devī, described as a divine mother.[3] It refers to Diddā by the masculine appellation of *deva* rather than *devī* (. . . *diddādeva rājye* . . .). B.K. Kaul Deambi suggests that Diddā's 'energy, political acumen and essentially masculine traits of character' caused people to view her 'more as a powerful king than as a mere queen'.

Similarly, the second inscription, which mentions a certain Dharmāṇika honouring his mother by dedicating some religious institution or charitable work in her name, is held as referring to Diddā as *rājan* rather than *rājñī*.[4] K.N. Sastri speculates that the appellation *rājan* was probably preferred by Diddā. He further wonders whether the practice of calling ruling queens by masculine epithets (*rājan, deva*) had a religious sanction.

However, the insistence on the word *rājan* by Sastri is puzzling because the actual word in the inscription is *rājñī*. Even Deambi seems to have made the same mistake: he translates the relevant word as *rājñī* but insists that Diddā is called *rājan*. J.N. Agrawal, too, makes the same error. Could this be an oversight on their part, or is it an instance of the usual cursory attention paid to women in history?

Kalhaṇa now talks of Diddā's involvement with Tuṅga, a lowly khaśa letter-carrier (*lekhahāraka*).[5] Once again, his ambivalence comes into play. He lambasts the 'fickle queen' Diddā for being 'deficient' in morality (succumbing to this infatuation) while, on the other hand, he appreciates Tuṅga for his successful Rājapurī expedition (*RT*, VI.351). Although Tuṅga is shown to subsequently strengthen the foundations of power given him by Diddā and become a recognized figure in politics, he is likened to the setting sun 'when the splendour of day departs' after Diddā's death (*RT*, VII.3–4).

At this juncture, it would be worthwhile to speculate on the presence of Prabhākaradeva (Sugandhā's lover), Naravāhana, and Tuṅga in the narrative. All three men served their sovereigns (and lovers) in matters of policy and in military expeditions. In a sense, therefore, men are shown serving women in the same way that women serve them. By extension, none of the women rulers of Kashmir seem to fit into the category of the 'warrior queen' who combined both elements of rule and martial leadership,[6] either on account of their supposed passivity (Yaśovatī and Sugandhā) or for more practical considerations (Diddā's lameness). Thus, battles were waged and won in Diddā's reign, but they were handled by Naravāhana or Tuṅga.

Finally, and most importantly, Diddā's act of bequeathing the throne to her nephew, Saṁgrāmarāja, had monumental repercussions. On the one hand, the throne passed in undisputed succession to her natal family from Lohara. This justifies the stress laid on the natal connections of the queens, in the narrative, and the possibility of them enabling the enhancement of the power of their maternal homes.[7] Thus, Diddā emphatically determined the future history of Kashmir through her maternal home[8] and demonstrated political sagacity by making Tuṅga and Saṁgrāmarāja vow not to harm each other.

On the other hand, the importance of Kalhaṇa's attitude for a gender analysis is highlighted. Thus, although he faults Diddā's selection procedure as being consonant with a woman's 'timid' nature (*RT*, VI.362–3), he equally lauds this change of dynasty at a woman's instance. His comment, which stresses his appreciation of the role of women in royal politics, has been cited in the previous chapter.

As with Sugandhā, Kalhaṇa's intentional ambivalence has prompted a variety of interpretations on Diddā, largely stereotypical and uncritical. U.N. Ghoshal, for instance, describes her as 'cruel and self-indulgent with a strong touch of feminine inconsistency'; S.C. Banerji dubs her 'a dissolute and monstrous queen', focusing on her cruel acts rather than considering details of her statesmanship, or in acknowledging the significant dynastic change she effects.[9] Likewise, P.V. Kane talks fleetingly of the reigns of 'the notorious queens'—Sugandhā and Diddā—as exceptions to the universal rule of male rulership, the notoriety, one presumes, stemming from their effrontery in exercising formal power.[10] In a similar vein, Beni Prasad dismisses these two rulers in a couple of pages.[11]

M.K. Dhar's *Royal Life in Ancient India* is another illustrative case with its overwhelmingly male focus, interspersed with factual errors relating to prominent women and a very arbitrary manner of acknowledging their presence.[12] Women rulers form a part of 'Social Conditions' where Diddā's motives for ruling are completely distorted, and Sugandhā finds no mention.[13] Additionally, details of succession and coronation rituals, as also the daily routine, are provided only with reference to male rulers. Likewise, Saroj Gulati who attempts a 'critical appraisal' of different social institutions in north India and 'their influence on the position of women' notes the contradictory aspects of *satī* and women rulers, but trivializes the latter by dint of factual errors, ambiguous references and dismissive statements.[14] B.N.S. Yadava, too, blames Kashmir's 'ambitious queens' rather than ambitious kings for vitiating the political atmosphere, omits the names of important women, and then talks of social decline in this period.[15]

Scholars who acknowledge Diddā's contribution are few, and their tone is mostly grudging. They stress Diddā's failings rather than her achievements—a ploy they do not usually adopt in their analysis of male rulers.[16] A stellar example is that of M.L. Kapur who calls Diddā 'the intelligent regent', 'a great judge of the human nature', and talks of her 'political and diplomatic talents' and 'wonderful capacity for organization', but hastens to add that she was 'uncommonly voluptuous, profligate and dissolute' with a 'limitless' lust 'for power'.[17] Furthermore, he seeks to conventionalize her by stressing that her 'first impulse' was to immolate herself on Kṣemagupta's death.[18]

And yet, Diddā seems no more cruel or ambitious than the average Kashmiri king striving to maintain his power and throne. In fact, Kalhaṇa uses her as a standard of comparison for male rulers like Salhaṇa (1111–12), implying his appreciation of the significance and vigour of her rule. As he puts it:

> On that (throne) on which even a lame queen (Diddā) had maintained herself for a long time in a spirited manner, he, though a man, had his mind distracted by fears (*RT*, VIII.419—*paṅgur-pyaṅkana kālaṁ krāntyā yatrātya-vāhayat, pumānpya-bhavattatra sādh-vasādh-vasta-dhīrrasau*).[19]

Admittedly, Kalhaṇa does tend to focus on dissent in Diddā's reign and her diplomacy is glimpsed only in so far as it relates to her survival tactics. However, he also examines, in detail, the ways in which she quells rebellions and she is shown to surpass most other rulers in this regard. Thus:

> Those treacherous ministers, who, during sixty years from the year (of the Laukika era three thousand nine hundred) seventy-seven (AD 901/2) onwards, had robbed sixteen kings, from King Gopāla(varman) to Abhimanyu, of their dignity, lives and riches—they all, together with their descendants and followers, were quickly exterminated by the angry

Queen Diddā with a mere terrifying frown, just as the great Asuras (were exterminated) by Durgā (*RT*, VI.256–8).

It is interesting to note that D.C. Sircar finds Diddā's attraction for men and her desire for power as a 'fatal weakness' in her character.[20] In contrast, Kalhaṇa applies the same standards to male and female rulers, criticizing Diddā and Sugandhā for their unconventional liaisons in much the same way as he does Cakravarman's involvement with ḍomba women, or Lalitāpīḍa's affair with Jayādevī (cited earlier).[21] In addition, though he often makes caustic remarks about Diddā, his outrage seems to be fuelled not by a woman's performance of the deeds, but by the cruelty of the deed. Besides, if Diddā is ambitious and ruthless, she is also shown as capable of exhibiting remorse, thus appearing in a realistic blend of good and bad qualities in much the same way as King Jayāpīḍa, for instance, is shown as brave and benevolent but also thoughtless and arrogant.

The significance of Kalhaṇa's account is undeniable for, as Sircar remarks, 'this is the only instance in the history of ancient India, wherein we have some details of the activities of a female ruler'.[22] While this may not be entirely correct, Kalhaṇa distinctly enables one to discern the crucial significance of Diddā's reign in several ways. As mentioned earlier, the most striking fact is the tenacity and extraordinary length of her rule by a consistent overcoming of obstacles.

Kalhaṇa gives due weight to the manner in which Diddā determined the future history of Kashmir. Not only is this evident in the ascension of the Lohara dynasty—which held sway until (and beyond) the date of the *Rājataraṅgiṇī's* completion—but also in the emergence of important rulers like Uccala, for instance, who justified his claim to rule by a specific reference to Diddā, her marriage to Kṣemagupta, and her selection of Saṁgrāmarāja as her heir, to demonstrate his impeccable ancestry.

And yet, as mentioned in the previous chapter, M.A. Stein is one who ignores this important sovereign in his 'Genealogical Tables of Kaśmīr Dynasties According to Kalhaṇa'.[23] Diddā is represented only as Kṣemagupta's wife here and not as a ruler. The dynastic line shows an abrupt end after her three grandsons—Nandigupta,

Tribhuvana, and Bhīmagupta. Diddā's rule is attested in the genealogical tables on the Lohara dynasty, however, but her marital status is prominently displayed here. This is an inexplicable omission on Stein's part since in his 'Introduction' he admires Diddā's political acumen and the length and significance of her rule.[24]

At this point, it would be worthwhile to ask as to what enabled the women of Kashmir to breach the ideological barrier, so emphatically highlighted in śāstric literature, which associated political authority with masculinity. Regrettably, there are very few secondary works on the specific conjunction of social and political circumstances, that created a space for women as political patrons,[25] but there are two ways of examining this problem. The first relates to the juxtaposition of prescriptions contained in the Dharmaśāstras with the actual exercise of political authority. The divergence of views among lawgivers itself strengthens the contention that there was scope for subversion. Female power in Kashmir can be traced to this gap between theory and practice.

What may also be kept in mind is that, exceptional though Sugandhā and Diddā may have been, they are not entirely unrepresentative of the situation in early historic India. Interesting parallels can be drawn with the Bhaumakara queens of early Orissa, and other notable dowagers like Prabhāvatīguptā of the Vākāṭaka family (fourth century AD) and Vijayabhaṭṭārikā of the Cālukya house (seventh century AD).[26] This evidence would indicate that women in ruling families received some military or administrative training.[27] S.C. Ray, for instance, acknowledges this as the factor behind the 'great success' of Sugandhā and Diddā.[28]

Similarly, Krishna Mohan, in her brief discussion of the women rulers, says the 'right of women to rule the realm was recognized in Kashmir from early times'.[29] However, as with most writers on Kashmir, they fail to understand the implications thereof. Thus, while Ray deals with the 'Position of Women' as part of the chapter on society with most of the discussion pertaining to peripheral issues, in a chapter on society Mohan sandwiches the 'Position of Women' between a discussion on caste and general aspects like the family.[30]

The second way of examining the problem relates to Cynthia Talbot's study of this aspect, which seeks to understand early medieval India in relation to the situation in early medieval Europe.[31] Talbot considers women political leaders from three regions between the ninth and thirteenth centuries: Sugandhā and Diddā of Kashmir, the six women rulers of the Orissan Bhaumakara dynasty, and the four women rulers of thirteenth-century Andhra. She draws parallels with medieval European women who possessed greatest political power in approximately the same period.[32] She talks of the decentralized nature of the medieval European polity that blurred the distinction between public and private spheres in the great aristocratic families who held power.[33]

Talbot claims that medieval Kashmir, Andhra and Orissa all resembled early medieval Europe in their lack of centralization. They only had a regional impact with a very loosely organized administrative apparatus. Women occupied a pivotal role in this decentralized situation where political power was personalized and could be embodied in marriage relations.

Thus, broadly, political authority was a right associated with particular families. Hence, the spheres of politics and kinship overlapped.[34] Women were allowed to exercise supreme political authority on occasions when it would ensure the retention of a throne within the immediate kin group. Sugandhā's reign is a case in point. Thus the centrality of the family in certain political cultures of this time could explain the phenomenon of ruling queens.[35]

In addition, regency provided an important justification for female authority.[36] However, as Talbot says, while the regent queen may have been the most acceptable type of woman ruler, her deviation from the societal norm of the good wife had to be vindicated. Thus, she foregoes the 'attractive' option of self-immolation due to her responsibilities towards her family and kingdom.[37] Yet, any echoes of the self-sacrificing woman, are put aside firmly in Kalhaṇa's text. Thus, both Sugandhā and Diddā use their period of regency as a stepping-stone to acquire power.[38]

Women's power in Kashmir, therefore, was a constantly fluctuating social process. Talbot stresses the flexibility of the prevalent gender ideology and of the construction of identity. She says the gap between theory and practice is reconciled through manipulation of gender imagery, privileging of maternal obligations and/or alteration of social memory. Once a woman becomes a ruler, a public persona could be constructed for her, to gloss over the incompatibility of her sex and gender role.[39] Thus one can speculate that the legendary justification for Yaśovatī's rule appeased the people and, perhaps, left such an impact on their minds that they tacitly accepted later women figures as legitimate wielders of power.[40]

There are, however, certain problems in applying Talbot's theory to Kashmir. For instance, Diddā's bestowal of the throne on the Loharas was unorthodox in that the rights of her natal family triumphed over that of the Yaśaskaras, with whom the sovereignty was associated. Thus, it was not her husband's family that was being privileged. The formation of the Kārkoṭa dynasty was similarly unusual in that the sovereignty was vested in the descendants of a king's daughter. Hence, Talbot's theory, though a useful one, is not wholly applicable here.[41]

FEMALE AGENCY IN THE DOMAIN OF MALE RULERS

As mentioned in the previous chapter, ruling power in early Kashmir, as revealed by the *Rājataraṅgiṇī*, was rarely an exclusively male prerogative: the power of women is shown to complement, parallel, and occasionally supersede, that of men in the court culture. The definitive political roles that a majority of the queens played underlined their emphatic presence and the exertion of much pressure/influence on male rulership, the very notion of which is permeated with assumptions and assertions on female agency in the text.

Queens

At the outset, one should note Kalhaṇa's deliberate ambivalence towards this important category of court participants. On the one hand, queens are often mentioned only at the conclusion of particular reigns for the purpose of introducing the succeeding ruler.[42] On the other hand, the significance that Kalhaṇa accords them is revealed in the following statement:

If during the day by one's presence, like a wanton woman by a jealous lover, it is possible to guard the sovereign from the incitements of backbiters, O, king! What the night tutor, the queen consort, coaches in private is a matter where a vigilant watch cannot be kept by those who do not know everything (*RT*, V.317–18).[43]

It would be worthwhile to examine this entire aspect with special reference to the post-Diddā phase of early medieval Kashmir in some detail.

QUEENS AS POWERS BEHIND THE THRONE

The *Rājataraṅgiṇī* provides general indications of the pivotal presence of queens, as in their joint coronation with the king (as per ancient Indian custom),[44] their independent treasuries and staff,[45] their guidance to the king, their inviolable written orders (*RT*, VII.1206, 1623), and their assumption of charge in critical (and frequently even normal) situations.[46] One can consider some specific examples below.

The best instance of a queen as the actual power behind the throne in the post-Diddā phase was Sūryamatī, the vigorous, self-willed and articulate wife of King Ananta (Lohara dynasty, AD 1028–63). In Kalhaṇa's account, the accent is largely on Ananta's ineffectual rule and character and Sūryamatī's capabilities, such that he is talked of as 'a mirror' reflecting his wife (*RT*, VII.179). Sūryamatī acquired supremacy by solving a financial crisis caused by Ananta with her independent resources and acumen, and thereby restoring the kingdom's prestige.[47] Thereafter, she took over the administration and gave orders to Ananta. This fact, coupled with Ananta's pragmatic acceptance of his inferiority, is a highly significant aspect of the narrative.[48] Kalhaṇa's comment on this reversal of roles in their relationship is refreshingly liberal. He says:

The husband's woman-like submission and her domination over her husband did not give occasion for blame, as their behaviour towards each other was irreproachable (*RT*, VII.200—*bhartur-nārī-vidheyatvaṁ tasyā bhartṛ-jayastatā, niṣ-kalaṅkena śīlena nānyonyaṁ gahāryatāmagāt*).

However, he details Ananta's virtues (*RT*, VII.201) to prove, perhaps, that he was otherwise a very worthy person.

Sūryamatī subsequently ordered Ananta to abdicate in favour of their worthless son, Kalaśa (1063–89), thereby precipitating an important chain of events. Kalhaṇa describes the 'simple-minded' Ananta succumbing to Sūryamatī's will as 'the opening for misfortune' (*RT*, VII.229). One should note here that Kalhaṇa and Stein differ on Sūryamatī's motives for Ananta's abdication. Stein represents Sūryamatī as wanting to put the rule in stronger hands,[49] whereas Kalhaṇa merely attributes her wishes to her blind love for her son.

Kalhaṇa describes the mental anguish of the couple at Kalaśa's promiscuous ways, and particularly dwells on Sūryamatī's frustration at being unable to imprison or punish her son (*RT*, VII.329–30). Yet, ironically, after secret negotiations, she obtained a respite for him from Ananta, thereby opening the doors for further harassment by Kalaśa. This state of affairs finally prompted Ananta to kill himself.

Interestingly, Ananta, prompted by Kalaśa's threats and Sūryamatī's taunts, apparently questioned the latter's domination—for the first and last time—just before his death. He laments:

> Pride, honour, valour, royal dignity, power, intellect, riches,—what is it, alas, that I have not lost by following my wife's (will)? (*RT*, VII.423—*abhimāno yaśaha śauryaṁ rājya-mojo matir-dhanaṁ, mayā jāyā-vidheyena hanta kiṁ kiṁ na hāritaṁ*).

At this juncture, Kalhaṇa enhances Ananta's aura of helplessness by reflecting that women, thought to be 'useless' accessories for men, actually use them as playthings, and that dominating women do not welcome their husbands' reproaches (*RT*, VII.424, 439).

Angered by Ananta's outburst, Sūryamatī labels him a pauper, mendicant, dullard, and inarticulate, reminding him that his condemnation of women would extend to his own female relatives (*RT*, VII.441). The accent now is on Ananta having outlived his usefulness, thereby prompting Kalhaṇa to view his death as a long-denied release from the machinations of his wife and son.[50] However, the highly uncharacteristic nature of this mutual outburst is shown in Kalhaṇa's reflection that Ananta killed himself 'in atonement for his breach of courtesy' (*RT*, VII.457), and that Sūryamatī's apparent gratitude for this expiatory act caused her to become the guardian of his interests again and later burn herself.

Sūryamatī played a definitive political role and clearly determined the future history of Kashmir. In fact, her influence was discernible even after her death. Kalaśa's son, Harṣa's initial survival in politics was due to Sūryamatī's sage advice (*RT*, VII.486–92). And yet, her role has not been fully appreciated or comprehended by scholars.[51]

In fact, the attempt to conventionalize the women figures, of which we have seen several examples in the previous pages, has been extended to Sūryamatī as well. Ghoshal, for instance, talks of Sūryamatī's 'fine womanly qualities' evident in her desire to see her son, Kalaśa, before burning herself.[52] However, Kalhaṇa tantalizingly speculates as to whether this desire sprang from maternal affection, or for 'some other reason' (*RT*, VII.468), hinting at Sūryamatī's anger with Kalaśa and echoing her earlier attempt to imprison and kill him.

Likewise, the poet Bilhaṇa's details on Sūryamatī in his *Vikramāṅkadevacaritam* are usually ignored in most secondary sources.[53] Bilhaṇa, who left Kashmir at the time of Kalaśa's nominal accession, devotes several verses to the praise of his hometown in Pravarapura, the women of Kashmir, and, most significantly, Sūryamatī, whom he calls by her other name, Subhaṭā.[54]

Bilhaṇa's statements on the linguistic abilities of Kashmiri women and their excellence in dramatics are often quoted. He remarks that '. . . in every house Sanskrit and Prakrit words sound charming like the mother-tongue of even women, not to speak of others' (Canto XVIII).[55] This is noteworthy in view of the fact that women were usually precluded from speaking Sanskrit, reserved for males and upper castes.[56] That the women of Kashmir could converse fluently in both languages is not only a pointer to their linguistic acumen, but also to the flexibility accorded them in this regard.

However, notably, the fact that Sūryamatī is the focus of at least seven verses (Canto XVIII, 40–6)—wherein her administrative and other abilities, as also her equation with her husband, Ananta, are revealed—is a fact that is wholly ignored and not alluded to by any writer who quotes from this text.[57] Bilhaṇa starts by calling her the 'climax of kindness, forgiveness and courtesy',[58] and then states that the king of Kashmir had 'acknowledged submission to her merits. . .'.[59] He then talks of the anxieties of Sūryamatī's co-wives on account of this. Sūryamatī also apparently enabled the learned to enjoy the storehouses, proclaimed free acceptance of land by the brāhmaṇas, and arranged 'for the protection of only the fame residing in the treasury of the earth. . .'.[60]

As is obvious, Bilhaṇa's statements are an important corroborative source for Kalhaṇa's information. Thus, the fact that Sūryamatī dominated over Ananta and directed various administrative activities is confirmed. In addition, the indications of harem rivalries on account of Sūryamatī's pre-eminence are doubly significant in view of Kalhaṇa's silence on this aspect. As Kalhaṇa's singular focus is on Sūryamatī, the fact of the existence of Ananta's other wives is interesting.[61] Whether Sūryamatī's dominance extended to her co-wives is a matter for conjecture. So, too, is the possibility of rivalry between her son, Kalaśa, and his other siblings.

However, these important details have been hitherto inexplicably disregarded, with the possible exception of the translators of the *Vikramāṅkadevacaritam* who, in their preface, mention the granaries built by Sūryamatī and the fact that she was conversant with state policy.[62] Any attempt at a gender analysis or an acknowledgement of the light thrown on the contemporary socio-political scene is, predictably, missing.

At this point, one can also consider some other prominent queens of the *Rājataraṅginī*, in the post-Diddā phase, who might not have wielded power on Sūryamatī's scale, but nevertheless exercised substantial influence—positive or otherwise—behind the throne. An example of a queen in the influential role of mediator is Kalhaṇikā, the wife of Jayasiṁha, who is shown to have successfully effected a reconciliation between her husband and his rebel cousin, Bhoja, thus preventing an incipient ḍāmara rebellion.[63] It would be worthwhile to examine her role in some detail.

At the outset, it is important to note that Kalhaṇikā is represented as having been made the chief queen as per the wishes of her father-in-law, Sussala (1112–20, 1121–8).

When the king was inaugurated, she had received the diadem of chief-queen desired for her by her father-in-law and the people (*RT*, VIII.3065—*śvaśureṇa prajā-bhiśca kṛtaṁ rājñobhiṣecane, āsāsyaṁ yā mahādevī-paṭṭa-bandhaṁ samādadhe*).

It is significant that Kalhaṇa takes the wish of the people as a legitimizing force for the appointment of queens, an aspect that surfaces often in the *Rājataraṅgiṇī*. It stresses the public and pivotal roles played by many of them.

Kalhaṇikā's role commenced with the rebel, Bhoja's desire to have her mediate between him and Jayasiṁha (*RT*, VIII.3063–9). Kalhaṇa's tone here presupposes such an arrangement to be commonplace, but he also describes Kalhaṇikā's exemplary virtues to justify her role in resolving the enmity between the cousins. He stresses the fact of her not being impulsive or weak-minded, despite her maternal love and desire to please her husband.

Interestingly, Kalhaṇikā's seemingly unstinted enthusiasm for her mission (*RT*, VIII.3070–2) appears in sharp contrast to Jayasiṁha's scepticism in that she even needed to convince him of the plan's efficacy. Admittedly, she eventually portrayed a more subdued and circumspect image, whereby she cautioned Jayasiṁha on the attendant dangers of the entire procedure (*RT*, VIII.3098). However, this coyness might have been a deliberate measure to preempt the possibility of Jayasiṁha being annoyed by her eagerness to mediate and abandoning the attempt. Nevertheless, it is remarkable that Jayasiṁha allowed her to negotiate with his arch-enemy at all—a mission so fraught with danger.

Kalhaṇikā's actual role, thereafter, is a trifle anticlimactic, confined to welcoming Bhoja and arranging for his comforts (*RT*, VIII.3180–2). Her presence seemed overshadowed by ministers like Dhanya who assumed the intricacies of the actual mediation with Bhoja. Even later, Kalhaṇikā was accorded a reception by Jayasiṁha only after he introduced Bhoja to Queen Raḍḍādevī. This is somewhat mystifying, as there is no prior indication of Jayasiṁha's preference for this queen.

And yet, the importance of Kalhaṇikā's contribution is obvious. On the one hand, she was instrumental in bringing one of Jayasiṁha's greatest rivals within his fold, preventing a potential ḍāmara rebellion that could have seriously threatened the king's position.[64] The importance of Kalhaṇikā's mediation is stressed, for instance, by the fact that Bhoja was reassured by her presence, apparently assuming Jayasiṁha to be a reflection of her and her virtues (*RT*, VIII.3182). On the other hand, Jayasiṁha is subsequently shown to accept the advice of his 'clever queen' regarding Bhoja (*RT*, VIII.3246–9), honouring her for vindicating his trust in her. At this point, it is interesting to note that Raḍḍādevī is described in terms of being 'proud' and 'delicate' (*RT*, VIII.3387, 3394), in contrast to the constant appellation of cleverness attributed to Kalhaṇikā, perhaps as an indication of her greater suitability for a task of policy.

Other prominent and powerful queens include Śrīlekhā, Ananta's own mother and King Saṁgrāmarāja's queen, who appears as a vigorous, vibrant and self-willed woman, almost cast in the mould of Sūryamatī. Initially, she is shown to take advantage of her husband's slipping power by indulging 'in licentious conduct' with her lovers (*RT*, VII.114). Seemingly 'very fond of accumulating wealth', Śrīlekhā obtained 'great power' by the king's favour (*RT*, VII.126). Thereafter, she apparently killed her son, Harirāja, by witchcraft and made an attempt to ascend the throne (*RT*, VII.133–5). This, however, proved to be an abortive bid, in that the court made Ananta the king to preempt her, prompting Kalhaṇa to speculate on the futility of Harirāja's murder (AD 1028—*RT*, VII.136–7).

Sussala's wife, Meghamañjarī, 'of exemplary virtues', who, interestingly, was raised like a son by her maternal grandfather, also appears to have wielded much influence over her husband (*RT*, VIII.204–5). Sussala shared his grievances regarding councillors with her and her fortune is cited as his support. Her sudden death traumatized him to the extent that he lost the desire to rule, and gave the throne (temporarily) to his son, Jayasiṁha (*RT*, VIII.1232).

In sharp contrast, there is an interesting reference to Śāradā, another wife of Sussala, who legitimized a rebel scheme, providing it the official sanction and material necessary to plunder the treasury (*RT*, VIII.1823), and, incidentally, proving the inviolability of the written orders of queens.[65] In similar vein was Harṣa's wife, Sugalā, who gained the support of her father-in-law, Kalaśa, and conceived an abortive plan to kill her husband (*RT*, VII.562–7). She later boldly staked her claim as Harṣa's chief queen (*RT*, VII.830).

Finally, Raḍḍādevī (cited earlier) is accorded a panegyric description by Kalhaṇa (*RT*, VIII.3382–6) who lauds her power in determining the treatment of princes and chiefs, consequent on Jayasiṁha's attachment for her (*RT*, VIII.3393—*sthir-prasāde bhūpāle nirgrahānugrahau kṣṇāt, bhū-bhujāmapi saṁvṛttā-vavichbhinnau tadichbhayā*). Raḍḍādevī also seemed to have had the influence to independently conclude politically sagacious marriage alliances for her daughters.

In conclusion, one can note the role of the harem, as a group entity, on the throne in the post-Diddā phase.[66] At the outset, one should note that the equation of most kings with their harems, which Kalhaṇa also holds as a reflection of their characters, seemed to be a conscious violation of stipulated norms and ideals. The *Rāmāyaṇa* and the *Mahābhārata*, for instance, advise the king to appease and protect his ladies but not to believe in their statements or to confide any secret to them.[67] However, the active participation of the harem in politics, as revealed by the *Rājataraṅgiṇī*, is an indication of the confidence reposed in many of its members.

In the pre-Diddā phase, the harem is shown as exercising a largely malignant influence on kings, as in prompting a drunk Lalitāditya Muktāpīḍa to give foolhardy instructions, or in being involved in Cakravarman's murder. This, and the fact that Kalhaṇa equates a big harem with degenerate royal characters, has perhaps provoked R.C. Majumdar to stress the 'evil influence of harem upon the king and the kingdom' among the several lessons that Kalhaṇa's history apparently teaches us.[68]

In the contemporary portions of Books VII and VIII, the harem's role seems to alternate between active political interference and passivity. Thus, for instance, the high-spirited wives of Kalaśa's harem spread disparaging rumours about the next king, Utkarṣa, to discredit him (*RT*, VII.758). The harem of Kalaśa's son, Harṣa, was constituted mostly of śāhī princesses, and seemed to have wielded much influence. On the one hand, some of them were involved in an abortive plot to kill Harṣa, instigated by the latter's rebel half-brother, Jayarāja (*RT*, VII.1016). On the other hand, they subsequently instigated Harṣa to murder Malla, the father of Uccala and Sussala, which proved to have fatal consequences for Harṣa (*RT*, VII.1469–70, 1484). They eventually burnt themselves, despite his pleas (*RT*, VII.1550–82). Interestingly, Harṣa's incompetence as a ruler is shown in his inability to control the members of his harem and their 'serious misconduct' (*RT*, VII.1142).[69]

The harem—as a group entity—in the later reigns seems to be marginal, and Kalhaṇa focuses on individual women instead. Thus, for instance, he talks of the general reversal of the status of women and forced prostitution in Uccala's reign, and of the women enjoyed by rulers like Salhaṇa and Bhikṣācara (*RT*, VIII.420, 867). Sussala's carefully nurtured distrust of women is dwelt upon (*RT*, VIII.1276–8), as also the fact of Jayasiṁha's association with his minister's wife. This, incidentally, speaks volumes for the objectivity of Kalhaṇa's stance in that, as Stein points out, he does not seek to hide the unsavoury aspects of Jayasiṁha's character, although he wrote in his time.[70]

QUEENS AND MATRIMONIAL ALLIANCES

That the queens of early medieval Kashmir had a definite political role to play is clearly exemplified in their almost consistent use, in the post-Diddā phase, to effect reconciliation, or to increase power, by the establishment of marital alliances.[71] Significantly, Kalhaṇa seems to concur with the efficacy and indispensability of such alliances in the political arena and, to this end, recounts them in painstaking detail.

It is important to note, however, that the woman is not always identified in these alliances. For instance, there is Bhikṣācara's alliance with two unnamed entities (*RT*, VIII.547, 878). Hence, their participation in such alliances seemed more a usage of their potential, rather than their exercise of an independent agency. This is underscored by the fact that the suitors changed with the shifting power equations, as in the ḍāmara Alaṁkāracakra giving his daughters to Jayasiṁha's sons instead of the rebel Bhoja, who was the original choice (*RT*, VIII.2953).

However, importantly, women are shown as the instigators of several such proposals.[72] Some notable examples are the ḍāmara Garga's wife, Chuḍḍā, who initiated the family's alliance with Sussala (*RT*, VIII.465), and Raḍḍādevī (Jayasiṁha's wife), who seemed to have independently decided to marry her daughter, Menilā, to Somapāla's son, Bhūpāla (*RT*, VIII.3394) and the other, Rājyaśrī, to King Prājidhara (*RT*, VIII.3398–9).

One should note again Kalhaṇa's purposeful ambivalence. Thus, on the one hand, he displays his conservatism by remarking that Saṁgrāmarāja lowered his 'royal fame' by 'unequal' relations (*RT*, VII.10), as in his daughter, Lothikā's marriage to a brāhmaṇa, Preman. Marriage alliances are, therefore, regarded as a measure of social prestige here. However, on the other hand, the alliances concluded between Sussala and the ḍāmara Garga's daughters (*RT*, VIII.459–60), are regarded with more flexibility, although this would rank as an alliance between unequals.

Marriage alliances are most profuse in Book VIII of the *Rāja-taraṅgiṇī*, especially from Uccala's reign. The language used by Kalhaṇa is highly illuminating. Uccala's daughter is a surety of lasting wealth and stability to her husband, Somapāla of Rājapurī (*RT*, VIII.290). Similarly, Lothaṇa increased his power 'through high connections' (*RT*, VIII.1915–24) by concluding two fresh alliances after his wife, Mallā's death.

It is important to note, however, that such alliances held no guarantee of peace. This was evident, for instance, in two of Jayasiṁha's brothers-in-law becoming his enemies, or in Sussala's liquidation of most of Garga's family, after overcoming the initial scruples of 'family affection' (*RT*, VIII.611–18). However, Kalhaṇa tempers Sussala's ruthlessness by a touching account of his grief at the death of his wife, Meghamañjarī's mother, Mallā, and grandfather (*RT*, VIII.618).

We can also consider the important issue of sibling rivalries for the throne. Kalhaṇa indicates a drastic change in succession rights, in the post-Diddā phase, in that the heir's right was contested by his real brothers, half-brothers, other ministers, and ḍāmaras, thereby setting aside the stipulations in the *Rāmāyaṇa* and the

Śukranītisāra that clearly favour the eldest son.[73] This scenario contrasted greatly with Avantivarman's reign, for instance, where he, 'being free from jealousy', is said to have granted permanent royal prerogatives to his uterine brothers and to his step-brother, Śūravarman, and his son (*RT*, V.42). Kalhaṇa's preference for this bygone age when royal families shared their possessions is seen, for instance, in his condemning Kalaśa as an 'unnatural son' for persecuting his parents for power (*RT*, VII.408–9).

Kalhaṇa uses evocative language to portray the enmity between brothers. Harṣa is thus wingless prey for his two falcon-like step-brothers, Vijayamalla and Utkarṣa, in the tussle for the throne (*RT*, VII.823).[74] Subsequently, Harṣa is shown to uproot his family with mixed feelings (*RT*, VII.1068, 1248–51). Likewise, blood brothers, Uccala and Sussala, clashed for the throne with no question of precedence between them until the birth of Sussala's son, Jayasiṁha, signalled an end to their enmity (*RT*, VIII.242). Kalhaṇa talks of Uccala's hostility to Sussala being 'mixed with tenderness' (*RT*, VIII, 295).

Sussala's reign and character form a sort of case study for Kalhaṇa's view of the disruptive effects of the throne on the king's relations with his sons, wives, brothers and servants. Interestingly, however, Kalhaṇa also specifies that Sussala's honour was sought to be upheld after his death, not by his male kinsmen but by his niece, Saubhāgyalekhā, who tried to prevent the disfigurement of his head by his enemies (*RT*, VIII.1464–5).

Dynastic Foundations and Women

Evidence of women of the Diddā and post-Diddā phase as dynastic destroyers can be discerned in a sequential fashion, as in the earlier phase. Thus, Abhimanyu 'withered' away like a flower owing to his proximity to the wickedness emanating from his mother, Diddā, and her companions. Diddā later destroyed the next three kings (and her grandsons)—Nandigupta, Tribhuvana and Bhīmagupta, by witchcraft or torture (*RT*, VI.311–12, 332), thereby paving the way for her accession to the throne.

Likewise, Queen Śrīlekhā apparently killed her son, Harirāja, by witchcraft to get the throne (*RT*, VII.133). Queen Sūryamatī is held responsible for Ananta's abdication (*RT*, VII.232–3) and eventual death by suicide (*RT*, VII.452–7). Her curse, incidentally, is cited as causing a spate of deaths among the followers of her son, Kalaśa (*RT*, VII.562–7). Kalhaṇa holds 'over-indulgence in sensual pleasures' responsible for Kalaśa's fatal illness (*RT*, VII.698). As for Harṣa, he survived a bid on his life by his wife Sugalā (*RT*, VII.695–87). Some of his other queens also plotted to kill him. Eventually, his śāhī queens convinced him to murder Malla (*RT*, VII.1469–70) which caused his defeat and death, the latter being specifically attributed to the curse of Malla's wife, Nandā (*RT*, VII.1490–4).

Uccala was waylaid and killed on his way to the apartment of his wife, Bijjalā, his senses dulled and alertness reduced at the prospect of a sensual evening (*RT*, VII.306–9). The death of Sussala's wife, Meghamañjarī, prompted him to give the throne to his son (*RT*, VIII.1232), thereby causing a (temporary) change in rulership. The wives of Lothaṇa and Sussala (Śāradā) both supported rebel schemes (*RT*, VIII.1820–3).

Thus, in a majority of cases, involvement with women did spell destruction for a king. Hence, the king as patriarch was not perceived of as invulnerable. His exercise of power had to be accompanied by constant watchfulness.[75] Nevertheless, Kalhaṇa, in keeping with his typical ambivalence, heavily underscores the role of women as creators, protectors and saviours as well, whereby, once again, by their intervention, women exerted a bearing on various dynasties.[76] Although there are stray instances of this in the earlier period, Kalhaṇa develops the theme more prominently in the post-Diddā phase.

Uccala was deluded in his bid to drown Bhikṣācara, a rival claimant and grandson of Harṣa, by the intervention of Āsamatī, a female relative of the śāhī princesses, who allegedly substituted another child in Bhikṣācara's place and enabled his escape to the 'Dekhan' (*RT*, VIII.224–7, 233). She thereby contributed to a future change of lineage in that Bhikṣācara assumed power at a later stage.[77] Her death was said to coincide with a fall in Bhikṣācara's fortunes (*RT*, VIII.552). The alleged involvement of Uccala's chief-queen, Jayamatī, in the rescue bid is highly significant. Thus, two women were involved in a dynastic change here but in a positive context. Incidentally, Stein, in his 'Introduction', does not mention Jayamatī's role in saving Bhikṣācara's life.

Likewise, a courtesan, Thakkanā, warned Uccala and Sussala about the threat to their lives from Harṣa (*RT*, VII.1252), and played an important role in saving them. Subsequently, when Harṣa was worsted by Uccala, he was deserted by all his male advisors, while women, significantly, seemed to support him with sound advice. A woman apprised him of the dangers to come (*RT*, VII.1624), while the wife of the minister Kapila offered him help on her own initiative, her behaviour thereby contrasting with that of her perfidious sons and husband (*RT*, VII.1613–14). Kalhaṇa seems to imply that had Harṣa heeded her advice, he could have survived and regained power, thereby changing the course of Kashmir's history.

Kalaśa faced the prospect of death twice, once in connection with an amorous adventure (*RT*, VII.307–13) and again at the hands of his irate mother, Sūryamatī (*RT*, VII.329–30). However, the intervention of his wife, Dilhā, who cleverly anticipated Sūryamatī's wrath and ensured Kalaśa's safety, was crucial in according Kalaśa a fresh lease of life and altering the course of events (*RT*, VII.331–3).

Women appear thus to have been involved in nearly every stage of a dynasty's progression—from its inception to its demise. Not only did women have a bearing on their foundation, they are also shown to have prolonged or curtailed the reigns and lives of various kings, in direct and indirect ways.[78]

ROLE OF COURTESANS/PROSTITUTES

The role of prostitutes and courtesans in the Diddā and post-Diddā phase in Kashmir can best be understood by an appraisal of the evidence in the *Rājataraṅgiṇī*, and Kṣemendra's *Samayamātṛkā*. The latter text is an invaluable source for the status of this important segment of society in the contemporary socio-political scenario. While its central idea may have been taken from Dāmodaragupta's *Kuṭṭanīmatam*, the scope it offers for a gender analysis is greater—both in regard to the development of the story as also in the overall characterization. It would be worthwhile to examine the evidence of both texts in this regard and assess the implications thereof, including obvious differences in the authors' perceptions.

The Evidence of the Rājataraṅgiṇī

Prostitutes and courtesans seemed to appear in greater profusion and play more palpable roles in the pre-Diddā phase of Kashmir, but a few notable examples can be cited of the Diddā and post-Diddā phase as well. Kalhaṇa's dislike of prostitutes and their 'low' origins did not prevent him from recording their rise to power and prominence.

The crucial role played by Thakkanā in saving the lives of Uccala and Sussala has already been cited. One can also consider the important role played by Uccala's chief queen, Jayamatī, a temple dancer's ward 'of unknown origin' who starts off as his mistress and later occupies 'one half of the throne'. Kalhaṇa's typical ambiguity is in evidence here. Thus, on the one hand, he stresses Jayamatī's immorality in having several lovers (*RT*, VII.1460–2). However, on the other hand, he appreciates her for having acquitted herself honourably as Uccala's wife, despite her 'common' birth, by dint of her kindness, courtesy, generosity, wisdom and so on (*RT*, VIII.82–3).

Significantly, Jayamatī was entrusted with the charge of Bhikṣācara (the previous king, Harṣa's grandson and a contender to the throne) by Uccala, thereby indicating the extent of his trust in her. Yet she played a crucial role in later allegedly masterminding Bhikṣācara's escape (cited earlier) and saving him from death at Uccala's hands. Jayamatī's contravention of Uccala's orders proved to be the cause of his subsequent disaffection for her. However, she was indirectly instrumental in enabling Bhikṣācara's accession to the throne at a subsequent stage (1120–1).

The Evidence of the Samayamātṛkā[79]

Kṣemendra's *Samayamātṛkā* deals with a prostitute, Kaṅkālī's ingenious means of survival and her timely adoption as a 'mother' by a young prostitute, Kalāvatī, whom she is instrumental in making wealthy by her judicious schemes. There are numerous references to places in Kashmir as part of a description of Kaṅkālī's travels, lending a tone of authenticity to the text. Moreover, importantly, there are references to Ananta and the usefulness of this text to him. To better understand these varied implications, it would be worthwhile to briefly outline the story.

The text commences with the plight of a young prostitute, Kalāvatī, after the death of her procuress 'mother'—her erstwhile guardian—thereby leaving her prey to all sorts of undesirable clients (*SM*, I.27, 32).[80] At this juncture, she is told of the advisability of adopting an old prostitute, Kaṅkālī, as her 'mother'. The suitability of the latter for the role is sketched in great detail, with special emphasis on her wily, shrewd nature and ability to capitalize on every situation.[81] It would be worthwhile to provide a brief account of Kaṅkālī's remarkably successful struggle for survival, during the course of which she changes several names, locales and professions.

Kaṅkālī, initially called Gargatikā, was sold at the age of seven to a woman in the market by her mother, Bhūmikā, who ran a travellers' lodge in Parihāsapura. The sale was enabled by the fact that Kaṅkālī was very articulate and able to entertain people with her talk even at that age (*SM*, II.3–4, 6). Subsequently, a merchant's son, Pūrṇik, was attracted to her but she decamped with his ornaments at night while he was asleep and raised an alarm, whereupon he ran away for fear of being discovered (*SM*, II.8–12).

Thereafter, Kaṅkālī moved to Śaṁkarapura with the jewels, under the name Mahlaṇā, where she associated with different men. She later repeated her feat of stealing jewels from an enamoured youth, Nandisoma, and moved to Pratāpapura (*SM*, II.19–20). She became the mistress of one Samarasiṁha, under the name Nāgarikā, and incited him to fight with his relatives in order to get rid of him. After assuming power in his household, she became the mistress of Samarasiṁha's son, Śrīsiṁha, which precipitated his downfall in that his absorption in her prompted the neighbouring king to attack him, upon which Kaṅkālī escaped with his wealth (*SM*, II.21–7).

Kaṅkālī now moved to the next town, under the name Mṛgāvatī, and assumed the guise of a high caste woman. While ostensibly engaged in ceremonies for her father on the river bank, she was able to attract a wealthy horse-owner, Bandhurasāra, whose business and income she came to control. On his sudden death, she made a pretence of wanting to burn herself, but was dissuaded by relatives and took over Bandhurasāra's possessions on the king's orders (*SM*, II.28–36).

Thereafter, she had an affair with the man in charge of the stables, sold his horses, and appropriated his wealth. Her stepsons' opposition to her selling the house resulted in a court case, whereupon she bribed the magistrates and won control over the property. She then sold the house and decamped with the money to the *Śāktamaṭha* where she dyed her hair black and pretended to be a businesswoman. She was eventually imprisoned for accepting stolen wealth, but managed to cut the jailer's tongue and escape (*SM*, II.40–51).

Kaṅkālī now established herself in Vijayeśvara, pretending to be the chief minister's daughter, under the name Anupamā. However, she eventually decided to become an ascetic to ward off the imminent prospect of begging, on account of her inability to attract clients to her visibly ageing self. She assumed the name Śikhā, befriended an ascetic, Bhairavasoma, and later decamped with his ornaments to the Kṛtyāśrama *vihāra* under the name Vajraghaṇṭā, where she occupied herself with advising various people (*SM*, II.52–64). She had a child by a man, Maṅgala, and thereafter became a nurse in the house of King Chitrasena's minister, under the name Ardhakṣīrā. She subsequently abandoned her son, appropriated his jewels and retired to a mountain village where she reared goats under the name of Dhanavatī (*SM*, II.65–74).

Thereafter, she reached Avantipuri, sold sweetmeats, and later begged for alms on the pretence of arranging for her companion's marriage. She now changed her name to Pañjikā and perfected the art of cheating at gambling outside gambling dens. After this, she changed her name to Mukulikā and sold religious icons but soon incurred debts and ran away (*SM*, II.77–81). Changing her name to Varṇā, she then pretended to be a great astrologer and became famous.

She subsequently robbed a minister of his silver vessels,[82] joined a tour, stripped unconscious travellers of their wealth after feeding them drugged food and went to Śūrapuram (*SM*, II.83–90). Braving inclement weather, she reached Baṁba where she accumulated wealth and honour by pretending to be a chaste brāhmaṇa woman, Satyavatī. She assured the king of a victory, but vanished before the fight, thereafter crossing borders with ease and duping rich men with her false talk and pretended abilities (*SM*, II.92–104).[83] Kaṅkālī finally returned home after her extensive travels (*SM*, II.105).

On subsequently agreeing to be the 'mother' of the prostitute, Kalāvatī, Kaṅkālī instructed the latter on the method of ensnaring rich clients and appropriating their wealth, and thoroughly appraised a prospective client, Śaṅkha. She encouraged Kalāvatī to implement her measures, which proceeded with clockwork precision.[84] Kaṅkālī is, thus, instrumental in making her protégée extremely wealthy, justifying her selection as Kalāvatī's 'timely mother' (*SM*, VIII.127—*iti samaya-mātṛkāyāha kaṅkālyā buddhi-saṁvibhāgena, bhuktvā vaṇijaha sakalaṁ kalāvatī pūrṇa-vibhavābhūt*).

It would be worthwhile to speculate on the implications of the *Samayamātṛkā* for an analysis of the society and polity. As is obvious, the text offers great potential in this regard, not only in revealing the specifics of a prostitute's status and profession but also Kṣemendra's attitude towards the profession, and the points of convergence and divergence with Kalhaṇa.

KṢEMENDRA'S MOTIVES AND THEIR IMPLICATIONS

Kṣemendra offers two important but completely varied motives behind the writing of this text. Initially, he states that the purpose of the *Samayamātṛkā* is to teach the prostitutes the secret of their trade (*SM*, I.3—*kṣemendreṇa rahasyārtha-mantra-tantropayoginī, kriyate vāra-rāmāṇāmiyaṁ samayamātṛkā*). This seemingly exaggerated claim is, however, corroborated by the exhaustive details he provides of this social group.

The business of prostitution and the machinations thereof are described somewhat in the nature of an eyewitness account.[85] For instance, Kaṅkālī identifies eighty types of lovers for Kalāvatī's benefit, and provides detailed and methodical instructions for ensnaring wealthy men, extracting their riches, and appraising the possibility of re-associating with them in the event of their regaining wealth.[86] The depiction of Kalāvatī, Kaṅkālī, and their companions, as also the milieu of their existence, strikes a realistic note.[87] The enumeration of specific aspects of the prostitute's trade, as in the indispensability of a procuress 'mother' in selecting the right client, speaks for an intimate knowledge of their life (*SM*, VIII.129).

The second motive is contained in the epilogue and is alternately significant and intriguing. Kṣemendra states that his purpose in writing the text is to provide the newly-crowned Ananta with a weapon against his enemies, in that it can offer ideas on the deployment of women in the enemy camp to effect the latter's downfall (*SM*, 4). Although this is clearly divergent from the earlier aim, it is strongly reminiscent of Kalhaṇa's comments on the destructive power of women and the power of prostitutes to ruin a ruler.

Admittedly, Kṣemendra voices his grievances against various 'dark aspects' of society in almost all his works and obviously, the *Samayamātṛkā* is intended to warn people about the threat posed by prostitutes by exposing the methods of their trade. The first motive, therefore, is a sarcastically worded one in that the effort is to teach the people, rather than the prostitutes, about prostitution. The purpose is, in all probability, to evoke a sense of revulsion towards the seemingly cold-blooded aspects of the trade and discourage association with it.[88]

However, one must consider the implications of the second motive as well. As the enemy's identity is not specified, one assumes that Kṣemendra is proffering general advice to Ananta and not alluding to a specific situation faced by him. Nevertheless, the novelty of his suggestion is significant in stressing the potential of women to effect changes in rulership, thereby distinctly echoing the *Rājataraṅgiṇī* in this regard, the accent being not the usefulness of prostitutes in aiding a political campaign, but the aura of destruction they bear and the desirability of utilizing it to one's advantage.

At this juncture, one can mention another intriguing reference, in the text, to women whose husbands died in battle, attacking the enemy king (*SM*, 4). Once again, as the context is not specified, one presumes the allusion is a generalized one. Kṣemendra seems to be educating Ananta on the potential value of women as a political weapon. The irony is that Ananta himself needed to be educated on political and other matters by his wife, Sūryamatī.

IMPLICATIONS OF KAṄKĀLĪ'S PORTRAYAL

Although Kṣemendra's aim is to portray the bawd, Kaṅkālī, as the epitome of moral degeneration, not only does she emerge as an unbelievably tough and shrewd character, she also embodies the possibilities and options open to a woman who is compelled by circumstances to live by her wits. Kaṅkālī is depicted as a complete survivor—aided by her ruthless reasoning—and being superior to men in terms of her astute wit and sagacity. In addition, she is also shown to possess pragmatism and discernment. Interestingly, this portrayal is an ironic outcome of Kṣemendra's stress on her rapacity and immorality that, however, clearly underlines her strength.

Kaṅkālī became a prostitute when her mother sold her at a tender age. However, she later provides a significantly novel justification for her adoption of the trade and successful deception of innocent clients, as having divine legitimization. Impressed by her steadfast determination to prosper by falsehood, the god Gaṇeśa apparently blessed her with prosperity (*SM*, IV.73–7). Hence, that a prostitute should shun truth so as not to jeopardize her existence, just as a businessman should shun generosity and a guru humility, is stressed (*SM*, IV.69–70). In addition, significantly, Kaṅkālī states her desire for wealth to be in conformity with social standards that equate it with respect and auspiciousness, thereby providing an added justification to her profession (*SM*, IV.74).[89]

Kaṅkālī's ability to outwit men in every aspect with consummate ease is an important feature of the text. Her arrogance is revealed in her contention that the brainless man is the means of survival for a prostitute, a spy, and a *viṭa* (rogue) (*SM*, IV.43). She was able to dupe men in her various guises, with false religious instruction (*SM*, II.99–100), or a pretended mastery of various skills, and so appropriate their wealth. As a result, she was able to change locales and cross borders with ease, the extent of her charm apparently spanning Kāmboja, Turuṣka, China, Trigarta, Gauḍa,

Aṅga and Vaṅga (*SM*, II.104). One of the interesting instances of her persuasive powers was in her ability to convince a man that she had not spat on his hand, although the reality was otherwise (*SM*, IV.38–42).

There are several other aspects to Kaṅkālī's personality, for instance, a probing and thoughtful mind. She questions some decisions taken by males like Rāma and Śiva, e.g. Rāma's pursuit of the golden deer and Śiva's combination of family life with asceticism.[90] She finds these foolish (*SM*, IV.24, 27, 34). Thereafter, she extends this into sympathy for (innocent) women who are obliged to survive on the mercy of male dullards (*SM*, IV.36).

Kaṅkālī's confidence and presence of mind is evidenced in her offering, at one stage, simultaneous advice to various categories of people. Thus, she counselled pious men on wisdom, housewives on skills, prostitutes on trapping men, businessmen on increasing wealth, and fools on getting work done through magical means (*SM*, II.63–4—*patvi maṇḍala-śikṣāyai praṇatānāṁ sadaiva sā, gṛhe gṛhe kula-strīnāṁ dadau dauha-śīlya-deśanāṁ; vaśya-prayogairveśyānāṁ vaṇijāmṛddhi-vardhanaiha, mantra-vādena mūrkhānāṁ sā paraṁ pūjyatāṁ yayau*).

Kaṅkālī's sharp, meticulous and coldly logical reasoning had important implications. It enabled her to enrich herself and her ward. On the other hand, it indicated the possibilities open to women who desired to lead unconventional lifestyles. Kaṅkālī's fluid adoption of various professions—most of which appear to be male prerogatives—underscores this.[91] Thus, she was alternately a businesswoman, a manager of horses, an astrologer, a gambler and a maker of metal. The fact that people accepted her in these roles is an important comment on the contemporary social scene and corroborates Kalhaṇa's evidence on the public presence of women in early Kashmir.

Was Kṣemendra, then, indicating an actual state of affairs in which certain women could opt for varied professions and travel extensively? One might argue that prostitutes usually command a greater degree of freedom than other women. However, it is important to note that Kaṅkālī's actual trade was *not* known to most of her associates, her strength lying in her ability to mask her real intentions. Therefore, to them she was an ordinary woman who was endeavouring to make a living. Hence, the sympathy and assistance accorded her, at various stages, is significant. It implies that women were, perhaps, accorded the same flexibility as men to choose their trade and that these liberal social mores dictated the acceptance of the same, such that a determined and shrewd individual like Kaṅkālī could succeed in her struggle for survival.

Admittedly, Kaṅkālī's beauty would have been crucial to her initial success, but, as Kṣemendra points out, it proved to be short-lived, forcing her to adopt other means to survive. As she pragmatically admits, wealth could only be obtained by intelligence or wisdom, and not by family, skills, beauty, or knowledge (*SM*, IV.19). It was her intelligence and resilience that enabled her to hold her own, making her one of the strongest women protagonists of the contemporary literature.

IMPLICATIONS OF KṢEMENDRA'S ATTITUDE

Kṣemendra's deep disapproval of prostitutes and their trade has implications not only on the fashioning of his characters, but also in highlighting important points of convergence and divergence with the *Rājataraṅgiṇī*. One may begin by noting that Kṣemendra in his *Deśopadeśa* includes the prostitute (*veśyā*) and the bawd (*kuṭṭanī*) among various categories of 'corrupt' persons, such as the wicked (*durjana*), miser (*kadarya*), voluptuary (*viṭa*), student (*chātra*) and so on, and subjects them to severe criticism, labelling them 'the blemishes of society'.[92] By extension, *veśyāvṛtta* or the way of a prostitute apparently constitutes one of the 'dark aspects' of the world, as per his *Kalāvilāsa*.[93]

Admittedly, there are several points of convergence with the *Rājataraṅgiṇī* in this regard. The condemnation of prostitutes and their ability to ensnare the minds of men, as also the inadvisability of capitulation to them, is common to both texts. Similarly, the aura of destruction that they seem to bear is another shared aspect. Just as men who associate with Kaṅkālī are shown to suffer ruin in one way or other, Kalhaṇa shows association with prostitutes to cause the ruination of several kings. Kṣemendra's final advice to Ananta (cited earlier) is in the same vein.

However, one should note several crucial points of divergence between the texts. For instance, fear of women and their apparent power over men seems to pervade the *Samayamātṛkā*, rather than the acceptance of it that is Kalhaṇa's attitude. Thus, Kṣemendra's stress is not so much on Kaṅkālī's resourcefulness and grit, as on her deviousness and unscrupulousness. Her various triumphs over men are not used to demonstrate her intelligence, but to stress the innocence of her victims and the general rapacity of the prostitute. This translates into his rather exaggerated depiction of Kaṅkālī's doings and his deliberately harsh portrayal of her character, without, apparently, a single redeeming feature. Her abandonment of her son and, by extension, her complete repudiation of motherhood, underscore this aspect.

On the other hand, most prostitutes in the *Rājataraṅgiṇī* appear in a realistic blend of good and bad qualities. Their power in the socio-political sphere is documented by Kalhaṇa in an even-handed manner. Their role as saviours and protectors, as in the case of Thakkanā and Jayamatī, is stressed on an equal level with their destructive potential. Besides, interestingly, while Kṣemendra discounts the possibility of prostitutes feeling genuine affection, the *Rājataraṅgiṇī* provides numerous examples of devotion and loyalty displayed by Jayamatī, Sahajā, and others.[94]

Thus, while Kalhaṇa acknowledges the power and influence of prostitutes in the contemporary socio-political scenario, Kṣemendra—the 'stern moralist'[95]—laments the destruction of people by prostitutes and their propensity to fall into the latter's trap (*SM*, VIII.128).[96] It is unclear as to which of the two represents the general social attitude in early medieval Kashmir. The bitterness of Kṣemendra's tone, when viewed in conjunction with his intimate knowledge of prostitution, may well stem from some kind of personal experience. The figure of Kaṅkālī could be based on an actual prostitute of Kṣemendra's acquaintance.

The absence of corroborative evidence precludes a more definite assessment in this regard. Nevertheless, the pivotal presence of prostitutes and the power exercised by them, as attested by both the *Samayamātṛkā* and the *Rājataraṅgiṇī*, is an undeniably important ingredient of early medieval Kashmir and a crucial topic for gender analysis.

In her work on prostitutes in the early medieval period,[97] Shalini Shah observes that they constituted a counter-culture with subversive potential and that patriarchal ideology was deeply suspicious of their non-marital and non-procreative sexuality. The recognition of their status and wealth by the state, therefore, implied their 'agency'.[98] Although Shah rightly critiques the portrayal of the prostitute as a victim of patriarchal oppression, she seems to err in questioning the image of the prostitute as a 'perfidious whore' whose sexuality threatened the patriarchal structure.[99] Lallā, Jayādevī and Kaṅkālī, for instance, definitely challenged the patriarchal structure in their unashamed use of sexual power to gain control over men. In any case, Shah herself points to the danger posed by prostitutes to patriarchy by virtue of their autonomous space and value systems.[100] Hence, the point of her critique is not immediately apparent. Nevertheless, her acknowledgement of the prostitutes' agency is very pertinent.

NON-ROYAL WOMEN

As mentioned in the previous chapter, although the *Rājataraṅgiṇī* deals almost exclusively with the royal court and its machinations, there are several references to non-royal women and their power and influence on courtly happenings, in direct or indirect ways. Their active participation in politics is in a parallel vein to their royal counterparts, whereby they often appear to overshadow their male counterparts.

The role of Āsamatī and Thakkanā in changing the course of royal politics has been cited. Apart from these, there are several instances of women mediators who played important roles. For instance, in the reconciliation between Jayasiṁha and Bhoja, the latter's nurse, Nonā, played a major part. She initially broached the issue to the king, acquainting him with Bhoja's desire to surrender (*RT*, VIII.3061). There is also the case of Mallārjuna's widowed mother, Sahajā, who mediated between him and Jayasiṁha's forces by attracting the commander, Koṣṭhaka, and his 'fickle-minded' troops by her feminine wiles (*RT*, VIII.1968–71).

The significant role of ḍāmara women can be gleaned not just from specific cases, but also from Kalhaṇa's periodic surveys of political equations. A noteworthy example is that of Chuḍḍā, the ḍāmara Garga's wife, who independently decided on the advisability of concluding a marital alliance between her family and Sussala's.[101] When Garga was hounded by Sussala's army, she and her daughter stepped in to conciliate Sussala. After Garga's execution, she carried on, undaunted, by becoming her son's guardian and protecting his interests (*RT*, VIII.1122, 1130). She eventually assumed such power that her murder was inevitable (*RT*, VIII.1138). Interestingly, a rival ḍāmara, Mallakoṣṭha, did not venture to return to his land until after her demise, owing to her formidable power base and her local support (*RT*, VIII.1153). There is also the case of the ḍāmara woman from Nīlāśva who, along with two other ḍāmaras from Devasarasa and Holaḍā, offered valuable loyalty and support to Jayasiṁha during Bhoja's rebellion, in contrast to their other counterparts.

One can also consider the contribution of Sillā, the ḍāmara Vijaya's mother, who commanded her son's troops in his absence and led them to safety from Vijayeśvara to Devasarasa (*RT*, VIII.1069–70) before being murdered, interestingly, by the same man (Tikka) who murdered Chuḍḍā. There is also the role played by the wife of Utpala, a professional killer, who offered him cold-blooded advice on the advantages of killing Sussala. This had great implications for the course of Kashmir's history as it led to Sussala's murder, thereby causing a change in rulership.

In conclusion, there are two important aspects to note here. First, it is obvious that non-royal widows do not seem to have been relegated to the margins of the contemporary socio-political scenario, thereby indicating an important point of convergence with some of their royal counterparts. The forceful and public presence of Chuḍḍā and Sahajā underscores this.

Second, one should note the implications of Kalhaṇa's portrayal of non-royal women. Admittedly, he maintains his ambiguity with regard to them in that he balances his description of female agency with stereotypical statements. Thus, for instance, Bhoja's nurse, Nonā, initiates an important reconciliation and yet is discredited for not possessing much intelligence on account of her sex (*RT*, VIII.3061)—though the fact of Bhoja reposing trust in her and her actions directly militate against this statement. However, Uccala's wife, Jayamatī, despised by Kalhaṇa for her low origin and her unwarranted intrusion into politics, is thereafter accorded a sympathetic treatment, especially in the aftermath of her thwarting Uccala's murderous designs on Bhikṣācara. So Kalhaṇa's portrayal of non-royal women is not in stereotypical or patronizing terms.

SATĪ: ROYAL AND NON-ROYAL

Self-immolation on the husband's death, another point of convergence in the lives of royal and non-royal women, particularly in the post-Diddā phase, warrants separate analysis. *Satī* was part of a value system that increased male domination over women and was seen as a means to overcome widowhood.[102] It was also linked to the socio-economic realities of a widow's life under patriarchy and the psychological conditioning that egged her on to the path of self-destruction.[103]

The ideal woman in Brahmanical texts was one imbued with the qualities of a *satī* or who epitomized *satītva*/the wifely power of the chaste woman.[104] By AD 700, the merit bestowed by *satī* was so great that it cut across the usual implications of karma for the husband and wife.[105] The *satī* was seen as making a conscious choice for her own sake and that of her family—both grounded in the power of the good woman.

Interestingly, Kalhaṇa uses *satī* to introduce both royal and non-royal women into the narrative. Additionally, he lauds it as 'the fitting course for a proud woman' (*RT*, VIII.448). His attitude parallels that of lawgivers like Aparārka, for instance, who praises it as the only *dharma* for widows,[106] and thereby sharply contrasts with Bāṇa's fierce opposition to the practice, as we shall see below.

The performance of *satī* is often shown to take the form of a competition between queens as, for instance, in the case of Uccala's queens, Jayamatī and Bijjalā: the latter, apparently eager to climb on the pyre, overtook the former whose reluctance was obvious (*RT*, VIII.363–7). Kalhaṇa reveals that Jayamatī was assaulted by robbers while ascending the pyre (*RT*, VIII.368). We do not know whether this was a common practice or an aberration.

Although Kalhaṇa does not often clarify whether the act of *satī* was prompted by force, social compulsion, or personal desire, he does indicate that the pressure to immolate was not always binding on the women. Thus, for instance, Utkarṣa's concubine, Sahajā, burnt herself on his death, whereas Kalaśa's concubine, Kayyā, chose to take another lover. Kalhaṇa's perspective on *satī* is best illustrated in the contrast he draws between these two. Sahajā apparently redeemed the dignity of womanhood by her decision to die on the pyre.

> The noble conduct which she then displayed makes women who are beloved by their husbands carry their heads higher even to this day (*RT*, VII.855—*tasyāstadānī-maucityaṁ nirvyūḍaṁ yena yośitaṁ, bhartṛ-prasāda-pātrāṇā-madyā-pyuccaistarāṁ śiraha*).

However, Kayyā, by opting to take a lowly village official as her lover, apparently disgraced 'the whole of womankind' (*RT*, VII.725). Kalhaṇa blames her 'lowly mind' for not cherishing Kalaśa's memory. As he puts it:

> If she did not remember that her lord had given her the foremost position in the whole seraglio, no matter, let her not remember it: because she was of low origin (*RT*, VII.726—*sarvā-varodha-prādhānya-pradānaṁ nāsmaradyadi, mā smāra-śīnnāma bhartustadanuccā-bhijanodbhavā*).

An interesting comment on birth is made by Kalhaṇa: Koṣṭhaka's wife who, born of a noble Rajput family, became a *satī* and entered the 'world of virtuous women' (*RT*, VIII.2335) is contrasted with the ḍāmara-wives who apparently preferred to outlive their husbands and have affairs with others.

The performance of *satī* by women from the non-royal strata of society, as revealed mostly by Book VIII of Kalhaṇa's text, is a departure from earlier passages where it is portrayed as largely a royal prerogative. Nandā, the mother of Uccala and Sussala, and widow of Malla, is introduced in connection with her self-immolation (*RT*, VII.1490–4). Interestingly, as with Sūryamatī, she acquired the power to curse on the pyre which, as in the former case, was apparently borne out.

Significantly, the death of a woman, too, seemed to precipitate the death of several men. Sūryamatī was followed by her male attendants on the pyre (*RT*, VII.481), while Meghamañjarī's cook, Teja, asserted his 'exceptional devotion' to her by killing himself on her death (*RT*, VIII.1224–5). Conversely, the deaths of both royal and non-royal men led to a spate of immolation by the women of their households. Eight of Kalaśa's queens and seventeen of Harṣa's became *satīs*, while, in the non-royal sphere, the death of Malla precipitated that of his consort, Kumudalekhā, sister-in-law, Vallabhā, two daughters-in-law, Āsamatī and Sahajā, and their six women attendants (*RT*, VII.1486–8). Similarly, governor Ānanda's mother, Gajjā, burnt herself on her son's pyre (*RT*, VII.1380), as did the sister of a minister, Dilhabhaṭṭāra, on his death (*RT*, VIII.448). Thus, death by burning was not limited to wives in either stratum of society.

In conclusion, one can note that Kalhaṇa's appreciative attitude towards *satī* appears at odds with his generally liberal perspective on women. And yet, even here, men are compared unfavourably to women. As Kalhaṇa remarks:

> Who is meaner than he who, though being a man, forgets that attachment to the master, the recollection of which makes women enter the pyre? (*RT*, VII.1412—*yoṣitopi viśantyagnim yaṁ dhyātvā vismṛtim vrajet, bhartṛ-sneha sa puṁsopi yasya konyastato-dhamaha*).

BUILDING ACTIVITIES OF MEN AND WOMEN

Building Activities of Kings

The linkage of power and glory with the buildings of kings continues from the earlier period. Male rulers are shown to concretize their political power and assert their ostentation through their buildings. However, an interesting variation is noticeable in that, for instance, Jayasiṁha's buildings are described not as an expression of his military prowess—as in the case of Lalitāditya Muktāpīḍa—but due to his diplomatic quelling of rebels, thereby pointing to a tangible change in issues of politics and political survival.

As in the earlier phase, Kalhaṇa's descriptions of these buildings often deliberately invoke and magnify the kings' glory and achievements. Jayasiṁha's powerful status was stressed by the pre-eminence of his *maṭha.* As Kalhaṇa puts it:

Then when the land had been embellished in all parts, the lord of kings built his own Maṭha which resembled the forehead mark (put on after affixing all other ornaments) (*RT*, VIII.2442—*evaṁ sarvāṅgamā-muktālaṁ-kṛteratha sa kṣiteha, viśeṣa-kābhaṁ bhūbhartṛ-vṛṣā svamakaron-maṭaṁ*).

Similarly, Harṣa's palaces testified to his wealth and desire for ostentation. Thus:

The very numerous palaces of the king shone forth with wonderful splendour, having golden Āmalaka ornaments and buildings which reached to the clouds (*RT*, VII.938—*sauvarṇa-mala-sārādyā rāja-dhānyo dharā-pateha, subharyo-bhrama-lihagṛhā bhrejire bhuvanādbhutāha*).

However, Kalhaṇa also shows piety and remorse as motives behind the building activities of certain kings. For example, with regard to Uccala, he says:

This pious (king), with whom the restoration of decayed (buildings) was a passion, put in order the famous sites of Cakradhara, Yogeśa and Svayambhū (*RT*, VIII.78—*śrī-cakradhara-yogeśa-svayambhū-sthāna-yojanaṁ, jīrṇoddhṛti-vyasaninā kṛtaṁ tena su-karmaṇā*).[107]

Furthermore, with reference to Kalaśa, he says:

This (king), whose doings were thus of a mixed character, built afresh the town and Śiva's stone temple at Vijayakṣetra, which had been burned down (*RT*, VII.524—*evaṁ śabalā-kṛtyena puraṁ tena navīkṛtaṁ, nirdagdhe vijaya-kṣetre śīlaveṣma na srūlinaha*).

Significantly, women also seemed to inspire male rulers to build, as largely evident in Book VIII of the *Rājataraṅgiṇī.* Thus, for instance, Jayasiṁha built a *maṭha* in honour of a deceased member of his harem. Thus:

In honour of Candalā, a moon-faced lady of his seraglio, who had died, he erected a Maṭha provided with ample means, from which door no guest was turned back (*RT*, VIII.3320—*avaro-dhendu-vadanāṁ mṛtāmuddiśya candalāṁ, pratya-ṣṭāpi maṭonūna-śrīr-dvāre-vāritā-tithiha*).

Similarly, Sussala built temples in the names of his wife and mother-in-law on the Vitastā's banks, along with one in his own (*RT*, VIII.579). Uccala built a *vihāra* in honour of his sister, Sullā (*RT*, VIII.248) but seemed to have equally honoured his male relatives in that he builds a *maṭha* 'to increase the merits of his father' (*RT*, VIII.243).

Building Activities of Women Rulers and Queens.

As in the earlier phase, there is a continued association of piety and atonement with the building activities of women rulers and queens. Thus, for instance, Diddā, the most prolific woman builder, confined this activity to the brief period of remorse and grief consequent on the death of her son, Abhimanyu.

> From that time forwards the wealth which she had acquired by evil acts, became purified through her astonishing deeds of piety (*RT*, VI.295—*tataha prabhṛtyadbhutā-bhistasyā dharma-pravṛtti-bhihi, kukarmabhirūpoḍāpi lakṣmīhi prāptā pavitratāṁ*).

Kalhaṇa lauds Diddā for her Diddāsvāmin temple, Diddāpura town and *maṭha*, a *vihāra* for foreigners, the Siṁhasvāmin shrine, her Viṣṇu images that 'sanctified the confluence of the Vitastā and Sindhu', and her reinforcement of temple walls (*RT*, VI.300–7). He remarks:

> Why enumerate (so) many pious works? It is related that she made sixty-four foundations in different localities (*RT*, VI.306—*teṣu teṣu pradeśeṣu kimuktairbhūribhihi srubhaiha, sā pratiṣṭā vyara-cayaccatuha-śaśtimiti srutihi*).

Diddā's building activity is thereby used as a standard against which prominent women builders in the *Rājataraṅgiṇī* are measured.

When royal women seemed to avoid valourizing their strength through their buildings, Kalhaṇa shows them allowing their male relatives to do just that. Thus, for instance, Bhīma Śāhī (Diddā's maternal grandfather) indicated his power by building the Bhīmakeśava temple in his granddaughter's adoptive country (*RT*, VI.178).

Kalhaṇa's ambiguous style is very much in evidence in his descriptions of the buildings of royal women. Though the exhibition of grandeur and power are not shown as the governing motives, these buildings are not necessarily depicted in humble or miniscule terms. This is clearly evident in the case of Ratnādevī (Jayasiṁha's wife) whose buildings were modelled on grand proportions that outranked others of the same type in size and splendour. As Kalhaṇa observes:

> When she had erected her Gokula, Śūravarman and others who had erected Gokulas (before), were held to be no better than those who eat (anything, even) grass (*RT*, VIII.2436—*gokulānāṁ vidhātāro gokule vihite tayā, gaṇitāha śūra-varmādyāha satṛṇābhya-vahārinaha*).[108]

Similarly, in a fashion reminiscent of Lalitāditya, her town in Dārvābhisāra in her name is said to have equalled 'the city of Indra' (*RT*, VIII.2440).

However, Kalhaṇa balances these overt indications of female grandeur with descriptions evoking the pious and noble sentiments that impelled such installations. He stresses Ratnādevī's kindness, evident in her foundations in honour of her dead servants (*RT*, VIII.2441), and attributes piety to her *maṭha* at Ratnāpura in a rather contrived manner. As he puts it:

> Her faultless Maṭha at Ratnāpura, which is a place of importance and has many gates, appears like an extensive cage for the swan of 'pious work' (*RT*, VIII.2434—*ratnā-pure bahu-dvāra-mahārghe niragho maṭaha, dhatte sukṛta-haṁsasya sphīta-vītamsa-vibhramaṁ*).

One should note that Kalhaṇa does not provide specific dimensional details of these buildings, as he does in the case of those of most male rulers. Thus he uses only general appellations to qualify these structures. For instance, merit is associated with most of Sūryamatī's buildings.

> She founded the (temple of Śiva) Gaurīśvara, and, having the second name of Subhaṭā, constructed the meritorious Subhaṭāmaṭha on the bank of the Vitastā (*RT*, VII.180—*subhaṭā-paranāmā sā gaurīśvara-vidhāyinī, puṇyaṁ vitastā-puline nirmame subhaṭā-maṭaṁ*).

Likewise, Diddā's buildings seemed to parallel her physical charm and beauty. As Kalhaṇa puts it:

> She of charming beauty built a Vihāra with a high quadrangle, as an abode for Kaśmīrians and foreigners (daiśika) (*RT*, VI.303—*cakre kāśmīrikāṇāṁ ca daiśikānāṁ samāśryaha, tayātyuchha-catuha-śālo vihāra-ścārū-saṁpadā*).

Similarly, the piety associated with Raḍḍādevī's buildings apparently enables her to outstep 'even the lame Diddā' (*RT*, VIII.3388).

It is significant that most royal women seemed to build to enhance the glory of their menfolk. Diddā, for instance, founded the Abhimanyusvāmin temple and Abhimanyupura town to 'increase her deceased son's merit' (*RT*, VI.299). She built Kaṅkaṇapura town 'to increase the eminence of the merit of her husband' (*RT*, VI.301) and erected the Siṁhasvāmin shrine in the name of her father, Siṁharāja (*RT*, VI.304).

Cynthia Talbot's view is that women, by offering the fruits of their activities to others, were complying with patriarchal norms of subservience, showing that their patronage of religion did not entail true independence of action.[109] Kalhaṇa's narrative, however, shows that this view cannot wholly be accepted with regard to Kashmir: there are instances of women building to perpetuate their own names, as in Diddā (Diddāpura town) and—from the pre-Diddā phase—Cakramardikā (Cakrapura town), Kamalā (Kamalāpura town), and Sugandhā.[110] There is also the case of Saṁgrāmarāja's daughter, Lothikā, who constructed a *maṭha* in the name of her mother, Tilottamā (*RT*, VII.120). Significantly, here a woman's memory was perpetuated by another woman. On the other hand, one can consider the case of Saṁgrāmarāja's queen, Śrīlekhā, an eager aspirant for the throne who even attempted, unsuccessfully, to crown herself. Kalhaṇa remarks:

> The lavish queen then built two Maṭhas in honour of her husband and son, and thought day and night of high treason (*RT*, VII.142—*maṭadvayaṁ tataha kṛtvā svasya bhartuha sutasya ca, tasthau vyaya-vatī rājñī rājya-drohodyatā-niśaṁ*).

Śrīlekhā can hardly be viewed as seriously endeavouring to concretize the glory of her menfolk!

Interestingly, the buildings of royal women often serve as a means for the introduction of other men into the narrative. Thus, for instance, Sūryamatī built a *maṭha* and *agrahāra* in her brother, Kallana's name, and two *maṭhas* in the names of her other brother, Sillana and her husband, Ananta (*RT*, VII.182–3).[111]

Finally, parallels can be drawn between the prolific building activity of the Kashmir queens and the Coḷa queens (tenth century AD), whose 'munificent religious activities' indicated their high position and their access to 'huge amounts of money or rich resources of income', enabling them to finance temple construction and make monetary donations.[112] In his study of the Candella queens, K.K. Shah, for instance, raises the possibility of queens having purchased land for purposes of donation from the cash held as part of their *strīdhana*.[113] This supposition could well be applied to some of the royal women donors of Kashmir in this period.[114]

Building Activities of Non-Royal Men

As shown in the previous chapter, the buildings, motives and patterns of donation in the case of non-royal males, though statements about prestige and power, were not as strongly defined as in the case of kings. At the outset, one should note that a large percentage of ministers who built in this phase belonged to Jayasiṁha's court. The numerous shrines, *agrahāras* and *maṭhas* erected by Jayasiṁha's minister, Rilhaṇa (*RT*, VIII.2408–13), and his brother, Sumanas (*RT*, VIII.3355–9), bear testimony to their influence in Jayasiṁha's court. Udaya (Jayasiṁha's commander-in-chief) also acquired fame in connection with his *maṭhas* and *agrahāras* (*RT*, VIII.2420), and Maṅkhaka (Jayasiṁha's minister of foreign affairs) is said to have established his pre-eminence by erecting a Śrīkaṇṭa shrine and *maṭha* (*RT*, VIII.3354).

One can also note the interesting case of an ascetic donor, Gagga, who seemed to have been a contemporary of Jayasiṁha. The Sri Pratap Museum fragmentary inscription of the year 21 (AD 1145) mentions the construction of a house at Tanārudramagra inside a temple, where two images were installed by Gagga.[115] However, whether this donation was motivated by a desire for fame or a purely religious compulsion is not known. There is, in addition, the stone slab inscription of the reign of Jayasiṁha of the year 25 (1149) that records the consecration of something by a *bhaṭṭa* Govinda.[116]

A significant proof of the common man's active participation in works of public utility is provided by the Dacchan stone inscription of (*laukika*) year 12 (1036), of the reign of (A)nantadeva, identified as Ananta. It records the construction of a bridge or an embankment (*setu*) by a certain Mahīmgupta.[117] However, there are no other details as to the financial resources of this individual that enabled the construction, or the motive.

As in the earlier phase, Kalhaṇa describes the buildings of non-royal males in a parallel fashion with that of kings, to evoke their grandeur and power. Thus, for instance, Rilhaṇa 'adorned' the cities with 'great maṭhas, bridges and numerous agrahāras', and 'excited wonder' by his Rilhaṇeśvara shrine (*RT*, VIII.2408–9), as did Udaya's 'splendid maṭha' which 'embellished the Padmasaras shore' (*RT*, VIII.2421).

As with kings, Kalhaṇa shows several non-royal males building in a woman's name. Thus, Dhanya constructed a *vihāra* in his dead wife, Bijjā's name (*RT*, VIII.3343–4), while Rilhaṇa built one in his wife, Sussalā's name, which later, interestingly, becomes known by her cat's name. As Kalhaṇa puts it:

> This man of merits had a Vihāra constructed at the place called Bhalerakaprapā, in honour of his deceased wife Sussalā. This (Vihāra) became known by the name of her cat which had followed her dead (mistress) into death, instead of forgetting her attachment as is the wont of animals (*RT*, VIII.2410–11—*lokāntara-gatāṁ kāntāṁ kṛtinoddiśya sussalāṁ, bhaleraka-prapā-sthāne vihārastena kāritaha; mārjāryā-stiryagucita-sneha-vismṛtya-pohataha, mṛtāmanu-mṛtāyāstan-nāmnā yaha khyātimā-gataha*).

The Srinagar inscription of Queen Diddā (992) that records Dharmāṇika's donation of some charitable work in honour of his mother is also significant in this regard. Thus, a (non-royal) woman's memory was perpetuated in a concrete manner by her son.[118]

It is interesting to note that Kalhaṇa's descriptions often hint at the builder's character, as in the case of Dhanya. Thus:

The Maṭhas and Agrahāras which Dhanya established under the name of his wife, did not get (known by) the desired appellation. Whence should fame (come) without merits? (*RT*, VIII.2419—*maṭāgrahārā dhanyena vallabhā-bhidayā kṛtāha, nābhīstaṁ lebhire nāma khyātiha puṇyairvinā kutaha*).[119]

In conclusion, one can note the tenth-century Buddhist image inscription of Śaṅkarasena and Devaśrīyā that records the consecration of the pious gift of an image of the Buddha by Śaṅkarasena, chief of the elephant corps (*mahāgajapati*), and by the princess Devaśrīyā, a Buddhist.[120] The mutual relations between the two are unclear but both are depicted on the pedestal in a worshipping attitude, by which it is presumed that they were a couple. Śaṅkarasena may have been a śāhī noble, since he is dressed in a Scythian costume and not a Kashmiri one,[121] while the identity of the princess remains unclear. However, it is significant that joint donations of the sexes—not necessarily of a strictly royal category—were also made and that they and, by extension, their religious preferences, could be represented on the image itself.

Building Activities of Non-Royal Women

Kalhaṇa details the buildings of only five non-royal women, four of them belonging to the Diddā and post-Diddā phase. This limited number precludes the possibility of a definitive analysis here. In a rather lukewarm similarity with their royal counterparts, Kalhaṇa associates the buildings of non-royal women with piety and nobility of character, as in the case of Sussalā, the minister Rilhaṇa's wife.

As Diddā among queens, so Sussalā among ministers' wives has secured the foremost rank by means of manifold religious foundations (*RT*, VIII.2414—*ārohati parāṁ kāṣṭāṁ pratiṣṭā-vividhādhvanā, diddā nṛpati-patnīśu mantri-strīśu tu sussalā*).

Sussalā indulged in reconstruction, as well as in 'all kinds of pious works' like building waterwheels, wells, student halls and so on (*RT*, VIII.2415–16).

The residual motives are varying. Cintā, the minister Udaya's wife, built a *vihāra* apparently to symbolize justice (*RT*, VIII. 3352–3).

The five buildings within her Vihāra appear as if they were the five high fingers of the upraised arm of Law (*RT*, VIII.3353—*prāsāda-pañca-kavyā-jāttadvihāra-sthitaha karaha, udasta iva dharmeṇa prottuṅgāṅgali-pañca-kaha*).

In addition, in an interesting attempt to perpetuate her name, Valgā (Diddā's porter-woman) erected the Valgāmaṭha (*RT*, VI.308—*krīḍā-caṅkra-maṇe rājñāha paṅgā vigraha-vāhinī, valgābhidha vaivadhikī valgā-maṭama-kārayat*). She, along with Sāmbavatī, Pārtha's courtesan (of the pre-Diddā phase) who built a Śiva shrine, indicate the existence of affluent professional groupings among city-based women of the lower echelons of society.[122]

Kalhaṇa does not provide details of the proportions of these buildings, except for a slight accent on the aesthetic aspect. Cintā's *vihāra* apparently 'adorned' the Vitastā's banks (*RT*, VIII.3352), while Sussalā's *vihāra* beautified the city. As Kalhaṇa puts it:

Her vihāra, which covered the whole ground of the residence of former royal dynasties, made the whole city a joy to look at (*RT*, VIII.2417—*pūrva-rājakulā-khaṇḍa-sthaṇḍila-vyāpinākhilaṁ, tad-vihārena nagaraṁ nītaṁ netrābhirā-matāṁ*).

Due to the paucity of details, it is difficult to ascertain patterns of donations by non-royal women.

In conclusion, it would be worthwhile to compare the situation in Kashmir with Cynthia Talbot's conclusions on the basis of her study of thirteenth-century Andhra inscriptions.[123] She observes, first, that since the performance of pious works was the only socially sanctioned public activity and prestige-enhancing opportunity available to royal women of medieval south India, they played a more prominent role as donors of temples and religious gifts than their menfolk. By extension, she also observes that though men might be lavish religious patrons, their pious works are never accorded the same degree of prominence as in the case of women.[124] Thus, men are mostly praised for their military accomplishments, whereas women are eulogized for their performance of pious works like temple construction.[125]

This inference, however, does not apply to early medieval Kashmir. Consider the narrative of the *Rājataraṅgiṇī*. It is clear that women—royal and non-royal—had manifold opportunities for public and political activity, and did not need to undertake construction activities to register their presence. That they engaged in this activity, of their own volition, under their own names, and in the same profusion as men, was an affirmation of their status.[126]

The power of women was made obvious in the physical landscape itself—in terms of the various shrines and buildings that usually bore their names and were, in all probability, constant reminders to the people about their achievements.[127]

Kalhaṇa glorifies kings largely for their aggression, but also for their piety. Although on the whole he largely associates piety and humility with women builders—either as a deliberate stereotypical stance or as a portrayal of public perception—he hints at the impelling force of several other motives besides these. So Talbot's analysis cannot wholly be accepted here. Kumkum Roy's contention that women's patronage of religious institutions can be viewed as statements of social identity has been demonstrated by my analysis.[128]

To conclude this chapter, one can reiterate that ruling power in early Kashmir was rarely an exclusively male domain, for women either exercised formal authority or were palpable influences behind the throne. In this context, Pāṇini's characterization of queens as *asūryampaśya*, or 'those who do not see the sun, that is, the wives of a king'—implying their rigorous seclusion—seems particularly inappropriate.[129] Thus, there is a clear divergence from, for instance, the *Arthaśāstra's* strictures regarding regulation of contact of the queen with outsiders, so as to prevent her access to alternative perspectives about the outer world.[130]

Although the edifice sought to be maintained in Kalhaṇa's work is a patriarchal one, he enables us to discern the 'non-patriarchal possibilities' within such an edifice.[131] And yet, regrettably, there are several attempts by writers to minimize or trivialize the status and agency of women, stressing the absence of a careful, interpretative analysis of Kalhaṇa's text or, alternatively, the existence of a bias. This, and the usual focus on the political, chronological and topographical details of the text, detract considerably from the potential of the *Rājataraṅgiṇī* for a gendered reconstruction of the social and political context of early medieval Kashmir.[132]

It is equally vital, at this point, to stress the liberal social mores that enabled the masterful presence of women here in this period.[133] Kumkum Roy's analysis of Medhātithi's (ninth century AD) commentary on the *Manusmṛti* in the altered locale of Kashmir is particularly relevant here.[134] Roy says there are indications that the context within which Medhātithi was functioning was characterized by the emergence and existence 'of alternative socio-political norms'. This is clear from his attempt to accord a limited recognition to women's control, within the household, over persons and things.

To Manu's injunction of marital consent being restricted to the father and brother (V.1.50), Medhātithi adds that the mother's consent is also necessary, as the daughter is owned by both parents. In addition, he concedes some degree of control over household resources to kinswomen, recognizes space for procreative women and accepts the possibility of less hierarchical relationships within the household—although attempting to conform to the *Manusmṛti's* framework of the *gṛha*.[135]

Roy suggests that the contradictions evident in Medhātithi's reworking of the *Manusmṛti* resulted from the context within which he was attempting to introduce certain values. There were constraints on the extent to which he could incorporate Brahmanical traditions and practices. Thus, he dismisses rituals that related to values central to the ordering of social relations in terms of a varṇa or gender hierarchy.[136] Despite his acceptance of patriarchal norms, therefore, Medhātithi could not (or did not) push this to its logical conclusion.[137]

Roy draws a parallel with Kalhaṇa's *Rājataraṅgiṇī* that, likewise, points to tensions inherent in reconciling śāstric norms with a situation which clearly did not conform to them.[138] Rulers were evidently located within a social context that was less closely structured in hierarchical terms than the śāstric ideal. Roy observes that the patrilineal (and patriarchal) ideal constituted only one of several contending power sources. Affinal kinsfolk could intervene to support/oppose rulers just as effectively as members of the patrilineage—and this was open to even relatively lower social categories like the ḍombas and cāṇḍālas.[139]

In such a situation, Roy opines, the rulers' conformity to śāstric ideals would be superficial; their household would have contrasted with śāstric norms at several levels. Thus, for instance, their women had independent access to resources and made endowments to perpetuate their names. This would have run counter to attempts to construct women as resources rather than as persons within the domestic context.[140] Roy also points to the formal assumption of power by these women and their influence in politics, presenting 'an obvious, highly visible challenge' to dharmaśāstric norms. She infers that domestic bonds/relations among non-ruling groups would have been similarly loosely structured and divergent from the patrilineal model.[141] The existence of alternative forms of household organization is, therefore, clearly evident in the relatively unstructured gender roles in early medieval Kashmir.[142]

NOTES

1. For more information on Bhīma Śāhī, D.R. Sahni, 'Dewai Stone Inscription of the Shāhī King Bhīmadeva', *Epigraphia Indica*, vol. XXI, 1892, pp. 298–9.
2. D.C. Sircar, *Studies in the Society and Administration of Ancient and Medieval India*, Calcutta, Firma K.L. Mukhopadhyay: 1967, 1, p. 243 mentions that the coins bearing Kṣemagupta's name alone are rare, whereas the other type with '*dī-kshemagupta de(va)*' are common. See A. Cunningham, *Coins of Medieval India: From The Seventh Century Down to the Muhammadan Conquests*, Varanasi, Oriental Books: 1967, p. 45. Also Devika Rangachari, 'Coinage and Gender: Early Medieval Kashmir', in *Coins in India: Power and Communication*, ed. H.P. Ray, Mumbai, Marg Publications: 2006, pp. 46–55.
3. B.K. Kaul Deambi, *Corpus of Śāradā Inscriptions of Kashmir*, Delhi, Agam Kala Prakashan: 1982, pp. 97–8. The inscription reads—*oṁ saṁ 65 śrā śu 25 śrā pra diddā-deva rājye, deya dharmoyaṁ rājānaka-upāsaka-bhīmaṭa-cāvata-putrasya tathā amara mātā gaṅgādevayā bhrātṛcaṅttu (tu) ṣṭyasya sakala sa.*
4. K.N. Sastri, 'Srinagar Inscription of Queen Diddā', *Epigraphia Indica*, vol. XXVII, 1956, pp. 153–5. It consists of ten lines in three verses. The text reads, . . . *sma dharmaparamo dharmāṅkanā(ma) sutaha, aṣṭaśaś-titamaṁśādhāma(ni) śu(cermasyasya) pakṣe site diddānāmani rājñī*

bhāva . . . (drā)ntarabhyāsajaha bhatyā yāṃ śritavāṅśica. Deambi, *Corpus of Śāradā Inscriptions*, pp. 100-1. See also J.N. Agrawal, *Inscriptions of Haryana, Himachal Pradesh, Punjab, Kashmir and Adjoining Hilly Tracts*, Delhi, ICHR/Pratibha Prakashan: 1999, p. 343.

5. He was previously a buffalo herdsman. Sally J.M. Sutherland, 'Seduction, Counter-seduction and Sexual Role Models: Bedroom Politics and the Indian Epics', *Journal of Indian Philosophy*, vol. 19, 1992, pp. 53–61 suggests that deformed female figures like Mantharā, the hunchback in the *Rāmāyaṇa*, are symbols of aggressive female sexuality. This reasoning could apply to the lame Diddā as well.
6. Cynthia Talbot, 'Rudrama-devī, the Female King: Gender and Political Authority in Medieval India', in *Syllables of Sky: Studies in South Indian Civilization in Honour of Velcheru Narayana Rao*, ed. David Shulman, Delhi, Oxford University Press: 1995, p. 398; Kathryn Hansen, 'The *Vīrāṅganā* in North Indian History: Myth and Popular Culture', in *Ideas, Images and Real Lives: Women in Literature and History*, ed. Alice Thorner and M.K. Raj, Mumbai, Orient Longman: 2000, pp. 283, 270, 261, talks of the woman who manifests heroism (*vīrāṅganā*) constituting an alternative paradigm of womanhood, repeatedly surfacing to challenge the patriarchal premises of north Indian society. The 'startling conjunction' of physical prowess, moral strength and sexual freedom with womanhood in the *vīrāṅganā* shows how 'extraordinarily and positively powerful' she is. Hansen also talks of evidence being derived from the historical record that documents the existence of 'outstanding queens in various regions of India since ancient times'. Note that the *vīrāṅganā* model cannot be applied to the Kashmiri royal women in entirety.
7. This includes Jayādevī and the other women dynastic founders in Kashmir. Note that Kalhaṇa repeatedly stresses the powerful family connections of Sugandhā and Diddā. Shalini Shah, *The Making of Womanhood*, New Delhi, Manohar: 1995, pp. 16–20, discusses matriliny and points out that a bilineal society, where matrilineal and patrilineal lineages/claims coexist, indicates a period of considerable change.
8. Contrast Diddā's action with, for instance, Thomas Trautmann's statement that when a woman marries, her husband's patrilineal ancestors become hers and she is cut-off from her natal ancestors and kin. See Thomas R. Trautmann, *Dravidian Kinship*, Cambridge, Cambridge University Press: 1981, p. 272.
9. U.N. Ghoshal, 'The Dynastic Chronicles of Kashmir', *The Indian Historical Quarterly*, vol. XVIII, 1942, p. 323; S.C. Banerji, *Cultural Heritage of Kashmir*, Calcutta, Sanskrit Pustak Bhandar: 1965, p. 51. Note that no other (male) ruler is described in such terms. In 'In Search of Our Past: A Review of the Limitations and Possibilities of the Historiography of Women in Early India', *Economic and Political Weekly*, 30 April 1988,

p. 7, Uma Chakravarti and Kumkum Roy raise the issue of distortions in 'the treatment of Diddā in Kalhaṇa's *Rājataraṅgiṇī*', but do not discuss this further. They also talk of the treatment of Kaikeyī in the *Rāmāyaṇa*, which probably reflects a tendency to condemn women who violated the 'proper' gender hierarchy. This argument could be extended to Diddā and her treatment.

10. P.V. Kane, *History of Dharmaśāstra*, Poona, Bhandarkar Oriental Research Institute: 1946, vol. III, p. 40. Perhaps the epithet 'notorious' is used for them because they ruled despite being widows. Notoriety can, in a limited way, be applied to Diddā because of her cruelty but in no sense can it be applied to Sugandhā. B.P. Mazumdar, 'Role of the Ḍāmaras in Medieval Kashmir', in *Essays in Indian Art, Religion and Society*, ed. K.M. Shrimali, Delhi, Munshiram Manoharlal: 1987, p. 27 clubs Sugandhā along with kings who were unable to rule 'because of their low instincts', or because they were 'tools in the hands of unscrupulous relatives or ministers'. The discussion on Sugandhā in Chapter III shows the inapplicability of this statement. In addition, Mazumdar talks of Sugandhā, Diddā and some other male rulers who could not assert their power because of powerful factions. This is wholly incorrect in Diddā's case.
11. Beni Prasad, *The State in Ancient India*, Allahabad, The Indian Press: 1974, pp. 327–8, prefaces this with a brief statement on women being barred from succession as a rule. S.C. Banerji omits to mention Sugandhā in his historical background of Kashmir (*Cultural Heritage of Kashmir*, pp. 6–14), nor does he mention Sūryamatī and Kalhaṇikā. Indra, *The Status of Women in Ancient India*, 2nd edn, Banaras, Motilal Banarsidass: 1955, p. 146 says that Sugandhā and Diddā came to power only because of the unsettled conditions of the time. Their desire to rule, or the people's acquiescence in their appointment, is not considered.
12. M.K. Dhar, *Royal Life in Ancient India*, Delhi, Durga Publications: 1991. See, for instance, p. 9 where he talks of the 'frequent and gruesome' involvement of queens in court plots, tracing this to their being neglected in large harems and their consequent desire for attention—a very simplistic observation!
13. Ibid. Diddā is referred to as a queen (unnamed, with no mention of Kashmir) who killed her three grandsons for power. Then, inexplicably, Dhar says that this must have been the direct outcome of her frustration due to the king's gross neglect and his bestowing favours on the principal queen and her children! This is a shocking misrepresentation of facts. As noted earlier, Diddā was Kṣemagupta's chief and most desired queen and, in fact, was a widow by the time she felt the need to dispose off her grandsons. Incidentally, this brief discussion is followed by a paragraph on royal amusements (pp. 44–5). Sugandhā finds a mention elsewhere (pp. 58–9) in a discussion on the 'Qualification of the king'. Here, she

and Diddā are mentioned as independent powerful queens but, again, the focus is completely androcentric. Ironically, Dhar refers to several women rulers in his discussion on 'Education and Marriage' (pp. 128–9) to show that education was given to female members of the royal household as well.

14. Saroj Gulati, *Women and Society: Northern India in the 11th and 12th Centuries*, Delhi, Chanakya Publications: 1985, p. 3. She dismisses the women rulers in one obscure line (p. 28) and refers to Dharmāṇika of the Srinagar inscription as Diddā's son (p. 39), thereby apparently showing that princes respected their mothers and engraved inscriptions in their honour! Gulati makes the amazing claim that, in most cases, queens were satisfied with the right to make a few donations for religious purposes. She also generalizes (p. 42) that women did not enjoy a particularly high status in the family or the society. After fleetingly mentioning examples of heroism by Diddā and of queens fighting with men, Gulati inexplicably observes (p. 216) that if there are fewer examples of seclusion of women, there are similarly few instances of 'queen rulers' in Kashmir. There is absolutely no analysis on the political scenario and the reasons for women's participation.
15. B.N.S. Yadava, *Society and Culture in Northern India in the Twelfth Century*, Allahabad, Central Book Depot: 1973, p. 9 alludes to the caste system but also talks of the frustration among upholders of the orthodox, established social order, generated partly by the gap between the norm and the reality. This could very well be applied to women who broke gender norms. Yadava also talks of Ananta's queen as an example of mutual rivalries among queens 'mixed with a love for power', that led to serious intrigues and fatal harem influences—but omits to mention her name (p. 124). Interestingly, while the ambitions of Diddā and Sugandhā seemingly corrupted Kashmir's politics, Yadava clearly does not see ambitious kings as an aberration.
16. An interestingly ambiguous assessment is made by S.C. Ray. While, on the one hand, he unhesitatingly refers to Diddā as a 'fickle minded queen', on the other hand, he states that despite the 'gross immorality and other defects of character', she was 'one of the ablest sovereigns of the valley'. He adds that while the 'lust for power' motivated her to perform 'acts of great cruelty', this does not indicate that she 'was lacking in humanity'—S.C. Ray, *Early History and Culture of Kashmir*, 2nd revd edn, Delhi, Munshiram Manoharlal: 1970, pp. 67–8. However, Ray omits to mention Diddā's transfer of the throne to Lohara (pp. 1–2). Banerji, *Cultural Heritage of Kashmir*, p. 11, calls Diddā 'a ruthless and immoral lady but nevertheless an able queen'. Ironically, the 'immorality' of the male rulers is never given overweening importance.
17. M.L. Kapur, *The History and Culture of Kashmir*, 2nd edn, Delhi, Anmol Publications: 1992, pp. 50, 53, 59–60. He labels Diddā a 'masterful

personality' but points out that she had 'absolutely no regard for morality'. Then he talks of Diddā's 'ability as a statesman' and concedes that while subsequent rulers were equally immoral, there were 'none as competent and able as Diddā'. He further concedes that Diddā's reign was significant, as it was rare for women to rule. In *Eminent Rulers of Ancient Kashmir*, Delhi, Oriental Publishers: 1975, p. 68, Kapur quotes M. Troyer to the effect that Diddā was 'the Messalina of Kashmir, was noted for her extraordinary profligacy rivaling anything that is recorded of Catherine of Russia'. (M.A. Troyer, 'Kashmir in Olden Times', *Calcutta Review*, 14, 1850, p. 214.)

18. Kapur, *History and Culture*, p. 45. Note here that though two separate chapters are devoted to Sugandhā and Diddā, respectively, the 'Position of Women' only forms a part of a chapter on 'Life and Culture Under the Hindu Kings: Some Aspects'. This, in turn, forms a part of 'Social Life' and comes after a detailed discussion on castes and classes in Kashmir.
19. Contrast this with G.M.D. Sufi's contention that Diddā 'misgoverned' the country for half a century and N.K. Gunrtoo's endorsement of Śrīvara's 'perfectly correct' claim that a kingdom ruled by women perishes in no time. G.M.D. Sufi, *Kashir: A History of Kashmir*, Delhi, Light & Life Publishers: 1974, vol. 1, p. 58 and N.K. Gunrtoo, 'Introduction', in *Śrīvara's Zaina Rājataraṅgiṇī*, tr. K.N. Dhar, Delhi, People's Publishing House: 1994, p. xix. Mazumdar, 'Role of the Ḍāmaras', in *Essays in Indian Art*, ed. Shrimali, p. 27, makes the inexplicable statement that Sugandhā and Diddā, along with Śūravarman I, Salhaṇa, and others, were incapable of asserting their power due to the existence of the tantrins, ḍāmaras, powerful ministers, and commanders-in-chief. This is wholly incorrect in Diddā's case.
20. Sircar, *Studies in the Society and Administration*, p. 245. For his part, H.C. Ray, *The Dynastic History of Northern India*, 2nd edn., Delhi, Munshiram Manoharlal: 1973, vol. 1, p. 133, says that this 'weakness' is exhibited in Diddā's failure of courage at Kṣemagupta's funeral pyre. He extends this into her liaisons with court officers, in much the same fashion as Sircar. It is not clear why reluctance to become a *satī* should be seen as a weakness in character and that too, by a modern writer. Besides, why should this have any bearing on her affairs? Gulati, *Women and Society*, p. 146, too links advocacy of *satī* with Diddā's case as an example of a widow running riot and harming the family and society.
21. Interestingly, when Kalhaṇa handles the liaisons of some of these royal women, he seems to underscore Kauṭilya's view (L.N. Rangarajan, ed. and tr., *Kauṭilya: The Arthaśāstra*, Delhi, Penguin Books: 1987, 4.13.33, p. 484) that those having relations with the queen need to be boiled alive. However, he also seems to underscore Varāhamihira's view. In his *Bṛhat Saṁhitā*, the latter says: 'Tell me truly, what faults attributed to women have not also been practised by men . . . ?' See Swami Madhavananda and

R.C. Majumdar, ed., *Great Women of India*, Almora, Advaita Ashrama: 1953, p. 23.

22. Sircar, *Studies in the Society and Administration*, 1, p. 243. That Diddā has not been a part of any research on powerful women figures in India is clear, for instance, from *Women in India: A Bibliography*, Nehru Memorial Museum & Library: 2001. It is seemingly exhaustive in its research but makes a straight jump from Yashodarā (*c.* 560 BC) to Razia Sultan (AD 1201), omitting several prominent women. Incidentally, the date provided for Razia is incorrect.
23. M.A. Stein, tr., *Kalhaṇa's Rājataraṅgiṇī*, 3rd rpt., Delhi, Motilal Banarsidass: 1989, vol. I, Appendix II, pp. 139–44.
24. Ibid., 'Introduction', p. 106. M.A. Stein, tr. *Kalhaṇa's Rājataraṅgiṇī*, 3rd rpt., Delhi, Motilal Banarsidass: 1989, vol. II, p. 20 records that it is still customary in Kashmir to name the eldest female member of a household 'Didd' after Diddā, in respectful recollection of 'the great queen'.
25. According to Hansen, 'The *Vīrāṅganā*', in *Ideas, Images and Real Lives*, ed. Thorner and Raj, p. 269, certain political and personal circumstances seem to foreshadow the emergence of queens in Kashmir, the south, Assam, and the tribal regions. She identifies as factors the support of a senior male to prepare them for the office, the absence of adult male heirs, and an external threat serving as a catalyst. She also includes 'personal inclination and talent' as 'significant if unchartable factors', enabling women to become powerful queens and warriors. Hansen's theory is of a very general relevance to the case of Kashmir.
26. Note that five of the Bhaumakara queens were kings' wives and one was a king's daughter. Here too, the people seem not to have viewed their rule with disfavour, and four of them were able to rule successively and successfully. Sircar, *Studies in the Society and Administration*, p. 237, discusses the reigns of Tribhuvana-Mahādevī and the others.
27. A.S. Altekar, *The Position of Women in Hindu Civilization*, 2nd edn, Delhi, Motilal Banarsidass: 1959, p. 21.
28. S.C. Ray, *Early History and Culture*, p. 114.
29. Krishna Mohan, *Early Medieval History of Kashmir*, Delhi, Meherchand Lachhmandas: 1981, p. 226.
30. S.C. Ray, *Early History and Culture*, p. 116 discusses marriage, *satī* and the 'literary evidence that testifies to the gross immorality and laxity of character prevailing among certain classes of women'; Mohan, *Early Medieval History*, p. 226. Talbot, 'Rudrama-devī, the Female King', in *Syllables of Sky*, ed. Shulman, pp. 396–7, notes that Rudrama-devī hardly figures in any secondary accounts of ancient Indian women or rulers. See also Chakravarti and Roy, 'In Search of Our Past', *Economic and Political Weekly*, p. 7 who say that Raziya has yet to receive her due place in history.
31. Talbot, 'Rudrama-devī, the Female King', in *Syllables of Sky*, ed. Shulman, pp. 393–423.

32. Note that she undertakes this exercise in trying to account for the 'unusually high frequency' of female rulers at the time (ibid., p. 410).
33. Ibid., pp. 410–11. Talbot points to the absence of strong, impersonal government institutions that enabled these royal families to assume political authority in various parts of Europe. She also talks of the zenith of female participation in politics and administration during the first feudal age that was ushered in by the collapse of the Carolingian empire in the late ninth century. European women had secure inheritance rights in the early medieval period, including control over landed property. As they were so influential within the family, women could exert their will on society at large. However, with the gradual strengthening of state and church institutions from the twelfth century onwards and with greater centralization, the independent political role of the European aristocracy became restricted. This led to the loss of female inheritance rights and the exclusion of women from political participation.
34. Ibid., pp. 411–12. Talbot says that kinship may have penetrated the political realm in medieval south Asia—as in medieval Europe—allowing women greater personal influence and enhancing their strategic importance as objects in marriage alliances. However, although women may have found more opportunities to wield political power, they could not lead their kin groups, given the patrilineal inheritance system, as stipulated in the Dharmaśāstra literature.
35. Ibid., p. 413. By family, Talbot means a small unit of male and female kin, both by birth and by marriage. That the immediate kindred, including women, took precedence, could undermine the patrilineage, that was apparently hegemonic. Talbot observes, therefore, that the rhetoric of patrilineal kinship was belied by the forms taken by social practice (pp. 414–15).
36. In the pre-Diddā period, there are three main instances of women regents apart from Yaśovatī and Sugandhā. Cakravarman was under the guardianship of his mother, Bappaṭādevī, for a while and then under that of his grandmother, Kṣillikā, for ten years (*RT*, V.290). Subsequently, Parvagupta is supposed to have installed the grandmother of Yaśaskara's son, Saṁgrāmadeva (948–9), on the throne as his guardian, and eventually assumed power himself (*RT*, VI.115–16).
37. Talbot, 'Rudrama-devī, the Female King', in *Syllables of Sky*, ed. Shulman, p. 408. Hansen, 'The *Vīrāṅganā*', in *Ideas, Images and Real Lives*, ed. Thorner and Raj, p. 263 says this could also imply a defiance of the code of female virtue in order to assume power.
38. Chakravarti and Roy, 'In Search of Our Past', *Economic and Political Weekly*, p. 6, discuss women regents who combined the mother-role with that of the ruler, being seen as less threatening to the patriarchal order than female rulers. Yet Sugandhā and Diddā completely reverse this notion, more so Diddā, whose behaviour militates against that of an ideal mother. Such a career also challenges the patriarchal ideology of

motherhood as the primary responsibility of women. See, for instance, J.A. Khan, 'Ideology of Motherhood in Ancient India', in *Women in Indian History: Social, Economic, Political and Cultural Perspectives*, ed. Kiran Pawar, Delhi, Vision & Venture: 1996, p. 49. A.S. Altekar, *State and Government in Ancient India*, 3rd edn, Delhi, Motilal Banarsidass: 1958, pp. 109, 487 says that at the succession of a minor heir-apparent, the administration was carried on by a council of regency. The evidence of the *Jātakas*, the *Pratijñāyaugandharāyaṇa*, and inscriptions show that dowager queens usually presided over such councils.

39. Talbot, 'Rudrama-devī, the Female King', in *Syllables of Sky*, ed. Shulman, pp. 409, 423, claims that one did not have to be a male to fulfil the masculine functions of a ruler. This identity could be achieved by performing suitable actions and assuming the appropriate social style. Talbot talks of Rudrama-devī being a female biologically but a male socially (p. 401).
40. It is, perhaps, in this vein that Śrīvara refers to Diddā's 'divine dignity' in his *Jaina Rājataraṅgiṇī*. See Dhar, tr., *Śrīvara's Zaina Rājataraṅgiṇī*, canto III, verse 176, p. 467.
41. Note, for instance, Talbot's contradictory and somewhat sweeping statement that although female power *did not* (italics mine) translate into formal political authority in India, the ideological barrier against ruling queens was breached on several occasions. Are we to assume, then, that Diddā did not wield formal political authority? See Talbot, 'Rudrama-devī, the Female King', in *Syllables of Sky*, ed. Shulman, p. 393. Another problem is with Talbot's view that ruling queens had to display heroic prowess to prove themselves as valid male substitutes, and that this was the only means by which they could turn their influence into authority (p. 421). However, none of the queens of Kashmir made any such conscious effort, focusing more on consolidating their power. Moreover, public approval for Sugandhā's rule was evident *before* she displayed any signs of heroism or ability.
42. For instance, *RT*, IV.660 where Lalitāpīḍa's mother, Durgā, is mentioned for the first time.
43. This translation is taken from R.S. Pandit, tr., *Rājataraṅgiṇī*, Delhi, Sahitya Akademi: 1935, p. 212, as Stein does not translate the verse. Incidentally, another significant verse of similar tone that Stein does not translate is—'The queen and the princes are the means which support the life of the king' (*RT*, VIII.3199)—p. 669.
44. K.P. Jayaswal, *Hindu Polity*, 2 vols., Patna, Eastern Book Depot: 1988, p. 201, quotes from the epics to prove the practice of joint coronation—from the Yuddha Kāṇḍa of the *Rāmāyaṇa* (128, 59) and the Śāntiparvan of the *Mahābhārata* (39, 11). Also Kane, *History of Dharmaśāstra*, III, p. 80 on the *Viṣṇudharmottara* (II.7) specifying the qualities of the principal queen and the need for her to be installed with the king.

45. Rangarajan, *Kauṭilya*, pp. 91, 289. The *Arthaśāstra* (Book V) fixes the salaries of queens, junior queens, queen dowagers, etc.
46. Altekar (*State and Government*, p. 161) notes that the *Yajurveda* and the Brāhmaṇas mention high state functionaries called *ratnins* who formed the king's council and consisted of royal relatives, departmental heads, and courtiers. The crowned queen and the favourite queen belong to the first of these categories and are invariably mentioned by all authorities. Hence, queens were not merely consorts in the Vedic sources but played a part in the administration. For his part, R.S. Sharma, *Aspects of Political Ideas and Institutions*, 2nd edn, Delhi, Motilal Banarsidass: 1968, pp. 134–5 talks of the *mahiṣī* (chief queen) being the third name among the eleven *ratnins*. He says the explanation in the *Śatapatha Brāhmaṇa* implies that the *mahiṣī* represents the goddess earth which, like a cow and mother, sustains men and fulfils all their desires.
47. Ananta's extravagance had caused him to incur heavy debt with foreign traders, one of whom even held the royal diadem and throne as pledges for a while. Sūryamatī used the savings of her own treasury to salvage the situation: *RT*, VII.190–8.
48. Chakravarti and Roy ('In Search of Our Past', *Economic and Political Weekly*, p. 7) point out that in sharp contrast to the acceptability of women wielding power on their sons' behalf, is the case of women acting on their husbands' behalf, like Nur Jahan and Jahangir. This could apply to Sūryamatī and Ananta as well. For historians, it has either represented the 'effete' rule of an 'emasculated' king, or a case of 'manipulation' by the wife, a power-hungry woman. Note that Sūryamatī was ably assisted by Haladhara, the son of a watchman at the Gaurīśa temple, whom she elevated to the rank of prime minister.
49. Stein, *Rājataraṅgiṇī*, 'Introduction', I, p. 110.
50. The description of Sūryamatī's outburst is a classic example of Kalhaṇa's ambiguous style. His stress on her vulgarity, at this point, is juxtaposed with a very logical and well-founded critique of Ananta and his attitude. Sutherland, in 'Seduction, Counter-seduction and Sexual Role Models', talks of Kaikeyī in the *Rāmāyaṇa* using her sexual power over Daśaratha to get her way. Since her focus is on the welfare of her only son, and she lets no other consideration stand in the way, she is reviled in Indian tradition. Sūryamatī and Ananta could form a parallel case.
51. In Prasad, *State in Ancient India*, pp. 327–8, Sūryamatī's role receives a cursory treatment, along with that of the female rulers of Kashmir.
52. Ghoshal, 'Dynastic Chronicles of Kashmir', *Indian Historical Quarterly*, pp. 325–6.
53. S.C. Banerji and A.K. Gupta, tr., *Bilhaṇa's Vikramāṅkadevacaritam*, Calcutta, Sambodhi Publications: 1965.
54. Ibid., verse 26, p. 277.
55. Ibid., verse 6, p. 272.

56. For instance, Sally J. Sutherland Goldman, 'Speaking Gender: *Vāc* and the Vedic Construction of the Feminine', in *Invented Identities*, ed. Julia Leslie and Mary McGee, Delhi, Oxford University Press: 2000, pp. 63, 76 notes that even French feminists like Luce Irigary and Helene Cixous feel that control over language—and thus, knowledge—is central to the preservation of patriarchal society. Robert P. Goldman, 'Language, Gender and Power: the Sexual Politics of Language and Language Acquisition in Traditional India', in ibid., pp. 85, 88 observes that language is regarded as a signifier of power and power relations in traditional India; while it is both gender and class specific in classical Sanskrit drama, high-status men and brāhmaṇa women sometimes speak Sanskrit. Low-status men and non-Brahmanical women speak one of a group of Prakrits. However, note that Bilhaṇa seems to imply that *all* the women in Kashmir at the time spoke Sanskrit (and Prakrit)—a highly significant fact in itself.
57. For instance, Yadava, *Society and Culture in Northern India*, pp. 241-2 quotes Bilhaṇa's thirty-two *ślokas* on Kashmir but fails to mention Sūryamatī, except for a fleeting reference to a temple built 'by Ananta-deva's queen'.
58. Banerji and Gupta, *Vikramāṅkadevacaritam*, verse 40, p. 281.
59. Ibid., verse 43, p. 282.
60. Ibid., verse 45, p. 282.
61. Agrawal, *Inscriptions of Haryana*, pp. 376–80 proposes that the badly damaged Hund White Marble Slab Inscription is most probably a reference to Ananta, and is connected with the Hund Inscription of Mahārājñī Kāmeśvarīdevī (AD 1019), that talks of the consecration of the temple of the chief queen Kāmeśvarīdevī, because it mentions the same categories of people. Agrawal, therefore, presumes a 'close blood-relationship' between Ananta and Kāmeśvarīdevī. Could the latter have been one of Sūryamatī's co-wives?
62. Banerji and Gupta, *Vikramāṅkadevacaritam*, p. 11.
63. This is not the first instance when a woman plays the role of a negotiator between two parties. There is the case of Queen Bhuvanamatī negotiating between her husband, Kalaśa, and Harṣa (*RT*, VII.680).
64. H.C. Ray, *Dynastic History of Northern India*, p. 173 where he acknowledges this contribution of Kalhaṇikā. See S.C. Ray, *Early History and Culture*, p. 89 for a similar acknowledgement; also Elise Boulding, *The Underside of History*, revd edn, Thousand Oaks, Sage Publications: 1992, vol. I, p. 46, who talks of the bonding role of a woman when she is sent as 'wife-diplomat' to the court of an opposing king. This could well apply to Kalhaṇikā's case.
65. For instance, Pandit, *Rājataraṅgiṇī*, p. 552 acknowledges the political importance of the queens of Kashmir in the use of Śāradā, an insignificant wife of Sussala, to legalize rebel activity by her sanction.

66. 'Seraglio' is the term that Stein uses. The terms that Kalhaṇa uses—used in early Indian works to describe the 'harem' or 'seraglio'—are the 'Inner Household'/*antaḥpura* or the 'Pure Interior'/*śuddhanta*). Somnath Dhar, *Kalhaṇa: The Poet Historian*, Delhi, Sahitya Akademi: 1978, p. 5 notes the lack of a specific Sanskrit term for harem. Although 'harem' is a culture specific term, it is used here for purposes of convenience. Note that the harem ranked as a treasure among the kings' possessions and was considered part of war booty (*RT*, IV.288; also *RT*, VI.88 and *RT*, VII.1388).
67. In D.C. Sircar, *Studies in the Political and Administrative Systems in Ancient and Medieval India*, Delhi, Motilal Banarsidass: 1974, p. 256, both these sources are cited—the *Mahābhārata*, 73 and the *Rāmāyaṇa*, 49, v.1.
68. R.C. Majumdar, *Ancient India*, 7th edn, Delhi, Motilal Banarsidass: 1974, p. 363.
69. Harṣa is supposed to have raped his cousin, Nāgā, as punishment for disagreeing with him (*RT*, VII.1147-8). The other prominent example is the rape by Cakravarman of a brāhmaṇa woman to purify himself of his association with the śvapāka women, Haṁsī (*RT*, V.400-2). Both these cases are cited as part of an account of the two rulers' shortcomings, the one as part of Cakravarman's depravity and the other as part of Harṣa's failing intellect.
70. Stein, *Rājataraṅgiṇī*, 'Introduction', I, p. 17.
71. Gerda Lerner, *The Creation of Patriarchy*, New York, Oxford University Press: 1986, p. 214, says that the first gender-defined social role for women was to engage in marriage transactions. Although she clarifies that men did the exchanging and defined the terms of the exchange, the evidence from early medieval Kashmir shows that the process was not always male-dominated.
72. Boulding, *The Underside of History*, I, p. 47 makes the interesting observation that in a diplomatic marriage the woman is not being used as a pawn. Both she and her spouse are manipulated, and she later becomes a manipulator when marrying off her offspring.
73. These stipulations have already been mentioned in the previous chapter. Also Mohan, *Early Medieval History*, pp. 82–3, on the 'interesting fluctuations in royal succession'; Romila Thapar, 'Genealogy as a Source of Social History', *Indian Historical Review*, vol. II, no. 2, Delhi, 1976, p. 274, on the close association of primogeniture with a society where land rights have been established. Any ambiguities relating to this form of succession would suggest a flexible situation in relation to land rights, or to divergent inheritance systems—like the establishment of a patrilineal system in an area with a matrilineal one. One could extend this reasoning to early medieval Kashmir in view of the unorthodox foundation of dynasties.

74. Incidentally, Vijayamalla is shown accompanied by his wife even while fighting on horseback (*RT*, VII.905–10).
75. Kumkum Roy, 'The King's Household—Structure/Space in the Śāstric Tradition', *Economic and Political Weekly*, 27, 24–31 October 1992, pp. 56–7.
76. In Sherry Ortner, 'Is Female to Male as Nature is to Culture?', *Feminist Studies*, 1, 1992, pp. 26–7, feminine symbols of transcendence are identified as 'Mother Goddesses' and 'merciful saviouresses'.
77. Āsamatī is also referred to as 'Diddā' (*RT*, VIII.224–7), apparently a respectful appellation stressing Diddā's influence on the people's minds.
78. Kathryn Hansen, 'The *Vīrāṅganā*', in *Ideas, Images and Real Lives*, ed. Thorner and Raj, p. 262, observes that the number of women 'who played prominent roles in the political history of north India is probably larger than is ordinarily acknowledged, especially if the influence of wives, mothers, and sisters upon ruling males is included'. Hansen comes closest to the truth here. Kumkum Roy, 'Where Women are Worshipped, there the Gods Rejoice', in *Women and the Hindu Right*, ed. Tanika Sarkar and Urvashi Butalia, Delhi, Kali for Women: 1995, p. 20 notes that *rājñī*, the feminine form of *rājan* (king), is virtually never applied to the wives of rulers who are either called *patnī* (wife) or *mahiṣī* (she-buffalo, a symbol of benevolent fecundity). The perpetuation of values embedded in such myths and rituals implied that any attempt by women to exercise direct control over political processes would have been construed as illegitimate. The queens of Kashmir obviously subvert this trend.
79. R.S. Tripathi, ed. and tr., *Samayamātṛkā of Makākavi Kṣemendra*, Varanasi, Chowkhambha Vidyabhavan: 1967.
80. Note that when Kalāvatī is questioned about the cause of her obvious worry, the questioning is in a sarcastic vein and stresses the deviousness of prostitutes like her. See, for instance, *SM*, I.23. Kalāvatī's 'mother', a procuress who had guarded her as vigilantly as a snake guards a treasure, had been murdered (*SM*, I.27–8).
81. The *nāpit* (barber) acts as Kalāvatī's informant; advising her to appoint Kaṅkālī as her 'mother' to retain control over her wealth, he offers to mediate between them (*SM*, II.107–8).
82. Her name, at this stage, is Kumbhādevı and she assumes all the practices of the Kāpālika sect—remaining naked, for instance—and so is revered by the minister, Kuladāsa (*SM*, II.86–7).
83. She pretends, for instance, to have visited many pilgrimage sites and to know the art of making gold and silver due to Sarasvatī's presence in her (*SM*, II.97, 103).
84. Kaṅkālī likens Kalāvatī's prospective client to a sacrificial animal (*SM*, VI.35). Acts VII and VIII of the text deal with the successful implementation of Kaṅkālī's measures.

85. For instance, *SM*, III.
86. Such instruction is evident throughout *SM*, V.
87. Shalini Shah, for instance, points to Kṣemendra's criticism of the *viṭa*, the cultured hanger-on in the prostitute's gathering, an indication of the eleventh-century scene in Kashmir. She says that this period saw the shrinkage of urban centres and urban economy in many parts of the country. Those institutions that drew their sustenance from a flourishing urban *nāgaraka* culture were also showing signs of degeneration. 'In the Business of *Kāma*: Prostitution in Classical Sanskrit Literature from the Seventh to the Thirteenth Centuries', *The Medieval History Journal*, vol. 5, no. 1, January–June 2002, pp. 132–3.
88. For Yadava, *Society and Culture in Northern India*, p. 331, 'the evil of prostitution' attained 'objectionable limits' by the eleventh century, this being seemingly apparent from Kṣemendra's writings. Yet he fails to analyse the various indicators of their prominence and political participation.
89. For instance, Kumkum Roy, 'The King's Household: Structure and Space in the Śāstric Tradition', in *From Myths to Markets: Essays on Gender*, ed. Kumkum Sangari and Uma Chakravarti, Delhi, Manohar: 1999, pp. 29, 36. Kumkum Sangari, *Politics of the Possible: Essays on Gender, History, Narrative and Colonial English*, Delhi, Tulika: 1999, p. 359 says that wealthier prostitutes in control of gifts/incomes raised the spectre of unfettered female individuation, as their wealth and upward mobility were not subject to marriage or familial patriarchal control.
90. She also poses profoundly philosophical queries on the ways of Gods, virtues and the universe (*SM*, IV.22–35).
91. I do not agree with Sukumari Bhattacharji, 'Prostitution in Ancient India', in *Women in Early Indian Societies*, ed. Kumkum Roy, Delhi, Manohar: 1999, pp. 211–12, that Kaṅkālī's 'lack of proficiency in any alternative profession' meant she had no other way to earn her livelihood. This is directly contradicted by the text.
92. Uma Chakraborty, *Kṣemendra: The Eleventh Century Kashmiri Poet*, Delhi, Sri Satguru Publications: 1991, pp. 70–6. He also includes the wife of an old man and other different types of people in contemporary Kashmir in this category.
93. Ibid., pp. 86-8. Kṣemendra refers to it as extremely treacherous and also includes love (*kāma*) in this category—as a man controlled by a woman is apparently doomed. Significantly, the first verse of the text is a salutation to Kāmadeva, while the second verse salutes Mahākālī and Mahāśakti (SM, I.1–2).
94. Shah's study of prostitution also considers the scope for love and pleasure in the work of the prostitute. 'In the Business of *Kāma*', *Medieval History Journal*, p. 121.

95. Chakraborty, *Kṣemendra*, p. 3.
96. Kṣemendra draws an evocative comparison here with a deer who sees other animals made captive but himself falls into a trap. Shah, for instance, labels the *Samayamātṛkā* a 'satirical tract' on prostitutes and a 'rabidly anti-prostitute text'. 'In the Business of *Kāma*', *Medieval History Journal*, pp. 124, 144.
97. Ibid., pp. 121–56.
98. Ibid., p. 138. Shah notes that prostitutes were regarded as autonomous subjects for the purposes of taxation, discipline, and punishment. They were virtually the only women who dealt with the state by themselves. In fact, Shah says that since the state was a beneficiary of tax from prostitutes, it had a vested interest in perpetuating the 'matriarchal' features of the prostitute household. She cites the *Arthaśāstra* to show that a prostitute's ornaments and wealth were to be given only to the daughter, sister, or mother, and not to the son.
99. Ibid., p. 121.
100. Shah says this is confirmed by the *Smṛti* literature that represents the patriarchal Brahmanical viewpoint. The exclusion of the *veśyā* from patriarchal domesticity and their consequent ostracism within the patriarchal universe ensured independence and autonomy (ibid., pp. 129–30).
101. Yadava, *Society and Culture in Northern India*, p. 151, points to the ḍāmaras as examples of the merger of political authority and property. What he does not acknowledge, however, is that ḍāmara women like Chuḍḍā ideally exemplify this combination of power and wealth. See also Mazumdar, 'Role of the Ḍāmaras', in *Essays in Indian Art*, ed. Shrimali, pp. 27–36. In the entire discussion on the ḍāmaras, there is absolutely *no* mention of Chuḍḍā and her politically prominent role—an inexplicable lapse on Mazumdar's part.
102. Julia Leslie, 'Suttee or *Satī*: Victim or Victor?', in *Institutions and Ideologies*, ed. David Arnold and Peter Robb, Surrey, Curzon Press: 1993, p. 47. The *Viṣṇusmṛti* (*c*. AD 100) is cited as recommending this custom as 'the widows can go the way of the departed soul by dying after him'. Also Julia Leslie, 'Suttee or *Satī*', in *Roles and Rituals for Hindu Women*, ed. Julia Leslie, London, Pinter Publishers: 1991, pp. 175–7 for a history of *sati* and its practice. It is derived from the Sanskrit word *sat* meaning 'goodness' or 'virtue' and denotes the practitioner and not the practice—the 'virtuous woman' who joins her husband in death. The term carries associations of great virtue, personal strength and religious autonomy. Common Sanskrit terms for it are *sahagamana* (going with), *anugamana* (going after) and *anumaraṇa* (dying after).
103. Gulati, *Women and Society*, pp. 123–4, says that when women were accorded property rights, it raised the problem of male control. This was solved by the method of *satī* that removed widows and evoked

religious and moral sanctity at the same time. See Shah, *The Making of Womanhood*, p. 93; Uma Chakravarti, 'Gender, Caste and Labour: Idealogies and Material Structure of Widowhood', *Economic and Political Weekly*, vol. XXX, no. 36, pp. 2248–50, says that widowhood is a state of social death and Brahmanical patriarchy institutionalized the marginalization in that widows have no recognized existence in the society.

104. Chakravarti, 'Gender, Caste and Labour', *Economic and Political Weekly*, p. 2250.

105. Leslie, 'Suttee or *Satī*', in *Roles and Rituals*, ed. Leslie, pp. 186–90. She says that as the concept 'woman' has negative connotations in Sanskrit religious law, the only answer to being female—in religious terms—is to become the perfect wife. *Satī* also becomes the ultimate and truly effective atonement for the bad wife as well.

106. Ashvini Agrawal, 'Economic Aspects of *Satī*', in *Women in Indian History*, ed. Pawar, p. 61. He talks of *satī* gaining full social and religious sanction between 900 and 1128.

107. Note that Kalhaṇa largely associates piety with reconstruction.

108. *Gokula* could mean, alternatively, a cow-house, a sanctuary, or a holy place.

109. Talbot, 'Rudrama-devī, the Female King', in *Syllables of Sky*, ed. Shulman, p. 405, says that most of their gift-giving was for the religious merit of their husbands or fathers. However, Leslie Orr, 'Women's Wealth and Worship: Female Patronage of Hinduism, Jainism and Buddhism in Medieval Tamilnadu', in *Faces of the Feminine in Ancient, Medieval, and Modern India*, ed. Mandakranta Bose, Delhi, Oxford University Press: 2000, pp. 124–30, notes that women's religious activities recorded in public and permanent inscriptions contradict the 'misleading' picture provided by normative texts that imply their lack of public presence. Records invariably refer to women as autonomous agents, capable of acquiring and alienating property without interference. Although Orr's analysis pertains to medieval south India, some of her contentions are applicable here.

110. In this context, one can consider the contribution of these women builders to urbanization—in laying the foundation of new towns and urban centres.

111. One can also consider the Wularhama Bath Inscription that records the construction of a sacrificial altar (*vedī*) by a lady described as proficient in the performance of religious acts and the wife or beloved of Ritibha, described as a king. There is no ruler of this name in Kashmir and hence this may be a reference to a local chief or outsider. The inscription is undated. Deambi, *Corpus of Śāradā Inscriptions*, pp. 145–7.

112. Harihar Singh, 'Women's Patronage to Temple Architecture', in *Women in Early Indian Societies*, ed. Roy, p. 291. Parallels can also be drawn

with the Cālukyas of Vātāpi and Kalyāṇī where women's patronage of religious institutions can be measured in terms of their access to positions of status within the political structure. Kanakalatha Mukund, 'Turmeric Land: Women's Property Rights in Tamil Society since Early Medieval Times', op. cit., p. 128, notes that as women of royal families were actively involved in the construction and maintenance of temples, the extent of their endowments precludes the 'facile assumption' that they were only using some kind of a personal allowance made to them. This is equally applicable to some of the women donors of early medieval north India. For interesting information on royal and non-royal women donors, Carol Radcliffe Bolon, 'Two Chalukya Queens and their Commemorative Temples: Eighth Century Pattadakal', in *Royal Patrons and Great Temple Art*, ed. Vidya Dehejia, Bombay, Marg Publications: 1988, pp. 61–76. Donors here, too, include queens and royal concubines.

113. K.K. Shah, 'Legal Rights of Women to Landed Wealth: A Case-Study of Candella Queens', in *Women in Indian History*, ed. Pawar, p. 76, notes that property rights, as accorded to women in theory, did have some substance in reality when she happened to be a queen or an aristocratic woman. In addition, there was no theoretical bar to women holding land under law as part of their *strīdhana* (p. 81).
114. For instance, Orr, 'Women's Wealth and Worship', in *Faces of the Feminine*, ed. Bose, p. 139, disagreeing with Vijay Nath's view that the identification of women in inscriptions as wives, mothers, or daughters shows their 'general economic dependance on menfolk in giftgiving'. Orr says this may throw light on their social family organization but not on their economic relationships.
115. Deambi, *Corpus of Śāradā Inscriptions*, pp. 143–4.
116. Ibid., p. 102.
117. Ibid., pp. 149–50. One could also include the restorations undertaken by Candramukha, a clerk's son in Saṁgrāmarāja's reign, in this category (*RT*, VII.115).
118. The third verse of the inscription is important not just for providing the date, as Sastri points out, but also because Dharmāṇika is said to honour his mother with the utmost devotion by dedicating charitable work to perpetuate her memory. Her name, however, is not traceable in the text. Sastri, 'Srinagar Inscription of Queen Diddā', *Epigraphia Indica*, vol. XXVII, p. 153.
119. Note that Kalhaṇa talks in a similar vein of Uccala's *vihāra* not attaining requisite fame (*RT*, VIII.247–8).
120. Deambi, *Corpus of Śāradā Inscriptions*, pp. 140–1.
121. Ibid. Deambi speculates that he may have been a noble of Kabul in the employ of a Kashmiri king.

122. Vijay Nath, *Dāna: Gift System in Ancient India: A Socio-economic Perspective*, Delhi, Munshiram Manoharlal: 1987, p. 70 talks of courtesans having emerged as an extremely affluent group of urban women donors.
123. Cynthia Talbot, 'Temples, Donors, and Gifts: Patterns of Patronage in Thirteenth-century South India', *Journal of Asian Studies*, 50, 2 May 1991, p. 328.
124. Talbot, 'Rudrama-devī, the Female King', in *Syllables of Sky*, ed. Shulman, pp. 402–5. Religious beneficence was considered desirable in a man but was not essential to his fame.
125. Talbot, 'Temples, Donors, and Gifts', *Journal of Asian Studies*, p. 328; George W. Spencer, 'When Queens Bore Gifts: Women as Temple Donors in the Chola Period', in *Śrīnidhīh: Perspectives in Indian Archaeology, Art and Culture* (K.R. Srinivasan Festschrift), ed. K.V. Raman et al., Madras, New Era Publications: 1983, p. 362, notes that these were important opportunities for royal women to play prominent public roles in support of religious and dynastic politics.
126. Three queens build for every five kings who did the same. However, one should also note that they form only 36.04 per cent of the royal women mentioned in the text. (These inferences also pertain to the period prior to the seventh century.) However, contrast these details with Gulati's unqualified assertion that queens only made gifts during the reigns of their husbands or grandsons, implying that they made none in their own! She also observes that laywomen were 'not allowed to make charitable donations' without their husbands' permission—a claim that flies in the face of the evidence (Gulati, *Women and Society*, p. 176).
127. Stein has documented, in painstaking detail, his efforts to trace these buildings—thereby corroborating the text. Stein, *Rājataraṅgiṇī*, I, II for details.
128. Kumkum Roy, 'Introduction', in *Women in Early Indian Societies*, ed. Roy, p. 42.
129. Indra, *Status of Women*, p. 73. He cites this from the *Aṣṭādhyāyī*, III, 2, 36. Pāṇini's time period is around 400 BC.
130. Rangarajan, *Kauṭilya*, p. 154.
131. Roy, 'The King's Household', *Economic and Political Weekly*, p. 59. Also Sangari, *Politics of the Possible*, pp. 384–6, who talks of female incitement, or women calling upon men to act, as a politically charged discursive unit that may mark the entry of women in the 'public' domain. Mani Kamerkar, 'History: Where are the Women?', in *Women's Studies in India*, ed. M.K. Raj, Bombay, Popular Prakashan: 1986, pp. 87–8, quoting Gerda Lerner, says it is in the selection of facts by historians that women are usually 'shortchanged'. Kalhaṇa distinctly steers clear of such a bias.

132. A rare avowal of their agency is Ashvini Agrawal's work that notes the 'significant role' played by women in the political life of Kashmir 'from time to time'. He observes that some of them carved a permanent place in the political niche by their own efforts and ability in the otherwise male-dominated sphere. He talks of Diddā's 'statesmanship' and 'political acumen', and of Sugandhā's role in ruling 'competently' when the 'situation demanded'. The role of Sugandhā, Diddā, Sūryamatī and Kalhaṇikā 'as king-makers, sovereigns, mediators and diplomats' is conceded. However, Agrawal's work is more a straightforward rendition of details than an analytic exercise. He does not consider the role of courtesans, or the wider implications of female rule. Besides, to talk in terms of a 'male-dominated sphere' in view of the enormous power wielded by women in Kashmir is questionable. See Ashvini Agrawal, 'Women in the Political Life of Kashmir (*c.* A.D. 650–1150)', in *Dimensions of Indian Womanhood*, ed. C.M. Agrawal, Almora, Shri Almora Book Depot: 1993, vol. I, pp. 87–8. Sangari, *Politics of the Possible*, pp. 385–6 argues that as women are primarily seen as having duties (as opposed to rights and duties for men), any claim to rights or personal and material interests is seen as an example of malign female agency and nature. This is because by staking a claim, women may 'expose' the material bases of a patriarchy and a large number of social values. Most writers on Kashmir (and, in fact, other regions as well) seem to reflect this bias in their treatment of powerful women figures.
133. Kapur, *History and Culture*, p. 93 tries to identify the factors that made culture in Kashmir 'distinctive'. He points to the mountainous barriers that restricted the flow of influences into the country, as also the 'peculiar' climatic conditions, as two vital factors. He also talks of the persistence of tribal survivals and their influence on Kashmiri society, and the interaction of complex historical forces from the time of the *nāgas* down to the Mughal invasion, that have largely contributed to the making of Kashmiri society. However, note that it is unclear whether unorthodox gender equations are the focus of Kapur's contention.
134. Kumkum Roy, 'Defining the Household: Some Aspects of Prescription and Practice in Early India', *Social Scientist*, vol. 22, nos. 1–2, January–February 1994, pp. 3–18.
135. Ibid., pp. 13–14. Medhātithi also attempts to safeguard *strīdhana* with various provisions. Roy says, in each case, his acquiescence in according space to women ran counter to his preoccupation with upholding patriarchal norms.
136. Ibid., pp. 10, 12–13.
137. Agrawal, *Inscriptions of Haryana*, p. 79 discusses Medhātithi's norms, which imply the husband's lack of dominion over the wife, who, additionally, has the right to maintenance. He then precipitately concludes that the 'lot of Indian womanhood' was not as hard as

assumed, without realizing that this specifically relates to Kashmir.

138. Roy, 'Defining the Household', *Social Scientist*, p. 16. She opines (pp. 14–15) that Kalhaṇa, like Medhātithi, is preoccupied with valourizing Brahmanical norms but recognizes the existence of alternatives, leading to 'sharply divergent opinions' about people being expressed in the same breath. However, this book also aims to show that the textual ambiguity stems from a desire to portray the agency of women and not to valourize orthodox norms. Roy herself points to the 'numerous references to relatively independent women' as a 'striking feature' of Kalhaṇa's account. She says the text enables one to explore the extent to which ruling families were organized around the norms laid down in the *Manusmṛti* and Medhātithi's work. These families were an extremely influential social stratum in Kashmiri society and were expected, as rulers, to ensure the implementation of the prescriptions and prohibitions outlined. However, Roy notes that though there are occasional references to rulers administering justice, there are, significantly, very few indications of attempts to enforce the norms of domesticity outlined.
139. Succession to the throne, ideally patrilineal, seems to have been rarely uncontested, as there are references to fratricide, participation of low status people in power struggles, and power being shared between rival kinsmen. Roy also talks of the natal kinsfolk of women playing a significant role in politics like Cippaṭajayāpīḍa's maternal uncles.
140. Note that though Roy refers to the women of ruling households here, non-royal women appear to have had similar access to resources and made similar endowments.
141. Ibid., p. 16. See also Roy, 'The King's Household', in *From Myths to Markets*, ed. Sangari and Chakravarti, p. 18. She says that the household was one of the most important institutions wherein and whereby gender relations were structured, enforced and perhaps possibly contested. Analyses of the varying relations within the household, and between the household and society, is related to the understanding of patriarchies.
142. Note an interesting statement in Shalini Shah, 'Gender and Sexuality in Ancient Punjab: A Case Study of the Karṇa Parva in the *Mahābhārata*', in *Breaking Out of Invisibility: Women in Indian History*, ed. Aparna Basu and Anup Taneja, Delhi, ICHR/Northern Book Centre: 2002, pp. 29–30. She cites the Anuśāsana Parva as referring to the sexual excesses of women in the northern quarter (*uttarādiśa*) which, as per Brahmanical description, is a land populated by licentious, self-willed women. Shah also cites the *Aitareya Brāhmaṇa* (eighth–seventh century BC) as stating that the people in the vicinity of the Himalaya have a *vairājya* type of state: a non-hierarchical, non-gendered social order. Though this may not pertain to Kashmir, the link between sexual freedom, independent women, and a loosely structured gendered order is significant.

CHAPTER V

Kashmir: Summary

I now survey some of the important points raised in the foregoing analysis on early medieval Kashmir. As is obvious, the overweening stress is on the information provided by Kalhaṇa's *Rājataraṅgiṇī*, since the epigraphic evidence is minimal and there are only a few other texts like the *Nīlamatapurāṇa* and Kṣemendra's *Samayamātṛkā* that offer some potential for a gendered reconstruction.

Kalhaṇa's text does not simply provide a list of rebellious or independent women[1] but, more significantly, conveys a sense of the interaction and tension between male rulers and female consorts, ruling queens and male advisors, and other protagonists in the royal court culture. One also gets a sense of the opportunities and constraints in the world of non-royal women as they seek to negotiate for their sons and husbands in the political arena. Finally, the common social ground occupied by royal and non-royal women can also be discerned.

The evidence of the *Rājataraṅgiṇī*, along with that of the *Nīlamatapurāṇa* and the *Samayamātṛkā* enables us to postulate a situation in early medieval Kashmir, where women—royal and non-royal—wielded formal and informal power. They clearly enjoyed a more equable status *vis-à-vis* men as compared to other parts of contemporary north India.

Obviously, Kalhaṇa's focus on the royal household would have been dictated not just by the fact that his was a chronicle of rulers, but that as this was a central institution from the perspective of both state and society. However, I have shown that power was not limited to the monarchs; it was as effectively exercised by women associated with them.[2] In addition, four of the six dynastic founders (that of the Kārkoṭa, Utpala, Yaśaskara and Lohara) owed their prominence to association with a woman or her family, whether of 'noble' birth or from the 'lower' strata of society, especially courtesans. This is a pointer to the political opportunities available to women in early medieval Kashmir. In this sense, the notion that kingship or the state was associated with the control of women and was an instrument of their subjugation[3] does not hold true for these women.

The inability of secondary writings on the *Rājataraṅgiṇī* to uncover its immense potential for a gendered reconstruction of the society and polity of early medieval Kashmir also needs to be reiterated. This is necessary owing to the text's pivotal position in a gender analysis of the relevant period and the fact that it is used almost exclusively as a source for this period in Kashmir. The *Nīlamatapurāṇa* and the *Samayamātṛkā*, in comparison, are used to a considerably lesser degree and the errors in their comprehension have been stressed in the course of the analysis.

Thus, when Krishna Mohan claims that the women of Kashmir held a generally 'respectable position', but were in 'no way equal or superior' to men—her view completely militates against the evidence.[4] She also talks of the apparent 'regret and remorse in Kalhaṇa's tone' when queens came to power. As the previous chapters reveal, this is a completely uncritical analysis. A more appropriate example is *The Role and Position of Women in the Social, Cultural and Political Life of Kashmir* by Vina Mathur where a monochromatic view of Kalhaṇa's attitude towards women is presented.[5]

However, clearly, Mathur's analysis is a sweeping and largely uncritical one. Kalhaṇa would not have focused so strongly on the role of women if he had been 'allergic' to them 'outstepping their limits'. In fact, he treats women as historically relevant figures, highlights the fluidity of roles in Kashmir's politics and also charts the rise of prostitutes/courtesans to power as queens and concubines. As noted earlier, the powerful role of prostitutes is corroborated by the *Samayamātṛkā* and the *Nīlamatapurāṇa*. While Kṣemendra portrays the involvement of prostitutes in public life and their ability to manipulate men to achieve their ends, the *Nīlamatapurāṇa* treats prostitutes as an indispensable part of the social and political milieu.

One can also consider R.C. Majumdar's claim that the *Rājataraṅgiṇī* stresses 'the evil influence of the harem upon the king and the kingdom'; 'the incredible sensuality of the kings and queens of Kashmir which brought untold sufferings upon the state', he writes, throws 'a lurid light on the manners and customs of the age', 'gives a rude shock to the fond illusion of benevolent despotism of our ancient rulers' and 'paints a ghastly picture of court life where debauchery reigns supreme'.[6] This is a highly exaggerated and inaccurate analysis. One does not see any misery arising out of Diddā's various amorous attachments, for instance. In fact, her lovers like Tuṅga actually help to quell rebellions and are appreciated by Kalhaṇa for this. The actual problems arise out of rival court factions jockeying for power and not because of the rulers' irresponsible sensuality.

Various reasons have been proffered for the striking presence and role of women in early medieval Kashmir that distinguishes it from other contemporary kingdoms in north India. The geographical features of Kashmir that largely insulated it from other areas is an important factor that enabled it to develop its own unique social and political system. Moreover, the persistence of tribal elements in Kashmiri society—as exemplified by the *Nīlamatapurāṇa* and its mores—is another contributory factor. Equally, other aspects—such as a decentralized polity and fluctuating social processes—contributed to create a situation of relatively unstructured gender roles that enabled Kashmiri women to subvert the patriarchal edifice time and again in a fairly consistent fashion. Women were tacitly accepted as legitimate wielders of power—on and behind the throne—and the patrilineal ideal was only one among several contending power sources.

NOTES

1. Kumkum Sangari, *Politics of the Possible: Essays on Gender, History, Narrative and Colonial English*, Delhi, Tulika: 1999, p. 382, says that feminist projects of retrieving the agency of women from past historical periods have often suffered from a degree of simplification produced by the anxiety to recover a roster of such women and enter them into liberatory schemas.

2. If power and authority are two different things and power is seen as the ability to influence people's actions and to enforce decisions, women in Kalhaṇa's text did exercise power.
3. Uma Chakravarti, 'Conceptualising Brahmanical Patriarchy in Early India: Gender, Caste, Class and State', *Economic and Political Weekly*, 3 April 1993, p. 582.
4. Krishna Mohan, *Early Medieval History of Kashmir*, Delhi, Meherchand Lachhmandas: 1981, p. 304. She says their field was mainly domestic, but talks in the same breath of ruling queens. Mohan's conclusions are based on her consideration of 'all the aspects of the social position of women in Kashmir'. She also says that Kalhaṇa either condemns queens for not performing *satī*, or 'quotes scandals about their relationships with their ministers', ignoring the fact that he discusses royal male liaisons in equal measure.
5. Vina Mathur, *The Role and Position of Women in the Social, Cultural and Political Life of Kashmir: 7th Century–16th Century A.D.*, Jammu, Doron Publication: 1985, pp. 102–3, 167, notes that Kalhaṇa 'did not like the dissolute conduct of certain queens, but there were kings who were equally immoral. Kalhaṇa has taken them to task individually but women as a class have been subjected to his criticism. He is harsh towards them. . . . He was an orthodox, conservative brāhmaṇ, allergic to women outstepping their limits.' In a similar vein, Tripat Sharma, *Women in Ancient India*, Delhi, Ess Ess Publications: 1987, p. 84, says that Kalhaṇa 'frequently criticises the foibles and frivolities of royal ladies'.
6. R.C. Majumdar, *Ancient India*, 7th edn, Delhi, Motilal Banarsidass: 1974, p. 363.

PART II

KANAUJ

CHAPTER VI

Kanauj: A Political Framework

(Seventh–Twelfth Century AD)

The present chapter provides a brief historical outline of Kanauj between the seventh and the twelfth century AD, as a precursor to a gender study of the polity and society of the time. This is a particularly well-documented period in Kanauj's history and coincides with its rise to prominence under the Maukharis, until the end of Govindaçandra's reign of the Gāhaḍavāla dynasty (*c.* 1154). The selection of Kanauj as a case study is due to the pivotal role it played in the political milieu of early medieval north India. The reintegration of women into a historical analysis of this kingdom would, therefore, be a fruitful exercise. Hence, while providing the framework, certain sources that are conducive to a gender analysis are identified.

The combined evidence of both literary and epigraphic sources has been taken into consideration to render this analysis a comprehensive one. The literary works in this study straddle differing genres—drama, historical biography, chronicle, and prose romance. Literary texts may provide a more powerful understanding of the ways in which society works to the disadvantage of women.[1] Most of the texts are in Sanskrit while two—Vākpati's *Gauḍavaho* (eighth century) and the *Karpūramañjarī* (tenth century)—are in Prakrit.[2]

There are obvious problems involved in using texts composed and compiled by men in order to reintegrate women into the history of the times. This study aims to examine the potentials and problems involved in such an exercise. The texts do not always work in ways that the genre to which they belong would suggest. Paradoxically, a historical chronicle like the *Gauḍavaho* contains 'as little history as possible', whereas a drama like Bhavabhūti's

Mālatīmādhava (eighth century) is rich in potential for a study of gender.

The inscriptions, numbering around eighty-eight, document information on the rulers of Kanauj: Harṣavardhana and his successors (AD 606–48), Yaśovarman's reign (*c.* 725–52), the Pratihāras (*c.* 810–1085) and finally, the Gāhaḍavālas (*c.* 1085–1197). The language of all the inscriptions under study is Sanskrit. The crucial importance of inscriptions, particularly in this period, is that they generally provide information on personages and events that are not known from any other source.[3] This is particularly true of the Madhuban inscription of Harṣa's reign (631) that provides rare details on the founders of the Puṣpabhūti/Vardhana dynasty to which he belonged.[4]

EARLY HISTORY OF KANAUJ

Although the analysis begins with the reign of Harṣa, as he was the inheritor of the legacy of the Maukharis, it becomes necessary to sketch the history of Kanauj under them. A crucially important marriage alliance was formed between Rājyaśrī, Harṣa's sister, and the Maukhari king, Grahavarman of Kanauj, which completely altered the political axis of the time. It would be difficult to appreciate the nuances of the society and polity of the time without an understanding of the factors that shaped these events.

The town of Kanauj in the Farrukhabad district of Uttar Pradesh was a city of strategic importance for communication and otherwise, situated as it was on a cliff of the right bank of the Gaṅgā.[5] A relatively obscure settlement during the time of the Mauryan dynasty, when it formed part of the northern dominions of that empire,[6] there are some early literary allusions that underline the character of Kanauj. The first mention of Kanauj as being of some historical importance is by the Chinese pilgrim, Fa-hian (fifth century), who gives some details along with the information that under the Guptas it was still relatively important.

The latter half of the fifth century witnessed great political ferment in north India, centered on a war between the imperial Guptas and the Puṣyamitras, followed by the Hūṇa invasions. The Maukharis, originally feudatories of the Guptas who were governing parts of Magadha, took advantage of the situation and established themselves at Kanauj as an independent power.[7]

Despite its rise to relative political prominence, the sources for the history of Kanauj under the Maukharis are very meagre. A few coins, epigraphic documents and casual literary references are all that are available. Among them are the seal of Sarvavarman found in Asirgarh, the Haraha inscription of Īśānavarman (both of the sixth/seventh century), the Later Gupta inscriptions, Maukhari coins from Bhitaura and the *Harṣacarita* of Bāṇabhaṭṭa (seventh century), a historical biography of Harṣa.[8]

Though the Maukhari records do not mention the kingdom over which they ruled, that Kanauj was their capital has been legitimately inferred from the *Harṣacarita.* If Kanauj had not been the Maukhari capital, there is no reason why Rājyaśrī should have later settled there with Harṣa (after Grahavarman's death), to whom the throne was apparently offered by the statesmen of Kanauj. This conclusion gains support from the large number of coins associated with Harṣa in Bhitaura near Kanauj.[9] Since the readings of the coin legends are various and uncertain, the Haraha inscription of AD 554 is taken as one of the starting points of the Maukhari chronology.

N. Ray argues that the Maukharis were of the *somavaṁśa* or the lunar race, on the grounds that Rājyaśrī, in the *Harṣacarita,* is said to have 'united the two brilliant lines of Puṣpabhūti and Mukhara . . . the sun and moon houses.'[10] He argues that the Puṣpabhūtis were of the solar race, sun-worshippers, and hence the Maukharis were lunar. However, Yuan Chwang, the Chinese pilgrim who visited India in the seventh century, says that Harṣa was a vaiśya ('fei she' caste),[11] so Bāṇa could have been merely comparing the two dynasties with the two famous legendary kṣatriya houses.

The background for the marriage alliance between Rājyaśrī and Grahavarman was the struggle for supremacy between the Maukharis, who had grown rich and prosperous in the fertile *doāb,* and the Later Guptas who were trying to reclaim their power. This contest forms 'the most arresting feature' of the sixth century, being a struggle between 'the waning glories of Magadha and the rising power of Kanauj'.[12] The feud finds expression not only in the Later Gupta inscriptions but also in coins where, as A. Cunningham has pointed out, the Maukhari king has his face turned to the left, in the opposite direction to that of the Gupta king.[13]

Initially, however, marriage alliances were concluded between the Maukharis and the Later Guptas to maintain relations. The Jaunpur inscription records the marriage of Ādityavarman and Devī Harṣaguptā, probably the sister of Harṣagupta, the Later Gupta king.[14] Similarly, Ādityavarman's son, Īśvaravarman, married Devī Upaguptā, also probably a Gupta princess. The Aphsāḍ inscription, however, records an open rupture between the two houses in Īśānavarman's reign, centering round his claims to imperial dignity and his defeat at the hands of Kumāragupta. The Deo-Baranārk inscription, however, indicates that Īśānavarman's son, Sarvavarman, annexed Magadha, the defeat having been only a temporary setback to the Maukharis.

The effect of the Maukhari–Gupta feud on the Vardhanas of Sthānvīśvara/Thānesar was profound. The Later Guptas began courting the Vardhana alliance. This finds support in a marriage alliance revealed by the Madhuban inscription of Harṣa's reign wherein Harṣa's grandfather, Rājyavardhana I, married Mahāsenaguptā, probably a Gupta princess and sister of the Gupta king, Mahāsenagupta.[15]

The *Harṣacarita*, while indicating that the Maukharis and the Vardhanas were on very cordial terms, notes that Avantivarman (Sarvavarman's successor) was succeeded by his eldest son, Grahavarman, who won the hand of Rājyaśrī in marriage. This was a very important alliance, linking the two powerful houses of the Maukharis of Kanauj and the Vardhanas of Thānesar, and was largely instrumental in shaping the course of history during that momentous period.[16] The Later Guptas who were courting the Vardhana alliance, broke off relations with them and formed an alliance with the Gauḍas. This worked well for the Guptas, for Devagupta of Mālwā advanced against Kanauj with the support of Śaśāṅka, the Gauḍa king, and murdered Grahavarman in 606.

The attack on Kanauj coincided with the death of Harṣa's father, Prabhākaravardhana, in Thānesar. Bāṇa says, 'On the very day on which the king's death was rumoured, his majesty Grahavarman was by the wicked lord of Mālwā cut-off from the living along with his noble deeds' (*HC*, VI.204). Kanauj was seized and occupied, and Rājyaśrī was thrown into a dungeon 'like a brigand's wife with a pair of iron fetters kissing her feet'.[17] Rājyavardhana, Harṣa's elder brother, successfully avenged his sister's humiliation by killing Devagupta in battle, but was, in turn, murdered by Śaśāṅka. These events form the background to the ascension of Harṣa to the throne of Thānesar and Kanauj.

HARṢAVARDHANA OF KANAUJ (AD 606–648)

The absorbing interest of Harṣa's reign is, D. Devahuti observes, due to the 'comparative abundance and reliability of source materials'.[18] It is important to note that the sources, both literary and epigraphic, are useful not just for reconstructing the events of his reign, but have immense potential for the reconstruction of gender in the society and polity of his time as well.

The epigraphic documents for Harṣa's reign are the Bānskherā copper-plate of the year 22 or AD 628, the Madhuban copper-plate of the year 25 or 631, the Sonpat copper seal and the Nālandā seals.[19] Interesting information is also provided by the inscriptions of his Cālukyan rival, Pulakeśin II, particularly the Aihole inscription.

The literary works of Harṣa's time comprise a historical biography, the *Harṣacarita*, written by his court-poet, Bāṇabhaṭṭa;[20] a prose romance, *Kādambarī*, by the same poet[21] and three plays authored by the king himself—the *Priyadarśikā*, the *Ratnāvalī* and the *Nāgānandam*. There is also the work of the Chinese pilgrim, Yuan Chwang—*Si-yu-ki* (*Buddhist Records of the Western World*)—based on his travels in India between 629 and 644—and *The Life of Yuan Chwang*, a biography by his disciple and companion, Shaman Hwui-li, based on details supplied by Yuan Chwang himself. In addition, Kalhaṇa's *Rājataraṅgiṇī* provides valuable information on the interaction between Kanauj and Kashmir. These works will be discussed in some detail.

The kingdom of Thānesar that Harṣa inherited had a very modest beginning, until enlarged in territory and influence by Prabhākaravardhana.[22] This is evident from the Bānskherā and Madhuban plates where his two immediate predecessors are simply called *mahārājas* whereas the Madhuban plate, for instance, calls him *mahārājādhirāja* and *paramabhaṭṭāraka*. The two plates also provide the correct genealogy of the dynasty, detailing the names of three rulers and their spouses that are not found in any other contemporary source.

The *Harṣacarita* as a factual source of Harṣa's reign has obvious limitations in that this Sanskrit prose work is a court-poet's panegyric and tends to weave together legend, myth, and fact in a very intricate fashion. It is here that Yuan Chwang's *Si-yu-ki* is particularly useful as a corroborative source. Though his mission was primarily Buddhist pilgrimage, his work taken in conjunction with Shaman Hwui-li's *The Life of Yuan Chwang* provides a very important eyewitness account of Harṣa's reign in Kanauj.[23] These three sources are linked in their bias towards Harṣa, and there is thus a need for careful analysis.

Despite these contemporary sources that supplement and corroborate each other on topics of general interest, various problems remain unsolved, such as the real political position of Harṣa at the start of his career and how he came to occupy the throne of Kanauj, being a mere prince of Thānesar. This also has implications on the nature of political succession—and the role of women within that—since it was through Rājyaśrī that Harṣa eventually obtained Kanauj and catapulted to importance.

It is here that the *Harṣacarita* proves particularly useful, detailing as it does Prabhākaravardhana's death, Rājya's reluctance to ascend the throne, and Harṣa assuming the reins of government on his brother's request. Subsequently, Rājya departed to avenge Grahavarman's death and was killed 'weaponless, confiding and alone' by the Gauḍa king.[24] Though Bāṇa does not name the kings involved, the Madhuban and Bānskherā inscriptions affirm that 'the kings Devagupta and others who resembled wicked horses, were all subdued with averted faces' by Rājya.[25] Yuan Chwang's testimony is similar. He talks of the involvement of the Gauḍa king, Śaśāṅka (She-shang-kia), the wicked king of Karṇasuvarṇa in east India, who persecuted the Buddhists and uprooted the sacred Bodhi tree.

Kanauj, having lost its sovereign Grahavarman—and the anticipated support of the Vardhanas—passed into Śaśāṅka's occupation. Probably to divert the army of Harṣa's cousin, Bhaṇḍi, that was pursuing him, Śaśāṅka released Rājyaśrī from detention. Meanwhile, Harṣa ascended the throne of Thānesar and began to devise means to mitigate the disaster. There is some controversy on the issue of his willingness or reluctance to ascend the thrones of both Thānesar and Kanauj and this will be discussed in greater detail in the next chapter.

When Harṣa's position became secure, he formally transferred his capital from Thānesar to Kanauj and declared himself the sovereign of Kanauj. The amalgamation of these two powerful northern kingdoms helped Harṣa extend the sphere of his influence and jurisdiction over other warring states in the north. The grandeur and power of Kanauj under Harṣa was apparently so great that, as per the *Cachnama*, long afterwards the expression 'you want Kanauj' passed into a proverb meaning 'you want the impossible'.[26]

As the *Harṣacarita* ends with the reunion of Harṣa and Rājyaśrī in the Vindhya forest and says no more on Harṣa's suzerainty, one needs to turn to Yuan Chwang, *The Life*, and the epigraphs, in order to understand how the power and influence of Kanauj was consolidated under Harṣa. The findspots of the Bānskherā and Madhuban plates show that Ahicchatra and Śrāvastī were divisions of the empire, while *śīlāditya* coins in the Bhitaura hoard indicate that Ayodhyā and Prayāga too were under him. Moreover, his title of 'king of Magadha' in the Chinese documents (along with the *Life's* testimony) shows that he exercised authority there. On the other hand, Yuan Chwang offers vague generalities like 'Śīlāditya mahārāja has conquered the nations from east to west, and carried his arms to remote districts'.[27]

Interestingly, R.K. Mookerji has concluded, on the basis of the *Life*, that Kashmir acknowledged Harṣa's suzerainty in that Harṣa is said to have appropriated a tooth of the Buddha, despite the ruler Durlabhavardhana's reluctance.[28] Furthermore, Yuan Chwang also mentions Pu-lo-ki-she (Pulakeśi) who defeated Harṣa in 634.[29] On the basis of all the evidence, it seems that Harṣa ruled a large empire comprising parts of eastern Punjab, almost the whole of Uttar Pradesh, Bihar, Bengal and Orissa.

One tantalizing feature that arises from a perusal of the sources (which will be examined in detail in the next chapter) is the personality and role of Rājyaśrī. Apart from being instrumental in her brother's rise to glory, the portrayal of her docility and submissiveness by Bāṇa is often at variance with her actual wilful decisions and with what can be gleaned from the Chinese accounts. These make some significant statements on Rājyaśrī's eager attendance at court and her intelligence, which is not made in any other contemporary work.[30]

The question of Rājyaśrī's influence on Harṣa's religious proclivities, leading him to strike an easy balance between Hinduism and Buddhism, is also discussed in the next chapter. Bāṇa indicates that Harṣa promised to embrace Buddhism at a later stage of his life along with his sister. The account of the assembly at Kanauj which led to Yuan Chwang being declared the 'Mahāyāna Deva' and the quinquennial charity distributions that revealed much of Harṣa's religious leanings is taken from Yuan Chwang's work and the *Life*, both desirous of stressing his Buddhist proclivities.[31] However, the Nandi symbol on the Sonpat seal, the *paramamāheśvara* epithet on the other seals, the Śaiva devices on his coins, and the granting of villages to brāhmaṇas indicate his Brahmanical, specifically Śaiva leanings.

Harṣa's interest in literature and his patronage of authors are particularly useful for the reconstruction of his reign.[32] On the one hand, he seemed to have continued the Maukhari tradition of liberal patronage. Bāṇa, despite an initial misunderstanding with Harṣa, was warmly accepted by the latter as his court poet. This probably explains the flattering tone of the *Harṣacarita* and an obvious attempt, as noted by Devahuti, to justify Harṣa's manipulations, particularly at the time of his accession.[33]

Bāṇa, often criticized for his ornate and verbose style, manages to infuse his works with a certain refreshing boldness of vision. Ostensibly a complex romance based on rebirth, the *Kādambarī*, for instance, is a valuable comment on the social life of the age, with significant glimpses into the lives of women ascetics and the options exercised by the women of the time.

On the other hand, Harṣa's own plays—the *Priyadarśikā*, the *Ratnāvalī* and the *Nāgānandam*—reveal much of his beliefs and his character. There is some controversy regarding the authorship of these three plays, said to have been composed by a king called

Harṣadeva whose identity has been a matter of speculation. However, by the process of elimination, only Harṣa of Kanauj meets the requirements.[34] It has been alleged that one Dhāvaka, Harṣa's literary protégé, was the actual author but ascribed these plays to Harṣa in return for wealth.[35] However, Dhāvaka as a poet is unknown to Sanskrit literature. Besides, Bāṇa states in the *Harṣacarita* that Harṣa 'in poetical contests . . . poured out a nectar of his own which he had not received from any foreign source'.[36] Jayadeva (twelfth century) mentions Harṣa's name in the *Prasannarāghava* along with Bhāsa, Kālidāsa and Bāṇa as well-known authors.[37]

The clinching testimony is, however, provided by the Chinese pilgrim I-tsing who in *A Record of the Buddhist Religion in India and the Malay Archipelago* (a quarter century after Harṣa's death), says that 'King Śīlāditya versified the story of Boddhisattva Jīmūtavāhana. . . . He had it performed by a band . . . and thus popularised it in his time.'[38] Moreover, the internal evidence of these plays is said to support Harṣa's claims to their authorship—in style, structure and diction. All three plays are believed to reveal some of the actual incidents in Harṣa's life, and his ideals and achievements. Hence, there is nothing 'intrinsically improbable' in the belief in Harṣa's authorship.[39]

That the dominant ideals and values of a culture are embedded in its stories is almost a truism.[40] For this reason, Harṣa's plays are valuable evidence on the general conditions of the times and a guide to his beliefs and character. Although the themes are not original, having been adapted from the *Bṛhatkathā* of Guṇādhya (first century AD),[41] he has introduced innovations in the matter of characters, detail and embellishments. Some of the themes are significant in themselves and are also suggestive of the ideas that went into the shaping of the original text. It would, therefore, be worthwhile to briefly examine the content of these plays.

The *Priyadarśikā* and the *Ratnāvalī* of Harṣa are both four-act plays with similar themes of the love intrigues of King Udayana of Kauśāmbī. The semi-legendary life of this ruler is given in the *Bṛhatkathā*, in Somadeva's *Kathāsaritsāgara*, and in Kṣemendra's *Bṛhatkathāmañjarī* (tenth/eleventh century).[42] He is believed to be the contemporary of the Buddha and of King Ajātaśatru of

Magadha, and many Buddhist, Jain, and Brahmanical traditions refer to him.[43] Where Harṣa is said to innovate is in making the heroine 'the main centre of the plot' in both plays.[44]

The *Priyadarśikā*, the older play, deals with Priyadarśikā, the daughter of King Dṛdhavarman of Aṅga, who is betrothed to Udayana but, owing to an invasion, is obliged to flee to safety and after several travails, arrives at the court of Udayana as Āraṇyikā. She is put in the care of Queen Vāsavadattā but after a brief encounter with the king, is smitten by him, as he is by her. The rest of the play deals with the machinations of the court jester and a maid to ensure the union of the two lovers in the face of Vāsavadattā's wrath. Eventually, Vāsavadattā accepts the marriage on learning that Āraṇyikā is actually her lost cousin, Priyadarśikā.[45]

The *Ratnāvalī*, another court comedy, is named after Ratnāvalī, a Siṁhala princess, whose union with King Udayana forms the theme of the play. Yaugandharāyaṇa, the chief minister of Udayana, desires Ratnāvalī for his master as her husband is prophesied to be a paramount sovereign. Yet, from fear of Queen Vāsavadattā, he adopts a devious scheme to unite the two. He circulates a rumour of Vāsavadattā's death to appease Ratnāvalī's father. However, Ratnāvalī is shipwrecked *en route* to Kauśāmbī, is rescued by a trader and hidden away in Vāsavadattā's harem by Yaugandharāyaṇa as Sāgarikā, a maid. Once again, the jester and a maid contrive to unite the two, braving Vāsavadattā's hostility. The latter reconciles to the marriage on learning that Ratnāvalī is her cousin.

A significant aspect of both plays is the portrayal of Vāsavadattā as a proud, articulate, and fiercely possessive woman, whom her husband is anxious to conciliate at every turn. In fact, the elaborate plots devised in both plays for the furthering of Udayana's love interests are aimed at evading Vāsavadattā's wrath. The obvious question comes up as to whether polygamy was actually the freely accepted norm of the day.

The stereotypical depiction of the bashful and ineffectual heroines only serves to highlight Vāsavadattā's strength and also, interestingly, the wit and resolve of the maids who are willing to take on the queen and resolve the love interest by clever planning. The ease of interaction between the sexes is another significant aspect of these plays.

The *Nāgānandam*, Harṣa's third play, is a Sanskrit drama in five acts with the theme of self-sacrifice and non-violence.[46] The kernel of this story, again, is taken from the *Bṛhatkathā*. This play is considered to be later than the others and an exemplification of Harṣa's apparent adoption of Buddhism at a subsequent stage of his reign. Thus, once again, the question of Rājyaśrī's influence on Harṣa's religion is raised.

The story revolves around Jīmūtavāhana, a *bodhisattva*, who sacrifices himself to save a *nāga*, Śaṅkhacūḍa, from Garuḍa, despite his devotion to his parents and his new bride, Malayavatī. He succeeds in making Garuḍa repent his animosity towards the *nāgas*. Finally, he is restored to life by Gaurī (Pārvatī) on Malayavatī's plea. One should note that Jīmūtavāhana differs markedly from Udayana, the hero of Harṣa's other plays and apparently a great conqueror, in his indifference to power and glory. Besides, Udayana's incorrigible lust for women can be contrasted with Jīmūtavāhana's detachment and indifference to worldly pleasures, his love for Malayavatī appearing to be almost contrived.

Malayavatī, in a fashion reminiscent of Harṣa's other heroines, is modest and submissive. Significantly, by propitiating Gaurī, she is instrumental in Jīmūtavāhana's resurrection. This again highlights the aura of religious co-existence (between the Brahmanical and Buddhistic streams) that the play seeks to depict, and which is perhaps a reflection of the reality in Harṣa's court. Thus, though the play is dedicated to the Buddha, it ends with a prayer to Gaurī for her benediction.

Maids are once again a prominent element of this play. Their intelligence and wit often find a ready target in the court jester. This is another thread that links the three plays in that most male courtiers, especially the court jester, are inferior to their female counterparts in wisdom and strategy. One could speculate that the writer, by making the jester look comic, portrays the brahmanic ideology as effete or ineffective.[47]

Devahuti believes that the *Nāgānandam*, of all Harṣa's plays, 'has an air of conviction about it'.[48] However, she stresses that all three jointly throw considerable light on the social, economic, and religious life of the period, as well as on the author's capabilities. It is interesting, in this context, that there is no mention of Harṣa's wife or children in any contemporary source. The *Harṣacarita* indicates that he was married and Yuan Chwang refers to Dhruvabhaṭṭa of Valabhī as his son-in-law, but there is no further information on his family.

YAŚOVARMAN OF KANAUJ (*c.* 725–752)

After Harṣa's death in 648, Kanauj witnessed a political upheaval. There are few sources of information for this period, but a Chinese writer, Matwan-lin (thirteenth century), talks of the chaos and the presence of a usurper—the minister, Aruṇāśva, whose bid for power was short-lived.[49] Interestingly, Aruṇāśva's queen and the remnant of his army apparently struggled on after his capture, but not only are there conflicting accounts in this regard, there is also no information on the identity of the queen in question.[50]

Bhāskaravarman of Kāmarūpa, one of Harṣa's feudatories, annexed Karṇasuvarṇa and adjacent territories, as is attested by the Nidhanpur plate. Several other powers in the west and north-west, like the Gurjaras of Rājputānā and the Kārkoṭas of Kashmir, asserted themselves, but all in all the period was a 'dark' one.

After Harṣa's death, the earliest monarch whose name has been recorded in literature and, perhaps, in an inscription, is Yaśovarman. His exploits form the subject of a contemporary Prakrit document, the *Gauḍavaho*, written by his court-poet, Vākpatirāja.[51] Some light is also thrown by Kalhaṇa's *Rājataraṅgiṇī* and Jain works like Rājaśekharasūri's *Prabandhakoṣa* and Prabhācandra's *Prabhāvakacarita* (thirteenth-fourteenth century).

The origin of Yaśovarman remains a mystery despite the relative abundance of source material. Vākpati praises him as 'an ornament to the lunar race', hence he was obviously of a kṣatriya family.[52] The *Bappabhaṭṭisūricarita* of the Jain Māṇikyasūri represents him as from 'the famous dynasty of Candragupta . . . of the illustrious family of the Mauryas.'[53] No other evidence corroborates this statement.

However, Kalhaṇa's *Rājataraṅgiṇī* helps to determine Yaśovarman's date and throws some light on certain aspects of his reign. It describes him as the lord of 'the land of Kānyakubja from the bank of the Yamunā to the Kālikā'.[54] Further references from this text reveal that Yaśovarman was a contemporary of the Kashmir king, Lalitāditya-Muktāpīḍa (724–60). Rājaśekhara's *Prabandhakoṣa* also reveals that a Jain saint, Bappabhaṭṭi, converted Āmarāja, Yaśovarman's son and successor, to Jainism and was raised to the dignity of *sūri* in 752, when Āma ascended the throne.[55] Hence, the dates of AD 725–52 for Yaśovarman fit in with the *Rājataraṅgiṇī's* information.

The title of Vākpati's work provides an important indication of Yaśovarman's aims and activities. The *Gauḍavaho* professes to deal with the killing of the Gauḍa king by Yaśovarman, but actually narrates the *digvijaya* or world conquest of the king. There are clear indications that Vākpati was vague on political events and their chronology. Thus, for instance, the Gauḍa king is unnamed, the causes of the clash are not mentioned, and the entire incident is dismissed in one verse. In addition, the lord of Magadha (*magahanāha*), the king of Vaṅga, and a Deccan king among others whom Yaśovarman apparently vanquished, remain unnamed.[56] Moreover, evidence of the south-eastern direction that he took can only be inferred from the reference to his halt to worship Vindhyavāsinīdevī, whose shrine is near modern Mirzapur in Uttar Pradesh.

George Bühler and S.P. Pandit believe the *Gauḍavaho* to be a prelude to a larger poem which remained unfinished, perhaps because of Yaśovarman's death and Vākpati's consequent lack of zeal.[57] This gets support from the last line of the text, which states that the life of the king 'will now be narrated'.[58] Alternatively, it could represent the major part of his work and only the detailed narration of the killing of the Gauḍa king was to be added to complete it. Incidentally, A.B. Keith and R.C. Majumdar regard the *Gauḍavaho* as more historical in character than the *Harṣacarita*. They point out that the *Harṣacarita* ends at the point of Harṣa's departure for conquests, while the *Gauḍavaho* provides details of Yaśovarman's conquests, as well as information on other aspects of his life.[59]

Interestingly, the Jain sources provide some factual information as part of an explanation of Vākpati's origin. The *Bappabhaṭṭisūricarita*, which calls Vākpati 'the head jewel of the kṣatriyas' and born of the Paramāra clan, states that Vākpati was initially at Lakṣmaṇāvatī, at the court of a Dharma of Bengal who was defeated and killed by Yaśovarman.[60] It is believed that the

Gauḍa king was actually the king of Magadha, in all probability Jīvitagupta II.[61] Vākpati was taken to Kanauj and imprisoned, and he composed the *Gauḍavaho* in captivity in order to please Yaśovarman. He achieved his purpose and, thereafter, became Yaśovarman's court-poet.[62]

Corroboration of Vākpati's account is received from epigraphic sources like the Nālandā stone inscription of Yaśovarmadeva. This document states that Mālāda, the son of Yaśovarman's minister, made certain gifts to the community of *bhikṣus* and to the temple erected by Bālāditya at Nālandā in honour of the Buddha. It extols Yaśovarman as the *lokapāla* (guardian of the world). The epigraph is undated and the king's ancestry is not mentioned, leading to controversies over its authorship.[63] It is generally ascribed to Yaśovarman of Kanauj and is significant in that it shows the extent of his dominions in the east and the north-west, thereby confirming Vākpati's account of the ruler's conquests. In addition, Yaśovarman is believed to have built the town of Yaśovarmapura to commemorate his victory over the Gauḍa king. This has been alternatively identified as the present town of Bihar by Cunningham or as Ghosrawa by F. Kielhorn.[64] Vākpati's account is also relevant for the question of Yaśovarman's coins.[65]

The *Rājataraṅgiṇī* reveals many aspects of the relation between Yaśovarman and Lalitāditya, which finds corroboration in the memoirs of Hui-ch'ao, a Korean Buddhist itinerant who visited both kingdoms at the time and mentions the clash between the two.[66] Kalhaṇa says that the 'thoughtful ruler of Kānyakubja' first 'showed his back to the fiercely shining Lalitāditya, and (then) made his submission'.[67] As a result, Kanauj came under Kashmir's sway and Kalhaṇa says that Yaśovarman was 'uprooted entirely'. This statement has also been used to determine the date of the completion of the *Gauḍavaho's* being before Lalitāditya's invasion, or before 725.[68]

However, elsewhere, Kalhaṇa says that Yaśovarman 'became by his defeat a panegyrist of his (Lalitāditya's) virtues'. Hence, Yaśovarman probably remained on the throne with nominal power. The fact that Kalhaṇa compares him to a mountain (*yaśovarmādri*) and that Hui-ch'ao talks of his 900 elephants as compared to Lalitāditya's 300, highlights Yaśovarman's prominence.[69]

Significantly, the *Rājataraṅgiṇī* has also been used to confirm

Yaśovarman's patronage of poets and of the literary activity at his court. Kalhaṇa states that Yaśovarman '. . . had been served by Vākpatirāja, the illustrious Bhavabhūti and other poets . . .' (*RT*, IV.144). This is confirmed by the literary tradition of the Jains and by Vākpati himself. Vākpati appears to have enjoyed more royal favour than Bhavabhūti, evident in his usage of the title *kairāya* (*kavirāja*). However, that Bhavabhūti was the more gifted of the two is a fact acknowledged by Vākpati himself. Thus, Rājaśekhara, a later tenth century poet, calls Bhavabhūti 'an incarnation of Vālmīki' in his *Bāla-Rāmāyaṇa*.[70] He is otherwise considered the best dramatist in the post-Kālidāsa era.

The three works of Bhavabhūti are the *Mahāvīracarita*, the *Mālatīmādhava*, and the *Uttara-Rāmacarita*. R.S. Tripathi cites Hertel as saying that all three of his plays 'must have been composed in Kanauj' for an 'audience of pilgrims in the temple of Kālapriyanātha (Mahākāleśvara),' evidently Yaśovarman's family deity.[71] The setting of two of his plays is determined by legend. Yet Bhavabhūti's plays are important sources for the eighth century and for the innovative themes he weaves into accepted legends, and the original and liberal observations he makes in the *Uttara-Rāmacarita*.

The *Mahāvīracarita* or *The Story of the Great Hero* is a re-telling in dramatic form of the major adventures of the epic hero, Rama. It can be examined along with the *Uttara-Rāmacarita* or *The Later Story of Rāma*, which deals with Rāma's renunciation of Sītā and their subsequent reunion. Bhavabhūti introduces certain aspects in the latter work that make it markedly different from the original *Rāmāyaṇa* of Vālmīki. He shows Rāma in the throes of anguish and guilt. The original Rāma does not spend his time in traumatized self-reproach as does Bhavabhūti's hero. The whole issue of Sītā's abandonment is tied up with the ideal of *prajānurañjana* (propitiation of the people), making it an important comment on the polity of the day.[72]

The *Mālatīmādhava* is a romantic drama spanning ten acts. It deals with the love of Mālatī and Mādhava, the children of powerful ministers—Bhūrivasu and Devarāta— which is brought to fruition and a successful conclusion by the Buddhist nun, Kāmandakī, a friend and fellow-student of the ministers. The play touches on significant aspects like the system of education and the freedom of choice available to students of both sexes. The vigorous and determined figure of Kāmandakī stands out as an intriguing and important creation of Bhavabhūti. She is willing to eschew the principles of worldly detachment dictated by her religion to fulfil the childhood vow of the ministers, to which she was a witness. The play shows her outwitting Mālatī's prospective suitors and even the king to achieve her goal. The servant girls of the convent, too, play important roles, as does the element of cross-dressing.

Mālatī is quite unlike contemporary heroines in her spirited questioning and rejection of her father's choice of suitor, and in her willingness to defy him. The ministers come across as shadowy, ineffectual figures, in visible dread of the king and his decisions. A parallel romance between the friends of the lead pair, Madayantikā and Makaranda, is depicted with a good deal of earthiness and passion, thereby distinguishing it from other contemporary works.

The play raises several questions on religion that, taken in conjunction with the information in the *Gauḍavaho*, makes for an interesting analysis. Vākpati stresses on Brahmanical deities and highlights, in tedious detail, the worship and rituals connected with the Vindhyavāsinī cult, an offshoot of the Śakti cult. However, the fact that Yaśovarman wrote the play *Rāmābhyudaya*, dealing with the story of the *Rāmāyaṇa* in six acts, is also proof of his devotion to Rāma.[73] Bhavabhūti, on the other hand, apparently highlights the closing gap between Buddhism and Brahmanism through the figure of Kāmandakī, foretelling the eventual merger between the two religions.[74]

Uncertain light is thrown on the period after Yaśovarman by Jain sources in that his son, Āma, is said to have succeeded him. Interestingly, it is revealed that Āma was born of Yaśodevī, Yaśovarman's chief wife, during her exile (engineered by the machinations of a co-wife).[75] The *Gauḍavaho* and other sources maintain an intriguing silence on this matter.

At this juncture, one should note that the next prominent dynasty of Kanauj is believed to be that of the Āyudhas, comprising three kings—Cakrāyudha, Vajrāyudha, and Indrāyudha.[76] The form of their names suggests that all three belonged to the same line. The sources for this dynasty are extremely meagre and, in fact, this has even led S.K. Aiyangar and G.C. Choudhary to contend that the Āyudha family was 'a concoction'.[77] They identify Vajrāyudha with Āma and say that since Indrāyudha is only known from the Jain *Harivaṁśa* of Jinasena, he is probably identical with the Rāṣṭrakūṭa king Indrarāja of the Baroda plates, which confirm Rāṣṭrakūṭa penetration in the north. Only Cakrāyudha can be located in Kanauj on the basis of Pāla[78] and Gurjara-Pratihāra records. Thus, they believe that the gap between Yaśovarman and the Pratihāras at Kanauj was filled in by Āma, negating the existence of the Āyudha dynasty.

However, one cannot discount the testimony of the *Harivaṁśa.* It clearly states that a king called Indrāyudha was ruling in Kanauj between 783 and 784.[79] Besides, Rājaśekhara says in his *Karpūramañjarī*, in connection with the travels of a merchant, Sāgaradatta—'to the capital of Vajrāyudha, the king of Pāñcāla, to Kanauj'. This statement confirms the existence of Vajrāyudha. Furthermore, Kalhaṇa's statement that Jayāpīḍa of Kashmir 'defeated the king of Kānyakubja in battle' is seen as either a reference to Vajrāyudha or Indrāyudha. So, in all probability, the Āyudha dynasty did rule Kanauj, albeit for a short period.

THE PRATIHĀRAS OF KANAUJ (*c.* 810–1085)

Āyudha rule was apparently cut short by the attack of Pratihāra Nāgabhaṭṭa II of Ujjain on Kanauj. There are around thirty-two epigraphic sources for the period of the Pratihāra dynasty, an abundance when compared to the preceding period. A very important feature of these inscriptions is that they provide valuable details on the male and female components of the Pratihāra genealogy, not yielded by any other source. The Daulatapura plate of Bhoja, the Dighwa-Dubauli plate of Mahendrapāla, and the Bengal Asiatic Society's plate of Vināyakapāla are among the notable inscriptions in this regard.

There are also several literary works of this period like those of Rājaśekhara, the *guru/upādhyāya* of kings Mahendrapāla I and Mahipāla of Kanauj,[80] who proudly traces his poetic descent from

Vālmīki and Bhavabhūti. Some of his works are the *Karpūramañjarī*, the *Kāvyamīmāṁsā*, the *Bāla Rāmāyaṇa* and the *Viddhaśālabhañjikā*.[81] Thus, analysed in conjunction with each other, the literary and epigraphic sources of this period hold great potential for the reconstruction of political and social history—both in totality and from a gender perspective.

Tripathi contends that the Pratihāras were a branch of the Gurjaras, one of the nomadic Central Asian tribes who entered India following the disruption of the Gupta empire. He cites the Rajor stone inscription (AD 959) of the reign of Mathanadeva, a feudatory of Vijayapāladeva of Kanauj, where he is described as belonging to the Gurjara–Pratihāra lineage.[82] However, links with the Ikṣvākus are proposed by Rājaśekhara.[83] In his *Bāla-Bhārata*, he calls his patron, Mahendrapāla I, *raghugrāmaṇī* (leader of Raghu's family). This clearly legendary connection was obviously incorporated to claim a respectable place in the Hindu polity.

The conquest of Kanauj gave the Pratihāras supreme power in the north and the Buckala inscription of Nāgabhaṭṭa (815) has full imperial titles for him like *mahārājādhirāja* and *parameśvara*. His kingdom comprised parts of Rajasthan, large parts of modern Uttar Pradesh and central India, and Kauśāmbī and nearby areas as its south-eastern limit. Marriage alliances like those between the Pratihāras and the Cāhamānas, attested to by the *Pṛthvīrājavijaya*, were concluded to cement their position.

The reign of Mahendrapāla's father, Mihira Bhoja (Bhoja I) {*c.* 836–85} is also of great significance. References in the *Rājataraṅgiṇī*, the Barah copper plate (836), the Partābgarh inscription of Mahendrapāla II (946), and some Rāṣṭrakūṭa inscriptions (like the Bagumra plates of Indra III of 905 that refer to the 'roaring Gurjara') talk of his military expansion.[84] There is no account of his administration except that of Suleiman, the Arab traveller (AD 851), who praises him for his control over law and order. He says—'There is no country in India more safe from robbers.'[85] This is a welcome change from Yuan Chwang's time where he complains of being robbed by brigands.

An interesting story lies behind Bhoja's abdication of the throne in favour of his son, Mahendrapāla I. H.C. Raychaudhuri cites the *Vastrāpatha Mahātmya* (a section of the *Skanda Purāṇa*), which says that Bhoja was informed by a warden of the forests about a doe-faced woman with a herd of deer in the forests at Raivataka.[86] When she was brought before the king, she informed him of the sanctity of the Suvarṇarekhā waters and of her previous births. Bhoja was so impressed by this that he decided to abdicate and go on a pilgrimage. Since the last-known date of Bhoja's reign as per the Pehoa inscription is 882, he probably died around 885, to be succeeded by his son Mahendrapāla by the queen, Candrabhaṭṭārikādevī.

The findspots of certain inscriptions at Rāmgayā and Guneriya show the success of Mahendrapāla's attempted conquest of Magadha and Bengal.[87] Another interesting source is a votive inscription from Itkhori in the Hazaribagh district of Jharkhand where the name of *Parameśvara Mahendrapāla* is incised on the pedestal of the image of Tārā, an obvious reference to this king. The *Rājataraṅgiṇī*, however, reveals that his kingdom suffered in the north-west where the territories originally seized by Bhoja were reclaimed by Śaṁkaravarman of Kashmir.

Rājaśekhara can, in a limited sense, be used as a source for the reign of Mahendrapāla, whom he refers to as Nirbhayarāja or Nirbhayanarendra in his plays. Unfortunately, unlike Bāṇa, he has not left any account of his patron's career. His writings reveal only faint traces of the position and importance of Kanauj and, by extension, that of his patroṇ. In the *Kāvyamīmāṁsā*, he says that this imperial city was a sacred place, where the people were 'elegant like new compositions' and the women were resplendent in 'adorable' dresses.[88] He extends this in the *Bāla Rāmāyaṇa*, claiming that the ornamentation, hair styles and speech of these women were being studied by women of other countries.

The *Karpūramañjarī* of Rājaśekhara is an important source for the study of gender, not only because the theme is harem intrigue, but also because of the poet's observations on women. He is believed to have said that genius is inherent in people, 'irrespective of the distinctions of sex', and to have lauded contemporary women poets. He quotes his wife, the gifted poet, Avantisundarī, thrice in his work, the *Kāvyamīmāṁsā*, being deeply appreciative of her skills.[89] The *Karpūramañjarī* was apparently produced at her behest.[90] This Prakrit verse play deals with harem intrigue in a fashion reminiscent of Harṣa's plays, yet differing from them in many ways. The story revolves around Karpūramañjarī, a princess of Lāṭa and Queen Vibramalekhā's cousin, who is introduced into King Caṇḍapāla's court by magical means, and their eventual marriage.

There is a significant departure from Harṣa's plays in the portrayal of the queen and her attitude towards the appearance of a rival on the scene. The open hostility and vocal disapproval of Queen Vāsavadattā towards Udayana's intrigues can be contrasted with the lukewarm and woefully inadequate resistance of Queen Vibramalekhā to King Caṇḍapāla's obvious fascination for Karpūramañjarī. She is completely outmanoeuvred by her maids, the jester, and the magician Bhairavānanda, who treats the female figures in the text with contempt. The queen has a very diluted voice in the play.

Once again, the maids are prominent for their superior wit and intelligence. Thus, for instance, Rājaśekhara lauds the poetic skills of Vicakṣaṇā, at the expense of the jester, and exalts her figure—a fact, incidentally, to which the translator of this work, N.G. Suru, pays scant regard.[91]

Rājaśekhara continued to be the court poet in the reign of Mahendrapāla's son, Mahipāla I, though how long he maintained his connection is unknown. As the last known date of Mahendrapāla is 907/8, he probably died around 910. There is an interesting dispute behind Mahipāla's succession that has implications for a gendered study of succession in the Kanauj polity. As per the Asiatic Society plate of Vināyakapāla[92] (931), Mahendrapāla was succeeded by his son, Bhoja (Bhoja II), whose mother was the queen, Dehanāgādevī. The Asni inscription (917), however, does not mention Bhoja but represents his half-brother, Mahipāla, born of Mahīdevī, as having come after Mahendrapāla. This omission could either be due to the shortness of Bhoja's reign or a battle for succession between the two contenders.

That Mahipāla faced a serious menace in the form of the Rāṣṭrakūṭas at the beginning of his reign is evident from the Cambay plates of Govinda IV (930) which say that Indra III 'completely devastated that hostile city of Mahodaya'.[93] However, Rājaśekhara indicates that he regained power: he is called the *mahārājādhirāja* of *āryavarta.*[94] In the *Bāla Bhārata*, he attributes victories to him in distant lands, but there is no epigraphic evidence to support these claims, and one must assume that by attributing 'world conquest' to his patron, the poet was only following a convention.

Interestingly, the Karhad plates (959) reveal that Mahipāla's victory over Govinda IV of the Rāṣṭrakūṭas was facilitated by the fact that the latter neglected governance in his fascination for women.[95] The testimony of the Arab traveller, Al Masudi, who visited India at the beginning of Mahipāla's reign and wrote his account in AD 943/4, testifies to the Rāṣṭrakūṭa–Pratihāra struggle, the characteristic feature of this epoch. He says—'This Baüüra (Pratihāra) who is the king of Kanauj is an enemy of the Balhara, the king of India'.[96]

On the basis of discrepancies in epigraphic information and centering around Mahendrapāla II and Devapāla, we can infer that another war of succession followed Mahipāla's death.[97] The renowned author, Somadeva, seems to have been a contemporary of Mahendrapāla II (940–8). He refers to him by name in the opening and concluding verses of the *Yaśastilaka Campu* and apparently composed the *Nītivākyāmṛtā* at his instance.[98]

The kingdom gradually declined, thereafter, with the rise of the Candellas and other states, and with the attack by Mahmud of Ghazni (1018) and its repercussions. Eventually, Kanauj was conquered by Candradeva Gāhaḍavāla in the last decade of the eleventh century.

THE GĀHAḌAVĀLA DYNASTY (*c.* 1085–1197)

The Gāhaḍavālas were the next important dynasty to rule Kanauj after an interim period of political upheaval and destructive raids. The source material for this dynasty includes around fifty-one inscriptions, significant in their recording of the power and presence of women. Here my analysis of the Gāhaḍavālas focuses on the epigraphic information alone.[99]

A significant percentage of these inscriptions provide information on powerful women administrators and donors. Among the more important inscriptions are the Benares grant of Govindacandra (AD 1105), the copper-plate grant of Madanapāla and Queen

Pṛthvī-Śrīkā (1107), and the Kamauli plate of Govindacandra and Queen Nayanakelidevī (1119). Finally, as specified earlier, the ambit of this study is limited to the early Gāhaḍavālas until AD 1154 (Govindacandra's last-known date and the end of his reign).

There is much speculation on the identity of the Gāhaḍavālas. Their charters expressly mention the name of the family/clan and call them kṣatriyas. They have been variously linked with the Rāṣṭrakūṭas, with a clan descending from the mythical Yayāti and with the *paurāṇik* Gahvara people or cave dwellers.[100] All these theories are far from conclusive and have not been detailed here.

As per the inscriptions, notably the Basahi plate (1104), Candradeva, the founder, Mahicandra's son, 'acquired the matchless sovereignty over the glorious Kānyakubja or Gādhipura,' and by his 'noble prowess' put an end to 'all distress of the people'.[101] His earliest-known date is 1090 and his last date is supplied by the Candrāvatī plates as 1099. The Basahi plate of his grandson, Govindacandra, says that his father, Madanapāla, was crowned in AD 1104. Hence, Candradeva probably died between 1100 and 1104.

Madanapāla's reign is intriguing on account of his apparent passivity and the evident delegation of responsibilities to his wives and son. The Sārnāth inscription of Govindacandra's wife, Kumaradevī, says that Madanapāla was 'a crest-jewel among impetuous kings . . . the lord who brought the circle of the earth under one sceptre. . . .'[102] Other charters too are full of such conventional and vague praise. However, Madanapāla seems not to have taken part in state affairs. Except for confirming the gift of Ahāuma village to a brāhmaṇa, Vāmanasvāmideva, no grants by Madanapāla are known, and those of his reign are executed on his behalf by the crown-prince, Govindacandra, and his two queens, Rālhadevī and Pṛthvī-Śrīkā. His inactivity could be attributed to preoccupation with wars, or the probability that he was an invalid. If the latter is true, then a medical treatise, the *Madana-vinoda-nighaṇṭu*, ascribed to a 'king Madana, lord of Kāśī', may have been written by him.[103]

Govindacandra succeeded Madanapāla between 1109 and 1114, between the latter's last-known date and the first charter issued in the former's name as ruling sovereign. His mother was the queen Rālhadevī, who gave her consent to a grant issued by him in his father's lifetime in 1105. The inscriptions reveal him to have four wives—Nayanakelidevī, Gosalladevī, Kumaradevī and Vasantadevī.[104] The *Prabandhakoṣa* says that his 'inner apartment' was 'peopled by 750 (damsels)'.[105] Govindacandra's reign is also marked by several works on law and procedure, notably the *Kṛtya-kalpataru*, by his minister, Lakṣmīdhara.

The Sārnāth inscription of Queen Kumaradevī indicates that Govindacandra effectively handled the danger posed by Masud III of Ghazni who sent an expedition against Kanauj, 'the capital of Hind', some time before 1109—as reported in the *Diwan* of Salman.[106] Thus, it says that Govindacandra gained fame as the incarnation of Hari 'who had been commissioned by Hara . . . to protect Baranasi from the wicked Turuṣka warrior. . . .'[107]

Literary and epigraphic records inform us of his other conquests.[108] The *Rambhāmañjarī* of Nayacandra, a Jain work that deals with Jayacandra, testifies that Govindacandra achieved a victory against Daśārṇa (eastern Mālwā) the day his grandson Jayacandra was born—which could account for the infant's name. The Rahan plate shows him making encroachments in Magadha, the Lār plates of 1146 prove that Mudgagiri (Monghyr) came under him, and the Gagaha plate represents him as having captured the elephants of the 'nine kings'. This indicates that he placed himself in the position of almost the leading monarch in *Jambūdvīpa*.[109]

The *Rājataraṅgiṇī* proves Govindacandra's alliance with King Jayasiṁha of Kashmir, who apparently 'made the rulers in Kānyakubja and elsewhere who were powerful owing to the possession of excellent territories, proud by his friendship'.[110] The coins of his reign, of which some copper and gold issues have been found, confirm the connections with the Cedis, since they are copied from the coins of Gāṅgeya-deva-cedi.

This concludes the brief political framework of Kanauj between the seventh and twelfth century before undertaking a gender analysis of its society and polity. Obviously, not all the sources are equally useful. The point of this analysis is to examine the visibility of women and not build on an assumption of their insignificance or passivity, as a surface reading of the available sources could convey. As mentioned at the outset, the subsequent chapters will problematize the issue, attempting to highlight the possibilities and the drawbacks inherent in such an exercise, and seeking to provide a far more nuanced picture of women's agency than has, hitherto, been available.

NOTES

1. For instance, Pam Morris, 'Literature and Feminism', in *Speaking of Gender*, ed. Elaine Showalter, London, Routledge: 1994, p. 7.
2. In the latter case, the choice of language by the author, Rājaśekhara, is deliberate so as to focus on the potential of languages other than Sanskrit. N.G. Suru, ed. and tr., *Karpūramañjarī*, Poona, Ruparel College: 1960, pp. lvii–lxii, stresses that the choice of Prakrit might stem from the need for this *saṭṭaka*/dance drama to appeal to the 'uncultured masses' as well.
3. For instance, D.C. Sircar, *Indian Epigraphy*, Delhi, Motilal Banarsidass: 1965, pp. 17–18.
4. For instance, it informs us that one Naravardhana founded a dynasty at Thānesar, 'immortalised by the deeds of Harṣa'. George Bühler, 'The Madhuban copper-plate of Harṣa', *Epigraphia Indica*, vol. I, 1892, pp. 67–75; R.S. Tripathi, *History of Kanauj to the Moslem Conquest*, rpt., Delhi, Motilal Banarsidass: 1989, p. 22. Note that the names Puṣpabhūti and Vardhana are used interchangeably for this dynasty.
5. Tripathi, *History of Kanauj*, p. 1. The present town is in the Fatehgarh district of U.P. J.N. Agrawal, *Inscriptions of Haryana, Himachal Pradesh, Punjab, Kashmir and Adjoining Hilly Tracts*, New Delhi, ICHR/Pratibha Prakashan: 1999, p. 45.
6. Tripathi, *History of Kanauj*, p. 16. Aśoka's son, Jalauka, is mentioned in Kalhaṇa's *Rājataraṅgiṇī* as having pushed his conquests as far as Kanauj in the east but the allusion is somewhat unclear.
7. Ibid., p. 22. The provenance of coins and inscriptions shows that the kingdom extended up to Ahicchatra and Thānesar on the west, to Nālandā on the east, up to the Tarai districts on the north and probably not beyond the southern boundaries of present Uttar Pradesh. Harivarman seems to have been the founder of the Maukhari house of Kanauj, as he is the first to be named in the dynasty's records.
8. Ibid., pp. 24–6. The Later Gupta inscriptions stress the Gupta-Maukhari relations, the last stages of their feud being narrated by the *Harṣacarita*. While the Maukhari coins furnish certain dates, the Nālandā seals are in a very fragmentary state and do not yield proper information. Regarding the genre of *carita* or historical biography, Romila Thapar ('Society and Historical Consciousness: The Itihāsa-Purāṇa Tradition', in *Situating Indian History*, ed. S. Bhattacharya and Romila Thapar, Delhi, Oxford

University Press: 1986, pp. 378-9) says that it focused on the king, the centre of formal political authority and the focus of the court.

9. The coins are associated with *śīlāditya pratāpaśīla*, the title Harṣa apparently assumed in Kanauj. Tripathi, *History of Kanauj*, p. 35.
10. Cited by Tripathi, p. 29. Also Baijnath Sharma, *Harṣa and his Times*, Varanasi, Sushma Prakashan: 1970, p. 34; E.B. Cowell and F.W. Thomas, tr., *The Harṣacarita of Bāṇa*, rpt., Delhi, Motilal Banarsidass: 1993, IV.161, p. 128. The relevant words are '. . . *soma-sūryavaṅśāviva puṣpabhūti mukharavaṅśau*. . . .'
11. Tripathi, *History of Kanauj*, pp. 29–30.
12. Ibid., p. 24.
13. Ibid., p. 45.
14. This has been concluded on the premise that it was common practice then for siblings to bear identical names with gender variations in the ending (ibid., p. 37). These two marriage alliances indicate that the Maukharis were getting more recognition.
15. Tripathi says that this fact, along with the *Harṣacarita*, provides some indication of the movements of the Later Guptas after the annexation of Magadha. Bāṇa says that Kumāragupta and Mādhavagupta are presented as Harṣa's cousins, the latter being held identical with the Mādhavagupta of the Aphsāḍ inscription. Bāṇa calls them *mālavarājaputra*, sons of the king of Mālwā. Thus, their father, the Gupta king, Mahāsenagupta (the son of Dāmodaragupta), probably retired to some part of Mālwā that still acknowledged his supremacy. Ibid., p. 46. Also Sharma, *Harṣa and his Times*, p. 30.
16. Tripathi, *History of Kanauj*, pp. 51, 43, terms it a 'diplomatic revolution'; K.K. Thaplyal, *Inscriptions of the Maukharis, Later Guptas, Puṣpabhūtis and Yaśovarman of Kanauj*, Delhi, ICHR/Agam Prakashan: 1985, p. 31.
17. This has, among other things, been said to point to the immoral laws of war in that age. Tripathi, *History of Kanauj*, p. 51.
18. D. Devahuti, *Harsha: A Political Study*, 2nd edn, Delhi, Oxford University Press: 1983, p. 1, says that the contemporary inscriptions prove a most trustworthy source. She echoes Vincent Smith's remark that 'our knowledge of the events of the reign of Harṣa far surpasses in precision that which we possess respecting any other early king, except Candragupta Maurya and Aśoka.' See Tripathi, *History of Kanauj*, p. 62 where Smith is cited.
19. The Madhuban grant restored land to the rightful donees after taking it away from a forger. See Devahuti, *Harsha*, pp. 272-4 for details of Harṣa's coins. Interestingly, the beautifully ornate signature of Harṣa in the Bānskherā plate is the only instance of a royal donor's signature on a seal (Thaplyal, *Inscriptions of the Maukharis*, p. 16).

20. Cowell and Thomas, *Harṣacarita*, p. xii claim to have used, for their translation, the Bombay text collated with the Calcutta and Kashmir editions. They have also consulted K.D. Sastri's translation (Benares, 1883), R.R. Kale's volume of English notes to it (Bombay, 1882) and G. Bühler's collation of all available manuscripts. A Hindi translation was made by Bal Govind Jha (ed. with Hindi tr., *Harṣa-Caritam of Bāṇabhaṭṭa*, Varanasi, Krishnadas Academy: 1994). For an interesting corroboration of the descriptions in the *Harṣacarita* with sculptural and other evidence, see V.S. Agrawala, *The Deeds of Harsha*, Varanasi, Prithivi Prakashan: 1969.
21. Bāṇa died before completing the *Kādambarī* and the text was completed by his son, Bhūṣaṇabhaṭṭa, in a style that is closely imitative of his father's. Bāṇa also wrote the *Caṇḍīśataka* and the *Pārvatīpariṇaya*. Mayūra, Bāṇa's alleged rival, was another poet at Harṣa's court, whose chief contribution was the *Sūryaśataka*. For details, Tripathi, *History of Kanauj*, p. 179. Also V.S. Pathak, *Ancient Historians of India*, 2nd impression, Gorakhpur, Purva Samsthana: 1984, p. 44. Interestingly, G.P. Quackenbos claims that Bāṇa apparently wrote the *Caṇḍīśataka* to appease his wife's anger. S.M. Sastri, 'Book Notice—The Sanskrit Poems of Mayūra and Bāṇa's *Caṇḍīśataka* by G.P. Quackenbos', *Indian Antiquary*, vol. XLVII, 1918, pp. 167–8.
22. Tripathi, *History of Kanauj*, pp. 78–80 for a discussion on the extent of the kingdom of Thānesar under Prabhākaravardhana. The poetic descriptions of his superiority over other rulers in the *Harṣacarita* such as him being 'a lion to the Hūṇa deer, a burning fever to the king of the Indus land . . .' and 'an axe to the creeper of Mālwā's glory' (*HC*, IV. 132) are, of course, exaggerated.
23. Yuan Chwang's account is also used to determine the status of the northern kingdoms that he visited or heard about. He refers to Kānyakubja (Kanauj) or Ka-no-ku-she, Ka-mo-lu-po or Kāmarūpa ruled by Harṣa's ally, Bhāskaravarman, and Valabhī whose ruler, Dhruvabhaṭa, was Harṣa's son-in-law. Tripathi, *History of Kanauj*, pp. 82–114 for a detailed list of the kingdoms mentioned by Yuan Chwang. Note that Yuan Chwang mentions the Suvarṇagotra country north of the Brahmaputrā, or 'the eastern woman's country', as ruled, significantly, by a succession of women. Samuel Beal, tr., *The Life of Hiuen-Tsiang* by Shaman Hwui-Li, Delhi, Academica Asiatica: 1973.
24. Harṣa learns that Rājya 'though he had routed the Mālwā army with ridiculous ease, had been allured to confidence by false civilities on the part of the king and then . . . despatched in his own quarters'. *HC*, VI.208; Tripathi, *History of Kanauj*, p. 65.
25. In Tripathi, *History of Kanauj*, pp. 65–6, an explanation is offered for this in that Bāṇa did not want to mention Devagupta's auspicious name (protected by the gods) owing to his foul deed. So he makes Harṣa

say—'My tongue seems soiled . . . as I take the miscreant's very name upon my lips' (*HC*, VI. 210). For Yuan Chwang's statement, Tripathi, *History of Kanauj*, pp. 66–7.

26. Tripathi, *History of Kanauj*, p. 150. Kanauj was apparently the centre of culture and crafts, power and politics, and religion and riches. Both Yuan Chwang and the *Harṣacarita* provide details of Kanauj's administration.
27. Ibid., p. 80. Yuan Chwang also credits Harṣa with extensive conquests and protracted military campaigns (p. 115). The *Life* describes Harṣa as a powerful monarch attended by numerous feudatories. The imperial titles given to Harṣa in the *Harṣacarita*, like 'king of kings' and 'sovereign of all continents' (*HC*, III. 99), and in his inscriptions, indicate his power.
28. Tripathi, *History of Kanauj*, p. 85. Apparently Harṣa learnt that Kashmir possessed a tooth of the Buddha, asked to worship it and, on being refused, carried it off by 'exercising force'. The question of Durlabhavardhana's reluctance is, however, open to contention.
29. This is supported by the Aihole Meguti inscription of Ravikīrti (AD 634), and the Nirpan, Karnul and Togarcedu grants that talk of Harṣa's defeat at Pulakeśin's hands when he tried to extend south. Ibid., pp. 107–8.
30. Beal, *Life*, pp. 176, 186–7.
31. Tripathi, *History of Kanauj*, pp. 157, 159, provides details of the 'curiously eclectic' religious services and shows how Harṣa apparently 'inclined' towards Buddhism through ceremonies, welfare measures, and the worship of relics. This is interesting as Yuan Chwang calls India 'the country of the Brāhmaṇas', p. 164.
32. Ibid., p. 175. Yuan Chwang says that Harṣa used to earmark a fourth of the revenue from crown lands for rewarding intellectual eminence. This patronage was apparently above religious considerations, as the *Life* records his generous gift of 'the revenue of eighty large towns' of Orissa to a Buddhist scholar, Jayasena, and munificent endowments to Nālandā.
33. Harṣa's step-brother, Kriṣṇa, apparently summoned Bāṇa to court and was instrumental in effecting a reconciliation between him and Harṣa.
34. Tripathi, *History of Kanauj*, pp. 180–1. Harṣa of Kashmir (1089–1101), Harṣa of Dhara (947–72), and Harṣa-Vikramāditya of Ujjain can be ruled out on chronological grounds, as these works are cited by earlier writers. Thus, Dāmodaragupta mentions in his *Kuṭṭanīmatam*, the story and performance of *Ratnāvalī*, which he ascribes to a king. The poet Māgha, too (700), speaks of the *Nāgānandam* in his *kāvya*: A.B. Keith, *A History of Sanskrit Literature*, London, Oxford University Press: 1920, p. 124.
35. Tripathi, *History of Kanauj*, p. 181 notes that Dhāvaka was apparently conversant with Harṣa's religious tendencies and life events, and could have ascribed the plays to him in return for gifts or honours. Tripathi quotes the Kashmiri poet, Mammaṭa (eleventh century), who talks of

gains from writing poetry, in his *Kāvyaprakāśa*, as in '. . . wealth—as to Dhāvaka and other poets, from Śrī-Harṣa and other kings'. However, he also points out that the language of the plays is simple, unlike Bāṇa's complicated style (pp. 185–7). See also G.C. Choudhary, *Political History of Northern India (from Jain Sources—c. 650 A.D. to 1300 A.D.)*, Amritsar, Sohanlal Jaindharma Pracharak Samiti: 1954, p. 17. The Jain poet, Svayambhu (eighth century), apparently mentions Śrī Harṣa as a well-versed poet. Hence, the Harṣa in question cannot have been a poet later than the eighth century AD.

36. Tripathi, *History of Kanauj*, p. 182; also *HC*, II.79.
37. Tripathi, *History of Kanauj*, p. 183. Jayadeva also mentions Mayūra's name. See also p. 182 where Soḍḍhala (eleventh century) is cited as having mentioned Harṣa in his *Udaya-sundarī-kathā* as a poet-king and patron of literature.
38. Ibid., p. 184. On this Tripathi cites J. Takasaku, tr., *A Record of the Buddhist Religion in India and the Malay Archipelago* by I-tsing, Oxford, 1896, pp. 163–4.
39. Tripathi, *History of Kanauj*, p. 187. However, he does not rule out the possibility that a protégé of Harṣa helped him polish up his dramas.
40. Meenakshi Mukherjee, 'Story, History and Her Story', *Studies in History*, vol. IX, no.1, 1993, p. 71.
41. For instance, C.H. Tawney, tr., *The Kathāsaritsāgara*, 3rd edn, Delhi, Munshiram Manoharlal: 1992, vol. I, pp. 97, 101–15.
42. Apart from these two Sanskrit versions of the original *paisāchi* text of one lakh verses, there is a third, a summary: the *Bṛhatkathā-śloka-saṅgraha* of Buddhasvāmin. However, only twenty-eight stanzas are extant. M.R. Kale, ed. and tr., *Priyadarśikā of Śrī Harṣadeva*, rpt., Delhi, Motilal Banarsidass: 1977, p. xxvii.
43. Udayana was apparently a very powerful ruler, renowned for his heroic deeds and romances. He was supposed to be a contemporary of King Pradyota of Avanti and was the fifth king in his line, as per the Purāṇas. Sharma, *Harṣa and his Times*, pp. 307–9; Kale, *Priyadarśikā*, Notes, pp. 5–6 for details of Udayana's origins; also p. xxx for a discussion on Udayana's marriage with Vāsavadattā. Udayana was apparently captured by King Caṇḍamahāsena and made to teach his daughter, Vāsavadattā, music. The king's covert design succeeded in that the two fell in love and escaped back to Kauśāmbī. Caṇḍamahāsena speedily gave his blessings to the union. Note that this marriage occurred not long before Priyadarśikā's appearance on the scene. S. Vats and Shakuntala Mudgal, eds., *Women and Society in Ancient India*, Faridabad, Om Publications: 1999, pp. 225–6 for information on the Buddhist women who married Udayana, thereby apparently proving his contemporaneity with the Buddha.

44. Sharma, *Harṣa and his Times*, p. 313; Kale, *Priyadarśikā*, p. ix says that the *Priyadarśikā* conforms to the rules of dramaturgy on broad lines (pp. ix, xxx). Kale says that though Harṣa does not show 'originality' in plots or skill in portraying characters, he shows it in the creation of situations necessary for dramatic action (p. xix). Ratnamayi Dikshit, *Women in Sanskrit Dramas*, Delhi, Meherchand Lachhmandas: 1964, pp. 172–7 finds that it is natural for these *nāṭikās* to be 'swamped with women'; there is not much originality in the plots, situations or characters, there being traces of borrowing from Kālidāsa as well. However, these similarities are confined to the literary or technical side of the plays, and not to the characters represented or the society reflected. M.R. Kale, ed. and tr., *The Ratnāvalī of Śrī Harṣa-Deva*, 2nd rpt., Delhi, Motilal Banarsidass: 1995, p. xxix, says that the plot resembles Kālidāsa's *Mālavikāgnimitram*. For a synopsis of the original story of Padmāvatī and Udayana in the *Kathāsaritsāgara*, see p. xxvii.
45. Note that Udayana's love for Priyadarśikā is absent in the *Kathāsaritsāgara* version. However, Udayana's intrigue with Bandhumatī, a captive princess, resembles this plot (Kale, *Priyadarśikā*, pp. xxv–xxvii). Harṣa might have taken this slim storyline and worked it up into the play.
46. Bak Kun Bae, ed. and tr., *Nāgānanda of Harṣa*, Delhi, Motilal Banarsidass: 1992, pp. vi–viii for a comparison of Harṣa's three plays.
47. For instance, Uma Chakravarti, *Everyday Lives, Everyday Histories: Beyond the Kings and Brahmanas of 'Ancient' India*, Delhi, Tulika Books: 2006, pp. 218–20. Romila Thapar, *Śakuntalā: Texts, Readings, Histories*, Delhi, Kali for Women: 1999, pp. 79–82 for the role of the *vidūṣaka* (jester) in romantic plays.
48. Devahuti, *Harsha*, p. 3.
49. For details of this period, Tripathi, *History of Kanauj*, pp. 188–92.
50. Devahuti, *Harsha*, pp. 226–9; B.P. Sinha, *Dynastic History of Magadha*, Delhi, Abhinav Publications: 1977, p. 156.
51. N.G. Suru, ed. and tr., *Vākpatirāja's Gauḍavaho*, Delhi, Munshiram Manoharlal: 1975, p. i. This *praśasti kāvya* consists of 1,209 *gāthās* in Prakrit in one long, continuous composition. The actual theme is cursorily dismissed in one verse, while the text abounds in detailed erotic descriptions of women and their lovers, of devastated enemy territory, of dead bodies, of gods, goddesses and mythical figures, and so on.
52. Tripathi, *History of Kanauj*, p. 193.
53. Choudhary, *Political History*, pp. 18–19; S.M. Mishra, *Yaśovarman of Kanauj*, Delhi, Abhinav Publications: 1977, p. 63, says that the cumulative evidence of the *Gauḍavaho*, the Mathurā inscription (seventh/eighth century) that mentions three Maurya kings, one of whom sacked Kanauj), and the Jain works seems to show that Yaśovarman belonged to the family of the later Mauryas of U.P. He either inherited Kanauj or won

it for himself. Cunningham believed Yaśovarman to be a descendant of the Maukharis due to the 'varman' ending of his name. For Suru, *Gauḍávaho*, p. li, Yaśovarman was a descendant of the Maukhari king, Avantivarman, Grahavarman's father. Kanauj was apparently restored later to some member of Grahavarman's family, of whom Yaśovarman was a descendant.

54. H.C. Ray, *The Dynastic History of Northern India*, 2nd edn, Delhi, Munshiram Manoharlal: 1973, vol. 1, p. 276. The verse cited from the *Rājataraṅgiṇī* is IV.145. The Kālikā may be identified with the present Kālīnadī that joins the Gaṅgā at a short distance below Kanauj: Tripathi, *History of Kanauj*, p. 202.
55. The religious conversion of Āma is also detailed in Prabhācandra's *Prabhāvakacarita*: Choudhary, *Political History*, p. 19. Moreover, Chinese authorities mention that a 'king of central India', I-cha-fou-mo (identified with Yaśovarman), sent a minister to China in AD 725 (Tripathi, *History of Kanauj*, p. 196).
56. *Magahanāha* means *magadhanātha* or 'the lord of Magadha'. The title *Gauḍavaho* implies that the vanquished king held sway over parts of Bengal too. Yaśovarman also defeated the *pārasikas* (Arab invaders) and the people on the Mandāra mountains (Tripathi, *History of Kanauj*, p. 199). Despite the lack of specific names in the text, the central theme was probably a historical reality, for the region of the vanquished king was under Kanauj, even under Harṣa and the Maukharis. Ibid., p. 200. Also Mishra, *Yaśovarman*, pp. 76–8 for details of Yaśovarman's conquests gleaned from the text.
57. Mishra, *Yaśovarman*, pp. 24–5. He also cites A.B. Keith and S.K. De's contention that it was an unfinished composition. Yaśovarman seems to have been vanquished by Lalitāditya before Vākpati could compose the subsequent part (p. 27).
58. Suru, *Gauḍavaho*, p. i. This—and the paucity of details—leads one to presume that the present poem is just a prelude. See p. xliii. Jacobi refutes this by saying that the extant form was all that Vākpati ever intended to write (Mishra, *Yaśovarman*, pp. 24–5).
59. Cited by Mishra, *Yaśovarman*, p. 24.
60. Choudhary, *Political History*, pp. 19–20.
61. Suru, *Gauḍavaho*, p. liii cites this contention of Dr. Mirashi.
62. Prior to the *Gauḍavaho*, Vākpati wrote a poem, *Mahu-maha-vijaya* (*Madhu-matha-vijaya*), probably about the killing of the demon Madhu by Viṣṇu. The text has not yet been discovered. Tripathi, *History of Kanauj*, p. 210.
63. Ibid., pp. 205-6; Hirananda Sastri, 'Nālandā Stone Inscription of Yaśovarmadeva', *Epigraphia Indica*, vol. XX, 1933, pp. 37–46, thinks it refers to Yaśodharman of the Mandasor inscriptions, the contemporary

of the Hūṇa chief, Mihirakula. On palaeographical grounds, however, the document is probably of a later date. The letters largely resemble the developed form of the Aphsāḍ inscription of Ādityasena (AD 627). See Mishra, *Yaśovarman*, p. 27.

64. Tripathi, *History of Kanauj*, p. 201.
65. Ibid., pp. 207–8. Crude coins of the Indo-Scythian type bearing the name Yaśovarma have been found in Punjab and Kashmir. From a numismatic point of view, they can be placed between Durlabhaka Pratāpāditya II and Jayāpīḍa. Thus, they are assigned to Yaśovarman of Kanauj, as the Kashmir list knows no such monarch. However, as neither the *Gauḍavaho* nor any other source mentions that Yaśovarman penetrated Punjab or Kashmir, these coins could also belong to an unknown minor king of the sixth/seventh century, rather than Yaśovarman of Kanauj.
66. Mishra, *Yaśovarman*, p. 32.
67. Tripathi, *History of Kanauj*, p. 201. The *Gauḍavaho* supports this statement by referring to a time 'when the corner of Yaśovarman's eye became twisted in consequence of a momentary shaking of his (kingly) position'. Jacobi holds this to be a reference to the invasion and narrows the date down to AD 733. See pp. 204–5.
68. Thus, the text was probably written between 700 and 725—after the Gauḍa battle and before the clash with Lalitāditya. Suru, *Gauḍavaho*, p. liii.
69. Mishra, *Yaśovarman*, p. 95.
70. Tripathi, *History of Kanauj*, p. 210; Mishra, *Yaśovarman*, p. 106. Bhavabhūti was also called Śrīkaṇṭa and was born in Padmapura (Vidarbha).
71. Tripathi, *History of Kanauj*, p. 209. Kālapriyanātha is usually identified with Mahākāleśvara whose shrine in Ujjain (in Mālwā) is also mentioned by Bāṇa. Michael Coulson, tr., *Three Sanskrit Plays: 'Śakuntalā' by Kālidāsa, 'Rākṣasa's Ring' by Viśākhadatta, 'Mālatī and Mādhava' by Bhavabhūti*, Harmondsworth, Penguin Books: 1981, p. 295; Michael Coulson, *A Critical Edition of the Mālatīmādhava*, Delhi, Oxford University Press: 1989.
72. Mishra, *Yaśovarman*, p. 135. See also Chapter VIII of this volume.
73. Mishra, *Yaśovarman*, p. 103. This play is not available in its original form but is quoted in some later works.
74. Ibid., pp. 21, 225.
75. Ibid., p. 115. Āma's mother is called both Yaśodevī and Suyaśā in the sources.
76. For more information on the dynasty, D.C. Sircar, *The Kānyakubja-Gauḍa Struggle*, Calcutta, The Asiatic Society: 1985, pp. 6-7, 10-19.
77. Choudhary, *Political History*, p. 28. Interestingly, S.M. Mishra (*Yaśovarman*, p. 125) claims that Choudhary has plagiarized the views

of S.K. Aiyangar regarding the Āyudhas. He also affirms that there is no evidence for presuming Indrāyudha and Vajrāyudha to be names of Āma.

78. R.D. Banerji, *The Pālas of Bengal*, Varaṇasi, Bhartiya Publishing House: 1973, pp. 8–12.
79. Tripathi, *History of Kanauj*, pp. 212–13. He presumes, on this basis, that Vajrāyudha must have ascended the throne around 770.
80. He represents himself as this in all the extant plays (ibid., pp. 253–4).
81. The *Bālarāmāyaṇa* or *The Rāmāyaṇa for Boys* narrates the whole story in ten long acts with 741 stanzas. The *Bālabhārata* or *The Mahābhārata for Boys* is not available in its complete form. Maurice Winternitz, *History of Indian Literature*, rpt., Delhi, Motilal Banarsidass: 1985, vol. III, part 1, pp. 267–8. For the English translation of the *Viddhaśālabhañjikā*, see the *Journal of African and Oriental Studies*, vol. 27, pp. 1–71.
82. Tripathi, *History of Kanauj*, pp. 221–2; Choudhary, *Political History*, p. 35.
83. Tripathi, *History of Kanauj*, p. 224. These links are also put forth by the Gwalior *praśasti* of Vatsarāja.
84. He extended the kingdom of Kanauj to the western boundaries of the Pāla dominions in the east, and in all other directions as well (ibid., p. 246). The Jain temple inscription at Deogarh (862) refers to Bhoja I as *paramabhaṭṭāraka mahārājādhirāja parameśvara*, indicating his full sovereignty and the feudal system of the reign. Choudhary, *Political History*, p. 42.
85. Tripathi, *History of Kanauj*, pp. 246–7.
86. Ibid., p. 245. The story is used as proof of Bhoja's authority in Saurāṣṭra/Kāthiāwār. Raychaudhuri finds confirmation for this story in the Āhār stone inscription (865).
87. For details of his conquests, ibid., pp. 248–52. Note that inscriptions from Unā (AD 893 and 899), recording grants of land by Mahendrapāla's feudatories, show his success in holding Saurāṣṭra (pp. 250–2).
88. Ibid., p. 254.
89. Suru, *Karpūramañjarī*, pp. lxxii–lxxiii.
90. Ibid., I.11.
91. For instance, ibid., p. xxix.
92. Mahipāla seems also to have been called Vināyakapāla, as this name occurs in the colophon of the *Bṛhat Kathākoṣa* of the Jain poet, Harisena. Choudhary, *Political History*, p. 43.
93. Tripathi, *History of Kanauj*, p. 259.
94. Ibid., pp. 262–4.
95. Ibid., p. 265.
96. Ibid., pp. 268–9.
97. Ibid., pp. 269–71 for details.

98. This is apparently declared in an anonymous commentary: Choudhary, *Political History*, p. 45.
99. Most of the later literary sources of Kanauj date beyond the period of this dynasty.
100. Tripathi, *History of Kanauj*, pp. 296–9. Some other scholars affirm that the Gāhaḍavālas were a branch of the Rāṣṭrakūṭas or Rāṭhors. The Sūrat grant of Trilocanapāla (1151), the Badaun stone inscription of Lakhanapāla and the Saheth-Maheth record have been used to prove that princes of the Rāṣṭrakūṭa lineage were ruling over Kanauj in the eleventh century.
101. Ibid., pp. 301, 295.
102. Ibid., p. 305. Also Sten Konow, 'The Sārnāth Inscription of Kumaradevī', *Epigraphia Indica*, vol. IX, 1908, p. 327.
103. Tripathi, *History of Kanauj*, p. 306.
104. Nayanakelidevī is called *paṭṭamahādevī* and *mahārājñī*. Gosalladevī, who is also called *paṭṭamahādevī*, was probably raised to this dignity after Nayanakelidevī's death. Kumaradevī was the daughter of Devarakṣita, the king of Pīṭhikā of the Cikkora clan. Vasantadevī is mentioned in a colophon of a manuscript of the *Aṣṭasahasrikā* (ibid., pp. 314–15). See F. Kielhorn, 'Plate of Govindacandra and his wife Nayanakelidevī', *Epigraphia Indica*, vol. IV, 1897, pp. 107–9; F. Kielhorn, 'Bangāvan Plate of Govindacandra and his queen Gosalladevī', *Epigraphia Indica*, vol. V, 1899, pp. 116–18; and Konow, 'Sārnāth inscription', *Epigraphia Indica*, vol. IX, pp. 319–28 for information on Govindacandra's queens.
105. Choudhary, *Political History*, p. 47.
106. Tripathi, *History of Kanauj*, pp. 307–8.
107. Note that Jain sources refer to Varanasi as the only capital of the Gāhaḍavālas, while the Brahmanical writers call them the rulers of Kanauj and Varanasi. The reason seems to be that the seat of the Gāhaḍavālas, Varanasi, did not lose its importance even after they occupied Kanauj (Choudhary, *Political History*, p. 51).
108. Tripathi, *History of Kanauj*, pp. 309, 311–12.
109. Govindacandra was succeeded by his youngest son, Vijayacandra, to whom the bardic text, the *Pṛthvīrāja-rāso*, credits several unauthenticated victories. Jayacandra, his son and successor, was the last great king of Kanauj whose power struck even Muslim historians like Ibn Asir who says in the *Kamil ut-Tawarikh* that he '. . . was the greatest king in India, and possessed the largest territory . . .' (ibid., p. 323). With Jayacandra's death in 1194, the kingdom of Kanauj ceased to exist as an independent Hindu state and soon sank into insignificance (pp. 333, 336).
110. Ibid., p. 312.

CHAPTER VII

Kanauj: A Gendered Perspective

(Harṣavardhana: Aspects of Polity, Religion and Literary Production)

As has been stated in the previous chapter, the epigraphic and literary sources for Harṣa's reign (AD 606–48) can be blended to form a largely composite picture. Thus, the focus of this chapter will be the gendered aspects of Harṣa's sovereignty, his religion, his plays and various other aspects relevant to the analysis. The task is to cull information from a mainstream tradition, looking through several authors' eyes and reading between the lines.

HARṢA'S SOVEREIGNTY

Harṣa's sovereignty is one of the most crucial aspects of the polity of the time, revolving round the question of Rājyaśrī's involvement in his ultimate accession to power and his pragmatic recognition of the same. This issue will be examined over several sections.

Genealogical Background

The inscriptions of Harṣa's reign provide straightforward genealogical details and are traditionally considered more valuable than Bāṇa's *Harṣacarita* in historical reconstruction. However, this section will attempt to show that such an assumption may be too simplistic. By extension, it will also question the usual reliance on inscriptions *vis-à-vis* textual data for reconstructing past histories.

Thus, a glaring lacuna in the inscriptions of Harṣa's reign is their total silence on Rājyaśrī, a crucially important figure at the time. Although information is provided on other women of the dynasty, they were obviously of lesser importance. Thus, for instance, the

Madhuban copper-plate grant of Harṣa dated *saṁvat* 25 (631) contains a detailed genealogy that reveals the names of three of Harṣa's female and male ancestors.[1] The summary of lines 1-4 reads as follows:

There was the illustrious Mahārāja Naravardhana. His son, from Vajriṇīdevī, was Mahārāja Rājyavardhana (I). His son, from Apsarodevī, was Mahārāja Ādityavardhana. His son, from Mahāsenaguptādevī, was Paramabhaṭṭāraka Mahārājādhirāja Prabhākaravardhana (. . . *mahā-rāja-śrī-nara-vardhanastasya putrastatpādānudhyātaha śrī-vajriṇī-devyāt-mutpannaha paramāditya-bhakto mahā-rāja-śrī-rājya-vardhanastasya putrastatpādānudhyātaha śrī-apsaro-devyāmutpanna paramād-itya-bhakto mahā-sena-guptā-devyāmutpannaś-catuha* . . . *parama-bhaṭṭāraka-mahā-rājādhi-rāja-śrī-prabhākara-vardhanastasya* . . .).

The Bānskherā plate of *saṁvat* 22 (628–9), the Nālandā clay seal of Harṣa and the Sonpat copper seal contain practically identical genealogical tables of Harṣa's family.[2]

The genealogical account that Bāṇa provides is at complete variance with the epigraphic information cited above but, in an important sense, it seems more relevant for a gendered re-construction. Bāṇa traces the genesis of the dynasty and Harṣa's birth to the goddess Lakṣmī. He focuses on Puṣpabhūti, the legendary founder of the dynasty, and talks with great conviction of this ambitious king and his unnamed queens. Harṣa's birth is traced to a boon given by Lakṣmī to Puṣpabhūti in the course of a sacrifice, at which the latter was assisting. She addressed him, 'almost overpowering him with an unabashedness at variance with her sex', and stated that he would be the 'founder of a mighty line of kings . . . wherein shall arise an emperor named Harṣa . . whose chowrie this hand, spontaneously abandoning the lotus, shall grasp' (*HC*, III.127).[3]

Rājyaśrī, too, is a definitive feature of Bāṇa's work, thus lending a considerably nuanced element to his account. Admittedly, Rājyaśrī is *not* the focus of the *Harṣacarita* but, apart from stray sentences in some Chinese sources, this is the *only* other source for her historical presence.

Similarly, although Harṣa's mother, Yaśovatī, has a presence in Harṣa's inscriptions, it is Bāṇa's treatment of her that is more palpable, thoughtprovoking and relevant. The Madhuban copper plate exemplifies the inscriptional picture. It states that it is meant for the increase of the merit of fame of Prabhākaravardhana, of 'the supreme deity and great queen, Yaśomatī'[4] and of Rājyavardhana. (Yaśovatī has *devī* prefixed to her name when referred to as Rājya's mother, but *paramabhaṭṭārikā mahādevī* when referred to as Harṣa's mother.[5] Thus, the Bānskherā plate calls her the *paramabhaṭṭārikā mahādevī rājñī yaśomatī*. The queens of Harṣa's predecessors, however, had only *śrī* prefixed to their names.)

On the other hand, there is Bāṇa's depiction of Yaśovatī which varies between a bold delineation and a stereotypical one. Thus, while she is 'intelligence's cloudless rain', she is also 'the penance purity of womanhood' (*HC*, IV.134).[6] In addition, Bāṇa gives us glimpses of a proud, determined, and somewhat aggressive nature in Prabhākaravardhana's chief queen.[7]

Yaśovatī's steely determination and obstinacy are revealed in the speech she makes to Harṣa in answer to his remonstrations, announcing her decision to burn herself before her husband dies of his illness. This provides a contrast to the narrative wherein she largely appears as a dutiful wife, obedient to her husband's commands and with not much sign of presumption. Her instant acquiescence in Prabhākaravardhana's choice of a husband for Rājyaśrī is a case in point.

Bāṇa's vagueness on Yaśovatī's maternal family has given rise to much speculation on her ancestry. Contemporary inscriptions, too, do not mention her family. In her farewell speech to Harṣa, she says—'I am the lady of a great house, born of a stainless ancestry . . . one bought with the price of valour . . .' (*HC*, V.186). Based on this claim, S.R. Goyal opines that Yaśovatī's family must have been a significant one.[8] R.K. Mookerji and Hoernle believe her to be the daughter of Yaśodharman of Mālwā, due to the similarity of names.[9] However, Yaśovatī's salutations to her living parents, in the same speech, belie this theory—Yaśodharman disappeared from the political scene soon after 533. One cannot rule out the possibility of Yaśovatī's maternal home being a humble one. As Devahuti remarks, had she belonged to an important family, Bāṇa would have noted the fact.[10] Thus, the ambiguity in the text could be deliberate.

Yaśovatī's pride in her position as Prabhākaravardhana's chief queen and of having borne the heirs to the throne is palpably evident. She calls herself the 'lioness mate of a great spirit . . . daughter, spouse, mother of heroes . . .' She further refers to having won 'the honourable fillet of chief-queen . . .', upon whose head 'have the subservient wives of countless feudatories poured coronation water,' who 'has been fanned by chowries waved by captive wives of foes' (*HC*, V.186).

One can posit a link between the indications of harem jealousies in the text and Yaśovatī's seemingly aggressive nature. For instance, she says 'upon the heads of rival wives have these feet been set.' Likewise, she apparently set her feet 'on the laps of her handmaids, on the heads of her co-wives' during her second pregnancy and 'would suffer no violation of her will' (*HC*, IV.139–40). Bāṇa justifies Yaśovatī's arrogance on the grounds that her mind reflected the thoughts of the unborn Harṣa, the future sovereign.

Much of this may be poetic license on Bāṇa's part, but the core idea of arrogance and wilfulness exists. Interestingly, these jealousies seemed to have been sunk at the time of her death for she bade a tearful farewell to four of her twenty co-wives, asking pardon for 'our love's quarrels' and even falling at their feet (*HC*, V.183–4).[11] Perhaps the most significant indication of Yaśovatī's position at court is provided in the midst of her farewells. Amid her largely directionless grief focused on her plants and animals, 'she was giving instructions to her husband's ministers' (*HC*, V.183). This underlines her power in court, the respect accorded her and the 'extraordinarily high status'[12] she seems to have enjoyed. In fact, the ministers seemed more bewildered and overwhelmed by grief about her 'certain resolution' than Yaśovatī herself. Much of their grief (and Harṣa's) could have been derived, therefore, from the prospect of losing a strong anchor at court.

Rājyaśrī and Harṣa's Sovereignty

The figure of Rājyaśrī, Harṣa's younger sister, is a pivotal one in the history of Kanauj. It is through her that Harṣa acquired sovereignty over the kingdom of Kanauj, which formed the basis for his power and glory. This fact needs highlighting, yet it is usually discussed in terms of great ambiguity and speculation. Moreover, except for V.S. Pathak, who talks of the historical 'diminution' of Rājyaśrī's personality,[13] the question of her near-invisibility in contemporary sources has hardly ever been raised. As has been noted, there is no mention of her in Harṣa's inscriptions. Then again, although she features in the *Harṣacarita*, it is as a dutiful, diffident, and bashful person who is largely inarticulate and wholly obedient. It is in the Chinese sources that we find important insights into her role and participation in power politics.

Rājyaśrī's importance in Bāṇa's scheme of things is evident, at the outset, when her birth (592) is dismissed in a few verses alone. This is in glaring contrast to the manifold verses devoted to the birth of Rājya and of Harṣa, in particular. Thus, Rājyaśrī 'added to the two sons formed a further ornament on Yaśovatī's necklace' (*HC*, IV.149). These cursory mentions continue through the text whereby she subsequently became an 'expert in song, dance and with all accomplishments' (*HC*, IV.155). Even Bhaṇḍi, Yaśovatī's brother's son, who is presented at the court as the princes' companion, is described in greater detail.

It is only during the description of Rājyaśrī's crucially important marriage to Grahavarman of Kanauj (603/4), that several verses are devoted to her and the preparations for the wedding. Her age, at this juncture, has given rise to much speculation on the status of the Puṣpabhūtis *vis-à-vis* the Maukharis of Kanauj. Shankar Goyal, for instance, opines that Thānesar was under the overlordship of the Maukharis when the marriage took place because of the great difference in the ages of the couple.[14] Rājyaśrī was twelve while Grahavarman must have been about thirty-five, since his middle-aged boyhood friend, Divākaramitra, was of this age. Goyal feels that Prabhākaravardhana's acquiescence in this alliance is 'eloquent proof' of his subordination to the Maukharis.

This assumption, however, is open to contention. Early Indian prescriptive texts recommended a sizeable age gap between the bride and groom. Besides, there was no trace of such a relation of subordination between the two families. Grahavarman apparently arranged the alliance himself, and Prabhākaravardhana revealed his eagerness to cement it and detailed the former's virtues to his wife. That such an alliance would be a politically crucial one to offset the Guptas' rising power is unstated but, nevertheless, obvious.

Rājyaśrī appears to have been used as a pawn to cement a political alliance and secure her family's fortunes. Thereafter, she became the silent mover of their destinies. Yet this fact remains largely unnoticed in Prabhākaravardhana's lengthy diatribe on the harsh necessity for marrying off one's daughters and Bāṇa's detailed description of the transformation of the court in view of the approaching nuptials.[15] Amid all this confusion, Rājyaśrī remains coy, fearful of the prospective event, and very much in the background. After marriage she does not make an appearance in the text until the very end, when Harṣa rescues her from a forest in the Vindhyas.

Before embarking on a study of Rājyaśrī, it is necessary to examine Harṣa's rise to prominence in his own kingdom of Thānesar. Not only does this provide a basis for his takeover of Kanauj, it is also used by scholars like D. Devahuti to examine his personality, his ambitions, and, by extension, his attitude to Rājyaśrī. Devahuti views Harṣa as an essentially calculating individual who might have had a hand in the murder of his elder brother, Rājya, and who, with a view to ruling Kanauj, desired the presence of Rājyaśrī by his side.[16] R.S. Tripathi, on the other hand, presents the conventional view of Harṣa's accession, based on the unaccountable tragedies in his family that forced him to take charge of Thānesar and Kanauj.[17] Thus, apparently, compassion for his sister made him rescue her and keep her by his side.

At the outset, the discrepancy between the epigraphic and literary evidence should be noted. Harṣa's inscriptions mention Rājya as his predecessor in rule, and this is seconded by Yuan Chwang's account.[18] Yet the *Harṣacarita* talks of Rājya's voluntary abdication of his rights to Harṣa and his eventual murder, thereby making Harṣa Prabhākaravardhana's immediate heir. Devahuti feels that from Prabhākaravardhana's illness, Bāṇa began to prepare the ground, in the text, for Harṣa's succession in preference to Rājya.[19] She says that the theme was pursued subtly but with great tenacity. Thus the dying Prabhākaravardhana was apparently not regretful at Rājya's absence but verbally proffered the sovereignty on Harṣa. He says—'Upon you my happiness, my sovereignty, my succession, and my life are set, and as mine, so those of all my people' (*HC*, V.175). Devahuti wonders at Prabhākaravardhana's motives in trusting Rājya with a Hūṇa campaign, but not trusting him to succeed to the throne.[20]

Subsequently, Rājya, grieved at his father's death, resolved to abdicate worldly concerns and leave the throne to Harṣa. 'Strange feelings of renunciation and aversion from worldly power' were apparently influencing both brothers at the time.[21] At this juncture, they were informed of their brother-in-law, Grahavarman's murder and Rājyaśrī's imprisonment.[22] Rājya set out to avenge the murder and succeeded in his aim but was killed, leaving Harṣa with no alternative but to mount the throne of Thānesar. Thus—

> He was embraced by the goddess of the royal prosperity, who took him in her arms and, seizing him by all the royal marks on all his limbs, forced him, however reluctant, to mount the throne,—and this though he had taken a vow of austerity and did not swerve from his vow, hard like grasping the edge of a sword (*anicchantaṁ balāt āropayitumiva siṁhāsanaṁ sarvāvayavesu sarvalakṣaṇaiha gṛhītaṁ gṛhīta brahmacaryaṁ āliṅgitaṁ rājyalakṣmya pratipannāsidhārā dhāraṇavrataṁ*).[23]

Harṣa, feels Tripathi, was, therefore, a victim of circumstance and his 'noble-minded' reluctance to supersede his brother's claims was genuine. Yet the text wavers between a show of reluctance and enthusiasm on Harṣa's part. When the general, Siṁhanāda, exhorts him to assume the reins of rule and punish the offender, calling him 'the only *śeṣa* left to protect the earth', Harṣa agrees and swears to take revenge or 'hurl my sinful self, like a moth, into an oil-fed flame.'[24]

Devahuti, on the other hand, raises several questions at this decision.[25] Why did Harṣa not make his anguish at being given the throne ever known? Why did he not reject the proposal? Did Rājya decide to punish Śaśāṅka, the Gauḍa king, only to increase his power and improve his inferior position *vis-à-vis* Harṣa? She concludes that the unusual twists in the story were inevitable owing to some episode uncomplimentary to Bāṇa's hero. This 'complex situation' seems to have been solved by Rājya's death. The idea that Harṣa could have been implicated in this murder is not ruled out. Bāṇa, too, refers to allegations of this nature that would soil his tongue to reveal.[26]

It is at this juncture that Rājyaśrī's role appears to develop. It is interesting that neither brother made any immediate attempt to rescue her or speculate excessively on her misfortune, though she was now an 'object of compassion' for them (*HC*, VI.204). Rājya, mainly enraged at Devagupta's temerity, came to Kanauj and defeated him, yet did not release Rājyaśrī immediately. Harṣa, too, spent time settling matters in his kingdom and waited for an auspicious day before setting out. Even then, his principal desire was to punish Śaśāṅka and not to release Rājyaśrī.

Shankar Goyal believes that since Rājyaśrī's imprisonment was in conformity with the 'war laws of the age', the brothers did not take it seriously.[27] Yet he speculates on Rājyaśrī's action, fleeing to the Vindhya forest with her train rather than going towards Thānesar, or making any attempt to find Bhaṇḍi who was nearby with Harṣa's army. He wonders whether she was displeased with her brothers' conduct and, furthermore, whether rumours of Harṣa's involvement in Rājya's murder had reached her, making her want to avoid him.[28]

Devahuti believes that Harṣa was also activated by political considerations in deciding to rescue Rājyaśrī and bring her back to Kanauj.[29] This became his principal aim once he learnt of her escape and the possibilities of her presence occurred to him. Although Shankar Goyal opines that Rājyaśrī had no claims on Kanauj due to her sex and the lack of an heir, it is obvious that her presence and the very act of rescuing her would strengthen Harṣa's claims against any of Grahavarman's kinsmen and win over the Maukhari nobles. It would give him the right to protect her and her husband's kingdom. Pathak, too, while acknowledging Harṣa's search for Rājyaśrī as that of 'an affectionate brother', says it was one of an 'astute politician' as well.[30]

Yet Tripathi prefers to focus on the humane considerations behind Harṣa's action. In 'fondness for his distressed sister', he postponed his march against Śaśāṅka and hastened to find her.[31] He tells Bhaṇḍi—'What care I for other seekers? Where she has gone, I myself, abandoning all other calls, will go' (*HC*, VII.254).

He eventually rescues Rājyaśrī just as she is preparing to burn herself, and enlists the aid of Divākaramitra, a Buddhist mendicant and Grahavarman's childhood friend, to persuade her to return to Kanauj, citing his desire to cherish her 'for a while' to compensate for her traumatic ordeals. He describes her as 'the sole link that keeps up my life, now that I have lost all my loved kindred' (*HC*, VIII.269). At this stage, he was 'melting with grief,' and 'greatly agitated'.

The actual mechanics of the takeover of Kanauj by Harṣa bore implications for Rājyaśrī's future as well. Initially, he indicated to Divākaramitra his desire to disregard royal duties to cherish her, probably indicating his preparedness to stay in Kanauj to settle its affairs.[32] Bhaṇḍi seemed to have prepared the ground for Harṣa's takeover of Kanauj by stressing his devotion and affection for his family, evident in his rescue of Rājyaśrī.[33] This fact—as also the intercession of Divākaramitra—could not have been overlooked by the grateful Kanauj populace.[34]

In addition, there was no serious claimant to the throne of Kanauj at the time except for Pūrṇavarman, a minor scion of the Maukhari line, whose claims were obviously inferior to Harṣa's. Speculation also centres round the Nālandā seal of a king whose name begins with the letter *su* and who was the son of Avantivarman, Grahavarman's father. This individual could have ruled briefly after Grahavarman's death, after which the throne went to Harṣa or, who a child at Grahavarman's death, could have got the throne after Harṣa.[35] Alternatively, it has been suggested that Grahavarman took Ṣuvratavarman as his second name to indicate his Buddhist leanings, Bāṇa calling him by his original name while the seal bore his chosen name.[36]

That Harṣa displayed some hesitation before ascending the throne is known.[37] Interestingly, Edward Pires feels that Harṣa was uncertain whether to ascend the throne or proclaim Rājyaśrī the queen dowager/sovereign of the Maukhari kingdom.[38] Tripathi speculates in similar fashion—'Should the crown therefore devolve upon the widowed queen Rājyaśrī, or was she to be doomed to obscurity, and her claims altogether ignored?' . . .[39] 'Should Harṣa then be asked to assume the burden of the state on Rājyaśrī's behalf?' He then cites several supporting reasons—that he had rendered signal service to Kanauj at a time of crisis, and that he had rescued Rājyaśrī and that 'the greatest fondness and attachment' existed between them.

Yet Tripathi, too, points to Harṣa's reluctance as stemming from the prospect of an 'additional burden and responsibility' involving permanent residence in Kanauj and the neglect of Thānesar, and the uncertainty of support of the Kanauj populace. Devahuti, however, traces it to Harṣa's deference to the custom of succession within a family and the Maukhari scion, Pūrṇavarman's presence.[40] Though he was offered the throne, he stressed his inadequacies and apparently referred the matter to the *bodhisattva* Avalokiteśvara who advised him to rule but not to use royal insignia like the lion throne or an imperial title.[41] Hence Harṣa assumed royal power under the name *kumāra* (prince) Śīlāditya.

So it was through Rājyaśrī that Harṣa acquired the prestigious throne of Kanauj. What should be noted here is the unusual circumstance of the throne passing to a queen's brother. This is not normally noted in discussions on Kanauj or Harṣa's takeover and needs to be given its due recognition as exemplifying female agency.[42] In early India wives did not usually succeed their husbands on the throne. The chief queen either adopted a boy whom she raised to the throne if she had no son, or the throne passed to the king's brother's son or a distant relation.[43] Hence, Harṣa's case was an unusual one.

Pathak, the only one to discuss Rājyaśrī's character in an analytical manner, says that her symbolic significance overshadows her historical personality. She is described as the fortune inherent in a monarch and her name is also used suggestively to indicate her symbolic significance.[44] The noteworthy reference, at the end of the *Harṣacarita*, to the bringing 'of a silvery seal of sovereignty by Rājyaśrī to Harṣa' seems to encapsulate her role as the one to confer glory and sovereignty on Harṣa by her association with him. The sunset is described in terms suggesting bloody wars and the fall of Harṣa's enemy, followed by the rising of the moon of Harṣa's glory (*HC*, VIII.290). Thus, Pathak argues against viewing the end of the *Harṣacarita* as an abrupt one, since Bāṇa intended to conclude his narrative by indicating Harṣa's acquisition of sovereign glory through his association with Rājyaśrī.[45]

Rājyaśrī—A Power Behind The Throne?

The key to Rājyaśrī's role in Kanauj seems to lie in the highly significant observation of the Chinese work, *Fang-chih*, that Harṣa 'administered the kingdom in conjunction with his widowed sister'.[46] This form of joint government, Devahuti notes, finds no reference in any Indian source.[47] Yet, instead of examining the possibilities of Rājyaśrī's exercise of power, she and other scholars concentrate on Harṣa's 'quiet usurpation' of control thereafter.[48]

The pertinent question at this juncture is whether Rājyaśrī could have assumed power at all. Most historians assume that her presence was important for Harṣa's takeover but say that she had no claim to the throne whatever, without seeing the contradiction in terms.[49] S.R. Goyal, for instance, dismisses any idea of her claims, believing Harṣa to have taken over Kanauj through 'diplomatic manoeuvres', when he might have exploited the people's sympathies for the widowed queen.[50] Tripathi, in turn, offers excuses for Harṣa's takeover of Kanauj instead of Rājyaśrī.[51] He says she was 'young and inexperienced', and 'under the shadow of a great bereavement and affliction'. Hence, she was perhaps 'unwilling to undertake the responsibilities and onerous duties of rulership'. Since she was also 'inclined' to the 'quietist' teachings of Buddhism, there was apparently 'little chance of her governing with vigour and success at this crisis'.

However, one needs to re-examine the problem. Admittedly, Rājyaśrī was at the tender age of fourteen years with no heir of her own. These two factors would definitely have limited her claims. Yet there was the precedent of Prabhāvatīguptā of the Vākāṭaka dynasty (third century AD), who took over the Vākāṭaka throne after the death of her husband, Rudrasena, despite having three sons.[52] Besides, Harṣa was only two years older than Rājyaśrī and could not have been vastly superior in terms of maturity and experience.

Furthermore, why did Rājyaśrī's presence become so crucial to Harṣa's calculations if she had no real claims? Why was her acquiescence in Harṣa's scheme so vital? Why was Divākaramitra's help enlisted to persuade her to accompany Harṣa to Kanauj? Despite the contentions of prescriptive texts and the time-honoured laws of succession, then, the absence of Rājyaśrī could have overturned Harṣa's claims altogether. This is a fact that needs to be acknowledged.

Rājyaśrī's feelings, at this point, would bear analysis. Her initial reluctance to accompany Harṣa back to Kanauj is intriguing. Though this is usually attributed to distress and a desire to embrace Buddhism, it could be that she envisaged future problems with Harṣa, revolving round the question of Kanauj and its rule. She could have yielded, subsequently, knowing that she had no other option and trusting Harṣa to deal with the situation diplomatically.[53] It is interesting that her decision to burn herself and her reluctance to accompany Harṣa show overtones of the determination and wilfulness of her mother, Yaśovatī.

At this juncture, Meenakshi Mukherjee's speculation that the projection of male valour could necessitate the depiction of female passivity in a text becomes relevant.[54] Harṣa's bravery and compassion is counterpoised by Rājyaśrī's coyness and subservience. She apparently receded into the background while Harṣa rose to greater heights of power and glory as the sole sovereign of Kanauj. This interpretation is a popular one, focusing on Harṣa's gradual change in status from a mere regent or guardian to joint ruler and thereon to sole ruler. He formally transferred his capital from Thānesar to Kanauj and exemplified his new sovereign status by assuming imperial titles in his inscriptions.[55] It is accepted that Rājyaśrī remained subservient in the background.[56]

Yet one wonders why the exercise of power should have been an either/or situation. Was it not possible for Rājyaśrī to have continued to collaborate with Harṣa on state matters? She may have preferred to maintain a low profile but need not have given up her initial status in Kanauj as Harṣa's advisor. She could even have been a member of his advisory council. After all, as Devahuti notes, they seemed to have made a practice of joint appearances, thereby showing 'extraordinary political foresight',[57] not only in court but also in periodic assemblies of various kinds attended by subordinate kings, courtiers and common people. Why should this have been so? Were they trying to make an important statement to the people? Was the intention to convey Rājyaśrī's importance in Harṣa's scheme of things?

Furthermore, what does the people's evident acceptance of their joint government imply for the polity of the age? Was a woman's participation in political affairs condoned/welcomed in contrast to the picture revealed by prescriptive texts that forbid/ condemn it? More importantly, why is this unusual aspect of joint government glossed over by most historians in their accounts of Kanauj's history?[58]

It is often assumed that women lack direct access to the public sphere and this circumscribes their power.[59] However, in Rājyaśrī's case, there seemed to have been a tacit understanding between her and Harṣa of her continued (but never overweening) presence in the court. She may not have exercised formal authority, but she could very well have exercised some amount of power.[60]

Rājyaśrī was, thus, an important person at Harṣa's court. The *Life* describes a scene thirty years later in Harṣa's court where his 'sister of great intelligence' was 'sitting behind the king' and reacting with enthusiasm to Yuan Chwang's discourse.[61] Since this event took place at Kajangala where Harṣa was temporarily encamped while on his way back from an Orissa campaign, it is obvious that Rājyaśrī had accompanied him there. Her appearance in the *mahāmokṣa pariṣad* or the sixth great quinquennial charity distribution at Prayāga is also documented—there she lent Harṣa a second-hand garment after he gave away all his possessions.[62]

All this heightens the contrast between the Rājyaśrī of the *Harṣacarita* and her actual personality and role. If she had faded into the background, as is usually presumed, why would she have participated so eagerly in court events or made her opinions known so volubly? Why would she have accompanied her brother on important military campaigns if she had relinquished her interests in state matters? Was there much more to her role than the paltry references in texts would imply?

This aspect of the polity in Kanauj has not received due recognition. So also, the fact that Rājyaśrī does not adhere to the model of the pious, ascetic widow provided by prescriptive texts.[63] Admittedly, the evidence is thin. Yet it is sufficient for a tentative picture of the role of Rājyaśrī. Devahuti does speculate that Rājyaśrī's ability, her connection with Kanauj, her unfortunate circumstances and her support for Harṣa may all have combined to secure for her 'a position uncommon for the female members of royalty', but declines to investigate this further.[64] Yet the assumption that Rājyaśrī could have been a power behind the throne cannot be lightly dismissed.

The Lack of Female Presence in Harṣa's Family

The other intriguing feature of Harṣa's history is that no source mentions his wife/wives. One would assume that such an important aspect of his life would feature at least in the *Harṣacarita*, but while Bāṇa waxes eloquent on elephants, horses, and minor court officials, for instance, he never specifically mentions Harṣa's spouses.[65] Though Harṣa indicates that he is married to more than one woman in his distressed speech after Rājya's death (*HC*, VI.206), they seem to have had no role in sharing his grief or in his future plans. They do not have a presence even in his inscriptions. Yet Harṣa's intimate knowledge of women and their behaviour, displayed in his plays, cannot have been that of a celibate.

Controversy surrounds Bāṇa's remark on Harṣa's reluctance to ascend the throne of Thānesar. He says that Harṣa was forced to mount the throne by the goddess of royal prosperity '. . . and this though he had taken a vow of austerity and did not swerve from his vow, hard like grasping the edge of a sword' (*HC*, II.78). The word 'austerity' is the wrong translation, for Bāṇa actually means celibacy here.[66] Thus, Shankar Goyal quotes Bāṇa's commentator, Śaṅkara, as saying that Harṣa vowed to remain celibate till he had conquered the world.[67] After twelve years, when he had accomplished his aim, he apparently told his queen, 'My vow is fulfilled.' Her angry retort was, 'Now I shall observe celibacy for twelve years.' This interesting and obviously popular account may, however, not be a factual one.

Likewise, there is no information on the identity of Harṣa's child/children. The presence of his daughter is indirectly documented by Yuan Chwang who refers to the reigning king of Valabhī as 'a son-in-law of the Śīlāditya reigning at Kānyakubja. His name was Tu-lo-po-po-ta (Dhruvabhaṭa) . . . of hasty temper, shallow views. . . .'[68] Thus, it is clear that Harṣa's daughter married Dhruvasena II Bālāditya (Dhruvabhaṭṭa) of Valabhī. Harṣa's child must have been born around 625 as Yuan Chwang visited Valabhī in 640. Thus, by extension, Harṣa would have married around this date.[69]

Yuan Chwang further says that this marriage was an act of 'great political astuteness' on Harṣa's part.[70] The security resulting from this connection disengaged Dhruvasena from the sphere of influence of the Cālukyan king, Pulakeśin II, secured the western extremity of Harṣa's empire and acquired the loyalty of the Maitrakas of Valabhī.[71] However, this is a classic case of female invisibility wherein the identity of the woman who achieved all this for her father remains unknown. It is tempting to speculate that Rājyaśrī could have had a hand in arranging this marriage but, in the absence of evidence, this would remain a mere supposition.

It is obvious, therefore, that the most important feature of the polity of Kanauj—Harṣa's ascendancy and eventual paramountcy—cannot be conceived apart from the role of his sister, Rājyaśrī. Thus, it is possible to cobble together information with the potential of altering the traditional view of the history of Harṣa's rule.

HARṢA'S RELIGION

The first issue revolves around the probable influence of Rājyaśrī on Harṣa's religious proclivities. On the one hand, it is believed that Harṣa, a Śaivite by faith, experienced a 'mighty religious transformation' and adopted Buddhism.[72] On the other hand, others insist that he remained a Śaivite, merely paying lip service to Buddhism.

Rājyaśrī's role in this seems to have suffered a historical 'diminution.' The point of relevance is not whether Harṣa formally adopted Buddhism but whether his obvious interest in it, and its propagation, could have been spurred by Rājyaśrī. So let us first examine her religious inclinations.

Rājyaśrī's Religion

While most historians are at pains to prove Harṣa's faith in Śaivism, the same rigorous analysis is not applied to Rājyaśrī. It is merely assumed that she was an ardent Buddhist. Rājyaśrī's interest in

Buddhism seems to have been triggered by her meeting with Divākaramitra in the Vindhya forest.[73] Prevented from burning herself by Harṣa's timely intervention, Tripathi says she was so impressed by the 'tranquil atmosphere' of the hermitage that she desired to assume the 'red garments' immediately.[74] The fact of her being 'so overwhelmed' by 'successive misfortunes' acted as a spur. Not that she was a stranger to Buddhism: her brother, Rājya, was a Buddhist and so was her husband, Grahavarman. The people of Kanauj, too, were partial to it.

Rājyaśrī was, however, frustrated in her aim since Harṣa prevailed upon Divākaramitra to turn down her request.[75] Harṣa promised to adopt the faith with her at a later stage and she was persuaded to return to Kanauj. Thereafter, the testimony of the *Life* reveals that she had kept her interest alive and followed the Hīnayāna school of Buddhism. She was 'distinguished for her knowledge of the Sammatīya school . . . and as she heard the Master of the Law (Yuan Chwang) extolling the doctrine of the Great Vehicle, and exposing the extreme poverty of the Little School of Doctrine, she was filled with joy and could not cease her praises.'[76]

On this basis, Diana Y. Paul concludes that Rājyaśrī was a Buddhist nun of the Sammatīya school.[77] She believes that Rājyaśrī's widowhood was not a time of 'passive retreat into the order of nuns' but for the 'active prosyletizing of her brother's interest'. She was the example of a nun who was a very strong member of her family, performing her role as a nun. This supposition is echoed by R.C. Majumdar—he also assumes that she was an actual nun.[78] These views indicate that a widow turning to religion and, furthermore, becoming a nun is more acceptable than to break with convention and portray Rājyaśrī as a widow active in state affairs with a deep interest in Buddhism.

However, the more important question is to consider if there is any evidence that indicates that Rājyaśrī wholly adopted the religion to the extent of becoming a nun. If it can be presumed that Harṣa was merely displaying interest in Buddhism without adopting it, why can the same reasoning not apply to her? Mere knowledge of a school of faith and enthusiastic response does not indicate a total conversion. The fact of Rājyaśrī's interest in Buddhism is undeniable, but the evidence would not warrant the assumptions of Paul and Majumdar. She could very well have been a strong member of the family but being a nun need not have been a precondition for it.

In a rare attempt to analyse Rājyaśrī's ideas, S.R. Goyal questions the notion that she who believed in the Hīnayāna school for thirty-five odd years could suddenly be filled with joy on hearing the poverty of her own doctrine exposed by Yuan Chwang, who extolled the Mahāyāna school! He calls the entire account of this incident 'fantastic' and avers that 'such miraculous conversions do not take place in real life'.[79] However, the question is not one of Rājyaśrī's conversion or otherwise, but rather of her interest in the faith. The speculation that she remained a Hindu with an abiding interest in Buddhism cannot be entirely discounted.

Rājyaśrī and Harṣa's Religion

Given Harṣa's involvement in Buddhism, it is tacitly assumed that this was *his* interest that Rājyaśrī chose to propagate. One cannot, however, dismiss the idea that *she* could have stimulated Harṣa's interest in the faith, in the first place. All the measures he adopted to propagate and extol this religion could have been undertaken at her behest. Thus, the question is: did Rājyaśrī fuel and sustain his interest in it? We may examine the evidence for and against this.

One should note, at the outset, the somewhat contradictory picture presented by both the epigraphic and literary evidence. The Bānskherā and Madhuban plates refer to Harṣa as *parama-māheśvara* (devout worshipper of the god Maheśvara/Śiva).[80] His Sonpat seal bears a reclining Nandi symbol and his coins bear Śaiva devices. In addition, the *Harṣacarita* refers to his worship of the 'adorable Nīlalohita' (Śiva) before embarking on his campaign, and cites his statement to Bhāskaravarman, his ally, that he would bow only before Śiva, if at all. All this can be adduced to prove Harṣa's faith in Śaivism.

But Harṣa's adoption of Śaivism did not follow a family precedent. Although the mythical Puṣpabhūti is said to have been an ardent Śaivite, all his other ancestors, principally Harṣa's father, Prabhākaravardhana, the *ādityabhakta*, were apparently sun worshippers.[81] The only exception is the *paramasaugata*,

Rājya, apparently a Buddhist. (The religions of the women are not mentioned.)

On the other hand, the *Harṣacarita* finds Harṣa making a somewhat ambiguous vow to adopt Buddhism in the unspecified future. He tells Divākaramitra of his desire to cherish Rājyaśrī for a while and 'at the end when I have accomplished my design, she and I will assume the red garments together'.[82] More importantly, he invited Yuan Chwang, the Chinese pilgrim, to Kanauj and convoked a grand assembly to publicize and refine the doctrines of the Mahāyāna school.[83] This is taken as irrefutable proof of his interest in Buddhism.

Furthermore, Harṣa built several monasteries, forbade the killing of creatures, considered sending emissaries to Orissa to establish the Mahāyāna doctrine, wrested the Buddha's tooth relic from Kashmir, patronized the Nālandā monastery, and provided for Buddhist monks at annual gatherings.[84] Besides, he apparently wrote the *Nāgānandam* to extol the glory of purposeful self-negation, forbearance and tolerance—the 'specific features of the Buddhist dogma'. Finally, he even seems to have deferred to the *bodhisattva* Avalokiteśvara in his decision to rule Kanauj.

However, one should note that most of the evidence cited above is provided by Yuan Chwang for obvious reasons. The Buddhist assembly at Kanauj undoubtedly exalted the Buddha and Yuan Chwang, whose superiority as the 'Master of the Law' was established. However, it seemed to have been convoked more to impress the gathering with Harṣa's power than from an avowedly religious purpose. In addition, Brahmanical gods were equally honoured during the proceedings, and not, as Tripathi believes, made to look inferior to the Buddha. The *Life* confirms that the assassination bid on Harṣa at the assembly was not made by 'disgruntled' Hindu heretics, as Yuan Chwang insists, but by adherents of the Hīnayāna, who had been worsted in debate.[85] Moreover, as Shankar Goyal argues, mere worship of a Buddha image by Harṣa does not prove his personal faith in the religion.[86]

The same holds true for Harṣa's quinquennial distribution of alms at Prayāga. Though Yuan Chwang once again stresses Harṣa's partiality to Buddhists, he seemed to have distributed his riches even, as Shankar Goyal points out, with a slight bias towards Hindus.[87] However, the proceedings did not seem to have had any particular religious affiliation, being, as Yuan Chwang himself remarked, part of a precedent set by Harṣa's ancestors.

As far as the *Nāgānandam* is concerned, there is nothing specifically Buddhist in its features or in its protagonist.[88] Jīmūtavāhana is an unworldly individual who believes in the greatness of sacrificing oneself for another's interests. These ideas could well belong to both the Hindu and the Buddhist religions. Although the play invokes the Buddha, it is Gaurī (Pārvatī) who eventually resolves the issue by resurrecting the hero and making him the emperor of the Vidyādharas.[89] It is also significant that the play is peppered with references to Hindu gods, the hero talking knowledgeably of Kāma, Sūrya, and so on. Even the central theme of the play—the hostility of Garuḍa towards snakes—is an aspect of Hindu mythology. Devahuti believes that it represents Harṣa's mixed religious beliefs, rather than exemplifying his faith in Buddhism alone.[90]

Pires suggests that the title *śīlāditya* was bestowed on Harṣa by Buddhist monks and was not his official one, as both his epigraphs and Bāṇa would testify.[91] His vow to Rājyaśrī was made, in all probability, on the spur of the moment in order to console her and wean her away from her decision to stay behind in the forest.[92] Divākaramitra's help was enlisted not only to persuade Rājyaśrī but also, probably, with the pragmatic realization that Kanauj was partial to Buddhists, more so one who was the dead king's friend.

S.R. Goyal thus speculates that Yuan Chwang misread Harṣa's respect for another religion as devotion to it.[93] Harṣa did not, as Tripathi believes, adopt both religions with 'a curious sort of eclecticism', but remained a Śaivite with an extremely liberal religious outlook.[94] Goyal points to the interdependence of polity, religion, society and economy and says that Harṣa's 'love' for Buddhism was more a matter of political expediency than faith.

Returning to the question of Rājyaśrī's influence, S.R. Goyal is categorical that she was too young to make any impact on the faith of Harṣa.[95] This is a questionable assumption. There was a difference of barely two years in their ages. If Harṣa could be decisive, calculating, and discerning at sixteen, why should Rājyaśrī be any less so? What was to prevent them from influencing each other? If Rājyaśrī had the determination and will to make decisions to burn herself and, further, to join Divākaramitra, and if Harṣa took these decisions seriously, why should her choice of religion not have had an effect on him? Conversely, if, at the age of fourteen, her mind could be developed enough to be 'inclined' to the 'quietist teachings of Buddhism', then could it not make an informed religious choice?

Admittedly, Harṣa may not have been sincere in his promise to Divākaramitra at the time. Nevertheless, to assume that Rājyaśrī's decision did not influence him at all would be to vastly minimize her role. After all, even Tripathi cursorily mentions that Harṣa's interest in Buddhism could have been stimulated by his fondness for his sister.[96] Yet, that Harṣa was merely indulging her interest in Buddhism without any corresponding fervour on his part cannot be ruled out. Perhaps he viewed it as a politically strategic manner of advancing his interests and impressing his people. Did Rājyaśrī acquiesce in this idea? Could they have used these mammoth, ostensibly religious, gatherings to enhance their power and popularity, and to demonstrate their riches and courtly splendour?[97] Alternatively, Rājyaśrī could alone have been behind the invitation to Yuan Chwang and the convocation of the grand assembly. Harṣa may have included Buddhists in his schemes of patronage at her insistence.

It is difficult to reach any terms of certainty due to the paucity of evidence on Rājyaśrī. Her presence is documented in the *mahāmokṣa pariṣad*—where Harṣa begs an ordinary, second-hand garment from her to cover himself—but not in the Kanauj assembly. However, she obviously participated in it in view of her eager responses to Yuan Chwang's discourse and obvious interest in Buddhism.

In conclusion, it is apparent that the attitude towards Rājyaśrī's religious choice exemplifies the tendency to define the religious needs of women more in terms of their 'emotional' nature and their dependence on others.[98] Rājyaśrī's choice is viewed as motivated solely by her sufferings and her natural inclinations, but Harṣa's choice is not as 'impulsive', being based on thought and calculation. However, as has been the purpose of this argument, it is important to view Harṣa's religion from a gendered angle and examine the light thrown by such a perspective.

HARṢA'S PLAYS

The gendered potential of Harṣa's plays is an aspect that has not been clearly appreciated or understood. This assumes importance because Harṣa's versions of the original stories could function as a form of validation for changing historical situations.[99] Thus, on the one hand, this section aims to redress such a lacuna in analysis. On the other hand, it will also highlight the attempt by certain secondary works to eclipse this aspect by an uncritical, stereotypical analysis and a refusal to consider women in unconventional moulds.

Harem Intrigue and Polygamy

The issue of harem intrigue, more specifically the competition among women for a man's sexual attentions, forms the focus of the 'sister plays', *Priyadarśikā* and *Ratnāvalī*.[100] As mentioned in the previous chapter, both deal with the loves of King Udayana of Kauśāmbī and the conflicts that ensue from his infatuations. The action centers around the chief queen, Vāsavadattā, who attempts to withstand the machinations of her maids, the jester, and the king.

The *Priyadarśikā* deals with Udayana's love for Āraṇyikā, a captive and an inmate of the harem, despite Vāsavadattā's displeasure. The various plots devised by the maids and the jester finally center round a mimic play that enables a clandestine meeting between the pair under the guise of acting.[101] Vāsavadattā discerns the plot, imprisons Āraṇyikā and finally releases her when she consumes poison. She consents to their union once she learns that Āraṇyikā is actually her cousin, Priyadarśikā, who was already betrothed to Udayana by her father.

The *Ratnāvalī* deals with Udayana's love for Sāgarikā who enters the harem after surviving a shipwreck. Braving Vāsavadattā's displeasure, once again, several maids and the jester contrive to arrange clandestine meetings, even disguising Sāgarikā as Vāsavadattā. The queen disrupts the plot, imprisons Sāgarikā and releases her only when her chambers seem to be on fire. It is revealed that Sāgarikā is actually Ratnāvalī, Vāsavadattā's cousin, whose hand was sought by the minister Yaugandharāyaṇa for Udayana, as she was destined to confer universal sovereignty on her spouse. Vāsavadattā consents to this union too.

The entire issue of harem intrigue could be better understood with a focus on Vāsavadattā, as envisioned by Harṣa, and the contrasting picture of her rivals in love—Priyadarśikā (Āraṇyikā) and Ratnāvalī (Sāgarikā). It is also important to examine the implications of how Vāsavadattā is portrayed in the plays. The question of the fluctuating loyalties of the maids who are vital actors in the harem intrigues will be dealt with in a separate section, since their visibility and presence has parallels in other texts as well.

THE PORTRAYAL OF VĀSAVADATTĀ

Harṣa's portrayal of Vāsavadattā forms a sharp contrast to the original in the *Bṛhatkathā*, and to any other version of her—as, for instance, in the *Pratijñāyaugandharāyaṇa* and Bhāsa's *Svapnavāsavadattā*.[102] In these texts, she is meek, submissive, and overawed by her husband. In Harṣa's plays, she overshadows every other personality and elaborate schemes are designed to circumvent her wrath. The resolution of both plays depends on her acquiescence, and even the king is shown awaiting her pleasure and decision. This is especially evident in the *Ratnāvalī*, the more dramatic of the two in terms of plot, dialogue, and characters.

What is immediately apparent about Vāsavadattā is not just her pride in her status and position, but also her determination to safeguard it. This is accompanied by a keenness of perception that enables her to discern the flaws in her husband's character, more particularly his philandering nature. This is seen most clearly in the *Ratnāvalī* where she recognizes the ability of her maids to attract Udayana; she laments with reference to Ratnāvalī,

> Oh the carelessness of my servants. She will fall within the view of him from whose range of sight she has been assiduously kept away

(*RV*, I.18—*aho pramādaha pari-janasya, yasyaiva darśana-pathāt-prayatnena rakṣyate tasyaiva dṛṣṭi-gocare patita bhavet*).

Significantly, she is not afraid to confront Udayana. Finding him in a compromising position in the *Ratnāvalī*, she rebukes him: 'I am truly Sāgarikā. But you with your heart entirely taken up by Sāgarikā, see everything as consisting of Sāgarikā' (*RV*, III.14). Her sarcasm is also evident in her words—'. . . I myself have been guilty towards him (the king), interposing an obstacle in his first meeting' (*RV*, III.14) and sweeping aside Udayana's fumbling lies—

> My husband, this is worthy of you; it befits you. Rise, my lord, rise. Why should you suffer trouble even now owing to the services of one naturally high-born? (*RV*, III.19—*ārya-putra yuktametat sadṛṣmetat, ārya-putra uttiṣṭa uttiṣṭa, kimadyāpi sahajā-bhijātāyāha sevayā dukha-manu-bhūyate*).

Furthermore, suspecting Udayana and the jester Vasantaka of hiding something, she remarks to her maid Kāñcanamālā, 'You simpleton . . . you do not understand his prevarication.' Likewise, in the *Priyadarśikā*, when she suspects the female playwright, Saṁkṛtyāyaṇī, of making unwelcome additions to the mimic play to further Udayana's love, she says—'Lady, this also has been overdone by you . . . *you* see the representation. I, for myself, cannot bear to see what is false' (*PD*, III.13). She also scathingly informs Vasantaka and the king, whom she discovers in a clandestine meeting with Priyadarśikā—'When I see this misbehaviour of you both, I am moved to laughter' (*PD*, III.14).

That Vāsavadattā is capable of fierce, largely unrelenting wrath is a crucial feature of both plays.[103] This has significant bearings on her equation with Udayana. He and the other characters are shown to be in perpetual and visible dread of her anger, which lies like a shadow upon them all. Thus, the jester, Vasantaka, remarks in the *Ratnāvalī*, 'Even now his (the king's) ears are grated with the harsh words of the ever-irate queen Vāsavadattā . . .' (*RV*, III.12). Udayana is well aware of her habit of concealing her anger under a visage of superficial calmness. When, for instance, he detects the first signs of her wrath in the *Priyadarśikā*, he says, 'I see that reconciliation is difficult to be brought about in this case. . . . So this your anger, though restrained with evident effort, is clearly seen' (*PD*, III.13). Similarly, he informs Vasantaka in the *Ratnāvalī* that 'the queen's persistent anger, concealed by her, through high-breeding, was not marked by you' (*RV*, II.21).

It is interesting to note that Vāsavadattā is capable of violence. Vasantaka's remark in the *Ratnāvalī* that 'we stand yet with our persons uninjured' (*RV*, III.15) despite the queen's obvious wrath is a telling one, as also Udayana's remark—'I do not so much think of myself . . . as of that poor Sāgarikā, come within the range of the sight of the queen, whose vehemence of anger was suppressed within' (*RV*, III.4). Vāsavadattā has no qualms in ordering Vasantaka to be tied and arrested, nor in causing Ratnāvalī to be bound in fetters and chained in a dungeon for daring to trifle with the king.[104] Ironically, she confesses to her treatment of Ratnāvalī, 'perishing, restrained with a chain by my cruel self' only when the prospect of her being burnt alive arises (*RV*, IV.16). And it is only when she discovers Ratnāvalī to be her cousin that she says, 'I am ashamed of this my cruelty, so remove her fetters' (*RV*, IV.20).

Likewise, in the other play, Vāsavadattā handles Priyadarśikā roughly and imprisons her, causing Udayana to remark, 'Excepting the queen's favour, there is no other means to procure her release' (*PD*, IV.1). As in the *Ratnāvalī*, she releases Priyadarśikā only when the prospect of her dying arises and then too, more from the fear that the people 'might, perchance, misjudge me' (*PD*, IV.8). In any case, it is the playwright, Saṁkṛtyāyaṇī, rather than the king who prevails upon Vāsavadattā to release Priyadarśikā. Her remorse, if any, seems largely superficial and, once again, actuated by the fact that Priyadarśikā is a relative.

More significantly, Udayana's attempts to placate Vāsavadattā, which often border on the ludicrous, completely reverse the traditional equation between husband and wife. The unusual reversion of custom in his falling at her feet time and again is a telling one. He does this in the *Priyadarśikā*, entreating her to 'be pleased, my dear, be pleased' (*PD*, III.14—*prasīda priye prasīda*). He even sits beside her on the ground in an abject fashion and laments, 'Why do you cherish this deep-seated anger when I have thus bowed to you?' (*PD*, IV.3).

Likewise, in the *Ratnāvalī*, he takes hold of the skirt of Vāsavadattā's garment and displays great confusion of mind at her implacability. This even prompts her maid, Kāñcanamālā, to say, 'Mistress, be favourably disposed. Going away, leaving the great king thus fallen at the feet, Your Highness is sure to feel remorse' (*RV*, III.15). To this Vāsavadattā retorts, 'Where is the reason either for favour or remorse in this case?' She rises languidly when she sees him later, indicating that her show of respect is purely perfunctory. When, in the *Priyadarśikā*, he talks in terms of being unworthy of her respect, she does not give a straightforward answer, but keeps him guessing at her state of mind. She is, thus, very much in control of the situation.

Perhaps the most revealing indication of Vāsavadattā's power over Udayana is that his union with Priyadarśikā/Ratnāvalī depends on her final consent. Thus, although the victory is his, it is evidently on Vāsavadattā's terms. For instance, in the *Priyadarśikā*, when she consents to the union, the king is shown in an uncomplimentary, vacillating light with his remark, 'What have I to do with her (Priyadarśikā)? You have been just now somehow conciliated' (*PD*, IV.11). Vāsavadattā retorts, 'Who are you not to take it (Priyadarśikā's hand)?' She forcibly draws their hands together, making the king remark, 'The queen is all powerful. Whence can we have power to do otherwise?' (*PD*, IV.11—*devī prabha-vati, kutosmāka-manyathā kartuṁ vibhavaha*). Even then, his feeling is more one of relief that Vāsavadattā is reconciled with him (*PD*, IV.11).

Likewise, in the *Ratnāvalī*, it is recognized that the queen is the 'chief authority' as to how to dispose of Ratnāvalī' (*RV*, IV.22). The king accepts Ratnāvalī as a favour to Vāsavadattā, since this is what she 'commands'. Thus, the resolution of both plays depends on Vāsavadattā's favour, thereby seeming to render redundant all the strategies devised by the maids and the jester to further the cause of the king's love.

Stephanie Jamison says a queen's power to give another in marriage is a direct role reversal.[105] The *Dharmaśāstras* define marriage as *kanyādāna* (gift of a maiden) and the giver is generally the father or a close male relative. The ability to 'give away' in marriage implies that the giver has dominion over the given. More importantly, it confers power on the giver, putting the receiver in his or her power. Jamison's analysis has important implications on Vāsavadattā's role. By conferring Priyadarśikā and Ratnāvalī on Udayana, she is stressing her power over both parties.

In stark contrast to Vāsavadattā are the portrayals of Priyadarśikā and Ratnāvalī. Both are highly ineffectual, colourless characters who are only remarkable for their beauty, thereby enabling them to catch the king's roving eye.[106] The intelligence, perception, and determination of Vāsavadattā find no corresponding echo here. Where Vāsavadattā is articulate and decisive, they are vacillating, weak, and unsure, preferring to indulge in love-sickness rather than actively resolving their problems.

Thus, for instance, Ratnāvalī, exhibiting a wholly gullible nature, assumes that Udayana is the god of love on account of his handsome face. By extension, she is completely ignorant of the identity of the king or the kingdom where she is residing. Furthermore, she constantly wishes to commit suicide in dejection or mourns her inability to do so. She laments, 'meritless that I am, I was not able to die even as I wished' (*RV*, IV.19). Vāsavadattā, in a similar situation, would have reacted with vigour, sarcasm, wrath and threats.

However, Ratnāvalī seems to be the slightly more articulate of the two. While Priyadarśikā, equally ignorant of the specifics of her surroundings, has nothing concrete to say on the turbulent course of her love, Ratnāvalī laments, 'Love for a person unattainable, [the sense of] shame very great and self under the power of another . . . this love is unequal' (*RV*, II.1). This holds true for their reactions to Vāsavadattā's final consent to their love. While Priyadarśikā dutifully but silently demonstrates her 'sisterly affection' for Vāsavadattā, Ratnāvalī is prompted by guilt to say, 'I have, indeed, given offence to the queen; so I cannot show my face to her' (*RV*, IV.20).

An interesting aspect of both characters is the curious reticence they maintain on their actual identities. Both have been thrust into the keeping of strangers by circumstances, yet they do not reveal any details which, ironically, could have resulted in them being restored to their families. Chafing at her position as Vāsavadattā's attendant, Priyadarśikā reflects,'That I, who was born in that sort of (so high a) race in that way and who lived commanding others, should now do the bidding of others. . . . Better even this than that I should lower myself by disclosing my illustrious race' (*PD*, II.4). Ratnāvalī, too, adopts her new name and identity, maintaining the same intriguing silence on her family. Perhaps this attitude was engendered by a sense of pride that we today cannot understand.

In conclusion, Harṣa's innovation is *not* in making the heroine 'the main centre of the plot', as is often assumed,[107] but in deflecting the attention to Vāsavadattā, clearly the main character in his plays, the heroines serving as a mere foil to her figure.

IMPLICATIONS OF VĀSAVADATTĀ'S PORTRAYAL

Vāsavadattā's portrayal has repercussions not just on secondary writings on Harṣa's plays, but also as regards the larger issue of polygamy and its acceptance at the time. It would be worthwhile to consider the views of Ratnamayi Dikshit in her *Women in Sanskrit Dramas*, not just because she uses Harṣa's plays as a reflection of contemporary womanhood, but also because of her analysis of Vāsavadattā's character.[108] However, as will be shown, Dikshit's refusal to consider women other than in their stereotypical presentations results in a classic case of pushing them out of sight. She ignores the immense potential that Harṣa's Vāsavadattā offers for a study of women's power.

Dikshit insists that Vāsavadattā, as depicted by Harṣa, 'is a sad commentary on womanhood as a whole.'[109] She apparently does not compare favourably with the Vāsavadattā of Bhāsa's *Svapnavāsavadattā* (alluded to earlier), 'that noble woman' who allowed herself to be presumed dead and became dependant on the princess who replaced her for the sake of 'the glory of her husband'.[110] The allusion is to a derivation of the original story of the *Bṛhatkathā* that deals with Udayana's absorption in Vāsavadattā to the detriment of his kingdom, thereby necessitating his marriage with Princess Padmāvatī of Magadha. Vāsavadattā lives in disguise under Padmāvatī's protection and eventually returns to the king.[111] As is obvious, the plot of the *Ratnāvalī* is somewhat similar.

Dikshit says that Harṣa's Vāsavadattā exemplifies the fact that women had less capacity for pure, selfless love than those of yore, the differences in portraits of Vāsavadattā being 'an eye-opener to the change' in society. She feels that the 'adorable queens' visualized by Kālidāsa (clearly meek, humble and self-effacing), seem to have disappeared by Harṣa's time, 'leaving only the second class ladies of the harem' for the poet to draw his ideals from. She traces the 'narrow mindedness' and 'jealousy' of harem intrigues, and the seemingly degenerate atmosphere of the harem, to the limited educational facilities and the growing seclusion of women that curbed their 'noble' qualities.[112]

By extension, she says that Vāsavadattā does not possess 'the dignity and broadmindedness required by her position as the chief queen' of 'a high and mighty king'. She apparently belongs to the *madhyā* type of heroines of Sanskrit dramaturgy, jealous, proud, easily angered or pleased—and it is this jealously unforgiving and prejudiced nature, which, to Dikshit, 'brings her down to a very low level'. Additionally, her anger is said to 'point to the very ordinary level of her character and culture'.[113] Therefore, the respect that Vāsavadattā commands is only due to her position and not because of any 'innate noble qualities'.[114]

And yet, it is clear that although the representation of Vāsavadattā adheres to a certain code of dramaturgy, the portrayal is that of a woman's fight for her dignity. This is a fact that Dikshit seems to have overlooked. Vāsavadattā's anger, jealousy and other supposedly negative attributes surface in reaction to a rival's appearance on the scene and the dread prospect of losing to her. Why should she necessarily be self-sacrificing and self-negating in such a situation? Why should Dikshit expect her to be liberal and generous to a rival, and fall short of supposedly feminine standards by not being so? This is, after all, an intelligent, articulate, and proud woman, intensely aware of the transient nature of her husband's attraction for her and desperate to maintain her position.

Moreover, that Udayana is actually pursuing her attendants and companions is an affront to Vāsavadattā's dignity. Her humiliation at being conspired against is revealed in her words to Saṁkṛtyāyaṇī in the *Priyadarśikā*: 'I was so made to be laughed at that it is with difficulty that I stand before your reverence through shame'.

In these circumstances, her words to Saṁkṛtyāyaṇī—'How he (Udayana), who cares no more for me, can care for mine?' (*PD*, IV.1) which, to Dikshit, reflects 'a very shallow and uncultured mind' is actually a perfectly legitimate doubt.[115]

Significantly, Udayana's behaviour is dismissed by Dikshit as that of a romantic, perhaps somewhat self-centered, mind. Mild statements are used to excuse his transgression—'Of course the behaviour of King Udayana also is no better,' apparently stemming from 'a discontented conjugal life.'[116] His familiarity with and dependence on the maids to further his love is glossed over and, ironically, Vāsavadattā's constant censure of Udayana is held responsible for their disrespectful teasing of him.[117] Yet it is significant that his flirtatious nature is actually made use of by his minister, Yaugandharāyaṇa, to conclude a desirable marriage alliance with Ratnāvalī.

The callousness of Udayana is seen not just in his disregard of Vāsavadattā's feelings but also by his selfish utterances. For instance, in the *Ratnāvalī*, his self-centered lament is—

Shall I think of that face of the queen robbed of its affectionate smile by long-cherished rage, or of Sāgarikā frightened by being rebuked with intense wrath; or of Vasantaka, bound and led away from here? Thus subjected to pain of every form, I do not experience ease even for a moment (*RV*, III.19—*kiṁ devyāha kṛta-dīrgha-rośa-mūśitata-snigdha-smitaṁ tan-mukhaṁ trastāṁ sāgarikāṁ susam-bhṛta-ruśā kiṁ tarjya-mānāṁ tayā, bandhā nītamito vasantaka-mahaṁ kiṁ cintayā-mītyaho sarvā-kāra-kṛta-vyathaha kṣaṇamapi prāp-nomi no nir-vṛtiṁ*).

When he hears that Sāgarikā has been taken away by the queen, he moans—'Oh! The queen's absence of regard for me!' (*RV*, IV.4). Furthermore, he informs Sāgarikā of her superior claims over the queen thus—'. . . thus all that was service on my part due to the queen's inborn nobility of mind (and nothing more); but what is (true) love, which has its flavour heightened by steady affection—that I have for *you* (alone)' (*RV*, III.18).

The extreme pathos of Vāsavadattā's situation is revealed, albeit unwittingly, by the king himself in the *Ratnāvalī*. He says:

Not indeed, by equivocal oaths, by endearing words, by ministering to her desire all the more, by the (manifestation) of great sense of shame, by prostrations at her feet, and by the constant exhortations of her friends, did the queen return to herself as she did, when by her weeping, anger was removed, of her own motion, having washed it off, as it were, with the waters of her tears (*RV*, IV.1).

Yet he ends by saying—'Now that the queen has been pleased, concern for Sāgarikā only troubles me' (*RV*, IV.2), thereby revealing a startling lack of conscience. Dikshit ignores this aspect of Udayana's character and concentrates instead on Vāsavadattā's inadequacies.[118]

At one level, the views of Minakshi Dalal, who discusses love conflicts in Sanskrit drama, seem to parallel those of Dikshit.[119] Dalal discusses the *khaṇḍitā* type of heroine whose jealousy and aggression on the appearance of a rival on the scene stems from the conflict of love and dignity. She is powerful but, despite her determination, weeps for her love. However, she qualifies that unlike the tragic anguish of Bhāsa's Vāsavadattā, Harṣa's Vāsavadattā appears like 'an ordinary queen struggling to retain her royal position'.

R.N. Dandekar's analysis of Bhāsa's portrayal of Vāsavadattā is also worth citing, at this juncture.[120] According to him, Vāsavadattā is one of the 'grandest' women characters in Sanskrit drama, and, given her nobility and self-sacrificial nature, is the real protagonist of the play. This poses an interesting comparison with Harṣa's Vāsavadattā who dominates his plays due to other reasons.

One should also briefly cite Dikshit's views on the heroine of Harṣa's *Nāgānandam*, Malayavatī, whom she rightly dubs a 'complete misfit' in the play with its philosophical tone.[121] Her only significance is in marrying Jīmūtavāhana, the hero, since he traces the success of his self-sacrificial endeavour to his marriage. As she believes Malayavatī to be propagating the ideal of complete devotion to the husband and in-laws, Dikshit concludes that the picture of women in the *Nāgānandam* is not wholly 'disappointing and discouraging'. However, she claims that all three of Harṣa's plays 'show a very unexhilarating condition of women in general'.[122]

In conclusion, one can cite Pathak's views on the *Ratnāvalī* and the implications of Harṣa's portrayal of its shadowy, submissive heroine.[123] He finds similarities between the *Harṣacarita* and the *Ratnāvalī*, as both describe the achievement of universal sovereignty. Pathak points to the supernatural factor in the form of the blessings that figure in both texts. Lakṣmī blesses Puṣpabhūti that he would be the ancestor of a universal ruler (Harṣa) and a sage prophesies Ratnāvalī's power through marriage, which prompts Yaugandharāyaṇa to seek her hand for Udayana.

In both cases, universal sovereignty is connected with a king's meeting with a woman—Rājyaśrī with Harṣa and Ratnāvalī with Udayana. This symbolic meeting is apparently in conformity with an established literary pattern. Pathak says that Bāṇa also records the present of a necklace by Divākaramitra to Harṣa after his meeting with Rājyaśrī. It is described as a 'banner which announces the coming of embodied imperial power'. Similarly, a jewel-necklace (*ratnāvalī*) forms a recurrent motif of Harṣa's play. It is a means of identifying Ratnāvalī who is named after it. Pathak then compares Rājya and Vāsavadattā as impediments to the achievement of universal sovereignty, and Grahavarman's murder and Ratnāvalī's shipwreck as paving the way for its attainment. On the basis of this argument, Pathak finally concludes that Bāṇa wrote the life of Harṣa on the model of the *Ratnāvalī*.

The purpose here is not to prove or disprove Pathak's contention, but to recognize that, implicit in his comparison of the texts, is the extension of the aspect of historical 'diminution' to the figure of Ratnāvalī as well. It also serves as an indicator of the use of women in marriage alliances to further a crucially important end. Comparisons may be drawn here with the politically strategic marriages of Rājyaśrī and Harṣa's daughter as well.

IMPLICATIONS ON THE ISSUE OF POLYGAMY

The second important implication of Vāsavadattā as she is portrayed is the issue of polygamy and its acceptance. Admittedly, Harṣa's plays reflect the social reality of this marriage system that was, essentially, a strategy for male desire and political consolidation, structurally integrated into kingship. Polygamy was a characteristic feature of a king's household that worked to enhance political power through marriage alliances with powerful rulers but also endangered smooth transitions of political power.[124] But was it as commonly accepted as we are led to believe? Were women as reconciled to this system as men? Do Harṣa's plays stress the actual reactions of women to polygamy that are usually suppressed in historical accounts?

Sweeping statements on polygamy as a social institution seem to be the norm in secondary sources. Dikshit says that it 'appears to have become the rule of the day', and Indra, too, remarks on it having become a widely accepted practice in later times,[125] chiefly sanctioned if the first wife was elderly or barren. There is no analysis on the reaction of the supplanted women, except to presume their acceptance of the situation. And yet, it is obvious that within a polygamous household, access to power and social status would necessarily be unequally available to the wives, leaving them insecure.[126]

M.R. Kale ignores the implications of Vāsavadattā's reactions on the issue of polygamy. Thus, he remarks with reference to the *Ratnāvalī*, 'We need not look askance at his (Udayana's) love-intrigue; polygamy was common in India among sovereigns in those days' and hence, it was 'excusable' if the king felt attracted by a new face.[127]

In addition, he quotes the rules of the *Sāhitya Darpaṇa* that dictate that the chief queen of such a play should be an adult woman, bold, and of a royal family. She should apparently bar the lovers from meeting and display indignation at every step so that the final union of the lovers should depend on her consent.[128] Then, in an obvious attempt to justify Udayana's transgression, Kale claims that Vāsavadattā, the chief queen, is 'elderly and majestic', also 'staid'.[129] Hence, Udayana's desire for Priyadarśikā/Ratnāvalī is justified.

However, Kale's assumption is baseless. Vāsavadattā, as borne out by the plays, is actually young and beautiful and had only recently married Udayana. This is clearly specified in the *Priyadarśikā* where Udayana calls her 'the jewel of women' (*PD*, I.6) and is obviously totally engrossed in her. In addition, she is described in terms that leave no doubt about her obvious beauty.[130] The king himself acknowledges that—

Our attachment has developed from day to day owing to the feeling of love being highly esteemed. So seeing that slip on my part, never committed before, that intolerant darling of me will surely give up life today, for a blundering when love reaches its climax, becomes intolerable (*RV*, III.15—*samā-rūḍa prītiha pranaya-bahūmānā-danu-dinaṁ vyalīkam vikṣyendaṁ kṛtamakṛta-pūrvaṁ khalu mayā, priyā muñcatyadya sphutama-sahanā jīvita-masau prakṛṣ-tasya premṇaha skhalitama-vishyaṁ hi bhavati*).

Kale admits that Vāsavadattā's love for Udayana is sincere and that her jealousy proceeds from this.[131]

Vāsavadattā's reaction to Udayana's new loves, however, questions a woman's tacit acceptance of polygamy. If polygamy were such a normal feature, why would she waste her time in censure and recriminations?[132] By extension, why would Udayana be so fearful of her reaction and conduct his affairs in such a clandestine manner? Why would the fulfilment of his other loves necessitate convoluted plots, taking the form of complicated intrigues? Finally, why would Ratnāvalī's father need to be deluded into thinking that Vāsavadattā was dead before he sent his daughter to Udayana as his future wife? If polygamy was the accepted norm, what objection could he have to Ratnāvalī joining Udayana's harem, or causing 'mental affliction' to Vāsavadattā?

In a traditionally polygamous alliance between noble families, benefits are expected. Yet both Priyadarśikā and Ratnāvalī are ostensibly maids and companions, and it is only later that they are revealed to be of royal blood. In the latter case, Ratnāvalī's true worth is known only to the minister, Yaugandharāyaṇa, and not to the king. Thus, Udayana has no practical reason to lust after either of them. Vāsavadattā is neither old nor ugly. Besides, she cannot be labelled as barren, for her marriage is a very recent one and if such had been the case, it would have found mention in the plays. Even the king muses in the *Priyadarśikā*,

Strange is the predilection for his new love of an amorous person, disregarding union with his own wife (*PD*, III.9—*aho kopi kāmi-janasya sva-gṛhiṇī-samāgame-pari-bhāvino janaṁ-abhinavaṁ prati pakṣapataha*).

His thoughts are echoed by Priyadarśikā: she asks Manoramā, the maid, how the king could be expected to stray when he was 'bound by the chains of the queen's virtues' (*PD*, III.1).

At this point, Kale's views on Vāsavadattā's 'magnanimity' in bestowing her rivals on Udayana assume significance.[133] This is not just an attempt to conventionalize her, but has bearings on the entire issue of the supplanted woman's consent in a polygamous situation. Referring to the *Priyadarśikā*, Kale points to the 'nobility' of Vāsavadattā's mind in bestowing the heroine on Udayana. Likewise, with regard to the *Ratnāvalī*, he claims that by 'willingly' accepting Ratnāvalī as her rival, Vāsavadattā appears 'in a generous and lovable light'. His views echo those of Dikshit on the rightness and advisability of a woman's submissive consent in such a situation.

However, the text shows that Vāsavadattā's acceptance of the situation was neither submissive nor willing, but stemming from a pragmatic survey of the realities of her position. It is her attempt to retain dignity and grace in a situation where she has been outmanoeuvred by the conniving of her husband, the maids and the jester. Last, it is a means of satisfying her husband and appeasing her uncles, the fathers of Priyadarśikā and Ratnāvalī. Any apparent 'magnanimity' on her part would have stemmed from the fact that her rivals were her cousins and, therefore, posed no serious outside threat to her position.

Besides, despite her acceptance of the situation, Vāsavadattā makes her continued resentment known. For instance, in the *Ratnāvalī*, she rather bluntly asks Yaugandharāyaṇa, 'Why don't you say clearly—"Give Ratnāvalī to him (the king)?"' (*RV*, IV.21—*ārya sphutameva kiṁ na bhaṇasi yatha prati-padayāsmai ratnāvalīmiti*).[134] It is only after this remark that she gives the bride away, saying—'Let this much at least, worthy of a sister, happen at my hands' (*RV*, IV.21—*etā-vadapi tāvanme bhagini-kānu-rūpaṁ bhavatu*).

Likewise, the *Priyadarśikā*, too, shows Vāsavadattā's grudging acceptance of the situation as the only reasonable option. In the garb of a reconciliatory speech, she subtly rebukes Priyadarśikā: 'O cunning one, come, now at least show your sisterly affection' (*PD*, IV.11—*ehyalīka-śīle, idānīṁ-api tāvad-bhaginī-snehaṁ daśaya*). These words can also be read: 'O one falsely observing reserve or affecting modesty etc. . . .'

Kale, however, chooses to disregard these indications, being overly anxious to bring Vāsavadattā within a stereotypical frame. He ignores the potential that such a spirited and obviously unconventional character has for the study of gender. Besides, neither he nor Dikshit note the important fact that Vāsavadattā completely subverts the traditionally projected polygamous situation, where enmity and anger is reserved for the co-wives alone.[135] Vāsavadattā directs much of her wrath on Udayana as well as on her rivals, and has no illusions about the fact that both parties are equally at fault.

The 'fearful picture of power struggles in the women's quarters', amply demonstrated in Harṣa's plays, has been discussed at length by Vātsyāyana in his *Kāmasūtra*.[136] He enjoins the senior wife to do her utmost to maintain her power and position, even to the extent of fomenting discord. The junior wife is expected to combine subservience with rivalry.[137] Interestingly, Vātsyāyana holds the senior wife to blame if her husband marries again. However, significantly, he says that a man could also be prompted by weakness of character in this decision.[138] This speculation could rightly be applied to Udayana.

At this juncture, one could consider Julia Leslie's views on polygamous situations. She says that, inevitably, the reasons given by Sanskrit religious law for marrying again convey a negative impression of the senior wife in that she is barren, old/sexually unattractive, bad-tempered or difficult to deal with, or lazy.[139] Yet Udayana does not seem in any way discomfited by Vāsavadattā's temper, for instance, until the appearance of her rivals.

For her part, Sally Sutherland says that the rejected woman is a common theme in literature, but specifies that, in the context of the ancient Indian world where polygamy was normative for certain sections of society, she was usually the virtuous, gentle, elder wife, while the new, younger wife was the aggressive one.[140] This character assessment obviously does not apply to Vāsavadattā and her rivals. Sutherland also suggests that the senior wife was more associated with the role of a mother by the husband, who was more comfortable with the younger wife's sexuality. This, again, does not apply in Vāsavadattā's case where there is no question of motherhood involved. Note that this itself raises the question of her age. Had she been elderly, as Kale presumes, her inability to bear a son would have been mentioned, motherhood being seen as crucial to a woman's identity.

In fact, the plurality of wives that is supposed to strengthen man's domination over women does not seem to have affected their mutual relations. Vāsavadattā's power remains intact and palpably evident in the *Ratnāvalī*, for instance, where she insists that Udayana pay deference to the relatives and emissaries of her maternal family.[141] She instructs him to stop a magic show on the arrival of her maternal uncle's chief minister, stating that Udayana 'should see him at once' (*RV*, IV.12).

In conclusion, one could consider Harṣa's plays under the general ambit of sexual politics,[142] the system of interpersonal power by means of which individual men dominated individual women, the relationship of domination and subordination being expressed in and through the medium of sexual relationships, loosely termed connections of love. However, the domination in this case is not confined to the male, for though his is the victory, it is a largely facile one in view of its dependence on a woman's favour and consent. The plays, thus, exemplify the fact that 'the subordination of women . . . requires the addition of more flexible terms since subordination in one sphere may be offset by power in another.'[143]

One could also speculate on the extent to which these plays mirror Harṣa's personal life. The intense resentment provoked among other rulers, in the *Priyadarśikā*, by the heroine's father verbally bestowing her on Udayana, can be said to reflect the tension that Rājyaśrī's marriage to Grahavarman caused. Additionally, the *Ratnāvalī* commences with the stage manager's wife bemoaning the fact of her daughter's betrothal to someone in a distant country and the inevitable pangs of separation to ensue. This, too, has echoes of Rājyaśrī's marriage and her departure to Kanauj.

More significantly, in view of the perceptive and intimate

knowledge of women and their feelings displayed in the plays, could Harṣa have modelled some of the female characters on his wife? Could Vāsavadattā be a reflection of his chief queen who was already rumoured to have a short temper and an acerbic tongue? Was he reflecting any situation of conflict in his own harem, or merely adapting the original story to suit his purpose?[144] Alternatively, did he want to convey the negative effects of polygamy and the anguish of a supplanted wife?

What, after all, could be the reason behind Harṣa's altered version of Vāsavadattā and his none-too-complimentary portrayal of Udayana? Admittedly, the core theme is not an original one but the conflict and dialogues are. It is through the dialogues, after all, that one grasps an idea of Vāsavadattā's power and her feelings. Was Harṣa seeking to heighten the dramatic element in his plays through his depiction of Vāsavadattā? Alternatively, could Harṣa's constant interaction with Rājyaśrī have given him a superior understanding of women and a desire to project it? If so, then why is the figure of Malayavatī so submissive and stereotypical in the *Nāgānandam*? Is it written from some other motive, or does it attempt to subscribe to conventional notions of a woman?

In view of the lack of corroborative evidence, one cannot answer these questions with any degree of certainty. Nevertheless, the gendered aspects of Harṣa's plays should be analysed, rather than merely focusing on Harṣa's authorship and technical similarities with other plays, as is the wont of most scholars with regard to Harṣa's literary output.

THE ROLE AND PRESENCE OF MAIDS[145]

One of the most significant features of the literary sources of this period is the power and influence that maids seemed to exercise in the royal court. This assumes added importance in view of the normally diluted voice of women in male-authored texts. Though their power is most amply exemplified in Harṣa's plays, there are parallel portrayals in Bāṇa's *Kādambarī*, for instance, in the interesting figure of a female companion or attendant to a prince. The purpose of this section is to examine these two aspects.

The Portrayal of Maids

At the outset, the views of Minakshi Dalal can be quoted once again. As part of her analysis on conflict in Sanskrit drama (cited earlier), she acknowledges the role of maids to some extent. They are said to be involved in the situation of 'psychological conflict' that is created in the plays.[146] However, the impression she creates is more of their unwitting involvement due to circumstances, rather than willing participation.

The most visible role of maids is in Harṣa's 'sister plays', where they enact a crucial role in the harem intrigues. They are the prime movers behind the plots and it is their scheming which eventually results in Udayana achieving his aim. In this, they are contrasted very favourably with the jester, Vasantaka, their male counterpart, whereby their intelligence and wit serve as a foil to Vasantaka's bungling.

A revealing example in the *Priyadarśikā* is the figure of Manoramā, who actively encourages the heroine's love for the king, despite her apprehension of Vāsavadattā's wrath. Her accurate assessment of Udayana's character is evident when she assures Priyadarśikā that 'he himself will be eagerly engaged in devising some means to see you' (*PD*, III.1). It is on Manoramā's suggestion that the king assumes his real identity in the mimic play to effect a clandestine meeting with Priyadarśikā. As she confidently informs him, 'This is the way to bring about another union.' In fact, it is this that leads the play to a climax, resulting in the eventual union of Udayana and Priyadarśikā.

Not only is Manoramā's intelligence on display, but also her presence of mind and her refusal to be cowed down by Vāsavadattā's disapproval. When, for instance, her complicity in the plot is uncovered, she immediately invents a plausible explanation and is able to convince Vāsavadattā of her innocence. Subsequently, though she laments the 'long continuity of the queen's anger' (*PD*, IV.1), she irrepressibly arranges a meeting with Vasantaka to inform the king of Priyadarśikā's imprisonment. She is, thus, able to anticipate Vāsavadattā's moves and outwit her at every turn.

Significantly, the male actors in the play are vastly inferior in terms of intelligence, charm, and wit. Udayana's total dependence on Manoramā's ideas and superior planning is obvious. Her power over him is aptly revealed by Vasantaka who remarks, 'Here, indeed, are kings made to dance (act) even by a maid-servant' (*PD*, III.6—*ete khalu rājano dāsyāpi evaṁ nartyante*). The same applies to Vasantaka who prides himself on his closeness to the king, but is inefficient and incapable of furthering the love affair. In fact, it is through his indiscreet babbling that Vāsavadattā learns of the plot centering round the mimic play. Thus, in every sense, he compares unfavourably to Manoramā.

The *Ratnāvalī*, which contains a profusion of maids, has the important figure of Susaṅgatā, Manoramā's counterpart. She plays a pivotal role in detecting Ratnāvalī's love for Udayana and, by drawing her portrait beside that of the king, exposes their mutual affections. Here, too, Vasantaka tries to take on the role of chief manipulator, but it is Susaṅgatā's superior planning that guides their actions and brings the play to a climax. Vasantaka remains the same bungling, ineffectual figure, chafing at Susaṅgatā's orders but with no alternative to offer.

Susaṅgatā's relations with the king have the same overtones of superior confidence as in Manoramā's case. This even enables her to fool the king by threatening to expose him and then saying, 'Sire, away with fear. (Emboldened) by your majesty's favour, I too played a joke' (*RV*, II.16). She even sits down in the king's presence and continues the conversation thus—a boldly disrespectful gesture. Subsequently, it is on her insistence that Ratnāvalī disguises herself as Vāsavadattā and has a clandestine meeting with the king. This has the important effect of acquainting Vāsavadattā with the affair and bringing the play to a climax, resulting in the union of the two lovers.

It is significant that the issue of fluctuating loyalties among Vāsavadattā's attendants resolves itself into a situation of women versus women, ranging round a man's sexual attentions. It is not just a question of Vāsavadattā's maids taking on her rival's cause, but also one of divisions within their own fraternity, causing them to take opposing sides in the intrigue. This explains the king's anxiety to hide Ratnāvalī's picture from Susaṅgatā, not knowing her complicity in the plot.

One such significant confidant, however, is the figure of Kāñcanamālā, in the *Ratnāvalī*, intensely loyal to Vāsavadattā and anxious that her image remains untarnished. 'Better be the king a bad person, but not the queen' (*RV*, III.18), she says. Her intelligent perception of the king's nature is as evident as Manoramā's and Susaṅgatā's. Seeing through Udayana's feigned illness, she remarks that he is 'concealing his love-sickness under the guise of indisposition' (*RV*, III.1). Clear indications of hostility towards him can be gleaned here, most probably on account of his insensitive treatment of her mistress.

The reason behind the involvement of the attendants in harem intrigues is not clear. It could have been prompted by a desire for excitement, as a novel variation from a humdrum existence. Equally, it could have been prompted by feelings of resentment towards the high-handed Vāsavadattā, tempting some girls to support the king's cause. It was obviously not done with a view to gaining royal favours. Udayana's uncertainty about the outcome of his love and the dread prospect of Vāsavadattā's retribution posed real disincentives to such an idea. The musings of Kāñcanamālā and Madanikā, another loyal maid, are not too illuminating in this regard. While both criticize Susaṅgatā for plotting against the queen, Madanikā declares—'Susaṅgatā, condemned are you that thus deceive the queen, who is, indeed, so kind to her attendants' (*RV*, III.1).

In the *Nāgānandam*, Caturikā and Navamālikā completely overshadow the submissive, shadowy heroine, Malayavatī. However, as the action is largely centered round the sacrifice of the hero, Jīmūtavāhana, the maids exert their influence only in furthering the love of the leading pair. Thus, Caturikā takes on the onus of effecting introductions between Jīmūtavāhana and Malayavatī, and ferrets out the latter's feelings with great dexterity, causing her to say, 'You are indeed a *caturikā* (sharp-witted). How can I conceal anything further?' (*NN*, II.1). Her involvement in the affair is of great significance since it culminates in their marriage, and Jīmūtavāhana later holds this responsible for bringing his dreams of self-sacrifice to fruition. The red garments presented by Malayavatī's parents to him, consequent on his marriage, resemble the slaughter garments of the *nāga*, Śaṅkhacūḍa, and enable him to sacrifice his body in place of the *nāga* to Garuḍa.

Once again, the jester, Ātreya, is compared unfavourably to the female court attendants. Not only is he ridiculed by Caturikā who squirts black juice on his face, but there is interaction between him and Navamālikā that speaks volumes on his comparative status. Knowing full well that he is 'a brahmin friend of the king' (*NN*, III.4), Navamālikā mocks him, challenges his position, and strips him of all vestiges of dignity.

When Ātreya begs to be released from a public ridiculing, Navamālikā demands that he 'fall prostrate' at her feet (*NN*, III.4—*yadi bhūmau sīrśaṁ niveśya pādayoha me patasi*). When Ātreya reacts angrily at the idea of falling 'before the feet of a slave-girl's daughter,' she threatens—'I will prostrate you'. Subsequently, when Navamālikā's lover makes her sit with Ātreya so that he 'might equally honour' both of them, she offers him wine that she has already tasted, and questions his brāhmaṇa status by asking him to recite some Vedic hymns. Admitting defeat, Ātreya says, 'What is the use of my arguing with you? This brahmin falls prostrate before your feet.' It is only at this juncture that Navamālikā relents and says she was only joking with him as a relative (*NN*, III.4). The very fact that she can claim kinship with such an exalted person is significant.

The implications of the depiction of maids are manifold. The original versions of the plays in the *Bṛhatkathā* do not contain such vigorous, high-spirited characters. Thus, Harṣa has innovated greatly in their depiction. Furthermore, by their intelligence, shrewdness, decisiveness and boldness, they cast the conventional heroines of the three plays into shadow. In the 'sister plays', therefore, the situation resolves itself into a contest between two sets of strong female characters—Vāsavadattā and the maids.

By extension, their power over the male characters is highlighted. Not only are they the prime movers in harem intrigues, their actual exchange of frivolities with the king and jester (and this applies to the *Nāgānandam* as well) shows their confident use of men as targets for venting their amusement and wit. Opportunities provided by the *madana* and other festivals, that enabled intermingling of the sexes without restraint, are very effectively used for this purpose.[147] This has great implications on the entire issue of gender. As R.C. Dwivedi briefly observes, even minor female characters (clearly maids) are treated with respect 'which they amply deserve', unlike the *vidūṣaka* who does not command much at all.[148]

Let us now examine the motives behind such a portrayal by Harṣa. Was he depicting a situation of reality? Was this based on an actual observation of the role of maids in the harem/court? Was their palpable role and presence the standard norm of the day? By extension, why does he constantly denigrate the male characters in their exchange with the maids? Did he want to attack the arrogance of brāhmaṇas by making unfavourable comparisons? Or did he merely want to break with a stereotype and introduce innovative figures of his own?

The comparative silence of most secondary works on this aspect is inexplicable. There are even cases of minimizing the role of maids, as in that of Kale who conveniently leaves out Manoramā from his discussion of 'the principal characters' of the *Priyadarśikā*. Vasantaka, whose role is not that crucial, is discussed. And yet, if one assumes the portrayal of maids to be a reflection of reality, is it not vital to analyse the role of women from this fresh perspective?

The Portrayal of Female Attendants

As noted earlier, the dividing line between maids and female attendants or companions in the harem is blurred in the sources. There were several categories of women at the early medieval court in Kanauj, some clearly menial servants, others playing a more ambiguous role. The necessity of treating them as separate categories arises as some well-defined female companions in the texts are clearly above the status of servants and have an important role to play in political and social affairs.

Though much of this evidence is obtained from the *Kādambarī*, one should note that both Priyadarśikā and Ratnāvalī of Harṣa's plays largely fall within the same category. Thus, Priyadarśikā is captured by Udayana's soldiers and introduced into the harem on Udayana's orders. He hands her over to Vāsavadattā's charge, to be taught 'singing, dancing, playing upon instruments and other accomplishments' fit for a maiden of high birth, and to be told when she reaches marriageable age. Ratnāvalī, too, enters the harem in a helpless condition after surviving a shipwreck. She is placed in Vāsavadattā's care and is, presumably, to be married off at a suitable time. Thus, on the one hand, they are little more than captive slaves and accompany their benefactor on regular errands. On the other hand, they are resentful of the enforced subservience, a fact recognized by their compatriots, who treat them with dignity and respect.

Patralekhā in the *Kādambarī* is somewhat similar to Harṣa's heroines. She is the daughter of a vanquished king and is raised by Queen Vilāsavatī, the mother of the hero, Prince Candrāpīḍa, in her harem. Bāṇa, however, provides an interesting twist by causing the queen to make her Candrāpīḍa's betel-bearer, 'to be admitted' to all his 'confidences' and to be cherished by him as a companion.[149]

Patralekhā's status as Candrāpīḍa's companion and confidant means that the usual fate of marriage or attending on a woman is not reserved for her. Bāṇa clearly breaks with tradition here. It is also significant that there are no sexual overtones to their relationship. While Patralekhā serves Candrāpīḍa with devotion and never leaves his side, he 'felt for her a great affection, beginning from his first glance at her, and constantly growing; he daily showed more favour to her, and counted her in all his secrets as part of his own heart'.[150] She accompanies him on his campaigns, sitting with him on his elephant and sleeping near him on the hard ground. Subsequently, she plays a crucial role in receiving the confidences of the heroine, Kādambarī, and conveying her love to Candrāpīḍa. So she resolves the 'conflicting signs' he had received and sets his doubts about Kādambarī to rest, thereby paving the way for their eventual union.[151]

The very significance of Patralekhā's role warrants a separate study, there being no such parallel figures in the *Kādambarī* or any other contemporary text. In ancient Indian prescriptive texts, the inadvisability of royal men confiding in women is clear; so her figure as Candrāpīḍa's confidant assumes added importance. However, it is interesting to note that Bāṇa seems to be contradicting himself. In the *Harṣacarita*, he makes the general, Siṁhanāda, instruct Harṣa at great length on the dangers posed by women confidants, citing several illustrative examples to prove his point.[152] Yet Patralekhā's role and presence is fleshed out in the *Kādambarī* and provides an instance of what Julia Leslie terms an 'ancient ambivalence' towards women in literary sources.[153]

The implications of Patralekhā's depiction are particularly noteworthy in view of the fact that most secondary works, once again, maintain a marked silence on this aspect. Admittedly, Bāṇa has taken the theme of the *Kādambarī* from the *Bṛhatkathā*. Nevertheless, the addition of and fleshing out of characters, as well as the revealing dialogues, are entirely his own. It is here that his unconventional views are evident.

Before examining Bāṇa's motives, one could consider two illustrative examples of his novel views. These can be seen in conjunction with his notable portrayal of Patralekhā. First, while describing a female courtier in a king's court, he shows her wearing a scimitar, 'a weapon rarely worn by women', and talks of her 'awe-inspiring' form that held 'the circle of kings in submission'.[154] This is a highly original depiction of a woman, hinting at her understated power and evoking a somewhat masculine aura.

The second case is significantly unorthodox in that a young cāṇḍāla woman is held to be the reincarnation of Lakṣmī.[155] Her beauty, despite 'the darkness of her hue', is described at great length. She is also compared to Durgā, and a king is made to criticise the gods for creating her 'in a race with whom none can mate'. She remains 'a Lakṣmī of the lower world'. Admittedly, Bāṇa is known to have a penchant for invoking goddesses as agents of comparison. He compares the 'strong' Vindhya forest to Durgā and his father's younger sister, Mālatī, to Sarasvatī (*HC*, II. 64). As part of his aim to show himself as a Vātsyāyana brāhmaṇa with Dadīcha-Sarasvatī associations, Bāṇa describes the intelligence and arrogance of Sarasvatī, as well as the power of Sāvitrī.[156] However, none of these parallel his radical rethinking of conventionally accepted Hindu mythology.

It is in this light that Bāṇa's portrayal of Patralekhā becomes clear. She is the creation of a man who is not averse to questioning accepted roles in society or to thinking innovatively. This could stem from his relatively unorthodox upbringing, being raised by his father, Citrabhānu, who 'acted a mother's part' and who evidently defied convention by later marrying a śūdra woman.[157] Additionally, Bāṇa seems to have consorted with varied friends—people 'of low birth', an ascetic widow, Cakravākikā, and a maid, Kuraṅgikā, among others (*HC*, I.47). This could have influenced his thinking and ideas.

Several of Bāṇa's statements seem to be based on actual observation. For instance, his description of Prince Candrāpīḍa's procession through the streets, which made the women's speech 'straightaway mirthful, confidential, confused; envious, scornful, derisive, coquettish, loving or full of longing',[158] might very well be based on Harṣa's effect on the female populace. The point is not whether this particular allusion is true, but that Bāṇa can be trusted to portray the actuality of contemporary situations.[159]

Admittedly, the story of the *Kādambarī* is a magical romance with no bearing on historical facts. Yet to portray a woman as a royal confidant and advisor makes an important statement about the socio-political milieu. Did Bāṇa have a particular woman in mind when he introduced Patralekhā's character? Could this woman have been Rājyaśrī? Or was he merely depicting a set-up in tune with his own ideas and thereby trying to show his approval of female intervention in political matters? More importantly, what prompted Bāṇa to dare to depict Lakṣmī in a despised social caste? Was this his way of questioning caste rules? Many of these questions remain unanswered.

CHOICES EXERCISED BY WOMEN

This section deals with the deliberate choices exercised by two women in Bāṇa's *Kādambarī* as regards the pattern of their lives. Thus, Mahāśvetā, a young princess of about eighteen years, decides to become an ascetic,[160] while Princess Kādambarī, her friend, decides to remain unmarried in sympathy for her. These decisions assume great significance, as by the Brahmanical norms which presumably affected most of the higher castes, a woman was not supposed to take any independent decisions about herself.[161] However, the text shows these women taking their decisions in the teeth of parental opposition and probable social condemnation. It would be worthwhile to examine these decisions and consider their implications.

The Choices Exercised

Mahāśvetā and Kādambarī shared a common fate at birth in that they were welcomed wholeheartedly by their parents, despite being girls. Mahāśvetā's birth was 'greeted' by her father 'with a great festival surpassing that for a son'.[162] Kādambarī, too, was a 'priceless daughter' and 'the very life of her parents'.[163] This is a highly novel departure from the usual preference for sons and sets the tone for their unconventional choices.

Mahāśvetā's decision is spurred by a heavenly assurance that her dead lover, Puṇḍarīka, would be eventually restored to her. Thus, she adopts a form of temporary asceticism while she waits for its fulfilment. She lives in a cave in a secluded forest, adopting all the outward trappings of asceticism (matted locks, bark robes and a bark bed). She gains confidence 'by the power of penance' which is apparent in her greeting Prince Candrāpīḍa without the slightest trace of fear, coyness, or uncertainty, although he is a complete stranger.[164] More importantly, she realizes 'the worthlessness of the world' and 'the harshness of destiny', learns 'the inconstancy of earthly things' and 'the frailness of all joys'. Her parents are 'disregarded', her kinsfolk and followers 'abandoned', the joys of earth are 'banished from her mind', and her 'senses held in firm restraint'.[165]

It is important to note that this decision is not the only proof of Mahāśvetā's self-willed nature. The very course of her love for Puṇḍarīka is dictated by boldness.[166] It is she who initially approaches Puṇḍarīka, despite knowing that he is an ascetic. Subsequently, though she briefly wrestles with questions of propriety, Mahāśvetā goes to seek Puṇḍarīka on her own at night, prompted by news of his love-sickness. 'This transgression against my parents would be a great wrong. But if . . . I follow duty, I shall in the first place accept death', she thinks.[167] It is when she learns of his death, soon after, that she takes her vow of asceticism.

Mahāśvetā's response to her parents' entreaties is not only indicative of her stubbornness, but challenges the very ideal of the submissive daughter. In addition, the fact that she is allowed to pursue her goal at all is entirely unconventional and unusual. Thus, though her father 'strove with all his might and by every means—prayers, admonitions, and tender words of every kind', he eventually 'understood' her 'firm resolve' and knew that she could not be swayed 'from that infatuation'.[168] It is interesting that force is not used as a means of persuasion, at this juncture. Of equal note is the fact that Taralikā, Mahāśvetā's betel bearer and her trusted confidant, becomes a 'sharer in the ascetic vow', and lives with her mistress in the forest without any sign of familial opposition.[169]

Kādambarī's case is a somewhat similar one. 'From sorrow' at Mahāśvetā's plight, she resolves not to marry while her friend is 'still in grief'. She takes this vow before her friends, declaring that if her father forced her to marry against her will, she would end her life 'by hunger, fire, cord, or poison'.[170] Stressing the implacability of her resolve, she informs Mahāśvetā—'. . . from love of thee I have . . . accepted an independent life contrary to the wont of maidens. I have despised noble breeding, transgressed my parents' commands, set at nought the gossip of mankind, thrown away modesty, a woman's grace; how, tell me, should such a one go back?'[171] She even feels guilty for staying at home while her friend languishes in the forest.

The reaction of Kādambarī's parents is unusual in that they seem to fear a direct confrontation with her on the subject. Her father learns of her resolve only through her attendants. He is deeply frustrated as she grows 'to full youth' but 'could say nothing to her, though he saw no other resource'. They eventually appeal to Mahāśvetā to convince her. Interestingly, when they later learn of Kādambarī's love for Candrāpīḍa, who is temporarily dead on account of a curse, they accept it with equanimity, stressing that they had never thought to see her wed, and were happy with her choice.[172]

A notable reflection on contemporary gender relations is provided when Mahāśvetā exhorts Kādambarī to 'lay aside diffidence, suspicion and shame' on account of Candrāpīḍa's presence, and 'behave to him as to me. He is thy friend, thy kinsman, and thy servant'.[173] Candrāpīḍa is allowed easy access into Kādambarī's quarters,[174] and Mahāśvetā blatantly encourages their romance before 'the sharp eyes of the harem' but without the knowledge of Kādambarī's parents.

Although both women are aware of the unorthodoxy of their

decisions and the unsavoury reactions they provoke, Mahāśvetā seems the stronger of the two in pursuing hers.[175] Kādambarī is prey to constant introspection and self-reproach on falling in love with Candrāpīḍa, since this is contrary to her vow of indefinite celibacy. Moreover, it is intriguing that though she is initially not deterred by the thought of parental opposition when taking her vow, she is now afraid of their reaction to her love for Candrāpīḍa. Her ironical lament is—'How should such as I . . . turn my thoughts on unmaidenly levity, acting thus without my father's will, or my mother's bestowal, or my elders' congratulations . . . ?'[176] She seems not to appreciate the boldness of her earlier stance, since she now shrinks from even sending a message to Candrāpīḍa on account of her sudden timidity. This is, perhaps, why Mahāśvetā terms Kādambarī's earlier resolve a 'foolish freak'.

Implications

As has been stated earlier, the fact of women taking decisions on the course of their lives is unusual and a definite break with traditional norms. Admittedly, this is a fictional work, yet Bāṇa's projections might very well be based on reality. Thus, it opens to debate the issue of the flexibility of choices open to women within the apparently rigid code governing their lives. It also raises questions on Bāṇa's motives and attitudes towards this aspect. The point here is not whether Mahāśvetā and Kādambarī actually took such vows, but whether one could portray women as being able to exercise such choices in a patriarchal milieu. As powerful ritual values characterized conventional social relations, any instances of women choosing to abjure these relations are doubly significant.[177]

How common was it for parents to condone their daughters' unorthodox choices at the time? What was the reason for their helplessness in this regard—recognition of the strength and toughness of their resolve, or perplexity at a show of independence so unusual in a royal family? Bāṇa presents quite the opposite picture in the *Harṣacarita*: on the issue of Rājyaśrī's marriage, Prabhākaravardhana gives a lengthy account of the necessity for a daughter's marriage at the correct time. Yaśovatī agrees with him, stating that mothers 'are to their daughters no more indeed than nurses, useful in rearing them. In their bestowal the father is the judge' (*HC*, 156). The startling contrast with the *Kādambarī* is intriguing.

At this juncture, one can consider the norms of textual tradition which indicated that a woman's religion is her family life, and that all notions of woman should be submerged in the ideal of 'wife'.[178] Women were expected to follow the social requirements of marriage, householdership, and religious practice focused on others' welfare. Yet Mahāśvetā deliberately flouts these conventions to embrace an ascetic's life without any formal initiation.[179] Admittedly, this is only a temporary withdrawal from the world. However, she could very well have waited at home for Puṇḍarīka's rebirth instead of embracing a difficult forest life. Thus, she undertakes asceticism for her own goals, making hers a somewhat self-centred decision in view of the self-negating nature usually expected of women.

Harṣa's *Priyadarśikā* contains the figure of Saṁkṛtyāyaṇī, a 'revered lady' of 'poetic genius' (*PD*, III.30). She is probably an ascetic with connections at court. Kale presumes her to be a lady of high rank and learning on the grounds that she speaks in Sanskrit and not Prakrit, the latter usually reserved for women and lower classes.[180] Nothing much is known about her lifestyle but this is another interesting case of a male author depicting a woman who opts out of a traditional life.

Similarly, Kādambarī's flouting of convention, although temporary, is also a noteworthy exercise. In her decision to challenge the convention of marriage, she is actually challenging the entire framework of traditional laws governing a woman's life. This show of independence is all the more significant in that it is spurred by another woman's distress.

Did Bāṇa, then, approve of women taking independent decisions regarding their lives? Was his awareness of an ascetic's life gleaned from his friend, the ascetic widow, Cakravākikā? Was his awareness of the social predicament of an independent woman based on her situation? Again, we do not know because of the lack of evidence.

SATĪ AND BĀṆA

To understand the significance of Bāṇa's opposition to *satī*, it would be worthwhile to reiterate some aspects of this practice. *Satī* was a social practice aimed at increasing man's power to demand/coerce and, thereby, typified a male-dominated and woman-demeaning society.[181] The desirability of this practice is echoed in several Brahmanical narrative and prescriptive works, as it was seen to bestow great merit on the performer and as constituting the perfect means for the ideal woman to overcome widowhood.

In these circumstances, the fiercely unequivocal resistance that Bāṇa offers to this practice is of vital importance. His views are most clearly exemplified in the *Kādambarī*, as part of Prince Candrāpīḍa's reassurance to Mahāśvetā on the rightness of her continuing to live after her lover, Puṇḍarīka's death.[182] He says:

> This following another to death is most vain! It is a path followed by the ignorant![183] It is a mere freak of madness, a path of ignorance, an enterprise of recklessness, a view of baseness, a sign of utter thoughtlessness and a blunder of folly, that one should resign life on the death of father, mother, friend or husband. If life leaves us not of itself, we must not resign it.

Candrāpīḍa follows this diatribe with several illustrative examples, mainly from the *Mahābhārata*, of women who did not follow their husbands into death. He mentions Ratī, Kuntī, Uttarā and Duhshalyā who 'made no resignation' of their lives when their husbands died. He also talks of the 'daughters of rākṣasas, gods, demons, ascetics, mortals, siddhas and gandharvas, who, when bereft of their husbands, yet preserved their lives'. He stresses that the practice is motivated by self-interest in the desire to avoid pain but brings 'no good' to the dead man whatsoever. By continuing to live, one can make offerings to the dead and keep his memory alive but 'by dying he helps neither—the dead man or himself'.

One should note that though Bāṇa does not specifically refer to the practice of *satī* by name, his meaning is obvious. The scathing language and the tone makes this a highly unconventional indictment of the practice and refreshingly so, at a time when it was considered to be the norm.[184]

Bāṇa's resistance to *satī* is very much in evidence in the *Harṣacarita* as well, but in a more subtle sense. As regards Yaśovatī's 'fixed resolution' to burn herself before Prabhākaravardhana's death, by itself 'an uncommon act',[185] he connects it to her pride. In answer to Harṣa's remonstrations, Yaśovatī talks of her position as chief queen and says—'. . . how otherwise could such a woman as I, whose price was valour, . . . act?' Harṣa finally deems her decision to be 'befitting a lady of rank' (*HC*, V.186–7).

As regards Rājyaśrī's attempt to burn herself, the remonstrances and arguments against it are lengthier and more persuasive.[186] Though Rājyaśrī apparently believes that for a woman without a husband or son, 'it is immodesty even to continue to live', her attendants lament her decision, call on her relatives to save her and curse the fire for preparing to burn her (*HC*, VIII.274–8). Emissaries are sent to seek help, and Rājyaśrī is eventually rescued from the pyre by Harṣa and Divākaramitra.

At this point, one could view the situation from an entirely new perspective. Is it possible that Rājyaśrī did *not* actually prepare to burn herself in the forest? After all, the only source of her decision to do so is Bāṇa's text. Could Bāṇa have invented this situation simply to include arguments against *satī* in his work? In fact, the utterance on the futility of living is actually made by Rājyaśrī's betel-bearer, Patralatā, and in the context of her desire to join Divākaramitra (*HC*, VIII.284).

It could very well be that Yaśovatī's act of burning herself was common knowledge and hence, Bāṇa had to mention it in his text. However, by including Harṣa's protests against it and Yaśovatī's lengthy justification, he could be trying to say that burning oneself, under these circumstances, need not be a logical act.[187] Significantly, in the subsequent descriptions of Prabhākaravardhana's death and the resultant grief at court, there is no mention of any of his other wives burning themselves. Could Bāṇa's silence here have been deliberate? Or did they actually not burn themselves?

In Rājyaśrī's case, Bāṇa could have taken liberties with the actual situation of her flight to the forest and her reunion with Harṣa there. The inclusion of her decision to burn herself would not only heighten the dramatic interest of the text, but also provide a chance for Bāṇa to air his disapproval of *satī*. By showing Harṣa's aversion to it on two occasions, he might have hoped that the king's attitude would influence that of his readers. It should be noted here that the only allusion to *satī* in the writing of Harṣa himself is in the *Nāgānandam* where Malayavatī resolves to burn herself on Jīmūtavāhana's disappearance, and her parents-in-law decide to join her on the pyre. Perhaps Harṣa had no definite views on the practice but allowed Bāṇa to depict his aversion to it all the same. After all, Bāṇa was his close friend and the poet might have tried to convince Harṣa of the rightness of his views.

Did Bāṇa, then, see himself as a social reformer of sorts? Furthermore, did his friendship with Cakravākikā have anything to do with his strong views on the subject? Was this merely Bāṇa's perspective or did a part of contemporary society actually view this practice with distaste?

I reiterate the importance of a gender analysis for the life and times of Harṣa. There is enough evidence provided of the role of particular women such as Rājyaśrī, and the role of other women in the intrigues of the court, to make this a fruitful area for investigation. It is also necessary to speculate on the reasons behind the authors' stance since their portrayal of society would reflect, consciously or otherwise, contemporary attitudes and cultural problems, though they may tend to transcend historical facts.

Thus, when Harṣa deliberately veers away from an original characterization and adds some novel touches of his own, his motives need to be analysed. Was this a factor of genre, audience, or author? By extension, when Bāṇa portrays his unconventional views on women, one could speculate that he was trying to resist the very 'constrictions' in social life to which Devahuti refers.[188] This holds true despite the fact that both writers were upper-class men and, thus, represented a highly exclusive class.[189] It is also interesting to note that none of the women in the texts examined above, except perhaps Yaśovatī, is judged from the perspective of motherhood, a traditionally crucial yardstick to define a woman's identity in a patriarchal social system.

Gender analysis is not always easy. Bāṇa's convoluted descriptions and his tendency to be sidetracked by minor characters and events, pose a substantial problem. As far as Harṣa is concerned, the contrasting picture of women provided by the 'sister plays' and the *Nāgānandam* is puzzling. And epigraphic evidence can be used only in a limited sense to corroborate the textual evidence. A careful interpretation of the textual and epigraphic evidence with an acknowledgement of the spaces for and voices of women is, therefore, crucial.

NOTES

1. George Bühler, 'The Madhuban Copper-plate of Harṣa', *Epigraphia Indica*, vol. I, 1892, pp. 67–75. It transfers the village of Somakuṇḍikā to two brāhmaṇas, Vāṭasvāmin and Śivadevasvāmin.
2. George Bühler, 'Bānskherā Plate of Harṣa', *Epigraphia Indica*, vol. IV, 1897, pp. 208–11. It grants the village of Markaṭasāgara to two brāhmaṇas, Bālacandra and Bhadrasvāmin. See also Hirananda Sastri, 'Nālandā Clay Seal of Harṣa', *Epigraphia Indica*, vol. XXI, 1932, pp. 74–6.
3. E.B. Cowell and F.W. Thomas, trs., *The Harṣacarita of Bāṇa*, 2nd rpt., Delhi, Motilal Banarsidass: 1993, pp. 96–7.
4. She is referred to as Yaśomatī in all the four inscriptions, whereas Bāṇa calls her Yaśovatī.
5. K.K. Thaplyal, *Inscriptions of the Maukharis, Later Guptas, Puṣpabhūtis and Yaśovarman of Kanauj*, Delhi, ICHR/Agam Prakashan: 1985, p. 92.
6. See *HC*, IV.134–5 for a detailed description of Yaśovatī. She is compared to various goddesses.
7. This is an aspect that has not received due recognition. For instance, B.N. Sharma, *Social Life in Northern India (A.D. 600–1000)*, Delhi, Munshiram Manoharlal: 1966, p. 26 dubs Yaśovatī 'an ideal lady' based on the qualities enumerated by Bāṇa, whereas reality suggests otherwise.
8. Shankar Goyal, *History and Historiography of The Age of Harsha*, Jodhpur, Kusumanjali Prakashan: 1992, p. 147 where he quotes S.R. Goyal's view.
9. Ibid.
10. D. Devahuti, *Harsha: A Political Study*, 2nd edn, Delhi, Oxford University Press: 1983, p. 74.
11. It is significant that the names of the other wives are revealed by Prabhākaravardhana in the course of his deathbed laments, wherein he seems to recall their names with perfect lucidity, asking each to assuage his pain in different ways (*HC*, V.177–8). Krishṇa, Harṣa's stepbrother and the one instrumental in bringing Bāṇa to court, might have been born from one of these subordinate wives of Prabhākaravardhana. See Devahuti, *Harsha*, p. 76.

12. Devahuti, *Harsha*, p. 75.
13. V.S. Pathak, *Ancient Historians of India*, 2nd impression, Gorakhpur, Purva Samsthana: 1984, p. 49.
14. Shankar Goyal, *History and Historiography*, pp. 141–2.
15. Interestingly, Bāṇa describes the joyful royal household now as 'the essence of freedom from widowhood'. See *HC*, IV.159.
16. Note, however, that much of Devahuti's reasoning on Harṣa's accession and Bāṇa's motives is derived from Pathak's analysis of the issue. See also Shankar Goyal, *History and Historiography*, p. 75.
17. R.S. Tripathi, *History of Kanauj to the Moslem Conquest*, rpt., Delhi, Motilal Banarsidass: 1989, pp. 63-77.
18. Samuel Beal, tr., *Si-Yu-Ki: Buddhist Records of The Western World*, 2nd edn, New Delhi, Munshiram Manoharlal: 1983, p. 210 where it is stated that after Prabhākaravardhana's death, Rājya 'ruled with virtue' till he was murdered. Also Devahuti, *Harsha*, p. 80.
19. Devahuti, *Harsha*, pp. 79–80. Note that R.C. Majumdar and V.S. Pathak have already speculated on the entire issue.
20. Ibid., p. 91.
21. Tripathi, *History of Kanauj*, p. 63.
22. Apparently Rājya's courtier, Saṁvādaka, arrives with this news. He also states the rumour that 'the villain, deeming the army leaderless', plans to invade Thānesar as well. At this, Rājya instructs Harṣa to remain behind and goes to avenge the loss with Bhaṇḍi as, 'This task is my royal house, this my kin, my court, my land . . . this day I go to lay the royal house of Mālwā in ruin. . . .'
23. Tripathi, *History of Kanauj*, p. 69. Tripathi feels that this is only a poetic way of describing Harṣa being favoured by destiny in that he had no prior claims to succeed his father but found himself in such a position through circumstances. He feels that Harṣa's previous reluctance and vow of austerity refers to 'his reluctance to avail himself of his father's preference for him'. Alternatively, the passage may refer to Harṣa's previous vow not to accept the crown when the grief-stricken Rājya wanted to abdicate in his favour. In any case, Harṣa's subsequent unhesitant accession apparently did not imply any swerving from his original vow of renunciation, as he was the only one left to resolve the crisis in both kingdoms. See p. 70.
24. Ibid., p. 68. Note that this is in keeping with his initial reaction on hearing the news of Rājya's murder when his 'aspect became terrific in the extreme' and he cursed the 'vilest of Gauḍas'.
25. Devahuti, *Harsha*, pp. 82–3, questions Harṣa's silence on Rājya's 'unusual decision' to abdicate. After all, he is believed to have protested on not being allowed to join Rājya's subsequent campaign of revenge.
26. Tripathi discredits K.M. Panikkar's view that perhaps Rāyja had an heir whom Harṣa 'scrupled to disinherit'. This apparently led to

'rebellious' feudatories initially spoiling his chances of securing Kanauj. Tripathi stresses Bāṇa's claims that the feudatories were loyal to Harṣa (*History of Kanauj*, p. 71). Shankar Goyal, *History and Historiography*, pp. 180–1 notes that Yuan Chwang refers to rumours regarding the alleged murder in which he implicates some of Rājya's ministers, probably even Bhaṇḍi.

27. Shankar Goyal, *History and Historiography*, p. 188.
28. Ibid., pp. 180–1. B.P. Sinha, *Dynastic History of Magadha*, Delhi, Abhinav Publications: 1977, p. 141 speculates that Rājyaśrī chose to go to the Vindhyas because it was a Maukhari territory and also harboured Grahavarman's friend, Divākaramitra. However, see R.C. Majumdar, 'Political History of South Bihar—550–750 A.D.' in *Comprehensive History of Bihar*, ed. B.P. Sinha, Patna, Kashi Prasad Jayaswal Research Institute: 1974, vol. I, part II, p. 235. His hypothesis on Rājyaśrī's puzzling flight to the Vindhyas rather than to Thānesar is that the Mālwā king, after being defeated by Rājya, retired to his own kingdom, taking Rājyaśrī with him, whereupon she escaped and entered the Vindhya forest.
29. Devahuti, *Harsha*, pp. 89–90 claims that Harṣa 'may have been dictated by considerations both humane and political'. She speculates that the unidentified 'Gupta' who released Rājyaśrī from prison could have been a member of the Kanauj household or a sympathizer from Śaśāṅka's camp. See also *HC*, VII.253.
30. Pathak, *Ancient Historians*, p. 51.
31. Tripathi, *History of Kanauj*, p. 72. It also appears that Śaśāṅka wanted to avoid an open conflict with Harṣa and withdrew from Kanauj. A compelling factor could have been the joint treaty signed by Harṣa and Bhāskaravarman of Assam.
32. Ibid., p. 73. Harṣa apparently says—'My sister, so young and so tried by adversity, must be cherished by me for a while, even if it involves the neglect of all my duties.'
33. Bhaṇḍi (usually identified with the Poni of Yuan Chwang's account) apparently told the statesmen of Kanauj—'I propose that he (Harṣa) assume the royal authority' and asked for everyone's opinion (ibid., pp. 74–5). Kanauj was in a 'hopeless state of confusion', needing 'a strong and guiding hand'. Devahuti too concedes that Bhaṇḍi was probably asked to prepare the psychological climate at Kanauj for the acceptance of Harṣa's leadership. He seems to have stressed Harṣa's affection for his family. See Devahuti, *Harsha*, p. 90.
34. Tripathi, *History of Kanauj*, p. 75. The chief ministers and magistrates of Kanauj apparently exhorted Harṣa to 'Reign, then, with glory over the land, conquer the enemies of your country; wash out the insult laid on your kingdom.'
35. Thaplyal, *Inscriptions of the Maukharis*, p. 32; Tripathi, *History of Kanauj*, p. 74 says that Harṣa talks of the 'disappearance of all her (Rājyaśrī's)

other relatives'. This could mean that Grahavarman's younger brother was either killed or had fled during the Gupta-Gauḍa disturbance.

36. Thaplyal, *Inscriptions of the Maukharis*, p. 35; Tripathi, *History of Kanauj*, p. 74 speculates that Grahavarman was called *sūnuragrajaḥ* to indicate that he was Avantivarman's eldest son. K.K. Dasgupta, 'Last Days of the Maukharis', *The Indian Historical Quarterly*, vol. XXXVIII, 1962, pp. 242–6, speculates that as the *Āryamañjuśrī-mūlakalpa* lists the name *suvra* after Grahavarman, this must have been his younger brother whom Harṣa had to oust.
37. Tripathi, *History of Kanauj*, p. 74 quotes V. Smith as saying that the nobles of Kanauj 'seem to have hesitated' before giving Harṣa the crown, and K.M. Panikkar's view that the inheritance was 'not a comfortable one'. Devahuti, *Harsha*, p. 83 notes Yuan Chwang's awareness of Harṣa's 'initial diffidence' in taking over Kanauj.
38. Edward A. Pires, *The Maukharis*, rpt., Delhi, Ramanand Vidya Bhawan: 1982, p. 116. Interestingly, Harṣa is treated as a Maukhari king in this work and not a Puṣpabhūti.
39. Tripathi, *History of Kanauj*, pp. 74–6.
40. Devahuti, *Harsha*, pp. 83, 92.
41. Tripathi, *History of Kanauj*, p. 76. Avalokiteśvara apparently promised Harṣa secret power to enable him to ward off his neighbours. See also Devahuti, *Harsha*, p. 94. It seems Avalokiteśvara told Harṣa to undo the harm done by Śaśāṅka to Buddhism.
42. Devahuti, *Harsha*, pp. 91–2, says that the brother of the widowed queen was expected to benefit by the absence of a strong male claimant. She further stresses that Harṣa's acquisition of Kanauj, *because of Rājyaśrī's presence* (italics mine), was beyond reproach. Yet the focus here is on Harṣa rather than Rājyaśrī. However, Pathak, *Ancient Historians*, p. 42, acknowledges that Harṣa obtained Kanauj through Rājyaśrī and acquired suzerainty.
43. D.C. Sircar, *Studies in the Society and Administration of Ancient and Medieval India*, Calcutta, Firma K.L. Mukhopadhyay: 1967, vol. 1, p. 237.
44. Pathak, *Ancient Historians*, p. 49. See also p. 42 where Pathak notes that *rājyaśrī* means 'the goddess of fortune manifested in sovereignty'. Thus, the statement about Rājyaśrī having united the two lines of the Puṣpabhūtis and the Maukharis has two meanings. Then again, Harṣa's initial reluctance to supersede Rājya's claims apparently makes him say—'Let sovereign glory (*rājyaśrī*) flee to a hermitage' (*HC*, V.190). The prophetic and symbolic value of this statement is underlined in Rājyaśrī's actual flight to the Vindhyan forest. See Tripathi, *History of Kanauj*, p. 70.
45. Pathak, *Ancient Historians*, pp. 30–1, 46, says that Bāṇa had been working to achieve this end and that the *Harṣacarita* was, therefore, 'a

complete and finished product of art'. Thus, the earlier notion that the text was fragmentary is untenable, as Bāṇa never intended to write beyond this stage. Pathak says that Bāṇa wanted to make Harṣa's meeting with the goddess of royal fortune appear inevitable and intelligible. Note that as the symbolic association of women with male sovereignty/glory is a convention of most *carita* works, Rājyaśrī's role could be seen in this light. However, the other indications of her power in the sources cannot be ignored.

46. Tripathi, *History of Kanauj*, p. 76; Thomas Watters, *On Yuan Chwang's Travels in India*, 2nd edn, Delhi, Munshiram Manoharlal: 1973, p. 345. This statement is not found in the *Life* or the *Records*.
47. Devahuti, *Harsha*, p. 91; Shankar Goyal, *History and Historiography*, p. 193, talks of Harṣa having 'usurped Kanauj by diplomacy' over three stages—first as a *kumāra* (or patron/regent), next as joint administrator with Rājyaśrī and, lastly, as sole ruler.
48. Tripathi, *History of Kanauj*, p. 77 says that after a 'modest guardianship or regency', Harṣa's was 'a sort of quiet usurpation' with the people's support, due to unusual circumstances. He also terms this a 'dexterous stepping into the shoes of the Maukharis'. Tripathi does speculate that Harṣa's 'unostentatious title' of *kumāra* definitely suggests that although, as per Bāṇa, he was already king of Thānesar, in Kanauj he was merely charged with the duty of keeping the government running. Hence, his political status there was no better than guardian or regent. However, he does not consider the implications of Rājyaśrī's role on Harṣa's status in Kanauj.
49. For instance, Devahuti, *Harsha*, pp. 90, 173. One could consider here Baijnath Sharma's interesting explanation for Bāṇa's silence on Harṣa's actual takeover of Kanauj. He speculates that Bāṇa 'like many others and, in accordance with the traditions of our country, did not find proper justification' for Harṣa's act of taking over Kanauj '*which rightfully belonged to his younger sister*' (italics mine). This statement raises many possibilities in that it acknowledges Rājyaśrī's right to power and questions a tacit acceptance of Harṣa's takeover. Ironically, Sharma himself does not consider these implications: Baijnath Sharma, *Harṣa and his Times*, Varanasi, Sushma Prakashan: 1970, p. 159.
50. Shankar Goyal, *History and Historiography*, p. 52.
51. Tripathi, *History of Kanauj*, pp. 74–5.
52. D.C. Sircar, *Studies in the Political and Administrative System in Ancient and Medieval India*, Delhi, Motilal Banarsidass: 1974, p. 33. Indra, *The Status of Women in Ancient India*, 2nd revd edn, Banaras, Motilal Banarsidass: 1955, pp. 146–57, talks of Daṇḍī Mahādevī (Orissa), Prabhāvatīguptā and the Kashmir queens (Diddā and Sugandhā) who succeeded to the throne as widows. However, there are problems with Indra's analysis. On the one hand, he says that although the political

rights of women in ancient India were limited, the political power they wrested for themselves needs to be examined. However, on the other hand, in Indra's analysis of women rulers in ancient India, there is no mention of Rājyaśrī's possible role in Kanauj's governance. Moreover, he makes an inexplicable statement on women being held inefficient as rulers, governors or counsellors, as a result of 'being light-hearted, whimsical and eccentric in their nature'.

53. Shankar Goyal, *History and Historiography*, pp. 180–1.
54. Meenakshi Mukherjee, 'Story, History and Her Story', *Studies in History*, vol. IX, no. 1, January–June, 1993, p. 72.
55. Tripathi, *History of Kanauj*, p. 77. Sharma, *Harṣa and his Times*, p. 162, makes the interesting speculation that Harṣa might have transferred his seat of government from Thānesar to Kanauj in deference to Rājyaśrī's wishes.
56. Pires, *The Maukharis*, p. 118, speculates that soon after Harṣa assumed full power (as exemplified in the Nālandā seal), Rājyaśrī passed away, or was gradually divested of all authority and receded into the background. Pires also hints that this could have been an unscrupulous takeover.
57. Devahuti, *Harsha*, p. 91.
58. D.C. Sircar does lament the lack of definite information regarding Rājyaśrī's part in Harṣa's administration (*Studies in the Society and Administration*, pp. 230–1).
59. Kumkum Sangari, 'Consent and Agency: Aspects of Feminist Historiography', in *Women in Indian History: Social, Economic, Political and Cultural Perspectives*, ed. Kiran Pawar, Delhi, Vision & Venture: 1996, p. 13; Shalini Shah, *The Making of Womanhood*, Delhi, Manohar: 1995, p. 162 refers to another aspect of the subordination of women—the creation of an artificial dichotomy between domestic and public, pertaining to women and men, respectively.
60. Power can also be seen as 'the ability to act effectively on persons or things, to make or secure favourable decisions which are not formally recognized as part of an individual's role'. This would include coercion, manipulation and other forms of influence. Leela Dube, 'Introduction', in *Visibility and Power: Essays on Women in Society and Development*, ed. Leela Dube, Eleanor Leacock and Shirley Ardener, Delhi, Oxford University Press. 1986, p. xxix; Shah, *The Making of Womanhood*, p. 15 cites M.G. Smith (from P.R. Sanday, *Female Power and Male Dominance: On the Origins of Sexual Inequality*, 1981, p. 114). Note that power is distinguished from authority, which is the right to make a particular decision and command obedience.
61. Devahuti, *Harsha*, p. 91; Watters, *On Yuan Chwang's Travels*, p. 345.
62. Samuel Beal, tr., *The Life of Hiuen-Tsiang* by Shaman Hwui-Li, Delhi, Academica Asiatica: 1973, p. 187; Tripathi, *History of Kanauj*, p. 160.
63. This—a form of social death—is apparently the only model provided.

Uma Chakravarti, 'Gender, Caste and Labour: Idealogies and Material Structure of Widowhood', *Economic and Political Weekly*, vol. XXX, no. 36, 9 September 1995, p. 2251; Uma Chakravarti, *Everyday Lives, Everyday Histories: Beyond the Kings and Brahmanas of 'Ancient' India*, Delhi, Tulika Books: 2006, p. 157.

64. Devahuti, *Harsha*, p. 184.
65. There is, however, an intriguing statement that Harṣa's magnificence was devoted 'to adorning the different quarters of the earth whose tribute he seizes, not the dolls which he calls his wives' (*HC*, II.61). See also *HC*, II.80 which says the rays of Harṣa's toe-nails were 'white like fine linen, as with the tiara of his chief queen'. Tripathi, *History of Kanauj*, p. 98 interprets Bāṇa's statement—'Here the supreme lord has obtained the hand of Durgā born in the snowy mountains'—as implying Harṣa's marriage with some hill-princess of a powerful family. Besides, Harṣa's remark, 'if you would have me watch over my wife, glory resides in your steel', is held as proof by Tripathi that he was married (*HC*, VI.206). Tripathi insists that Bāṇa is 'quite explicit' about Harṣa's marriage and wonders why Beni Prasad says, 'Neither Bāṇabhaṭṭa nor Yuan Chwang nor any of the contemporary inscriptions refers to any wife of Harṣavardhana, or to the fact of his marriage' (Beni Prasad, *The State in Ancient India*, Allahabad, The Indian Press: 1974, p. 385). In fact, Prasad is completely justified in his remark for, except for some vague allusions by Bāṇa, there is no specific information on Harṣa's marriage or wife in any contemporary source.
66. S.R. Goyal, *Harsha and Buddhism*, Meerut, Kusumanjali Prakashan: 1986, p. 145. Note, however, that Bāṇa talks of Harṣa's imperial splendour being 'eclipsed by the women' in his camp who are further described without any names (*HC*, II.82–3).
67. Shankar Goyal, *History and Historiography*, p. 64. He also says that Harṣa was a celibate when Bāṇa composed his biography. Therefore, the *Harṣacarita* must have been composed before AD 625.
68. Tripathi, *History of Kanauj*, p. 109. Yuan Chwang qualifies, however, that he was a 'sincere believer in Buddhism'.
69. Shankar Goyal, *History and Historiography*, p. 64.
70. Devahuti, *Harsha*, p. 62. Note that she does not speculate on the identity of Harṣa's wife/wives or any other possible heirs. His daughter is only cursorily mentioned. Devahuti speculates that the marriage must have taken place in 632.
71. Tripathi, *History of Kanauj*, pp. 111–12 for a discussion on whether Valabhī was a feudatory state of Kanauj and its bearing on this marriage; B.P. Sinha, *The Decline of the Kingdom of Magadha* (*c. 455–1000 A.D.*), Patna, Motilal Banarsidass: 1954, p. 61, notes that Dhruvasena became a firm ally of Harṣa and even attended his Prayāga assemblies.
72. Tripathi, *History of Kanauj*, p. 163.

73. The exact area where this occurred is unclear. Divākaramitra was a follower of the Maitrāyaṇi *śākhā*. He was initially a leading brāhmaṇa teacher but later adopted Buddhism. See *HC*, VIII.261.
74. Tripathi, *History of Kanauj*, p. 73.
75. Divākaramitra might have been motivated by fear of Harṣa in dissuading this 'wise woman' from adopting his religion. He tells Rājyaśrī that 'though sorrow has made a wide inroad, is not thy elder brother to be regarded by thee, who is as a guru and as a father? . . . He now stops thy desire . . . thou must only do what he commands . . . thou must in any case obey his decree' (*HC*, VIII.287).
76. Beal, *Life*, p. 176.
77. Diana Y. Paul, *Women in Buddhism*, 2nd edn, California, University of California Press: 1985, p. 103.
78. R.C. Majumdar, ed., *The Classical Age*, Delhi, Bharatiya Vidya Bhawan: 1954, p. 390.
79. S.R. Goyal, *Harsha and Buddhism*, p. 92.
80. Tripathi, *History of Kanauj*, p. 163 terms this evidence a 'most important testimony'. See also S.R. Goyal's argument in support of Harṣa's Śaivism in S.R. Goyal, *Harsha and Buddhism*, pp. 3, 9–15. He criticizes the view that Harṣa's interest in Buddhism spanned two phases—when he was merely interested in it and when he finally adopted it—since this is based on Yuan Chwang's testimony which is questionable. See pp. 72–3. For a detailed argument on this issue, Thaplyal, *Inscriptions of the Maukharis*, pp. 71–2. However, note that there is no mention of Rājyaśrī's influence on Harṣa's religion whatsoever. Shankar Goyal, *History and Historiography*, p. 124 notes that the word 'Ṣthānvīśvara' (Thānesar) is derived from *sthānu* and *īśvara*, meaning either the abode of Śiva or a *sandhi* of both words meaning Śiva.
81. *HC*, IV.135. This epithet is used for him and the other male ancestors in the Madhuban and Bānskherā inscriptions.
82. Harṣa also tells him that he has surrendered his soul to 'righteous vengeance'. He desires that Rājyaśrī remain by his side 'and be comforted with your righteous discourses and your advice . . .' (*HC*, VIII.288).
83. Tripathi, *History of Kanauj*, pp. 151–7 for a detailed description of the grand assembly in Yuan Chwang's account and the *Life* which involved Buddhist priests, brāhmaṇas and *nirgranthas*, priests of Nālandā, and kings of twenty countries. The Buddha, the Dharma and the Sangha were worshipped.
84. Ibid., p. 133: Tripathi quotes Yuan Chwang as saying that viands were provided for 1,000 Buddhist monks and 500 brāhmaṇas at the royal lodges everyday. There were also apparently 100 Buddhist monasteries containing over 10,000 brethren. Yuan Chwang, however, concedes that non-Buddhists were several thousands in number. Thus Buddhism flourished in comparison to the fifth century when Fa-Hsien found only two monasteries in Kanauj (p. 167).

85. Beal, *Life*, pp. 179–80. According to Yuan Chwang, an assassination bid on Harṣa was apparently made by a 'heretic' who, when questioned, voiced the resentment of his ilk who 'have scarcely been spoken to, while Harṣa devoted himself to the *śramaṇas*'. 500 brāhmaṇas were arrested, Harṣa punishing the chief plotters and sending the others into exile. Beal, *Buddhist Records*, pp. 220–1; Tripathi, *History of Kanauj*, pp. 155, 164–5. S.R. Goyal, *Harsha and Buddhism*, pp. 96–7 suggests that Yuan Chwang, realizing that the Hīnayānist plot against him would look adverse in his *Records*, concocted a brāhmaṇa plot to kill Harṣa. S.R. Goyal argues that the very fact of Harṣa giving alms to brāhmaṇas in Prayāga shortly after invalidates this plot. Hence, there is nothing in the Kanauj assembly proceedings that would prove Harṣa's faith in Buddhism.
86. Shankar Goyal, *History and Historiography*, p. 322: if Bhāskaravarman could participate in the worship of the Buddha in the Kanauj assembly and yet be regarded a Śaiva, why not Harṣa?
87. Ibid., p. 324. Shankar Goyal cites the *Life* that Harṣa gave gifts to Buddhists on the first three days and to brāhmaṇas for the next twenty days. This is not mentioned by Yuan Chwang in his *Records*, as it proves that Harṣa was not expressly Buddhist. Tripathi, *History of Kanauj*, pp. 157–61 for a detailed description of the proceedings. Devahuti, *Harsha*, pp. 180–1, says that these quinquennial assemblies were in the Buddhist tradition but held at the holy Hindu site of Prayāga, thereby further attesting Harṣa's mixed religious beliefs. However, Shankar Goyal (*History and Historiography*, p. 323) says that they had no particular Buddhist affiliation. Yuan Chwang also indicates that this was the sixth such ceremony held since 617.
88. Note that it is nowhere overtly mentioned that Jīmūtavāhana is a Buddhist. Thus, Garuḍa's statement, towards the end, that 'I have really slaughtered a *bodhisattva*' seems a trifle disjointed in that Jīmūtavāhana is only described as being a renowned Vidyādhara prince throughout. Bak Kun Bae, ed. and tr., *Nāgānanda of Harṣa*, Delhi, Motilal Banarsidass: 1992, p. 153.
89. Note that the play begins with an invocation to the Buddha but Malayavatī is a worshipper of Gaurī (Pārvatī) throughout. Significantly, her marriage to Jīmūtavāhana is foretold to her in a dream as a sign of the goddess' favour (*NN*, I.14–17). The play ends with everyone prostrating themselves at Gaurī's feet. The *Priyadarśikā* opens with salutations to Pārvatī and then to Śiva. Kale's interesting explanation for this order is that Pārvatī is 'the more respectable of the two, as being the mother of the world' (M.R. Kale, ed. and tr., *Priyadarśikā of Śrī Harṣadeva*, rpt., Delhi, Motilal Banarsidass: 1977, p. 1).
90. Devahuti, *Harsha*, p. 180.

91. Thaplyal, *Inscriptions of the Maukharis*, p. 72; Beal, *Buddhist Records*, p. 212.
92. Shankar Goyal, *History and Historiography*, p. 62 stresses that Harṣa did not follow his vow even after Śaśāṅka's death and the conquest of his dominion.
93. Ibid., p. 50.
94. Tripathi, *History of Kanauj*, pp. 70–1, 163–5. Tripathi qualifies that Harṣa maintained the 'eclectic character of his public worship', officially honouring Hindu gods in Prayāga, for instance.
95. S.R. Goyal, *Harsha and Buddhism*, p. 78.
96. Tripathi, *History of Kanauj*, p. 163, also mentions Harṣa's fondness for the Buddhist Rājya as a similar motivating factor.
97. Interestingly, Tripathi (ibid., 162) treats 'Harṣa's religion and devotion' separately from his 'benevolent activities' (as at Prayāga).
98. Paul, *Women in Buddhism*, p. 60; J.A. Khan, 'Idealogy of Motherhood in Ancient India', in *Women in Indian History*, ed. Pawar, p. 54.
99. Romila Thapar, 'The *Rāmāyaṇa*: Theme and Variation', in *India: History and Thought*, ed. S.N. Mukherjee, Calcutta, Subarnarekha: 1982, p. 245.
100. Kale, *Priyadarśikā*; M.R. Kale, ed. and tr., *The Ratnāvalī of Śrī Harṣadeva*, 2nd rpt., Delhi, Motilal Banarsidass: 1995.
101. Kale, *Priyadarśikā*, p. xxxi for a description of the *garbhanāṭaka* or an act with a play in it.
102. Bhāsa's date is between the third century BC and third century AD. Both plays are about Udayana. The first deals with his marriage to Princess Padmāvatī and the second with his marriage to Princess Vāsavadattā. The hero in both plays is actually the minister, Yaugandharāyaṇa. Ratnamayi Dikshit, *Women in Sanskrit Dramas*, Delhi, Meherchand Lachhmandas: 1964, pp. 40–1 for a brief summary of the plays. Kale, *Priyadarśikā*, p. xxv for a discussion of Udayana's marriage with Vāsavadattā.
103. For instance, knowing Vāsavadattā's irate temperament, the king wishes to tease her. He says, 'Today I shall certainly make the queen's face purple with anger, gazing upon this garden-creeper as upon another woman in love' (*RV*, II.4).
104. However, note that Vāsavadattā, exhibiting a somewhat mercurial temperament, repents very quickly. She releases him and feeds him sweets.
105. Stephanie W. Jamison, 'Giver or Given?: Some Marriages in Kālidāsa', in *Jewels of Authority: Women and Textual Tradition in Hindu India*, ed. Laurie L. Patton, Delhi, Oxford University Press: 2002, pp. 69–73, 79, cites the *Mālavikāgnimitram*, where the queen gives her ex-servant to the king for their union, as also the *Vikramorvaśī*. Although she does not mention any of Harṣa's plays, she mentions Kāmandakī in Bhavabhūti's *Mālatīmādhava*.

106. Kale, *Ratnāvalī*, Introduction, p. xxxv, acknowledges the inadequacies of Ratnāvalī's portrayal by Harṣa.
107. Sharma, *Harṣa and his Times*, p. 313.
108. Dikshit, *Women in Sanskrit Dramas*, pp. 183–8.
109. Ibid., p. 183.
110. Dikshit draws a parallel here with the ideals upheld in the *Rāmāyaṇa* and by Kālidāsa in that the wife should safeguard her husband's name with dignity and respect. Ibid., p. 184.
111. Yaugandharāyaṇa's idea is to fake Vāsavadattā's death to induce Udayana to marry Padmāvatī. Vāsavadattā reluctantly agrees to disguise herself and live with Padmāvatī for her husband's sake. It is only after the marriage that she reveals herself to the couple. There is a fleeting mention of Padmāvatī (and some other wives) in the *Ratnāvalī* but she is obviously marginal to its plot (*PD*, III.28).
112. Dikshit, *Women in Sanskrit Dramas*, pp. 184, 188.
113. Ibid., p. 184.
114. Ibid., pp. 186–7. In fact, the same could be said of Udayana: while he is lusting after Priyadarśikā, Vāsavadattā is, ironically, engaged on a fast for his welfare.
115. The allusion is to Vāsavadattā's maternal uncle and Priyadarśikā's father, King Dṛdhavarman of Aṅga, who has been displaced from his throne. Vāsavadattā's mother had written asking for Udayana's help. However, Udayana is already engaged in restoring Dṛdhavarman to his throne, proving thereby that despite his preoccupation with Priyadarśikā, he is also engaged in state affairs. This could also be interpreted as significant evidence of Udayana's love for Vāsavadattā in that he exerts himself on behalf of her relatives.
116. Dikshit, *Women in Sanskrit Dramas*, pp. 185–6.
117. Ibid., p. 185. Dikshit says that Vāsavadattā does not care if her husband is disgraced before the harem servants. Predictably, she does not consider Vāsavadattā's humiliating predicament wherein her husband is actually cavorting with the maids. Note here that Udayana has apparently 'set aside the affairs of state' to devise a means to obtain his love. Vāsavadattā's battle-lines are, therefore, more than justified (*PD*, III.27).
118. N.K. Singhi, 'Gender Theme: Issues and Perspectives', in *Women Images*, ed. Pratibha Jain and Rajan Mahan, Jaipur, Rawat Publications: 1996, p. 61, makes the point that societal values are different for men and women whereby chastity, virginity and faithfulness provide the framework of norms for female sexual relationships.
119. Minakshi Dalal, *Conflict in Sanskrit Drama*, Bombay, Somaiya Publications: 1973, pp. 138, 260. Harṣa's three plays, as also Bhavabhūti's works, are included in the twenty plays she surveys.

120. R.N. Dandekar, 'The Svapna-Episode in the Svapnavāsavadattā', in *The Age of the Guptas and Other Essays*, ed. R.N. Dandekar, Delhi, Ajanta Publications: 1982, pp. 175-90.
121. Dikshit, *Women In Sanskrit Dramas*, pp. 193-4 qualifies that Malayavatī does not show much individuality but is a creation that satisfies social dictates regarding the ideal wife and daughter-in-law. Note that even in the throes of love, Malayavatī still views Jīmūtavāhana 'with a mingled feeling of joy and fear' and cannot be near him 'out of excessive fear'. In this, she differs markedly from Priyadarśikā and Ratnāvalī who are clearly eager for the consummation of their love. See *NN*, II.6.
122. Dikshit, *Women in Sanskrit Dramas*, p. 194, says that Harṣa upholds the ideals of two religions in this play—the Buddhist ideal of self-sacrifice of man, and complete devotion to the husband for women propagated by Hinduism. Dikshit also points to two contradictory trends in social thought towards women—one denouncing them as the root of all evil, the other trying to uphold their greatness—running in tandem for a long time (p. 170). Jasbir Jain, 'Cinderella's Stepmother: An Analysis of a Counter-Image', in *Women Images*, ed. Jain and Mahan, p. 80, says that negative images of women in literature are created by a society that seeks scapegoats and women readily fall prey to it because of their deeprooted insecurity.
123. Pathak, *Ancient Historians*, pp. 41–3.
124. Chakravarti, *Everyday Lives, Everyday Histories*, p. 233; Saroj Gulati, *Women and Society: Northern India in the 11th and 12th Centuries*, Delhi, Chanakya Publications: 1985, p. 259.
125. Dikshit, *Women in Sanskrit Dramas*, p. 188; Indra, *Status of Women*, pp. 58 and 53–64 for a history of polygamy and references to it in ancient texts. Gulati, *Women and Society*, p. 29 for Manu's rules about polygamy (Manu IX.81): a barren wife could be superseded in the eighth year; one whose children die, in the tenth year; the mother of daughters in the eleventh year; and one of harsh speech, immediately. As per Devala, for a man abandoning his wives 'through infatuation . . . no expiation can be prescribed' (pp. 73–4). This is interesting in the context of Udayana's behaviour in Harṣa's plays. Medhātithi's contention, too, is significant in that the husband should apparently consult a devoted wife before marrying another woman. Note that there is no doubt about Vāsavadattā's devotion to Udayana in the plays.
126. Chakravarti, *Everyday Lives, Everyday Histories*, p. 268. Also C.M. Ridding, tr., *Bāṇabhaṭṭa's Kādambarī*, Bombay, Jaico Publishing House: 1956, pp. 149–50 for a highly significant comment on polygamy. Prince Candrāpīḍa remarks, albeit with reference to two birds, 'For women feel that a shared wifehood is the bitterest matter for indignation, the chief cause for estrangement, and the greatest possible insult'. This

not only highlights Bāṇa's attitude but also raises the question of a woman's acceptance of the system. There is another boldly unorthodox view on the philandering male. Candrāpīḍa contends that if a woman becomes reconciled to one, then 'shame on her'. Note that these views are expressed by the hero.

127. Kale, *Ratnāvalī*, p. xxxiii; Kale, *Priyadarśikā*, p. xxxvi. Ironically, the king is vested with the authority to punish errant wives, while he indulges his sexual desires through the guise of polygamy. Uma Chakravarti, 'Conceptualising Brahmanical Patriarchy: Gender, Caste, Class and State', *Economic and Political Weekly*, vol. 28, no. 14, 3 April 1993, p. 584.
128. Kale, *Priyadarśikā*, p. ix.
129. Ibid., p. xxxvii; Kale, *Ratnāvalī*, p. xxxv.
130. *RV*, I.20–2, 25.
131. Kale, *Priyadarśikā*, p. xxxvii.
132. For an interesting and related analysis, see Julia Leslie, 'Śrī and Jyeṣṭhā: Ambivalent Role Models for Women', in *Roles and Rituals for Hindu Women*, ed. Julia Leslie, London, Pinter Publishers: 1991, p. 126, who contends that the goddess Jyeṣṭhā (the sister of Śrī-Lakṣmī) evokes the 'deadly fury' of the superseded wife. Leslie believes that the 'curious ambivalences' in the images of these sister goddesses are reflected in the traditional image—positive and negative—of the Hindu wife. Śrī-Lakṣmī, identified with virtuous women, represents the power of good fortune but is also unstable and fickle. Similarly, the negative image of Jyeṣṭhā has a positive appeal in its human counterpart—the compensation of power. Thus, the senior wife is mocked yet feared, domesticated yet in control, inauspicious and yet the acknowledged power in the home. Shah, *The Making of Womanhood*, p. 110 speculates that the unanimous condemnation of Lakṣmī's nature might reflect the sexual autonomy of the Mother Goddess who later settles down as Viṣṇu's consort. After all, one of patriarchy's major concerns is the control of female sexuality, perceived as dangerous unless appropriately harnessed.
133. Kale, *Ratnāvalī*, pp. xxxv, xxxviii.
134. Vāsavadattā comments—'I have, indeed, been made (to act like) a wicked woman by minister Yaugandharāyaṇa by whom, although knowing, nothing was told' (*RV*, IV.20). However, Kale notes that she knew about Yaugandharāyaṇa's plan but not about the identity of the proposed bride (p. 245). Interestingly, the common people were apparently aware of Yaugandharāyaṇa's attempt to unite Ratnāvalī and Udayana, for a merchant of Kauśāmbī recognizes the shipwrecked Ratnāvalī and brings her to the city, knowing the reason for her presence.
135. For instance, Shah, *The Making of Womanhood*, p. 79. In this situation,

the husbands are not perceived as guilty, and enmity is generated among the women.

136. Leslie, 'Śrī and Jyeṣṭhā', pp. 124–5, quotes verses 4.2.1–23 and 4.2.24–38 of the *Kāmasūtra*.
137. Note that the senior wife is seen as something of a bully, causing dissension and suspicion all around her to safeguard her position. Her status and authority are directly related to the degree she can control the co-wives and female servants (ibid., pp. 125-6). Sally J.M. Sutherland, 'The Bad Seed: Senior Wives and Elder Sons', in *Bridging Worlds: Studies on Women in South Asia*, ed. Sally J.M. Sutherland, Delhi, Oxford University Press: 1992, p. 25 says it is no accident that *sapatnī* (co-wife) also means rival.
138. He qualifies, however, that a man could marry again from personal inclination or because the first wife produced no son. But, in both cases, the implication casts aspersions on the wife's femininity.
139. Leslie, 'Śrī and Jyeṣṭhā', p. 124.
140. Sutherland, 'The Bad Seed', p. 25.
141. Shah, *The Making of Womanhood*, p. 79, says that the first wife's constant insecurity is a feature of such a household. In Vāsavadattā's case, the insecurity is centred round Udayana's love for her and not on any apprehensions of losing power. See, for instance, *RV*, I.16 where, while conveying a message to the king, the maids say 'the queen commands' and then change it to 'respectfully submits'. The king, however, wants to know 'what the queen commands'. Also Leslie, 'Śrī and Jyeṣṭhā', pp. 123–4 on the image of the senior wife in Sanskrit religious law as largely powerful and positive. The only negative attribute is the fact that she has been superseded and the obvious implication that she has been deemed at fault. Thus, though she may be rejected sexually for several reasons, her religious status in the household and her accompanying authority is secure. The junior wives owe her authority and 'her power in the house is unquestioned'.
142. H. Eisenstein, *Contemporary Feminist Thought*, England, Unwin Paperbacks: 1984, p. 12, cites Kate Millet on sexual politics being a 'major pillar of patriarchy'.
143. Shah, *The Making of Womanhood*, p. 146, quoting from Renee Hirschon, ed., *Women and Property: Women as Property*, 1984, p. 19.
144. Interestingly, Bāṇa indicates some sort of harem jealousy while describing the women in Harṣa's camp: *HC*, II.83. See also Ridding, *Kādambarī*, p. 139 where Bāṇa provides information on ranks in a harem. Kādambarī's mother, Madirā, was given the title of chief queen by King Citraratha, 'bearing with it cowrie, sceptre and umbrella, marked by a golden throne and placing all the harem below her—a woman's rarest glory!' He does this as he is 'charmed by her countless virtues'.

145. The word 'maids', in this context, refers to a category of women servants who attended on the queen. They are to be distinguished from women attendants who were of a slightly higher rank and were seen as friends of the queen or royal personage in question. However, the dividing line between the two is rather ambiguous.
146. Dalal, *Conflict in Sanskrit Drama*, pp. 164, 139.
147. *RV*, I.10-16.
148. R.C. Dwivedi, 'Women in Classical Sanskrit Literature', in *Women Images*, ed. Jain and Mahan, p. 53.
149. Ridding, *Kādambarī*, p. 75.
150. Ibid., pp. 75–6.
151. Ibid., pp. 170–8. She even reproaches Candrāpīḍa for his inaction in this matter. Note that Madalekhā, Kādambarī's maid, complements Patralekhā's role in mediating between Candrāpīḍa and Kādambarī. Candrāpīḍa praises her for being 'clever' and for her 'skill in oratory' (p. 157).
152. *HC*, VI.224 on the 'blunders of heedless men arising from women'. He quotes this from Kāmandakīya's *Nītisāra*. Also G.C. Choudhary, *Political History of Northern India (from Jain sources—c. 650 AD to 1300 AD)*, Amritsar, Sohanlal Jaindharma Pracharak Samiti: 1954, p. 340 for interesting details in the *Nītisāra* regarding a king's personal safety. The king was to be protected first from women, then from claimants, and then from the sons. Women are depicted as sources of evil and bundles of hypocrisy. However, interestingly, Choudhary reiterates that the sphere of influence of queens was 'limited' to the palace, without considering the wider ramifications of the strictures (p. 339). Note here that Kalhaṇa sounds a similar warning in his *Rājataraṅgiṇī*.
153. Leslie, *Roles and Rituals*, p. 67.
154. Ridding, *Kādambarī*, p. 9. The queens of King Śūdraka's court are, however, only fleetingly mentioned and do not intrude into the narrative, thereby raising questions on the disproportionate attention paid to a female courtier.
155. Ibid., pp. 11-13. Lakṣmī apparently took this form 'to avoid contact with mankind', while she looked after her son, Vaiśampāyana, who was reborn as a parrot owing to a curse (p. 201).
156. *HC*, I.43–6. After bearing a son, Sārasvata, to Dadhīca, Sarasvatī returns to the heavens, necessitating a foster-mother, Akṣamālā, for the infant. Akṣamālā's son, Vatsa, was of the same age as Sārasvata and acquired all the latter's knowledge. Bāṇa was apparently a descendant of Vatsa. See also Pathak, *Ancient Historians*, p. 33. See *HC*, I.9–12 where goddess Sarasvatī, who bore a Brahmanical thread, is cursed by the sage Durvāsas for smiling at his mistake in chanting the Vedas and banished to the world of men. Her arrogance is also evident in her mocking of herself

on falling in love with a mortal, Dadhīca. Sāvitrī is described as 'the great goddess' in ascetic form. She rebukes Durvāsas in scathing terms and, more significantly, would have 'answered curse with curse' had not Sarasvatī intervened on the plea that brāhmaṇas deserve respect. Sāvitrī, subsequently, accompanies Sarasvatī to the earth for the duration of the curse. Shah, *The Making of Womanhood*, p. 145, says that the use of Sarasvatī as a legitimating authority for human enterprises and as an image of woman as the creator of culture might be treated as a kind of lingering evidence of an earlier, more public role for women.

157. *HC*, I.47, II.57. Bāṇa's mother's name was Rājadevī. Note that Bāṇa's step-brothers were Candrasena and Mātṛsena, in charge of the army and feudatory chiefs, respectively. Bāṇa's brothers are described as *bhrātarau pārāśavau*, a term indicating mixed parentage.
158. Ridding, *Kādambarī*, p. 68.
159. Note that some of Bāṇa's perceptive statements underline his reliability as an impartial observer. For instance, he says that 'all service is hateful . . . , and a court is full of dangers' (*HC*, II.62). Yet the security and prestige of his position as Harṣa's court poet is obvious (*HC*, II. 91).
160. Ridding, *Kādambarī*, pp. 95-7, 134 for Mahāśvetā's description.
161. For instance, Sanjukta Gupta, 'Women in the Śaiva/Śākta Ethos', in *Roles and Rituals*, ed. Leslie, p. 194.
162. Ridding, *Kādambarī*, p. 102.
163. Ibid., p. 139.
164. Ibid., pp. 97-8.
165. Ibid., p. 133. However, Mahāśvetā is not a typically non-sexual ascetic; she is merely containing her sexuality for a brief period.
166. Note that she fights her love for an ascetic but eventually approaches Puṇḍarīka, because he, 'being an ascetic and regretful of his love and timid by reason of his youth', would not take the initiative. Ibid., p. 120.
167. She weighs her options: '. . . like a base-born maiden, I cast away shame, relinquish self-control, desert modesty . . . transgress good behaviour, trample on conduct . . . without my father's leave, or my mother's approval, I were to go to him myself and offer him my hand' (Ridding, *Kādambarī*, p. 122).
168. Ibid., pp. 133–4.
169. Taralikā plays the same role of trusted advisor to Mahāśvetā as Patralekhā to Candrāpīḍa. Significantly, she advises Mahāśvetā to ignore her parents in the cause of her love (ibid., p. 123).
170. Ibid., p. 139.
171. Ibid., p. 141.
172. Ibid., p. 192. Note that Kādambarī undertakes to nurture Candrāpīḍa's body until the curse ends and he regains life. So she too adopts a form of asceticism in the forest.

173. Ibid., p. 146.
174. This indicates that the harem was not as isolated as it was supposed to be. On the one hand, the *strīniveśa* (the women's place) was to be in the deep interior of the royal residence, as per the *Arthaśāstra* (1 20.10). (Kumkum Roy, 'The King's Household: Structure/Space in the Śāstric Tradition', *Economic and Political Weekly*, vol. 27, nos. 43 and 44, 24-31 October, 1992, p. 56.) On the other hand, the *Harṣacarita* shows an ascetic, Bhairavācārya, and his messenger entering King Puṣpabhūti's harem and the king placing 'himself, his harem, his court and his treasury at the ascetic's disposal' (*HC*, III.118). However, the *Priyadarśikā* indicates that Udayana does not seem to have access to every member of the harem. He is obliged to ask Vasantaka for suggestions to meet Priyadarśikā (*PD*, II.22).
175. In response to her berating herself for being 'shameless', 'cruel', etc., Candrāpīḍa reminds her of the greatness of her sacrifice (Ridding, *Kādambarī*, pp. 135-7). Bāṇa uses a man's arguments to justify Mahāśvetā's resolve.
176. Ibid., p. 175.
177. Lynn Teskey Denton, 'Varieties of Hindu Female Asceticism', in *Roles and Rituals*, ed. Leslie, p. 216.
178. Leslie, *Roles and Rituals*, p. 11, observes that women ascetics deliberately flout the traditional religious duties of women (*strīdharma*) and social requirements of marriage/householdership. See also Julia Leslie, '*Strīsvabhāva*: The Inherent Nature of Women', in *Oxford University Papers on India*, ed. N.J. Allen et al., Delhi, Oxford University Press: 1987, vol. I, part 1, pp. 28–58. She talks of the 'total lack of interest in the woman except as wife', and notes that all fear and condemnation is directed at women as biological creatures, representatives of wild/untamed nature (pp. 43, 52).
179. However, S. Vats and Shakuntala Mudgal, eds., *Women and Society in Ancient India*, Faridabad, Om Publications: 1999, p. 104 cite the *Mītākṣara* as quoting the lawgiver, Baudhāyana, to the effect that some *ācāryas* did allow women to adopt the ascetic mode of life. See also Suvira Jaiswal, 'Female Images in the Arthaśāstra of Kauṭilya', *Social Scientist*, vol. 29, nos. 3–4, March-April 2001, pp. 57–8. She notes that Kauṭilya projects female ascetics as a significant element in female sociability, providing support to women at critical points. Jaiswal says that though law does not ordain an ascetic life for women, they may have adopted it as a resistance to patriarchal norms.
180. Kale, *Ratnāvalī*, p. 190. He says that judging by the use of Prakrit by women and minor characters in the dramas, it appears to have been in common usage by the fifth century BC. It was first used by women of even the higher classes, and by uneducated people generally.
181. Singhi, 'Gender Themes', in *Women Images*, ed. Jain and Mahan, p. 63

points out that this value system stems from a situation of differential social ideals for men and women. Mandakranta Bose, 'Satī: The Event and the Ideology', in *Faces of the Feminine in Ancient, Medieval, and Modern India*, ed. Mandakranta Bose, Delhi, Oxford University Press: 2000, pp. 23–4 notes that the tradition of validating *satī* in religious law did not begin till the early medieval times or the eighth century. See also Julia Leslie, 'Suttee or *Satī*: Victor or Victim?', in *Roles and Rituals*, ed. Leslie, pp. 177, 180.

182. Ridding, *Kādambarī*, pp. 135–6. Candrāpīḍa's view is that 'nothing makes a woman more despised' than to kill herself 'by poison, fire, or famine' (p. 150).
183. The verse reads—. . . *yadetadanumaraṇam nāma tadātiniśphalaṁ* . . . or 'a form of escape upheld only by fools'.
184. Note that Medhātithi too (*c.* 900), opposes *satī* and calls it a form of suicide. Ashvini Agrawal, 'Economic Aspects of Satī', in *Women in Indian History*, ed. Pawar, p. 60.
185. Devahuti, *Harsha*, p. 74.
186. *HC*, VIII.271–5 for a detailed description of Rājyaśrī's distress preparatory to mounting the pyre.
187. Dikshit, *Women in Sanskrit Dramas*, p. 192, states that burning oneself to death is not sanctioned by the lawgiver, Manu. Widows could either become celibate or ascetic.
188. Devahuti believes Harṣa's era to be significant for its political equilibrium and for the stresses inherent in the social tradition that started a trend towards constrictions in family and community life. It is possible to speculate on the role of women in this socio-political scenario. Devahuti, *Harsha*, p. ix.
189. W.F. Menski, 'Marital Expectations as Dramatized in Hindu Marriage Rituals', in *Roles and Rituals*, ed. Leslie, p. 52, qualifies that though it may not always be posssible to determine the thoughts of individual writers, they do give us the views of a particular elite which is valuable.

CHAPTER VIII

Kanauj: A Gendered Perspective

(The Reign of Yaśovarman, the Pratihāras and the Gāhaḍavālas)

We shall now consider the sources of the reign of Yaśovarman (*c.* AD 725–52), the Pratihāras (*c.* AD 810–1085) and the Gāhaḍavālas (*c.* AD 1085–1197).[1] As stressed in Chapter VI, it is not always possible to combine the information of the literary and epigraphic sources of this period to form a composite picture. However, despite this, reconstruction is enabled by a separate evaluation of the two parallel streams of information.

In this chapter, the sources will be considered in a sequential manner, pertaining to their relevant periods. This is necessary in order to seek out the changes that occurred in Kanauj over time. In addition, certain themes are particular to a source or its author, thus making it difficult to consider the same theme over the entire time-span.

YAŚOVARMAN OF KANAUJ

The information yielded by the epigraphic sources for Yaśovarman's reign can, at no point, be corroborated by the literary evidence, yet it has possibilities of its own. The Nālandā stone inscription of Yaśovarmadeva, undated though it is, and whose protagonist is the son of Yaśovarman's minister, offers possibilities of a gender analysis. The object of the inscription is to record that Mālāda, son of Yaśovarmadeva's minister, made certain gifts to a temple that King Bālāditya erected at Nālandā, to honour the Buddha.[2]

Notably, Mālāda is identified with reference to his mother and sister, in this inscription, and not his father or brother. Thus, while his father is called *mārgapati* and *udīcīpati*, merely indicative of his designation, and not by his actual name, Mālāda is described as the son (literally 'gladdener') of Bandhumatī, obviously his mother. Thus, verseș 3-4 read, '*hitaha śrīmānu-dārāśayaha putro mārga-pateha pratītatikinodicī-pater-mantriṇaha, mālādo bhuvi nandanori-damano yo vabandhumatyā-suadhordīnā-śāparipūrṇai.*'

It is further stated that the gift has been made by 'him who is the brother of Nirmmalā.' (v. 11—*yaśasā bhuvi nirmalāyā bhrātrā vyadhayi śaradindu-vibhānanāyāha*...); the gift was made 'for the sake of the welfare and longevity of the parents, brother, wife, sister, son and friends of Mālāda' (v. 12).

The implications of this inscription are many. That Mālāda is mentioned only with reference to the female members of his family is significant. That the names of his father and brother are missing is intriguing. This omission could have been a conscious decision on Mālāda's part. Alternatively, the inscriber of the record might have felt the need to highlight the female names alone. More significantly, it could be indicative of a general trend wherein the female members of non-royal families begin to feature in inscriptions. Thus this inscription departs from the conventions of the royal inscriptions of Harṣa's reign and could well indicate the growing visibility of non-royal women in public life.

However, the inscription has not been subjected to this sort of analysis. Stress is usually laid on the identity of the king and on other technical aspects. H. Sastri, for instance, only speculates that the names of the women are Sanskritic and could apply to ladies of foreign descent, too.[3]

For a comprehensive gender analysis, however, a focus on the literary works of Yaśovarman's period is essential. What now follows is entirely based on Bhavabhūti's *Uttara-Rāmacarita* and the *Mālatīmādhava* whose potential for gender study is momentous. The novel innovations of Bhavabhūti and the clear analytical articulation of his unconventional ideas make his work crucially significant.

The importance of Bhavabhūti's works as a reflector of gender issues is in contrast to Vākpati's *Gauḍavaho*. Vākpati's treatment of women as an ambiguous, amorphous whole is striking. Thus, Yaśovarman's dalliance with his 'enemies' captive wives' (*GV*,

105, 839–43, 1069), 'courtesans' (*GV*, 161–6) and 'the band of beauties' (*GV*, 207, 787, 1125) is described in detail, along with 'the love-sports of the wives of the army' (*GV*, 694). This leads to much erotic verse, with no mention of any specific woman.[4] Incidentally, this omission has not been really seen as a problem. S.M. Mishra, for instance, accepts Vākpati's silence without speculating on the identity of Yaśovarman's wife/wives, and only briefly deals with the king's 'amorous sports' under the heading 'His Pastimes and Amusements.'[5]

The lack of mention of any specific woman is all the more mystifying in view of the apparent intrigues in Yaśovarman's harem that are revealed by Jain sources. The *Bappabhaṭṭisūricarita* states that Yaśovarman's son, Āma, was born of his chief queen, Suyaśā, during her exile at Rāmasainya due to the intrigues of a co-wife.[6] The duo was subsequently restored to their positions and though Āma was a spendthrift, thereby angering Yaśovarman, he was eventually appointed Yaśovarman's successor, so that the machinations of Suyaśā's unnamed rival were finally thwarted. Yet the identity of this woman and the nature of the intrigue remain unknown.

The Uttara-Rāmacarita

The *Uttara-Rāmacarita* represents Bhavabhūti's attempt to reinterpret the latter portion of the original *Rāmāyaṇa* of Vālmīki. It centres round Sītā's abandonment by Rāma due to rumours regarding her chastity and the implications of his decision. The text has been seen as an exercise in a psychological analysis of Sītā's predicament[7] and a novel interpretation of the ethics behind Rāma's decision. By extension, it is seen as an attempt to 'redraw' the relations between this couple.[8] This rethinking of an accepted tradition has bearings not just on Bhavabhūti's perspective, but also on the entire process of social thought regarding a woman's chastity.

Romila Thapar suggests that variations on original epic forms facilitate assimilation from classical tradition to local culture.[9] What is pertinent to the local culture can be incorporated into the epic through fresh episodes. There are thematic parallels, but also crucial differences in certain episodic embellishments. In the process, much is revealed of contemporary thought in the socio-political milieu, as is the case with the *Uttara-Rāmacarita*. To understand the potential of this text, Sītā's abandonment will be viewed not just by its political associations, but also through the perspective of the principal characters.

THE POLITICAL IMPLICATIONS OF SĪTĀ'S ABANDONMENT

The most crucial feature of Bhavabhūti's *Uttara-Rāmacarita* is not Rāma's perception of Sītā's abandonment as a politically sagacious move, but the decision becoming the subject of a public debate. The palpable regret and uncertainty that surrounds Rāma's resolve is forcibly expressed by way of a public debate on Sītā's plight. This is a clever innovation that has momentous bearings on the question of gender.

A fact of primary significance is that Sītā is sacrificed in accordance with the *prajānurañjana* ideal of pleasing the people.[10] At the outset, Rāma states—

> Should I be required to give up affection, mercy and happiness, or even Jānakī (Sītā), in order to propitiate the people, I will have no pangs (*UR*, I.12—*sneharh dayārh ca saukhyarh ca yadi vā jānakīmapi, ārādhanaya lokasya muṅcato nāsti me vyathā*). Queen . . . have mercy! This calumny may last till the end of your life. The people who are hard, have to be propitiated by those who treasure their family (*UR*, I.14).

Subsequently, when he hears the people's rumours and resolves to abandon Sītā, he says, 'For dutiful men, propitiating the people by whatever actions, is a vow. If . . . a scurrilous scandal were to descend owing to my connection, woe! Fie on my wretched self!' (*UR*, I.41–2). When Lakṣmaṇa remonstrates with him, he retorts, 'How dare you say that the citizens and village-folk are bad men!' (*UR*, I.44). He even justifies their doubts regarding the fire ordeal since it had taken place in faraway Laṅkā, the place of her abduction by Rāvaṇa. In this sense, the *Uttara-Rāmacarita* follows the tone of the original.

However, significantly, the very act of deferring to the people on this matter is subjected to in-depth questioning in the text. Thus, that such a decision is taken against Rāma's personal inclinations and faith in Sītā's purity is clearly stated. Rāma says, 'Why these stray means of purification for her who was absolutely pure even in her birth? . . . Whatever evil is spoken by us is surely not deserved by you (Sītā)' (*UR*, I.13, 14). He also angrily comments, 'Fie on this stay in a stranger's house!' (*UR*, I.40) . . . 'The worlds are holy because of you but unholy are the utterances of people about you!' (*UR*, I.43) Recalling his succumbing to the 'sovereign subjects of the city and village', he cries aloud—'Please forgive!' (*UR*, III.32). There cannot be a sharper contrast with the original Rāma who stoically stands by his decision and refuses to be swayed by emotional afterthought.

Likewise, Bhavabhūti uses the figure of Janaka, Sītā's father, to question the need for yielding to public opinion:

> . . . Who is this fire to purify our progeny? . . . Already insulted by Rāmabhadra, we are given a fresh insult by these people indulging in such talk' (*UR*, IV.11—*āha koyamagnir-nāmāsmat-prasūti-pari-shodhane, kaṣṭamevam-vādinā janena rāma-bhadra-paribhūtā api vayaṁ punaha pari-bhūyā-mahe*).

He further laments 'the hard-heartedness of the wicked citizens' and the 'rashness of King Rāma' to which Arundhatī, Sage Kaśyapa's wife, lamely replies that the people 'though beggarly, have to be protected' (*UR*, IV.24). It is clear, therefore, that Rāma's action cannot be easily condoned by him or by others, even though it is politically prudent.

At this juncture, the interplay staged by heavenly nymphs to depict Sītā's plight assumes significance. It provides a logical culmination to the doubts voiced throughout the text, and brings Rāma's decision within the scrutiny of the principal characters. It is also a means of demonstrating Sītā's anguish to the public, thereby prompting them to reconsider the logic of their condemnatory stance.[11]

The conversation between Pṛthvī, Sītā's mother, and Bhāgīrathī, the family deity of the Ikṣvākus, encapsulates it all. Pṛthvī's scathing comment on Rāma runs thus—

> He did not care for the authority of the hand which he as a child grasped in his childhood. He did not care for my authority or that of Janaka; nor

for the proof of the fire, nor that of her obedience, nor of the family's continuance (*UR*, VII.5—*na pramāṇī-kṛtaha pāṇirbālye bālena pīditaha, nāha na janako nāgnirnānu-vṛttīrna santatihi*).

She further chides Sītā for referring to Rāma as 'my noble lord', demanding, 'What is he to you?' (*UR*, VII.6).[12] However, Bhāgīrathī's response stresses Rāma's dilemma and the difficulty of his decision. She says,

> That the entire people ought to be propitiated, this is the family treasure to the Ikṣvākus. Therefore, in this difficult position, what could that child (Rāma) do? (*UR*, VII.6—*ikṣvākū-nāṁ kula-dhanaṁ-idaṁ yat-samārādhanī-yaha kṛtsno lokasta-diti viśame kiṁ sa vatsaha karotu*.)

The people's view is clearly targeted when Sītā's purity is stressed in blatant terms by Pṛthvī and Bhāgīrathī, causing Rāma to say, 'Let the people hear, if they care to' (*UR*, VII.9). Subsequently, when Arundhatī proclaims Sītā's 'holy and chaste character' to the 'people of the cities and villages', she adds, 'What is your opinion about accepting her back?' Lakṣmaṇa then points out that 'all the citizens and villagers and the entire crowd of creatures, receiving this rebuff from the noble Arundhatī, are bowing down before the noble queen' (*UR*, VII.19). He, too, bows to Sītā, acknowledging his complicity in Rāma's plan (*UR*, VII.20). On Arundhatī's orders, Sītā is appointed Rāma's 'religious companion' (*UR*, VII.19), thereby proclaiming his faith in her purity.

Thus, very significantly, it is the combined persuasion of women which restores Sītā to her original status, questions the stance of the people, and ensures a show of unanimous regret. In the process, a cherished political ideal is criticized and the involvement of a woman's character in the issue shown to be completely unwarranted. By doing so, Bhavabhūti subverts the original story where Sītā's abandonment is shown to be sad but inevitable.[13]

In addition, Bhavabhūti introduces the added effect of reuniting the couple, a departure from the original where the resentful Sītā re-enters the earth after her purity is proclaimed. At the end of Bhavabhūti's play, Sītā dramatically rises from the waters, escorted by Pṛthvī and Bhāgīrathī, and revives the swooning Rāma by her touch. Though the reunion has been termed a bold step, one beyond the scope of contemporary imagination,[14] it actually lends a curiously conventional ending to a hitherto unorthodox rendering. However, it has been speculated that Bhavabhūti was desirous of showing the idealistic oneness of the duo and used their reunion as a means to show it.[15]

In conclusion, it is also important to consider the composition of the 'people' who had cast aspersions on Sītā's purity. Janaka says that the subjects are mainly 'brahmins, children, old and infirm, people and a host of females!' (*UR*, IV.25). So 'people' is a very loose term, making it difficult to pinpoint the actual culprits. However, that 'a host of females' is said to be involved is interesting. Could this mean that Bhavabhūti indirectly indicts women for Sītā's ordeal? Or does he deliberately ensure that Sītā is strongly supported by women to show that not all of them thought alike on the matter? What he establishes beyond doubt is the error of deferring to the people on the issue of Sītā's purity.[16] The public stance is convincingly shown as unworthy, doubly so when a sovereign succumbs to it.

The Figure of Rāma and its Implications

To highlight the ethics of Rāma's decision, Bhavabhūti cleverly innovates in projecting him as an unusually sensitive and emotional figure. This is a sharp contrast to the decisive and implacable Rāma, the king *par excellence*, for whom the law and duties assume precedence over everything else. Bhavabhūti's Rāma is fragile enough to question his own decisions and regret their implications. His mental anguish even precipitates fainting spells.

The regret is nowhere more evident than in Rāma's lament: 'I have turned myself into a murderer, my action is thoroughly disgusting!' (*UR*, I.45—. . . *ati-bībhatsa-karmā nṛśansosmi samvṛttaha*). Furthermore, he reflects—'. . . What right have I, an untouchable sinner that I am, to profane the queen? . . . I have become an outcaste by this unprecedented performance!' (*UR*, I.46). He even addresses his right hand in sarcasm, saying—'You are Rāma's limb, who was clever in exiling Sītā . . . How can you have mercy?' (*UR*, II.10). He refers to himself as one who has 'destroyed his darling, and is full of sin and all alone' (*UR*, II.28).[17]

This entire aspect of self-introspection and regret is a novel addition. The reaction of the original Rāma is significantly different. Beyond tearfully stressing that a man cannot live in infamy, he does *not* respond in such a strong, self-condemnatory vein. Nor does he speculate on the ethics of his decision after his initial distress. However, in Bhavabhūti's *Uttara-Rāmacarita*, the words 'sinner', 'crime', and 'murderer' are used, pointing to the gargantuan proportions of Rāma's regret. He even informs his mother, Kauśalyā, that he is a sinner and that after what he did to Sītā, he has lost his right to pity or mercy (*UR*, VI.42—*janakā-nāṁ raghū-nāṁ ca yatkṛtsnaṁ gotra-maṅgalaṁ, tatrāpya-karuṇe pāpe vṛthā vaha karuṇā mayi*). Even when Sītā is finally restored to him, he remains overwhelmed by the enormity of his crime and the mercy nevertheless shown him (*UR*, VII.19).[18]

Bhavabhūti shows, therefore, that in pandering to the people's whims and abandoning Sītā, Rāma is actually abandoning a part of himself. This is in keeping with his notion of an ideal couple in that the two are incomplete without each other. However, his more important aim is to portray Rāma's decision as an unwarranted and unethical one, amply proved by his anguished regret.

THE IMPLICATIONS OF SĪTĀ'S PORTRAYAL

To appreciate the implications of Rāma's decision, it would be worthwhile to examine the portrayal of Sītā in the *Uttara-Rāmacarita*. What is immediately apparent is that Bhavabhūti's Sītā is more submissive and forgiving than the original one. This is possibly a deliberate variation keeping in mind the desired result of her eventual reunion with Rāma.

At the outset, appreciating Rāma's willingness to sacrifice her to please the subjects, Sītā says—'Just for this reason is my noble Lord the foremost of the family of Raghus!' (*UR*, I.12). Subsequently, when speculation assumes reality and Lakṣmaṇa abandons her in the forest, she reacts with total dispiritedness and is taken away by Pṛthvī and Bhāgīrathī (itself a significant variation) in the throes of labour.

The original Sītā, paradoxically, is more spirited in her reaction. She stresses her purity, charges Lakṣmaṇa to convey this to Rāma and points to her condition as laughable. She further talks of drowning as a preferable option and is deeply upset that Rāma acted on the words of some strangers. This resentment eventually causes her to reject the possibility of a reunion with him, preferring to re-enter the earth instead.[19]

In a limited sense, Bhavabhūti's Sītā is also conscious of the fact that she was abandoned 'without cause or mercy' (*UR*, III.13). Yet though her life 'pricks with the dart of an unreasonable abandonment' (*UR*, III.15), she gives priority to her concern for Rāma's well-being and his loneliness. She even feels embarrassed by her 'persistent attachment' to Rāma, in spite of everything (*UR*, III.43). Thus, when she encounters Rāma in the Pañchavaṭī forest after twelve years and in an invisible state—another important innovation—she is deeply moved by his anguish. She laments her 'luckless' state which has brought 'torture' and agony to Rāma (*UR*, III.43).

Any trace of resentment is removed when Sītā hears of her golden image being used by Rāma for his sacrifice and in the play's conclusion, her joy at being appointed Rāma's religious companion is expressed: 'My noble husband knows how to wipe out Sītā's sorrow' (*UR*, VII.20). All this conveys the impression that the actual fact of abandonment was more hurtful to her than the fact that Rāma was responsible for it. Once the outward trappings of her position are restored, she is wholly satisfied, choosing not to reflect too deeply on Rāma's culpability.

PORTRAYALS OF OTHER WOMEN AND THEIR IMPLICATIONS

That Sītā is the only truly conventional female figure in Bhavabhūti's text is obvious. Her stereotypical reactions can be sharply contrasted with the fierce condemnation of Rāma indulged in by her own mother, Pṛthvī, and by the sylvan deity, Vāsantī. An original creation of Bhavabhūti's, Vāsantī plays the significant role of relentlessly reminding Rāma of old associations and ridiculing his decision of abandoning Sītā. Addressing Rāma by his formal title (to indicate her disapproval), she bluntly asks, 'O, Your Majesty, why are you so dreadfully cruel?' (*UR*, III.26) . . . 'O ruthless, it's true that you love fame! But could there be a more terrible infamy than this?' (*UR*, III.27).

This prompts Rāma to justify his agony at great length. However, in keeping with her portrayal, Sītā continually berates Vāsantī for tormenting Rāma who 'deserves loving treatment from everybody' (*UR*, III.26). Unwilling to acknowledge the searing truth of her statements, she begs Vāsantī to stop and is angry with her for aggravating Rāma's anguish.

The figure of Kauśalyā, too, seems more spirited in comparison with Sītā. Her appearance, at this juncture, is in any case an innovation. In the *Uttara-Rāmacarita*, Kauśalyā, the other queens and Arundhatī are attending a sacrifice at the time of Sītā's abandonment. They 'subsequently refuse to re-enter Ayodhyā 'which is robbed of the daughter-in-law' and determine to live in Vālmīki's penance-grove instead. Whether their anger is directed towards Rāma or the people is unclear.

Much of Kauśalyā's reaction to Rāma's decision is revealed in her talk with Sītā's father, Janaka.[20] She is reluctant to face Janaka in the knowledge of Sītā's plight. Subsequently, in another novel departure, Janaka actually taunts Kauśalyā by asking her if she is well, prompting the chamberlain to intervene on her behalf and say, '. . . it's not appropriate for you to torture the queen, who is already under heavy sorrow and who, out of the same angry grief, has long since discarded the sight of the moon-like face of dear Rāma' (*UR*, IV.11). In fact, Janaka's belligerence at this point terrifies Kauśalyā and she begs Arundhatī to appease his anger.[21] This, again, contravenes the original where Janaka's reaction is not really dwelt upon and he never shows any signs of wrath or aggression. Nor is there any such strained meeting between him and Kauśalyā.

At this point, Janaka makes certain interesting remarks on his affinal kin that have no parallel in the original. He reveals that though custom demanded that the bride's parents worship the son-in-law's relatives, in his relations with Daśaratha 'it became exactly opposite', and Daśaratha 'endeavoured to propitiate' Janaka (*UR*, IV.17). More significantly, he reminisces about the time when he would be the one 'to bring reconciliation or to vent the anger' of Daśaratha and Kauśalyā (*UR*, IV.15). In the original *Rāmāyaṇa*, Kauśalyā neither quarrels with Daśaratha nor does Janaka assume such overweening importance in their lives.

OVERALL IMPLICATIONS OF THE TEXT

There has been much speculation on the main theme of the text and the actual purpose behind Bhavabhūti's variations. While Minakshi Dalal feels that 'love-in-separation' is its essence, R.G. Harshe says that the central idea is not Sītā's abandonment but the conflict between two duties.[22] Thus, it attempts to show 'how the husband Rāma suffered by the dutifulness of the king Rāma'. On the other hand, R. Dikshit[23] and S.M. Mishra believe that Bhavabhūti was influenced by the general political disintegration in the eighth century, consequent on the Arab invasions. Thus, not only does he present Rāma as an ideal ruler, he also effects his reunion with Sītā to encourage and legitimize the contemporary practice of accepting back into families women who had been raped or captured by Muslim invaders from Sindh.[24]

All these inferences may well have an element of truth in them. However, it is clear that the single crucial significance of the *Uttara-Rāmacarita* has not been discerned. This is the attempt to show that a woman's purity cannot be made the subject of public debate, and that a ruler should not defer to public opinion on this matter. All the variations that Bhavabhūti makes work towards this aim.[25]

Thus when Beni Prasad says that the text 'dares to criticize' Rāma's action, but admits the regard that the king must pay to public sentiment, he is completely missing the point.[26] The text does *not* condone Rāma's propitiation of the people in this matter. He is shown to bitterly regret his decision and the public is made to change its views. Likewise, when A. Borooah calls the interplay 'grand', 'effective', 'interesting' and 'touching', he misses its actual role as a forum for a public debate on Rāma's action.[27] It is all that he brands it and much more besides.

Bhavabhūti's stance assumes crucial importance in a patriarchal milieu that judges a woman by her purity and sets exacting standards for it. The centrality of this issue in Brahmanical patriarchy, we have seen, was because the purity of caste was contingent upon it.[28] That Bhavabhūti questions an unthinking acceptance of Sītā's abandonment based on her apparent lack of purity is vitally unconventional. The fact that he shows the fury of the women, making them the means of Sītā's resurrection, has, again, momentous implications. Mishra admits that the women of the *Uttara-Rāmacarita* are not conventional or replicas of their counterparts in the original *Rāmāyaṇa*,[29] but he should also note that the very unconventionality of their portrayal is designed for a specific purpose.

Finally, there are two statements in the text that encapsulate Bhavabhūti's stance towards and understanding of women. At the outset, he says,

> As about the purity of women, so about the goodness of compositions, people are malicious (*UR*, I.5—*yathā strīṇāṁ tathā vācaṁ sādhutve durjano janaha*).

Furthermore, he makes Arundhatī say:

> Virtues alone are the source of worship in a virtuous person, neither sex nor age! (*UR*, IV.11—*guṇāha pūjā-sthānaṁ guṇiśu na ca liṅga na ca vayaha*).

The impression conveyed is that of a man impatient with loose talk on female chastity and believing in the fundamental equality of the sexes. Thus, it is true that Bhavabhūti 'pursued psychological introspection to a point unprecedented in his cultural environment', but that he pursued it in the cause of women has an important bearing on a gender study of his time.[30]

In conclusion, it is interesting to note that the *Candrāvatī Rāmāyaṇa* by a poet, Candrāvatī, in sixteenth-century Bengal is a hitherto 'silenced' text that is considered incomplete and of poor literary value, as it focuses entirely on Sītā and her life-story. Rāma is on the periphery and is projected as a poor king, husband, brother, father, and a jealous personality. This 'personal interpretation' of Rāma seen from the wronged woman's perspective is significant, although it is outside the purview of this study.[31]

The Mālatīmādhava

The *Mālatīmādhava* needs to be viewed in conjunction with the *Uttara-Rāmacarita* for a complete enunciation of Bhavabhūti's unconventional views on women. This original, romantic play revolves around the female Buddhist mendicant, Kāmandakī, whose potential has, hitherto, not been assessed properly. Though she is the prime mover and determinant of the action, her role has been seen as answering certain religious questions alone. To understand the implications of her portrayal on the contemporary society and polity, it is necessary to focus on her actual role, as also the motives behind her creation. Other gendered aspects of the text will also be examined in the course of this analysis.

Before embarking on an analysis of Kāmandakī's portrayal, however, it would be pertinent to give a brief summary of the story. Kāmandakī is desirous of effecting a match between Mālatī, the daughter of the minister Bhūrivasu, and Mādhava, the son of the minister Devarāta. This is in pursuance of a childhood vow taken by the two men that they would conclude an alliance between their children, and which was witnessed by their fellow students, Kāmandakī and Saudāmanī. The king poses a problem by wanting Mālatī for his friend, Nandana. However, Kāmandakī is able to frustrate Nandana's designs, and fulfil her friends' vow by marrying off Mālatī and Mādhava. One can now consider the various implications of her role.

THE IMPLICATIONS OF CO-EDUCATION

Since the entire action of the play revolves around a vow taken in a co-educational set-up, it would be worthwhile to examine the implications of this aspect. It is generally conceded that Bhavabhūti's works afford 'the earliest clear descriptions of co-education'.[32] Thus, one has the example of Ātreyī in the *Uttara-Rāmacarita*,[33] and that of Kāmandakī, Saudāmanī, Bhūrivasu and Devarāta in the *Mālatīmādhava*. This has been viewed by some as a reflection of the educational pattern of Bhavabhūti's time. Yet Borooah argues against the presumption that the education in this period was either general or openly conducted.[34]

However, it is clear that both these views are concerned with a very limited perspective. The really significant point is that Bhavabhūti develops the potential of the co-educational set-up in such a manner that it is shown to have influenced the life and ambition of a woman who participated in it. Among other things, this is evident from the manner in which Kāmanadakī is influenced by the 'lasting bond of friendship' formed with her fellow students.[35] This bond impels her to make the fruition of her friends' vow her overriding ambition, relegating her religion and even her life to second place.

Thus, Kāmandakī openly acknowledges her determination to fulfil her friends' 'desires', even 'by sacrificing my life or my vows' (*MM*, prelude to I.9). Questions posed by her disciple, Avalokitā, for instance, on how she could 'commit' herself when she has rid her mind 'of worldly attachments', wears 'a mendicant's robes' and lives 'by the begging bowl' (*MM*, prelude to I.8) do not deter her. That Bhūrivasu trusts her implicitly in this matter is to her 'the strongest proof of his regard', spurring her desire to be worthy of it.

It is also highly significant that in pursuance of her aim, Kāmandakī is shown to subvert traditional notions of womanly fickleness and helplessness. There is a certain cold-blooded intent and ruthlessness in her planning and execution. Not only does she involve her disciples and the servant-girls of the monastery in her plan, she also subtly develops the love between Mālatī and Mādhava to the desired end without betraying her actual interest in it. She effectively performs the role of a trusted go-between. Her plan is so well-conceived that she envisages and finally effects the marriage of Makaranda (Mādhava's friend) and Madayantikā (Nandana's sister) as well.[36] Here she practices a form of 'benevolent despotism' on them (*MM*, VI.7).

Moreover, in pursuance of her aim, Kāmandakī indirectly challenges the king and completely frustrates his plans regarding Mālatī. Her boldness in this regard contrasts sharply with the fearful compliance of Bhūrivasu and Devarāta with the king's desires, though these are at complete variance with their own. Thus, Mālatī's father, Bhūrivasu, tells the king that he is free to decide about his daughter's future. Kāmandakī bases her attack on the crucial meaning of Bhūrivasu's ambiguous words. She proclaims them to be 'essentially false', since to defer to a king in determining a daughter's marriage 'has no sanction in either morality or custom' (*MM*, IV.4).

Not only is the unconventionality of this utterance striking, it also depicts the wit and sagacity of Kāmandakī. Significantly, the king later accepts the marriage of the lead pair with equanimity, thereby proving the rightness of Kāmandakī's stance and showing her in a more courageous and persevering light than the shadowy ministers. Thus, though she later attributes her success to Mādhava's merit, her plans and her 'pupils' labours', Mādhava and Makaranda rightly credit it to 'the unswerving strategy of the mighty' (*MM*, X.23), a clear allusion to her efforts.[37]

One should also note that it is actually the combined efforts of two women that bring their male friends' vow to fruition. The fourth member of the quartet, Saudāmanī, rescues Mālatī from a sorceress. Her role is appreciated by Kāmandakī: 'It is you the world must salute, whose miraculous power is shown in such deeds beyond even a *bodhisattva's* encompassing' (*MM*, X.21). Although Saudāmanī's level of involvement was nowhere as intense as Kāmandakī's, she was equally concerned about the welfare of her fellow students. This is evident in her displaying satisfaction at the 'cherished desire' of her old friends achieving fruition (*MM*, X.23).

At this juncture, one could examine a secondary implication: the co-educational set-up is shown to impel women towards unconventional life choices. Bhavabhūti is stressing the great potential of such a system for women. Thus, while their male friends adopt conventional career choices, both Kāmandakī and Saudāmanī eschew the paths normally prescribed for women and adopt those of their own liking. Though both adopt Buddhism, Saudāmanī later changes her faith to Śaivism and acquires magical powers. She lives alone with her own set of disciples and acquires fame for her supernatural skills. Nowhere are these choices viewed with suspicion or disfavour.[38] This easy acceptance may not have been an actual fact of the contemporary patriarchal society but even so, is significant in itself.

A final, highly significant implication of the co-educational set-up is reflected in Kāmandakī's views on marriage and the equality of sexes implicit in it. In her advice to the newly-married Mālatī and Mādhava, she says that a husband and wife are 'like a dear friend, like all one's kin, like all desires, like a fortune, like life itself to each other'.[39] She adds, 'That is the truth I would have you learn in each other' (*MM*, VI.18). There is no hint of a submissive relationship here but rather one of reciprocity and equality. Kāmandakī's participation in a system of equality of education could well have helped shape her views. Consequently, Bhavabhūti's views on marriage and the relations between the sexes are clear.

The idealistic note is, however, tempered by a sensitive and strongly pragmatic observation on the aftermath of marriage from a woman's perspective. Lavangikā, Mālatī's companion, remarks on the 'rankling darts, bitterly remembered till life's end, which make living in another's house so hateful—the fearful indignities which make a family dread the birth of a girl' (*MM*, VII.1).[40] Such a remark could only come from one who is acutely aware of a woman's place in society and has a sympathetic understanding towards it. Needless to say, such an observation is not paralleled in any other contemporary work that, instead, lauds the husband's home as the right place for a woman.

In conclusion, one should note that the education of women, whether co-educational or otherwise, was encouraged for a limited span of time in early India. The Vedic sources bear testimony to this, as also the *Bṛhadāraṇyaka Upaniṣad* that mentions rituals by which a person prays for the birth of a daughter who would be a *paṇḍitā* or learned lady.[41] With the growing rigidity of caste society and the accent on women's sexuality, however, female education was either curtailed or limited to arts that would serve them for marriage purposes. Contemporary sources talk of singing, dancing and painting as the accomplishments that girls needed to master, not logic or metaphysics, nor Hindu scriptures and the folklore that Kāmandakī and Saudāmanī are shown pursuing.[42] In such a context, therefore, Bhavabhūti's views are intriguingly unorthodox.

And yet, Borooah's view that it is 'blindness' to admit that Hindu women and men could mingle freely, as Bhavabhūti would have us presume, is too extreme.[43] If this were so, why did Bhavabhūti choose to portray such a set-up at all? Did he want to show the sexes equal in every sense, including educational matters? Did he want to indicate the possibility of women leading independent lives on the strength of their educational base? More significantly, did he want to show that friendships between the sexes need not necessarily have sexual undertones? These possibilities considerably enhance the potential of the co-educational element in the text beyond being a comment on a possibly contemporaneous situation.

IMPLICATIONS OF KĀMANDAKĪ'S PORTRAYAL ON RELIGION

It is generally conceded that the *Mālatīmādhava* 'rather novelly' highlights the lapses and laxities in Buddhism that sapped its strength and paved its way for its merger with the Brahmanical religion.[44] In this sense, Bhavabhūti apparently reflects his epoch that marked the resurgence of neo-Hinduism and the decadence of Buddhism in India.[45] To concede this, one needs to examine the implications of Kāmandakī's portrayal on contemporary religion and on the apparent shrinking of differences between the two faiths.

That Kāmandakī and her disciples, Avalokitā and Buddharakṣitā, represent the Mahāyāna school of Buddhism is stated at the outset. However, that Kāmandakī's sole object is the marriage of Mālatī and Mādhava and not *nirvāṇa* is considered proof of the laxities in Buddhism that enabled a female mendicant to indulge such a worldly involvement.[46] Not only do her disciples evince surprise at her desire, she herself acknowledges the influence of 'this very friendship so at variance with my mendicant's garb' (*MM*, II.5). Her commitment is so intense that it becomes the driving ambition of her life and even prompts her to consider taking her life, at a later stage, when Mālatī is abducted by the sorceress, Kapālakuṇḍalā, and feared dead.[47] This is obviously at variance with the behavioural dictates for a Buddhist nun. Furthermore, the willing involvement of Kāmandakī's disciples and other inmates of the convent in her scheme is considered additional proof of the same laxity in discipline.

The knowledge displayed by Kāmandakī and her disciples of Hindu mythology and tradition is taken as proof of the closeness between Buddhism and contemporary Brahmanism. Kāmandakī cites the examples of Śakuntalā and Ūrvaśī, and the authority of Aṅgīra, to advise Mālatī on the course of her love. Similarly, Buddharakṣitā quotes the *Kāmasūtra* with reference to the treatment of married ladies. Furthermore, Kāmandakī worships in the shrine of Śiva and continually prays to 'the Gods' for success (*MM*, VI.7), a phrase that would apply more to the Hindu pantheon than to Buddhism. Finally, Kāmandakī's fulsome praise of the Śaivite Saudāmanī indicates her appreciation of the latter's powers, holding them to even surpass a *bodhisattva's* comprehension. Hence, it would appear on the strength of all this evidence, that Kāmandakī's role has, largely, implications on the contemporary religious sphere.

However, one should reflect more closely on Kāmandakī's portrayal. Could it be that Bhavabhūti does *not* use her to depict the lapses in the practice of the faith, but only to show that friendships could often transcend religious considerations? This supposition is strengthened by the fact that he does not specifically target Buddhism anywhere in the text. Even Borooah points out that his introduction of female Buddhist ascetics without a word against them was unlike other contemporary writers who unhesitatingly ridiculed the religion.[48]

Furthermore, no specific information is revealed of the Buddhist way of life or of the requirements of the monastery, apart from the fact that mendicants were not supposed to involve themselves in worldly matters. Such a stipulation, however, could apply to a mendicant of any religion and not just Buddhism. By extension, this could show that Bhavabhūti lacked a detailed knowledge of Buddhism and that he never intended the religious question to be the focus of his text.[49] M. Winternitz is one of the few who recognize that Kāmandakī has 'so little to do with religion' that it is only because it is expressly mentioned in the prelude that her identity as a Buddhist nun is known.[50]

Bhavabhūti could have made Kāmandakī a Buddhist ascetic to portray the unconventionality of her actions without completely outraging the tenets of contemporary Brahmanical patriarchy. In this sense too, though his choice of her religion is deliberate, it has nothing to do with denigrating Buddhism. Had she been shown as a Hindu woman, he might have had to dilute the nature and content of his plot to show at least some outward signs of conformity. However, by making her a Buddhist, he effectively extends the scope and freedom of his play.

Thus, it is clear that there can be more than one reason for

Kāmandakī's centrality of presence, not merely the religious factor. This is highly significant inasmuch as the *Mālatīmādhava* has hitherto been analysed largely from the religious point of view. The validity of the religious argument is not being wholly discounted, but it is vital to acknowledge other factors that could stem from the contemporary socio-political milieu.

We should note that Bhavabhūti uses the figures of Saudāmanī and her one-time disciple, Kapālakuṇḍalā, to reflect the increasingly popular Śakti cult of his time.[51] The bloodthirsty desire of Kapālakuṇḍalā and her new mentor, Aghoraghaṇṭa, for human sacrifice before the shrine of Karālā (Cāmuṇḍā) has a parallel in the *Gauḍavaho* where the worship of Vindhyavāsinī, another element of the Śakti cult, is seen to be associated with similar rituals.[52] It is this, rather than Buddhism's declining state, that Bhavabhūti seems to take 'special cognizance' of.[53]

IMPLICATIONS OF SOME OTHER PORTRAYALS

It would be worth our while to examine the portrayals of Mālatī and Mādhava with the intriguing blend of conventional and unconventional elements conjured by Bhavabhūti. Mālatī's spirited response to the alleged selection of Nandana as her suitor by her father, Bhūrivasu, is striking. The indignation displayed is at complete variance with the weeping and resigned compliance of other heroines.

It is important to note, however, that Kāmandakī provides much of the instigation. She deviously hints that Bhūrivasu has promised Mālatī to win 'the friendship of that crony of the king's' (*MM*, II.7). Thus, Mālatī demands—'What, Father sacrificing me to the king? Father thinks less of his own daughter than of pleasing the king' (*MM*, II.7). Later, when her match with Nandana is apparently finalized, she remarks, 'by his hardness Father has shown himself an ogre' (*MM*, IV.7). Such resentful statements are contrary to the norm of unquestioned obedience expected in such matters. Moreover, that such displeasure could be openly expressed has significant undertones in the entire question of a woman's response to the choice of her marriage partner in a patriarchal society.

Yet Mālatī's spirited resistance on this issue remains the sole trace of unconventionality in her character. When her friend,

Lavangikā, implies that Mādhava was willing to marry her secretly, she coyly remarks—'Oh heavens, she is suggesting things that no young girl may contemplate', upon which Kāmandakī upbraids her for being a 'timid daughter' (*MM*, VI.14).[54]

That Mālatī subsequently marries Mādhava in a secret ceremony without her parents' knowledge is not proof of her daring but of her highly suggestible temperament, a fact gauged well by Kāmandakī and used to her purpose. It is Kāmandakī's constant prompting that enables Mālatī to challenge her parents and the king, and fulfil her heart's desire. Thus, Kāmandakī gives her examples of defiance in the name of love, but cleverly brands them 'reckless escapades and by no means to be recommended' (*MM*, II.7).

Additionally, she affects helplessness to thwart Bhūrivasu's apparent design, saying that fathers and fate usually determine a girl's future (*MM*, II.7).[55] Thereafter, she shrewdly reflects, 'She (Mālatī) now dislikes the other suitor, and doubts her father, and old tales have shown her the path that she must take' (*MM*, II.12-13). This enables her to encourage Mālatī's clandestine love for Mādhava and push their marriage through in the teeth of opposition.

The portrayal of Mādhava, too, is interesting for its combination of stereotypical and unconventional elements. Initially, he is shown as a dreamy, romantic individual, weaving garlands with effortless ease, a rather unorthodox accomplishment for a hero. The garland he weaves out of *bakula* flowers is used to convey his love for Mālatī who, in turn, sees it as a proxy for his presence.

However, Bhavabhūti bows to conventionalism, thereafter, in stressing Mādhava's 'manly' attributes of physical strength. A tussle with an escaped tiger is introduced in a contrived manner to show that Mādhava could tackle such dangers as easily as he wove garlands. Subsequently, he boldly sojourns in a graveyard, rescues Mālatī from a sorceress[56] and vanquishes a mob of angry guards with Makaranda's help. Thus, he is very much the conventional hero at the end.

Among the other gendered aspects of the text, the element of cross-dressing constitutes a boldly unconventional feature and plays an important part in the plot. It forms part of Kāmandakī's remarkably audacious plan for the marriage of Mālatī and Mādhava, necessitating the mock marriage of Makaranda and Nandana,

Mālatī's other suitor. For this purpose, Makaranda is made to dress in Mālatī's clothes and spends a great deal of time in this guise. Not only does he get 'married' to Nandana before Mālatī's parents, he also resists his advances in the bedchamber, causing Nandana to berate his 'wife' in no uncertain terms. Makaranda is also able to fool Madayantikā into believing in this false identity, making her confess her love for him in the process.

Once again, it is important to note that it is Kāmandakī who persuades the others. Her bold determination about this cross-dressing venture contrasts with their apprehension. When Mādhava, for instance, is nervous about the dangers that the disguised Makaranda could face, Kāmandakī retorts, 'Who are you to worry about that?' (*MM*, VI.18).

Finally, we may consider the views of Dikshit and Mishra. While Mishra believes that Bhavabhūti's female figures betray the characteristic features of his period, Dikshit specifically talks of Mālatī and Madayantikā as 'models of maidens' of the aristocracy of the times.[57] There is a hidden irony in such views, obviously hitherto overlooked.

If these women are truly representative of Bhavabhūti's period, then are we to assume that their unconventional actions and utterances were normal? By extension, would women of aristocratic families of the time view parental authority on marital issues as high-handedness, and rebel against it, whatever the instigation? Additionally, what does one make of Madayantikā's comments that reflect a strong yearning for the consummation of her passion for Makaranda (*MM*, VII)? Were women allowed to express their sexual desires so freely? Usually women are shown to lament their love-sickness but never openly express their desire for sex. Coulson remarks that the 'traditionally stronger' sexual appetites of women are usually eclipsed in literary works.[58] Hence, that Bhavabhūti should boldly depict this is an important feature of his text.

Mishra qualifies that the women of this period were in an 'unenviable' situation, with hardly any education, no say in their marriage, and dominated by men and social prejudices.[59] If that is so, how does one explain female education and the unconventional life choices in the text? If, as Mishra says, the women figures are 'realistic and representative', how could their position actually be so low?

At this juncture, one can consider Dikshit's view that the *Mālatīmādhava* was written because of criticisms of the *Uttara-Rāmacarita*.[60] The text indicates that Bhavabhūti was not a popular writer in his time.[61] That he was criticized for his unconventional portrayal of women is a very strong possibility. However, Dikshit says that it is for this reason that the *Mālatīmādhava* is 'full of female characters all belonging to the upper middle class *with no special individuality of their own*' (italics mine).[62] This is to my mind an incorrect appraisal of the text. The preceding discussion has shown the great potential of Kāmandakī, and the other unorthodox aspects in the play. If Bhavabhūti had been so bothered by social attitudes, why would he have introduced such elements in it?

One must concede that Bhavabhūti was an individualistic writer with an open mind about women.[63] This led him to question social values and to portray the possibilities of female power. His views on women would obviously be unpopular in a Brahmanical patriarchal milieu.

Further, that Bhavabhūti had strong moral scruples regarding relations between the sexes is clear. In fact, N.G. Suru speculates that the 'abject moral degradation' that Sanskrit poets reduced their royal patrons to perhaps 'disgusted' Bhavabhūti to the extent that he portrayed Rāma and Mādhava in 'the fullness of their sublime monogamous love', rather than using intermediaries to further it.[64] It is important to consider all these aspects before hastily concluding that Bhavabhūti's female characters represent his period. They seem to represent not his period but his views on their position.

That Bhavabhūti was undeterred by criticism is obvious. His confidence in his stance and in his skills is revealed in a rather arrogant remark at the beginning of the *Uttara-Rāmacarita*, where, answering his critics, he arrogates to himself the position of 'an overlord whom the goddess of speech follows like an enslaved woman' (*MM*, I.1). It is clear that his texts afford great potential for a gender analysis.[65]

THE PRATIHĀRAS

In this section, the analysis is broken up into two streams of information. The first is based on the thirty-two extant inscriptions of the Pratihāras. In the second section, the analysis shifts to the literary source, the *Karpūramañjarī* of Rājaśekhara. As in the case of the preceding period, the epigraphic and literary sources of the reign of the Pratihāras yield disparate streams of information.

Epigraphic Sources

Of the thirty-two extant inscriptions of the Pratihāras, only nine or ten are useful for a gendered reconstruction of the times. These are the Buckala inscription of Nāgabhaṭṭa (AD 815); the Barah copper-plate (836), the Daulatapura plate (843), the Āhār stone inscription (865), the Vaillabhaṭṭasvāmin temple inscription at Gwalior (875), the Gwalior *praśasti* and the Barton Museum Bhāvnagar inscription—all of Bhoja's reign; the Dighwa Dubauli plate of Mahendrapāla I (898); the Bengal Asiatic Society's plate of Vināyakapāla (Mahipāla/931); and the Partābgarh inscription of Mahendrapāla II (946).

FEMALE AND MALE GENEALOGICAL CONNECTIONS

A vital feature of five of these inscriptions is the accurate and comprehensive information they provide on the male and female ancestry of the Pratihāras. Contemporary literary sources do not yield such details. The epigraphic information, therefore, not only enables one to reconstruct the Pratihāra history with a tolerable degree of certainty, but also indicates the possibilities of fratricidal wars of succession.

The Daulatapura plate of Bhojadeva I of Mahodaya, whose purpose is to renew a grant, reveals that the Mahārāja Devaśaktideva had a son, Vatsarājadeva, from his wife, Bhūyikādevī. Vatsarāja and his wife, Sundarīdevī, had a son, Nāgabhaṭṭadeva. Nāgabhaṭṭa's wife, Īṣaṭādevī, had Rāmabhadradeva whose wife, Appādevī, gave birth to Bhojadeva.[66] The identical genealogy is mentioned in the Barah copper plate of Bhojadeva as well (lines 2–6—*mahārāja-*

śrī-deva-śakti-devastasya putrastat-pādānudhyātaha śrī-bhūyikā-devyāmutpannaha . . . mahārāja-śrī-vatsa-rāja-devastasya putrastatpādānudhyātaha śrī-sundarī-devyāmutpannaha . . . mahārāja-śrī-nāga-bhaṭṭa-devastasya putrastatpādānudhyātaha śrīmad-īṣaṭā-devyāmutpannaha . . . mahārāja-śrī-rāma-bhadra-devastasya putrastatpādānudhyātaha-śrīmad-appā-devyāmutpannaha . . . mahārāja-śrī-bhoja-devaha).[67]

The Dighwa-Dubauli plate of Mahendrapāla I (Bhoja's son) adds one more name to the list: that of the king's mother (and Bhoja's wife), Candrabhaṭṭārikādevī.[68] The Bengal Asiatic Society's plate of Vināyakapāla (Mahipāla) carries the genealogy further, in that it mentions two wives of Mahendrapāla I, Dehanāgādevī and Mahīdevīdevī, who gave birth to Bhoja (II) and Vināyakapāla, respectively.[69]

The possibility of a war of succession after the death of Mahendrapāla I is suggested by the Partābgarh inscription of Mahendrapāla II.[70] This inscription provides the same genealogical details up to Mahendrapāla I but thereafter mentions only Vināyakapāla, not Bhoja II or his mother. It states that the son of Mahendrapāla I and Mahīdevīdevī was Vināyakapāladeva. This is further enhanced by the fact that the Asni inscription (917) does not mention Bhoja II, but represents his half-brother Mahipāla, born of Mahīdevī, as having come after Mahendrapāla I.

The implications of this discrepancy are significant. Either Bhoja II died early and it was considered unnecessary to mention his name or that of his mother, or he was a claimant to the throne who was eventually ousted by Mahipāla. This points to a probable fratricidal war and, by extension, to possible rivalries among the queens over their sons' claims.

One could also speculate that Dehanāgādevī might have been lower in the harem hierarchy than Mahīdevīdevī and this could have influenced the outcome of the fight. Although there is no concrete evidence to support this theory of harem rivalry, it cannot be wholly rejected. R.S. Tripathi feels that, initially, Mahipāla did not want to mention the name of his rival, Bhoja II, but eventually included him in the genealogical list.[71] As the Haddala grant of Mahipāla's feudatory, Dharaṇīvarāha, mentions him as ruling in AD 914, the approximate date of Mahipāla's accession could be 912.

Significantly, another war of succession seems to have followed Mahipāla's death. The Partābgarh inscription reveals that Mahipāla was succeeded by Mahendrapāladeva (II), his son by Queen Prasādhanādevī of the Devathāddhi family. However, the Siyadoni inscription of 948 describes Devapāla as Mahipāla's immediate successor. Hence, either the reign of Mahendrapāla II was very short or there were hostile relations between the different claimants as before.[72]

Once again, the question of harem rivalries cannot wholly be ruled out. Perhaps the ranking of the respective mothers in the harem influenced the outcome of this struggle.[73] This speculation is supported by the wording of the Partābgarh inscription wherein there is a double meaning lent to the word *prasādhana* in that the queen mother, Prasādhanādevī, is complimented by being called the 'ornament of the family of her birth.'[74] This extra touch to her description points to her evidently exalted status.

PRESENCE OF NON-ROYAL WOMEN IN EPIGRAPHS

The heightened visibility of non-royal women in some Pratihāra inscriptions is a significant continuation of an earlier trend. This is usually evident in inscriptions issued by feudatories of the Pratihāras. Yet it is important that the wives and other female relatives of these donors are mentioned in a parallel vein to the Pratihāra queens. The documentation of their presence in such an emphatic manner is a pointer to their role and presence in contemporary society.

At the outset, one should note that wives of feudatory rulers, though aristocrats, are considered in this section on non-royal women to distinguish them from the imperial Pratihāras. Thus, for instance, the first inscription of the Vaillabhaṭṭasvāmin temple at Gwalior built by Alla, the guardian of the Gwalior fort under Bhoja I, refers to Alla's wives as well as those of his father, Vaillabhaṭṭa.[75] Vaillabhaṭṭa is said to have taken 'the virtuous and noble Jajjā, the daughter of Kāsarakīya-Viṣṇu' for his wife. She is thereafter exalted: 'As Viṣṇu Lakṣmī, as Śiva the mountain-daughter and as Indra Sacī' (line 9).

Alla's other wives are described thus:

This great and passionless man who had married Vavvā, the daughter of Kanhuka and mother of (his) favourite daughter Somaṭā, further Goggā, the daughter of Bhaṭṭa, then Gaurī, the daughter of Mahādeva, Sillā, the daughter of Govardhana, and Īṣaṭā, the daughter of Nannaha, built . . . this temple of Viṣṇu. . . . (v. 25)

Details of their ancestry are thus revealed. Similarly, the Buckala inscription of Nāgabhaṭṭa refers to the Queen Jayāvalī, the daughter of Jajjaka, setting up something after building a temple in the village of Rājyaghaṅgakaṁ. Her husband must have been some kind of feudatory chieftain of Nāgabhaṭṭa, holding Rājyaghaṅgakaṁ.[76]

Clear references to non-royal women are provided by two inscriptions of the reign of Bhoja I: the fragmentary Barton Museum Bhāvnagar inscription that mentions Manikā (the faithful wife of a very charitable man, Gogga) and the Āhār stone inscription that records mainly the acquisition of land with a temple.[77] The latter mentions several non-royal women involved in the transaction and this will be considered below.

Not only are non-royal women given a presence in the inscriptions, but at least one of the grants in question is designed for their welfare and merit. Thus, the Vaillabhaṭṭasvāmin temple inscription talks of Alla building the temple 'for the increase of the spiritual merit of Vavvā, etc., and of himself'. This is somewhat reminiscent of the inscriptions of the imperial Pratihāras, notably the Dighwa-Dubauli plate of Mahendrapāla and the Bengal Asiatic Society plate of Vināyakapāla, that grant villages 'to increase the religious merit' of the royal donors' parents. It is interesting that while the Pratihāra rulers make grants for the sake of their parents' merit—not their wives'—their feudatories (notably Alla) seem to be concerned with both aspects.[78]

NON-ROYAL WOMEN AND DONATIONS

Documents demonstrating instances of women holding or disposing of landed property are few and, therefore, significant.[79] This is where the Āhār stone inscription of Bhoja's reign assumes great importance. It consists of ten separate documents, recorded at different dates, of which seven record the acquisition of land and houses with the revenue of the temple of the goddess Kanakadevī/Kāñcanadevī, situated in the town of Tattānandapura.[80]

Document V states that the *goṣṭī* purchased part of a building site from Bhaṭṭa Īśvara 'with the consent of the mother, Iyaṭṭā' and gave it to the temple.[81] Likewise, Document VII records that the Sauvarṇika *mahājana* acquired an *āvārī* from Bhaṭṭa Divākara in the orchard of Sutarnāka 'with the consent of the mother Bhaṭṭinī Mahādevī'.[82] Finally, Document VIII mentions some kṣatriyas, as also Lacchikā, the wife of Devanāga, and Sampat, the wife of Mādhava, who made over the entire rent of a house by a deed of ninety-nine years to the goddess.[83]

That the consent of women in such business transactions was not a mere formality is indicated by the record of their presence in the procedure. Could this mean that property, of whatever kind, could not be disposed off without the final consent of the women in the family? If so, what does this say for the status of women in the contemporary milieu? If their consent was token, why was it sought in the first place? Obviously, non-royal women had some say in determining the use and disposal of land or property. In view of the lack of exact information, one cannot say for certain whether their royal counterparts enjoyed the same power. Yet that such power existed for women at any level of society is significant.

Thus, we can stress the importance of the epigraphic evidence for a gendered reconstruction of this period. Admittedly, the number of inscriptions pertinent to gender is a very small proportion of the whole. Yet it is possible to glean much information by subjecting them to a systematic analysis. Their importance is heightened by the fact that the various implications discussed above, especially the visibility of non-royal women and their role *vis-à-vis* property, have been hitherto largely ignored. Admittedly, genealogical details are extremely important for a historical reconstruction but by concentrating on them and not on other aspects, one misses out much of the potential offered by these inscriptions, as I have endeavoured to show.

Rājaśekhara's Karpūramañjarī

This section will deal with the *Karpūramañjarī* of the poet, Rājaśekhara, a contemporary of King Mahendrapāla I and an active court participant. The focus on this text may seem misplaced, but it is important not only because of its theme—harem intrigue—but also because Rājaśekhara's observation of court culture from close quarters has led to his works being considered 'valuable source material for the study of early medieval society'.[84] His birth in a brāhmaṇa household and his personal connections on account of his father, an important court functionary, rendered him 'eminently suited to assess the courtly culture of his period'.[85] In fact, Caṇḍapāla, the hero of his *saṭṭaka* or dance drama, is believed to be a 'thin and transparent veil for Mahendrapāla', the words Nirbhara/Nirbhaya used for the king being suggested by the word Caṇḍa(pāla).[86]

Let us determine the ways in which the *Karpūramañjarī* can be used for a gendered reconstruction of the socio-political milieu of Rājaśekhara's time (855–930). This will be done over several sections.

THE ISSUE OF HAREM INTRIGUE

The theme of the *Karpūramañjarī* can be seen as a continuation of Harṣa's 'sister plays' in that it, too, revolves around a harem intrigue. There are certain resemblances with the plot of the *Ratnāvalī*, but the contrasts in character delineation and other aspects in Rājaśekhara's text completely outweigh these. The variations, which will be analysed below, are significant not only as a pointer to changed conditions, but also as a reflection of Rājaśekhara's motives and personality.

As regards the plot, Karpūramañjarī, the Kuntala ruler's daughter, is introduced into King Caṇḍapāla's court by the magician, Bhairavānanda. The mutual attraction between her and the king is in no way diminished by the fact of her proving to be Queen Vibramalekhā's cousin. Bhairavānanda, in the knowledge that Karpūramañjarī would confer sovereignty on her future spouse, tricks Vibramalekhā into thinking that a match has been arranged between one Ghanasāramañjarī, who has the same power, and Caṇḍapāla. The naïve queen consents to the match for her husband's benefit, and it is only after the ceremony that she realizes Karpūramañjarī and Ghanasāramañjarī to be the same person.

Interestingly, Suru speculates that this plot of an oppositional marriage was a reflection of Rājaśekhara's own marriage with Avantisundarī, the daughter of a Cauhāna feudatory of the Pratihāras, whom the poet met through his father.[87] This unconventional union was obviously a happy one since Rājaśekhara describes himself as the *tilaka* on the forehead of his family, chiefly because of Avantisundarī.[88] Furthermore, it is revealed that it is

> Avantisundarī, the crest-wreath of the Cāuhāṇa family, the wife of the great poet Rājaśekhara, who desires this (drama) of her husband to be enacted on the stage (*KPM*, I.11—*cāuhāṇa-kulamoli-māliaā rāasehara-kaīndagehiṇī, bhattuṇo kiim-avanti-sundarī sā paunjai-ume-amichhai*).

However, the resemblance with Harṣa's plays seems to be more pronounced in the *Karpūramañjarī* than with any real life story. As S.K. De remarks, there is an 'unmistakable' influence of Harṣa's *Ratnāvalī*, but so is Rājaśekhara's 'flat' rehandling of the theme, the plot 'poorly managed', and the characterization 'distinctly feeble'.[89] The nature of these variations needs now to be examined.

CHANGES IN PORTRAYAL OF THE CHIEF QUEEN

One of the most significant variations from Harṣa's plays is the portrayal of the chief queen in the *Karpūramañjarī*. The naïve, gullible and wholly ineffectual Vibramalekhā forms a strong contrast to the formidable and aggressive figure of Vāsavadattā. Admittedly, both queens are outmanoeuvred in the course of the plays, but Vāsavadattā's forceful reactions are in sharp contrast to Vibramalekhā's weak resistance to her husband's philandering.[90]

What is most immediately apparent is the scant respect that Vibramalekhā seems to command from the male figures in the text. Her equation with Caṇḍapāla is an adequate indicator of this. Where Vāsavadattā is treated with polite consideration and deference by Udayana, Caṇḍapāla is not particularly affected by Vibramalekhā's presence. On Karpūramañjarī's magical intrusion into the court, he indulges in lewd remarks, despite the queen's presence and the knowledge that the two are cousins.

Vibramalekhā's reaction to this is characteristically lukewarm. She merely inquires after Karpūramañjarī's family after a long interval and then begs leave to attend to her cousin. In fact, Karpūramañjarī herself is moved to wonder at the king's lustful behaviour 'even when with his beloved' (*KPM*, I.29), an aspect that does not seem to outwardly affect the queen. Needless to say, Vāsavadattā's reaction in a similar situation would have been one of justifiable wrath and sarcasm. Her very presence would have been a deterrent to such behaviour on the part of the king.

Vibramalekhā's reaction to the romance is almost wholly muted. Where Vāsavadattā makes an articulate declaration of her resentment, Vibramalekhā never openly voices her anger to Caṇḍapāla, or shows any visible signs of wrath. Her hostility is only indirectly implied through the clandestine meetings of the couple by means of an underground passage.[91] That Karpūramañjarī is confined in a prison-house by the queen is, again, revealed only by the jester, Kapiñjala, who informs the king of the formidable security arrangements made by her. Hence, though Vibramalekhā goes to great lengths to prevent the duo from meeting, it is curious that she never openly communicates her disapproval.

By extension, Caṇḍapāla's view of Vibramalekhā's resistance is seen in his paying lip service to her cleverness. He remarks on 'the shrewd queen' being 'outwitted' at one point (*KPM*, II.30), but pursues his love with no real fear or apprehension, knowing that he could very well brush aside any obstacle that she poses. This is in sharp contrast to the very real fear and awe of Vāsavadattā's reactions that pervades Harṣa's plays.

That no deep attachment exists between Caṇḍapāla and Vibramalekhā is obvious not only in the course of the play, but also in the eagerness with which the king accepts Karpūramañjarī's hand at the end. By contrast, Harṣa's Udayana seems often genuinely troubled by Vāsavadattā's grief and only accepts his new love on Vāsavadattā's capitulation. However, Caṇḍapāla deliberately ignores Vibramalekhā's dejection, glibly remarking on his satisfaction with his new bride, the emperor's title, and the fact that 'even though she has a rival', the queen 'is not now mentally disturbed by anger' (*KPM*, IV.23). His response stems from a total indifference to Vibramalekhā's feelings, whereas Udayana's happiness is complete only when Vāsavadattā has shown herself to be wholly appeased.

Conversely, unlike Udayana, Caṇḍapāla makes no effort whatsoever to appease Vibramalekhā. This is ironic in view of the fact that the play opens with a benediction to Rudra (Śiva) who is engaged in 'frequent prostrations' before Pārvatī 'to appease her jealous wrath' (*KPM*, I.4). By extension, when the jester, Kapiñjala, questions the king on his sudden love for Karpūramañjarī after his 'love for the queen has now developed into a deep attachment', he refuses to answer (*KPM*, III.9). Udayana, however, is sincerely fond of Vāsavadattā despite his other loves and is well aware of her virtues. His character, therefore, appears in a more endearing light that that of Caṇḍapāla.

Another notable variation is the fact that Vibramalekhā's awareness of her relationship with Karpūramañjarī does not prompt her into consenting to the match. Unlike Vāsavadattā, who learns of the identity of her rivals only at the end (thereby prompting her to view them in a slightly more charitable light), Vibramalekhā is aware of her rival's identity from the start but does not allow this fact to lessen her hostility. This is intriguing in view of the fact that she has no objection to the king marrying an unknown Ghanasāramañjarī, 'who would be the queen of an emperor'. Thus, she is willing to sacrifice her interests in this case but not in the case of her cousin. The prospect of her husband's future glory through Karpūramañjarī does not seem to comfort her for she remains distressed at the end. Thus, it seems that it is the prospect of her cousin as rival that upsets the queen. Had the rival been a stranger, it would not have mattered.

It is important to note that Caṇḍapāla's attitude of casual disrespect apparently percolates to the other male characters in the text. The jester is able to talk in disparaging terms of Vibramalekhā even before the king, labelling her 'the old cat' (*KPM*, II.30). (In Harṣa's plays, though the jester and maids talk about Vāsavadattā in a sarcastic vein, their words never assume the brazen overtones of the *Karpūramañjarī*.) The attitude of the magician, too, is a case in point. Throughout the text, he treats the female characters with a contempt that he makes little effort to hide. Yet despite his drunkenness and uncouth mannerisms, Vibramalekhā persists in treating him with reverence and gratitude for uniting her with her cousin.[92]

The queen's intriguing deference towards Bhairavānanda, and her highly gullible nature, ultimately lead to her downfall. Thus, her consent to the match with Ghanasāramañjarī is obtained by the wily magician as a gift for consecrating the image of Pārvatī. Not only does he deceive her in a most audacious manner, there is no trace of fear or guilt in his attitude. This is unlike the schemers against Vāsavadattā who spend their time apprehending her wrath and have a respectful dread of it. The contrast is most clearly exemplified in Bhairavānanda's triumphantly cruel remark to the queen at the end: 'You have been very nicely tricked (by me)!' (*KPM*, IV.21). Even at this juncture, Vibramalekhā evinces no reaction but only 'looks in dejection'. This forms another clear variation from Harṣa's plays in that though Vibramalekhā's dejection is shared by Vāsavadattā, the latter's sarcastic barbs continue to punctuate her remarks in a clear display of her resentment.

What is the reason behind Rājaśekhara's portrayal of Vibramalekhā as a shadowy, ineffectual figure, and for developing the element of conflict 'on a very subdued key'?[93] The contrast with the vibrant, aggressive Vāsavadattā and her passionate response in a similar predicament could not be greater. Is Vibramalekhā's figure, then, a reflection of the diminished status of the chief queen? Is her diluted visibility and shadowy presence a pointer to an actual state of affairs?

If Caṇḍapāla is actually a cover for Mahendrapāla I, then does one presume that the text reflects a real harem intrigue? Or did Rājaśekhara merely borrow a popular theme and fashion a dance drama out of it? Even so, one can legitimately presume that there is some reflection of reality in his work. Hence, could there have been some sort of rivalry between Mahendrapāla's queens—already hinted at in the inscriptions? Or is the poet highlighting a general situation and the utter helplessness of women in this regard? After all, there is great pathos in Vibramalekhā's silence in the face of her husband's open preference for another and the treachery she has encountered.

The *Karpūramañjarī* seems to imply that in Rājaśekhara's time the chief queen could be treated with indifference and be accorded minimal powers. Then there is obviously a change in attitudes towards women from the seventh century, where the chief queen is portrayed as a formidable figure commanding respect and awe even from her husband. That she is ousted in the matter of her husband's love assumes secondary importance in view of the fact that her consent and appeasement is still considered vital.

At this juncture, one can cite Suru's views on Vibramalekhā handing over her cousin to Caṇḍapāla in a fashion similar to Vāsavadattā. That, despite her reduced powers, Vibramalekhā could arrange a match for her husband without consulting him is in itself significant. That, despite her being deceived and outmanoeuvred, her consent, however grudging, is awaited, is another significant aspect. Despite the other variations from Harṣa's plays, this one aspect remains unchanged and, therefore, needs to be duly appreciated.

Regardless of a chief queen's powers and influence, her consent to a polygamous situation was vital. And yet, Suru chooses to disregard this aspect in his denigration of Caṇḍapāla for 'brazenly' submitting to 'the dictation of his wife who does the *kanyādāna* to him'.[94] His indignation at a woman daring to exercise such independence is palpable. He thereby ignores all the other implications of this issue for a gender analysis.

In conclusion, if one assumes that Vibramalekhā reflects a changed status for women in the harem, how does one explain the liberal portrayal of women by Bhavabhūti in the preceding period? Was there a sudden change in social mores, or was Bhavabhūti, as speculated earlier, merely reflecting a fanciful situation, there actually being a marked deterioration in the status of women from Harṣa's times? Once again, in view of the paucity of evidence, one cannot do much more than pose this as a problem.

CHANGES IN PORTRAYAL OF THE HEROINE

A notable feature of the *Karpūramañjarī* is the element of what may be termed 'vulgarity' that seems to pervade it.[95] The very entry of the heroine on the stage is a case in point. Karpūramañjarī is spirited away from her home in the middle of her bath and appears in Caṇḍapāla's court in wet, clinging garments. This provides an occasion for an open exchange of lewd remarks by Caṇḍapāla and his jester. Subsequently, the king elicits from and discusses intimate details of Karpūramañjarī's ornamentation, and the bodily attributes of beautiful women, with a servant maid. Such overtones are not to be found in Harṣa's plays. Udayana might not be averse to seeking a maid's counsel, but he does not exceed the limits of decency. Both Priyadarśikā and Ratnāvalī are treated with respect throughout.

Karpūramañjarī's reaction to her situation exemplifies boldness verging on brazenness. Although she is exposed to the eyes of the court in a state of semi-nudity, she does not appear ill at ease or embarrassed in any way. She answers questions posed to her in a composed manner and even laughs and jokes. In fact, it is Vibramalekhā who begs leave to dress her properly, as she is 'in such a condition' (*KPM*, I.35). Her attitude, therefore, is a strong contrast to that of the coy, shrinking heroines of Harṣa's plays.

Furthermore, unlike the uncertainty displayed by Harṣa's heroines, Karpūramañjarī is sure of the king reciprocating her love, and writes him a letter hinting at her feelings—a rather bold step (*KPM*, II.8). Where Harṣa's heroines have to be coaxed into clandestine situations, Karpūramañjarī shows no fear in breaking bounds and meeting Caṇḍapāla secretly. Besides, she willingly engages in a ludicrous game of hide-and-seek to trick Vibramalekhā and effect her own marriage. Her eager acquiescence in Bhairavānanda's plans shows her shrewd realization of her cousin's hostility and the need to circumvent it. Here again, she differs from Priyadarśikā and Ratnāvalī and their feeble lamentations.

However, despite her somewhat bold delineation, one should note that Karpūramañjarī's character also suffers diminution in the text in that her thoughts and reactions are rather cursorily noted. Moreover, in a fashion reminiscent of the *Ratnāvalī*, it is made clear that Caṇḍapāla marries her 'to gain the rank (and title) of the sovereign king' (*KPM*, I.12). She is used as a pawn by Bhairavānanda to further his ends. Nevertheless, the little evidence provided of her boldness and candour makes it worthwhile to speculate on this reversion of portrayal wherein, unlike in Harṣa's plays, the heroine is actually tougher and livelier than the chief queen.

We could speculate that, over time, women of the harem acquired a certain visible boldness and decisiveness. This is what makes Karpūramañjarī so different from either Priyadarśikā or Ratnāvalī. Alternatively, Karpūramañjarī's persona could have been modelled on that of Rājaśekhara's wife, Avantisundarī. This again raises the question of the poet's plot having been modelled on his real life story. Avantisundarī's boldness in desiring an unconventional love match is, perhaps, reflected in Karpūramañjarī's general boldness of response.

The very introduction of a young girl into a harem for political considerations probably reflects the political realities of the day. In this sense, the *Karpūramañjarī* is no different from the *Ratnāvalī*. However, that Karpūramañjarī does not mind being the object of lustful gazing is a novel departure. Was this a growing contemporary reality? It is also intriguing that with an increase in the heroine's boldness, there is a corresponding dilution in the personality and presence of the chief queen. In this sense, women as depicted in Harṣa's time seem to have had a more palpable and inspiring presence than in the time of the *Karpūramañjarī*.

THE PRESENCE AND ROLE OF MAIDS

A notable feature of the *Karpūramañjarī* is the influence exerted by maids in the harem intrigue and in court life, in general. Once again, there are divisions between them as regards their loyalty to the queen. These are significant aspects of continuity with Harṣa's plays.

The prime mover in the harem intrigue in Rājaśekhara's text is the maid, Vicakṣaṇā. Her cleverness and importance are stated, at the outset, as if to justify Caṇḍapāla's subsequent trust in her to further his clandestine affair. A significant interchange between Vicakṣaṇā and the jester Kapiñjala not only establishes her poetic ability, but also confirms her superiority and intelligence over the latter. Thus, Vicakṣaṇā challenges Kapiñjala to a poetic contest to demonstrate her facility with words. It is interesting that this near-hostile exchange takes place in the royal couple's presence and, even more so, that they take Vicakṣaṇā's side and are agreed on her obvious talent. Vibramalekhā tells Vicakṣaṇā, '. . . you have (always) been uppish with pride for your great poetic gift' (*KPM*, I.20). Her poetic response to the jester's verse impresses Caṇḍapāla so much that he says, 'Truly Vicakṣaṇā is *vicakṣaṇā* (clever) by her cleverness of expression and diversity of diction . . . she stands as a crest-gem of poets!' (*KPM*, I.21).

Vicakṣaṇā's cool contempt towards Kapiñjala almost parallels Bhairavānanda's attitude towards the female characters in the text. Not only does she upbraid him in sarcastic terms, she indicates a desire to kick him and pound his face (*KPM*, I.21). More significantly, she even advises the royal couple not to placate him when he storms out in anger. This is a notable variation from the maids of Harṣa's plays who, although contemptuous of the jester, observe certain limits in their speech and behaviour with him.

Although Kapiñjala displays anger and jealousy, he is eventually compelled to acknowledge Vicakṣaṇā's superior intelligence. Thus he petulantly condemns the royal court 'where a slave-girl is seen, head in line with a brahmin' (*KPM*, I.21) and says that he would be better off at home doing service at the feet of his wife, Vasundharā. However, subsequently, when there is talk of Vicakṣaṇā's elder sister, Sulakṣaṇā, an equally gifted poet, he remarks, 'So, this Vicakṣaṇā is a goddess of Learning on the earth. And her eldest sister, too, is a goddess of Learning of all the three worlds! With them, therefore, I shall have no competition' (*KPM*, II.11).

Vicakṣaṇā's arrogance obviously extends to the king. She indulges his curiosity about Karpūramañjarī and imposes on herself the task of furthering his love. Not only is her shrewd appraisal of Caṇḍapāla's abilities evident, her mocking attitude is also clearly displayed in discussions with Kapiñjala about the king's love for Karpūramañjarī with an irreverence and levity not to be found in Harṣa's plays (*KPM*, II.43). One should also note that Vicakṣaṇā does not fear the queen's reaction. Unlike Susaṅgatā and the other conniving maids who have a lively dread of Vāsavadattā's wrath, Vicakṣaṇā seems almost indifferent to Vibramalekhā's presence.

At this juncture, it is important to note that Vicakṣaṇā's presence in the text continues to a midway point. There is no explanation for Rājaśekhara's sudden silence on her presence, and for the appearance of insignificant maids like Kuraṅgikā and Sāraṅgikā thereafter. As she seems set to play such a crucial role, her sudden absence in the text is inexplicable. One can only hold the inconsistencies of Rājaśekhara's writing accountable for it.

Significantly, there are fluctuating loyalties of the maids to the queen in the *Karpūramañjarī* as well. Vicakṣaṇā seems the sole conniver, for Vibramalekhā employs a veritable army of women to guard Karpūramañjarī and bar her access to Caṇḍapāla. The prison-house is guarded by five female chowrie-bearers with swords and shields, five ladies-in-waiting with bows and arrows, five betel bearers with lances, five maids in charge of the bath with swords and shields, and five maids who recite witty sayings as supervisors, staffs in their hands (*KPM*, IV.10). This revelation is important not only as an indicator of the categories of harem maids, but also to highlight the ironic failure of the queen's painstaking efforts.

Rājaśekhara innovates by investing maids with poetic talent. This is a deviation from Harṣa's plays where the maids display intelligence and shrewdness but no poetic proclivities whatever. The most reasonable explanation for this seems to be tied up with Rājaśekhara's appreciation of poetic abilities in women, his wife, in particular.

Consider, then, Avantisundarī and the influence she exerted on Rājaśekhara. She was obviously a poet and scholar of some repute. Her views on poetics are voiced three times by Rājaśekhara in his *Kāvyamīmāṁsā*. Additionally, she is quoted by the poet Hemacandra (1088-1178) in his *Deśīnāmamālā* to illustrate the meaning of certain Prakrit expressions as used in her works.[96]

Rājaśekhara had the opportunity to study a talented poet closely. That he was deeply appreciative of her abilities and learning is clear in his references to her views, and in staging the *Karpūramañjarī* at her behest. By extension, her facility with Prakrit could have influenced his choice of language for the text. This was obviously unconventional in view of the prevailing preference for Sanskrit, and the relegation of Prakrit to women and low-caste characters in texts.[97] Rājaśekhara justifies his decision at the beginning of the *Karpūramañjarī*:

Sanskrit compositions are harsh, while a composition in Prakrit sounds so soft. The difference between the two is as much as there is between man and woman! (*KPM*, I.7—*parusā sakka-ambadhā pāuambadho vi hoi saumāro, purisa-mahilāṇaṁ jetti-ami-hantaraṁ tettiami-māṇaṁ*).

One can consider a refreshingly insightful observation of Rājaśekhara, at this juncture. He believes that genius inheres in men and women equally. Thus, both can be designated by the same term *kavi* (poet).[98] He says—'It is heard and seen that princesses, daughters of ministers, courtesans and concubines are possessed of extensive knowledge of the *śāstras* (scriptures) and poetic genius.'[99] He insists that Sarasvatī must be dark in complexion like Vijayāṅkā, since this poet is 'Sarasvatī incarnate'.[100] Such a novel comparison ranks with Bāṇa's portrayal of Lakṣmī as a cāṇḍāla woman, in the *Kādambarī*, and is as noteworthy.

Rājaśekhara's sincere appreciation of women and their intellectual abilities needs to be kept in mind while subjecting his works to a gender analysis. One could speculate that he chose the figure of Vicakṣaṇā as the ideal protagonist for his views, thereby making her presence doubly significant. Rājaśekhara's views, however, differ considerably from those of Suru, who chauvinistically remarks that Vicakṣaṇā is 'too clever and unbelievably poetic'.[101] Such a statement serves to underline the liberality of Rājaśekhara's views.

What was the reason for the continued importance of maids in harem intrigues over time? Rājaśekhara's period could not have possessed the same elements as those of the seventh century. Yet the influence of the maids remains. This must be reflective of reality and cannot be attributed to mere coincidence or textual imitation. It is, therefore, obvious that their presence in court was vibrant and vital, and continued to be so over a span of time. Additional qualities like brashness and abrasiveness might have been assumed in degrees, but the central essence of their pivotal role remains unchanged.

The overall implications of their role, intelligence and creative talent are noteworthy. It argues considerable knowledge and exposure on their part if, in every case, their superiority is established over their male counterparts. In this context, sweeping statements like those of R.S. Shukla, for instance, that 'girls of ordinary families' were 'usually uneducated' seem untenable.[102] Furthermore, that their visibility and importance is taken for granted in court is also a significant pointer to contemporary social attitudes and mores.

THE RELIGIOUS FACTOR AND WOMEN

Before concluding this analysis of the *Karpūramañjarī*, we need to consider the curious interlink between the religious aspect in the text and the denigration of women. In a pioneering analysis, B.D. Chattopadhyaya talks of the trends in religion, 'a vital part of the social orientations of this period', being reflected in the text 'at least at the level of royalty'.[103] He stresses the significance of Bhairavānanda as introducing the element of the supernatural. He further states that the text 'firmly establishes' the *kaula dharma* to which Bhairavānanda is affiliated, thereby confirming the emergence of new sects and the growing sectarian separation in this period.[104]

However, what is significant is that though Bhairavānanda's supernatural power makes the king attain the status of a *cakravartī*, it involves the complete denigration of the women concerned. Karpūramañjarī is produced in court in the middle of her bath as a demonstration of Bhairavānanda's powers. Moreover, the latter has already determined her marriage with Caṇḍapāla and sets about effecting it with ruthless determination. That the heroine acquiesces in his plan is beside the point.

Similarly, Bhairavānanda callously bends Vibramalekhā to his will, and is the prime mover behind her eventual failure and dejection. This is intriguing in view of the fact that Tantrism is supposed to lend a measure of liberality to women.[105] And yet, the queen fashions her own downfall by pleading with Bhairavānanda to consecrate the image of Pārvatī and agreeing to Caṇḍapāla's match with Ghanasāramañjarī in return for it. Thus, admittedly, the play does facilitate an understanding of the early medieval religious world and contemporary attitudes to it.[106] Yet one should also consider this intriguing interplay of women and the protagonist of this new sect. Why, for instance, did Vibramalekhā revere Bhairavānanda to such an extent? By extension, how does he acquire the power to manipulate the chief queen of a powerful king? Was Vibramalekhā motivated by fear of his powers, or was she herself drawn to his faith? Does this, therefore, imply the exercise of religious freedom on her part?

Moreover, if Caṇḍapāla is a veil for Mahendrapāla I, then does one presume this to be the actual state of affairs in his court? In fact, Chattopadhyaya speculates that Rājaśekhara tries to offer an explanation for the closeness of Tāntric elements to the royalty through the figure of Bhairavānanda.[107] Did one of Mahendrapāla's queens venerate a member of the *kaula dharma*, thereby prompting Rājaśekhara to portray it? Besides, Rājaśekhara handles Bhairavānanda with a mixture of disdain and fear, implying that he has modelled this figure on an actual person in court.[108] And yet, there is no corroborative epigraphic information on this aspect. Nevertheless, one must acknowledge the religious implications of the text on the issue of gender.

To conclude this analysis of the *Karpūramañjarī*, the palpable discrepancy between Rājaśekhara's text and his attitude needs to be considered. Suru's speculation on works on harem intrigue is relevant here. He believes that these plays were written to flatter kings by giving 'literary sanction' to their 'polygamous love', while encouraging chastity and 'jealousy-free subservience on the part of their wives' to preclude their rebelling against such situations.[109]

This view could partly apply to Rājaśekhara, in that his work was probably aimed at obtaining Mahendrapāla's approval. However, significantly, he does not particularly exhort 'jealousy-free subservience', but rather stresses the utter futility of female opposition in these matters. Thus, though the theme of the text is ostensibly similar to Harṣa's plays, it is less complimentary to women. Admittedly, Vāsavadattā is frustrated in her aim but the aura of respect, power and authority that surrounds her contrasts sharply with the diluted, ineffectual presence of Vibramalekhā. This aspect is intriguing in view of Rājaśekhara's general appreciation of women and their abilities.

One wonders at the treatment of women by Rājaśekhara. As in the case of Harṣa's plays, one can speculate whether the differing representations of women in this play are attributable to the demands of the genre, or to the audience. The intriguing question remains as to why Rājaśekhara projects women in such a poor light when he is otherwise appreciative of them and refreshingly so? Is this an unconscious discrepancy? After all, if one reads this text without any knowledge of Rājaśekhara's other remarks on women or his respect for his wife, one would wrongly conclude that his views are stereotypical. Alternatively, is he projecting an actual state of diminished power and visibility of the women in his time? Does he deliberately veer away from Harṣa's plays to show the changed contemporary socio-political milieu? Once again, in view of the lack of corroborative evidence, it is difficult to say for certain.

THE GĀHAḌAVĀLAS

The final section of this chapter, dealing with the sources of the Gāhaḍavāla dynasty of Kanauj, differs from the preceding ones in that it focuses on epigraphic information alone. This is necessitated by the fact that the overall ambit of this study on Kanauj extends approximately up to 1154, the end of the reign of King Govindacandra. Most literary sources of the Gāhaḍavālas date after this period and, therefore, fall outside the purview of this study. Moreover, the epigraphic information of this limited period is so rich in data that it provides a sufficient base for a fruitful gender analysis.

Of the 51 Gāhaḍavāla inscriptions up to AD 1154, around 16, or approximately 31.3 per cent, are conducive to a gendered reconstruction of the contemporary society and polity. These are the Candrāvatī plates of Candradeva (AD 1092/3), the Bengal Asiatic Society grant of Candradeva and Madanapāla (1097), the Benares grant of Govindacandra (1105), the copper plate grant of Madanapāla and Queen Pṛthvī-Śrīkā (1107), and the Rahan grant of Madanapāla and Govindacandra (1109). These grants of Govindacandra were issued while he was a *yuvarāja* (crown prince).

The other grants of Govindacandra were issued after he ascended the throne, most of which refer to him as *paramabhaṭṭāraka mahārājādhirāja parameśvara govindacandradeva*. These are the Kamauli plate of Govindacandra and Queen Nayanakelidevī (AD 1119), the Don Buzurg plates of Govindacandra (1119), the Saheth-Maheth plate of Govindacandra (1129), the Pāli plates of Govindacandra and his mother Rālhadevī (1133), the plate of Govindacandra and the *yuvarāja mahārājaputra* Āsphoṭacandra (1134), two other Kamauli plates of Govindacandra (both dated

1141), the plate of Govindacandra and the *mahārājaputra* Rājyapāla (1146), the Bangāvan plate of Govindacandra and Queen Gosalladevī (1151), the Hathiyadah pillar inscription (1151), and the Sārnāth stone inscription of Queen Kumaradevī (undated). All the inscriptions mentioned relate to grants of land.

While the Pratihāra inscriptions merely address the assembled officers without naming any specific category, the Gāhaḍavāla grants include the *rājñī* (queen) as second in the list of land grant executors.[110] The potential of these inscriptions is not just in revealing the important female personages associated with Govindacandra and his father, Madanapāla, but also in indicating their role in the exercise of power and in the realm of donations and religion. Their value for a gender analysis is, therefore, greater than the other inscriptions dealt with in the course of this study.

Visibility of Female Personages

The most notable feature of the Gāhaḍavāla inscriptions is that, unlike the Pratihāra inscriptions, there is a complete absence of royal female members in the few genealogical lists provided of the dynasty. Instead, significantly, the presence of women is made known through grants of land made by them and by others in their name. This has implications on their visibility, status, and donative powers.

The visibility of women is most pronounced in the reigns of Madanapāla and his son, Govindacandra. Pṛthvī-Śrīkā and Rālhaṇadevī/Rālhadevī, the two wives of Madanapāla, are known through their respective grants. Additionally, there were grants made in Rālhadevī's memory by her son, Govindacandra. Likewise, Nayanakelidevī, Gosalladevī and Kumaradevī, three of the four wives of Govindacandra, are known through their grants of land and their installations.[111] All these grants will be considered in detail in the following sections.

The importance of these inscriptions for a comprehensive reconstruction of the Gāhaḍavāla lineage is obvious. The names of the royal women are not mentioned in any other contemporary work. Moreover, interestingly, the genealogy contained in the Sārnāth inscription of Kumaradevī only mentions the male ancestors of the Gāhaḍavāla line.[112] In these circumstances, the very fact that the royal women chose to mark their presence through inscriptions is significant. This can be said to represent the peak of the trend of according visibility to female personages in inscriptions.

Female Power and the Gender Equation

A crucial feature of the reign of Madanapāla was his apparent delegation of responsibilities to his two wives and son. Not only is this tied up with a situation of enhanced female visibility, it also necessitates a re-examination of the issue of actual political power wrested by women in early India where their formal political rights were either limited or non-existent. By extension, this also has a bearing on traditional gender equations in society.

Of the four grants issued in Madanapāla's reign, the only one made by him alone is the reconfirmation of a grant made by his father, Candradeva. Thus, the copper plate grant of Candradeva and Madanapāladeva records the former's grant of the village of Ahāuma to the brāhmaṇa, Vāmanasvāmiśarman.[113] The other grants are one by Pṛthvī-Śrīkā and two by Govindacandra, one of them made with Rālhadevī's permission.

The appearance of Madanapāla's name on Pṛthvī-Śrīkā's grant seems a formality in that the wording suggests it to have been an independent donation by the queen.[114] It records that the *mahārājñī* Pṛthvī-Śrīkā, after bathing in the Gaṅgā at Benares, granted the village of Bahuvarā in the Bhailavata *pattalā* to the *purohita* Devavara and other brāhmaṇas. There is no mention of the king's prior consent here, nor is his presence at the time noted.

Of equal significance is the Benares copper plate grant of Govindacandra whereby he bestows the village of Kṣithā in the Jīāvatī *pattalā* to one Vīlhākāya Dīkṣita. He makes this grant with the consent of the queen mother, Rālhadevī (*jananī rālhadevī*), as well as that of the *pratihāra* Gautama, the *purohita* Jāguka and the *mahattaka* Vālhana.[115] Rālhadevī is also called the *mahāmātṛ-rājñī śrī-rālhaṇadevī* here. Once again, there is no mention of the king's consent.

The implications of these inscriptions are immense. Women everywhere seem to hold some measure of influence or informal power.[116] On the other hand, they imply that the king's control was subject to challenge from within—from sons and wives in particular.[117] Thus, the appearance of a consistent monolithic edifice of patriarchal norms and practices might often have been a facade.

That Pṛthvī-Śrīkā and Rālhadevī were handling administrative affairs in conjunction with Govindacandra is fairly obvious. Why else would there be no specific mention of Madanapāla's contribution, or more grants issued by him? Even the Sārnāth inscription of Kumaradevī praises him in very vague, conventional terms—as in his being a 'crest jewel of impetuous kings', and so on. Yet the credit for all the victories in Madanapāla's reign is given to Govindacandra. The reasons for Madanapāla's passivity are unknown. Explanations centering on a possible illness or literary preoccupation have been offered.

H.C. Ray, for his part, attributes Madanapāla's silence to the 'masterful personality' of his son.[118] He points out that three of the four grants in Madanapāla's reign were issued by Govindacandra, and that the credit for all victories in his father's reign was given to him. However, one should note that Govindacandra only issued two grants at the time, one with his mother's consent and one with his father. Moreover, if Ray's views were to be accepted, one would not only be overlooking Pṛthvī-Śrīkā's grant but also dismissing the role of Madanapāla's queens. Admittedly, Govindacandra's role as a crown prince was vigorous but what about that of the two royal women?

That Pṛthvī-Śrīkā and Rālhadevī were masterful personalities in their own right as well is a very real possibility. In fact, Madanapāla's passivity could have stemmed from a realization of this, and there are two sides to it. On the one hand, Madanapāla could have been disinterested in an active role, for whatever reason, and willingly allowed his wives and son to shoulder his responsibilities. On the other hand, power could have been wrested from Madanapāla in degrees by either of the queens, or both of them acting in conjunction, with the ready support of Govindacandra. Govindacandra's masterful nature could, therefore, have reflected that of his mother.

That Rālhadevī exerted a substantial influence on her son is revealed in the grants made by him as a king in her name after her death.[119] In these, she is called 'the great queen' (*bṛhadrājñī* or *mahārājñī*) and they commemorate a particular day, either that of her birth or death, which remains unspecified (*bṛhad-rājñī-rālha-devī-divase*). The first of these records that Govindacandra, 'on the day of the great queen Rālhadevī', granted the village Laṅkacūḍa in the Navagāma *pattalā* to the *dīkṣita* Jāguśarman. The second records his grant of a village to Jāguśarman in the Avimukta *kṣetra* of Benares, 'on the day of the great queen', who remains unnamed, though this is an obvious reference to Rālhadevī. There are no grants in Pṛthvī-Śrīkā's memory but the independent tone of her single grant is indicative of her importance.

Thus, significantly, this situation implies an inherent reversal of gender equations. Not only is it evinced in the role of the queens in the administration, but also, and more importantly, in the co-operation that seems to have existed between them and Govindacandra. At least, there is no evidence to the contrary in this regard. Madanapāla's acceptance of the situation can be legitimately presumed from the fact of Govindacandra's battles and his grants.

This aspect has significant implications on Govindacandra's attitude as well. His acceptance of a situation wherein he had to defer to his mother, and possibly to Pṛthvī-Śrīkā as well, is seemingly not laced with any kind of resentment, at least as far as the former is concerned. This is obvious in his grants in Rālhadevī's memory, as well as the respectful tone of the Don Buzurg plates recording the grant of Vaḍagrāma village to the brāhmaṇa Tultaica-Śarman, for the increase of merit and fame of Govindacandra's parents and himself.[120] One should also note that Rālhadevī, as confirmed by the Pāli plates, witnesses many years of her son's reign. Hence, it is reasonable to presume that she continued to exert an influence on him and his administration, until her death.

Interestingly, Govindacandra's wives, too, seem to have enjoyed much freedom and visibility. Not only is this apparent in their donations but also, most convincingly, in the religious freedom displayed by Queen Kumaradevī that establishes her as a Buddhist in the Sārnāth inscription. All these aspects will be considered in detail in subsequent sections, but it is important to view them as a logical extension of Govindacandra's association with women during his early administrative experience.

Before concluding this section, we may note that there is no evidence on relations between Pṛthvī-Śrīkā and Rālhadevī. These might have been amicable or otherwise. Pṛthvī-Śrīkā seems not to have had a child who might have posed a threat to Govindacandra. This could have had a bearing on her probable acceptance of Rālhadevī as her superior. However, all this is based on the conjecture that Maḍanapāla had only two wives. Alternatively, it is possible to speculate that Madanapāla had other wives, who existed in the shadow of the two more prominent ones. In such a situation, harem rivalries between the two sets of queens might have arisen naturally.

In the case of Govindacandra's wives, however, the Sārnāth inscription of Kumaradevī seems to imply mutual rivalries stemming from harem ranking. It is crucial to note that this inscription is actually a *praśasti* (eulogy) to Kumaradevī, claiming that her praises were sung in the three worlds.[121] It establishes Kumaradevī's high status 'in the splendid harem of that king', where she was 'like the streak of the moon amongst the stars' (vv. 19-20—. . . *ahaha kumara-devī tena rājñā prasiddhā nṛi-jagati pariginī tā śrī-rivehācyutena, pra-vilasada-varodhe tasya rājñonnānaṁ niyata-mamṛta-raśmer-lekhikā tāra-kāsu* . . .). Additionally, she 'was the permanent abode of luck, annihilated sin, and took her pride in abundant virtues, being famous with that king (Govindacandra) like Śrī with Viṣṇu. . . .' Kumaradevī might, therefore, have enjoyed a more favoured position than her co-wives. From this, one can legitimately presume some amount of rivalry directed towards her.

Lending strength to this contention is the fratricidal war that seems to have followed Govindacandra's death. That Govindacandra's chosen heir was to be either Āsphoṭacandra or Rājyapāla is clear from the fact that both made grants with him and, so, were obviously participating in the administration.[122] However, intriguingly, it is an unknown son, Vijayacandra, who eventually ascended the throne, thereby raising the question of a possible palace intrigue or war between the three contenders. Furthermore, the identity of their mothers is not revealed in any inscription. Hence, harem rivalries could quite possibly have centred round this succession issue with, perhaps, the less prominent queens' heirs being ousted. The lack of evidence precludes one from making a more definite statement in this regard.

Grants by Queens and their Implications

There are several notable aspects to the grants made by the Gāhaḍavāla queens. On the one hand, as stated earlier, it reflects their heightened visibility, contrasting with the Pratihāra queens whose presence is registered only in genealogical lists. On the other hand, it reflects the queens' motives, as well as the resources enabling them to make grants. All these aspects will be considered in detail below.

DONATIONS AND ACCESS TO RESOURCES

An integral aspect of donations by queens would be the resources supporting such grants. In his study of the Candella queens and their rights to landed wealth, K.K. Shah concluded that donations by queens could only be made if they had specific personal rights over movable and immovable forms of property.[123] It would be interesting to examine the tenability of this theory in the case of the Gāhaḍavāla queens.

On the one hand, it would appear that the queens derived their resources from the king in order to make grants. Thus, the Pāli plate of Govindacandra states that he made over to his mother, the *mahārājñī* Rālhadevī, ten *nālukas* of land in the Guduni village of the Goyara *pattalā*, as a gift for the *ṭhākkura* Jayapālaśarman.[124] Additionally, the Bangāvan plate of Govindacandra records that his queen, the *paṭṭamahādevī mahārājñī* Gosalladevī, 'endowed with all royal prerogatives, after bathing in the Gaṅgā at Benares . . . with the king's consent', gave the village of Gatiara in the Bhīmamayūtāsa *pattalā* to the *ṭhākkura* Aṇataśarman.[125] Likewise, the Kamauli plate of AD 1119 makes it known that Govindacandra's queen, the *paṭṭamahādevī mahārājñī* Nayanakelidevī, 'endowed with all royal prerogatives, after bathing in the Gaṅgā, with his consent' gave the village of Daravali in the Kothotakoṭiāvarahottara district to the *purohita* Jāguśarman.[126]

The king's 'consent' is, however, a somewhat ambiguous issue. Prior permission might have been necessary for the making of a grant. If the queen lacked independent resources, as the above grants seem to imply, then the king's consent was obviously an important prerequisite. Alternatively, the king's consent could have been a formality, merely serving to enhance the status of the grant.

This notion is strengthened by the Kamauli plate (AD 1119), that opens as if it were meant to record a grant made by the king (*śrīmad-govinda-candra-devo vijayi . . .*), but confirms Nayanakelidevī as the actual donor. In this case, the king's consent could be interpreted in quite another way. Even in the case of the Pāli plates, it is unlikely that a person of importance like Rālhadevī was wholly devoid of control over resources and needed help from her son in this regard. The grant could imply a specific situation wherein the resources required exceeded her own, thereby necessitating the transfer of land to effect it.

By extension, there are two instances of grants issued independently by queens that make no mention of the king's consent. This could imply that they had rights over some kind of property that enabled them to make these grants. Whether such property was specifically designated for the purpose of making grants, or whether it was left to the queen's discretion to apportion her property for this purpose, is uncertain. Pṛthvī-Śrīkā's grant (described earlier) is thus relevant.

Of equal note is the Sārnāth inscription of Kumaradevī that records the construction of a *vihāra*. The independent tone of this grant is supported by the statement that Kumaradevī 'found a noble satisfaction in bestowing gifts' (v. 13), and that she 'excelled the creepers of the wishing tree' (v. 9).[127] Moreover, had Govindacandra sponsored the grant, neither would it have taken the form of Kumaradevī's *praśasti*, nor would a lengthy account of the queen's natal family of Pīṭhī have been included along with the Gāhaḍavāla genealogy.

Shah's suggestion cannot be confirmed or denied with any degree of certainty. That queens had access to resources is obvious, but their degree of control over it and the size and nature of their holdings remain unclear. It is also unclear as to whether control over property was limited to some queens on the basis of harem ranking, or whether all were equal in this regard and only a few apportioned their resources for making grants.

DONATIONS AND THEIR MOTIVES

Queens may have made donations with the compelling motive of registering their presence. In the case of Madanapāla's queens, the need to acquire public status through grants might also have had political overtones. Pṛthvī-Śrīkā's grant is a case in point. She probably needed to make her presence felt more than Rālhadevī who could afford to maintain a low profile in view of her son being the appointed heir.

Significantly, some of Govindacandra's grants also serve to highlight the female presence. This is particularly true of those made in Rālhadevī's memory. Additionally, that Govindacandra's wives were allowed to make donations with him, or in their own name, indicates his contribution to female visibility. One can take note of the Hathiyadah pillar inscription here.[128] It records the excavation of a tank by several *ṭhākkuras*, the chief among them being Bellana *ṭhākkura*, the *bhāṇḍagārika* of Gosalladevī, the *mahārājñī* of King Govindacandra. Not only is this testimony to Gosalladevī's attendants and thereby her own status, but also to the fact that individuals could derive their public identity on the basis of service to the queen/s.

Another crucial motivating factor behind donations by queens could have been rivalries at court. This might explain the grants made by Govindacandra's queens, particularly the Sārnāth inscription of Kumaradevī that serves to buttress her status.[129] Not only does the inscription convey Kumaradevī's religious proclivities, it also eulogizes her and reveals more details of her parents' ancestry than of her husband's, thereby proving the many uses to which an inscription can be put. It is revealed that her father, Devarakṣita of Pīṭhī, married Śaṅkaradevī, the daughter of his one-time vanquisher, Mahaṇa. Other details are also given regarding the two men and their rise to power. Interestingly, the eulogy was composed by a friend of the king, Śrīkuṇḍa of Vaṅga. Additionally, verse 22 refers to one Jambukī, who was made the foremost of all *paṭṭalikas* by Kumaradevī after preparing this grant.

One should note, in conclusion, that all these conjectures are premised on a study of a few relevant inscriptions. It cannot be concluded that motives behind donations revealed here apply to the entire gamut of Gāhaḍavāla inscriptions.[130] Nevertheless, the implications of this study for a gendered reconstruction of the time are undeniable.

Religious Flexibility and Women

One of the most significant aspects of the Gāhaḍavāla inscriptions is the overall implication on the realm of religion. The Sārnāth inscription of Kumaradevī indicates the measure of religious freedom enjoyed by this royal female donor, an aspect that does not find a parallel in the Pratihāra or earlier inscriptions (where it is tacitly assumed that the queens follow the religions of their royal spouses). It also forms a point of contrast with the grants issued by other Gāhaḍavāla queens due to its overtly religious motive. The religious beliefs of these queens are not publicised through their grants whose wording is almost entirely secular, and the fact of the beneficiaries being brāhmaṇas seems merely incidental.

In order to assess the importance of the Sārnāth inscription, it is necessary to briefly examine the religious beliefs of the early Gāhaḍavālas. The Candrāvatī plate of Candradeva begins with an invocation to Śrī (Lakṣmī),[131] while the copper-plate grant of Candradeva and Madanapāla, as well as the grant of Madanapāla and Govindacandra, hail Lakṣmī in the opening verse.[132]

In these circumstances, the Sārnāth inscription assumes importance in that it hails the Buddhist goddess, Ārya-Vasudhārā, and then records the construction of a *vihāra* with the image of this goddess by Kumaradevī. She is also stated to have restored the *śrīdharmacakrajina* image of the Buddha and placed it in this *vihāra*, or had another one constructed for the purpose.[133] Thus—

> This Lord of the turning of the Wheel was restored by her in accordance with the way in which he existed in the days of Dharmāśoka . . . and even more wonderfully, and this *vihāra* for that *sthavira* was elaborately erected by her. (vv. 22, 23)

That Kumaradevī was a Buddhist is clearly revealed by her activities in this inscription. The wording is also definite on this point in that she is apparently 'full of mercy like Tārā' (v. 9), and that 'she bowed down to the Buddha' (v. 13). Her mind 'was set on religion alone; her desire was bent on virtues' and she 'had undertaken to lay in a store of merit' (v. 13).

In a milieu where femininity was often associated with the secular, this inscription assumes momentous importance. As remarked earlier, the presumption is that queens followed the faith of their husbands. However, here is the instance of a Buddhist queen of a sovereign who evidently followed the Brahmanical faith and Kumaradevī was not only allowed to pursue her faith in Buddhism but to also publicly acknowledge the fact. Furthermore, as has been shown, this inscription even served the purpose of enhancing her status in several ways, proving that an ostensibly religious grant could be used in other ways.[134]

The religious freedom accorded to Kumaradevī raises several pertinent questions. Was it extended to her alone or to the other queens as well? Furthermore, does it reflect Kumaradevī's superiority in the court? Or did it suit some political purpose of Govindacandra to accord this measure of flexibility to Kumaradevī? After all, she came from a politically prominent family, as the grant clearly demonstrates, and he might have felt the need to indulge her in such matters.

However, at this juncture, one can cite an interesting speculation regarding the Saheth-Maheth plate of Govindacandra, by which he restored six villages to the *vihāra* of the Buddhist establishment at Jetavana. It is felt that the grant was made at Kumaradevī's instance, since of the two Buddhist ascetics mentioned—Śākyarakṣita and Vāgīśvararakṣita—the latter came from the Coḷa dominions near Pīṭhī (Kumaradevī's original home).[135] It is possible that she introduced him to Govindacandra and persuaded him to make the grant.

Govindacandra's acceptance might have been fuelled by political necessity, as suggested above, or it may have sprung from a desire to please his wife. It is even possible that he was not rigid in religious matters, in the first place, and did not mind making such overtures.[136] Once again, the lack of corroborative evidence prevents a definitive conclusion. Nevertheless, the importance of this aspect for a gender analysis is undeniable.

In conclusion, it is important to note that if a comprehensively analytical approach is taken, even a reliance on one type of source material can yield richly significant matter. This is amply proved by the potential of the epigraphic evidence of the early Gāhaḍavālas for a gendered reconstruction of the contemporary society and polity. Such evidence is conducive to manifold interpretations and should be analysed accordingly, avoiding its use as a mere list of rulers in a dynasty.

NOTES

1. As specified in Chapter VI, we will take this study to the end of the reign of the Gāhaḍavāla king, Govindacandra, AD 1154.
2. Hirananda Sastri, 'Nālandā Stone Inscription of the Reign of Yaśovarmmadeva', *Epigraphia Indica*, vol. XX, 1933, pp. 37–46.
3. Sastri only speculates, in passing, on the omission of the name of the noble family of which Mālāda is a scion. See also K.K. Thaplyal, *Inscriptions of the Maukharis, Later Guptas, Puṣpabhūtis and Yaśovarman of Kanauj*, Delhi, ICHR/Agam Prakashan: 1985, pp. 189–93. In the discussion on Yaśovarman's epigraph, no mention is made of Mālāda's mother and sister.
4. N.G. Suru, ed. and tr., *Vākpatirāja's Gauḍavaho*, Delhi, Munshiram Manoharlal: 1975. Some of the erotic verses in the text are—*GV*, 163, 165, 186, 188, 202–5, 321, 365, 368, 690–3, 731–6, 750, 754–9, 762–71, 773, 775–6, 780, 782, 795–6, 1003, 1127–63 and 1172. After his victory, Yaśovarman apparently halted all other activities to concentrate on the pleasures of love and dalliance (*GV*, 737). Suru notes that 169 *gāthās* are devoted to describing Yaśovarman's love sports and that there is too much 'wallowing in the flesh' (pp. lxxviii, lxxx). See also p. lxxix where he provides a topic-wise distribution of these verses.
5. S.M. Mishra, *Yaśovarman of Kanauj*, Delhi, Abhinav Publications: 1977, pp. 110–11.
6. Ibid., pp. 115–16 where this Jain work is quoted. Āma was apparently fostered by a Jain saint, Siddhasena, at Modherakapura in Gujarat and Mishra talks of other stories about Āma in Jain works.
7. Minakshi Dalal, *Conflict in Sanskrit Drama*, Bombay, Somaiya Publications: 1973, p. 226, says that the text makes an effort to understand the psychological side of Sītā's abandonment.
8. Ratnamayi Dikshit, *Women in Sanskrit Dramas*, Delhi, Meherchand Lachhmandas: 1964, pp. 207–8, states that Bhavabhūti wanted to

redraw the picture of Rāma and Sītā as the ideal he saw, namely—the identical life of husband and wife.

9. Romila Thapar, 'The *Rāmāyaṇa*: Theme and Variation', in *India: History and Thought*, ed. S.N. Mukherjee, Calcutta, Subarnarekha: 1982, pp. 221, 235.
10. Mishra, *Yaśovarman*, p. 135 talks of this ideal being edified in the *Uttara-Rāmacarita*. Ironically, Sage Aṣṭāvakra's advice to Rāma on the *prajānurañjana* ideal is absent in the original *Rāmāyaṇa*, but it is implicit that Sītā is being abandoned in order to establish the sovereignty of the people. Bhavabhūti wanted, perhaps, to give clear enunciation to this political ideal, so as to highlight the contrast between duty and personal inclination evident in the text. See G.K. Bhat, ed., *Bhavabhūti's Uttara-Rāmacarita*, Surat, The Popular Book Store: 1953, I.11.
11. Note that the play starts with Sītā's predicament in the forest on being abandoned (*UR*, VII.2).
12. Pṛthvī eventually changes her stance, blaming her anger on her 'affection' and holding 'fate' responsible for leading Rāma to abandon Sītā.
13. For instance, Mishra, *Yaśovarman*, p. 169 where reference is made to Bhavabhūti's comparison of the cruel nature of the saunika and cāṇḍāla professions with Rāma's banishment of his wife.
14. Dikshit, *Women in Sanskrit Dramas*, p. 209.
15. Ibid., p. 210. Mishra, *Yaśovarman*, pp. 192–3 says that Bhavabhūti's projection of marital relationships is obviously an ideal and does not reflect the reality of his time.
16. It is intriguing that the subjects who authored this 'dreadful calumny' are so easily exonerated. Thus, Pṛthvī reflects that Rāma is kept alive by his courage 'and the holy merits of his subjects' (*UR*, VII.7).
17. He even puts his head on the sleeping Sītā's feet at one point (*UR*, I.50), a clear reversion of prevailing custom.
18. He says—'What a great crime I committed and both the Goddesses have shown me mercy!' (*UR*, VII.19). (At this point, he is overwhelmed by the care extended to Sītā by Pṛthvī and Bhāgīrathī.)
19. Wendy Doniger, *Splitting the Difference: Gender and Myth in Ancient Greece*, Chicago, University of Chicago Press: 1999, p. 23, acknowledges that Sītā has 'some agency' in Vālmīki's text, for she leaves Rāma in the end. In addition, Rāma himself admits that Rāvaṇa could not have raped Sītā as she was protected by her own energy.
20. In this text, Janaka is supposed to have become a hermit after Sītā's 'death' (*UR*, IV.2). He apparently practices penance in the penance-grove of Candradvīpa. (In the original *Rāmāyaṇa*, he was of an unworldly temperament all along.)
21. He says, 'Oh, the hard-heartedness of the wicked. Oh, the rashness of King Rāma! . . . it is time my anger suddenly blazed forth, either with

bow or with curse!' (*UR*, IV.24). Kauśalyā thereon urges Arundhatī to—'. . . Save us, save us! Appease the angry Royal sage' (*UR*, IV.24).

22. Dalal, *Conflict in Sanskrit Dramas*, p. 228; R.G. Harshe, *Observations on the Life and Works of Bhavabhūti*, Delhi, Meherchand Lachhmandas: 1974, p. 28.
23. Dikshit, *Women in Sanskrit Dramas*, p. 210. Apparently Bhavabhūti shows that by exiling Sītā, Rāma was actually banishing himself.
24. Ibid., p. 214; Mishra, *Yaśovarman*, p. 129.
25. For instance, Padmini Rajappa, 'Bhavabhuti's Sita: A Woman of Substance', *The Times of India*, New Delhi, 22 May 2001, p. 7 observes that Bhavabhūti's *Uttara-Ramacarita* is 'outstanding for its rare sensitivity, that treats Sita with dignity as a woman whose feelings count'. She talks of Bhavabhūti's 'humanism and modernity' and notes that he 'stands tall in the world of Sanskrit literature for making Sita count as an individual'. However, this is one of the very few gender-sensitive appraisals of the text.
26. Beni Prasad, *Theory of Government in Ancient India*, Allahabad, Central Book Depot: 1968, p. 285.
27. A. Borooah, *Bhavabhūti and his Place in Sanskrit Literature*, Assam, Publication Board: 1971, p. 44.
28. Uma Chakravarti, 'Conceptualising Brahmanical Patriarchy: Gender, Caste, Class and State', *Economic and Political Weekly*, vol. 28, no. 14, 3 April 1993, pp. 579, 582–4; Kumkum Roy, 'The King's Household: Structure/Space in the Śāstric Tradition', *Economic and Political Weekly*, vol. 27, nos. 43 & 44, 24–31 October 1992, p. WS–56.
29. Mishra, *Yaśovarman*, p. 183.
30. Michael Coulson, tr., *Three Sanskrit Plays: 'Śakuntalā' by Kālidāsa, 'Rākṣasa's Ring' by Viśākhadatta, 'Mālatī and Mādhava' by Bhavabhūti*, Harmondsworth, Penguin Books: 1981, p. 299. An instance of this is apparently provided by Bhavabhūti's 'ideal of human partnership'. Coulson says that this might not be a new idea but it is given analytical articulation in the *Uttara-Rāmacarita*.
31. Nabaneeta Dev Sen, 'Candrāvatī-Rāmāyaṇa—Feminizing the Rāma-Tale', in *Faces of the Feminine in Ancient, Medieval, and Modern India*, ed. Mandakranta Bose, Delhi, Oxford University Press: 2000, pp. 189–90. For other divergent versions of the *Rāmāyaṇa*, Uma Chakravarṭi, *Everyday Lives, Everyday Histories: Beyond the Kings and Brahmanas of 'Ancient' India*, New Delhi, Tulika Books: 2006, pp. 222-52.
32. Mishra, *Yaśovarman*, pp. 184–5. Also R.S. Shukla, *India as known to Haribhadra Suri*, Meerut, Kusumanjali Prakashan: 1989, p. 102.
33. Ātreyī is a female ascetic wanting to learn from Sage Agastya. See *UR*, II.3. She cites the presence of Lava and Kuśa (Sītā's children) as distracting elements to her study in Vālmīki's *āśrama*.

34. Borooah, *Bhavabhūti and his Place*, p. 41 specifically refers to the figure of Ātreyī in the *Uttara-Rāmacarita* but his remarks apply to education in Bhavabhūti's period in general.
35. Coulson, *Three Sanskrit Plays*, pp. 310–11. Note that while most scholars record Bhavabhūti's mention of co-education, hardly any stress the fact that Kāmandakī carries her childhood friendship forward to form her life's ambition. However, Harshe, *Observations on the Life*, p. 69, acknowledges that ties of friendship impel Kāmandakī to violate her religion, vows, and reputation, and even prepare to lose her life.
36. Note here that among the persons Vātsyāyana considers suitable for arranging liaisons between courtiers (*nāyakas*) and independent women (*nāyikās*) are bald-headed women, obviously female monks. Daud Ali, 'From *Nāyikā* to *Bhakta*: A Genealogy of Female Subjectivity in Early Medieval India', in *Invented Identities*, ed. Julia Leslie and Mary McGee, Delhi, Oxford University Press: 2000, p. 163. Ali notes that Buddhist monks/nuns perform similar functions in Sanskrit dramas. This reasoning could apply to Kāmandakī as well.
37. Significantly, it is Kāmandakī who bestows Mālatī on Mādhava (*MM*, VI.15). Also, interestingly, Kāmandakī prepares to fall at Mādhava's feet to beg him to treat his wife with 'love' and 'understanding' (*MM*, VI.16).
38. Note here that along with the principal male characters, Kāmandakī and Saudāmanī also speak in Sanskrit. Perhaps female religious figures were exempt from the general rule of women using Prakrit. See Mishra, *Yaśovarman*, p. 183.
39. This is somewhat reminiscent of the ideal relationship portrayed between Rāma and Sītā in the *Uttara-Rāmacarita*.
40. She says this with reference to Nandana's 'hateful, scorching words' to 'Mālatī' (actually the disguised Makaranda) on 'her' resisting his advances (*MM*, VII.1). However, note that Nandana's sister, Madayantikā (who is unaware of the deception and is inclined to sympathize with her brother) says, 'Whatever he is like, you will have to comply with his whims, because he is the husband' (*MM*, VI.1).
41. Dikshit, *Women in Sanskrit Dramas*, p. 5. The reference from the *Bṛhadāraṇyaka Upaniṣad* is iv.4, 17. See also Mishra, *Yaśovarman*, p. 192 on *Smṛti* writers from AD 400 to 700 applauding this in glowing terms.
42. For instance, Mishra, *Yaśovarman*, p. 184. Interestingly, in the *Harṣacarita*, when Bāṇa returns to his village, he asks whether '*the boys* pursue their studies at the proper time' (italics mine). See *HC*, III.93.
43. Borooah, *Bhavabhūti and his Place*, p. 37.
44. Mishra, *Yaśovarman*, p. 225.
45. Harshe, *Observations on the Life*, p. 68, says that the text makes it appear that there never existed great differences between Buddhists and Hindus.

46. Dikshit, *Women in Sanskrit Dramas*, p. 243, says that Kāmandakī represents the 'deteriorated condition of the Buddhist nuns'. Also Mishra, *Yaśovarman*, p. 225.
47. Note that she plans to kill herself along with Mālatī's friends, Lavangikā and Madayantikā—her partners in sorrow (*MM*, VII.7).
48. Borooah, *Bhavabhūti and his Place*, p. 25.
49. For instance, although the prime mover in the play is a Buddhist, it is dedicated to Śiva and Gaṇeśa.
50. Maurice Winternitz, *History of Indian Literature*, rpt., Delhi, Motilal Banarsidass: 1985, vol. III, part 1, p. 263.
51. Sanjukta Gupta, 'Women in the Śaiva/Śākta Ethos', in *Roles and Rituals for Hindu Women*, ed. Julia Leslie, London, Pinter Publishers: 1991, p. 205. Madhu Khanna, 'The Goddess-Women Equation in Śākta Tantras', in *Faces of the Feminine*, ed. Bose, p. 114, notes that Śākta tantras do not consider women subordinate to men but view them as the goddess's physical counterpart on earth.
52. Mishra, *Yaśovarman*, pp. 23, 218 talks of the grim rituals associated with the worship of Vindhyavāsinī. Note, however, that in his benediction, Vākpati addresses almost all the Gods of the Hindu pantheon, including some forms of Pārvatī and Lakṣmī.
53. Mishra, *Yaśovarman*, p. 217.
54. Lavangikā, who boldly approaches Mādhava in the initial stage and who is obviously privy to Kāmandakī's plans, takes the place of the clever maid of the earlier plays.
55. Note that she also casually mentions Mādhava and his virtues to ignite Mālatī's curiosity. She later remarks in satisfaction, 'Excellent! Without betraying my interest, I have carried out the duties of the entrusted go-between . . . I have praised in passing the nobility, in birth and character, of my dearest Mādhava—and all that remains is to bring them together' (*MM*, II.12–13). And, 'I have worked successfully upon Mālatī, until she treats me as her confidante' (*MM*, III.1).
56. The sorceress, Kapālakuṇḍalā, is frustrated in her aim of sacrificing Mālatī to goddess Karālā. She vows revenge on Mādhava for killing her master, Aghoraghaṇṭa, during the rescue and for despising her 'as a woman'. To show him the power of her anger (*MM*, prelude to VI), she abducts Mālatī. However, Saudāmanī foils her plans.
57. Mishra, *Yaśovarman*, p. 183; Dikshit, *Women in Sanskrit Dramas*, p. 204.
58. Coulson, *Three Sanskrit Plays*, p. 297.
59. Mishra, *Yaśovarman*, p. 192. The specific social prejudices he mentions are the popularity of *satī* and the bias against widow remarriage. He further states that Bhavabhūti's concept of equality in marital relations is, therefore, obviously an ideal and does not reflect his times. See also p. 183.
60. Dikshit, *Women in Sanskrit Dramas*, p. 203.

61. For instance, Borooah, *Bhavabhūti and his Place*, p. 19. It is believed that Bhavabhūti's critics were Bāṇa's son and admirers, owing to their differing literary styles. Alternatively, his critics might have been his own family, friends and relatives who did not appreciate his career choice or creative output: G.K. Bhat, 'The Detractors of Bhavabhūti', *Annals of the Bhandarkar Oriental Research Institute*, vol. LX, parts I–IV, 1979, p. 151.
62. Dikshit, *Women in Sanskrit Dramas*, p. 203.
63. Ibid., pp. 197–202 for a discussion on Bhavabhūti's *Mahāvīracarita* and its liberal portrayal of Dravidian women, as compared to the 'oppressed Āryan noblewomen' of the north.
64. N.G. Suru, ed. and tr., *Karpūramañjarī by Kavirāja Rājaśekhara*, Poona, Ruparel College: 1960, p. xv.
65. This is notwithstanding opinions like that of Borooah who tries to detract from their importance in his anxiety to show that Bhavabhūti did not portray women too liberally, despite the overwhelming evidence to the contrary (for instance, *Bhavabhūti and his Place*, p. 37).
66. F. Kielhorn, 'The Daulatapura plate of Bhojadeva I of Mahodaya', *Epigraphia Indica*, vol. V, 1899, pp. 208–13.
67. Hirananda Sastri, 'Barah Copper-plate of Bhojadeva', *Epigraphia Indica*, vol. XIX, 1928, pp. 15–19. Dated 836, its object is to grant Valāka *agrahāra* in Kānyakubja *bhukti* to brāhmaṇas of the family of Bhaṭṭa Kācharasvāmin.
68. J.F. Fleet, 'The Dighwa-Dubauli Plate of the Mahārāja Mahendrapāla I', *Indian Antiquary*, vol. XV, 1886, pp. 105–13. The purpose of the inscription is to record the grant of Pānīyakagrāma village in Śrāvastī *maṇḍala* to Bhaṭṭa Padmāsana.
69. J.F. Fleet, 'The Bengal Asiatic Society's Plate of the Mahārāja Vināyaka-pāla', *Indian Antiquary*, vol. XV, 1886, pp. 138–41. It grants the village of Tikkarikāgrāma in Varanasi *viṣaya* to Bhaṭṭa Bhullaka. Both sons of Mahendrapāla are referred to as *mahārāja* here.
70. G.H. Ojha, 'Partābgarh inscription of King Mahendrapāla II', *Epigraphia Indica*, vol. XIV, 1918, pp. 176–88. The date is 946.
71. This is apparently supported by the Bilhari inscription which says that Kokalladeva I, whose help Bhoja seems to have sought, 'set up two . . . columns of his fame . . . that well-known Kriṣṇarāja (in the south) and (in the north) Bhojadeva, a store of fortune'. So Bhoja probably first ousted Mahipāla but the latter fought back with the help of the Candella king, Harṣadeva. As per the Khajurāho inscription No.1, Harṣadeva is said to have helped place a Kṣitipāla on the throne of Kanauj, thereby increasing the power and prestige of his own house. Kṣitipāla has been identified with Mahipāla, as the terms are synonymous. See R.S. Tripathi, *History of Kanauj to the Moslem Conquest*, rpt., Delhi, Motilal Banarsidass: 1989, pp. 255-7.

72. Ibid., p. 271.
73. Shalini Shah, *The Making of Womanhood*, New Delhi, Manohar: 1995, pp. 78–9, notes that the polygamous household established a hierarchy among wives with the chief queen exalted above the others. Co-wives engendered insecurity and enmity and step-children became targets of their hostility.
74. Ojha, 'Partābgarh inscription', *Epigraphia Indica*, vol. XIV, p. 178 for this speculation.
75. E. Hultzsch, 'The First Inscription of the Vaillabhaṭṭasvāmin temple at Gwalior', *Epigraphia Indica*, vol. I, 1892, pp. 154–9. The temple was apparently consecrated in the year 932.
76. The purpose of this grant is a little unclear. Note the significance in males like Jajjaka acquiring a presence in inscriptions on account of their female relatives. Thus, Jajjaka's ancestry is also provided in the grant. See D.R. Bhandarkar, 'The Buckala inscription of Nāgabhaṭṭa', *Epigraphia Indica*, vol. IX, 1908, pp. 198–200. The date is 815.
77. D.B. Dishalkar, 'Barton Museum Bhāvnagar inscription of Bhoja's reign', *Epigraphia Indica*, vol. XIX, 1928, pp. 174–7; D.R. Sahni, 'The Āhār Stone Inscription of Bhoja's reign', *Epigraphia Indica*, vol. XIX, 1928, pp. 52–62.
78. The Rājor inscription of Mathanadeva, probably that of a feudatory of Vijayapāladeva of Kanauj, refers to the grant of Vyāghrapāṭaka village to the temple of Lacchukeśvara Mahādeva (Śiva), named after his mother (Lacchukā), on the occasion of the temple's consecration. F. Kielhorn, 'Rājor Inscription of Mathanadeva', *Epigraphia Indica*, vol. III, 1897, pp. 263–7.
79. K.K. Shah, 'Legal Rights of Women to Landed Wealth: A Case-Study of Candella Queens', in *Women in Indian History: Social, Economic, Political and Cultural Perspectives*, ed. Kiran Pawar, Delhi, Vision & Venture: 1996, p. 77 where he observes this. He also notes that epigraphic evidence of cash donations by queens and non-royal women is readily available.
80. The dates are between 864 and 904. The inscription mentions several goddesses, Nandā-Bhagavatī (Document II), Gandhadevī (Document VI), Sarvamaṅgaladevī (Document VII) and Kaṇakadevī (Documents II, IV, V, VI, VII, VIII, IX, X). B.D. Chattopadhyaya, 'Historiography, History, and Religious Centers: Early Medieval North India, circa A.D. 700-1200', in *Gods, Guardians, and Lovers: Temple Sculptures from North India A.D. 700-1200*, ed. Vishakha N. Desai and Darielle Mason, New York, The Asia Society: 1993, pp. 40–1 notes that north Indian guilds of this period were associated with important political and urban centres and then cites this inscription as showing the wealth and status of the donor community of goldsmiths in Tattānandapura. Chattopadhyaya points to

the multiple social groups, the complex cultural-ideological milieu and the resultant diverse pattern of patronage of religious establishments.

81. Michael D. Willis, 'Religious and Royal Patronage in North India', in *Gods, Guardians, and Lovers*, ed. Desai and Mason, p. 56, notes that grants to religious establishments by ordinary people were growing after the seventh century, evidenced by the increasing mention of administrative boards or committees/*goṣṭīs* that were set up to manage endowments.
82. Sahni, 'Āhār Stone Inscription', *Epigraphia Indica*, vol. XIX, p. 56.
83. This deed was apparently made in consideration of payment out of the funds of the temple by the Sauvarṇika *mahājana* (ibid).
84. B.D. Chattopadhyaya, 'Rājaśekhara, His Royal Household and its Religion: A Study of Some Aspects of the *Karpūramañjarī*', in *Religion and Society in Ancient India: Sudhakar Chattopadhyaya Commemoration Volume*, ed. Pranabananda Jash, Calcutta, Roy & Chowdhury: 1984, p. 274.
85. Ibid., p. 273. Chattopadhyaya says that even if one does not consider Rājaśekhara as primarily a commentator of the politics or culture of his time, his awareness of key politico-cultural areas of his period is revealed in his repeated references to contemporary *janapadas* and their linguistic, literary, and cultural traits (pp. 273–4). For details on Rājaśekhara, B.D. Chattopadhyaya, *The Making of Early Medieval India*, Delhi, Oxford University Press: 1994, pp. 223–32.
86. Suru, *Karpūramañjarī*, p. xiii.
87. Ibid., pp. lxx–lxxi. Rājaśekhara's father was apparently an important functionary in the courts of Bhoja and Mahendrapāla I and was probably the king's representative in Unā. The two must have met there, resulting in an inter-caste marriage. (Avantisundarī was a Rājpūt/kṣatriya princess of a Cauhāna family, while Rājaśekhara was a brāhmaṇa *upādhyāya*.) Suru feels that Rājaśekhara could have been inspired by a story in the *Daśakumāracarita* in which a miracle-maker, Vidyeśvara, effects the marriage of Prince Rājavāhana and one Princess Avantisundarī, despite much opposition (ibid., pp. lxxi–lxxii).
88. Ibid., p. lxxi. This is stated in the *Bālarāmāyaṇa* I.6.
89. De says that the text is 'weakly imitative' of the *Ratnāvalī* (ibid., p. xxii).
90. Note another significant departure from Harṣa's plays in the portrayal of the king. Caṇḍapāla does not seem to be occupied in any state affairs and spends all his time pursuing Karpūramañjarī, whereas Udayana had tempered his love interests with a simultaneous sifting of power equations and seemed aware of political problems to a greater degree.
91. The development of this hostility and the usual lamentations of the heroine on her enforced separation from the king are missing in the *Karpūramañjarī*, robbing it of dramatic content. This is another obvious difference from Harṣa's plays.
92. Chattopadhyaya, "Rājaśekhara', in *Religion and Society in Ancient*

India, ed. Jash, p. 275 speculates on the queen's intriguing veneration of Bhairavānanda, despite his uncouth and treacherous behaviour.

93. Suru, *Karpūramañjarī*, p. xvi.
94. Ibid., p. xxxvi. He also denigrates Caṇḍapāla for submitting to the dictates of his jester and the maids.
95. Admittedly, what is regarded as 'vulgar' or 'decent' varies according to context. Here, the use of the term is based on a comparison with Harṣa's plays, and also on reactions of the women figures at Caṇḍapāla's court.
96. D.C. Sircar, *Studies in the Society and Administration of Ancient and Medieval India*, Calcutta, Firma K.L. Mukhopadhyay: 1967, vol. 1, pp. 254–5; Suru, *Karpūramañjarī*, pp. lxxii–lxxiii.
97. Suru, *Karpūramañjarī*, pp. lvii speculates that this 'dance-drama' was meant to appeal to the uncultured masses as well, hence the choice of language. See pp. lvii–lxii. See also Chapter VI.
98. R.C. Dwivedi, 'Women in Classical Sanskrit Literature', in *Women Images*, ed. Pratibha Jain and Rajan Mahan, Jaipur, Rawat Publicaions: 1996, p. 53.
99. Padmini Sengupta, *The Story of Women of India*, Delhi, Indian Book Company: 1974, p. 81. This is a quote from the *Kāvyamīmāṁsā*.
100. Sircar, *Studies in the Society and Administration*, p. 255. Rājaśekhara apparently mentions five women poets apart from Avantisundarī in verse in Jalhaṇa's *Sūktimuktāvalī*. They are—Vijayāṅkā, Śīlābhaṭṭārikā, Vikaṭanitambā, Prabhudevī and Subhadrā. It is presumed that Śīlā-bhaṭṭārikā, whose verses Rājaśekhara praises as comparable with Bāṇa's, was associated with Bhojarāja, probably the king of Kanauj (836–85). She is said to have composed a verse in the course of her play with Bhoja, as per the *Śāraṅgadharapaddhati* (1363).
101. Suru, *Karpūramañjarī*, p. xxix.
102. Shukla, *India as Known to Haribhadra Suri*, p. 103.
103. Chattopadhyaya, 'Rājaśekhara', in *Religion and Society in Ancient India*, ed. Jash, p. 274.
104. Ibid., p. 275. B.N.S. Yadava, *Society and Culture in Northern India in the Twelfth Century*, Allahabad, Central Book Depot: 1973, p. 326 notes that 'licentiousness and other anti-social practices' in the name of the Tāntric religion was attributed to the followers of the *kaulācāra* system, as in the case of Bhairavānanda.
105. For instance, Khanna, 'The Goddess-Women Equation', in *Faces of the Feminine*, ed. Bose, p. 116, notes that in Tāntric texts, 'for the first time in Hindu religion', an attempt was made to actualize the divinity of women on the social plane to introduce an ethos of equality and reverence for them. For details on Tāntricism, Yadava, *Society and Culture in Northern India*, p. 380. R.S. Sharma, *Early Medieval Indian Society: A Study in Feudalisation*, Kolkata, Orient Longman: 2001,

p. 14 notes that Tāntrism is the best example of the integration of tribal cults into a pan-Indian Brahmanical cult based on the worship of the mother goddess. It originated as a result of land grants to brāhmaṇas in outlying areas inhabited by tribal and non-Brahmanical people. Women were some of its greatest exponents. See pp. 232, 235.

106. Chattopadhyaya, 'Rājaśekhara', in *Religion and Society in Ancient India*, ed. Jash, p. 278. For instance, he points out that the swing festival of Gaurī normally has Vaiṣṇavite associations but the *Karpūramañjarī* indicates the existence of its Śaivite counterpart (*KPM*, II).
107. Ibid., p. 276. Also Devangana Desai, 'Art Under Feudalism in India (*c.* A.D. 500-1300)', in *The Feudal Order: State, Society and Ideology in Early Medieval India*, ed. D.N. Jha, Delhi, Manohar: 2000, p. 493. She notes that the portrayal of Tāntric *ācāryas* in relation with women and in aristocratic company is a popular motif in temple art after AD 900.
108. Chattopadhyaya traces a similar attitude in Bāṇa and Bhavabhūti with regard to the Śaiva ascetic, Bhairavācārya, in the *Harṣacarita*, and the sorceress, Kapālakuṇḍalā, and her mentor, Aghoraghaṇṭa, in the *Mālatīmādhava*, respectively. 'Rājaśekhara', in *Religion and Society in Ancient India*, ed. Jash, p. 276.
109. Suru, *Karpūramañjarī*, p. viii.
110. For instance, the Kamauli plates of Govindacandra of AD 1126 and 1114 inform the *rājā-rājñī-yuvarāja-mantrī-purohita* and so on. See F. Kielhorn, 'Twenty-One Copper Plates of the Kings of Kanauj', *Epigraphia Indica*, vol. IV, 1897, pp. 99–103. The Pāli plates of Govindacandra and Rālhaṇadevī of 1133 and the Machhlishahr plate of Govindacandra of 1143 are other examples. See F. Kielhorn, *Epigraphia Indica*, vol. V, 1899, pp. 113–16. Also note that there is no mention of the *rājñī* in Harṣa's Bānskherā plate, for instance. See George Bühler, 'Bānskherā Plate of Harṣa', *Epigraphia Indica*, vol. IV, 1897, pp. 208–11.
111. Vasantadevī was the fourth wife of Govindacandra. For details, H.C. Ray, *The Dynastic History of Northern India*, 2nd edn, Delhi, Munshiram Manoharlal: 1973, vol. 1, p. 532. Tripathi, *History of Kanauj*, pp. 314–15 notes that Vasantadevī's name appears in a colophon of a manuscript of the *Aṣṭasahasrikā*.
112. Sten Konow, 'The Sārnāth inscription of Kumaradevī', *Epigraphia Indica*, vol. IX, 1908, pp. 319–28. The inscription has four parts—the invocation, the details on Kumaradevī's ancestry, the genealogy of the Gāhaḍavāla family and, finally, a specification of Kumaradevī's gifts and her praise.
113. F. Kielhorn, 'Copper-plate Grant of Candradeva and Madanapāladeva', *Indian Antiquary*, vol. XVIII, 1889, pp. 9–14. The date is 1097.
114. Ray, *Dynastic History of Northern India*, p. 512.
115. A. Venis, 'The Benares Copper-plate Grant of Govindacandra of Kanauj',

Epigraphia Indica, vol. II, 1894, pp. 358–61. It corresponds to 1105. Also Ray, *Dynastic History of Northern India*, pp. 519–20.

116. Eleanor Leacock, 'Women, Power and Authority', in *Visibility and Power: Essays on Women in Society and Development*, ed. Leela Dube, Eleanor Leacock and Shirley Ardener, Delhi, Oxford University Press: 1986, p. 107.
117. Roy, 'The King's Household', *Economic and Political Weekly*, p. WS–59. In this context, one could note an interesting and completely contradictory statement in G.C. Choudhary, *Political History of Northern India (from Jain Sources—c. 650 A.D. to 1300 A.D.)*, Amritsar, Sohanlal Jaindharma Pracharak Samiti: 1954, p. 339, that the 'sphere of influence of the queens' was 'limited to the palace'. The sweeping/uncritical nature of this statement, as also a disregard for its unstated implications, is obvious.
118. Ray, *Dynastic History of Northern India*, p. 513.
119. Both are Kamauli copper-plate grants of Govindacandra dated 1141. Kielhorn, 'Twenty-One Copper Plates', *Epigraphia Indica*, vol. IV, pp. 113–14.
120. D.R. Sahni, 'The Don Buzurg Plates of Govindacandra', *Epigraphia Indica*, vol. XVIII, 1926, pp. 218–24; Ray, *Dynastic History of Northern India*, p. 512.
121. Significantly, the inscription declares that even the people sang her praises. This could be an indirect reference to Kumaradevī's popularity among them.
122. The grants alluded to are the Plate of Govindacandra and the Yuvarāja Mahārājaputra Āsphoṭacandra (AD 1134), and that of Govindacandra and the Mahārājaputra Rājyapāla (1146): F. Kielhorn, *Epigraphia Indica*, vol. VIII, 1905, pp. 155–8. Ray, *Dynastic History of Northern India*, pp. 532–3 comments on the intriguing emergence of Vijayacandra, as also the likelihood of a fratricidal war between him, Āsphoṭacandra and Rājyapāla.
123. Shah, 'Legal Rights of Women', in *Women in Indian History*, ed. Pawar, p. 76.
124. F. Kielhorn, 'Three Copper-plate Inscriptions of Govindacandra of Kanauj', *Epigraphia Indica*, vol. V, 1899, pp. 112–15. The king is referred to as *paramabhaṭṭāraka parameśvara govindacandradeva* here.
125. Ibid., pp. 116–18.
126. Kielhorn, 'Twenty-One Copper Plates', *Epigraphia Indica*, vol. IV, pp. 107–9. This is granted on the occasion of a solar eclipse on 11 May 1119.
127. Note that there is no mention of Govindacandra's consent for this grant. Contrast this, for instance, with Saroj Gulati's claim that Kumaradevī possibly got the donated image constructed in her husband's lifetime 'but not in the capacity of an independent queen': *Women and Society:*

Northern India in the 11th and 12th Centuries, Delhi, Chanakya Publications: 1985, p. 177. Where is the proof for such an illogical assumption?

128. Ray, *Dynastic History of Northern India*, pp. 526–7.
129. Harihar Singh, 'Women's Patronage to Temple Architecture', in *Women in Early Indian Societies*, ed. Kumkum Roy, Delhi, Manohar: 1999, p. 292 talks of the 'pious and charitable' Kumaradevī and observes that she 'obviously' had 'great influence on her husband'.
130. B.N.S. Yadava refers to the queen of a vassal chief granting a village to a Buddhist monastery in Madanapāla's reign in *c.* 1157. It is unclear which inscription he is referring to, because the date mentioned is much after that of Madanapāla, the Gāhaḍavāla king, and, in any case, there is no grant made in his or subsequent reigns that fits this description (*Society and Culture in Northern India*, pp. 253–4).
131. It confers the *pattalā* of Kathehali on 500 brāhmaṇas: D.R. Sahni, 'The Candrāvatī Plates of Candradeva', *Epigraphia Indica*, vol. XIV, 1918, pp. 192–209. The reference here is to the first of the two Candrāvatī plates (1092/3). The second document is dated 1156.
132. F. Kielhorn, 'The Copper-plate Grant of Madanapāla and Govindacandra', *Indian Antiquary*, vol. XVIII, 1889, pp. 14–19. This seems a variation from the earlier period in that though a goddess is invoked, she is not a manifestation of Pārvatī/Śākti and has Vaiṣṇavite associations. However, note that the official title of the Gāhaḍavālas was *parama-māheśvara*. See Yadava, *Society and Culture in Northern India*, p. 352. Tripathi, *History of Kanauj*, pp. 306–7 mentions the bull emblem on coins that testify this fact. Their records often invoke the blessings of Śrī (Lakṣmī) and Dāmodara (Gaṇeśa), and the representations of Garuḍa and the conch-shell on the seals of copperplates indicate their leanings towards Vaiṣṇavism (p. 351).
133. The wording of the grant is not quite clear on this point. Note that the moon is invoked along with Vasudhārā.
134. The gendered aspects of the grant have not always been acknowledged. For instance, Yạdava, *Society and Culture in Northern India*, p. 343, cites the Sārnāth inscription not to show religious flexibility or Kumaradevī's prominence, but to prove the continued existence of Buddhism in several parts of north India.
135. D.R. Sahni, 'The Saheth-Maheth Plate of Govindacandra', *Epigraphia Indica*, vol. XI, 1912, pp. 20-6. Note that Pīṭhī is identified with Pīṭhapuraṁ in the modern Godavari district. Kumaradevī probably sent for these two Buddhist ascetics to effect the grant.
136. Sectarian boundaries were not as sharply defined as often assumed. Hence, patronage of diverse sects need not necessarily represent tolerance but rather strategies of legitimation in situations where several sects existed.

CHAPTER IX

Kanauj: Summary

It would be worthwhile to provide a summation of some important points raised in the course of this analysis of early medieval Kanauj. One of the most significant aspects is the necessity for according due weight to literary and epigraphic sources. The usual reliance on the testimony of inscriptions over literary texts can often prove to be unwarranted. Thus, for instance, the inscriptions of Harṣa's reign are wholly silent on the pivotal figure of his sister, Rājyaśrī, and provide information on other, less important, women in Kanauj.

Bāṇa's *Harṣacarita*, a considerably nuanced account, treats Rājyaśrī as a historically relevant figure and enables us to trace Harṣa's acquisition of Kanauj through her. This is vitally important in that Harṣa owed his sovereignty and glory to Rājyaśrī, a fact that militated against prescribed succession norms. Another significant aspect is the issue of the invisibility of women that needs to be viewed in conjunction with the kind of visibility that they had.[1] This is related to the enormous variability in power, authority and decision-making prerogatives that they seemingly had—both in relation to men as individuals and to their society as a whole.[2] Thus, Rājyaśrī may appear to be a coy, submissive figure in the *Harṣacarita*, but there are enough indications of her influencing Harṣa in matters of politics and religion, and perhaps being a power behind the throne. Similarly, the Gāhaḍavāla queens, who have no presence in genealogical lists, made grants of land to affirm their political positions.

This is an important pointer to the socio-political milieu of the time that allowed women to participate in contemporary matters and proclaim their capacities in a distinct manner. This single fact proves that the 'position' of women cannot be relegated to a part of 'the various aspects of social life' like varṇas, dresses, food and so on, as R.S. Shukla, for instance, seems to think.[3] His attitude parallels the attempts of several scholars to ignore the potential of most of these sources for a gendered analysis.

By extension, it appears that role expectations for men and women prescribed by religious and political elites were not necessarily clearly defined, or without competing options.[4] Thus, the fact of Rājyaśrī's widowhood does not seem to have deterred her from making independent religious and political choices. Similarly, Rālhadevī and Pṛthvī-Śrīkā, the wives of the Gāhaḍavāla king, Madanapāla, seem to have reversed traditional roles and taken an active part in the administration. In addition, though women were traditionally expected to follow their husbands' religion, Kumaradevī, the wife of Govindacandra Gāhaḍavāla, was a proclaimed Buddhist.

In a similar vein, women figures like Mahāśvetā and Kādambarī, in Bāṇa's *Kādambarī*, are shown to take independent decisions about their lives, in direct contravention of prescribed patriarchal laws. Likewise, the Buddhist ascetic, Kāmandakī, in the *Mālatīmādhava*, even flouts the king's wishes to fulfil her friends' goals. Women also seem to have reacted adversely to polygamous situations, as is evident in the plays on harem intrigue, thereby disproving the assumption of their tacit acceptance of this custom.

Thus, our sources preclude any uni-dimensional theory of a progressive decline in the position of and attitudes towards women in this time-span. That women exercised influence in varied forms is reflected not just in the visibility of women in inscriptions and literature but also in the examples cited above. One should also note the refreshingly liberal views of poets like Bhavabhūti and Bāṇa who question accepted traditions and social practices in their works. While Bhavabhūti subverts a portion of the *Rāmāyaṇa* to stress the heinousness of Sītā's abandonment, Bāṇa portrays Lakṣmī as a cāṇḍāla woman and launches a fierce diatribe against *satī*.

As regards the issue of female donations, non-royal women of the Pratihāra period and the royal women of the Gāhaḍavālas played a prominent role. In fact, it is only through the donations of the Gāhaḍavāla queens that their presence as integral players in the polity was registered. While the Pratihāra royal women figure prominently in genealogical lists, their role as donors is not documented, whereas their non-royal counterparts seem to have had a voice in the control/disposal of property and in some transactions.

It has been speculated that the Pratihāras were not involved in actual temple building, although they were active patrons of brāhmaṇas and notable temples.[5] This was, apparently, a part of their conscious policy to avoid localization of power and particularization of identity that temple-building and divinity-naming implied, as it would impede their efforts to control the nobility of north India. If one accepts this view, the absence of royal Pratihāra women donors becomes understandable.

Finally, one should caution against the assumption that our source material is always openly conducive to a gender analysis. Individual authors/ inscriptions may pose exceptions, but a general overview reflects the need for a very careful study of the sources to glean even a little bit of information. This forms a striking contrast to the patently gendered potential of the sources of Kashmir that formed the theme of the previous section.

NOTES

1. Shirley Ardener, 'The Representation of Women in Academic Models', in *Visibility and Power: Essays on Women in Society and Development*, ed. Leela Dube, Eleanor Leacock and Shirley Ardener, Delhi, Oxford University Press: 1986, p. 3.
2. Eleanor Leacock, 'Women, Power and Authority', in *Visibility and Power*, ed. Dube, Leacock and Ardener, p. 107.
3. R.S. Shukla, *India as Known to Haribhadra Suri*, Meerut, Kusumanjali Prakashan: 1989, p. 83.
4. Diana Y. Paul, *Women in Buddhism*, 2nd edn, California, University of California Press: 1985, p. xi.
5. Michael D. Willis, 'Religious and Royal Patronage in North India', in *Gods, Guardians, and Lovers: Temple Sculptures from North India A.D. 700–1200*, ed. Vishakha N. Desai and Darielle Mason, New York, The Asia Society: 1993, pp. 56–9.

PART III

BENGAL–BIHAR

CHAPTER X

Bengal–Bihar: Political Framework (Seventh–Twelfth Century AD)

This chapter surveys literary and epigraphic sources that can be used for a gender study of Bengal and Bihar between the seventh and the twelfth century AD. This period spans the reigns of Śaśāṅka and the Pāla–Sena rulers, along with several minor dynasties. The selection of the Bengal–Bihar region as a case study is not only due to its pivotal position in early medieval north India, but also due to its close interaction with the kingdoms of contemporary Kashmir and Kanauj—the first two case studies of this book. This results in common sources and themes, and concurrent historical events, and, inevitably, involves a certain amount of repetition in the analysis. A focus on the space and agency accorded to women during the stipulated time period would be an important and significant historical exercise and the effort in this section will be to identify the problems and potential of such a study.

While the stress in the Kanauj section was on the combined evidence of epigraphic and literary sources, and the focus was on literary sources in the study of Kashmir, it is epigraphic evidence that is more useful with regard to the kingdoms located across early medieval Bengal and Bihar, as there is no really comprehensive written account of the history of this region at the time.

The inscriptions, numbering about 110, provide information on Śaśāṅka, the Later Guptas, the Khaḍgas, the Pālas, the Candras, the Varmans and the Senas in Bengal and Bihar. All are in Sanskrit and are largely donative in nature. The literary evidence ranges from the *Rāmacarita* of Sandhyākara Nandi (*c.* tenth century)—a historical chronicle with a distinct male focus and very little information on women—to some references in the Buddhist *Āryamañjuśrī-mūlakalpa*. The *Harṣacarita* of Bāṇa and the account of Yuan

Chwang are also useful.[1] Although, in addition, there are several technical treatises on law and medicine, they do not easily lend themselves to a gender analysis.

There is also a body of religious texts, the Upapurāṇas (eighth–thirteenth centuries), such as the *Devībhāgavatapurāṇa* (eleventh/twelfth century) and the *Brahmavaivarttapurāṇa*.[2] These are amenable to a conventional religious analysis, which, however, is not the focus of this work. It should be noted, however, that no text is particularly useful for a comprehensive gender reconstruction on the scale of the *Rājataraṅgiṇī*.

EARLY HISTORY OF BENGAL–BIHAR

Bengal had three main divisions—the Rājshāhī division north of the Gaṅgā, of which the most important part was the ancient land of Puṇḍravardhana; west of the Gaṅgā was Vardhamānabhukti whose main territory was Rāḍha; and the central region of Bengal constituted ancient Vaṅga and a part of Samataṭa.[3] Gauḍa was under the jurisdiction of the Pālas and, even before that, was a very important historic city mentioned in the *Arthaśāstra* and the *Kāmasūtra*. Varāhamihira's *Bṛhat Saṁhitā* distinguishes the Gauḍa territory from Puṇḍra (north Bengal) and Vaṅga and Samataṭa (south-east Bengal).[4] However, Gauḍa and Vaṅga seemed to have been interchangeable names for Bengal as a whole and, as Niharranjan Ray points out, the whole of Bengal may have been called Gauḍa at certain points of time.[5]

There are no references to Bengal in the *Ṛg Veda*, but the *Aitareya Brāhmaṇa* refers to the Puṇḍras as *dasyus* and the *Aitareya Āraṇyaka* talks contemptuously of Vaṅga. The *Baudhāyana Dharmasūtra* (*c.* fifth century BC) quotes older authorities while prescribing penance for those visiting Puṇḍra and Vaṅga.[6] However, the *prācyas* or easterners gradually became more familiar to later Vedic/post-Vedic literature and constituted a definite factor in the politico-cultural history of India before the Mauryan period.[7]

Concurrent with the gradual expansion of what may be called Brahmanical culture in Bengal–Bihar between the fourth century BC and the fourth century AD are references to it in the *Rāmāyaṇa* and the *Mahābhārata*, the latter indicating Magadha to be a great power and the division of Bengal into many states, nine of which are specifically mentioned.[8] The fortunes of Bengal were closely linked with Magadha, evidence being provided not just by texts like the *Mahābhārata* and the *Aitareya Āraṇyaka* but also by subsequent political realities.[9] The history of Bengal between the fall of the Mauryas and the rise of the Guptas (*c.* 200 BC–AD 350) is rather obscure.

In the fourth century, most of Bengal was incorporated in the Gupta empire and epigraphic records show that northern Bengal was an important administrative unit of the empire under the name Puṇḍravardhanabhukti.[10] The fall of the Gupta empire witnessed the establishment of Vaṅga and Gauḍa as two independent kingdoms in Bengal (sixth-seventh century), as also the rise of independent powers like the Puṣpabhūtis of Thānesar, the Maukharis of Kośala, and the Later Guptas of Magadha and Mālwā.

The Farīdpur plates (sixth century) provide the names of three *mahārājādhirājas*—Gopacandra, Dharmāditya, and Samācāradeva—who seem to have formed a dynasty. It is possible that Gopacandra supplanted Gupta authority in Bengal, and that Bengal was invaded by the Maukhari king, Īśānavarman, and the Cālukyan king, Kīrtivarman I, probably during the reigns of these three kings.[11]

ŚAŚĀṄKA (*c.* SEVENTH CENTURY)

Śaśāṅka is the first known independent king of Bengal who extended his suzerainty far beyond its geographical limits,[12] his chief centre being Gauḍa with the capital at Karṇasuvarṇa. N. Ray points out that it is from his time that an attempt can be traced to bring different settlements of Bengal under a common name, a process completed under the Pāla-Sena kings.[13]

Śaśāṅka's history is, remarkably, almost entirely reconstructed from 'hostile sources'.[14] The *Harṣacarita* refers to him as *gauḍādhama* (vilest of Gauḍas), *duṣṭagauḍabhujaṅga* (wicked Gauḍa serpent) and other derogatory terms, owing to Śaśāṅka's enmity with Bāṇa's patron, Harṣa. The account of Yuan Chwang echoes Bāṇa's dislike of Śaśāṅka. In addition, there are a couple of epigraphs and coins, and some references in the *Āryamañjuśrī-mūlakalpa*, a 'pseudo-prophetic' Buddhist text of dubious historical value, since it refers to personages by their initials and is an often garbled account.[15]

The lineage and early history of Śaśāṅka is obscure and there is no clear information on how he occupied the throne of Gauḍa. A seal matrix cut in the rock of the Rohtāsgaṛh hill fort records the name of *śrī mahāsāmanta śaśāṅka* (the illustrious great vassal Śaśāṅka), from which it is presumed that he was probably subordinate to Mahāsenagupta, the Later Gupta king.[16] R.C. Majumdar speculates that Śaśāṅka was in charge of the eastern dominions and made himself the independent ruler of Gauḍa soon after. Mahāsenagupta's weakening power in the east might either have been the cause or the effect of Śaśāṅka's rise to imperial power.[17]

That Śaśāṅka was a great political figure ruling over a vast territory is indirectly indicated by Bāṇa, Yuan Chwang, and the *Āryamañjuśrī-mūlakalpa.* Thus, Yuan Chwang calls him the king of Karṇasuvarṇa, while Bāṇa talks of the *śaśāṅkamaṇḍala* or circle of states headed by him.[18] There is epigraphic evidence of Śaśāṅka's suzerainty over Daṇḍabhukti and Utkala (Oḍra/Orissa) in the form of his Midnapur copper plates. In addition, the Gañjam plates of Mādhavarāja II of the Śailodbhava dynasty of Koṅgoda (AD 619) names Śaśāṅka as the suzerain.[19] Śaśāṅka's coins have been found at Nālandā and Gayā. He was, thus, the sovereign of much of north India including parts of modern Uttar Pradesh, the whole of Bihar, Orissa and a very large part of Bengal. Hence, he was at the height of his power at the time of Harṣa's accession in Kanauj in 606.

Śaśāṅka's clash with Harṣa has already been detailed in the section on Kanauj. His role in this imbroglio—specifically his encounter with Rājya—has fuelled a series of controversies. What is highly significant is that precedence has been given to the extent of Śaśāṅka's culpability in Rājya's murder, rather than a focus on Rājyaśrī's contribution in transforming the political scenario, or any analysis of the marriage alliance with which Śaśāṅka was allegedly luring Rājya, before his death. Attempts have been made by several historians to either defend Śaśāṅka or to cull evidence to prove his crime—in the course of which the role of the women at the time has been conveniently ignored. All this will be discussed in detail in the next chapter.

Interestingly, although Bāṇa records Harṣa's preparations to invade Gauḍa and his tactical alliance with Bhāskaravarman of Kāmarūpa, there is no subsequent evidence of any clash/war between him and Śaśāṅka.[20] Śaśāṅka seems to have been in possession of Magadha at the time of his death (*c.* 637–8), as Yuan Chwang—travelling in Magadha in those years—talks of Śaśāṅka having recently cut down the Bodhi tree. Harṣa could only acquire Magadha after Śaśāṅka's death, and it is presumed that the latter's dominions were conquered by Harṣa and Bhāskaravarman between 638 and 642.[21]

In conclusion, it should be noted that Śaśāṅka's persecution of Buddhists, as revealed by Yuan Chwang's account, seems to have had a political motive rather than a religious one. R.D. Banerji, for instance, feels that the Buddhists persecuted by Śaśāṅka at Bodhgayā and Kuśīnagara were probably sympathetic to Harṣa, accounting for Śaśāṅka's hostilitv towards them.[22]

THE LATER GUPTAS

The unstable period after Harṣa's death in 646 saw the rise of the Later Guptas in Magadha.[23] Although the Aphsāḍ inscription of Ādityasena (seventh century) provides a genealogy of the Later Guptas from Kṛṣṇagupta (fifth century), I shall discuss the reigns of only those rulers who fall within the relevant time-span, the dividing line being provided by Mahāsenagupta, Harṣa's contemporary. The sources are around six inscriptions that also contain the names of queens and their donations, a few coins, and stray references in the *Harṣacarita* and Yuan Chwang's account.

As cited in the section on Kanauj, the Later Gupta ruler, Mahāsenagupta, became an ally of the Puṣpabhūtis of Thānesar because of the marriage of his sister, Mahāsenaguptā, to Ādityavardhana Puṣpabhūti. This alliance was meant to act as a deterrent on the Maukhari policy of aggression but failed in its aim and Mahāsenagupta was forced to retire to Mālwā after sending his sons, Mādhavagupta and Kumāragupta, to the court of Ādityavardhana's son, Prabhākaravardhana, at Thānesar around 602/3.[24]

Under circumstances that remain unclear, it appears that Mādhavagupta subsequently acquired power in Magadha. He was succeeded by Ādityasena, his son by Queen Śrīmatīdevī. Ādityasena's reign and that of his three successors—from the latter half of the seventh century to the early eighth century AD—is known from six inscriptions from Bihar.[25] They were all evidently powerful rulers as their adoption of imperial titles suggests.

Ādityasena seems to have ruled over a fairly extensive territory. His inscriptions at Aphsāḍ, Shāhpur and Mandaragiri indicate that Magadha and Aṅga (modern south Bihar) were under him, and he is credited with the westward expansion of the kingdom.[26] Ādityasena is referred to as the lord of Magadha in the Paśupati temple inscription of Jayadeva of Nepal (eighth century) that, significantly, talks of the Maukhari king, Bhogavarman, marrying the daughter of Ādityasena. Ādityasena's wife, who features prominently in inscriptions, was Koṇadevī/Kośadevī.

Ādityasena was succeeded by Devagupta, his son by Koṇadevī. Devagupta (680–700) was, in all probability, the paramount ruler of northern India (*sakalottara-patha-nātha*) referred to in Cālukyan inscriptions as having been defeated by Vinayāditya around 695/6.[27] Devagupta was succeeded by his son, Viṣṇugupta, by Kamaladevī (700–15), who is known from the Mangraon inscription. Viṣṇugupta was succeeded by his son by Ijjādevī, Jīvitagupta II, the last-known ruler of this dynasty. The Deo-Baranārk inscription of this king was issued from his victory camp near Gomatikoṭṭa on the banks of the Gomatī and recorded the grant of the Deo-Baranārk village.[28]

The history of the Later Guptas after Jīvitagupta II is obscure, the centre of gravity shifting from Magadha to Kanauj. An example of this obscurity is the defeat of the Gauḍa king by Yaśovarman of Kanauj (725–35) that forms the next crucial event in the history of Bengal. As cited earlier, the *Gauḍavaho* of Vākpati refers very incidentally to the slaying of the lord of Magadha who fled before Yaśovarman in the Vindhyan region before being killed, and the identity of the slain Magadhan ruler (*magadhanātha*) is presumed to be the same as the Gauḍa ruler (*gauḍādhipati*).[29] However,

Yaśovarman's defeat at the hands of Lalitāditya of Kashmir shortly after 736 put paid to his rule in this region.

An important corroborative source for this juncture of history is the *Rājataraṅgiṇī* of Kalhaṇa, and Bani Roychoudhuri points to two incidents discussed here that lead to the presumption of the Gauḍa king acknowledging Lalitāditya's suzerainty.[30] First, Kalhaṇa mentions an elephant troop from Gauḍa-maṇḍala joining Lalitāditya, implying that the Gauḍa king was sending troops to help his suzerain. Second, Kalhaṇa talks of the Gauḍa king being forced to visit Kashmir at Lalitāditya's command, and of his murder there. Lalitāditya had apparently calmed the former's apprehensions about his safety by dint of swearing by a Viṣṇu image that he would be unharmed. However, he eventually murdered the Gauḍa king at Trigrāmī. The fact of this forced journey alone indicates the Gauḍa king's submission to Lalitāditya.

In addition, Kalhaṇa provides some interesting indications of the public perception of this deed. He talks of the loyal adherents of the Gauḍa king swearing to avenge his murder and entering Kashmir disguised as pilgrims, whereupon they attacked the temple and broke what they thought to be the Viṣṇu image. Although they were killed soon after by Lalitāditya's soldiers, Kalhaṇa lavishes praise on their bravery and says, 'to this day the world is filled with the fame of the Gauḍa heroes'.[31] This reveals his objectivity and, perhaps, public opinion on this matter.

The *Rājataraṅgiṇī* also talks of the connection of Lalitāditya's grandson, Jayāpīḍa, with Bengal. We have seen that after being exiled, Jayāpīḍa reached Puṇḍravardhana ruled by Jayanta, a vassal chief of the Gauḍa kings, and married his daughter, Kalyāṇadevī.[32] He then apparently defeated the five Gauḍa chiefs and made Jayanta their overlord. The implications of this marriage alliance will be specified in the next chapter, but one should note here that the reference to five kings indicates political disintegration in the region.[33]

THE PĀLA DYNASTY (*c.* 765–1162)[34]

The period from the eighth to the twelfth century in Bengal is generally called the 'Pāla–Sena' period. However, as will be evident from the following discussion, the Pālas ruled for more than 400 years and controlled significant areas of Bengal and Bihar, while the Senas had a much shorter rule of about 100 years and ruled far less substantial regions.[35]

The establishment of the Pāla dynasty marks an epochal event in the history of Bengal–Bihar in that this has been described as 'one of the longest known heritages of a single monarchy in India'.[36] Their order of succession is precisely known and the chronology can be fixed with a tolerable degree of certainty. Notwithstanding such a secure chronology and such a detailed knowledge of royal succession, there is a near-total silence on the 'significant others' of these kings. Royal women are practically invisible, although some of them were involved in crucially significant marriage alliances.

This contrasts, on the one hand, with the records of contemporary Kanauj and Kashmir, as also with the records of the Later Guptas, Varmans, Candras and Senas. On the other hand, secondary sources on Pāla ḥistory reflect a lack of interest in this lacuna. The silence is all the more inexplicable when the prominent presence of non-royal women in the Pāla period—as donors, landowners and on genealogical lists—is discerned from the sources.

The Pāla period is a fairly well-documented one, evidence being provided by around 82 epigraphs, as well as texts like Sandhyākara Nandi's *Rāmacarita* and the *Āryamañjuśrī-mūlakalpa*.[37] The *Rāmacarita* of 215 Sanskrit verses is divided into four cantos and is written in *double entendre* throughout—a fact that effectively obscures much of its meaning.[38] On the one hand, it is an account of Rāma's rescue of his wife, Sītā, from the *rākṣasa*, Rāvaṇa. However, on the other hand, it is an account of Rāmapāla's (a later Pāla king) recovery of his kingdom of Varendra from a family of Kaivarta usurpers. The author's father, Prajāpati Nandi, was apparently the *sāndhivigrahika* (minister of peace and war) of Rāmapāla, thereby bolstering the value of the text as a largely objective, eyewitness account.[39] The *Rāmacarita* was probably completed in the reign of Madanapāla, one of Rāmapāla's sons, as the work ends with a wish for the long reign of that king. Thus, it provides a history of the Pālas from 1070–1120.[40]

However, one should note the inherent problems of this ostensibly historical account. As H.C. Ray points out, the text is so difficult to understand that it is more or less unintelligible, except for the 50 verses of Canto I and 36 verses of Canto II for which a commentary exists.[41] The latter yields much historical information on Rāmapāla's reign and hence, according to R.D. Banerji, 'the principal value of the discovery lies in the commentary'.[42] In addition, D.C. Sircar stresses the lack of order in the description of events relating to Pāla history, as also the repetition and insufficient detail.[43] Moreover, the poet's preoccupation with making a parallel with the *Rāmāyaṇa* results in the text being 'practically a failure as a historical *kāvya*' in that its historical data need to be gathered with great circumspection.

Another Sanskrit text is the *Rāmacarita* of Abhinanda (ninth century) but there is some controversy regarding the author's identity. Abhinanda apparently enjoyed the patronage of a Pāla prince, Hāravarṣa, of the family of Vikramaśīla—the latter name being held to be that of Dharmapāla.[44] However, there is no corroborative evidence for this. The *Subhāṣita-ratnakoṣa*, an anthology of Sanskrit poems compiled in the late eleventh/early twelfth century by a Buddhist scholar, Vidyākara, can be used to reconstruct village life in early medieval Bengal as some poets of the Pāla period are quoted in it.[45] There are also a few technical treatises like Pālakāpya's *Hastyāyurveda* on the ailments of elephants and the Buddhist grammarian, Candragomin's works on grammar and logic—whose limited value in this analysis has been noted.[46]

Some foreign literary sources also contain several details pertaining to this period as, for example, the Tibetan lāmā, Tāranātha's *Tibetan History of Buddhism in India* (1608). Providing some popular legends of the time, the author, however, names only those rulers who patronized Buddhism.[47] In addition, Arab treatises such as *Silsil ut Tawarikh* by the trader Suleiman (951) provide information on Chinese and Buddhist travellers in the Pāla period.[48]

Interestingly, Susan Huntington points to the 'almost embarrassing abundance of dated images' in the sculptural tradition of Bengal and Bihar from the eighth to twelfth centuries, the art production apparently being supported by 'a very active lay community'.[49] The Pāla period is also held to have initiated a new school of art simultaneously cultured in Bihar and Assam. Thus, Tāranātha talks of the skilled sculptors, Dhīman and Bitpāla of Varendra, in the time of Dharmapāla and Devapāla, who took the initiative in this regard.[50]

In view of the long rule of the Pālas and the extent of their kingdom, the lack of currency constitutes an 'intriguing problem'.[51] The Bodhgayā inscription of Dharmapāla talks of *dramma* coins, but neither the epigraphs nor the literary sources associate the later Pāla kings with coins.[52] Thus, for instance, Suleiman states that under the Pālas, cowries were used extensively in business, despite sufficient gold and silver in the royal treasury.[53]

There is no definite information on the origin of the Pālas for, unlike other contemporary records, the Pāla inscriptions do not claim any 'mythical pedigree'.[54] The Khalimpur inscription of Dharmapāla says that the family sprang from one Dayitaviṣṇu who is called *sarva-vidyāvadāta* (sanctified by all sorts of knowledge), and whose son was Vapyaṭa/Bappaṭa.[55] This points to a humble ancestry for the dynasty. The Kamauli plate of Vaidyadeva talks of the Pālas belonging to the solar dynasty (*mihirasya-vaṁśa*) and, along with the *Rāmacarita*, refers to Varendra (northern Bengal) as the *janakabhū* (fatherland) of the Pālas.[56]

Gopāla I (*c.* 765–70), the son of Vapyaṭa, was the first known ruler of the Pāla dynasty. He is only known through later literary references and genealogies, as in the Khalimpur plate.[57] The circumstances that enabled his acquisition of the throne—as revealed by later records and Tāranātha—are intriguing and highly significant. Gopāla was apparently elected to end the 'reign of fishes' (*mātsya-nyāya*) {swallowing up of smaller principalities by larger, more aggressive ones} that marked the politics of Bengal after the collapse of Śaśāṅka's empire in the seventh century.[58] Gopāla was apparently elected by the *prakṛtis* (or leading chiefs) to end this anarchical situation.[59] On the other hand, it is important that Tāranātha's account talks of Gopāla having to overcome a woman to get the throne. This might be a fanciful account, but the implications for a gender history are obvious and will be considered in the next chapter.

Dharmapāla (*c.* 775–810), Gopāla's son by Queen Deddadevī, was involved in a tripartite struggle with the Rāṣṭrakūṭas and Pratihāras, and simultaneously brought much of Bihar and Bengal under his direct control.[60] He was the first Pāla ruler to assume full imperial titles in his inscriptions, and the *Udayasundarīkathā* of Soḍḍhala (eleventh century) refers to him as *uttarāpathasvāmin* or 'lord of Uttarāpatha'.[61] The Monghyr plate states that he married Raṇṇādevī, daughter of the Rāṣṭrakūṭa king, Parabala—a politically strategic alliance.

Dharmapāla's most notable achievement, however, seems to have been the defeat of Indrāyudha of Kanauj and the raising of Cakrāyudha to the throne. His installation of Cakrāyudha in Kanauj seems to be borne out by the Gwalior inscription of the Pratihāra king, Bhoja (876), who says that his grandfather, Nāgabhaṭṭa II (815–33), defeated 'Cakrāyudha whose lowly demeanour was manifest from his dependence on others'.[62] However, that Dharmapāla himself may have suffered defeat is shown by the Rādhanpur copper plate that talks of the Pratihāra ruler, Vatsarāja, defeating the Gauḍa king and taking away the two white umbrellas of the Pāla kingship.[63] The Sanjan plates of Amoghavarṣa also record that the Gauḍa king was defeated by the Rāṣṭrakūṭa king, Dhruva, 'as he was fleeing between the Gaṅgā and the Jumnā'.[64]

There is some ambiguity over Dharmapāla's successor. As the Khalimpur plate mentions Tribhuvanapāla as the *dūtaka* (executor) of the grant, it is presumed that he was Dharmapāla's eldest son and heir. However, as it is Devapāla who is mentioned as Dharmapāla's son and successor in subsequent inscriptions, it is believed that Tribhuvanapāla died in his father's lifetime. The Monghyr grant (v. 12) states that Devapāla succeeded to his father's dominions without any trouble.

Devapāla (*c.* 810–47) is generally considered to be the mightiest Pāla ruler. The Bādal pillar inscription claims that owing to the advice of his ministers, Darbhapāṇi and Kedāramiśra, Devapāla 'eradicated the race of the Utkalas, humbled the pride of the Hūṇas, and scattered the conceit of the rulers of Draviḍa and Gurjara'.[65] He thus 'made tributary' the land between the Vindhya and the Himalaya. The Monghyr grant talks of Devapāla's elephants reaching the Vindhyas, while his cavalry roamed about in the Kāmboja country (v. 13).[66]

In addition, the Bhāgalpur inscription states that Devapāla's cousin, Jayapāla, was responsible for securing the submission of Utkala and Prāgjyotiṣa (Assam).[67] One should note here that

Devapāla is supposed to have been defeated by Mihira Bhoja (836–85), as per the latter's claims, but the Pāla records say that Devapāla 'brought low the arrogance of the lord of Gurjara'.[68]

Also, the question of Devapāla's successor remains unclear.[69] The Bādal pillar inscription says that Śūrapāla succeeded Devapāla, while the Bhāgalpur plate places Vigrahapāla I between Devapāla and Nārāyaṇapāla. Hence it is presumed that Śūrapāla was another name of Vigrahapāla or, alternatively, that Śūrapāla died childless and his brother, Vigrahapāla, succeeded him, or else that there was a tussle for the throne. The implications of this alleged 'palace revolution'[70]—as a possible offshoot of harem rivalries—will be considered in the next chapter.

One should note here that F. Kielhorn believes Vigrahapāla/Śūrapāla to be the son of Devapāla's cousin, Jayapāla, and the grandson of Vākpāla, the second son of Gopāla I.[71] This view is supported by the fact that the names of Vākpāla and Jayapāla are absent in the inscriptions of Dharmapāla and Devapāla but appear regularly in the inscriptions of Vigrahapāla's descendants, implying that they were the grandfather and father of that king.[72] Thus, the issue of rival claimants to power is raised once again.

Vigrahapāla I (*c.* 860–1) seems to have been the king of Aṅga, Vaṅga and Magadha who paid homage to the Rāṣṭrakūṭa king, Amoghavarṣa, as per the latter's Sirur and Nilgund inscriptions.[73] He married Lajjādevī, a Haihaya (Cedi) princess of Tripurī—a strategic alliance probably designed to win over Kalacuri friendship. That Vigrahapāla seems to have abdicated in favour of his son, Nārāyaṇapāla, is borne out by the latter's Bhāgalpur grant: 'Let asceticism be mine and the kingdom thine'.[74]

Even in Nārāyaṇapāla's case (*c.* 861–917), as H.C. Ray points out, there is no real evidence of military success, but 'plenty of vague praise' instead.[75] The Kahala plates of Soḍhadeva (1077) say that the Kalacuri chief, Guṇāmbodhideva, received land from the Pratihāra Bhoja and took away the sovereignty from the Gauḍa king.[76] There is definite proof of a Gurjara Pratihāra success in Bengal and Bihar in the form of the Pratihāra king, Mahendrapāla's inscriptions in Nālandā, Gayā and Itkhaurī in Bihar, and Pahārpur in north Bengal.[77] Nārāyaṇapāla was apparently defeated by the

Rāṣṭrakūṭa king, Kṛṣṇa II. Although he seems to have wrested Magadha and north Bengal from the Pratihāras between 910 and 916, Nārāyaṇapāla's reign is seen as the decline of the 'first' Pāla empire.[78]

Rājyapāla (*c.* 917–52), Nārāyaṇapāla's son, made a crucially important marriage alliance with the Rāṣṭrakūṭas by marrying Bhāgyadevī, the daughter of the Rāṣṭrakūṭa king, Tuṅga, and thereby effecting a temporary cessation in hostilities. He was succeeded by Gopāla II (*c.* 952–72). The Pāla rule now seems to have reached a critical juncture. D.C. Sircar notes the claim of Śrīcandra of Vikramapura (925–75) of having installed Gopāla on the throne and returning the captured Pāla queen to her husband,[79] a fact that is not really elucidated by the available sources.

In addition, the evidence of the Rāmgaṛh, Guneriā, and Itkhaurī inscriptions shows that some parts of Magadha were included in the Pratihāra empire. Likewise, the Khajurāho inscription of the Candella ruler, Yaśovarman (954), records his defeat of the Gauḍa king, while another Khajurāho inscription of 1001 states that the wives of the kings of Andhra, Rāḍha and Aṅga were imprisoned by Yaśovarman's son, Dhaṅgadeva (954–1002).[80]

More significantly, two independent kingdoms were set up in south-eastern and south-western Bengal by the Candras and the Kāmbojas, respectively. The Dinajpur pillar inscription shows that a Gauḍa king belonging to the Kāmboja family conquered northern Bengal in the time of Gopāla II.[81] The combined testimony of this record and the Irda copper plate show that the Kāmboja Pālas ruled for at least two generations in western and northern Bengal, while south Bihar was under the imperial Pālas. The Irda plate, issued from Priyaṅgu, talks of a Rājyapāla and his two sons, Nārāyaṇapāla and Nayapāla, by his queen, Bhāgyadevī, thereby leading many scholars to assume a connection between the two sets of rulers. However, as P.L. Paul concludes, one must assume the existence of a separate line of independent kings of the *Kāmboja-vaṁśa* with, admittedly, a remarkable coincidence of names between them and the Pālas.[82]

However, Gopāla's successor, Mahipāla I (*c.* 977–1027), is credited—by his own and subsequent inscriptions—with the restoration of the Pāla kingdom, thereby creating the 'second Pāla empire' after the Pratihāra (and Kāmboja) interregnum.[83] Thus, verse 12 of the Bāngaṛh grant mentions his recovery of his paternal kingdom that had been snatched away by people who had no claim to it.[84] The revival of Pāla power under this 'second founder of the fortunes of the Pālas' is also seen in the restoration of religious buildings in Nālandā—as revealed by the Bodhgayā image inscription, while the Sārnāth inscription refers to 'hundreds of pious works' undertaken by him.[85]

At the same time, Mahipāla was presumably defeated by the northern incursion of Rājendra Coḷa I between 1021 and 1023, as per the Tirumalai inscription of the Coḷa king which states that he seized Daṇḍabhukti, Dakṣiṇa-Rāḍha, Uttara-Rāḍha and Vaṅgala.[86] Mahipāla was also defeated by the Kalacuri ruler, Gāṅgeyadeva, around 1026.

Nayapāla (*c.* 1027–43), Mahipāla's son, also had to contend with the rising Kalacuri threat in the form of Gāṅgeyadeva's son, Lakṣmīkarṇa (1041-72). The Bherāghāṭ inscription of Alhaṇadevī, the queen of Lakṣmīkarṇa's grandson, Gayākarṇa, says that before him the Vaṅga 'trembled with the Kaliṅga'.[87] In addition, the Karanbel stone inscription of Jayasiṁhadeva says that his great-grandfather, Lakṣmīkarṇa, was waited upon by Gauḍa and other princes. However, Tibetan sources reveal that the monk, Dīpaṅkara Śrījñāna, intervened between Nayapāla and Lakṣmīkarṇa and secured peace.[88] Yet the *Rāmacarita* indicates that Lakṣmīkarṇa launched another campaign against the Pālas. The text also points to a subsequently significant alliance in that Nayapāla's son, Vigrahapāla III, managed to defeat Lakṣmīkarṇa and marry his daughter, Yauvanaśrī.

Vigrahapāla III, the next king (*c.* 1043–70), seems to have married a sister of Mathaṇadeva of Aṅga apart from Yauvanaśrī. He seems to have been defeated soon after by the Cālukyan king, Vikramāditya VI, during his northern incursion. Bilhaṇa's *Vikramāṅkadevacaritam* refers to the kings of Gauḍa and Kāmarūpa being defeated by his patron, Vikramāditya, some time before 1068.[89] Thus, the Pāla territories were reduced considerably with the loss of eastern, western, and southern Bengal.

The period after Vigrahapāla's death was marked by the rivalry of his three sons—Mahipāla II, Śūrapāla II and Rāmapāla—and their successive reigns. The history of Mahipāla's reign and the subsequent period is almost entirely derived from the *Rāmacarita*, although one needs to note that it is biased in Rāmapāla's favour and, therefore, not wholly objective. The text talks of Mahipāla II (*c.* 1070–1) imprisoning his other brothers in the belief that they were plotting for the throne.

The oppressive and intolerant Mahipāla was eventually defeated and killed by the Kaivarta Divya, who took over the throne, followed by his brother, Ruddoka, and then the latter's son, Bhīma. Divya is described as a subordinate or servant who had risen to a high position, thereby implying that he was probably a governor or subordinate ruler of the Pālas.[90] In this connection, one should note that Divya's revolt seems to have had popular support—on account of Mahipāla's arbitrary rule—and hence, the commentary describes the Kaivarta takeover as an act of giving protection to the people.[91]

How, then, was the kingdom recovered by Rāmapāla from the Kaivartas? Apparently, in a desperate bid to win over his recalcitrant feudatories, Rāmapāla travelled to the principalities of his *sāmanta-cakra* and lured the chiefs over with promises of land and wealth.[92] The detailed list of these fourteen chiefs and their allies is of great historical importance, as it provides an idea of Rāmapāla's strength and of the political dismemberment of Bengal by the fall of the Pāla power. Most of them seem to have been located in portions of west and north Bengal, and Bihar, as the list provided by the *Rāmacarita* reveals.[93]

Thus, with their help and that of his maternal uncle, Mathaṇa of Aṅga, Rāmapāla crossed the Gaṅgā on a bridge of boats, defeated the Kaivartas under Bhīma, and recovered his dominions. Hari, a friend of Bhīma, endeavoured to rally forces after the latter's capture but was overpowered and executed along with Bhīma, thereby extinguishing all remnants of the Kaivarta challenge.[94]

Rāmapāla (*c.* 1072–1126) apparently came to power after the brief rule of his brother, Śūrapāla II (*c.* 1071–2). Interestingly, the *Rāmacarita* does not mention Śūrapāla as having ascended the throne, but the Manahali grant of Madanapāla refers to him as *narapati*. H.C. Ray suggests the murder of Śūrapāla by Rāmapāla, thus prompting this deliberate omission on the court historian's part.[95] At the time of Rāmapāla's accession, Pāla authority was limited to a part of western Bengal, as Magadha was out of their control, Aṅga was under the Pīṭhīs, and Yakṣapāla, the governor of Gayā, seems to have ignored Pāla overlordship by not mentioning the king's reign in his inscriptions.[96] In addition, the Gāhaḍavālas of Kanauj had occupied Kāśī and were threatening the western region of south Bihar.

Rāmapāla is the only Pāla king known to have definitely ruled for at least forty-two years, as is shown by the Chandimau image inscription dated in his forty-second regnal year and dedicated by a merchant, Sādhu Saharaṇa, son of Sādhu Bhadulva of Rājgīr.[97] He built his capital at Rāmāvatī whose beauty is lauded in the *Rāmacarita* and is identified with the latter day Rāmauti in the Sarkar Lakhnauti of the *Ain-i-Akbari*.[98] He later overran Utkala, Kaliṅga and Kāmarūpa after consolidating his territories. The *Rāmacarita* states that a king of the eastern country (*prāgdeśrīya*) 'who held the title of Varman' sought Rāmapāla's protection, surrendering his elephants and chariots (*RC*, III.44). It has been rightly assumed that this was the Varman ruler of eastern Bengal, probably Harivarman or his son.[99]

Rāmapāla apparently entrusted the kingdom to an unnamed son, possibly Rājyapāla, and eventually drowned himself in the Gaṅgā at Monghyr in grief at the news of his uncle, Mathaṇa's death.[100] At this juncture, one should note that the revival of Pāla supremacy under Rāmapāla was temporary, as his successors were weak and could not arrest the decline. Problems were posed by assertive feudatories, the Senas on the east and the Gāhaḍavālas on the west.[101]

The *Rāmacarita* talks of three more kings after Rāmapāla. The Manahali grant says that Rāmapāla's son, Kumārapāla, succeeded him (*c.* 1126–8) but his reign is dismissed in just one verse in the *Rāmacarita*. The Kamauli grant of Kumārapāla's minister, Vaidyadeva, indicates that the latter practically asserted his independence by assuming imperial titles, suppressing recalcitrant ministers and achieving a naval victory in Vaṅga and over Tiṁgyadeva of Kāmarūpa.[102]

Kumārapāla was succeeded by his son, Gopāla III (*c.* 1128–43), who was succeeded, in turn, by his uncle, Madanapāla, the son of Rāmapāla and Madanadevī (*c.* 1143–61). The Manahali grant (v. 18) and the *Rāmacarita* (*RC*, IV.12) imply that Gopāla died in his youth, probably at the hands of Madanapāla.[103] However, this is a matter of dispute. Madanapāla's chief queen—as the Manahali grant reveals—was Citramatikā. Madanapāla is the only Pāla ruler whose accession date is known with certainty, on account of the Valgudar inscription that is dated in his eighteenth regnal year and also bears the date of the *śaka* year 1083, eleventh *Jyaiṣṭha*, corresponding to 4 May 1161. So he must have ascended the throne in 1144/5.

A victory in Kaliṅga is claimed for Madanapāla, but it appears that north Bengal passed into the hands of Vijayasena of the Sena dynasty during his reign. The *Rāmacarita* refers to a fierce battle near Madanapāla's capital that almost certainly refers to Vijayasena's invasion of Gauḍa and is corroborated by the Deopārā inscription of Vijayasena.[104] The Jayanagar image inscription shows, however, that Madanapāla ruled for at least nineteen years in Bihar.

After Madanapāla's death, Pāla sovereignty ceased over western, southern, and eastern Bengal, and over western and northern Bihar.[105] Although there are subsequent kings in Bihar like Govindapāla (*c.* 1161–5) and Palapāla (*c.* 1162), their relationship with the imperial Pālas has not been established.[106] Hence, Madanapāla is considered the last king who is definitely known to have belonged to the Pāla dynasty.

INDEPENDENT/SEMI-INDEPENDENT KINGDOMS IN THE PĀLA PERIOD

At this juncture, a brief survey of a few minor independent/semi-independent kingdoms before/during the Pāla period is provided, not just to establish a continuity in history but also because it offers several points of interest for a gender analysis. The kingdoms considered are those of the Khaḍgas, Candras and Varmans.

The Khaḍga Dynasty (c. 625–725)

The Khaḍga dynasty apparently ruled over parts of eastern and southern Bengal, specifically the Dhaka and Tippera districts, between 625 and 725. Their history is reconstructed from two copper plates found at Ashrafpur (near Dhaka) and a record on a Śarvvāṇī image at Deulbāḍī.[107] The inscriptions reveal the names of four rulers—Khaḍgodyama, Jātakhaḍga, Devakhaḍga and Rājarājabhaṭṭa—but yield no real historical information beyond mere conventional praise. The Ashrafpur plates were issued by Devakhaḍga from Karmāntavāsaka, while the Deulbāḍī inscription was by Prabhāvatī, Devakhaḍga's chief queen.

The origin of the Khaḍga dynasty is unknown but the Deulbāḍī inscription refers to Khaḍgodyama as *nṛpādhirāja* or 'great conqueror'. Similarly, Jātakhaḍga is said to have defeated enemies, while Devakhaḍga, 'a lordly maker of donations' (*dānapatiḥ*), donated land to the Buddhist monastery of Saṁghamitra for the longevity of his son, Rājarājabhaṭṭa, who confirmed the grant after his accession. Corroborative evidence of Rājarājabhaṭṭa's rule is provided by the account of the Chinese pilgrim, I-tsing, who cites a Buddhist priest, Sheng-Chi's discovery of a Rājabhaṭa ruling over Samataṭa—who is identified with Rājarājabhaṭṭa of the Khaḍga dynasty.[108] The inscription mentions four monasteries, thereby providing important proof of the existence of Buddhism in east Bengal at the time. The history of the dynasty after Rājarājabhaṭṭa is not known.

The Deulbāḍī inscription is also of great importance because it is the first to have been issued by a queen in the history of Bengal–Bihar in the period of this study. The significant fact of Prabhāvatī reverencing a Durgā image while her husband was a devout Buddhist is an aspect of note. Furthermore, the Ashrafpur plate talks of Prabhāvatī owning some land that was later given in donation by the king.

At this juncture, one should note the evidence of the Tipperah copper-plate grant of a *sāmanta* Lokanātha that reveals a line of feudatory chiefs in east Bengal around Tipperah.[109] The grant refers to a fight between Lokanātha and his suzerain, and between Lokanātha and Jayatuṅgavarṣa. As palaeographic evidence assigns the inscription to the seventh century, it is presumed that Lokanātha was a feudatory of the Khaḍga dynasty, and that Jayatuṅgavarṣa was the title of either Khaḍgodyama or Jātakhaḍga.[110]

The Candra Dynasty (c. 900–1050)

The Candras ruled eastern Bengal and the coastal regions of southern Bengal from the tenth to the eleventh century, and constituted one of the most important independent/semi-independent powers of the area during the Pāla period. R.C. Majumdar's reconstruction of the Candra genealogy suggests that they ruled continuously in east Bengal for at least 111 years.[111] The sequence of the Candras is Pūrṇacandra (before 900), Suvarṇacandra (before 900), Trailokyacandra (about AD 900), Śrīcandra (929–75), Kalyāṇacandra (975–1000), Laḍahacandra (1000–20) and Govindacandra (1020–50).[112]

Both Pūrṇacandra and Suvarṇacandra seem to have been petty chieftains under the Pālas, but Trailokyacandra was an independent sovereign with the title *mahārājādhirāja*.[113] He seems to have been successful during the weak succession of Rājyapāla or Gopāla II. Śrīcandra assumed full imperial titles and his conquests are known from the Maināmatī plates of Laḍahacandra and the Dacca plate of Kalyāṇacandra. As noted earlier, the Dacca plates indicate that he helped Gopāla II to get the throne at one point, and returned his captured queen to him. The identity of the Pāla queen in question remains unknown.

The submission of the Gauḍa king to Kalyāṇacandra is indicated by the Maināmatī plates, which say that he 'made the face of the king of Gauḍa bend down under the weight of shame for a long while'. There is also a reference to an invasion of the *mlecchas* repulsed by Kalyāṇacandra that saved the Pālas from further humiliation but made the Pāla king wholly subordinate to him. This indicates the position of the Candras *vis-à-vis* the Pālas. During Kalyāṇacandra's rule, the Candra power was extended over Kāmarūpa and the deltaic region of Bengal.

Kalyāṇacandra was succeeded by Laḍahacandra, his son by Kalyāṇadevī, the daughter of a merchant[114]—itself a significant fact. Laḍahacandra was succeeded by Govindacandra, his son by Queen Saubhāgyadevī. The Tirumalai inscription of Rājendra Coḷa refers to Govindacandra as the ruler of Vaṅgaladeśa in 1021–3 whom he defeated.[115] The Candra inscriptions do not mention Govindacandra's successors and they seem to have been ousted by the Varmans, although Kalacuri records show that the Candra kingdom bore the brunt of their invasions.[116]

The Varman Dynasty (c. 1050–1150)

The Varman dynasty succeeded the Candras in eastern Bengal and, like the latter, constituted one of the most important independent powers in Bengal during the Pāla period. The history of this dynasty is largely reconstructed from the Belāva copper plate of Bhojavarman that states their descent to be from a branch of the Yādava dynasty of Siṁhapura and contains the complete genealogy.

Jātavarman seems to have laid the basis for the greatness of the Varman dynasty and to have been the first independent ruler, because his father, Vajravarman, is not referred to as a king but as a poet and scholar. The Belāva record states that Jātavarman conquered Aṅga after defeating its ruler, probably taking advantage of the confusion caused by the Kaivarta Divya's revolt, to which it makes a significant allusion.[117] In addition, he launched a successful campaign against Kāmarūpa and concluded an important alliance by marrying Vīraśrī, the daughter of the Kalacuri ruler, Lakṣmīkarṇa. This synchronism is important for setting the date of the Varmans and the Pālas as Jātavarman, by this alliance, became the brother-in-law of the Pāla king, Vigrahapāla III.[118]

Jātavarman was succeeded by Sāmalavarman, his son by Vīraśrī. However, the Vajrayoginī plate of Sāmalavarman suggests that it was Harivarman who succeeded Jātavarman, leading to the speculation that Harivarman was the elder brother and predecessor of Sāmalavarman.[119] It is speculated that Harivarman is to be identified with the chief Hari, to whom prominence is accorded in the *Rāmacarita*, and who initially allied with the Kaivarta Bhīma and then sought Rāmapāla's protection by propitiating him with gifts of chariots and elephants.[120] Bhojavarman, the son of Sāmalavarman by Queen Mālavyadevī, was the next Varman ruler and assumed the titles of *parama-vaiṣṇava* and *mahārāja*. The Varman dynasty did not rule for very long, as it was ousted from east Bengal by the Senas immediately after Bhojavarman's reign.[121]

THE SENA DYNASTY (*c.* 1050–1280)

At the outset, one should note that although the Sena dynasty continues well into the thirteenth century, this book will focus on their history until the end of Lakṣmaṇasena's reign (AD 1206), since this falls within the relevant time period. As in the case of the Pālas, the epigraphic evidence—comprising around eleven inscriptions—is more fruitful for purposes of historical reconstruction than the available literary evidence.[122] It is also important that the Sena inscriptions, unlike those of the Pālas, provide a lot of information on the royal women of the dynasty.

The Senas originally belonged to the Karṇāṭa country, evident from their official records. The Deopārā *praśasti* of Vijayasena and the Mādhainagar grant mention a Deccan king, Vīrasena—of doubtful identity—as the remote ancestor of the Senas.[123] R.D. Banerjee feels that the ancestors of the Senas came to Bengal in the train of the Coḷa invasion, while R.P. Chanda believes their origins to be connected with the exploits of the Cālukyan king, Vikramāditya VI, in that they might have formed a principality in Rāḍha (west Bengal) in the confusion caused by the latter's expedition.[124]

The founder of the dynasty, Sāmantasena, is described as belonging to 'the family of the moon' (*dākṣiṇātya-kṣaurīndra*) and 'the head-garland of the karṇāṭa-kṣatriyas', perhaps implying that the Senas were initially brāhmaṇas but later adopted the military profession and became kṣatriyas.[125] The Deopārā inscription indicates that Sāmantasena was the first of the Karṇāṭa–Sena family to migrate to Bengal and, along with the Naihāti inscription, implies that though he was engaged in military campaigns in the south, probably in the service of a Karṇāṭa prince, he was already settled in Rāḍha in west Bengal.[126] It is presumed that Sāmantasena made his family very powerful as his son, Hemantasena (late eleventh century)—for whom only vague praise is recorded—is the first to take royal epithets such as *mahārājādhirāja* in records like the Barrackpore inscription of Vijayasena. His 'great queen', Yaśodevī, is referred to in the Deopārā inscription. He was probably just a chief with an independent principality in Rāḍha.[127]

The real founder of the political fortunes of the Senas in

Bengal was Hemantasena's son, Vijayasena (*c.* 1095–1158), who made many territorial acquisitions. Vijayasena originally seems to have been a feudatory of the Pālas. However, his marriage with Vilāsadevī, a princess of the Śūra family of Apara-mandāra, apparently catapulted him from a mere independent chief of Rāḍha to political greatness. The Khalimpur inscription states that, at a later stage, the Sena king 'impetuously assailed' the lord of Gauḍa, generally identified with Madanapāla.[128] That Vijayasena drove out the Pālas from northern Bengal is proved by this record and by the Barrackpore plate of the sixty-second year of his reign. He also sent a fleet against a combination of powers against him and a list of chiefs with whom Vijayasena came into conflict is provided.[129]

Vijayasena was succeeded by his son, Vallālasena (*c.* 1158–79).[130] The Naihāti plate does not ascribe any concrete military achievements to him but he is credited with defeating Govindapāla of Magadha in 1162.[131] Vallālasena married Rāmadevī, the daughter of the Cālukyan king, Jagadekamalla II—an important political alliance. The Mādhainagar grant of his son, Lakṣmaṇasena, states that the latter—when a crown prince—seized the fortune of the Gauḍa king and made war on Kaliṅga and Kāśī. His dominions probably included Aṅga, Varendra, Rāḍha, Bāgḍi and Mithilā.[132] Interestingly, the *Vallālacarita* records Vallālasena's attempts to borrow money from the great banker, Vallabhānanda, the father-in-law of the Magadhan king, on account of the financial problems caused by the long-drawn war with the Pālas.[133]

Lakṣmaṇasena (*c.* 1179–1206), Vallālasena's son by Rāmadevī, was the last important ruler of the Sena dynasty. The *Tabaqat-i-Nasiri* (thirteenth century) claims that he was around sixty years of age at the time,[134] and inscriptions state his wife to have been Tādādevī/Candrādevī. As stated above, he vanquished the kings of Gauḍa and Varanasi before coming to power, and made expeditions against Kāmarūpa and Kaliṅga, thereby largely extending the Sena power.[135] After the completion of the conquest of Gauḍa, he renamed it Lakṣmaṇavatī and was the first Sena ruler to assume the title of *gauḍeśvara*, as revealed by the Mādhainagar copper plate that also contains an account of his conquests.[136]

As per his sons' inscriptions, Lakṣmaṇasena erected monuments in Puri and Prayāga to celebrate his victories.[137] Interestingly, his court poets, Śaraṇa and Umāpatidhara, also describe the expeditions of an unnamed king who conquered Gauḍa, Kaliṅga, Kāśī, Magadha and Prāgjyotiṣa—a probable allusion to him, while the *Pavanadūta* of Dhoyi, another court poet, talks of Lakṣmaṇasena reaching Malaya (Travancore hills) in the course of his conquests.

Contemporary inscriptions talk of the danger posed to north India by the invasions of Muhammed Ghori, who had defeated the Cauhana king, Pṛthvīrāja, and the Gāhaḍavāla king, Jayacandra.[138] Lakṣmaṇasena was eventually overrun by Ghori's general, Muhammad Bakhtyar Khalji, after a surprise raid on his capital, Nadiya, in 1199 whereby he lost all his possessions. He fled to eastern Bengal and ruled from Vikramapura until around 1206.[139] Although the Sena kings continued to rule here for another fifty years, the Muslims established their authority over south-west and north Bengal in the thirteenth century. However, the decline of Sena power was precipitated not just by the Turkish invasion, but also by neighbouring kingdoms and rebellious feudatories that grew powerful at the cost of the Sena territory.[140]

N. Ray feels that the harmony and synthesis in religion, society and culture of the Pāla period was completely abandoned in the Sena era where the kings rearranged castes to their own liking and not as per *Smṛti* rules.[141] However, Paul notes the improvements they instituted in the economic sphere, for instance, whereby the minute description of land in the Sena grants, as per different standards of measurement in different areas, indicated a general system of land survey/measurement in Bengal under the Senas.

This concludes the political framework of the kingdoms across Bengal and Bihar. The focus, in the subsequent analysis, will largely be on the epigraphic evidence and, to a limited extent, the *Rāmacarita*, in an effort to provide a gendered reconstruction of the relevant period.

NOTES

1. Bāṇa, for instance, indicates the general advancement of Sanskrit in Bengal in the seventh century while referring to poetic styles. He claims that 'in the Gauḍas, there is pomp of syllables'. Jhunu Bagchi, *The History and*

Culture of the Pālas of Bengal and Bihar (c. 750 A.D.–c. 1200 A.D.), New Delhi, Abhinav Publications: 1993, p. 142. R.C. Majumdar, *History of Ancient Bengal*, Calcutta, G. Bharadwaj and Company: 1971, p. 351, says that this disparaging remark probably stems from Bāṇa's dislike for Bengal. Rājaśekhara, too, refers, in his *Kāvyamīmāṁsā*, to the popularity of Sanskrit in Gauḍa/Bengal.

2. Majumdar, *History of Ancient Bengal*, pp. 416–17 says that although the *Brahmavaivarttapurāṇa* and the *Bṛhaddharmapurāṇa* may be said to belong to Bengal, it is difficult to be certain. Both texts are not much later than the thirteenth century (pp. 574–5). Kunal Chakrabarti, 'Texts and Traditions: The Making of the Bengal *Purāṇas*', in *Tradition, Dissent and Ideology: Essays in Honour of Romila Thapar*, ed. R. Champakalakshmi and S. Gopal, Delhi, Oxford University Press: 1996, pp. 56, 64 admits the difficulty of fixing the chronology of the Bengal purāṇas 'with even an approximate degree of certainty'. Jayadeva's *Gīta Govinda* (twelfth century)—an erotic celebration of the love between Rādhā and Kṛṣṇa—also pertains to this period but is, surprisingly, a very inadequate source for a gendered reconstruction (for instance, Lee Siegal, *Sacred and Profane Dimensions of Love in Indian Traditions as Exemplified in the Gītagovinda of Jayadeva*, Delhi, Oxford University Press: 1978).
3. Bani Roychoudhuri, *The Political History of Bengal to the Rise of the Pāla Dynasty*, Calcutta, Sanskrit Pustak Bhandar: 1990, p. 2. References to various places in Bengal, pp. 2–5, 14–23.
4. Majumdar, *History of Ancient Bengal*, p. 7.
5. Gauḍa seems to have implied both a city and an area. Niharranjan Ray, *History of the Bengali People (Ancient Period)*, tr. J.W. Hood, Calcutta, Orient Longman: 1994, pp. 95. Ray notes (pp. 80–1) that Vaṅga, Gauḍa and Puṇḍra were all communities that lived in regions later named after them. The kingdom of Puṇḍravardhana emerged in the seventh century and was called Puṇḍravardhanabhukti under the Pāla–Sena kings.
6. Majumdar, *History of Ancient Bengal*, p. 25; Roychoudhuri, *Political History of Bengal*, pp. 15, 22; P.L. Paul, *The Early History of Bengal*, Calcutta, The Indian Research Institute: 1939, vol. I, p. 1. Note that indigenous tribes like the Vaṅgas, Suhmas, Śabaras, and Puṇḍras are known as *dasyus* in the time of the *Dharmasūtras*, but as kṣatriyas in later literature. Majumdar also talks of the Jain *sūtras* representing the people of Rāḍha as savage/uncultured.
7. Roychoudhuri, *Political History of Bengal*, p. 22. Bengal also seems to have been a part of the Mauryan empire: Yuan Chwang saw many Aśokan topes at Puṇḍravardhana, Karṇasuvarṇa, and Tāmralipti. See Paul, *Early History of Bengal*, I, p. 5. However, note that this should be treated with caution because Yuan Chwang did not understand the difference between Mauryan and other *stūpas*.
8. Majumdar, *History of Ancient Bengal*, pp. 26–9.

9. R.S. Tripathi, *History of Ancient India*, 3rd rpt., Delhi, Motilal Banarsidass: 1967, p. 354; Roychoudhuri, *Political History of Bengal*, pp. 27–8; N. Ray, *History of the Bengali People*, pp. 81–2.
10. Majumdar, *History of Ancient Bengal*, pp. 38, 40, 41. This was so under the Gupta king, Kumāragupta I and, except for Samataṭa, indicates the end of the independence of the region.
11. The Haraha inscription of Īśānavarman (554) talks of the warlike activities of the 'Gauḍas living on the seashore' (*samudrāśrayaṇa*), while the Mahākūṭa inscription (602) states that Kīrtivarman defeated the kings of Aṅga, Vaṅga and Kaliṅga: Paul, *Early History of Bengal*, I, pp. 15–16; Bagchi, *History and Culture of the Pālas*, p. 72.
12. Majumdar, *History of Ancient Bengal*, p. 49.
13. N. Ray, *History of the Bengali People*, p. 96. He says that from the earliest historical times to about the sixth/seventh century, Bengal was divided into the settlements of Puṇḍra, Gauḍa, Rāḍha, Suhma, Samataṭa and Vaṅga, each being distinct and independent. When Śaśāṅka established his reign in Gauḍa, these regions achieved a form of political unity. The historical significance of the name 'Gauḍa' was enhanced whereby the Pāla kings, although 'lords of Vaṅga', liked to be known as 'lords of Gauḍa' (*gauḍeśvara*). Ray says that from the eighth century, the three settlements that became synonymous with Bengal as a whole were Puṇḍravardhana, Gauḍa, and Vaṅga. New divisions came to be subsumed under the name of Gauḍa, as were settlements of several parts of Bengal (pp. 96–7).
14. Roychoudhuri, *Political History of Bengal*, p. 131.
15. Majumdar, *History of Ancient Bengal*, p. 53; Susan L. Huntington, *The 'Pāla-Sena' Schools of Sculpture*, Leiden, E.J. Brill: 1984, p. 31.
16. R.C. Majumdar, 'Political History of South Bihar (550-750 A.D.)', in *Comprehensive History of Bihar*, ed. B.P. Sinha, Patna, Kashi Prasad Jayaswal Research Institute: 1974, vol. I, part II p. 230. B.P. Sinha, *Dynastic History of Magadha*, Delhi, Abhinav Publications: 1977, pp. 131–5 speculates on the identity of a Jayanāga of Gauḍa assigned to this time and his relationship with Śaśāṅka. See also L.D. Barnett, 'Vappaghoṣavāṭa Grant of Jayanāga', *Epigraphia Indica*, vol. XVIII, 1926, pp. 60-4.
17. Majumdar, *History of Ancient Bengal*, p. 48, says the rise of an independent Gauḍa was probably facilitated by Mahāsenagupta's apparent defeat by the Kalacuris, forcing his two sons to live in Prabhākaravardhana's court. This is uncertain but could explain the rise of the Gupta-Magadha kingdom and Śaśāṅka's political equations.
18. This indicates Śaśāṅka's influence in the political field. Śaśāṅka's date of accession is not known but since he was a contemporary of Mahāsenagupta, he probably rose to power at the beginning of the

seventh century. Roychoudhuri, *Political History of Bengal*, pp. 115, 121–2.

19. Majumdar, *History of Ancient Bengal*, p. 50; Tripathi, *History of Ancient India*, p. 354.
20. Roychoudhuri, *Political History of Bengal*, pp. 125–6, cites Barua's speculation that the alliance between Harṣa and Bhāskaravarman was 'disastrous for Śaśāṅka' who fled to Orissa. She also cites the *Āryamañjuśrī-mūlakalpa's* reference to a defeat of Soma (Śaśāṅka) by 'H' (Harṣa). However, there are doubts regarding this. Bāṇa refers to Harṣa's victory over Sindh and Himalayan countries but not over Gauḍa, while Yuan Chwang, despite his bias against Śaśāṅka, does not mention his defeat at Harṣa's hands. Majumdar, *History of Ancient Bengal*, p. 53 speculates that it was only after Śaśāṅka's death that Harṣa could resume his eastern campaign.
21. Evidence is provided in the form of Bhāskaravarman's Nidhānpur grant from his victory camp at Karṇasuvarṇa, as also the *Life*'s account of him meeting Harṣa at Kajangala with 30,000 ships and 20,000 elephants, indicating his suzerainty in that area. In addition, Yuan Chwang calls him the king of 'eastern India' who promised him safe conduct up to Tāmralipti. Majumdar, *History of Ancient Bengal*, pp. 71–2, notes that Harṣa himself had returned from a victorious campaign in Koṅgoda, formerly under Śaśāṅka. Roychoudhuri, *Political History of Bengal*, pp. 128, 136–7; Paul, *Early History of Bengal*, I, p. 26; P.B. Vidyavinoda, 'Nidhānpur Copper Plates of Bhāskaravarman', *Epigraphia Indica*, vol. XII, 1914, pp. 65–79. Śaśāṅka's death was apparently followed by a period of confusion. Yuan Chwang talks of Pūrṇavarman, Harṣa's feudatory, who succeeded Śaśāṅka in Magadha.
22. Roychoudhuri, *Political History of Bengal*, p. 130. Also T. Watters, *On Yuan Chwang's Travels in India*, 2nd edn, Delhi, Munshiram Manoharlal: 1973, pp. 115–16, 183–4. Śaśāṅka, a Śaivite, apparently cut down and burnt the Bodhi tree of Gayā, replaced Buddhist icons with Śiva images, and drove monks out of a monastery at Karṇasuvarṇa in a seemingly anti-Buddhist purge. However, ironically, Yuan Chwang also talks of the flourishing state of Buddhism in Śaśāṅka's own capital, Karṇasuvarṇa, referring to the magnificent Raktamṛttika monastery and several others. His account also indicates the flourishing state of Buddhism in Puṇḍravardhana, Tāmralipti and other places under Śaśāṅka. Note that there is no mention of any fanatical anti-Buddhist acts in Karṇasuvarṇa itself.
23. B.P. Sinha, *The Decline of the Kingdom of Magadha (c.455–1000 A.D.)*, Patna, Motilal Banarsidass: 1954, pp. 132–3 notes that the lineage of the Later Guptas is not known from epigraphic records and their connection with the imperial Gupta dynasty is uncertain. They were probably

feudatories of the imperial Guptas (Tripathi, *History of Ancient India*, p. 355).

24. This, incidentally, explains the term of *mālavarājaputra* used for the two brothers in the *Harṣacarita*: Sinha, *Decline of the Kingdom of Magadha*, p. 176. Note that the Aphsāḍ inscription corroborates the close relationship between Mādhavagupta and Harṣa. Besides, their contemporaneity provides a fixed point in the chronology of the Later Guptas, as Harṣa's dates are clearly known (Sinha, *Dynastic History of Magadha*, p. 80).
25. Majumdar, 'Political History of South Bihar', in *Comprehensive History of Bihar*, ed. Sinha, pp. 223–4 notes that Magadha was the central seat of authority of these last four kings, as all their records are found here.
26. Aphsāḍ is in the Gayā district of Bihar. For details, Roychoudhuri, *Political History of Bengal*, pp. 146–8. It is presumed that Ādityasena was a subordinate ruler under Bhāskaravarman of Kāmarūpa and assumed power after the latter's death. K.K. Thaplyal, *Inscriptions of the Maukharis, Later Guptas, Puṣpabhūtis and Yaśovarman of Kanauj*, Delhi, ICHR/Agam Prakashan: 1985, p. 160.
27. Roychoudhuri, *Political History of Bengal*, pp. 149–50; Sinha, *Dynastic History of Magadha*, pp. 162–5.
28. The description of the camp suggests that Jīvitagupta had a military campaign, probably against Yaśovarman of Kanauj, and he might have died fighting him. Roychoudhuri, *Political History of Bengal*, pp. 150–1. See also J.F. Fleet, *Corpus Inscriptionum Indicarum—Inscriptions of the Early Gupta Kings and Their Successors*, vol. III, 3rd revd edn, Varanasi, 1970, p. 214.
29. Only five of the 1,209 verses of the text (*GV*, 354, 414–17) deal with this event, and verse 1194 alone refers to the slaying. Majumdar, *History of Ancient Bengal*, p. 75. H.C. Ray, *The Dynastic History of Northern India*, 2nd edn, Delhi, Munshiram Manoharlal: 1973, vol. I, p. 277 thinks that the king of Magadha–Gauḍa defeated and killed by Yaśovarman was probably a Śaila king or a Khaḍga ruler.
30. Roychoudhuri, *Political History of Bengal*, 152–3. She points out, however, that Kalhaṇa's account has no direct reference to Lalitāditya invading any part of Bengal. *RT*, IV.148 and IV.323–30 for the references.
31. *RT*, IV.332, 335.
32. N. Ray, *History of the Bengali People*, p. 258 mentions Kalhaṇa's account of the opulence of the citizens of Puṇḍravardhana at the time. Majumdar, *History of Ancient Bengal*, p. 455 cites an interesting reference in Kṣemendra's *Deśopadeśa* to students of Gauḍa who came to Kashmir with frail bodies but soon became overbearing and arrogant. This is another notable instance of the interaction between the two early medieval kingdoms.

33. Majumdar, 'Political History of South Bihar', in *Comprehensive History of Bihar*, ed. Sinha, p. 242, notes that the successive invasions of Yaśovarman of Kanauj and Lalitāditya of Kashmir completed the political disintegration of Magadha and Gauḍa in the mid-eighth century. However, the Pāla empire rose out of these ruins and united these regions of Bengal and Bihar once again.
34. There is a clear discrepancy regarding dates for the Pāla rulers given by various historians, since some of them believe in the existence of ambiguous rulers like Śūrapāla I. The dates provided here are those outlined by Jhunu Bagchi, for not only is her work a fairly comprehensive one, she has also consulted earlier works on this area for her analysis: *History and Culture of the Pālas*, pp. 8–28. However, Bagchi's dates for Gopāla I (*c.* 750–5) appear to be too early in the Pāla context, and *c.* 765–70 seems more appropriate.
35. Thus, Susan Huntington talks of the term being a more 'conventional designation' than an accurate reflection of political realities (*'Pāla-Sena' Schools of Sculpture*, p. 73).
36. Bagchi, *History and Culture of the Pālas*, p. 5. She talks of the Pāla administration being noteworthy for its long and stable government in Bengal (p. 56).
37. Ibid., p. 5. Bagchi discusses the copper plates, stone epigraphs and image inscriptions. Huntington, *'Pāla-Sena' Schools of Sculpture*, pp. 29–31 says, however, that the evidence is often contradictory and incomplete, probably due to the repetition of names and the non-specific references of image inscriptions.
38. Huntington, *'Pāla-Sena' Schools of Sculpture*, pp. 31–2, talks of this *śleṣa* form producing two levels of meaning simultaneously. She adds that though this text is biased in Rāmapāla's favour, it is one of the main sources of Pāla history. Bagchi, *History and Culture of the Pālas*, p. 144, says it is, perhaps, the only *kāvya* of Bengal origin.
39. Haraprasad Sastri, ed., *Rāmacarita: A Historical Record of the Pāl Dynasty by Sandhyākara Nandi*, Varanasi, Bhartiya Publishing House: 1973, p. 1, talks of Rāmapāla's access to court knowledge on this account. This is why Paul talks of his text and the commentary as being 'of unique importance' for Bengal's history in the last half of the eleventh century (Paul, *Early History of Bengal*, I, p. 57).
40. An interesting aspect of the text is that it is inspired by the *Rāmāyaṇa*, although the Pālas were Buddhists. Thus, while stating that he belongs to Vṛhadvati attached to Puṇḍravardhana in Varendra, the author dubs his work a *kaliyuga-rāmāyaṇa* and himself a *kaliyuga-vālmīki*. N. Ray, *History of the Bengali People*, p. 480 calls it a valuable eyewitness account but an imitation of the poem *Rāghavapāṇḍavīya* (*c.* 1123–40).
41. H.C. Ray, *Dynastic History of Northern India*, pp. 346–7. In fact, Haraprasad Sastri who has translated the text has not been able to tackle it in entirety, as it is 'difficult to explain' (*Rāmacarita*, p. 1).

42. R.D. Banerji, *The Pālas of Bengal*, Varanasi, Bhartiya Publishing House: 1973, pp. 53–4 thinks that the commentary is older than the text and was probably written by Sandhyākara Nandi himself.
43. D.C. Sircar, 'Introduction', in A.K. Maitreya, *The Fall of the Pāla Empire*, Darjeeling, University of North Bengal: 1987, p. iv. See also p. 38.
44. Hāravarṣa is, therefore, often identified with Devapāla, Dharmapāla's son: Bagchi, *History and Culture of the Pālas*, pp. 144, 161.
45. Shahanara Husain, 'Village Life in Early Medieval Bengal: A Study Based on the Subhāṣitaratnakoṣa', in *History and Society*, ed. D. Chattopadhyaya, Calcutta, K.P. Bagchi & Company: 1978, pp. 311–12. The text is an anthology of 1,738 verses and poets like Rājaśekhara and Bhavabhūti have been quoted in it. However, it has a preponderance of Bengali poets, most of whom flourished in the Pāla period.
46. Bagchi, *History and Culture of the Pālas*, p. 145, talks of other works by Buddhist grammarians that were popular in Bengal, but there is not enough evidence that they originated there.
47. It provides incomplete data. See Huntington, *'Pāla-Sena' Schools of Sculpture*, p. 31. Majumdar, *History of Ancient Bengal*, p. 166 says that the text preserves many Buddhist traditions regarding India's political history. It also provides names of successive generations of kings of Vaṅgala (southern/eastern Bengal).
48. Bagchi, *History and Culture of the Pālas*, p. 2, specifies, however, that most of Tāranātha's descriptions and those of other foreign historians are imaginary accounts with incorrect names of kings.
49. This, according to Huntington, *'Pāla-Sena' Schools of Sculpture*, pp. 37, 69, is unusual among Indian art schools.
50. Bagchi, *History and Culture of the Pālas*, pp. 132-3, 127. Bitpāla was Dhīman's son and they excelled in stone carving, metal work, and painting. Huntington, *'Pāla-Sena' Schools of Sculpture*, p. 166, talks of the Pāla school of art and notes that the number of images in Bengal show that until around 1025, Bihar and Bengal were in close contact, either transporting images and artisans from place to place, or having artists trained in near-identical styles. Devangana Desai, 'Art Under Feudalism in India (*c*. A.D. 500-1300)', in *The Feudal Order: State Society and Ideology in Early Medieval India*, ed. D.N. Jha, Delhi, Manohar: 2000, pp. 490–1 notes that numerous local centres of art grew between 650 and 900.
51. B.S. Verma, 'Archaeological Excavation and Sites (320–1200 A.D.)', in *Comprehensive History of Bihar*, ed. Sinha, p. 554; B.D. Chattopadhyaya, 'Currency in Early Bengal', *Journal of Indian History*, vol. LV, part III, December 1977, pp. 50–1 says that though the general paucity of coins between the seventh and thirteenth centuries is explained in terms of decline in trade and consolidation of a feudal economy, the gap is wider in and truer of Bengal than of other areas of north India. However, he says there are several familiar coin-names in the Pāla epigraphs. Also

M.R. Tarafdar, 'Trade and Society in Early Medieval Bengal', *Indian Historical Review*, vol. 4, no. 2, January 1978, pp. 274–5 on a natural economy under Pāla–Sena rule.

52. R.S. Sharma, 'Social and Economic Conditions (500–1200 A.D.)', in *Comprehensive History of Bihar*, ed. Sinha, p. 372. However, there is evidence of the comparative richness and luxury of the towns. See, for instance, Majumdar, *History of Ancient Bengal*, p. 340. He cites the *Rāmacarita's* description of Rāmāvatī as 'a city of rows of palaces'.
53. Bagchi, *History and Culture of the Pālas*, p. 88. However, Kunal Chakrabarti stresses the importance of agriculture under the Pālas. He says that traders and artisans were prominent until the seventh century, but from the eighth, powerful landowners became important (*Religious Process: The Purāṇas and the Making of a Regional Tradition*, Delhi, Oxford University Press: 2001, p. 39).
54. Majumdar, *History of Ancient Bengal*, pp. 97–9 says this was because the Pālas were Buddhists and did not care for Brahmanical traditions of this sort.
55. F. Kielhorn, 'Khalimpur plate of Dharmapāladeva', *Epigraphia Indica*, vol. IV, 1897, p. 245. H.C. Ray, *Dynastic History of Northern India*, pp. 282–3, says this indicates that Dharmapāla came from an educated family.
56. Paul, *Early History of Bengal*, I, pp. 34–5. The sources alternatively refer to Varendra as Varendrī. N. Ray, *History of the Bengali People*, p. 88 cites the *Rāmacarita* as indicating that Varendra was the royal seat of the Pāla kings, locating it between the Gaṅgā and the Karatoā. However, Tripathi, *History of Ancient India*, pp. 362–3 asks whether the Pāla capital was Mudgagiri (Monghyr), from where the kings issued several grants.
57. Huntington, '*Pāla-Sena' Schools of Sculpture*, p. 39 notes that there are no inscriptions or monuments definitely ascribable to his reign. However, the Monghyr grant of Devapāla says that Gopāla conquered the world up to the sea. In addition, Tāranātha attributes the Odantapurī monastery (in modern Bihar) and the revival of the Nālandā monastery to him, along with lavish gifts to the Buddhist clergy (Bagchi, *History and Culture of the Pālas*, p. 96).
58. Majumdar, *History of Ancient Bengal*, p. 82; Huntington, '*Pāla-Sena' Schools of Sculpture*, p. 39. *Mātsya-nyāya* is a technical term used in political treatises to indicate a situation where there is no established central authority, resulting in a chaotic state where local chiefs assume royal authority and might alone is right.
59. Paul, *Early History of Bengal*, I, pp. 111–12 says Gopāla's election by the *prakṛtis* has been taken to mean an election by the people. However, *prakṛti* is a technical term meaning principal officers, of which the *Śukranīti* gives ten names like the minister, the judge, etc. Hence, Gopāla was probably placed on the throne by the officers of state.

60. Majumdar, *History of Ancient Bengal*, p. 102; B.P. Sinha, 'Political History of South Bihar (750-1200 A.D.)', in *Comprehensive History of Bihar*, ed. Sinha, p. 251.
61. Majumdar, *History of Ancient Bengal*, p. 104. The Khalimpur grant issued by *paramasaugato mahārājādhirāja śrīmad-dharmapāladeva* and dated in Dharmapāla's thirty-second year refers to his extensive conquests in northern India. In addition, there are clay seals found in Pahārpur bearing the name *śrī-dharmapāladeva* (H.C. Ray, *Dynastic History of Northern India*, pp. 285, 289–90).
62. This settlement was 'readily accepted' by the leading contemporary states of north India like Gandhāra, Avantī, Kuru, and so on. For details, Tripathi, *History of Ancient India*, p. 356; Kielhorn, 'Khalimpur plate', *Epigraphia Indica*, vol. IV, pp. 243–54; H.C. Ray, *Dynastic History of Northern India*, p. 286.
63. Sinha, 'Political History of South Bihar', in *Comprehensive History of Bihar*, ed. Sinha, p. 247. Vatsarāja was later defeated by the Rāṣṭrakūṭa Dhruva who captured the umbrellas.
64. Paul, *Early History of Bengal*, I, p. 37 says this is confirmed by the Baroda and Surat plates of Karkarāja. The Sanjan plates further testify that Dharmapāla and Cakrāyudha submitted to Govinda III Rāṣṭrakūṭa (794–814). Nāgabhaṭṭa is supposed to have seized Kanauj from Cakrāyudha and though Dharmapāla was angered at the dethronement of his protégé, they both suffered defeat at Mudgagiri. See Tripathi, *History of Ancient India*, p. 356.
65. F. Kielhorn, 'Bādal Pillar Inscription of Nārāyaṇapāla', *Epigraphia Indica*, vol. II, 1894, p. 163. Verse 13 reads—*utkāli totkalakulaṁ hṛta-hūṇa-garva kharvīkṛta-draviḍa-gurjara-nātha-darpa gauḍeśvaraścira-mupāsya dhiyaṁ yadīyāṁ*. Majumdar, *History of Ancient Bengal*, p. 115 speculates that the Draviḍa ruler whose pride Devapāla curbed was most probably the Pāṇḍya ruler, Śrī-Māraśrī Vallabha.
66. H.C. Ray, *Dynastic History of Northern India*, p. 290.
67. Paul, *Early History of Bengal*, I, p. 45 thinks this might be a reference to Harjaravarman whose Tezpur rock inscription is dated 829.
68. Sinha, 'Political History of South Bihar', in *Comprehensive History of Bihar*, ed. Sinha, p. 253.
69. Paul, *Early History of Bengal*, I, pp. 46–8. Note, however, that the *yuvarāja* (crown prince) Rājyapāla is mentioned as the *dūtaka* of the Monghyr grant of Devapāla's reign. As he is not mentioned subsequently, it is presumed that he died in his father's reign. Also H.C. Ray, *Dynastic History of Northern India*, pp. 296–7; V.A. Smith, 'The Pāla Dynasty of Bengal', *Indian Antiquary*, vol. XXXVIII, 1909, p. 243. Note that Bagchi provides dates of *c*. 847–60 for Śūrapāla I.
70. H.C. Ray, *Dynastic History of Northern India*, p. 295.
71. Ibid., p. 297.

72. Huntington, '*Pāla-Sena' Schools of Sculpture*, p. 35.
73. Majumdar, *History of Ancient Bengal*, p. 121.
74. This was issued in Nārāyaṇapāla's seventeenth regnal year and records his grant of a village in Mudgagiri to a Śiva shrine: Tripathi, *History of Ancient India*, p. 358. Paul, *Early History of Bengal*, I, p. 48 speculates that Vigrahapāla's decision to become an ascetic might have been due to these foreign invasions.
75. H.C. Ray, *Dynastic History of Northern India*, p. 301.
76. Sinha, 'Political History of South Bihar', in *Comprehensive History of Bihar*, ed. Sinha, p. 256; Majumdar, *History of Ancient Bengal*, p. 121 speculates that Bhoja, who rewarded the services of the feudatory Kalacuri chief against the Pālas by a grant of land, was encouraged by the recent defeat of the Pālas by the Rāṣṭrakūṭas (Sirur inscription), and the pacific disposition of Vigrahapāla and Nārāyaṇapāla.
77. Sinha, 'Political History of South Bihar', in *Comprehensive History of Bihar*, ed. Sinha, p. 258; Tripathi, *History of Ancient India*, pp. 358–9.
78. Huntington, '*Pāla-Sena' Schools of Sculpture*, p. 48. Nārāyaṇapāla apparently took advantage of the fratricidal struggle between Bhoja II and Mahipāla and recovered Uddaṇḍapura.
79. Sircar, 'Introduction', in Maitreya, *Fall of the Pāla Empire*, p. ix.
80. Ibid., p. 51. Majumdar, *History of Ancient Bengal*, pp. 125, 182.
81. Sinha, 'Political History of South Bihar', in *Comprehensive History of Bihar*, ed. Sinha, p. 259. It records the building of a Śiva temple by a Gauḍa king of the Kāmboja family.
82. Paul, *Early History of Bengal*, I, p. 82. Priyaṅgu, the Kāmboja capital, was in south-west Bengal.
83. Huntington, '*Pāla-Sena' Schools of Sculpture*, pp. 55–6.
84. Sinha, 'Political History of South Bihar', in *Comprehensive History of Bihar*, ed. Sinha, pp. 260–1, says this may be a reference to victory over the Kāmboja Pālas. Also R.D. Banerji, 'Āmgachi grant of Vigrahapāla III', *Epigraphia Indica*, vol. XV, 1920, pp. 299–300.
85. H.C. Ray, *Dynastic History of Northern India*, p. 316, says it is evident from the number and distribution of Mahipāla's records that he was a successful king. The Sārnāth inscription, which records repairs effected by Mahipāla through his brothers, provides one of the fixed points of Pāla chronology by stating the *vikrama saṁvat* date 1083, AD 1026.
86. Majumdar, *History of Ancient Bengal*, pp. 132–3; R. Mukherji and S.K. Maity, *Corpus of Bengal Inscriptions Bearing on History and Civilization of Bengal*, Calcutta, Firma K.L. Mukhopadhyay: 1967, p. 28.
87. H.C. Ray, *Dynastic History of Northern India*, p. 326.
88. Bagchi, *History and Culture of the Pālas*, p. 2 notes that Dīpaṅkara Śrījñāna was a Buddhist preacher who went to Tibet from the Pāla kingdom. Tripathi, *History of Ancient India*, p. 361 talks of Cedi records boasting of Nayapāla's submission.

89. Majumdar, *History of Ancient Bengal*, pp. 140–1 says it is difficult to assess the exact nature of Vikramāditya's success, although it seems to have coincided with the establishment of the Senas in Rāḍha (West Bengal), and the Varmans in Vaṅga (East Bengal). Paul, *Early History of Bengal*, I, pp. 56–7 refers to the inscriptions of Someśvara I and II, along with those of Vikramāditya VI, stating that the Cālukyas shattered the pride of Gauḍa and Vaṅga. Note that the Pālas' reduced power in Magadha is shown by four inscriptions from Gayā that glorify one Śūdraka and his son as protectors of Gayā, and of being honoured by 'the lord of Gauḍa' (Majumdar, *History of Ancient Bengal*, pp. 142–3).

90. Sircar, 'Introduction', in Maitreya, *Fall of the Pāla Empire*, p. xvi; Majumdar, *History of Ancient Bengal*, pp. 144–5 speculates that Divya probably took advantage of the weakness of the central authority and dissension between the brothers to kill his master and seize the throne. He says that, interestingly, there is no specific reference to Divya having headed the rebellion, or of his having taken part in the encounter. Not much is known of his activities but he must have been a highly placed officer who made his position secure, as three members of his family ruled in succession.

91. The *Rāmacarita* also praises Bhīma's character and the peace he effected in Varendrī through his policies (*RC*, II.21–7), thereby providing a significant tribute to Sandhyākara Nandi's objectivity. B.N.S. Yadava, *Society and Culture in Northern India in the Twelfth Century*, Allahabad, Central Book Depot: 1973, p. 106 talks of the Kaivarta takeover as an important example of a powerful peasant revolt.

92. Paul, *Early History of Bengal*, I, p. 152 points to the changed attitude of the *sāmantas* in Rāmapāla having to meet them personally, and implore their help with promises of more territory and money.

93. Majumdar, *History of Ancient Bengal*, p. 147; H.C. Ray, *Dynastic History of Northern India*, p. 344.

94. Sircar, 'Introduction', in Maitreya, *Fall of the Pāla Empire*, p. xx, says that this is a reference to Harivarman (1073–1127) of the Varman dynasty. Corroborative evidence of the struggle is provided by the Kamauli plate of Vaidyadeva and the Manahali plate of Madanapāla.

95. H.C. Ray, *Dynastic History of Northern India*, p. 338.

96. Sinha, 'Political History of South Bihar', in *Comprehensive History of Bihar*, ed. Sinha, p. 267.

97. Huntington, *'Pāla-Sena' Schools of Sculpture*, pp. 68, 78. H.C. Ray, *Dynastic History of Northern India*, p. 346 cites the Bihar stone image inscription recording a dedication by Bhaṭṭa Icchara in the second year of Rāmapāla's reign. (Paul, *Early History of Bengal*, II, p. 6: Rāmapāla is also supposed to have built the Jagaddalavihāra, the last great Buddhist monastery.)

98. *RC*, III.31–3, 37, 39, 48; Majumdar, *History of Ancient Bengal*, p. 150. R.S. Sharma, 'Problems of Peasant Protest in Early Medieval India', in *Land System and Rural Society in Early India*, ed. B.P. Sahu, Delhi, Manohar: 1997, p. 352 notes that Rāmapāla built several Śiva temples in Rāmāvatī after his victory to pacify the people who were obviously Kaivartas. Thus, he gives a religious dimension to the Kaivarta revolt, as the Pālas were Buddhists and the Kaivartas were Śaivites.
99. H.C. Ray, *Dynastic History of Northern India*, p. 345.
100. Ibid., p. 348. Majumdar notes that apart from Rājyapāla, Kumārapāla and Madanapāla who are mentioned as Rāmapāla's sons in the sources, Tāranātha refers to another son, Yakṣapāla, who ascended the throne three years before his father's death and ruled for a year. His identity remains uncorroborated, however.
101. Tripathi, *History of Ancient India*, p. 362. The Pāla authority was now confined to a portion of Bihar.
102. Banerji, *Pālas of Bengal*, p. 61 says that the naval victory was probably over Anantavarman Coḍagaṅga.
103. H.C. Ray, *Dynastic History of Northern India*, pp. 350–1.
104. Sinha, *Dynastic History of Magadha*, p. 227.
105. Majumdar, *History of Ancient Bengal*, p. 159. Note that there are specific references in the *Raghuvaṁśa* and in foreign inscriptions to Bengal as a sea-power with a formidable naval force. In addition, the Pālas are supposed to have had the largest elephant force (Paul, *Early History of Bengal*, I, pp. 142–3). However, as Paul points out, the rise of the Candras, Varmans, Khaḍgas and Senas shows that Pāla power was more firmly rooted in northern Bengal and Bihar than in Vaṅga and Rāḍha (p. 85).
106. For instance, Govindapāla of Gayā—who was destroyed in 1162—assumed full imperial titles like 'lord of Gauḍa' in his inscription, but it is unclear whether he was the last Pāla ruler in the Gayā region (Majumdar, *History of Ancient Bengal*, p. 159). However, Sinha, 'Political History of South Bihar', in *Comprehensive History of Bihar*, ed. Sinha, pp. 271–2 speculates that either Vallālasena or Vijayacandra Gāhaḍavāla violently overthrew Govindapāla, as the term *vinaṣṭa rājye*/ *gaṭa rājye* of the Gayā inscriptions seems to indicate.
107. Roychoudhuri, *Political History of Bengal*, pp. 155–7; Majumdar, *History of Ancient Bengal*, pp. 78–9.
108. Roychoudhuri, *Political History of Bengal*, pp. 158–9.
109. Majumdar, *History of Ancient Bengal*, p. 88; Paul, *Early History of Bengal*, I, p. 27. The first of these chiefs was Ādimahārāja who was followed by his son, Śrīnātha. Śrīnātha's son was Bhavanātha, who became an ascetic. Lokanātha, whose exploits the grant describes, was in charge of the administration, but it is unclear whether he was the son

or nephew of Bhavanātha. This grant is also referred to as the Tripura grant.

110. Majumdar, *History of Ancient Bengal*, p. 88. However, R. Basak, 'Tipperah Copper-plate Grant of Lokanātha', *Epigraphia Indica*, vol. XV, 1920, p. 304, says that as Lokanātha is only described as *nṛpa/ kumārāmātya*, he was probably a feudatory chief under Ādityasena of Magadha.

111. Majumdar, *History of Ancient Bengal*, p. 195 does this on the basis of the Bharella Inscription of Laḍahacandra, the Rāmapāla copper plate, the Kedārpur copper plate, and the Dhulla and Edilpur plates of Śrīcandra. Also Mukherji and Maity, *Corpus of Bengal Inscriptions*, pp. 21–3.

112. Mukherji and Maity, *Corpus of Bengal Inscriptions*, p. 22. The Candras seem to have been Buddhists, as the Buddha is invoked in all their grants and the rulers have the epithet of *parama-saṅgha* applied to them (pp. 24–5).

113. Ibid., pp. 25–6.

114. A.H. Dani, 'Chandras of East Bengal', *Indian History Congress Proceedings*, part I, 23rd session, Aligarh, 1960, p. 43. The earliest known sculpture bearing the Candra name is that of a Śiva Naṭarāja image dated in the eighteenth year of King Laḍahacandra (tenth/eleventh century AD). Huntington, *'Pāla–Sena' Schools of Sculpture*, p. 62.

115. Mukherji and Maity, *Corpus of Bengal Inscriptions*, pp. 23, 28.

116. Kokkalla claims to have raided the treasuries of Vaṅga. Hence, the Candras could have been destroyed by the invasions of Lakṣmīkarṇa as well. Majumdar, *History of Ancient Bengal*, p. 196.

117. Mukherji and Maity, *Corpus of Bengal Inscriptions*, pp. 29–30; R. Basak, 'Belāva Copper-plate of Bhojavarmadeva', *Epigraphia Indica*, vol. XII, 1914, p. 42.

118. Mukherji and Maity, *Corpus of Bengal Inscriptions*, p. 235. As Lakṣmīkarṇa's last-known date is 1073, Bhojavarman's reign must be placed at the end of the eleventh century and beginning of the twelfth century (pp. 235–6).

119. Ibid., pp. 30–1.

120. Majumdar, *History of Ancient Bengal*, p. 202.

121. Mukherji and Maity, *Corpus of Bengal Inscriptions*, p. 32. The Varmans adhered to the Brahmanical faith with, however, the same sort of tolerance as demonstrated by the Pālas. For instance, the Vajrayoginī plate of Sāmalavarman records his donation to the Buddhist shrine of Prajñāpāramitā to please his patron deity, Viṣṇu: N.K. Bhattasali, 'Vajrayoginī Plate of Sāmalavarman', *Epigraphia Indica*, vol. XXX, 1958, p. 262.

122. The limitation of Jayadeva's *Gīta Govinda*, in this regard, has already been pointed out. Bagchi, *History and Culture of the Pālas*, p. 88 notes that no coins of the Sena dynasty have been found.

123. Paul, *Early History of Bengal*, I, p. 86; F. Kielhorn, 'Deopārā Stone Inscription of Vijayasena', *Epigraphia Indica*, vol. I, 1892, p. 305.
124. Paul, *Early History of Bengal*, I, pp. 87–8; N. Ray, *History of the Bengali People*, p. 31 speculates that the military commanders/soldiers who accompanied the Cālukyan expedition into Bengal and Bihar, later set up the Sena dynasty in Rāḍha and Vaṅga.
125. Tripathi, *History of Ancient India*, p. 364. This is indicated by the Mādhainagar grant.
126. H.C. Ray, *Dynastic History of Northern India*, p. 355 cites the Deopārā Inscription that Sāmantasena 'slaughtered the wicked robbers of the wealth of Karṇāṭa'. He speculates that Sāmantasena or one of his predecessors came in the train of Vikramāditya Cālukya when he invaded north-east India in the reign of his father, Someśvara I (1044–68). R.D. Banerji, 'Naihāti grant of Vallālasena', *Epigraphia Indica*, vol. IV, 1897, pp. 156–63: it talks of Sāmantasena's forefathers ornamenting the Rāḍha country.
127. Majumdar, *History of Ancient Bengal*, pp. 223–6. Their early land grants were all issued from Vikramapura, the capital city of Vaṅga.
128. For details, Tripathi, *History of Ancient India*, pp. 364–5.
129. Some of these were Nānyadeva of Tirhut and the kings of Kāmarūpa and Kaliṅga. For details, Paul, *Early History of Bengal*, I, pp. 90–1.
130. H.C. Ray, *Dynastic History of Northern India*, p. 364: the Barrackpur grant of Vijayasena indicates that Vallālasena was already associated in the government of the state. Vallālasena is supposed to have compiled the *Dānasāgara* and the *Adbhutasāgara* but apparently left the latter incomplete.
131. Mukherji and Maity, *Corpus of Bengal Inscriptions*, p. 35 note Vallālasena's claim in the *Adbhutasāgara* that he was engaged in warfare with the *gauḍarāja*, identified with Govindapāla. They include Govindapāla in the Pāla dynasty.
132. Majumdar, *History of Ancient Bengal*, p. 217.
133. Paul, *Early History of Bengal*, I, p. 93. Vallabhānanda was siding with the Pālas. Vallālasena is supposed to have reorganized the caste system and instituted 'kulinism' in Bengal but there is no epigraphic corroboration of his social reforms (Tripathi, *History of Ancient India*, p. 365). Attempts seem to have been made to blacken Vallālasena's reputation by those adversely affected by this system.
134. Majumdar, *History of Ancient Bengal*, p. 217. The text was written by Minhaj-ud-din Abu-Umar-i-Usman.
135. Ibid., pp. 231–3; Mukherji and Maity, *Corpus of Bengal Inscriptions*, p. 35.
136. Majumdar, *History of Ancient Bengal*, p. 226. Vijayasena and Vallālasena did not assume the title of *gauḍeśvara* in their records—it was attributed to them in the grants of their successors.

137. Mukherji and Maity, *Corpus of Bengal Inscriptions*, p. 36; Majumdar, *History of Ancient Bengal*, p. 221.
138. Mukherji and Maity, *Corpus of Bengal Inscriptions*, pp. 36-7.
139. Lakṣmaṇasena was succeeded by his sons, Viśvarūpasena and Keśavasena, but there are no detailed accounts of their reigns or that of their successors. Majumdar, *History of Ancient Bengal*, p. 227 cites the *Tabaqat-i-Nasiri* as saying that Lakṣmaṇasena's descendants ruled in Bengal up to 1245, and probably until 1260.
140. Majumdar, *History of Ancient Bengal*, p. 227. The Sẹnas promoted the Brahmanical religion. Vijayasena was a Śaivite and so was Vallālasena whose Naihāti grant bears the title *niḥśaṅka-śaṅkara*. Majumdar, *History of Ancient Bengal*, pp. 218–19, 231; P.L. Paul, *The Early History of Bengal*, Calcutta, The Indian Research Institute: 1940, vol. II, p. 51.
141. N. Ray, *History of the Bengali People*, p. 355; Sushila Mandal, *History of Bengal: The Middle Age*, Calcutta, Prakash Mandir: 1970, part I, p. 21 praises the Pālas but criticizes the Senas for the 'religious degeneration, social stagnation and political sterilization' of Bengal.

CHAPTER XI

Bengal–Bihar: A Gendered Perspective

A gendered reconstruction of the society and polity of the kingdoms that were located across Bengal and Bihar between the seventh and the twelfth centuries is now attempted in this chapter. As noted earlier, this analysis spans the reign of the Pālas, Senas, and other minor dynasties like the Later Guptas, the Khaḍgas, the Candras, and the Varmans. It also discusses the rule of Śaśāṅka.

Unlike the other two sections, the discussion here does not follow a chronological sequence. This is because the bulk of the source material pertains to the Pāla–Sena period of around 400 years. Other dynasties like the Khaḍgas, Candras, and Varmans ruled for much shorter periods and, besides, there are very few sources pertaining to their rule. For example, the history of the Varman dynasty is essentially reconstructed through a single inscription, the Belāva plate of Bhojavarman. Therefore, I have chosen to focus on the Pāla–Sena period first and subsequently analyse the other kingdoms.

As mentioned in the previous chapter, the focus is largely on the information provided by around 100 inscriptions due to the paucity of relevant literary sources, with the notable exception of Sandhyākara Nandi's *Rāmacarita* (eleventh century)—a useful source for the Pālas.

WOMEN AND THE PĀLA RECORDS

To begin with, one should note that the inscriptions of the Pāla period maintain an almost complete silence on the royal women of the dynasty, the reconstruction of their presence being largely a process of inference and deduction. This lacuna is striking on account of the fact that the Pāla rule spanned 400 years and seventeen kings, and yet only six of their queens have a presence in the records, the rest being unnamed, shadowy figures. The silence is even more accentuated when one considers the forceful and vigorous presence of the royal women of the kingdoms of contemporary Kanauj and Kashmir—especially the latter—that we have seen.

In addition, the palpable presence of non-royal women of the Pāla period poses a sharp contrast to the seemingly insubstantial role of their royal counterparts. Predictably, these aspects are glossed over in most secondary sources on Bengal and this, too, will be discussed. The analysis is spread over several sections that span a reconstruction of the identities of the royal Pāla women, as also the role/presence of non-royal women.

Royal Women and the Genealogical Line

Before attempting a survey of the royal Pāla women—in as sequential a manner as possible—there are two important points to take note of. First, the Pāla queens are not included in the list of important court functionaries who are informed of the various grants. This, as will be shown in subsequent sections, is radically different from the inscriptions of the Senas, Candras, and Varmans, where queens figure prominently in the list of executors of land-grant transactions, thereby attesting to their prominence. Second, only those queens who were involved in politically strategic marriage alliances find mention in the Pāla records. Most of these alliances seem to have been made with the Rāṣṭrakūṭas in an obvious attempt to solve political differences.[1]

A paradoxical feature of the Pāla grants is that most of them were made for the increase of merit and the fame of the parents of the royal donors, but few of the mothers invoked are named. Thus, for instance, the Belwā plate of Mahipāla I does not mention a single woman in the genealogical list but is intended for the merit of the king and his parents.[2] This is similar to the Belwā plate of Vigrahapāla III, the Bāngaṛh grant of Mahipāla I, and the Nālandā copper-plate grant of Devapāla. References to the royal Pāla women in other contexts are, at best, fleeting, and, at worst, oblique and obscure.

As regards the first Pāla ruler, Gopāla, R.C. Majumdar points to a subtle reference to the royal family of his wife, Deddadevī, in the Khalimpur copper-plate of Dharmapāla, their son (ninth century).[3] Verse 5 states, 'the illustrious Deddadevī, a daughter of the Bhadra king, became the queen of that brilliant ruler of the earth, to him a source of joy'. It further compares Deddadevī to the wives of deities like the moon, Viṣṇu and Śiva, the word *bhadrātmajā* being used after Bhadrā, the name of Kuvera's wife. F. Kielhorn views it as an epithet qualifying Deddadevī, translates it as 'a daughter of the Bhadra king', and sees Bhadra as a tribal or family name.[4] A.K. Maitreya, however, takes the reference to mean 'daughter of a gentleman'.[5]

Dharmapāla's marriage with Raṇṇādevī, the daughter of a Rāṣṭrakūṭa prince, Parabala, is an illustrative case of a politically imperative marriage bond.[6] Dharmapāla probably sought the help of the Rāṣṭrakūṭas when he was defeated by the Pratihāra ruler, Nāgabhaṭṭa II.[7] However, although the Rāṣṭrakūṭa king, Govinda III, defeated Nāgabhaṭṭa, the possibility of the Pratihāras attempting to recover power could not be ruled out. B.P. Sinha hypothesizes that Dharmapāla's awareness of this future Pratihāra threat prompted him to forge an understanding with the Rāṣṭrakūṭas through the marriage alliance with Raṇṇādevī in about 798, even at the advanced age of 45 years.[8]

The Monghyr copper-plate inscription of Dharmapāla's son, Devapāla, states,[9]

> Entering into the life of a householder that ruler of the earth (Dharmapāla) married Raṇṇādevī, daughter of Śrīparabala, the foremost of the Rāṣṭrakūṭas (verse 9—*śrī-parabalasya duhitṛhi kṣitipatina rāṣṭrakūṭa-tilakasya, raṇṇā-devyāha paṇirjagṛhe gṛha-medhinā tena*).

Verse 11 talks of this 'praiseworthy' and 'devoted' wife of Dharmapāla giving birth to Devapāla.

There is no information on the wives of Devapāla in any epigraphic source. Ironically, however, his Nālandā copper-plate grant provides details on another woman—Tārādevī, the mother of Bālaputradeva, the Śailendra ruler of Suvarṇadvīpa. The inscription records Devapāla's grant of villages Nandivanāka, Maṇivātaka, Natikā, and Hastigrāma in Rājagṛha *viṣaya*, along with Pālāmaka in Gayā *viṣaya*, to Bālaputradeva through an ambassador for the upkeep of the monastery built at Nālandā by the former.[10] Verse 30 refers to Bālaputra's mother, Tārā, the queen consort of Bālaputra's father, the king of Yavabhūmi. Tārā is described as the daughter of the great ruler, Dharmasetu, and compared to the goddess of that name. Interestingly, the grant of villages was apparently made at her behest.

This inscription has generally been used only to show Devapāla's interaction with Bālaputra,[11] although it is unique in the sense that a royal woman from another country is behind the grant, and details of her ancestry are clearly revealed. Paradoxically, no similar light is thrown on the women associated with Devapāla.[12] Considering that the grant was made in the thirty-ninth year of his reign, one would expect his marriage to have taken place long before this—and yet, the women of his court remain deeply in shadow.

The next significant alliance was the one between Vigrahapāla I and Lajjādevī, the daughter of the Haihaya king of Tripurī, probably designed to win over the Kalacuri friendship.[13] The Bhāgalpur copper-plate inscription of Nārāyaṇapāla states:

> Vigrahapāla had a spouse named Lajjā, the ornament of the race of the Haihayas, who purified the families of her father and husband by her pure conduct (v. 9—*lajjeti tasya . . . patnī babhūva kṛta-haihaya-vaṁśābhūṣā, yasyāha śucī ni caritāni pituśca vaṁśe patyuśca pāvana-vīdhiha paramo babhuva*).[14]

Corroborative reference to this marriage is made in the *Rāmacarita* (*RC*, I.9).

The most momentous marriage alliance of the Pāla dynasty seems to have been the one between Rājyapāla, the sixth Pāla king, and Bhāgyadevī, the daughter of the Rāṣṭrakūṭa king, Tuṅga.[15] As mentioned in the previous chapter, Rājyapāla ruled at a time when the Pāla power was at a critical stage, faced with the strong Pratihāras of Kanauj who occupied northern Bihar and Bengal. The matrimonial alliance was obviously for strengthening purposes, while also having the effect of causing a temporary cessation in hostilities between the Pālas and the Rāṣṭrakūṭas.[16]

The significance of this alliance can be gauged from the fact that it is given prominence in every official record of the Pālas after

Rājyapāla. For instance, Bhāgyadevī is the only woman included in the genealogy provided by the Āmgachi grant of Vigrahapāla III and the Bāngaṛh grant of Mahipāla I.[17] Verse 8 of the Bāngaṛh inscription refers to Bhāgyadevī as 'the daughter of the high-crested Tuṅga, the moon of the Rāṣṭrakūṭa family' (*tasmāt-pūrvvakṣiti-dhrānnidhiriva mahasāṁ rāṣṭrakūṭānvayendos-tuṅgasyottuṅga-maulerddubitari tanayā bhāgya-devyāṁ prasūtaḥ*).

Other politically strategic marriages obviously paled in comparison to this one. Dharmapāla's marriage with Raṇṇādevī is only known from the Monghyr and Nālandā grants of Devapāla, while the marriage of Vigrahapāla I with Lajjādevī is only known from the Bhāgalpur grant of Nārāyaṇapāla. Bhāgyadevī, on the other hand, features in every genealogical account of the Pālas thereafter, thereby underscoring the great political importance of this alliance.[18]

Significantly, Bhāgyadevī's presence is useful in another aspect of historical reconstruction, centering round the Kāmboja interregnum in the later part of the tenth century. As noted earlier, the Irda copper-plate of one Nayapāladeva refers to Rājyapāla, Nārāyaṇapāla, and Nayapāla—also names of Pāla rulers.[19] The inscription also mentions a Bhāgyadevī, thereby posing a striking similarity with the Pāla line. While some scholars question the very existence of the Kāmboja rule, B.P. Sinha stresses the differences between the two sets of rulers despite the similarity in names. He points out that Bhāgyadevī of the Pāla records is always mentioned with the Tuṅga/Rāṣṭrakūṭa connection, whereas this is not true of the Bhāgyadevī of the Irda plate.[20] Hence the Bhāgyadevī of the Irda plate was not the same as her royal Pāla namesake and, therefore, belonged to a completely different dynastic line.

There is, however, another argument to show that the Irda plate belonged to a different line of kings—and this is an aspect that has, hitherto, not been considered by any scholar. The Irda inscription mentions the queen (*mahiṣī*) as the first category of executors of the grant.[21] This is in complete contradistinction to the Pāla grants where the queens do not even figure in the list of executors. The Irda plate would therefore have belonged to a different line of kings, whose women were accorded prominence in the public domain.

The identity of subsequent Pāla queens is largely ambiguous.[22] As mentioned in the previous chapter, there is an interesting but cryptic reference in the Khajurāho Inscription (AD 1001) to the queens of Rāḍha and Aṅga who were apparently imprisoned by the Candella king, Dhaṅga, as part of the ongoing Candella crusade against the Gauḍas.[23] However, the identity of these women remains unclear, there being no corroborative reference in the Pāla records.

One can also consider the Dacca plates of Kalyāṇacandra of the Candra dynasty that claim that Śrīcandra (925–75) installed Gopāla II on the throne, at one point, and returned the captured Pāla queen to her husband.[24] Thus, 'he was great in the great festivity of reinstating Gopāla, was a protector of sacrifices in returning the Pāla queen, who was defeated at ease and captured'. The identity of this queen, and the reasons for her capture, remain shrouded in mystery, as there is no corresponding mention in the Pāla records. One could speculate that she might have acted as Gopāla's surety—in a fashion similar to Kalhaṇikā of the Kashmir section—and was released on his reinstatement.[25]

The marriage alliance between Vigrahapāla III and Yauvanaśrī, the daughter of the Kalacuri king Lakṣmīkarṇa (1041–70), figures next in the line of crucial matrimonial connections. As mentioned in the previous chapter, the struggle between the Pālas and the Kalacuris was a protracted one that spanned the reigns of Mahipāla I and Nayapāla—the immediate predecessors of Vigrahapāla III—and finds mention in Tibetan sources, Kalacuri records, and the *Rāmacarita*. Nayapāla's clash with Lakṣmīkarṇa, the son of the Kalacuri ruler, Gāṅgeyadeva, was particularly fierce. However, the *Rāmacarita* indicates that Vigrahapāla III defeated Lakṣmīkarṇa and married his daughter, Yauvanaśrī, in a probable attempt to cement an alliance.[26]

Alternatively, as suggested by P.L. Paul, Lakṣmīkarṇa's motive was to achieve lasting peace with the Pālas.[27] The threats posed by the Cālukyas and Paramāras in the south and west, as well as the rising power of the Candellas, might have impelled him to make an alliance. In either case, however, the strategic importance of this marriage lent an added significance to the figure of Yauvanaśrī. Yauvanaśrī's sister, Vīraśrī, was also involved in another politically vital marriage alliance—with the Varman king, Jātavarman. This will be discussed in a subsequent section.

Significantly, Vigrahapāla III concluded another highly important marriage alliance that witnessed the continuation of the Pāla-Rāṣṭrakūṭa bond. Although this is not mentioned in any inscription, the *Rāmacarita* indicates that he married a sister of Mathaṇadeva of the Rāṣṭrakūṭa branch of Magadha.[28] As will be shown below, Mathaṇa, along with his sons and nephews, rendered signal service to Vigrahapāla's son, Rāmapāla, in regaining the Pāla kingdom from the Kaivartas.

Moving on to the reign of Rāmapāla's son, Madanapāla, one of the most significant inscriptions is now the Manahali copper-plate grant.[29] Issued in the king's eighth regnal year, it records the gift of a village in Koṭivarṣa *viṣaya* in Puṇḍravardhanabhukti to Vaṭeśvarasvāmiśarman, as his fee for chanting the *Mahābhārata* at the request of Citramatikā, Madanapāla's chief queen (v. 44–46— . . . *paṇḍita-bhaṭṭa-putra-śrī-vaṭeśvara-svāmi-śarmaṇe paṭṭa-mahādevī-citramatikayā veda-vyāsa-prokta-prapāṭita-mahābhārata-samutsargigata-dakṣiṇātvena bhagavantaṁ buddha-bhaṭṭārakamuddiśya śāsanīkṛtya pradattosmābhihi*). Not only does this inscription reveal the name of Madanapāla's mother, Madanadevī, its ambiguous wording seems to indicate that Citramatikā might actually have been the donor.[30] On the other hand, the word *asmā* or 'by us' could also imply that this was a joint donation of the royal couple.

Considering the significance of the information provided in this verse, it is surprising that in the translation provided by R. Mukherji and S.K. Maity, the vital verse regarding Citramatikā has not been subjected to a detailed translation like the other verses. More stress is laid, for instance, on the announcer, Bhīmadeva, and the artist, Tathāgatasara, than on the only probable royal Pāla female donor.[31]

Verse 18 talks of Madanapāla's parents thus: 'After Gopāla, his uncle Madanapāla, a son of Rāmapāla and born of the womb of Madanadevī . . . protected the earth.' The *Rāmacarita* indicates that Rāmapāla eventually gave the throne to his son and in his last days was accompanied by an unnamed queen whose company he enjoyed for long (*RC*, IV.1–2). It is unclear whether this is a reference to Madanadevī or some other queen. Additionally, her fate after Rāmapāla drowned himself is another matter for conjecture. There is, likewise, no information on the mothers and wives of Kumārapāla, Madanapāla's brother, or Gopāla III, Madanapāla's nephew, who were his predecessors on the throne.[32]

From these details, a few general points emerge that can be understood within a broader context. To begin with, the importance of royal women is foregrounded by the fact of their strategic marriage alliances. However, these alliances were not always binding sureties in that they did not deter the Rāṣṭrakūṭas from undertaking campaigns against the Pālas or claiming suzerainty over them.[33] Similarly, Devapāla apparently defeated a Rāṣṭrakūṭa king, although his mother belonged to that line. Nevertheless, matrimonial alliances—and the royal women who were part of such alliances—were integral to the Pāla foreign policy.

This in itself raises the issue of their comparative invisibility in the official records. Why, for instance, does Bhāgyadevī only figure in genealogical accounts and not as a donor? Did she not desire more prominence when she obviously knew how indispensable her connections were? By extension, were the other Pāla queens (Raṇṇādevī and Lajjādevī) content with their involvement in crucial marriage bonds and no more? Why, in the 'extensive' Pāla administrative structure and 'expanded bureaucracy',[34] was there apparently no role for women?

A parallel could, perhaps, be drawn with the Vijayanagara empire, at least as regards the non-participation of royal women in donations. Kanakalatha Mukund notes the sharp decline in references to women during the Vijayanagara rule after the fourteenth century and opines that the culture of the rulers might have discouraged the public display of rights through recorded endowments.[35] The Pālas might have been similarly restrictive with regard to women's property rights and donations. Yet this does not satisfactorily explain the general invisibility of royal Pāla women.

And yet, interestingly, archaeological evidence suggests that these women *did* have a public presence. B.S. Verma makes a fleeting reference to the site of Patharghāṭa in Bhāgalpur (Bihar) that has sculptures on the rocky hills and caves. Among these are 'wrestling scenes witnessed by the king and the queen', belonging to the Pāla period.[36] The implication here—that Verma, incidentally, does not consider—is that the queens obviously had a public presence that would seem to be at variance with the epigraphic evidence.

Similarly, it is entirely possible that the Pāla royal women influenced the religious activities of the rulers. It becomes necessary, therefore, to have some idea of the religious preferences of the Pālas. The Pāla kings were Buddhists and nearly all the Buddhist icons and temples discovered in Bengal belong to their period.[37] They founded the Odantapurī, Somapur, and Vikramaśīlā monasteries, and were patrons and supporters of Nālandā. However, equal respect was accorded to the Brahmanical religion in the form of land grants, the mention of Brahmanical deities and temples in royal inscriptions, and the permeation of ideas from the *Rāmāyaṇa*, the *Mahābhārata*, and the Purāṇas in these records.[38] In fact, Nārāyaṇapāla's Bhāgalpur plate does not even address him as *parama-saugata* as was usual. It appears from his donations that he worshipped Śiva whereby he built a thousand temples for Śiva-bhaṭṭāraka.[39] In addition, the Pāla kings upheld the Brahmanical caste system, proved, for instance, by the Āmgachi inscription of Vigrahapāla III that describes him as the guardian of the four varṇas.[40] Furthermore, there is evidence of Pāla kings attending the sacrificial ceremonies of their brāhmaṇa ministers.[41]

Most of the Pāla kings appear to have married princesses of brāhmaṇa families. The influence of these Hindu queens could, perhaps, be a partial explanation behind the religious toleration of the Buddhist Pālas, despite their assiduous promotion of Buddhism. Haraprasad Sastri points to the probable influence of Dharmapāla's Hindu queen, Raṇṇādevī—the daughter of the Rāṣṭrakūṭa Parabala who had erected a Vaiṣṇava temple at Paithan—in his endowing a Viṣṇu temple.[42] Furthermore, some of the Pāla donations were inspired by wholly Brahmanical causes as, for instance, the donation of land for the rendition of the *Mahābhārata* for Madanapāla's wife, Citramatikā.[43]

Finally, do secondary works on the Pāla dynasty take cognisance of its gendered aspects? The answer is definitely in the negative, for the gender blindness of most of these works is as marked as those pertaining to Kaṣhmir and Kanauj. Thus, for instance, in *The Pāla Dynasty of Bengal*, V.A. Smith provides a list of inscriptions, a dynastic list, and the Pāla genealogy, but omits to mention Rāmapāla's wife, Madanadevī, in the genealogy and refers to only three Pāla queens—Raṇṇādevī, Bhāgyadevī, and Citramatikā.[44] This is reminiscent of M.A. Stein's omission of the names of queens Sugandhā and Diddā from the genealogical table of rulers in Kashmir.

One can also mention Verma's failure to discuss the importance of the Pāla royal women, despite his fleeting references to their having contributed to strategic political alliances and influencing religious faiths in his *Socio-Religious, Economic and Literary Condition of Bihar (From A.D. 319-1000)*. Maitreya seems to adopt a slightly more balanced attitude as seen by his brief comments on the interesting ways in which queens are alluded to in the Pāla records. He talks of Devapāla referring to his father's marriage with Raṇṇādevī, of Nārāyaṇapāla mentioning his mother, Lajjādevī, and of Mahipāla I stating that his grandfather was born of Bhāgyadevī.[45] Yet he seems to take cognisance of only three Pāla queens here.

R.S. Sharma is one of the very few to notice the silence on royal women in the Pāla records.[46] He says that in pre-Pāla times, women were evidently important, the queens figuring in the genealogical tables of the Later Guptas, Maukharis, Vardhanas, and Pratihāras. Sharma also suggests, from their absence in Pāla genealogies, that women in ruling families had a low position under the Pālas. He feels, therefore, that this could suggest matrilineal traces among pre-Pāla dynasties while the Pālas were completely patrilineal. Sharma contrasts this with the contemporary situation in Orissa where women played an important part in the administration, probably on account of the tribal background.

One should note here that this situation could also be fruitfully contrasted with the kingdoms of contemporary Kashmir and Kanauj where, as discussed in earlier sections, royal women had a palpably visible and significant role, clearly documented by epigraphic and literary sources. The reasons behind their relative invisibility in the Pāla context remain unclear in view of the lack of substantial evidence. Yet it is possible to speculate that the royal Pāla women did enjoy a more significant role than that revealed by the inscriptions, as we shall see below.

Sibling Rivalries and Contested Successions

A significant feature of the Pāla records is that several instances of sibling rivalries can be gleaned from them. This in turn could be a reflection of harem rivalries in that—as with the kingdoms of contemporary Kashmir and, particularly, Kanauj—the son of the most powerful queen could often triumph over his other sibling contenders for the throne. While there are no clear indications of the involvement of royal Pāla women in court politics (unlike the case of royal participants in harem rivalries in Kashmir and Kanauj), certain useful inferences can be drawn from the available evidence.

One of the most significant indications of harem rivalry can be discerned in the Monghyr copper-plate grant that talks of Dharmapāla's marriage with Raṇṇādevī, the daughter of the Rāṣṭrakūṭa, Śrīparabala. Verse 10, that indicates Raṇṇādevī's rivalry with the other unnamed wives of Dharmapāla, states:

> Is this lady an embodiment in human form of royalty or earth itself, put into human shape or an incarnation of the king's fame or the presiding deity of his household—creating these doubts in the minds of his subjects, she (Raṇṇādevī) of pure conduct defeated with her really great virtues the whole harem (*dhṛtatanuriyaṁ lakṣmīha sākṣāt kṣitirṇu śarīriṇī kimavanipateha kīrttimūrttāthvā gṛha-devatā, iti vidadhatī śucyācārā vitarka-vatīha prajāha prakṛti-guru-bhiryā śuddantaṁ guṇairakarodadhaha*).[47]

It is possible to make the reasonable guess that Raṇṇādevī was able to quell the other women of the harem on account of her politically strategic family connections. The successor of Dharmapāla, Devapāla taking the throne could then be seen as a concrete manifestation of her superior position and probable influence.

Indications of sibling rivalry too are revealed in Devapāla's accession to the throne and in that of his successor. The Bhāgalpur inscription refers to Dharmapāla's younger brother, Vākpāla, who 'carried out the commands of his elder brother' (v. 4). It further reveals that Vākpāla's son, Jayapāla, was a 'conqueror' who vanquished enemies and 'thus caused his elder brother (*pūrvaja*) Devapāla to enjoy the pleasures of the kingdom of the world' (v. 5).[48] Jayapāla's son is identified as Vigrahapāla (v. 7) and he is seen as Devapāla's succesor. Thus, as Smith points out, Devapāla seems to be the nephew of Dharmapāla and not his son, thereby contradicting the Monghyr inscription that talks of him as Dharmapāla's son and successor.[49]

These inscriptions raise the possibility of sibling/harem rivalry on two levels. On the one hand, it is unclear whether Dharmapāla's mother, Deddadevī, was Vākpāla's mother as well. If she was, that could explain Vākpāla's compliance with his elder brother's orders. Alternatively, Vākpāla might have had a different mother and his submission might be seen as a practical acceptance of Dharmapāla's greater power. Once again, Deddadevī's probable superiority on account of her important connections might have ensured this state of affairs.

On the other hand, it appears that the successors of Vākpāla and Jayapāla—rather than those of Devapāla—are involved in the furtherance of the Pāla line, thereby showing a disregard for the laws of primogeniture. This not only allows the possibility of two genealogies but also, as per H.C. Ray, raises the spectre of a 'palace revolution' in the accession of both Devapāla and Vigrahapāla I.[50] It is important to note here that although the Pāla records do not make any clear statement about this, there are many subtle references that hint at the same.

As noted earlier, the parentage of Devapāla's successor, Vigrahapāla I, appears to be a controversial aspect. Although the Bhāgalpur plate seems to indicate that he was born of Devapāla, the subject of the relevant verse is Jayapāla.[51] It is important to note here that there is no mention of Vākpāla or Jayapāla in the grants of Dharmapāla and Devapāla, but they appear regularly in the grants of Vigrahapāla's descendants, where the victories of the reigns of Dharmapāla and Devapāla are attributed to them. Hence, this strengthens the possibility of their direct connection with Vigrahapāla and his son, Nārāyaṇapāla.[52]

The *Rāmacarita* provides several significant details on another rivalry, between the three sons of Vigrahapāla III: Mahipāla II, Śūrapāla II, and Rāmapāla. The text describes Mahipāla's imprisonment of Śūrapāla II and Rāmapāla on his accession to the throne. Maitreya concludes that Rāmapāla was the king-elect but that Mahipāla claimed the throne by the law of primogeniture. He was apparently spurred by the fear of Rāmapāla's popularity and his probable designs on the throne.[53]

As noted earlier, Rāmapāla eventually won back the kingdom with the help of his maternal uncle, Mathaṇa. This fact, in itself, accords great significance to the figure of Rāmapāla's mother and Mathaṇa's sister—who, however, remains unnamed in the records. Perhaps the rivalry between her and Yauvanaśrī, the other wife of Vigrahapāla III, translated into the rivalry between their sons—although the identity of Mahipāla's mother remains unclear.[54]

There are indications of rivalry on another front as well. The Manahali copper-plate grant of Madanapāla indicates that Śūrapāla II ascended the throne, at some stage, referring to him as *narapati*. However, the *Rāmacarita* does not provide tangible information on him, either during Rāmapāla's exile and struggle or the aftermath of the quelled Kaivarta rebellion, giving the impression that the throne passed from Mahipāla II and the Kaivartas to Rāmapāla. This has led R.D. Banerji to speculate that Rāmapāla murdered Śūrapāla II to get the throne.[55] R.C. Majumdar contests this theory, claiming that Śūrapāla II probably played no part in the recovery of Varendrī and that Rāmapāla succeeded him on the throne after his death.[56]

It should be noted that the Bangāon plate of Vigrahapāla III names the *dūtaka* as the *mantrin* Prahasitarāja, described as a son of the king.[57] One can presume another fratricidal palace intrigue here, as this son of Vigrahapāla is entirely unknown and does not have the usual 'pāla' name ending. Interestingly, D.C. Sircar believes that he was born of a concubine, which would explain the name and his relative obscurity.[58] If so, it is highly significant that a son of a mere concubine was accorded prominence in an official record and in court, thereby reflecting the influence probably wielded by his mother.

Significantly, there seems to have been some rivalry between the three sons of Rāmapāla as well. The sources indicate that

Kumārapāla succeeded Rāmapāla but the *Rāmacarita* dismisses his reign without an explanation as to why he superseded his brother Rājyapāla (*RC*, IV.14–15). After all, the text refers to Rāmapāla having discussions with Rājyapāla, who assisted in the recovery of Varendrī, and who also seems to have been the unnamed son to whom Rāmapāla entrusted the kingdom in his old age (*sūnusamarpitarājya*—*RC*, IV.1).[59] There is no evidence, besides, that Rājyapāla died young, enabling Kumārapāla to take over the throne.

The text also does not indicate why Kumārapāla's son and successor, Gopāla III, was succeeded by his uncle, Madanapāla. Interestingly, Banerji suggests that Madanapāla murdered Gopāla on the grounds that both the *Rāmacarita* (*RC*, IV.12) and the Manahali grant (v. 17) indicate Gopāla's unnatural death as an infant.[60] However, the Rajibpur image inscription talks of the installation of a Sadāśiva image by one Purṣottamadeva in the fourteenth year of Gopāla's reign, thereby disproving the view of his having died in childhood.[61]

The Pāla royal records, therefore, provide a highly variegated picture. They accord very limited space to the royal women, implying their complete marginalization in the socio-political milieu. However, they also provide evidence of sibling and/or harem rivalry that implies the involvement of some of these women in court politics. This raises the possibility of a more active role for them than is usually presumed.

The indiference of secondary sources to these gendered inferences is, of course, a familiar, marked factor. Ironically—and predictably—the identity of the rulers' sons and the possible reasons for the insertion or omission of their names becomes the subject of painstaking and detailed analysis, while there is hardly any speculation on the near-total absence of royal women from the records.

Gopāla's Accession

Tāranātha provides a curious yet significant account of Gopāla's accession in *Tibetan History of Buddhism in India* (1608) in that a woman was apparently involved in the process. Tāranātha talks of the previous contenders to the throne having to deal with 'a strong and ugly Nāga woman', who assumed the form of an earlier king's queen (either Govicandra or Lalitacandra of the previous Candra dynasty) and killed every elected king.[62] Thus a new king was killed every night, and the body thrown out at dawn by this woman.

After several years of this situation, the lot fell to the son of a family whom a devotee of goddess Cuṇḍā was visiting. The guest offered to take the son's place for money and was elected king by the leaders. At midnight, when the *nāga* woman approached him, he struck her with the wooden club sacred to his deity, and killed her. The people were amazed to find him alive in the morning and he offered to take the place of those whose turn was next. Thus, he was elected king seven times in seven days and was finally elected a permanent king by the people who gave him the name Gopāla. Tāranātha adds that Gopāla was the son of a kṣatriya woman who lived near Puṇḍravardhana. He was apparently directed by Cuṇḍā in a dream to the *vihāra* of Ārya Khasarpana, where he prayed for a kingdom. He was then asked to proceed to the east, and his expectations were duly fulfilled.

There are several significant aspects to Tāranātha's account that have been largely glossed over in secondary sources. For instance, Bani Roychoudhuri recounts the story in detail but does not bother to analyse or even mention the woman's alleged role or that of the goddess in her analysis of Tāranātha's account. She merely talks of the story revealing the confusion in Bengal due to the lack of a central authority, this being largely corroborated by epigraphic evidence.[63] Roychoudhuri points to the Khalimpur grant of Dharmapāla stating that Gopāla was elected king by the *prakṛtis* or principal officers to end the state of anarchy in Bengal. The relevant verse reads,

> His (Vapyaṭa's) son was the crest-jewel of the heads of kings, the glorious Gopāla, whom the people made take the hand of fortune, to put an end to the practice of fishes . . . (. . . *mātsyanyāyaṁ apohituṁ prakṛtibhirtakṣmyāḥ karaṅgrāhitaḥ śrī-gopāla iti kṣitīśa-śīrasāṁ cūḍāmaṇistat-sutaḥ*. . .).

If, as Roychoudhuri says, Tāranātha's story 'contains some historical truth',[64] what is the role of the mystery woman, her identity, and the reasons behind the introduction of this element in the narrative? What, after all, were his sources, and were they part of popular legend? Why is this element not taken into consideration in secondary accounts of Gopāla's election and Bengal's political history? Could there have been an actual female personage who desired the throne and, therefore, harmed the other contenders? Why, significantly, should she have manifested herself as Govicandra or Lalitacandra's wife? Perhaps the story has some exaggerated elements. However, it is surprising that though Tāranātha is often quoted as a source on other aspects of Bengal's history, this particular account of his is summarily dismissed.

There is another important aspect to Tāranātha's account that has not been commented upon so far by any secondary source, and that links the histories of contemporary Kanauj and Kashmir to Bengal. As narrated above, a goddess is shown to be involved, in a significant way, in Gopāla's accession. Thus, it is important that the Pāla dynasty's inception is covertly attributed to a goddess's intervention in much the same way as Lakṣmī is linked to the formation of the Vardhana kingdom of Thānesar in Bāṇa's account, and Pārvatī is linked to the formation of Kashmir in Kalhaṇa's account. Admittedly, the stories in these literary accounts might be largely fabricated. Yet why does no secondary source speculate on this aspect that links the legends of the three contemporary polities?

In fact, this dismissive attitude is evident in several secondary works. Thus, for instance, Maitreya does not choose to comment on Tāranātha's account of Gopāla's accession.[65] Similarly, Majumdar talks of Gopāla's election being 'a very intriguing problem in the administrative and constitutional history of Bengal' and a 'bloodless revolution', but dubs Tāranātha's account a 'fine illustration of historical myths'.[66] The account might definitely be lacking in historical veracity, but does it not merit a more detailed analysis?

Non-Royal Ministerial Women and the Pāla Records

There were two sets of hereditary ministers during the Pāla regime, a practice seemingly inherited from the imperial Guptas.[67] The first set of five ministers served kings Dharmapāla to Nārāyaṇapāla, while the second set of three ministers served kings Vigrahapāla

III to Kumārapāla. The formidable power of these men, especially the first five, is distinctly attested in the inscriptions. However, the most crucial point to note, at this juncture, is that the names of the ministers' wives are meticulously mentioned in the records, in the fashion of royal genealogical charters. The prominence accorded to these non-royal women is not only significant in itself but also heightens the contrast with the royal Pāla women whose absence from the charters, as discussed above, is highly conspicuous.

The most significant evidence in this regard is provided by the Bādal pillar inscription of Nārāyaṇapāla's reign (ninth/tenth century) that records the erection of a pillar by the brāhmaṇa Rāma Guravamiśra, but is actually a laudatory account (*praśasti*) of Guravamiśra and his ancestors.[68] The inscription furnishes the names of four Pāla kings who were served by some of these men.[69] Thus, Garga, the founder of the family, served Dharmapāla, while his son, Darbhapāṇi, and grandson, Someśvara, served Devapāla. Someśvara's son, Kedāramiśra, served Śūrapāla and Nārāyaṇapāla, while his son, Guravamiśra, served Nārāyaṇapāla alone.

Importantly, the names of the women associated with each of the five ministers are specifically cited, often with conventional statements of praise—again reminiscent of standard royal charters. Thus, for instance, verse 3 says,

> His (Garga's) wife was Icchā, like love dwelling in his heart. By nature pure and tender, she was like the beauty of the moon (*patnīchha nāma tasyā-sīdichhevāntar-vivarttinī, nisarga-nirmala-snigdhā kāntiścandra maso yathā*).

Verse 4 talks of their son, Darbhapāṇi, 'the illustrious chief of the twice-born'.

In a similar vein, verse 8 states of Darbhapāṇi:

> To him was born, of the illustrious Śaṅkaradevī, the twice-born Someśvara, the illustrious, a favourite of the supreme lord, as the moon had sprung from Atri (*tasya śrī-śaṅkara-devyāmatreha moma iva dvijiha, abhūt-someśvaraha śrīmān parameśvara-vallabhaha*).

Verse 10 follows the same trend by stating of Someśvara:

> Desirous of attaining the state of a householder, he in due form took the hand of Rallādevī, a suitable spouse, even as Śiva had done of

Śivā, and Hari of Lakṣmī (. . . *śiva iva karaṁ śivāya haririva lakṣmīyā gṛhāśramapretsuva, anu-rūpāyā vidhivat rallā-devyāha sa jagrāha*).

The next verse talks of Kedāramiśra having taken his birth 'from them'—indicative of equal importance accorded to both parents. The details of Kedāramiśra's wife are revealed in verse 15: 'His wife was Vavvā, born at Devagrāma, unlike the fickle Lakṣmī and the childless Satī' (. . . *deva-grāma-bhavā tasya patnī vavvābhidhā-bhavat*).

Verses 17 and 18 state that 'she bore to him a son', Rāma, called Guravamiśra.

It would be worthwhile to enquire, at this point, into the purposeful inclusion of the names of the ministers' wives in this inscription. A feasible and logical presumption is that the ministers deliberately promoted this format of writing to add to their fame in the public eye and to stress their power amongst the Pāla kings. Thus, by adopting the standards of most contemporary royal charters, they were probably attempting to pose a parallel to the royal power. Moreover, the ministers' powers seems intentionally accentuated by the contrast of them according equal value to their wives in their charters, unlike their royal patrons.

That the ministers were a powerful political force is amply highlighted by the Bādal pillar inscription. Garga apparently made Dharmapāla the lord of the east, and the tract between the Himalayas and the Vindhyas. Likewise, verse 7 of the grant contains an interesting allusion to Darbhapāṇi's power. It states that though the prince Devapāla 'resembled the king of the gods' and had subdued 'sundry kings', he first offered a chair of state to Darbhapāṇi and then 'ascended his own throne with trembling'.[70] Similarly, verse 9 talks of Darbhapāṇi's son, Someśvara, displaying 'unlimited prowess' and showering 'riches upon suppliants'.

Verse 13 has often been cited as evidence of Devapāla's power, but is actually a veiled reference to the influence of Someśvara's son, Kedāramiśra, 'of irresistible great might' (v. 11), indicating that the former's glory stemmed from the latter. It states, 'Attending to his wise counsel, the lord of Gauḍa long ruled the sea-girt earth, having eradicated the race of the Utkalas, humbled the pride of the Hūṇas, and scattered the conceit of the rulers of Draviḍa and Gurjara.'

Finally, the prestige and authority associated with the 'famous and compassionate' son of Kedāramiśra, Guravamiśra, 'who caused pleasure to the king', is clearly outlined in verse 19: 'Since the illustrious prince Nārāyaṇapāla, desirous of victory, skillful in discerning excellent qualities, held him in high esteem, what need is there of further eulogy?' Verse 28 underscores Guravamiśra's eminence: 'Having roamed to the furthest ends of the world, and hence descended even to the bottom of the lower regions, his spotless fame has risen here in the guise of this Garuḍa with a serpent in his mouth.' As a corollary, verse 27 draws a parallel between the Garuḍa pillar and Guravamiśra's ambitions. Thus, the pillar 'like his own aspiration rises to an unparalleled height and is firm like his affection'.

Admittedly, the claims made in this inscription are exaggerated—as is the case with most eulogistic records. However, as Majumdar points out, the fact of the Bādal record being a public document supports the theory that there is an element of truth in it.[71] Besides, its mention of the ministers' wives is what is striking in relation to the Pāla royal charters. Possibly, as noted earlier, the purpose of introducing women as a vital element of the record was to underline the power and prestige associated with this 'formidable generation of ministers'.

That the Bādal pillar inscription does not constitute a stray example is proved, although in a slightly diluted sense, by the Kamauli copper-plate grant of Vaidyadeva (*c.* 1142) that deals with the second set of hereditary ministers.[72] The inscription provides the names of three successive Pāla kings who were served by these men. Yogadeva served Vigrahapāla III and his son, Bodhideva, served Rāmapāla. Bodhideva's son, Vaidyadeva, was Kumārapāla's minister and was apparently the ablest of the three. The inscription records the grant of villages Śāntipāṭaka and Mandāra in Kāmarūpa *maṇḍala* to a brāhmaṇa, Śrīdhara, by Vaidyadeva, who was later appointed ruler by Kumārapāla in place of Tiṁgyadeva in Kāmarūpa.

In a fashion reminiscent of the Bādal pillar inscription, verse 6 states of Vaidyadeva's father, Bodhideva:

His wife was Pratāpadevī, the resting-place of virtue, good fortune and good report, whose beauty was boundless, and who was the embodiment of her husband's joy (*asya pratāpa-devī patnī dharmanikītti-viśrāntiha viśrāntiha, āsī-dasīmakantiha santoṣa-syādṛtiha patyūha*).

Although the wives of the ministers Yogadeva and Vaidyadeva are not mentioned in this inscription, names of other non-royal women are provided. Thus, verses 23 and 24 mention Yudhiṣṭhira and Pāī 'of boundless beauty', the parents of the donee, Śrīdhara. Furthermore, verse 33 mentions Murāri and Padmā, the parents of the *praśasti* composer, Manoratha. The inclusion of these names is highly significant as yet again highlighting the visibility of various categories of non-royal women in the Pāla period.

As in the case of the ministers of the Bādal record, here, too, there seems to be a connection between ministerial power and the mention of women. The *Rāmacarita* claims that Rāmapāla always consulted his ministers before deciding on his course of action against the rebellious Kaivarta chiefs.[73] In addition, there are several concrete indications of Vaidyadeva's power in the Kamauli plate itself in that, as noted earlier, he appears to have asserted his independence by quelling rebellious ministers and by a naval victory in southern Bengal (*RC*, V.11).[74]

There are several other inscriptions pertaining to the women of ministerial/feudatory families and it would be worthwhile to examine them in the same context.[75] A significant example is the undated Bhaturiya inscription of Rājyapāla's time that records the dedication of village Madhuśraṇa to Vṛṣabhadhvaja (Śiva), installed by his minister, Yaśodāsa.[76] The important aspect of this inscription is the mention of Yaśodāsa's mother, Sarasvatī, the wife of Saṅghādāsa (v. 5), and her parents, Sūryakuṇḍa and Durvāyī (v. 4), as part of Yaśodāsa's genealogy.

In a similar vein, the Rāmgunj copper-plate inscription of Īśvaraghoṣa of Dhekkari, a feudal chief (*mahāmaṇḍalika*) of Rāmapāla, refers to his parents, Dhavalaghoṣa and Sadbhāvā, while tracing his genealogy.[77] Although Īśvaraghoṣa has no title of paramount sovereign, he nevertheless arrogates all the privileges to himself. The inscription records the grant of village Diggāsodikā in Piyollamaṇḍala to one Bhaṭṭa Śrīnibbokaśarman and, significantly, includes the queen as one of the persons to be informed, in the fashion of the Sena and Varman charters.[78]

Another example is the Ārmā inscription of Madanapāla's time (*c.* 1157) that records the grant of village Khaṇḍapāṭakagrāma to a Buddhist monastery, Dhavalasaṅgha, by Sārthadevikā, the queen (*rājñī*) of *mahāmaṇḍalika* Jaśkapāla, probably a petty local chief.[79] Importantly, Sārthadevikā seems to have purchased the village from the ruling authority, as it is stated that she 'made (it) a unit permanently attached to her own land'.

Similarly, the Lai inscription of Vikramadevī, dated in the thirty-second year of an unnamed ruler, records the fact that the image on which the inscription is engraved was made by Vikramadevī, the chief queen (*paṭṭarājñī*) of *rāṇaka* Yaśaḥpāla, probably on his behalf (*siddhaṁ dāna-pati-vāsāgārika-rāṇaka śrī-yaśaḥpāla-paṭṭarājñāḥ śrī-vikrama-devyāh saṁ 32 varṣa*).[80] As *rāṇaka* is well known as a title of feudatory rulers, it is presumed that Yaśaḥpāla was probably a scion of the imperial Pālas.

In conclusion, it is important to note that the visibility accorded to these non-royal women has not been deemed a relevant theme of analysis in most secondary sources. A notable exception is U.N. Ghoshal who speculates on the title *devī* attached to the name Śaṅkara.[81] He says that it is 'of special interest', as it has long been known in literary and historical records as the title of a queen, especially a consecrated queen or *agramahiṣī*. Ghoshal then draws a comparison with Raṇṇādevī and Lajjādevī.

Another exception seems to be H.C. Ray who, however, only depicts this aspect in the form of a short table from which one presumes the identity of the women as ministerial spouses thus—'Darbhapāṇi–Śaṅkaradevī, Someśvara–Rallādevī and Kedāramiśra –Vavvā'.[82] One wonders why such a significant aspect does not merit a coherent statement in itself but must, instead, be presented in this confusing and ambiguous fashion. Additionally, there is no mention of Garga's wife. All this clearly hints at the gender bias operating in most secondary sources.

Other Non-Royal Women in the Pāla Period

In almost complete contradistinction to their royal counterparts, the non-royal women in the Pāla period not only enjoy a vastly greater visibility in the inscriptions, but are often shown to be donors and builders as well. This serves the dual purpose of underscoring their importance in society and implying their possession of independent resources or, alternatively, their ability to tap them. Interestingly, their donations were in the same area as those of the Pāla rulers—north Bengal and, particularly, Bihar.

The Nālandā metal image inscription of the third year of Devapāla's reign (early ninth century) refers to Vikhākhā (Viśākhā?), the sole wife of the 'destroyer of the Kalacuris' (*kalacuri-antaka*), resident of Purika village in Rājagṛha, installing the image along with the people.[83] Vikhākhā's unnamed husband must have been a great warrior who defeated the Kalacuris at some point. Another significant record from Nālandā is the Balarāma image inscription of Devapāla's reign that records the dedication of the image at Nālandā in the *devapāladeva-haṭṭa* or 'the mart of Devapāladeva' by Nisiṅgha(?)kā, the wife of Śoujjeka (*śrī-nālandāya śrī-devapāla-deva-haṭṭe malaporasya śoujjekasya vadū nisiṅghakāya deva dharmmaya pratīpādīttaḥ*).[84]

The Valgudar inscription of Dharmapāla's reign[85] states,

> (The God) Madhuśreṇika (is installed) at the city of Kṛmilā during the reign of the illustrious Dharmmapāladeva; this meritorious gift is caused to be made by Ajhukā who is the wife of Sālo (*śrī-dharmma-pāla-deva-rājye krimilādhisthāne madhuśreṇikaḥ, sālo-dharmma-patnī-ajhukena deva-dharmmoyaṁ kāritaḥ*).

Interestingly, the same name figures again in the Balarāma image inscription from Kurkihār in the ninth year of Devapāla's reign, which records the gift of the image to Mallapore (monastery?) by Ajhukā, the wife of Śiṅgeka, resident of Saddhu village in Vāhiravaṇa and probably the village chief.[86]

In a similar vein, the Kurkihār bronze image inscription of the thirty-first year of Rājyapāla's reign records the religious gift of a Karā-Maheśvara image by one Mūlakā, the wife of Mahiāru, resident of the Āpaṇaka monastery.[87] Another Kurkihār bronze image inscription of the thirty-second year of Rājyapāla's reign records the religious gift of an image of Vasudhārā by one Va(ṭu)kā, the wife of Gopālahīno of the Āpaṇaka monastery. Gaukā, another wife of Gopālahīno, is shown to dedicate an image of Vasudhārā in the same year.

A notable epigraph is the Kurkihār bronze image inscription of the nineteenth year of the reign of Vigrahapāla III. It records the religious gift of a Buddha image by Pekhokā, the wife or daughter-in-law of the Mahattama Dūlapa.[88] A further record of the reign of Vigrahapāla III—the Naulāgaṛh image inscription—is dated in his twenty-fourth regnal year and mentions the construction of an image on behalf of Aśokā, the wife of Dhammaji (Dharmajit) and the daughter of a vintner of Kṛmilā named Mahāmati. Similarly, the inscription on an image of Tārā in the first/second regnal year of Rāmapāla records the gift of the image by Sonikā, the wife of the merchant, Vāmbha.[89]

The Nongaṛh inscription of Madanapāla's time (AD1144) is also a very important one in that it shows a man's vow being fulfilled by his wife.[90] It states that the image on whose pedestal the record was engraved was the *devadharma* of *dānapati* Śīja and his wife, Aśokā, at Dakā. The wording implies that the vow was made by Śīja but the image was dedicated for installation by Aśokā (. . . *deva-dharmmoyaṁ dānapatiśe jasya dakāyāṁ vadhū-aśokāyā jayadrata puṇaṁ* . . .).

Instances of non-royal male donors are also available but these grants are nowhere as abundant or detailed as those pertaining to non-royal women. A case in point is an image of Cuṇḍā from Kurkihār of the thirty-first year of Mahipāla's reign, the gift of the son of a goldsmith, Keśava.[91] The fact that the male donor remains unnamed is noteworthy and heightens the contrast with the profusion of names of non-royal women donors provided by the inscriptions.

A related and notable aspect is the mention of non-royal women in the inscriptions of non-royal male donors—either by name or by other allusions. An interesting example is the Tārā image inscription from Hilsā in the year 25 or 35 of Devapāla's reign, recording the religious gift of Gaṅgādhara, 'a great lay devotee of Sakka (Buddha)', that refers to the importance of the teacher (*ācārya*), mother and father.[92] Likewise, the incomplete Bodhgayā image inscription of the eleventh year of Mahipāla I records the donation of two temples for the benefit of the unknown donor's mother and father.[93] The equal importance accorded to both parents in both these cases is noteworthy. Similarly, the Gayā Inscription of

Nārāyaṇapāla's seventh regnal year, recording the dedication of a *vāsa* (house) at Gayā for ascetics by one Bhānudeva, mentions his mother, Vallabhadevī, and his father, Bappadeva (v. 5).[94]

Another case is the Ghoṣrāvān stone inscription of Devapāla's time, which records the erection of an edifice for a diamond throne (*vajrāsana*) by a Buddhist monk, Vīradeva.[95] Verse 4 mentions Vīradeva's father, Indragupta, and his mother, Rajjekā, the latter being apparently very devoted to the former. Additionally, the merit from Vīradeva's endeavour was meant to accrue to 'all persons', including his parents. The Bangāon plate of Vigrahapāla III issued in his seventeenth regnal year—recording the grant of land to one Ghānṭūkaśarman by a private individual, Ghaṇṭīśa, an officer of the king—is also significant.[96] Thus, though it omits to mention Ghaṇṭīśa's mother's name, it records the name of his great-grandmother and her ancestry instead. Ghaṇṭīśa is described as the son of Yogeśvara and grandson of Vivada, the latter being born of Iddhahalā, daughter of Gohaṇaka and granddaughter of Kāccha, originally of Kroḍāñca/Kolāñca.

One may note, at this juncture, that the extant sculptures and images have been used largely as sources of the art and sculptural traditions of the Pāla period. In the process, the gendered evidence of their inscriptions has been completely ignored. Thus, for instance, the donations by the residents of the Āpaṇaka monastery have been used to prove the existence of a common artistic community with stylistic similarities, and to show that the monastery probably patronized a particular workshop in that area. However, there is no analysis on the significant fact that the donors were women. An example is Susan Huntington who talks in terms of the 'three images' donated by 'people' to prove her point about a common workshop and artistic styles, but she does not specify, in this particular analysis, that all three donors are women.[97]

Another example is Jhunu Bagchi who does not involve non-royal women in her analysis, despite profuse references to their significant contributions in contemporary records. She states, for instance, that 'new constructions and maintenance of the monasteries were undertaken by Pāla monarchs regularly'.[98] What about the non-royal women involved in construction activities? Why is this activity shown as being confined to the Pāla rulers alone?

Bagchi subsequently talks of women too 'having the right to dedicate those images and also accomplish other religious acts'—a very ambiguous statement—and then dismisses all the evidence in one paragraph alone.[99] She focuses, instead, on the contribution of the Pāla kings and the Buddhist monks in this regard.

Furthermore, Bagchi notes that several images of Buddhist *and* Brahmanical nature were dedicated by people of different professions (merchants, goldsmiths, and others), thereby showing 'the good economic life' of the people.[100] There is no mention of women, although the epigraphic evidence clearly points to their involvement in donations. Bagchi adds that Pāla art and sculpture was sponsored not so much by the court but by rich individuals, and that while these had no actual connection with the society or life of the people, they reflected past religious experience.[101] This statement errs on several counts.

If one were to speculate on the economic life of these people, then it is obvious that non-royal women donors were either in possession of some amount of resources that enabled them to make donations or that they had access to their husbands' resources in this regard. One cannot talk in terms of rich individuals without acknowledging this fact. Thus, when Huntington talks of 'a very active lay community' rather than royal patronage that 'supported religious establishments' and patronized art production,[102] it is obvious that non-royal women form a crucial part of this category—as the inscriptions testify.

Hence, to say that all this had no connection with the actual practical life of the people is highly questionable. The images *per se* might have reflected religious traditions, but the identities and motives of their various donors is a distinct statement on the contemporary society. After all, it is extremely significant that non-royal women had the freedom to donate and build, and clearly state the fact of having done so in the records. If certain workshops and styles were being patronized, then women could well have had some say in the output.

This requires that non-royal women be viewed as important actors in contemporary Pāla society, and is all the more crucial in view of their largely inconspicuous royal Pāla counterparts. Sharma, for instance, notes the fact that many votives in Bihar were donated by women, mostly of the merchant class.[103] An interesting parallel can be drawn here with women donors of medieval south India. Leslie Orr points out that the wives of landowners/ merchants, brāhmaṇa women and palace women were 'especially active as donors' from the ninth to the twelfth century.[104]

Thus, clearly, the social mores of the Pāla period allowed a certain measure of freedom and agency to non-royal women rather than the royal—but whether this was a part of dictated state policy is difficult to determine. Kunal Chakrabarti talks of the stress on agriculture rather than trade in the eighth century, and the rise of powerful landowners under the Pālas.[105] This 'stratified and hierarchized' socio-economic structure of early medieval Bengal might explain the prominence of non-royal women as a logical reflection of their husbands' growing power.

FEMALE PRESENCE IN THE SENA INSCRIPTIONS

In almost complete contrast to the Pāla inscriptions, the inscriptions of the Sena rulers document the presence of royal women, both as part of the genealogical line and as donors. This does not mean that all Sena inscriptions mention them, for some of them provide an exclusively male genealogy. However, by analysing the evidence, one can reconstruct the presence of royal women as meaningful figures. More importantly, irrespective of their inclusion/exclusion in the main subject of the inscriptions, the queens are always included in the categories who are to be informed of the various land grants. In contradistinction to the Pāla epigraphs, though, there are no inscriptions recording the presence of non-royal Sena women.

The focus here is on eleven inscriptions of three of the five main Sena rulers—Vijayasena (*c.* 1095–1158), Vallālasena (1158–79) and Lakṣmaṇasena (1179–1206), there being no inscription of Vijayasena's father, Hemantasena (late eleventh century), or of his grandfather, Sāmantasena. The Sena rulers after Lakṣmaṇasena are not included in the analysis because they fall outside the relevant time span of this study.

A very important aspect of the Sena inscriptions is the inclusion of queens in the category of land grant executors. They are placed third in the list after the vassal kings and feudatory chieftains, and this is the procedure followed in almost all the Sena grants. Thus, for instance, the Tarpanadīghi copper-plate grant of Lakṣmaṇasena records the gift of Velahiṣṭī village in Puṇḍravardhanabhukti to Īśvaradevaśarman for the enhancement of the merit and fame of himself and his parents, informing all the assembled kings, feudatories, queens, princes and so on (v. 8—*samupāgata-śeṣa-rājā-rājanyaka-rājñī-rāṇaka-rājaputra* . . .).[106] Not only does this form a point of distinction with the royal Pāla grants, it establishes the royal Sena women as substantial and respected figures in the contemporary polity and society.

At the same time, it is necessary to remember that not all the Sena grants mention the royal women in the genealogy. For instance, Vilāsadevī is the only Sena queen mentioned in the Naihāti grant of Vallālasena, while Rāmadevī is the only queen mentioned in the Mādhainagar inscription of Lakṣmaṇasena. Likewise, the Anuliā copper-plate grant of Lakṣmaṇasena provides an exclusively male genealogy with no royal woman being mentioned at all, although, ironically, the gift is for the merit of Lakṣmaṇasena's parents and informs the queens as usual.[107]

An interesting comparison can be drawn here with the Pratihāra inscriptions of Kanauj that precisely mention all the royal women of the genealogical line. However, as Paul points out, although the actual political influence exercised by the chief queen was not known, her influence was 'considerable'.[108] The presence of the royal Sena women in genealogical lists, in donative inscriptions, and in the list of land grant executors amply corroborates the above statement.

None of the Sena inscriptions mention the wife of Sāmantasena, the acknowledged founder of the dynasty, or of Vīrasena, his remote mythical ancestor. What is known about them is based on Ānanda Bhaṭṭa's *Vallālacarita* (sixteenth century) that traces the Sena ancestry to the epic hero, Karṇa. The text treats the Senas of Bengal as descendants of his great-grandson, Vīrasena. It claims that Vīrasena married Somaṭā, the daughter of a Gauḍa brāhmaṇa.[109] The names and identities of the wives of the other Sena rulers are, however, duly recorded.

The Sena inscriptions reveal that nearly all the marriage alliances concluded by the rulers were politically strategic ones. Significantly, although the *Dharmaśāstras* prescribe isogamy or the marriage of status-equals, in most of these politically strategic marriages, the wife's status was often higher than that of her husband's.[110] This challenges the Brahmanical concept of the inferiority of wife-givers to wife-takers.

Consider, for instance, the Deopārā Inscription of Vijayasena that records his building of the Pradyumneśvara temple and talks of his grandfather, Sāmantasena, migrating to Bengal from Karṇāṭa and establishing the Sena family.[111] This probably happened—as speculated in the previous chapter—in the wake of the Cālukyan invasion of Vikramāditya VI. There is no mention of Sāmantasena's wife, nor is there any speculation about this lacuna in secondary sources.

Sāmantasena's son, Hemantasena, married Yaśodevī, who is referred to as 'the great queen' (*mahārājñī*) in the Deopārā inscription. From this, it is presumed that Hemantasena had some pretension to royal dignity and claimed to be a chief of some importance.[112] This is corroborated by the imperial title of *mahārājādhirāja* accorded him in the Barrackpur plate of Vijayasena.[113] Although Hemantasena remains a shadowy figure, Yaśodevī is described in the Deopārā plate in the following way: her feet 'were brightened by a series of rays of the lines of the crest-jewels of the wives of princes, both friendly and hostile' (v. 14).[114]

Nevertheless, it is Hemantasena's son, Vijayasena, who is regarded as the real founder of the Sena fortunes in Bengal. It was his marriage with Vilāsadevī, a princess of the Śūra family of Apara-Mandāra, which seems to have catapulted him into political greatness. Vijayasena was, initially, an independent chief in Rāḍha, whose help was sought by Rāmapāla against the Kaivartas. H.C. Ray suggests that he be identified with the Vijaya of Nidrābala who, as per the *Rāmacarita*, helped Rāmapāla in his mission and seems to have been a mere feudatory of the Pāla king.[115]

Vijayasena conquered nearly all of Bengal on the strength of his newfound power.[116] The Naihāti grant of Vijayasena's son,

Vallālasena, dated in his eleventh year,[117] states with reference to him, 'Vilāsadevī was the principal queen (and) the crest-jewel of the ladies' quarter of this lord of the earth' (v. 10).

The Barrackpur grant of Vijayasena provides more details about Vilāsadevī:[118] 'Vilāsadevī was his (Vijayasena's) queen, the moonlight of the ocean-like race of Śūra' (v. 7—*abhavad-vilāsa-devī śūra-kulām-bhodhi-kaumudi tasya* . . .). A Śūra chief—ruler of an important principality in south Rāḍha—also figures in the list of Rāmapāla's *sāmantas* and hence this matrimonial alliance would have undoubtedly improved Vijayasena's power.

The importance of Vijayasena's marriage to Vilāsadevī is, in fact, acknowledged in most secondary sources. Majumdar says that it is 'probable' that the marriage helped Vijayasena 'to attain political greatness', and Paul admits that it 'might have raised his political and social status'.[119] In fact, Vijayasena's victories over the kings of Gauḍa, Kāmarūpa and Kaliṅga, and the kings Nānya and Vīra—for which he is eulogized in the Deopārā *praśasti*—is held by a range of historians as being a consequence of his marriage with Vilāsadevī. It is also possible to speculate that Vijayasena's assumption of the imperial titles of *parama-māheśvara parama-bhaṭṭāraka mahārājādhirāja* and *arirāja-vṛṣabha-śaṅkara* was a reflection of his exalted status after his marriage. Note that the Pradyumneśvara temple, too, might be a reflection of his standing.

Vijayasena's son, Vallālasena, who is credited with the conquest of Magadha and Mithilā, also seems to have made a politically important marriage. He married Rāmadevī, the daughter of a Cālukyan king, probably Jagadekamalla II. The Mādhainagar copper-plate inscription of Lakṣmaṇasena mentions Rāmadevī as the wife of Vallālasena and Lakṣmaṇasena's mother:[120]

> Rāmadevī, a crest-gem of the harems of all kings, a moon, belonging to the family of Cālukya kings, and respected (equally) even by the Goddess of fortune and the Earth was his (Vallālasena's) spouse (v. 9—*tasyā priyābhūdvahumāna-bhūmi-lakṣmī-pṛthīvyorapi rāmadevī*...).

The India Office Plate of Lakṣmaṇasena (1197) also refers to Rāmadevī in a similar vein.[121] Thus, verse 9 states, 'Rāmadevī, the crest-jewel of far and near harems, the crescent moon of the family of the Cālukya princes . . . was his (Vallālasena's) consort.'

Majumdar talks of the alliance between Vallālasena and Rāmadevī proving the growing prestige of the Senas as a political power, while simultaneously showing their continued contacts with their ancestral land of Karṇāṭa.[122] It is also possible to speculate that Vallālasena's conclusive victories were a logical consequence of his marriage connections with a powerful ally, thereby underscoring the significance of Rāmadevī's role.

Verse 10 of the India Office grant mentions Lakṣmaṇasena as the son of Rāmadevī and Vallālasena.[123] An interesting but uncorroborated tradition about Rāmadevī states that she kept herself suspended with head down and legs bound for two hours, so that Lakṣmaṇasena could be born at a time propitious for the longevity of his reign.[124] (She died immediately afterwards.) This sacrifice, however, is not mentioned in the inscriptions.

It is speculated, on the basis of records, that Lakṣmaṇasena had four wives—Śrīyādevī, Kalyāṇadevī, Alhaṇadevī and Tāḍādevī.[125] Thus, verse 14 of the Madanapāda copper-plate grant of Lakṣmaṇasena's son, Viśvarūpasena (end of the twelfth century) states that the 'illustrious Viśvarūpasena . . . sprang from Lakṣmaṇasena and his consort Tāḍādevī.'[126]

In the previous chapter, attention was drawn to the surprise raid on Lakṣmaṇasena's capital in 1199 by Muhammed Bakhtyar Khalji, the general of Muhammed Ghori. Sources talk of Lakṣmaṇasena's queens falling into the hands of these Muslim invaders, along with his treasure, maids, and attendants. This blanket statement, echoed in almost all secondary sources, does not identify the queens involved or even speculate on their fate after capture, although information is provided on Lakṣmaṇasena's re-establishment after his escape.[127]

Another noteworthy aspect of the Sena grants is the evidence provided of royal women donors. The Barrackpur grant of Vijayasena issued in the thirty-second year of his reign is crucially important in this context, as it records the donations of Vilāsadevī whose prominence has already been stressed. The inscription refers to the grant of land in Khāḍī *viṣaya* of Puṇḍravardhanabhukti to Udayakaradevaśarrman. The grant was made inside the palace at Vikramapura as the *dakṣiṇā* of the *homa* performed by the donee—on the occasion of the golden *tulāpuruṣa* gift performed by *mahāmahādevī* Vilāsadevī on the occasion of a lunar eclipse.[128]

Vilāsadevī's motives seem to be clearly stated in verses 9 and 10. Vijayasena enabled her to make various gifts, since she had borne 'the illustrious Niḥśaṅkaśaṅkara', another name for Vallālasena. The grant, however, was for the merit of Vijayasena's parents and himself.

Another important evidence that serves to buttress Vilāsadevī's status is provided by the Naihāti grant of Vallālasena. The inscription records the grant of village Vālḷaḥiṭṭhā of Varddhamānabhukti by Vallālasena as the *dakṣiṇā* of the golden horse gift made by Vilāsadevī, the king's mother, to a brāhmaṇa, Ovāsudevaśarman. 'While giving a golden horse on the day of solar eclipse, his mother granted a deed of gift and the king . . . assigned it to learned Ovāsu . . . (v. 14).'[129]

One could infer that her contribution to Vijayasena's political glory prompted Vilāsadevī to adopt a more visibly prominent role. This raises the question of the resources at her disposal. In this context, Paul's observations could prove to be useful.[130] He talks of the 'very high' position of the queen-consort, and the third place customarily accorded to her in the list of officers and feudatories. He further talks of Kauṭilya placing her in the first grade of officers with the *mantrin* and *purohita*, drawing 48,000 *paṇas* from the state treasury, the same amount being allocated to the queen mother.

Paul then points specifically to the religious ceremony performed by Vilāsadevī, and the lands granted to the sacrificial priest as *dakṣiṇā*, as an illustrative case. It is thus possible to suggest that Vilāsadevī drew on her own resources to make donations that would register her role and presence. As mentioned in the inscription, she granted the gift, Vallālasena merely assigned it. An interesting parallel could be drawn here with Rālhadevī of the Gāhaḍavāla dynasty of Kanauj, whose vigorous presence can be gleaned from her donations as a queen and queen mother.

Additionally, Paul observes that the Pāla–Sena kings conferred lands as per the traditional royal policy outlined in the *Arthaśāstra* (that the king should reward learned men, or those who rendered services to kings/queens).[131] He distinguishes this from the Gupta and post-Gupta periods when private persons/officials gifted land in their personal capacities. However, the point to note here is that the policy was being followed not just by the kings, but also by some royal women, in this case Vilāsadevī.

The Sena inscriptions normally record grants made by the rulers for the increase of their fame and that of their parents.[132] However, a notable exception is posed by the India Office Plate of Lakṣmaṇasena, which records his gift of land in Puṇḍravardhana-bhukti to Padmanābhadevaśarman to earn merit for his wives, 'Mahādevī . . . pādevī' and the 'Mahādevī Kalyāṇadevī'.[133] This is a crucial departure from the usual merit-seeking for parents and self in that it marks the first instance of a king bestowing something for the spiritual benefit of his consorts.

In conclusion, one should note the absence of non-royal Sena women in the epigraphic records, thereby constituting a vital point of distinction with the Pāla records in which they have a vibrant presence. Thus, the only relevant reference to non-royal women in the Sena period is in the Deopārā *praśasti* that talks of brāhmaṇas growing in wealth as a result of Vijayasena's favour, and of their wives being taught the identification of jewels by the wives of the townspeople.[134]

FEMALE PRESENCE IN OTHER DYNASTIES

The Later Gupta Inscriptions

Although the Later Gupta inscriptions at Aphsāḍ and Deo Baranārk provide a list of eleven kings of the dynasty—Kṛṣṇagupta, Harṣa-gupta, Jīvitagupta, Kumāragupta, Dāmodaragupta, Mahāsenagupta, Mādhavagupta, Ādityasena, Devagupta, Viṣṇugupta and Jīvitagupta II—this analysis is only concerned with the last four who ruled from Magadha.

The history of Ādityasena (*c.* seventh century) and his successors is known from six inscriptions found in Bihar. For purposes of a gender analysis, there are two important aspects to these Later Gupta inscriptions. First, the royal female presence can be clearly gleaned from the grants. Second, female titles figure prominently and, once again, this suggests that the titles accorded to queens mirror the political growth of the kings. It would be worthwhile to examine this in some detail.

The Deo Baranārk inscription of Jīvitagupta II (first half of the eighth century) provides a comprehensive genealogy with the female presence intact—from the time of Mādhavagupta and Śrīmatīdevī to Jīvitagupta II.[135] The son of Mādhavagupta and Śrīmatīdevī was Ādityasena who married Koṇadevī. Their son, Devagupta, married Kamaladevī and had a son, Viṣṇugupta. Viṣṇugupta's son, by Ijjādevī, was Jīvitagupta II. One should note here that the wife of Jīvitagupta II is not mentioned either in contemporary inscriptions or in Vākpati's *Gauḍavaho*, but nowhere is this considered a matter for discussion.

As part of the Later Gupta genealogy, one can also mention the contemporary Kaṭrā copper-plate inscription of Jīvagupta.[136] It records the grant of three localities in Tīrabhukti to the Cāmuṇḍā-bhaṭṭārikā temple for the merit of Jīvagupta's parents (Rāmagupta and Rāmabhaṭṭārikā). Judging by the imperial titles of father and son, they could have belonged to the Later Guptas of Magadha.[137]

The inscription suggests that Rāmagupta was born of a Queen Tārā (*śrīmaṭṭā(rā)-bhaṭṭārikāyāṁ-utpannasya parama-bhaṭṭāraka-mahārājādhirāja-parameśvara-śrī-rāmagupta-devastasya*). Interestingly, Rāmagupta is called the son of Tārā alone in the inscription, there being no mention of his father. However, K.K. Thaplyal, who translated the grant, does not mention either of these facts in the abstract of the record. Furthermore, although Tārā is mentioned later in Thaplyal's list of names provided by the inscriptions, that of Rāmabhaṭṭārikā, the wife of Rāmagupta, is omitted.[138] This shows the usual trend of scrupulous attention accorded to the male figures, and disregard of the women.

As regards donations by women in the Later Gupta period, the Aphsāḍ stone inscription of Ādityasena is particularly important. It records the building of a Viṣṇu temple by Ādityasena, a religious college or monastery by his mother, Śrīmatīdevī (vv. 23–4: *tajjannyā mahādevyā śrīmatya kārito maṭaha, dhārmikebhyaha svayaṁ dattaha suraloka-gṛho-pamaha*), and the excavation of a tank by his wife, Koṇadevī (v. 25: *khānitamādbhutaṁ sutapasā pepiyamānaṁ janaistasyaiva priya-bhāryayā narapateha śrī-koṇadevyā saraha*).[139] Koṇadevī's presence is also confirmed by the Deogaṛh temple inscription recording the erection of a Nṛhari temple by Ādityasena, and the Mandār hill inscriptions that record the excavation of two tanks by her.

Concerning the Aphsāḍ inscription, Thaplyal makes the interesting observation that Śrīmatīdevī and Koṇadevī are the only queens mentioned in it, although it provides the names of rulers from Kṛṣṇagupta to Ādityasena.[140] He also notes that the two queens are mentioned only in the narrative of the acts of charity and not in the genealogical part, thereby distinguishing it from the Deo Baranārk inscription and posing a parallel with the Gāhaḍavāla grants of Kanauj. This is an important indicator of the space accorded to the Later Gupta women, although their visibility is definitely greater than that of their royal Pāla counterparts. By extension, one could reflect on the donations of the two queens. Were they sponsored by independent resources or by Ādityasena? If the former, then it is an obvious reflection of the donors' status.

One could reflect on the undated Mandār hill inscriptions here, recording the construction of a tank by Koṇadevī. It is unclear whether the reference is to two tanks or the same one.[141] However, the word *kīrtti* used in this connection implies that the act would confer fame on the performer (. . . *parama-bhaṭṭāraka-mah(ā)r(ā)j(ā)dhirāja-śrī-āditya-sena-deva day(i)tā, parama-bhaṭṭārik(ā) r(ā)jñī-mahādevī-śrī-k(o)ṇadev(ī) puṣkariṇī-kīrttimim(ā)n-kāritavatī*). Hence this could be seen as Koṇadevī's attempt to acquire fame and an exalted status.

Alternatively, Ādityasena might have been seeking to elevate his own status through that of his wife, and hence sanctioned the tank construction. In either case, the motivating factor is highly significant. Koṇadevī's exalted status is also revealed by the Deogaṛh temple inscription, that records her arrival with Ādityasena from 'the Coḷa city' and the performance of three *aśvamedha* sacrifices by them.[142] It is possible to extend this line of reasoning to Śrīmatīdevī as well. Could her religious college have been intended for the Buddhists rather than brāhmaṇas—as an expression of religious freedom? We have no information to make a definite statement in this regard.

The question of a wife's titles reflecting the growth in status of a king is significant. Thus, for instance, Majumdar derives the fact of Mādhavagupta assuming imperial titles from the Deo Baranārk inscription, which states that Ādityasena's mother (Mādhavagupta's wife, Śrīmatīdevī) was given imperial titles like *paramabhaṭṭārikā* and *mahādevī*.[143] Ādityasena was the first king of the Later Gupta line to claim imperial titles. He is referred to as *kṣitīśacūḍāmaṇi* and *lokapāla* in the Aphsāḍ inscription. The Mandār hill inscription designates him *parama-bhaṭṭāraka mahārājādhirāja*, and his queen, *parama-bhaṭṭārikā rājñī mahādevī koṇadevī*.[144] However, in the Deo Baranārk inscription, he is *parama-bhāgavata-śrī* and not *mahārājādhirāja*. The imperial titles are similarly missing in the Shāhpur inscription (AD 672) that records the gift of a private individual at Nālandā. Here, the king is just *śrī-ādityasenadeva*.[145]

The Kaṭrā plate of Jīvagupta, for its part, forms an exception to this trend. It refers to Rāmagupta and his son, Jīvagupta, by the imperial titles of *parama-bhaṭṭāraka-mahārājādhirāja-parameśvara*, while Jīvagupta's mother is only *bhaṭṭārikā*.[146] Here, it is only the king who takes grandiose titles.

Finally, it is interesting to note that Nepal inscriptions talk of Ādityasena's daughter marrying the Maukhari king, Bhogavarman, son of the sister of King Aṁśuvarman of Nepal. Bhogavarman's daughter, Vatsadevī (and Ādityasena's granddaughter), became the queen of the Nepal king, Śivadeva, at a later stage. It is speculated that the references to these marital alliances in the official records of Nepal imply the high political and social status of the Later Gupta kings in eastern India.[147] It is also believed that the desire to cultivate good relations with the Maukharis precipitated the marriage of Ādityasena's daughter.[148] However, there is no information on her name or on the identity of her mother—nor, it must be stressed time and again, are the secondary sources particularly interested in this aspect.

Śaśāṅka

Śaśāṅka's rule provides an important parallel with the history of contemporary Kanauj. There are certain aspects of Śaśāṅka's history, specifically, his entanglement with the Vardhanas of Thānesar, that are of relevance for a gender study and reveal, in the process, a significant lacuna in most secondary sources.

As stated earlier, Śaśāṅka began as a *mahāsāmanta* of unknown background who successfully challenged the combined power of the northern states of Kanauj, Thānesar, and Kāmarūpa, and retained the independence of his vast realm till his end.[149] His clash with Rājya and Harṣa of Thānesar has already been detailed. Most secondary sources on Śaśāṅka selectively focus on his origin, the means he employed to rise to power, and his culpability in Rājya's murder. Such a focus proves to be inadequate on two counts.

First, there is hardly any speculation on Rājyaśrī's role in forcing Śaśāṅka to rethink his political equations and thereby precipitating a chain of events that crystallized in his enmity with Harṣa. Second, there is no speculation on the identity of Śaśāṅka's wife/wives and daughter. This becomes all the more glaring in view of the possibility—raised by Śaṅkara (fourteenth century), a commentator on the *Harṣacarita*—of the connection of Śaśāṅka's daughter with Rājya's death. Apparently, she was offered to Rājya by Śaśāṅka, in an attempt to lull the former's suspicions, and that led to his murder. It would be worthwhile to examine all this in some detail.

The depth of analysis on Śaśāṅka's origin has already been noted. Majumdar's view that Śaśāṅka was a *mahāsāmanta* under Mahāsenagupta, the Later Gupta king, has been cited.[150] D.C. Ganguly, however, relying on the Deo Baranārk Inscription, believes that Śaśāṅka was a feudatory of the Maukhari king, Avantivarman.[151] As for Banerji, he feels that Śaśāṅka belonged to the Gupta dynasty of Magadha on the basis of the similarity of the weight, fabric, and provenance of the coins of Śaśāṅka and the later Guptas.[152] Sinha's views on the identity of Śaśāṅka's overlord have already been cited in the previous chapter in some detail.

The debate on Śaśāṅka's alleged hand in Rājya's murder is equally vigorous. Most scholars either cite Bāṇa's claim that Śaśāṅka lured Rājya to his death, or Yuan Chwang's claim that Śaśāṅka 'hating the superior military talents of Rājya, made a plot and murdered him'.[153] The ambiguous comment of the Madhuban Inscription of Harṣa that Rājya 'in consequence of his adherence to a promise gave up his life' further complicates the issue. Thus, C.V. Vaidya and R.G. Basak feel that Śaśāṅka was guilty of treachery.[154]

However, Majumdar and Banerji doubt the accounts of Bāṇa and Yuan Chwang, both obviously biased in favour of Harṣa.[155] Majumdar, in particular, attempts to portray Śaśāṅka as a misunderstood hero and blames his ministers for any plot to kill Rājya, pointing out that Harṣa himself does not level any murder charge on Śaśāṅka. N. Ray, on the other hand, provides a more balanced picture and stresses that there is 'no need to try to absolve Śaśāṅka' of his 'misdeeds'.[156]

However, crucially, the figure of Rājyaśrī in Śaśāṅka's political calculations remains, at best, understated and, at worst, ignored. At best, Majumdar grudgingly admits that Śaśāṅka's prospects became 'gloomy' with the politically strategic marriage alliance of Grahavarman and Rājyaśrī, prompting him to devise an alliance with Devagupta of Mālwā.[157] The treatment of Rājyaśrī here is as an invisible part of the marriage alliance. Similarly, Roychoudhuri talks of Grahavarman being 'impelled by fear' of Śaśāṅka's might in asking for Rājyaśrī's hand.[158]

Yet the clear connection of Rājyaśrī with the first firm challenge to Śaśāṅka's power—thereby shaking him out of his complacency, forcing him to seek Devagupta's support and thereafter curbing his power—is glossed over, the constant stress on the 'marriage alliance' reducing her figure to a disembodied entity. Interestingly, Paul's surmise on Rājya's death again highlights the importance of Rājyaśrī. He believes that Rājya was allegedly asked to relinquish the Maukhari alliance by Śaśāṅka. Rājya could not do so because of Rājyaśrī's involvement in the marriage alliance, and this paved the way for his murder.[159]

A similarly indifferent treatment is extended to Śaśāṅka's wife and daughter. There is absolutely no reflection on Śaśāṅka's wife, even though the *Āryamañjuśrī-mūlakalpa* states that Śaśāṅka's son, Mānava, ruled briefly after him.[160] The identity of Mānava's mother and the possibility of Śaśāṅka having more than one wife are not issues of interest for most historians. Another significant aspect is the outright dismissal of Śaṅkara's claim that Śaśāṅka's daughter was offered to Rājya as an eventual ploy to murder him.[161] Admittedly, Śaṅkara's sources for this view are unclear. Yet could there have been some truth in his claim?

Why does no secondary source display any interest in Śaśāṅka's daughter? There is no analysis—on a scale accorded to his origin/career—on whether she was a historical personage, or whether she shared the same mother as Mānava, and so on. The paucity of reliable sources extends to most of Śaśāṅka's history—and yet there is no dearth of speculation on other aspects of his career. To cite an example, the 'strong element of vagueness and obscurity' pervading the issue of Rājya's murder does not prevent Majumdar, for instance, from indulging in an in-depth analysis to prove Śaśāṅka's innocence.[162]

The Khaḍga Inscriptions

As mentioned in the previous chapter, the history of the Khaḍga dynasty is reconstructed on the basis of three inscriptions—two copper plates from Ashrafpur and an inscription on an image of Śarvvāṇī (Durgā) at Deulbāḍī. It is the Deulbāḍī Inscription that assumes importance in this analysis, as it boldly confirms the presence and importance of Prabhāvatī, the wife of the third king, Devakhaḍga, and also indicates the extent of religious freedom she enjoyed.[163]

The inscription mentions Khaḍgyodama, the overlord of kings, whose son and grandson were Jātakhaḍga and Devakhaḍga, respectively. It then states that 'Prabhāvatī, the queen-consort of this king (Devakhaḍga), out of reverence for Śarvvāṇī, covered her image with gold' (*rājñastasya mahādevī mahiṣī śrīprabhāvatī śarvvāṇī-pratimāṁ bhaktyā hema-liptāṁakārayat*). It is significant, therefore, that Prabhāvatī honoured a Brahmanical goddess and stressed this fact in her inscription, even though her husband was a devout Buddhist. Additionally, one of the Ashrafpur plates indicates that Prabhāvatī owned some land that Devakhaḍga gave away to the Buddhist monasteries.[164] This again indicates that she was a prominent figure with the power to determine her religious choices and an obvious access to resources.

At this juncture, one can mention some interesting aspects of the Tipperah copper-plate grant of Lokanātha, a feudatory of the Khaḍgas.[165] The inscription mentions the names of several female members of this line of feudatories, while recording the grant of land to *mahāsāmanta* Pradoṣaśarman in Suvvaṅga *viṣaya* for making a temple. It talks of Śrīnātha and Bhavanātha who forsook royalty for their brother's son. The latter's wife, Gotradevī, was the mother of Lokanātha. Thus, verses 5–7 make a significant mention of Gotradevī, her mother, Aṣṭāyikā, and three generations of maternal grandparents.

Interestingly, Lokanātha's maternal grandfather, Keśava, is described as a pāraśava by caste, indicating that his brāhmaṇa father married a śūdra woman.[166] Incidentally, this seems to have been a common practice in the Pāla–Sena period.[167] Majumdar points out that as Keśava was placed in charge of the army and was generally respected, these marriages obviously did not provoke any condemnation, despite the disapproval of Manu, for instance.[168]

Verses 16–21 of the Tipperah plate talk of prince Lakṣmīnātha, whose mother was the brāhmaṇa lady, Suvacanā, the daughter of Bṛhaspatisvāmin. Suvacanā had a reputation for bestowing desirable gifts on her supplicants (v. 19). Thus her importance and popularity are clearly indicated and, besides, the statement implies that she possessed some means of her own to endow her supplicants. These could have been independently owned, or Suvacanā could have induced her husband to disburse his wealth in this manner. In both cases, her significance is confirmed.

The Candra Inscriptions

The genealogy of the Buddhist Candras, as constructed by Majumdar, spans the reigns of Pūrṇacandra, Suvarṇacandra, Trailokyacandra, Śrīcandra, Kalyāṇacandra, Laḍahacandra, and Govindacandra. At the outset, it is important to note that the queen is included as one of the categories to be informed of the grants, as in the Rāmapāla copper-plate inscription of Śrīcandra (v. 18) and the Dhulla plate of the same king. In fact, the latter grant mentions her as the first category in this regard (*rājñī-rāṇaka-rājaputra . . .*).[169]

The Rāmapāla plate of Śrīcandra enumerates the royal women in the Candra line, while recording the grant of land in Puṇḍrabhukti to Pītavāsaguptaśarman by the king.[170] This does not mean that such a faithful recording can be found in other inscriptions. For instance, the Kedārpur copper plate of the same king traces the genealogy from Pūrṇacandra to Trailokyacandra but omits to mention the women.[171]

The Rāmapāla grant mentions Pūrṇacandra's wife (and Suvarṇacandra's mother) but without her name (v. 4). However, Trailokyacandra's wife is clearly identified: 'This king (Trailokyacandra), whose authority was acknowledged by all, had a wife, Śrīkāñcanā by name, who was as beautiful as gold.' Śrīkāñcanā, it is stated, gave birth to Śrīcandra. The Dhulla plate of Śrīcandra also mentions Śrīkāñcanā. The Maināmatī plates of Laḍahacandra state that he was born of Kalyāṇadevī, the daughter of a merchant. Łaḍahacandra's queen is named as Saubhāgyadevī, the mother of Govindacandra, the last-known Candra king.

As stated earlier, Śrīcandra is supposed to have restored the Pāla ruler, Gopāla II, to the throne and returned his captured queen to him. Most secondary sources are unanimous in stressing this as an indicator of the power equations between Gopāla II and Śrīcandra.[172] There has been hardly any discussion on the issue of Gopāla's unnamed wife or the reasons behind her capture. Who was the woman in question, and how and why was she captured? Was her eventual release a part of a deal or was she a surety for Gopāla? Why does this important event not find mention in the Pāla inscriptions?

The Varman Inscriptions

There are several important gendered aspects of the Varman inscriptions that have so far been overlooked by historians. The female members of the Varman genealogical line are mentioned in the inscriptions, as in the records of contemporary minor kingdoms. In addition, the wives of ministers have a clear presence—as in the Pāla records. There is, moreover, an intriguing stress on a daughter, without parallel in contemporary grants.

One of the most significant inscriptions is the Belāva copper-plate Inscription of Bhojavarmadeva, the fourth king of the Varman dynasty, recording his grant of the village Upgalikā in Puṇḍrabhukti to the priest, Rāmadevaśarman, for the merit of his parents and himself.[173] The queen is mentioned in the first few categories of persons to be informed about the grant. The inscription claims that Jātavarman, Bhojavarman's grandfather, laid the foundation for the dynasty's greatness and married Vīraśrī, the daughter of the Kalacuri king, Lakṣmīkarṇa. There are indications that this marriage was instrumental in Jātavarman's rise to power. That Jātavarman's political status was connected with his marriage is evident in verse 8, which says he manifested 'his sovereign royal dignity' by marrying Vīraśrī. The other ways in which he apparently manifested this dignity were in humiliating Kāmarūpa, extending his royalty in the Aṅgas, subduing Divya, and distributing riches to brāhmaṇas. His marriage with Vīraśrī is, then, ranked on a par with other strategic political decisions.

Paul points to the stress laid on Jātavarman's marriage with Vīraśrī that seems to have something to do with his military conquests. He speculates, from the way in which the words *kalacuri* and *mātṛvaṁśa* occur in the broken Vajrayoginī plate of Sāmalavarman, Jātavarman's son (it talks of the Kalacuri family as the *mātṛvaṁśa* or mother's lineage of Sāmalavarman's brother, Harivarman), that the marriage was perhaps a great factor in determining the political fortunes of the Varman family.[174]

The Belāva plate states that Vīraśrī gave birth to Sāmalavarman who succeeded Jātavarman. Interestingly, the Vajrayoginī plate, issued in Sāmalavarman's reign, suggests that it was Harivarman who succeeded Jātavarman.[175] It is speculated that Harivarman was Sāmalavarman's older brother and predecessor, although the portion of the record that indicates their relationship is missing.

Another significant aspect of the Belāva plate is the mention of Mālavyadevī, Bhojavarman's mother and Sāmalavarman's chief queen. Verse 12 states,

> Although the harem (of Sāmalavarman) was full of daughters of many kings, yet it was Mālavyadevī who became his chief queen (*pūrṇepya-śeṣa-bhūpāla-putrī-ṇāmavarodhane, tasyāsīdagramahiṣī saiva sāmala-varmanaha*).[176]

This seems to imply that Mālavyadevī was not the daughter of a king. Despite this handicap, however, she seems to have ousted the others in capturing Sāmalavarman's affections and, by extension, the top rank at court. Some sort of harem rivalry would have been a logical consequence of this, but there is no evidence. Verse 13 contains another noteworthy statement: 'They had a son Bhojavarman by name who resembled them and was the illuminator of both the families.' The equal weightage accorded to both parents is largely unparalleled in contemporary inscriptions.

One of the most notable aspects of the Belāva plate is that the name of a ruler's daughter is given prominence.[177] Verse 11 states:

> Through Mālavyadevī, he (Sāmalavarman) had a daughter, Trailokyasundarī, by name. She was, as if, the banner of Cupid, the hero in the conquest of the whole world (*tasya mālavyadevyāsīt kanyā trailokyasundarī, jagadvijayamallasya vaijayantī manobhuvaha*).[178]

Interestingly, verse 10 merely mentions that Sāmalavarman had a son who waged battles, but does not reveal his name (Udayin) until later. Unfortunately, there is no corroborative information from any other source on the noteworthy reference to a daughter, and, predictably, hardly any present-day historian is interested in this aspect.[179]

Another significant record is the Bhuvaneśwar inscription of Bhaṭṭa Bhavadeva, the minister of war and peace for King Harivarman.[180] As mentioned in the previous chapter, Harivarman is often identified with the Hari of the *Rāmacarita* who initially aided the Kaivarta Divya and later propitiated Rāmapāla. The record forms a parallel with some of the Pāla ministerial grants in that women connected with the minister's family have a clear presence in the inscription, perhaps in imitation of royal records and as a probable affirmation of their status.

The inscription traces Bhavadeva's ancestry to his grandfather, Ādideva, chief minister of the 'king of Vaṅga', probably Jātavarman, and mentions Ādideva's wife, Devakī, and their son, Govardhana. Verse 13 states that Govardhana 'married Sāṅgokā, the foremost of all ladies—an adorable and pious daughter of a Vandyaghaṭīya brāhmaṇa'. Verse 14 mentions Sāṅgokā's son, Bhavadeva. Thus, the careful detailing of the place of the women in this ministerial family seems a deliberate and familiar device to underline their importance.[181]

No secondary work has debated on the various issues raised in this analysis, beyond stating bare factual details, thereby revealing a clear propensity to ignore the women of the Varman history. However, as can be discerned from the above analysis, the royal women of the dynasties preceding or concurrent with the Pālas seem to enjoy a greater visibility and presence in the records than their Pāla counterparts. This, again, intensifies the inexplicably shadowy presence of the Pāla queens. After all, there cannot have been such a drastic change in the socio-political milieu that allowed a measure of freedom and agency to one lot of royal women and to have denied this to another. It should be noted here, however, that non-royal women seem to have a palpable presence only in the Pāla period and not in any other.

In conclusion, one can draw attention to Chakrabarti's analysis of the worship of the goddess in Bengal, since this appears to be linked with the issue of religious flexibility in this period.[182] He talks of the Brahmanical initiative in reorganizing the social structure and religious mores of the indigenous people of Bengal through the codification of the Upapurāṇas during the early medieval period.[183] Chakrabarti claims that the Bengal Purāṇas constructed a plausible genealogy for the goddess, attaching her manifestations to the important male members of the Brahmanical pantheon to ensure authenticity and a proper place for her in the divine hierarchy, thereby making this one of the major symbols of Bengal's cultural tradition.[184] Thus, by appropriating and transforming the local goddesses, the Brahmanical attempt at achieving social dominance in Bengal was articulated.[185] However, there seems no obvious correlation between this aspect and the religious freedom that women like Prabhāvatī and Citramatikā seem to have enjoyed.

OTHER GENDERED ASPECTS OF THE PĀLA–SENA PERIOD

This section will examine certain gendered themes that span one or more sections and do not necessarily adhere to a chronological format. Most of this analysis is derived from points that have been raised fleetingly in secondary sources on Bengal–Bihar, but that have been ignored, thereafter.

The Role of Maternal Bonds

The significance of maternal bonds and connections in Rāmapāla's recovery of the throne is a crucial aspect of Pāla history and warrants a separate discussion for two main reasons. First, the central role played by Rāmapāla's maternal uncle, Mathaṇa/Mahaṇa, a feudatory of Aṅga, in helping Rāmapāla achieve his aim is important. Second, a vital connection is revealed between the histories of Kanauj and Bengal–Bihar in that Kumaradevī, the Buddhist queen of the Gāhaḍavāla king, Govindacandra of Kanauj, was the granddaughter of Mathaṇa, and her marriage itself seems to have been engineered in Rāmapāla's interest.

As mentioned earlier, the *Rāmacarita* reveals that Rāmapāla's elder brother, Mahipāla II, was ousted by the Kaivarta revolt, thereby forcing Rāmapāla to seek aid from his feudatories and eventually regain his kingdom. The important point here is that Rāmapāla's uncle, the Rāṣṭrakūṭa Mathaṇa, fashioned and directed his success against the Kaivartas, and was the single most crucial factor in his acquisition of the kingdom. Although most secondary sources provide plentiful details of Mathaṇa's assistance in this regard, none of them stress its implications for a gendered history.[186]

By extension, although the fact of Mathaṇa being Rāmapāla's maternal uncle is tacitly acknowledged, there is hardly any specific statement that he was the brother of an unnamed wife of Vigrahapāla III except, perhaps, for a passing reference by Sircar.[187] Moreover, predictably, there is no debate on the identity of Rāmapāla's mother except, perhaps, for H.C. Ray who feels that as Mathaṇa is described as a Rāṣṭrakūṭa in the *Rāmacarita* (*RC*, II.8), one could assume that Vigrahapāla III married a Rāṣṭrakūṭa princess.[188] Thus, Rāmapāla was the son of this queen and not of Vigrahapāla's other wife, the Kalacuri, Yauvanaśrī. Banerji, too, makes a note of this fact.[189]

The *Rāmacarita* reveals that after seeking shelter with his maternal relatives (*matri-bāndhavāḥ*—*RC*, I.40), Rāmapāla's first task in exile was to seek the help of his feudatories (*sāmanta-cakra*), through a measure of bribery and coercion over particularly rebellious ones. As the entire process of recovery was apparently dictated by Mathaṇa, it is reasonable to assume that this initial task was devised by him as well. However, the defeat of a formidable adversary, Devarakṣita of Pīṭhī, by Mathaṇa seems to have been an important ingredient of the latter's plans to aid his nephew—by enlisting Pīṭhī's help—and also exposes the connection with Kanauj.[190]

The mention of this incident in the *Rāmacarita* (*RC*, V.8) finds corroboration in the Sārnāth inscription of Kumaradevī of Kanauj. The inscription states, 'In the Gauḍa country there was a priceless warrior . . . the Aṅga king Mahaṇa, the venerable maternal uncle of kings. He conquered Devarakṣita in war and maintained the glory of Rāmapāla, which rose in splendour because the obstruction caused by his foe was removed' (v. 7).[191] Subsequent verses talk of Mathaṇa marrying his daughter, Śaṅkaradevī, to Devarakṣita of Pīṭhī and of their daughter, Kumaradevī, who was married to Govindacandra of Kanauj. As the conquest of Devarakṣita is so prominently mentioned, it appears that he was an important feudatory of the Pālas and that Mathaṇa clearly relieved Rāmapāla by defeating Devarakṣita. Thus, 'the lord of Pīṭhī' (*pīṭhīpati*) is placed first in the list of Rāmapāla's *sāmantas* in the *Rāmacarita*.[192]

It appears that Mathaṇa won over Devarakṣita after his defeat by concluding a marriage alliance between him and his daughter, Śaṅkaradevī. Banerji wonders at the reason behind this: either Devarakṣita defeated Mathaṇa and peace was concluded after this marriage, or Śaṅkaradevī was given to Devarakṣita to draw him to the camp of Mathaṇa and Rāmapāla.[193] The latter suggestion appears more plausible as even H.C. Ray points to this 'combination of force with diplomacy' as being 'eminently successful' in that the *pīṭhīpatis* henceforward helped Rāmapāla materially in his campaign against the Kaivartas.[194]

There are indications, in the *Rāmacarita*, of Mathaṇa's financial aid to Rāmapāla—another aspect that has not been specifically noted. The text talks of Rāmapāla travelling to the principalities of his *sāmanta-cakra* and of forest chiefs to win them over with the distribution of land and wealth (*RC*, I.43). Taken in conjunction with the fact of Rāmapāla having sought refuge with Mathaṇa, one can presume that the resources in question—both for undertaking this arduous, extensive mission and for purposes of bribery—were those of Mathaṇa and not of the exiled Rāmapāla. Thus, Mathaṇa's willingness to proffer financial, as well as mental and physical aid to his nephew, is highly significant.

The support provided by other maternal relatives of Rāmapāla is no less significant. A case in point is that of *mahāpratihāra* Śivarāja, Mathaṇa's nephew and Rāmapāla's cousin, who conducted an important reconnaissance mission in Varendra prior to the actual attack on the Kaivartas, now led by Bhīma. This *rāṣṭrakūṭamāṇikya* or 'jewel of the Rāṣṭrakūṭa family' (*RC*, I.47) was able to crush Bhīma's defences to such an extent that it seemed as if Varendra was already liberated and encouraged Rāmapāla to launch his final invasion. Śivarāja apparently also made a careful survey of the villages and *viṣayas* to ensure the safety of the properties of the temples and brāhmaṇas (*RC*, I.50).

In addition, Mathaṇa's sons, the *mahāmaṇḍalika* Kāhnuradeva and Suvarṇadeva, led the vanguard of Rāmapāla's army along with Śivarāja in the eventual battle with Bhīma that enabled Rāmapāla to recover his *janakabhū* or paternal kingdom (*RC*, II.6–11, 21–31).[195] These maternal relatives of Rāmapāla are mentioned at the bottom of the list of supportive feudatories in the *Rāmacarita*, along with Rāmapāla's eldest son, Rājyapāla, who predeceased him.

The enormity of Mathaṇa's endeavour is highlighted by the fact that despite the Kaivarta revolt being called an unfortunate civil revolution (*dharma-viplavaṁ anikaṁ*) in the *Rāmacarita* (*RC*, I.24), it is clear that it had popular support and that Rāmapāla's accession was by no means a unanimous desire. Mahipāla II seems to have been an oppressive ruler and, hence, the occupation of Varendra by the Kaivarta Divya is described as an act of giving protection in the people's best interests.[196] There are indications that even the feudal chiefs rallied around Divya, viewing him as their protector (*RC*, II.21–7). Hence Rāmapāla's eventual victory over the Kaivartas was not based on the willing submission of the people, but on the success of his superior mercenary force through Mathaṇa's help.

The bond between Mathaṇa and Rāmapāla seems to have endured. When Rāmapāla ascended the throne in AD 1077, his authority was limited and tenuous, and large parts of the erstwhile

Pāla empire were not in his control.[197] However, Mathaṇa seems to have assisted him in the painstaking resumption of power. An important example of this is seen in the Rahan grant of Madanapāla of Kanauj (1109) that describes Madanapāla's son, Govindacandra, as 'terrific in cleaving the frontal globes of arrays of irresistible mighty large elephants from Gauḍa'—seen as an obvious reference to Rāmapāla. Majumdar says that the result of this conflict is, perhaps, indicated by the term *dhṛta-madhyadeśa-tanimā* (*RC*, III.24) to describe Varendra's political condition, or that Rāmapāla kept in check the growing power of *madhyadeśa*—indicating the Gāhaḍavāla kingdom.[198]

Significantly, this is partly attributed to the 'diplomatic marriage' of Govindacandra and Kumaradevī, the princess of Pīṭhī, who, as mentioned earlier, was the granddaughter of Mathaṇa.[199] Majumdar speculates that it was probably engineered by Mathaṇa to cement the alliance between the Pālas and Gāhaḍavālas. Thus, Mathaṇa's constant desire to ensure a peaceful rule for Rāmapāla and his willingness to achieve this by any means is palpably significant. The symbiotic relationship between uncle and nephew is finally underscored by the fact that Rāmapāla apparently drowned himself in the Gaṅgā at Monghyr in 1130, 'overwhelmed' with grief at the news of Mathaṇa's death (*RC*, IV.8–11).

In concluding this section, three relevant points can be made. The first is a reiteration of the importance of Mathaṇa's intervention in the fortunes of the Pāla dynasty. Had he not involved himself so wholeheartedly in Rāmapāla's struggle, the continuation of the Pāla rulers would have remained a doubtful proposition. In fact, conclusive evidence of Mathaṇa's power over Rāmapāla and the fortunes of the Pāla dynasty is seen again in the collapse of the kingdom under the weight of disaffected vassals after Rāmapāla's death. Thus, the fact that the kingdom was regained and revitalized on the strength of a maternal bond is vitally significant, and its importance for a gendered history of the kingdom needs to be acknowledged.

It is also pertinent that Rāmapāla's son, Madanapāla, was helped, at a subsequent stage, by Candradeva of Aṅga and Mathaṇa's grandson, in his war against the Gāhaḍavālas.[200] Candradeva apparently made the arrangements for Madanapāla's coronation, and seems to have brought about an alliance between Madanapāla and either Govindacandra or Vijayacandra of Kanauj. All this underscores the continuation of the matrilateral bond and its pivotal role in ensuring the stability of the Pāla rule.

In this context, Thomas Trautmann's views are pertinent.[201] He notes that under the Indo-Aryan marriage rules, new marital alliances are forged in each generation and old ones are allowed to grow cold, whereby old allies are replaced with fresh ones. However, as per the Dravidian rules, the affines become a hereditary group with a correspondingly greater and now permanent interest in the succession. One can draw a parallel with the Rāṣṭrakūṭas who followed the Dravidian pattern of cross-cousin marriage and Mathaṇa's interest in the Pāla empire.

The second point is another interesting connection that can be drawn between Kanauj and Bengal–Bihar in that Harṣa, too, seems to have shared a close relationship with his uncle—a factor whose gendered relevance is usually overlooked, although its details are tacitly accepted. As cited in the section on Kanauj, the Gupta king, Mahāsenagupta, in his search for allies, married off his sister, Mahāsenaguptā, to the Puṣpabhūti ruler, Ādityavardhana. This alliance was welcome to the Vardhanas, as marriages into the Gupta family had stimulated the political ambitions of different families.[202]

Thus, Sinha points to the first assumption of imperial titles by Prabhākaravardhana, Mahāsenaguptā's son and Harṣa's father, thereby stressing the recurrent motif of a woman's hand in the assumption of titles and assertion of status. This alliance, however, failed in its design of stemming Maukhari aggression and Mahāsenagupta was forced to retire to Mālwā, thereby explaining Bāṇa's term of *mālavarājaputra* for his two sons, Kumāragupta and Mādhavagupta.[203] On Mahāsenagupta's subsequent defeat by the Kalacuris, his sons were sent to Prabhākaravardhana's court and were appointed companions to Harṣa and Rājya, although Majumdar cautions that they might have been given refuge for humanitarian rather than kinship reasons.[204]

Mādhavagupta shared a very close bond with Harṣa—who was actually his nephew, although they were of nearly similar age. His closeness to Harṣa is expressed in the Aphsāḍ inscription of his son, Ādityasena, that talks of Mādhavagupta's eagerness for Harṣa's company (v. 15).[205] Apparently Mādhavagupta was always by Harṣa's side, even accompanying him in his quest for Rājyaśrī, and was eventually crowned the ruler of Magadha by Harṣa. However, there are several divergent views on this event. For instance, the *Harṣacarita* refers to the anointment of *kumāra* as king by Harṣa and this is seen as a reference to Kumāragupta being made a sovereign by Harṣa. Therefore, it is speculated that Mādhavagupta succeeded his brother or, alternatively, that in the scramble for power after Harṣa's death, one of the two brothers seized the throne of Magadha.[206] However, the significant point here is that, as in the case of Rāmapāla and Mathaṇa, the uncle supported the nephew consistently. Yet this interesting parallel has not been, hitherto, noticed or commented upon.

The third interesting point is a continuous parallel drawn in the *Rāmacarita* between the kingdom of Varendra and Sītā, the wife of the epic hero, Rāma. To this end, Sandhyākara Nandi uses the term *janakabhū* frequently to indicate both Sītā for whom Rāma fought with Rāvaṇa, and Varendra for whom Rāmapāla fought with the Kaivartas (*RC*, I.38–41, 28, 31; III.15–25).[207] Similarly, certain expressions simultaneously imply the guarding of Varendra and Sītā from covetous eyes.[208]

Interestingly, the Kamauli plate of Vaidyadeva continues this parallel imagery by talking of Rāmapāla and Rāma gaining glory by repossessing Varendra and Sītā, respectively (verse 4).[209] Banerji reminds us that comparisons of Rāma with Rāmapāla seem habitual in the eleventh century.[210] However, the parallel between Sītā and Varendra implies that women were equated with possessions that needed to be guarded stringently. This, in a sense, parallels the low profile of the royal Pāla women and their seemingly circumscribed existence in the confines of the harem.

Courtesans/Prostitutes in the Pāla–Sena Period

Not much information can be gleaned from the literary and epigraphic sources of the Pāla–Sena period on the role of prostitutes and courtesans. However, there are significant indications—in texts like Kalhaṇa's *Rājataraṅgiṇī*—that they played a somewhat prominent role in the contemporary society and polity. An important distinction can be drawn with contemporary Kashmir here in that the visibility accorded to these women in the Pāla–Sena sources is extremely limited, as compared to their masterful presence in the sources of Kashmir. The distinction extends to their role as well, in that while they wielded great political influence in Kashmir, the role of their counterparts in Bengal–Bihar remains largely ambiguous and inscrutable.

The earliest, most significant reference to temple girls and courtesans in Bengal pertains to the eighth century and is provided by Kalhaṇa's *Rājataraṅgiṇī*. The details have already been cited in the discussion on Kashmir and in the previous chapter, but it would be worthwhile to recount them briefly. The exiled Jayāpīḍa of Kashmir apparently sought shelter in Puṇḍravardhana with a temple girl, Kamalā, who intelligently penetrated his disguise. This precipitated a chain of events that led to Jayāpīḍa's marriage with Kalyāṇadevī, the daughter of King Jayanta, a vassal of the Gauḍas, and the eventual recovery of his kingdom. Kamalā later accompanied the royal couple back to Kashmir.

These details have been used by most scholars to prove the existence of temple prostitutes in Bengal at the time.[211] Additionally, Chakrabarti talks of the songs of prostitutes featuring on ocasions of collective festivity, while N. Ray describes the sensual opulence of Lakṣmaṇasena's court with prostitutes performing dramas such as Jayadeva's *Gīta Govinda* through dance.[212] On the other hand, Majumdar talks of their existence as reflecting the low moral standards of society, tracing this to the influence of Tāntric doctrines, and the tenets of Buddhism and Brahmanism of the eleventh and twelfth centuries.[213]

Some of the wider implications of Kalhaṇa's details have not been considered. Kalhaṇa gives significant indications of Kamalā's sagacity and shrewdness. Not only did she discern Jayāpīḍa's royal background, she also lent him her firm support and eventually marked her presence in Kashmir by building towns and temples. She was, thus, able to parallel Kalyāṇadevī's presence who, significantly, was made an official functionary—the *mahāpratihārapīḍa*—at Jayāpīḍa's court and similarly built to concretize her name, thereby showing a clear contrast with her royal counterparts in Bengal. Thus, Kalhaṇa shows both the temple prostitute and the royal woman—both from Bengal—enjoying a near-similar status and wielding much influence in Kashmir. Admittedly, his account of Jayāpīḍa's exploits might have a legendary basis but the several important inferences that can be drawn from it have, hitherto, been glossed over.

One can cite N. Ray's views as an illustrative case.[214] Ray notes that Kalhaṇa's details corroborate the reference to temple prostitutes in the *Rāmacarita.* He then concludes, from Kalhaṇa's praise of Kamalā and Sandhyākara Nandi's favourable mention, that dancing girls were not disreputable in the society of the contemporary urban nobility in whose circles 'dancing girls, paramours, women of the court and temple girls' were seen as an 'indispensable element'. He further states—with reference to temple prostitutes—that 'their enjoyment was not very widespread' in the Pāla period but later spread due to 'southern influence' so that in the Sena–Varman periods, temple girls dominated the thoughts and fancies of the upper levels of society, as seen in the Deopārā eulogy of Vijayasena. The reference here is probably to verse 30 of the record that talks of Vijayasena's provision of a hundred beautiful female attendants 'for the husband of only half a wife'—an intriguingly ambiguous statement.[215]

There are several implications of this statement, beginning with Ray's attempt to club together dancing girls, temple girls, and women of the court in one category. Does this mean that all the women associated with the court were necessarily dancing or temple girls, there being no other role for them? Further, where is the evidence that they were an 'indispensable element' of the milieu of the urban nobility? After all, they do not have a presence in the inscriptions and, besides, the clinching evidence is largely provided by the Kashmiri text, the *Rājataraṅgiṇī*, rather than a source from Bengal.

Additionally, what is this ambiguous 'southern influence' that seems to have increased the popularity of temple prostitutes in the Sena–Varman period? If we are meant to presume that this category of women was not really well known in Bengal before, what do we make of the evidence provided by Kalhaṇa that pertains to the eighth century? Not only does Ray ignore the ramifications of his statements and Kalhaṇa's evidence, he also chooses to talk of temple prostitutes as some sort of commodity in his reference to the 'enjoyment' of them.

To conclude this chapter, I cite some notable cases of gender-blindness in certain secondary sources dealing with the Pāla–Sena period. Majumdar's views regarding the presence of women in the inscriptions of the relevant period is a case in point.[216] He notes that the Sena grants include the queen 'who does not figure in similar lists of even a single record of the Pāla kings'. Majumdar speculates whether the addition signifies the greater political importance of the queen, but observes that as the Candras, Varmans, Kāmbojas, and Senas—whose records bear the addition—all originally belonged to territories outside Bengal, 'the innovation might be due to foreign influence'.

Notably, the very next line says, 'More significant, however, is the inclusion of the Purohita in the grants of the Kāmboja, Varman, and Sena kings', as it indicates the great importance of the religious and social aspects of administration. Interestingly, this fact is not mentioned in the discussion of the Pālas, but as a sort of incidental point of interest in an analysis of the period of the Senas and other minor dynasties. All this is deeply reflective of Majumdar's own interests and priorities. The very fact that the reference to women is termed an 'innovation' here is suggestive of a bias. Is the inclusion of women in the Kanauj inscriptions, for instance, a novelty rather than being a legitimate part of the genealogical information?[217]

By extension, if the inclusion of women in the category of land-grant executors is seen as an innovation, then how does this reconcile with the exalted status of the queen as given in Kauṭilya's *Arthaśāstra*, for instance? Why does Majumdar not dwell on the very limited presence of the royal Pāla women in the official records, such that the very mention of a queen in subsequent grants is termed an innovation?

Equally inexplicable is another sweeping statement of Majumdar as regards the previously cited Rāmgunj copper plate of Īśvaraghoṣa, a Pāla feudatory. He notes that the grant faithfully imitates the style of the Pāla, Varman, and Sena dynasties of independent kings, the same categories of people having to be informed like the *rājan, rājanyaka, rājñī* and so on.[218] However, he errs in saying that these categories of executors 'closely correspond' to those of the Guptas, Pālas, and Senas because queens are clearly *not* included in this list in the Pāla records. Majumdar evidently does not apply his otherwise critical and methodical standards of analysis to gender issues.

Ironically, Majumdar's views on gendered aspects appear more critical and discerning than those of N. Ray. Ray claims that the inscriptions of the Pāla–Sena period show that the aim of women was to be faithful, productive, and to bear comparison with the female characters of the epics.[219] It is difficult to derive the sources for these rather far-fetched conclusions. No inscription makes any statement to this effect, the aims seeming to reflect Ray's expectations from women rather than a reflection of reality.

Paradoxically, Ray points to the fact that women either donated with men or set up images and gave alms alone. Why does he not consider the implications of women as donors and their access to and disbursal of resources? In fact, the admirably clear reasoning that Ray brings to bear on several other issues of the history of Bengal–Bihar—such as his balanced appraisal of Śaśāṅka's career and alleged misdeeds—only serves to highlight his lack of rigorous analysis on gender issues. There are several other examples of this.[220]

In a similar vein, Verma displays an almost complete indifference to women, except for a brief note on the forms of marriage/ remarriage, prostitutes and women's household duties, that constitute a mere seven pages of his total analysis of 184 pages.[221] Women also feature briefly in his discussion on the dress and ornaments of this period, the entire aspect being seen as a part of 'Social Condition'.[222] The painstaking details that Verma provides of educational norms, admission procedures to the universities and the curriculum do not include any references to female education, or even the minimum requirements of study for royal women.

In addition, despite Verma's fleeting references to various Pāla queens having led to strategic political alliances or to them having influenced religious choices, there is absolutely no speculation/ analysis on the role of women in the Pāla period. Likewise, although B.C. Sen indulges in a lengthy analysis of the categories mentioned in the grants of this period and admits the fact that the *rājñī* figures in them, he does not discuss this aspect or the absence of the queen in Pāla records.[223]

The process of invisibilizing the identities of women is continued apace by H.C. Ray, despite the fact of his otherwise analytical and intelligent analysis. In a manner reminiscent of M.A. Stein, he omits to mention certain key women figures like the Pāla queen Madanadevī, and the Candra queen, Kāñcanā, in the Genealogical Tables that he provides of the respective dynasties.[224] The fact that he mentions women of the other dynastic lines displays a very half-hearted attention to gender information.

This arbitrary approach is also seen in certain statements of Paul.[225] Thus, for instance, while claiming that the position of the queen-consort was very high and that she figures third in the list of land-grant executors, Paul does not clearly distinguish the Sena records—to which this applies—from those of the Pālas. The administration of the Pālas and Senas cannot be clubbed together as one amorphous category in this sense. Moreover, Paul talks of the 'considerable' influence of the chief queen, although her actual political influence was not known. Once again, this holds true only for the Sena queens and not the Pāla ones. Paul cites Vilāsadevī's ceremonies as an illustrative example but does not clearly specify the crucial distinction to be made here between the two sets of royal women. However, this seems to be more a case of oversight on Paul's part than a deliberate lack of attention to gender issues.

Royal women in the Pāla period obviously did not enjoy the same prominence and power as the women of the contemporary kingdoms of Kanauj and, especially, Kashmir. The reasons are not very clear, particularly when one considers the rather considerable role played by some royal women of the Senas and other minor dynasties in this period, as well as that of non-royal women of the Pāla period itself.

One could presume that the inscriptions do not accurately reflect the agency of women or, alternatively, that women were not accorded prominence in the socio-political milieu of early medieval Bengal. However—as seen above—the matter is complicated further by the attempts of several writers to minimize the presence of women through their uncritical and biased analysis.

NOTES

1. P.L. Paul, *The Early History of Bengal*, Calcutta, The Indian Research Institute: 1939, vol. I, p. 71, notes that the Rāṣṭrakūṭa alliance was the 'corner-stone' of the Pāla foreign policy as the Rāṣṭrakūṭas, directly or indirectly, rendered great service to the Pāla empire from its foundation to its demise. Also D.C. Sircar, *Studies in the Society and Administration of Ancient and Medieval India*, Calcutta, Firma K.L. Mukhopadhyay: 1967, vol. I, p. 29.
2. D.C. Sircar, 'Belwā Plate of Mahipāla I', *Epigraphia Indica*, vol. XXIX, 1957, pp. 1–9.
3. F. Kielhorn, 'Khalimpur Plate of Dharmapāladeva', *Epigraphia Indica*, vol. IV, 1897, pp. 243–54. The incription records the grant of four villages—Krauñcaśvabhra, Māḍhāśānmatī, Pālītaka and Gopippalī—to the temple of Nunnanārāyaṇa by Dharmapāla, as per the request of *mahāsāmantādhipati* Nārāyaṇavarman who had founded it. Also R.C. Majumdar, *History of Ancient Bengal*, Calcutta, G. Bharadwaj and Company: 1971, p. 97.
4. R.D. Banerji, *The Pālas of Bengal*, Varanasi, Bhartiya Publishing House: 1973, p. 7 notes that the Bhadras are variously placed in middle, eastern, or southern India in the *Bṛhat Saṁhitā*.
5. Majumdar, *History of Ancient Bengal*, p. 97. While inclining to Kielhorn's view, he notes that Dharmapāla is described as *rājabhaṭādi-vaṁśa-patita* in a commentary to the *Aṣṭasāhasrikā Prajñāpāramitā* composed by Haribhadra in his reign. Attempts have been made to link this with Rājabhaṭa, the son of Devakhaḍga of the Khaḍga dynasty and, therefore, the Pālas and Khaḍgas who were both Buddhists. Majumdar points out that although *patita* means 'fallen' or outcast, it can also mean 'descended by the female line'.
6. Parabala is known from the Pathari pillar inscription of 861: F. Kielhorn, 'Pathari Pillar Inscription of Parabala', *Epigraphia Indica*, vol. IX, 1908, pp. 248–56; H.C. Ray, *The Dynastic History of Northern India*, 2nd edn, Delhi, Munshiram Manoharlal: 1973, vol. I, p. 288.
7. The Sanjan plates show that the Rāṣṭrakūṭa king, Govinda III, subdued Nāgabhaṭa II. Dharmapāla apparently submitted to him of his own accord, as did Dharmapāla's protégé, Cakrāyudha of Kanauj. See Paul, *Early History of Bengal*, I, p. 69. Every Rāṣṭrakūṭa campaign against the Pratihāras was indirectly of great political advantage to the Pālas (p. 70).
8. B.P. Sinha, 'Political History of South Bihar (750-1200 A.D.)', in *Comprehensive History of Bihar*, ed. B.P. Sinha, Patna, Kashi Prasad Jayaswal Research Institute: 1974, vol. I, pt II, p. 250; B.P. Sinha *The Decline of the Kingdom of Magadha (c. 455–1000 A.D.)*, Patna, Motilal Banarsidass: 1954, p. 345. Sinha talks of the distinct political advantage of this alliance

in offsetting the renewal of Pratihāra hostility and gaining Rāṣṭrakūṭa support. The *Rāmacarita* refers to Dharmapāla's son, Devapāla, as *samudra-kula-dīpa* or 'descended from the ocean'. In this connection, Majumdar talks of an old text, the *Dharmamaṅgala* of Ghanarāma, on Dharmapāla's queen, Vallabhadevī, being banished to the forest for having no son. She subsequently liaised with the ocean and had a son. Majumdar also cites Tāranātha's account of Gopāla being succeeded by a son whom the sovereign of the ocean begot on his younger queen. He then dismisses both these 'silly' stories outright (Majumdar, *History of Ancient Bengal*, p. 98).

9. It records the grant of Meṣikā village in Kṛmilā *viṣaya* to Bihekarātamiśra. R. Mukherji and S.K. Maity, *Corpus of Bengal Inscriptions Bearing on History and Civilization of Bengal*, Calcutta, Firma K.L. Mukhopadhyay: 1967, pp. 114–31.
10. Hirananda Sastri, 'Nālandā Copper Plate of Devapāladeva', *Epigraphia Indica*, vol. XVII, 1924, pp. 310–27 for details. Sastri notes that the *dūtaka* of the grant, Balavarman, is described as the 'overlord of Vyāghrataṭīmaṇḍala' and hence, he was obviously an official of the king of Magadha entrusted with the arrangements of the grant (p. 326). R.S. Tripathi, *History of Ancient India*, 3rd rpt., Delhi, Motilal Banarsidass: 1967, pp. 357–8.
11. Jhunu Bagchi, *The History and Culture of the Pālas of Bengal and Bihar (c.750 A.D.–c.1200 A.D.)*, Delhi, Abhinav Publications: 1993, p. 59.
12. This is ironic in view of the interesting reference in verse 33 to Devapāla being 'the preceptor for initiating into widowhood the wives of all the enemies'. D.C. Sircar mentions a copperplate grant of Devapāla's son, Śūrapāla, which talks of a queen, Māhaṭā (apparently Devapāla's wife and Śūrapāla's mother), building a temple at Varanasi and installing a Śiva liṅga there. It seems Devapāla granted four villages at her request. However, the identity of Śūrapāla is an ambiguous issue and besides, this queen is not named in any other source. Interestingly, Sircar cites this not as proof of the queen's existence but to show that the Pālas were in occupation of Varanasi at the time. D.C. Sircar, *The Kānyakubja-Gauḍa Struggle*, Calcutta, The Asiatic Society: 1985, p. 54; Susan L. Huntington, *The 'Pāla-Sena' Schools of Sculpture*, Leiden, E.J. Brill: 1984, pp. 210–11, 45–6.
13. Majumdar, *History of Ancient Bengal*, p. 123 speculates that Vigrahapāla's queen was a daughter of the powerful Kalacuri king, Kokkalla.
14. The inscription records the grant of Makutikā village in Kakṣa *viṣaya* to Śiva: Mukherji and Maity, *Corpus of Bengal Inscriptions*, pp. 163–84. The next verse refers to Nārāyaṇapāla, the son of Lajjā and Vigrahapāla.
15. Paul, *Early History of Bengal*, I, p. 70, says N.N. Vasu identifies Tuṅga

with Kṛṣṇa II, who had the title 'Tuṅga'. However, Banerji, *Pālas of Bengal*, p. 22 identifies Tuṅga as Tuṅga Dharmmāvaloka.

16. Paul, *Early History of Bengal*, I, p. 70; Majumdar, *History of Ancient Bengal*, p. 124. The Bāngaṛh grant refers to the 'illustrious' Rājyapāla who, by erecting temples 'whose sides were as high as the ridges of the principal mountains, had become famous' (R.D. Banerji, 'Bāngaṛh grant of Mahipāla I', *Epigraphia Indica*, vol. XIV, 1918, p. 329).
17. R.D. Banerji, 'Āmgachi Grant of Vigrahapāla III', *Epigraphia Indica*, vol. XV, 1920, pp. 293–301. It records the gift of villages in Puṇḍravardhanabhukti to Khoduladevaśarman in the king's twelfth regnal year. The Bāngaṛh grant records the donation of Kuraṭapallikā village in Puṇḍravardhanabhukti by Mahipāla I in his ninth regnal year to the brāhmaṇa, Kṛṣṇādityaśarmman. Banerji, 'Bāngaṛh Grant', *Epigraphia Indica*, vol. XIV, pp. 324–30 for details. Note that both these grants provide an almost identical genealogy from Gopāla I to Vigrahapāla III.
18. For instance, Paul, *Early History of Bengal*, I, p. 70; and 'Relations of the Pālas and Senas of Bengal with the Other Provinces', *The Indian Historical Quarterly*, vol. XII, 1936, p. 635.
19. It records the gift of Bṛhat-chattivannā village of Varddhamānabhukti to paṇḍit Aśvatthaśarmman, issued in the king's thirteenth regnal year. N.G. Majumdar, 'Irda Copper Plate of the Kāmboja King Nayapāladeva', *Epigraphia Indica*, vol. XXII, 1938, pp. 150–9 for details. See also J.C. Ghosh, 'Notes on the Irda Copper Plate Grant of King Nayapāladeva', *Epigraphia Indica*, vol. XXII, 1938, pp. 43–7 where he questions N.G. Majumdar's analysis of the Kāmboja rule.
20. Sinha, 'Political History of South Bihar', in *Comprehensive History of Bihar*, ed. Sinha, pp. 259–60; Sinha, *Decline of the Kingdom of Magadha*, p. 399.
21. N.G. Majumdar, 'Irda Copper Plate', *Epigraphia Indica*, vol. XXII, vv. 22–3, p. 159. R.C. Majumdar, *History of Ancient Bengal*, p. 313 notes the mention of the *mahiṣī, yuvarāja* and *ṛtvika* as executors of the grant. However, he does not speculate further on this.
22. H.C. Ray, *Dynastic History of Northern India*, pp. 324–5 cites the colophon of a manuscript in Nayapāla's reign. It was apparently written on the instructions of *pravara-mahāyāna-yāyinī paramopāsikā-rājñī-uddākā* in the year 14 of the *vijayarājya* of the Pālas under *mahārājādhirāja paramabhaṭṭāraka nayapāladeva*. The identity of this queen remains unclear, there being no other corroborative source.
23. Dhaṅga's dates are *c.* 954–1002. Note that he also imprisoned the queens of Kāñcī and Andhra. Paul, *Early History of Bengal*, I, p. 51.
24. D.C. Sircar, 'Introduction', in A.K. Maitreya, *The Fall of the Pāla Empire*, Darjeeling, University of North Bengal: 1987, p. ix.

25. Huntington, '*Pāla-Sena*' *Schools of Sculpture*, p. 217 for the reference to a donation by Gopāla and his wife that could, alternatively, be seen as a reference to a goddess. It is pertinent to note here that although Gopāla's successor, Mahipāla I, is subsequently seen as having restored the Pāla fortunes in the tenth century and is lauded for the same, the inscriptions do not reveal anything about his marital status.
26. Majumdar, *History of Ancient Bengal*, p. 139; H.C. Ray, *Dynastic History of Northern India*, p. 330 says that the *Rāmacarita* also indicates that Vigrahapāla did not completely uproot Lakṣmīkarṇa. He thinks that the marriage with Yauvanaśrī was the result of an alliance between the two powers.
27. Paul, *Early History of Bengal*, I, p. 56 finds that Lakṣmīkarṇa was obviously not compelled to give Yauvanaśrī to Vigrahapāla.
28. Ibid., p. 71: Paul notes this fact and that this branch of the Rāṣṭrakūṭas rendered great service to the Pāla cause at a critical point (pp. 70–1). Also H.C. Ray, *Dynastic History of Northern India*, p. 337.
29. Mukherji and Maity, *Corpus of Bengal Inscriptions*, pp. 209–19.
30. Bagchi, *History and Culture of the Pālas*, pp. 24–5 claims that it was Citramatikā who made the gift and not Madanapāla.
31. Mukherji and Maity, *Corpus of Bengal Inscriptions*, p. 219.
32. Note that the *Rāmacarita* makes certain gendered allusions after Rāmapāla's reign (*RC*, IV.21–3, 25) but they are too ambiguous to be very useful.
33. Paul, *Early History of Bengal*, I, p. 71. The Muslim traveller, Suleiman, for instance, confirms that they compelled 'every prince . . . to pay homage to themselves'.
34. Niharranjan Ray, *History of the Bengali People (Ancient Period)*, tr. J.W. Hood, Calcutta, Orient Longman: 1994, p. 282.
35. Kanakalatha Mukund, 'Turmeric Land: Women's Property Rights in Tamil Society since Early Medieval Times', in *Women in Early Indian Societies*, ed. Kumkum Roy, Delhi, Manohar: 1999, p. 134
36. B.S. Verma, 'Archaeological Excavation and Sites (300–1200 A.D.)', in *Comprehensive History of Bihar*, ed. Sinha, p. 540. Patharghāṭa (also known as Vaṭeśvarasthāna) is in the Bhāgalpur district of Bihar on the banks of the Gaṅgā near village Antichak, the site of Vikramaśīlā. There is a big rocky hill on which there are numerous relief sculptures and a few caves. Apart from the scenes cited, the sculptures also represent a few of Viṣṇu's *avatāras*.
37. Ibid., p. 182; Bagchi, *History and Culture of the Pālas*, pp. 96–8.
38. N. Ray, *History of the Bengali People*, p. 182. An interesting example is Devapāla's Nālandā grant which ends with an expression for the continuance of the grant 'as long as the Ganges has her limbs agitated by the extensive plaited hair of Hara'—a typically Brahmanical allusion. H.C.

Ray, *Dynastic History of Northern India*, p. 295. Devapāla's Monghyr grant compares him to various epic heroes (Bagchi, *History and Culture of the Pālas*, p. 154).

39. B.P. Mazumdar, 'Religion and Philosophy (500-1200 A.D.)', in *Comprehensive History of Bihar*, ed. Sinha, p. 404. Bagchi, *History and Culture of the Pālas*, pp. 98–9 cites the Mūrtiśiva *praśasti* from Bāngaṛh of Nayapāla's time that talks of Bengal being influenced by Śaiva ascetics in the tenth/eleventh century. She notes, therefore, the 'obviously religious liberality' prevalent in medieval India. Banerji, *Pālas of Bengal*, p. 18 notes that Devapāla's brother, Jayapāla, too, was a Hindu by inclination.
40. Likewise, the Monghyr copper plate of Devapāla mentions Dharmapāla's scrupulous regard for the rules of caste. B.S. Verma, *Socio-Religious, Economic and Literary Condition of Bihar (From A.D. 319-A.D. 1000)*, Delhi, Munshiram Manoharlal: 1962, p. 2.
41. Majumdar, *History of Ancient Bengal*, p. 517.
42. Haraprasad Sastri, ed., *Rāmacarita: A Historical Record of the Pāl Dynasty by Sandhyākara Nandi*, Varanasi, Bhartiya Publishing House: 1973, p. 6. The Keśava *praśasti* at Bodhgayā of the twenty-sixth year of Dharmapāla records the establishment of Mahādeva's image at the Campeśa temple at Mahābodhi and the gift of a tank for religious purposes by Keśava, son of the sculptor, Ujjvala. The king expended 3,000 silver coins for the tank's excavation. H.C. Ray, *Dynastic History of Northern India*, p. 288. Dharmapāla also founded the Vikramaśīlā monastery that is sometimes called *śrīmad-vikramaśīlādeva-vihāra* after his title (P.L. Paul, *The Early History of Bengal*, Calcutta, The Indian Research Institute: 1940, vol. II, p. 26).
43. Paul, *Early History of Bengal*, II, pp. 47–8 contends that although the Pāla kings were following the traditional policy of rewarding learned and pious brāhmaṇas with land, the building of new monasteries, the reconstruction of old ones, and 'huge expenses' on Buddhist establishments indicate where their sympathies actually lay. He also notes that Jainism was losing ground in the Pāla period, as very few Jain images of this time have been found (p. 71).
44. V.A. Smith, 'The Pāla Dynasty of Bengal', *Indian Antiquary*, vol. XXXVIII, 1909, p. 244. B.P. Sinha, too, omits Madanadevī's name in his Genealogical Tables on the Pālas (*Dynastic History of Magadha*, Delhi, Abhinav Publications: 1977, p. 256).
45. Maitreya, *Fall of the Pāla Empire*, p. 1.
46. R.S. Sharma, 'Social and Economic Conditions (500-1200 A.D.)', in *Comprehensive History of Bihar*, ed. Sinha, p. 366.
47. Mukherji and Maity, *Corpus of Bengal Inscriptions*, pp. 122, 117.
48. This is reiterated in the Bāngaṛh Grant of Mahipāla I.
49. Smith, 'Pāla Dynasty of Bengal', *Indian Antiquary*, vol. XXXVIII,

p. 247 contradicts his own conclusions by identifying the three sons of Dharmapāla as Tribhuvanapāla, who was crown prince but died, Devapāla who succeeded him, and Vākpāla whose progeny became kings.

50. H.C. Ray, *Dynastic History of Northern India*, pp. 296–7. He notes that the Monghyr grant of Devapāla refers to the *yuvarāja* or crown prince, Rājyapāla, as its executor. Ray presumes that Rājyapāla predeceased Devapāla. Mukherji and Maity point out that the existence of this son of Devapāla is not known from any other source and hence, he might have assumed the name of Vigrahapāla I after ascending the throne. Mukherji and Maity, *Corpus of Bengal Inscriptions*, pp. 126, 131.
51. Hoernle inclines to the view that Vigrahapāla was Devapāla's son, while Kielhorn and Banerji feel that he was Jayapāla's son. H.C. Ray, *Dynastic History of Northern India*, p. 297.
52. Paul, *Early History of Bengal*, I, p. 48. The Bādal *praśasti* says Śūrapāla succeeded Devapāla, while the Bhāgalpur plate says that Vigrahapāla I succeeded him. H.C. Ray and Banerji presume that Vigrahapāla I and Śūrapāla were the same person. H.C. Ray, *Dynastic History of Northern India*, pp. 296–7. However, Sinha, 'Political History of South Bihar', in *Comprehensive History of Bihar*, ed. Sinha, pp. 255–6, says that Śūrapāla was either a son of Devapāla or of the *yuvarāja* Rājyapāla. Sinha believes, like Ray, that the succession to the throne after Devapāla's death was not peaceful and that Rājyapāla might have ascended the throne only to be ousted by Śūrapāla. Śūrapāla, however, had to deal with the rising family of Vākpāla, Dharmapāla's brother, and was eventually overthrown by Vigrahapāla, Jayapāla's son. Alternatively, one could presume that they were brothers and that Śūrapāla died childless, enabling Vigrahapāla to succeed him. See Smith, 'Pāla Dynasty of Bengal', *Indian Antiquary*, vol. XXXVIII, p. 243.
53. Maitreya extends Paul's observation ('Rāmapāla, the Last Great Pāla King', *The Indian Historical Quarterly*, vol. XIII, 1937, p. 40) that Rāmapāla is referred to as *sarvasammata* or 'accepted by all'. Although the Kaivarta rebellion and subsequent usurpation of Varendrī seems to have been precipitated by Mahipāla's oppressive rule, it could be seen as a repercussion of this sibling rivalry as well.
54. The identity of the mother of Śūrapāla II is unclear, too, but on account of his imprisonment by Mahipāla, one can presume that they did not share the same mother.
55. *RC*, I.33 seems to refer to Śūrapāla. The verse talks of the 'other brother' having to spend time in the forest (prison?) as well. The silence of the *Rāmacarita* on this issue seems, therefore, to form a parallel with the silence in the *Harṣacarita* on Harṣa's alleged desire to get rid of his brother, Rājya, a view corroborated by H.C. Ray (*Dynastic History of Northern India*, p. 338).

56. Majumdar, *History of Ancient Bengal*, pp. 142–7. This is part of his palpably obvious attempt to deny the existence of murders or devious acts in Bengal's history. For instance, he embarks on a heated and rather unnecessary defence of Mahipāla II to contest the *Rāmacarita*'s claim that he was an oppressive ruler, despite the detailed description provided of his lack of wisdom and hardheartedness (*RC*, I.22, 31, 36–7, 39). Majumdar's denial of Rāmapāla's desire for the throne is another debatable issue. Admittedly, Sandhyākara Nandi's account may be biased in favour of Rāmapāla, but one cannot wholly dismiss the indications of his ambition or desire for power that may well have crystallized into this form of sibling rivalry.
57. D.C. Sircar, 'Bangāon Plate of Vigrahapāla III', *Epigraphia Indica*, vol. XXIX, 1957, p. 51.
58. Sircar, *Studies in the Society and Administration*, pp. 22–3.
59. Paul, *Early History of Bengal*, I, p. 113 cites the *Rāmacarita* on discussions between Rāmapāla and Rājyapāla. Paul seems to assume that Rājyapāla was entrusted with the task of governing in Rāmapāla's old age. Banerji, *Pālas of Bengal*, p. 52 believes that although Rājyapāla helped recover Varendrī, he died and Kumārapāla took over. H.C. Ray, *Dynastic History of Northern India*, p. 350, notes that although the grant was issued in the fouth year of Kumārapāla, scholars feel that he had a short reign, as he is the subject of only one verse.
60. Banerji, *Pālas of Bengal*, p. 62. However, D.C. Sircar, 'Nimdīghi Inscription Mentioning Gopāla', *Epigraphia Indica*, vol. XXXV, 1962, pp. 228–33 records the construction of a Śaiva shrine by one Bhāvakadāsa. Sircar says the grant refers to Gopāla III, as it mentions him having died fighting some enemies near the record's findspot, thereby corroborating the *Rāmacarita's* details. Interestingly, Gopāla's trusted officer, Aidadeva, seems to have followed him in death, after receiving his father's consent to do so. Note that a parallel can be drawn here with the *Rājataraṅgiṇī* that records deaths precipitating other deaths in reaction.
61. Paul, *Early History of Bengal*, I, pp. 67–8; N.K. Bhattasali, 'The Rajibpur Sadāśiva-image Inscription of Gopāla III of Bengal', *The Indian Historical Quarterly*, vol. XVII, 1941, pp. 217–22. Majumdar, *History of Ancient Bengal*, pp. 155–6, wonders why there is no explanation for Gopāla III being succeeded by Madanapāla, and acknowledges the 'dark hints' in the *Rāmacarita*. Predictably, he dismisses this in view of the lack of 'positive evidence', without considering that it could reflect Madanapāla's probable rivalry with Kumārapāla (and his progeny), and the fruition of his desire to acquire the throne.
62. Bani Roychoudhuri, *The Political History of Bengal to the Rise of the Pāla Dynasty*, Calcutta, Sanskrit Pustak Bhandar: 1990, p. 163. Also E. Lyall, tr., 'Tāranātha's account of the Magadha kings', *Indian Antiquary*, vol. IV, 1875, pp. 366–7.

63. Roychoudhuri, *Political History of Bengal*, pp. 163–4: *mātsya-nyāya* indicates a situation where there is no established government, prompting every strong man to aggrandize himself at the cost of his weaker neighbours. Also Kielhorn, 'Khalimpur Plate', *Epigraphia Indica*, vol. IV, pp. 248, 251.
64. Roychoudhuri, *Political History of Bengal*, p. 163.
65. Maitreya, *Fall of the Pāla Empire*, p. 15.
66. Majumdar, *History of Ancient Bengal*, pp. 309, 95, 168, says that the leading chiefs' choice was probably endorsed later by the people. Interestingly, Paul draws a comparison between Gopāla's election and Yaśaskara's election by the brāhmaṇas in Kashmir (cited in the Kashmir section). He quotes Kalhaṇa as saying that the election of a king 'is tantamount to lunacy' (*RT*, V.456) {*Early History of Bengal*, I, p. 111}.
67. Bagchi, *History and Culture of the Pālas*, pp. 56–7.
68. F. Kielhorn, 'Bādal Pillar Inscription of Nārāyaṇapāla', *Epigraphia Indica*, vol. II, 1894, pp. 160–7.
69. Kielhorn says that it is 'of some value' for this reason. Ibid., p. 161.
70. Darbhapāṇi's diplomacy enabled Devapāla to exact tribute from the whole of northern India from the Himalaya to the Vindhya and from the eastern to the western seas.
71. Yet Majumdar notes that the Khalimpur grant of Dharmapāla and the Monghyr inscription of Devapāla do not associate their victories with their ministers. Majumdar, *History of Ancient Bengal*, pp. 305–6.
72. A.Venis, '(Kamauli) Copperplate Grant of Vaidyadeva, King of Kāmarūpa', *Epigraphia Indica*, vol. II, 1894, pp. 347–58 for details. He notes that the inscription also throws light on the relations between the rival Pāla–Sena dynasties.
73. Bagchi, *History and Culture of the Pālas*, p. 58.
74. Verse 9 talks of Vaidyadeva being 'the minister after his own heart of the famous king Kumārapāla', while verse 12 claims that the latter loved Vaidyadeva 'dearer even than life' and entrusted the empire to his generalship. These verses might have been been a covert way of indicating Vaidyadeva's power over Kumārapāla. Vaidyadeva's suppression of a revolt by the disaffected Tiṁgyadeva in Kāmarūpa seems to have led to his assumption of independent imperial titles like *parama-māheśvara* and *parama-bhaṭṭāraka*, thereby being indicative of his growing power. It is interesting that Vaidyadeva's younger brother or nephew, Budhadeva, is introduced at the end of the record, probably to mark him as the ministerial heir (v. 20). Paul, *Early History of Bengal*, I, p. 67.
75. N. Ray, *History of the Bengali People*, p. 337 says the Pāla inscriptions and the *Rāmacarita* show numerous feudal kings or chiefs in the central government, feudalism being the political basis of the Pāla state. Interestingly, he talks of *satī* as a characteristic practice of the feudal era

that spread towards the end of the Pāla period and Sena times. Ray cites the *Bṛhaddharmapurāṇa* which encourages brāhmaṇa widows to burn themselves (p. 338).

76. D.C. Sircar, 'Bhaturiya Inscription of Rājyapāla', *Epigraphia Indica*, vol. XXXIII, 1963, pp. 150–4. The fact of Yaśodāsa having built a huge temple with eight other shrines is mentioned. This parallels his eulogy and is an obvious statement of his power.
77. Majumdar, *History of Ancient Bengal*, pp. 361–70. Evidence has been culled from the *Rāmacarita* to show that Īśvaraghoṣa was a vassal king under Pāla suzerainty.
78. N. Ray, *History of the Bengali People*, p. 283: the grant mentions the queen and the principal queen as executors of the transaction, neither of whom is mentioned in Pāla inscriptions as royal officials.
79. D.C. Sircar, 'Ārmā Inscription of Madanapāla's Time', *Epigraphia Indica*, vol. XXXVI, 1964, pp. 42–4.
80. D.C. Sircar, 'Lai Inscription of Vikramadevī', *Epigraphia Indica*, vol. XXX, 1958, pp. 82–4. Sircar presumes that the unnamed ruler is Palapāla (*c.* 1165–1200) who ruled over the Monghyr region near Lai. One can also consider, in this category, a rather ambiguous inscription of Devapāla's reign that refers to the installation of a Hārītī image by a prince and princess of the Rājagṛha *viṣaya* whose names are not clear: Bhagwant Sahai, *The Inscriptions of Bihar*, Delhi, Ramanand Vidya Bhawan: 1983, p. 71; Huntington, '*Pāla–Sena' Schools of Sculpture*, p. 207.
81. U.N. Ghoshal, 'The Position of the Brāhmaṇas in Ancient Bengal', *Annals of the Bhandarkar Oriental Research Institute*, vol. XLVI, pts I–IV, 1965, p. 79.
82. H.C. Ray, *Dynastic History of Northern India*, p. 291.
83. Sahai, *Inscriptions of Bihar*, pp. 70–1; Huntington, '*Pāla–Sena*' *Schools of Sculpture*, pp. 206–7. The word can either be read as *jananī* (mother) or *janāni* (people).
84. Huntington, '*Pāla–Sena*' *Schools of Sculpture*, p. 207. She notes that Nālandā underwent its most active phase under the Pālas (p. 108).
85. D.C. Sircar, 'Valgudar Inscription of Dharmapāla's Reign', *Epigraphia Indica*, vol. XXVIII, 1958, pp. 137–45.
86. Kurkihār was a Buddhist monastic site in the Gayā district of Magadha. Huntington, '*Pāla–Sena' Schools of Sculpture*, pp. 208, 42, 102, talks of the disputed identity of the site and notes that it seems to have been a major art-producing centre of religious and artistic importance in the Pāla period.
87. Sahai, *Inscriptions of Bihar*, pp. 82–4. Huntington, op. cit., pp. 52–3, says that the exact identification of the Āpaṇaka monastery is unknown. She notes that the inscriptions from Kurkihār belonging to Rājyapāla's reign indicate the presence of donors from Kāñcī, thereby providing important evidence of contact between eastern India and the south for religious and trading purposes.

88. Sahai, *Inscriptions of Bihar*, pp. 95–6. The other two sculptures from Kurkihār were donated by Tikūka and Utīmarāka, the sons of Dūlapa.
89. Huntington, '*Pāla–Sena*' *Schools of Sculpture*, p. 68.
90. D.C. Sircar, 'Nongaṛh Inscription of Madanapāla's time', *Epigraphia Indica*, vol. XXXVI, 1964, pp. 41–2. Nongaṛh is in the Monghyr district of Bihar.
91. Huntington, '*Pāla–Sena*' *Schools of Sculpture*, p. 60. For other examples, pp. 211–13.
92. Ibid., pp. 209, 43. Hilsā is in the Patna district of Bihar.
93. Sahai, *Inscriptions of Bihar*, pp. 85–6.
94. D.C. Sircar, 'Gayā Inscription of the Time of Nārāyaṇapāla', *Epigraphia Indica*, vol. XXXV, 1962, pp. 225–8 for details. One can also consider, in this category, the Gayā inscription issued in Nayapāla's fifteenth regnal year that records the construction of a Viṣṇu temple by the brāhmaṇa Viśvāditya. The record does not mention any women—except for an interesting remark in verse 19 that the eulogy should reside 'for ever in the heart of good men like a lady, the sole source of happiness springing from love and friendship'. Mukherji and Maity, *Corpus of Bengal Inscriptions*, pp. 141–50.
95. Mukherji and Maity, op. cit., pp. 136–8. Ghoṣrāvān is 12 km south-east of Biharsharif, the chief town of Nālandā in the Patna district. Verse 10 talks of Vīradeva constructing two places of worship 'which were like crest-jewels on the crown'. Additionally, verse 14 says that his buildings resembled 'his mind in elevation'. It is interesting, therefore, that even a Buddhist monk's buildings are a concretization of his fame.
96. The grant is represented as a royal gift because the king, as per legal procedure, had to ratify the creation of a rent-free holding by any of his fief-holders. Sircar, 'Bangāon Plate', *Epigraphia Indica*, vol. XXIX, p. 51; D.C. Sircar, *Studies in the Political and Administrative Systems in Ancient and Medieval India*, Delhi, Motilal Banarsidass: 1974, p. 226.
97. Huntington, '*Pāla Sena*' *Schools of Sculpture*, p. 53. Huntington also points out that the Brahmanical subject of Umā Maheśvara donated by Mūlakā, Mahiāru's wife, is handled in a virtually identical manner to the two Buddhist images of Vasudhārā donated by Vāṭukā and Gaukā. This suggests the existence of a common artistic community and workshop, perhaps at Kurkihār itself.
98. Bagchi, *History and Culture of the Pālas*, p. 69.
99. Ibid., p. 77.
100. Ibid., pp. 89–90.
101. Ibid., p. 127.
102. Huntington, '*Pāla–Sena*' *Schools of Sculpture*, p. 69.
103. Sharma, 'Social and Economic Conditions', in *Comprehensive History of Bihar*, ed. Sinha, p. 366.

104. Leslie Orr, 'Women's Wealth and Worship: Female Patronage of Hinduism, Jainism, and Buddhism in Medieval Tamilnadu', in *Faces of the Feminine in Ancient, Medieval, and Modern India*, ed. Mandakranta Bose, Delhi, Oxford University Press: 2000, p. 132.
105. Kunal Chakrabarti, *Religious Process: The Purāṇas and the Making of a Regional Tradition*, Delhi, Oxford University Press: 2001, pp. 39–40.
106. Mukherji and Maity, *Corpus of Bengal Inscriptions*, pp. 295–302. See also the Naihāti grant of Vallālasena (v. 14), and the Mādhainagar, Anuliā and India Office grants of Lakṣmaṇasena.
107. It records the gift of land in Mātharaṇḍiya village in Puṇḍravardhanabhukti to the scholar, Raghudevaśarman. Ibid., pp. 302–12.
108. Paul, *Early History of Bengal*, I, p. 112.
109. H.C. Ray, *Dynastic History of Northern India*, p. 354.
110. Thomas R. Trautmann, *Dravidian Kinship*, Cambridge, Cambridge University Press: 1981, pp. 272, 274, 401.
111. F. Kielhorn, 'Deopārā Stone Inscription of Vijayasena', *Epigraphia Indica*, vol. I, 1892, pp. 305–15.
112. Paul, *Early History of Bengal*, I, p. 89; H.C. Ray, *Dynastic History of Northern India*, pp. 357–8.
113. R.D. Banerji, 'Barrackpur Grant of Vijayasena', *Epigraphia Indica*, vol. XV, 1920, pp. 278–6.
114. This is held as being indicative of Hemantasena's status and evidence of feudalism. H.C. Ray, *Dynastic History of Northern India*, p. 358.
115. Note that there are no epithets like *bhūpāla* or *rājā* that would indicate that Vijayasena was a *sāmanta* of high importance. Paul, *Early History of Bengal*, I, p. 89 notes that verses 17–19 of the Deopārā *praśasti* refer to the part played by Vijayasena in helping Rāmapāla recover Varendra from the Kaivartas.
116. The Deopārā inscription records Vijayasena's victorious expeditions to the north, east, and south. Paul, *Early History of Bengal*, I, p. 91, notes that the defeated chiefs Vīra, Vardhana and Rāghava can be identified with Vīraguṇa and Govardhana of the *Rāmacarita*, and the son of the Kaliṅga king, Coḍagaṅga, respectively.
117. R.D. Banerji, 'Naihāti Grant of Vallālasena', *Epigraphia Indica*, vol. IV, 1897, pp. 156–63.
118. Banerji points to its 'vital importance' in being the only inscription to note Vilāsadevī's descent from the Śūra family. Hence, he concludes that the majority of genealogical works of Bengal are 'not reliable sources of historical information'. Banerji, 'Barrackpur Grant', *Epigraphia Indica*, vol. XV, p. 279.
119. Majumdar, *History of Ancient Bengal*, p. 224; Paul, *Early History of Bengal*, I, p. 92. Paul, *Early History of Bengal*, II, p. 56, notes that the Śūras were supporters of the Brahmanical religion, as were the Senas.

Hence, the alliance was of political significance in more ways than one.

120. It records the gift of Dāpaṇiyāpāṭaka village in Puṇḍravardhanabhukti to Govindadevaśarman: Mukherji and Maity, *Corpus of Bengal Inscriptions*, pp. 277–89. The grant describes Rāmadevī as *cālukya-bhūpālapāla-kulendralekhā.*
121. H.N. Randle, 'India Office Plate of Lakṣmaṇasena', *Epigraphia Indica*, vol. XXVI, 1952, pp. 1–13.
122. Majumdar, *History of Ancient Bengal*, pp. 216, 229. Paul, *Early History of Bengal*, II, p. 56, notes that Vallālasena's reorganization of society as per the principles of *kulinism*, making some socially higher than the others, was impelled more by political reasons than socio-religious ones. Recipients of *kaulinya* rank were royal favourites who had helped the establishment of Sena rule and on whom they could rely for support.
123. Majumdar, *History of Ancient Bengal*, p. 230 says that as the *Adbhuta-sāgara* was left incomplete by Vallālasena, who apparently left with his queen to Nirjarapura, it is presumed that they drowned themselves, as the word *nirjara* implies 'heaven'. However, Majumdar says that it could also indicate retirement in that particular locality.
124. H.C. Ray, *Dynastic History of Northern India*, p. 372.
125. Randle, 'India Office Plate', *Epigraphia Indica*, vol. XXVI, p. 9.
126. The name can be read as Tāndradevī or Cāndrādevī. Viśvarūpasena's Sāhitya-pariṣad copper-plate grant contains the name 'Taṭṭana', while the Edilpur plate talks of the queen Cāndrādevī. Mukherji and Maity, *Corpus of Bengal Inscriptions*, pp. 318, 321, 342. Sircar, *Studies in the Political and Administrative Systems*, p. 200 claims that the name of Viśvarūpasena's mother was Alhaṇadevī and not Tāḍādevī.
127. For instance, Mukherji and Maity, *Corpus of Bengal Inscriptions*, p. 37 note that all Lakṣmaṇasena's 'wives, maidservants, attendants and women fell into the hands of the invader'.
128. Banerji, 'Barrackpur grant', *Epigraphia Indica*, vol. XV, pp. 280, 284. Vikramapura was the capital city of Vaṅga. Vijay Nath, '*Mahādāna*: The Dynamics of Gift-economy and the Feudal Milieu', in *The Feudal Order: State Society and Ideology in Early Medieval India*, ed. D.N. Jha, Delhi, Manohar: 2000, p. 421, provides a list of rulers who performed *tulāpuruṣa mahādāna* that is, however, exclusively male. Nath notes that all of them were trying to stake their claim to political power and if so, Vilāsadevī's performance of this ceremony acquires added significance. The purpose of the *mahādāna* was, apparently, to provide ritual validation for the power and social status of political aspirants of tribal and obscure origins. This is evident from the fact that it was performed mostly by founders of new dynasties of tribal antecedents, seeking to augment their newly-won political power (p. 437).

129. Banerji, 'Naihāti grant', *Epigraphia Indica*, vol. IV, p. 158; Maity, *Corpus of Bengal Inscriptions*, p. 267.
130. Paul, *Early History of Bengal*, I, p. 112.
131. Paul, *Early History of Bengal*, II, p. 42.
132. Some illuminative examples are the Govindapur, Tarpanadīghi, Mādhainagar, Anuliā, and Sunderban copper-plate grants of Lakṣmaṇasena.
133. Randle, 'India Office Plate', *Epigraphia Indica*, vol. XXVI, pp. 3, 12.
134. Kielhorn, 'Deopārā Stone Inscription', *Epigraphia Indica*, vol. I, p. 314; Majumdar, *History of Ancient Bengal*, p. 340. The women had to be trained to distinguish pearls, emeralds, and silver coins from cotton-seeds, bottle-gourd flowers and so on. It might also be pertinent to note that Jīmūtavāhana asserts the widow's right to inherit her husband's property in the absence of a male issue, and supports her claim over that of the brother/other male relations. This could imply that non-royal women had access to resources that might have been used for donative purposes, although there is no real evidence in this regard. As Jīmūtavāhana himself points to the conflicting views on the subject, it is not clear whether the socio-political milieu in the Sena period actually accorded women this measure of liberality, or which section of women it pertained to (p. 456).
135. It records the reconfirmation of the grant of village Vāruṇikā in Nagara *bhukti* to the shrine of Varuṇavāsin: K.K. Thaplyal, *Inscriptions of the Maukharis, Later Guptas, Puṣpabhūtis and Yaśovarman of Kanauj*, Delhi, ICHR/Agam Prakashan: 1985, pp. 171–3. Note that it mentions three earlier rulers—Bālāditya of the imperial Gupta dynasty, and Śarvavarman and Avantivarman Maukhari—who had confirmed the grant. It also mentions several officials of different categories.
136. Ibid., pp. 174–6.
137. Sahai, *Inscriptions of Bihar*, pp. 56–7.
138. Thaplyal, *Inscriptions of the Maukharis*, pp. 118–21.
139. Ibid., p. 164.
140. Ibid., p. 166.
141. Ibid., p. 167 for details.
142. Roychoudhuri, *Political History of Bengal*, p. 147, notes the inscription's claim that they returned from 'the Coḷa city' with much wealth. She says that no other inscription of Ādityasena mentions this event and it is improbable that he had such authority. Roychoudhuri, therefore, agrees with B.P. Sinha that Ādityasena went on a pilgrimage and returned with presents from various rulers. Also Thaplyal, *Inscriptions of the Maukharis*, p. 45.
143. R.C. Majumdar, 'Political History of South Bihar (550-750 A.D.)', in *Comprehensive History of Bihar*, ed. Sinha, p. 239.
144. Roychoudhuri, *Political History of Bengal*, p. 148 notes that Koṇadevī's

title is that of the spouse of a paramount sovereign. Ādityasena's title, too, indicates that he was a powerful king.

145. Majumdar, 'Political History of South Bihar', in *Comprehensive History of Bihar*, ed. Sinha, p. 239. Sinha, *Dynastic History of Magadha*, pp. 157–8, says that either the assumption of imperial titles had no meaning in the Later Gupta dynasty, or they undertook extensive conquests only after AD 672/3. He feels (p. 86) that the titles were probably adopted out of deference to the imperial Gupta family.
146. Thaplyal, *Inscriptions of the Maukharis*, p. 91.
147. Majumdar, 'Political History of South Bihar', in *Comprehensive History of Bihar*, ed. Sinha, pp. 237–8.
148. Sinha, *Dynastic History of Magadha*, pp. 161–2.
149. N. Ray, *History of the Bengali People*, pp. 309–10 notes that the subsequent war between Gauḍa and Kanauj for north Indian sovereignty can be traced to Śaśāṅka's reign, and in his catapulting Bengal to political greatness. Ray adds that this was a period of the gradual extension of Brahmanism and its culture throughout Bengal.
150. He presumes that the Later Guptas were in possession of Magadha and Gauḍa, and that when Śaśāṅka became the ruler of Gauḍa, he inherited the rivalries of the Later Guptas as well. Majumdar, *History of Ancient Bengal*, pp. 45–8.
151. Roychoudhuri, *Political History of Bengal*, p. 111. Roychoudhuri notes that despite the mutual struggle between the Later Guptas and the Maukharis for Gauḍa and Magadha, neither was successful. Śaśāṅka's identity as a Maukhari subordinate is not supported by any concrete evidence.
152. Ibid., pp. 111–12. Banerji further claims that Śaśāṅka and Devagupta of Mālwā tried to restore the Gupta prestige after Prabhākaravardhana's death. However, there is no real basis for this view. The alliance between Devagupta and Śaśāṅka need not suggest blood connections, nor the similarity in coins prove any family relationship. Thus, Śaśāṅka's coins have the symbol of a *nandīdhvaja* rather than the Gupta *garuḍadhvaja*. Besides, the inscriptions would definitely have mentioned any blood connections between the two. In addition, Roychoudhuri cites K.L. Barua's view that Śaśanka's alleged persecution of Buddhists is irreconciliable with the Gupta policy of religious toleration.
153. Ibid., pp. 123–4; Samuel Beal, tr., *The Life of Hiuen-Tsiang by Shaman Hwui-Li*, Delhi, Academica Asiatica: 1973, p. 83.
154. Paul, *Early History of Bengal*, I, p. 20. Vaidya and Basak also accept Bāṇa's view that Rājya's death was due to his carelessness.
155. Majumdar, *History of Ancient Bengal*, pp. 60, 63; Roychoudhuri, *Political History of Bengal*, p. 124.
156. N. Ray, *History of the Bengali People*, p. 351 admits Śaśāṅka's animosity towards Buddhism and the reasons for it.

157. Majumdar, *History of Ancient Bengal*, pp. 50–1. The presence of Mahāsenagupta's sons at the Thānesar court was an added factor.
158. Roychoudhuri, *Political History of Bengal*, p. 122.
159. Paul, *Early History of Bengal*, I, p. 22, justifies the silence of Bāṇa and Yuan Chwang on the specificities of this issue as stemming from a desire to protect Rājya's reputation and cover up his probable lack of political wisdom. Hence, they have made general remarks on the folly of carelessness instead.
160. For instance, Roychoudhuri, *Political History of Bengal*, p. 140. Mānava apparently ruled for eight months and was succeeded by Jayanāga. Paul cites the *Āryamañjuśrī-mūlakalpa's* interesting reference to Śiśu, apparently one of Śaśāṅka's successors, in whose brief reign the influence of women would be felt. There is no other corroborative evidence for this (*Early History of Bengal*, I, pp. 29–30).
161. Roychoudhuri, *Political History of Bengal*, p. 125 says that Rājya was probably compelled to enter Śaśāṅka's camp to arrange a truce, and died due to foul play. There is no mention of Śaśāṅka's daughter in this connection.
162. Majumdar, *History of Ancient Bengal*, pp. 60–2 contests Basak's theory that Śaśāṅka murdered Rājya and that Bāṇa deliberately concealed the details of the allurement offered. He also queries Śaṅkara's theory regarding the offer of Śaśāṅka's daughter to Rājya.
163. N.K. Bhattasali, 'Deulbāḍī Śarvvāṇī Image Inscription of Mahādevī Prabhāvatī, queen of Devakhaḍga', *Epigraphia Indica*, vol. XVII, 1924, pp. 357–59. Majumdar, *History of Ancient Bengal*, p. 550 clarifies that Śarvvāṇī is the feminine form of Śarva (Rudra/Śiva). The figure at Deulbāḍī was an eight-armed deity.
164. Roychoudhuri, *Political History of Bengal*, p. 157.
165. R. Basak, 'Tipperah Copper Plate Grant of Lokanātha', *Epigraphia Indica*, vol. XV, 1920, pp. 301–15 for details.
166. Basak says it was important that the rule continued through him. In addition, he draws a parallel with Bāṇa's father who also married a śūdra woman. Note that pāraśava refers to the son of a brāhmaṇa male and a śūdra female who, according to Manu, is equivalent to a corpse. Saroj Gulati, *Women and Society: Northern India in the 11th and 12th Centuries*, Delhi, Chanakya Publications: 1985, p. 77.
167. N. Ray, *History of the Bengali People*, p. 203 notes that Bhavadeva writes of the cultured śūdra wives of brāhmaṇas, while Jīmūtavāhana describes the rules of inheritance for one born of such a union. However, Ray says that marriage with a śūdra woman gradually became socially disreputable.
168. Majumdar, *History of Ancient Bengal*, pp. 423–4 also notes that Lokanātha is referred to as a karaṇa—but whether he was degraded to this caste because of his mother, or whether the term was used

as an official designation (probably a scribe) and not a caste name, is unknown. Puspa Niyogi, *Brahmanic Settlements in Different Subdivisions of Ancient Bengal*, Calcutta, Indian Studies—Past and Present: 1967, p. 46 sees the grant as proof of the flexible caste rules in Bengal. For a divergent view, see Gulati, *Women and Society*, pp. 78, 81. She cites Lokanātha's inscription as evidence that such a marriage was not appreciated. However, she talks of Candrasena and Mātṛsena, the two sons of a śūdra wife of Bāṇa's father, as holding important positions without seeing the contradiction in terms.

169. D.C. Sircar, 'Dhulla Plate of Śrīcandra', *Epigraphia Indica*, vol. XXXIII, 1963, pp. 134–40. It grants land to a brāhmaṇa, Vyāsagaṅgaśarman, for the merit of Śrīcandra's parents and himself.
170. Mukherji and Maity, *Corpus of Bengal Inscriptions*, pp. 221–9. This grant was for the welfare of his grandparents, parents, and himself.
171. N.K. Bhattasali, 'Kedārpur plate of Śrīcandradeva', *Epigraphia Indica*, vol. XVII, 1924, pp. 188–92.
172. A.H. Dani, 'Chandras of East Bengal', Indian History Congress Proceedings, 23rd Session, Aligarh, 1960, part I, p. 40.
173. R. Basak, 'Belāva Copper Plate of Bhojavarmadeva', *Epigraphia Indica*, vol. XII, pp. 37–43; Mukherji and Maity, *Corpus of Bengal Inscriptions*, pp. 238, 241–2.
174. Paul, *Early History of Bengal*, I, p. 79; N.K. Bhattasali, 'Vajrayoginī Plate of Sāmalavarman', *Epigraphia Indica*, vol. XXX, 1958, pp. 259–63. Sāmalavarman made donations to a Buddhist shrine to please his patron deity, Viṣṇu.
175. Mukherji and Maity, *Corpus of Bengal Inscriptions*, pp. 30–1.
176. Ibid., pp. 242, 238.
177. A parallel can be drawn with the Nālandā stone inscription of Yaśovarmadeva, which mentions the sister of the donor, Mālāda, and the minister's daughter. A similar comparison can be made with the Vaillabhaṭṭasvāmin temple inscription at Gwalior that refers to the Pratihāra feudatory chief, Alla's 'favourite daughter', Somaṭā
178. Mukherji and Maity, *Corpus of Bengal Inscriptions*, pp. 242, 237–8. Contrast this with the fact that although Prabhāvatīguptā, the daughter of the Later Gupta king, Devagupta, made a crucial marriage alliance with the Vākāṭaka ruler, Rudrasena II, her role finds no mention in the inscriptions/sources of Bengal–Bihar.
179. However, this segment of the Varman history has been subject to differing views in the limited analyses available. For instance, H.C. Ray, *Dynastic History of Northern India*, pp. 332, 336 claims that Mālavyadevī was the daughter of Udayin, a great warrior whose identity is uncertain. Basak, 'Belāva Copper Plate', *Epigraphia Indica*, vol. XII, pp. 38, 42 echoes this view. He feels that Udayin was the son of the poet's master. In addition, Basak says *trailokyasundarī* is a reference to Mālavyadevī's

beauty (the most beautiful lady in the three worlds), not a reference to her daughter. The ambiguous wording of the inscription precludes a definite statement on this aspect.

180. Majumdar, *History of Ancient Bengal*, pp. 349–61.
181. This is echoed by verse 16, which states, 'Being assisted by the power of counsel of this minister, King Harivarmadeva attained lawful victory and ruled the kingdom for long'. The subsequent verses that talk of Bhavadeva's building activities and donations serve to underline his status. For instance, 'his highly charming palace' seemed to 'enter into rivalry with the Kailāśa mountain' (verse 28).
182. Chakrabarti, *Religious Process*, pp. 33, 165. He says the basic impulse behind this was apparently 'non-Brahmanical, non-Sanskritic, indigenous'.
183. Kunal Chakrabarti, 'Cult Region: The *Purāṇas* and the Making of the Cultural Territory of Bengal', *Studies in History*, vol. XVI, no.1, New Delhi, January–June 2000, p. 2. The Upapurāṇas offered a balance between the purāṇic Brahmanical tradition and exclusively regional local traditions.
184. Ibid., p. 4; Chakrabarti, *Religious Process*, p. 34; N. Ray, *History of the Bengali People*, p. 422. Ray notes that the *Devīpurāṇa* talks of the worship of the Śākta goddess with Tāntric rites by men in collaboration with women in Rāḍha, Varendrī, and Kāmarūpa. Śākta worship developed in Bengal before the seventh/eighth century. Madhu Khanna, 'The Goddess-Women Equation in Śākta Tantras', in *Faces of the Feminine*, ed. Bose, p. 121, says that the Śākta tradition is a rare instance of a gender-inclusive *dharma* with a theology of male-female equivalence.
185. Chakrabarti, *Religious Process*, p. 165; Chakrabarti, 'Cult Region', p. 13. He says that the cult of the regional goddesses, conceived and promoted by the Bengal Purāṇas, helped to create a common focus and to integrate a highly stratified rural society. Manasi Dasgupta and Mandakranta Bose, 'The Goddess-Woman Nexus in Popular Religious Practice: The Cult of Manasā', in *Faces of the Feminine*, ed. Bose, p. 148, talk of the Śakti cults, centred on the idea of powerful female deities, as a striking cultural phenomenon of medieval eastern India, especially Bengal.
186. Majumdar, *History of Ancient Bengal*, pp. 147–50. R.S. Sharma, *Early Medieval Indian Society: A Study in Feudalisation*, Kolkata, Orient Longman: 2001, pp. 210, 212 talks of the kin-based solidarity evidenced at the time of the Kaivarta revolt in Mathaṇa's support to Rāmapāla. This is a more appreciative statement but does not clearly enunciate the role of the matrilateral bond in question.
187. Sircar, *Studies in the Society and Administration*, p. 136, notes that one of the queens of Vigrahapāla III was the sister of the Rāṣṭrakūṭa Mathaṇa

of Aṅga. Paul, 'Relations of the Pālas and Senas', *Indian Historical Quarterly*, vol. XII, p. 635.

188. H.C. Ray, *Dynastic History of Northern India*, p. 337.
189. Banerji, *Pālas of Bengal*, p. 43, speculates that Mathaṇa was the maternal uncle of Mahipāla II and Śūrapāla II, as well as of Rāmapāla. Banerji says that besides these, the sons of Mathaṇa's other sisters might have been reigning in other parts of the country too. The relationship between Mathaṇa and Rāmapāla is explicitly mentioned in the commentary on *RC*, II.8.
190. Paul, *Early History of Bengal*, I, p. 103 notes that the history of Pīṭhī in the eleventh/twelfth century is known from contemporary records, and can be identified as the southern portion of Magadha. Sircar, 'Ārmā Inscription', *Epigraphia Indica*, vol. XXXVI, p. 43, notes the mention of *pīṭhīpati* Devasena as the ruler of a territory including Ārmā in western Monghyr.
191. Banerji, *Pālas of Bengal*, p. 46, notes that, interestingly, the *Rāmacarita* does not refer to the enmity between Devarakṣita and Rāmapāla that is otherwise evident from the Sārnāth Inscription.
192. The *pīṭhīpati* of the list of fourteen *sāmantas* is Bhīmayaśas, presumed to be Devarakṣita's successor. He is also said to have overthrown the army of Kanauj, probably that of Candradeva Gāhaḍavāla: H.C. Ray, *Dynastic History of Northern India*, pp. 339–41. Apart from these fourteen rulers whose names are mentioned, there are some other allied chiefs who remain unnamed. The list is given in *RC*, II.
193. Banerji, *Pālas of Bengal*, p. 46.
194. H.C. Ray, *Dynastic History of Northern India*, pp. 339–40.
195. Bhīma's queen was probably captured later. *RC*, II.31; Sircar, 'Introduction', in Maitreya, *Fall of the Pāla Empire*, p. xix.
196. Maitreya, *Fall of the Pāla Empire*, pp. 46, 48, 50.
197. Ibid., p. 50: Maitreya notes that the Kaivarta revolt caused a change in the configuration of states of the Pāla kingdom, causing Rāmapāla to conquer land and other provinces.
198. Majumdar, *History of Ancient Bengal*, pp. 153–4; H.C. Ray, *Dynastic History of Northern India*, p. 345 notes that Rāmapāla apparently conquered Utkala, Kaliṅga, and Kāmarūpa as well. He cites *RC*, II.45, 47.
199. Majumdar, *History of Ancient Bengal*, p. 154; Sinha, *Dynastic History of Magadha*, p. 223 notes that this marriage must have taken place in the last years of Rāmapāla's reign.
200. Sinha, *Dynastic History of Magadha*, pp. 224–5.
201. Trautmann, *Dravidian Kinship*, pp. 426, 431–2.
202. Sinha, *Dynastic History of Magadha*, p. 111; *Decline of the Kingdom of Magadha*, p. 175.

203. Sinha, *Decline of the Kingdom of Magadha*, p. 176. Roychoudhuri, *Political History of Bengal*, p. 110, says that Mahāsenagupta may have tried to establish his suzerainty over Magadha but Śaśāṅka's rise forced him to turn back to Mālwā.
204. Majumdar, 'Political History of South Bihar', in *Comprehensive History of Bihar*, ed. Sinha, p. 231. Sinha, *Dynastic History of Magadha*, p. 102 speculates that Mahāsenagupta might have died in the battle against the Kalacuris and that Prabhākaravardhana rescued the orphans, Kumāragupta and Mādhavagupta, around 602/3, just before he died.
205. Thaplyal, *Inscriptions of the Maukharis*, p. 163.
206. Majumdar, 'Political History of South Bihar', in *Comprehensive History of Bihar*, ed. Sinha, p. 237. Roychoudhuri, *Political History of Bengal*, p. 143 speculates that it was Mādhavagupta who ascended the throne because his name is mentioned in the Aphsāḍ inscription.
207. Mikael Aktor, 'Untouchables, Women and Territories: Rituals of Lordship in the *Parāśara Smṛti*', in *Invented Identities*, ed. Julia Leslie and Mary McGee, Delhi, Oxford University Press: 2000, pp. 133, 148, 152, points to a particular relation between women and land in Indian texts whereby they are the two most important domains of lordship. They are metaphorically interchangeable—women are fields while land is a woman/mother/goddess. As women are compared to the soil, adultery is likened to the appropriation of a territory. Mary McGee, 'Introduction', in ibid., p. 19, notes that to pillage either land or women is to threaten lordship.
208. *RC*, I.39, II.31, IV.2.
209. The inscription further notes that Rāmapāla killed Bhīma as Rāma killed Rāvaṇa, and crossed the ocean of war as Rāma crossed the ocean: Venis, '(Kamauli) Copper Plate Grant', *Epigraphia Indica*, vol. II, p. 355.
210. Banerji, *Pālas of Bengal*, p. 55.
211. Majumdar, *History of Ancient Bengal*, p. 465, admits the *Rājataraṅgiṇī* evidence and claims that lax sexual morality led to the propagation of evil customs like keeping female slaves and dedicating girls to the temple.
212. Kunal Chakrabarti, 'Texts and Traditions: The Making of the Bengal *Purāṇas*', in *Tradition, Dissent and Ideology: Essays in Honour of Romila Thapar*, ed. R. Champakalakshmi and S. Gopal, Delhi, Oxford University Press: 1996, pp. 76–7. He says this must have been a popular custom and was retained by the Bengal Purāṇas, thereby illustrating their assimilative process. N. Ray, *History of the Bengali People*, p. 516, says that the father of Jayadeva's wife, Padmāvatī, wanted to give her as a temple girl. Padmāvatī would apparently dance to Jayadeva's songs.
213. Majumdar, *History of Ancient Bengal*, p. 465.
214. N. Ray, *History of the Bengali People*, pp. 258, 377–8.

215. Kielhorn, 'Deopārā Stone Inscription', *Epigraphia Indica*, vol. I, p. 315. This is part of a eulogy on how the Senas support the poor.
216. Majumdar, *History of Ancient Bengal*, pp. 280–83, 318.
217. Sharma, *Early Medieval Indian Society*, p. 166, cites the commentator, Viśvarūpa (800–50), to the effect that a royal charter relating to land grants should bear the name of the royal officer/*dūtaka*, the name of the royal military camp, the family tree for three generations (including the names of women), and verses indicating the consequences of making and receiving the gift. Hence, women featuring in grants is certainly not an 'innovation'. It may also be noted here that, elsewhere, Majumdar discusses the 'Position of Women' before the section on 'Food and Drink', as part of the several aspects of social life (*History of Ancient Bengal*, pp. 455–7).
218. Majumdar, *History of Ancient Bengal*, p. 275.
219. N. Ray, *History of the Bengali People*, pp. 380–1.
220. For instance, Ray is somewhat inattentive to details regarding women, as in his statement that Mahāsenagupta's father gave his daughter, Mahāsenaguptā, to be Prabhākaravardhana's queen. In fact, she was Prabhākaravardhana's mother. One could also consider Ray's statement that Jayāpīḍa fell in love with Kalyāṇadevī and married her when Kalhaṇa clearly shows that she was given to him as part of a political alliance (ibid., pp. 308, 317).
221. Verma, *Socio-Religious, Economic and Literary Condition*, pp. 11-18.
222. Ibid., pp. 1–58. However, Verma does make the interesting observation that festivals were socially licensed occasions for people to indulge their otherwise repressed instincts.
223. B.C. Sen, 'Administration Under The Pālas and The Senas', *Indian Culture*, vol. VII, no. 2, October–December 1940, p. 212.
224. H.C. Ray, *Dynastic History of Northern India*, pp. 384–5.
225. Paul, *Early History of Bengal*, I, p. 112.

CHAPTER XII

Bengal–Bihar: Summary

This chapter is a brief survey of some of the important points raised in the gender analysis of early medieval Bengal and Bihar. The relative invisibility of royal women in the official records of the Pālas constitutes an important issue. Ironically, some of them are shown to be involved in marriage alliances of strategic import and yet, do not even feature as executors of official grants. Their absence forms a point of contrast with the royal women of the Sena dynasty, and those of minor dynasties like the Later Guptas, Khaḍgas, Candras, and Varmans whose presence is attested in the genealogical context, as also in the realm of donations. In fact, royal women of minor dynasties seemed to have a more visible role than either the Pāla or Sena royal women.

Another notable feature is that the non-royal women of the Pāla period are shown to have a vibrant public presence through their varied donations and are, even otherwise, accorded weight in inscriptions. Significantly, the presence of non-royal women of the Sena and other dynasties is limited and negligible. Thus, it is important to note that two sections of women in the same period are subject to varied treatment in the sources, whereby one has a shadowy presence while the other is accorded tangible freedom.

At one level, the near-total absence of Pāla royal women in inscriptions could be related to the emergence of a regional, dynastic state structure in Bengal, the hallmarks of which were a hierarchical political order and tenuous bonds with political allies.[1] B.D. Chattopadhyaya talks of the crystallization of a regional state from the early Pāla period that witnessed crucial changes in rural society and economy.[2] New categories of landholders emerged and the administrative apparatus at the local level was expanded.

It could be argued, therefore, that as the Pālas were attempting to establish their fledgling empire, strict control was maintained over the royal women to garner and buttress popular support. Hence, the attempt might have been to control/screen the public image of these women, thereby explaining their near-invisibility and, conversely, the relative prominence of non-royal women. However, such an explanation is not entirely satisfactory. Clearly, dynasties such as the Senas did not use such means to establish themselves, although faced with a similar struggle. Moreover, as cited earlier, archaeological evidence suggests that the Pāla royal women *did* have a public presence. The paucity of sources poses a real obstacle for us.

Susan Fischler's study of the Roman empire poses an interesting parallel.[3] She notes that the image of the Roman imperial women became weighed down by the expectations and fears of the male elite and thus acquired added significance and symbolic meaning. The presentation of these women was symbolic of the state of the realm. Hence, careful attempts were made by those in power to control these images and limit public displays that implied female power within the imperial order. At the same time, the image of these women as symbols of the new political order was also promoted.

Christiane Klapisch-Zuber's work on genealogical accounts of fourteenth to fifteenth century Florence provides another significant parallel.[4] She finds that relationships between men and women as they are prescribed, codified, and subjectively experienced within a society play a significant role in the elaboration of a genealogy and in the way it depicts kin relationships. She then notes that women appeared in significant numbers in these accounts only when the inquiry extended to marital alliances. However, their inclusion hinged more on the concern with delineating the role that alliances with other houses played in the family's fortune than on any desire for genealogical completeness. This is somewhat reminiscent of the Pāla royal genealogical accounts.

As with Kanauj and Kashmir, secondary sources on Bengal and Bihar are marked by a general indifference to gender issues, and a distinct tendency to overlook the role and presence of women in the social and political sphere. To cite one example, Puspa Niyogi's painstaking analysis on the extension of Brahmanism in Bengal under the Pālas is at variance with her remark that three generations are mentioned in the Pāla–Sena inscriptions.[5] On the one hand, she does not note the relative absence of the royal women in the Pāla epigraphs. On the other, she does not differentiate these records from the Sena grants where women are treated differently.

A gender analysis of early medieval Bengal–Bihar also suggests that there is no direct equation between the worship of goddesses and an exalted position for the women of that society.[6] Although this has been noted in the section on Kashmir, it should be reiterated here in the context of the strong tradition of goddess worship in this area and to correct the assumption of a correlation between the two factors. Kunal Chakrabarti, for instance, points out that there is no necessary logical equivalence in any society between exalted female objects of worship and a high position of women to the extent that the sacred cosmos mirrors everyday reality. Yet he says that 'a certain social flexibility for women may be assumed'.[7]

One can contest this assumption on two grounds. First, any 'social flexibility' obviously pertained to non-royal Pāla women and royal women of the Sena and other dynasties, but *not* to the royal Pāla women. Chakrabarti does not indicate which category of 'women' he is referring to. Second, there may have been social flexibility of a sort, but whether this stemmed from religious factors alone is a contentious issue.[8] Chakrabarti admits to a 'fundamental duality' in the characterization of women in the Bengal Purāṇas whereby they are alternatively sacred and vilified objects.[9]

Kumkum Sangari and Uma Chakravarti's views are more useful. They speculate that the new agrarian relations and intensification of the processes of stratification in Bengal in the sixth/seventh century might have contributed to a new ideological formation at the junction of the Brahmanical and the local, paradoxically making the former more flexible and the latter more constrictive for women.[10] This could explain the relative insignificance of the royal Pāla women in the contemporary milieu. On the whole, however, a gendered survey of early medieval Bengal and Bihar shows the presence and role of women to be fairly diluted as compared to the contemporary kingdoms of Kashmir and Kanauj, thereby showing the impossibility of making sweeping generalizations on women in early medieval north India.

NOTES

1. B.D. Chattopadhyaya, 'State and Economy in Northern India: 4th Century–12th Century', in *Recent Perspectives of Early Indian History*, ed. Romila Thapar, Bombay, Popular Prakashan: 1995, pp. 313–14. He says that there was reduced control over *janapadas* and that *sāmantas/ mahāsāmantas* represented the hierarchical order. Chattopadhyaya notes the emergence of a new economic order as well, characterized by a local, agrarian economy, largely devoid of commercial enterprise.
2. B.D. Chattopadhyaya, *Aspects of Rural Settlements and Rural Society in Early Medieval India*, Calcutta, Centre for Studies in Social Sciences: 1990, p. 129, says the shift from the expansive Gupta empire to a regional power centre in post-Gupta Bengal coincided with these changes. Sushila Mandal, *History of Bengal: The Middle Age*, Calcutta, Prakash Mandir: 1970, pt I, pp. 21–4 says that the awakening of Bengal as a state was the greatest contribution of the Pāla kings. She adds that the feudal basis of the Pāla state was its strength and weakness, and that there was a new force at the time representing regional dynasties/kingdoms who asserted their right to self-determination.
3. Susan Fischler, 'Social Stereotypes and Historical Analysis: The Case of the Imperial Women at Rome', in *Women in Ancient Societies*, ed. Leonie J. Archer, Susan Fischler and Maria Wyke, London, Macmillan: 1994, pp. 127–30.
4. Christiane Klapisch-Zuber, 'Family Trees and the Construction of Kinship in Renaissance Italy', in *Gender, Kinship, Power*, ed. M.J. Maynes, et al., Great Britain, Routledge: 1996, pp. 101–13.
5. Puspa Niyogi, *Brahmanic Settlements in Different Subdivisions of Ancient Bengal*, Calcutta, Indian Studies—Past and Present: 1967, pp. 13–14.
6. Gerda Lerner, *The Creation of Patriarchy*, New York, Oxford University Press: 1986, p. 142 finds it remarkable that in societies that subordinate women economically, educationally and legally, the spiritual and metaphysical power of goddesses remains active and strong.
7. Kunal Chakrabarti, 'Divine Family and World Maintenance: Gaṇeśa in the Bengal Purāṇas', in *From Myths to Markets: Essays on Gender*, ed. Kumkum Sangari and Uma Chakravarti, New Delhi, Manohar: 1999, p. 58.
8. For instance, ibid., pp. 65–6: Chakrabarti talks of the puranic adoption of the mother goddess as its central character in Bengal. Paradoxically, he

says the idea was to create a divine paradigm that would encourage a social order directly antithetical to the exalted position of women in society. Hence, to undermine the status of the goddess while formally acknowledging her position, the Purāṇas introduced an ambiguity in her character. If the aim was, then, to lower the status of women in a subtle way, how did religion create social flexibility for women?

9. Ibid., pp. 73–4.
10. Kumkum Sangari and Uma Chakravarti, 'Disparate Women: Transitory Contexts, Persistent Structures', in *Myths to Markets*, ed. Sangari and Chakravarti, p. xxvi.

CHAPTER XIII

Conclusion

The focus of my book, the early medieval period in north India between the seventh and twelfth century AD, is a time of pivotal importance in more ways than one. This period has been discussed around several debates that focus on the vibrant changes that marked it and that offer alternative perspectives for analysis. One of the cardinal ways of viewing this period is from the gender angle—an aspect, however, that has not been adequately tackled by secondary sources.

I have attempted to fill this lacuna in understanding this period through a gender study of prominent—but representative—regional kingdoms located in Kashmir, Kanauj and Bengal–Bihar. At the same time, there has been an attempt to show how the same set of sources can be interpreted in different ways to provide new gendered meanings and depth to the period. The analysis endeavours to be as comprehensive as possible within the limitations of the sources. The variegated picture of women's agency that arises, as a result, is largely dependent on the specific regional, social and political circumstances, as also on the type of source material available.

Gender historians have often stressed that historical events affect the lives of women and men in very different ways so that women cannot be excluded from or marginalized in any historical inquiry. It is for this reason that accepted schemes of periodization are often questioned to verify the implications of such convenient nomenclature on the lives of women.[1] Such an exercise could easily be extended to the early medieval period in north India—a period that has been, hitherto, almost exclusively assessed from the perspective of men.

The near-unanimous attempt by secondary sources to in-visibilize the role and experiences of women in this time-span is a very conspicuous factor. For instance, fierce debates range around the issue of whether the age was feudal or not, but there is hardly any debate on whether women's lives were impinged in any way. In fact, women do not form the subject at all in studies of this period. They do not form a reference point for any of the changes in polity, society or economy that occurred at the time. Their place is on the periphery as a non-reactive, non-participatory group whose position mechanically changed to reflect larger changes around them.

Obviously, this provides a partial, truncated view of the period and of the role of women in it, particularly when the evidence reveals the myriad forms of power exercised by the latter in the kingdoms under review. If the vantage point is shifted to reflect the role of women, it reveals a varied, richer and more comprehensive picture. The problem of the invisibility of women is a complex one because it is linked with the kind of limited visibility accorded to them in both primary and secondary sources. The focus of this work, therefore, is to identify the problems and possibilities of a gender interpretation.

One of the most significant issues is that of women's power, exercised in formal and informal ways in different regional contexts but, particularly, in Kashmir. Female rulership in Kashmir was an aspect that cut across time-spans and dynasties, and was, additionally, culturally acceptable. The throne was a source of legitimate authority for *both* royal and non-royal women, either as direct rulers or as regents. This, naturally, posed a distinct challenge to prescriptive norms of succession that favoured the male and denied women access to public roles of authority.

Sugandhā and Diddā, the two most prominent women rulers of Kashmir, commenced their pursuit of power as regents and were backed by strong public approval, particularly in the former case. Their growth to political maturity involved confrontations with rebellious factions and scheming contenders. It was here that Diddā emerged triumphant, quelling the opposition with a sure hand and ruling Kashmir for over fifty years in a competent and assured manner. Both rulers were responsible for important dynastic changes, Sugandhā by enabling her lover's family to gain prominence, and Diddā by bequeathing the throne to her natal kin from Lohara. Female rulership, therefore, was a strikingly significant feature of early medieval Kashmir.

Additionally, power was exercised by royal and non-royal women of Kashmir in a range of situations—as queens, courtesans, court participants, mediators, dynasty makers and destroyers, and in other capacities. Prominent among the powerful queens were Sūryamatī, who solved a financial crisis, handled the administration, and made crucial political decisions, and Kalhaṇikā, who dispelled a rebel threat by her mediation. Raḍḍādevī devised politically strategic marriage alliances for her daughters. Śrīlekhā made an abortive bid for the throne, and Śāradā legitimized a rebel scheme.

Royal and non-royal women of Kashmir appear, therefore, to have wrested a largely autonomous space for themselves in political and social circles. Clearly, the patriarchal order in Kashmir was capable of being subverted or transgressed—and this, interestingly, seemed to have been largely tolerated. It is necessary, however, to note the manner and extent to which patriarchal norms were subsumed since deviations are inherently significant.

As regards Kanauj, the absence of women rulers here does not imply that some royal women could not be independent or instrumental. Rājyaśrī, for instance, was pivotal in enabling Harṣa to obtain the throne of Kanauj. Used as a pawn in a strategic marriage alliance, Rājyaśrī later became so important in Harṣa's calculations that her presence was essential for him to stake his claim to Kanauj. Indications of her active participation in Harṣa's court, thereafter, and her possible influence on Harṣa's religious choices, are pointers to the power she must have wielded.

There are other prominent instances of powerful women in Kanauj. The Pratihāra genealogical lists, for instance, accorded clear visibility to the royal women. At the same time, there are unmistakable indications of the involvement of some of them in harem rivalries, manifested in succession wrangles among sibling contenders. The rivalry between Bhoja II and Vināyakapāla, the sons of Dehanāgādevī and Mahīdevīdevī, respectively, is a case in point. The Gāhaḍavāla queens, Pṛthvī-Śrīkā and Rālhaṇadevī, who seemed to jointly handle the administration in conjunction with the latter's son, Govindacandra, are subsequent examples of powerful women whose presence is documented not in genealogical lists but in donation charters.

The corresponding evidence from Bengal–Bihar appears to be at immediate variance. The Pālas, who constituted the most important dynasty with the longest rule, do not seem to have accorded any space to their royal women, who are almost invisible in contemporary records. This is a puzzling factor in view of the fact that some of them, such as Raṇṇādevī and Bhāgyadevī, were obviously involved in court politics and rivalries, apart from participating in vital marriage bonds. Hence, they evidently played a more active role in politics than the sources would convey. Yet they do not feature as donors or as land grant executors, as do the royal women of preceding and succeeding dynasties in Bengal–Bihar. The Sena royal women, for instance, featured in inscriptions as part of the genealogical line on account of their important marriage alliances. The strategic marriage tie between Vilāsadevī of the Śūra family and Vijayasena that catapulted the latter to greatness is a case in point.

One can argue that as the Pālas were struggling to establish a fledgling state, they maintained strict control over their women to garner and buttress popular support. However, the Pratihāras and other contemporary dynasties were similarly engaged in legitimizing and consolidating their rule—and the agency accorded to women varied in each case.

Interestingly, while the Dharmaśāstras prescribe isogamy or the marriage of status equals, in several politically crucial marriages, hypogamy prevailed—the wife's status was higher than that of her husband. Vijayasena's marriage with Vilāsadevī is an illustrative case. By extension, the Brahmanical concept of hypergamy—the inferiority of wife-givers to wife-takers, was regularly challenged. The importance of Diddā's family and that of Vilāsadevī, Bhāgyadevī, and a range of other queens was reiterated time and again in the inscriptions. Additionally, the extent to which diverse marriage alliances correspond with or diverge from possibilities of gift-exchange/subordination can also be discerned.

The importance of natal ties in enabling, for instance, Diddā's maternal grandfather, Bhīma Śāhī, to build in his granddaughter's adoptive country and her bequest of the throne to her own family of Lohara, was a marked factor. In fact, a woman's identity seemed made up, in equal measure, of her own family and her in-laws—a fact that is stressed in the inscription of the Gāhaḍavāla queen, Kumaradevī, at Sārnāth, which accords much space to her natal family and, thereby, reveals the power equations involved in the marriage alliance. Incidentally, non-royal women represent a similar ambivalence in the records.

The role of non-royal women as a prominent socio-political grouping is another significant aspect of this time-span. Their influence was manifested in varying degrees in all the three kingdoms under survey. Once again, it was Kashmir that witnessed the vigorous participation of non-royal women in court politics on an almost equal plane with their royal counterparts. The diverse origins of queens indicate that political power was a legitimate quest for non-royal women. In addition, the role of the powerful ḍāmara-woman, Chuḍḍā, for instance, in charting political equations, challenging Sussala's might, and consolidating her son's power is noteworthy. Āsamatī, who changed the course of royal politics, Nonā, who initiated an important reconciliation, and Sillā, who assumed military command, were similarly prominent non-royal women who actively engaged in political affairs.

The participation of non-royal women and men, on an equal plane, in socio-political functions, as also their relatively unrestricted intermingling, point to a degree of freedom and liberality for non-royal women in Kashmir that corroborated their agency on the political plane. One could, perhaps, trace their relative prominence to the structure of the royal household that was a likely model for the rest of the society. The non-patriarchal elements within the royal household in Kashmir could have influenced non-royal households and activities as well, leading to the public presence of non-royal women.

The presence of non-royal women is somewhat dilute in Kanauj. However, they were accorded space in several inscriptions like the Vaillabhaṭṭasvāmin temple inscription and the Nālandā stone inscription of Yaśovarmadeva, as part of the male donors' genealogy. In addition, posing an interesting parallel to the maids of Unmattāvanti's court in Kashmir who procured and named their own candidate to the throne, the maids that feature in harem intrigues in Kanauj literature seem to have a measure of power. For instance, Manoramā and Susaṅgatā, of Harṣa's *Priyadarśikā*, are the prime movers behind the harem intrigue and successfully circumvent the chief queen's wrath to fulfil the king's desire. Several other non-royal women are mentioned in connection with land transactions and donations, and these will be considered in a subsequent discussion on women donors.

Interestingly, the presence of non-royal Pāla women in Bengal–Bihar was an indubitably vibrant one and posed an immediate contrast to the shadowy presence of their royal counterparts, as also those of the Senas and other minor kingdoms of whom very little is known. Not only did they form a conspicuous donor category (which will be discussed subsequently), but their presence in genealogical lists was another notable factor. For instance, the meticulous mention of the wives of the two sets of hereditary ministers under the Pālas, in the fashion of royal genealogical charters, could be a way of acknowledging the power of the latter. Women feature in several male donation charters as well. These could pertain to ministerial/feudatory families (as, for instance, the Bhaturiya inscription that mentions the name of the minister, Yaśodāsa's wife and both her parents), or to lay people (such as the Buddhist donor, Vīradeva, whose parents are named in the Ghoṣrāvān stone inscription). In either case, the public presence of non-royal women is clear.

The role of women as donors was another significant aspect of this period. The kingdoms under survey show different patterns of female donations and different levels of involvement in this activity. This issue was intimately linked to ownership of resources and to public status. Interestingly, epigraphic evidence of women as donors is available in an almost unbroken chain until the seventh century AD in north India. This includes the Mauryan and post-Mauryan periods, as also that of the Guptas.[2] Hence, obviously, donations by women between the seventh and twelfth century were the continuation of an existing trend—a fact that is overlooked in almost all the secondary sources.

Once again, there is a profusion of royal and non-royal women in Kashmir who donated, on an equal plane with their male counterparts, to assert their power and presence. The buildings of Sugandhā, Diddā, Sūryamatī, and other powerful queens like Ratnādevī, for instance, concretized their political power on the land, constant reminders to the people about their roles. These are paralleled, to some extent, by the buildings of non-royal women, prominent examples being the buildings of Sussalā, the minister Rilhaṇa's wife, and the Valgāmaṭha of Diddā's porter-women, Valgā. Yet neither royal nor non-royal women in Kashmir needed building activities to register their presence, as manifold opportunities for public/political activity were open to them. Their involvement in this activity, therefore, in the same profusion as men and under their own names, was an affirmation of their status.

The evidence from Kanauj presents a variegated picture. While royal Pratihāra women do not appear as donors, the Āhār stone inscription reveals the involvement of several non-royal Pratihāra women in land transactions, and in the acquisition and disposal of property. Conversely, the power wielded by Gāhaḍavāla queens like Rālhadevī and Pṛthvī-Śrīkā is discerned only from donations, as they do not otherwise feature in genealogical lists. For instance, Rālhadevī's role is gleaned from the independent tone of her donations, the grants made by her son, Govindacandra, with her consent, as well as donations made in her memory. This is a manifestation of the influence she otherwise exerted on the administration during the reign of her husband and son.

There were several other instances of Gāhaḍavāla queens making independent grants that argue the possession of ample resources, as well as the desire for a public status. The Sārnāth inscription of Kumaradevī, for instance, served to enhance her status by praising her extravagantly, stressing her family connections, and revealing the extent of religious freedom she enjoyed in that she was allowed to venerate Buddhist gods although her husband, Govindacandra, followed the Brahmanical faith.

The corresponding picture in Bengal–Bihar is uneven. While royal Pāla women did not donate, their counterparts under the Senas and other minor dynasties did. For instance, the donations of the Sena queen, Vilāsadevī, and her performance of the *tulāpuruṣa* ceremony (usually performed by seekers of universal power) were a logical consequence of the political influence accruing from her family connections. The donations of the Later Gupta queens,

Śrīmatīdevī and Koṇadevī, whose titles, incidentally, mirror changes in the king's status, were similarly important. Noteworthy evidence is also provided by the Deulbāḍī Śarvvāṇī inscription of the Khaḍga queen, Prabhāvatī. Not only is it the only inscription issued by a royal woman from this area, it also poses a parallel to the Sārnāth inscription in that Prabhāvatī venerated a Brahmanical goddess, even while her husband was a Buddhist.

Interestingly, as regards non-royal women donors, it is only those under the Pālas who appear as a very conspicuous donor category. Not only were there donations by wives of Pāla feudatories as, for instance, Sārthadevikā, the wife of a local chief who purchased land for the purpose, but there were also instances of donations by affluent urban-based women. Prominent examples are the dedication of an image in a mart by Nisiṅghakā, the wife of Śoujjeka, and the installation of an image in a city by Ajhukā, the wife of Śālo. The Kurkihār inscriptions that record the religious gifts of various women are vitally important. The significance of non-royal women in making grants and financing building construction does not need to be spelt out. Their prominence could, perhaps, be linked to the rise of new social classes to dominance, who were willing to disburse their resources in this manner.

Thus, interesting variations in social identity, motives behind donations, and control over resources are obtained in different historical contexts. The size of some of the donations implied the use of resources over and above personal allowances. Could a part of state funds have been kept aside for royal women to bestow at will? If so, it is significant that they were allowed to choose diverse donees. Equally, the ownership of resources by non-royal women argues a greater autonomy for them in economic affairs than is usually assumed. Women donors, therefore, were obviously not constrained by the norms of the *Dharmaśāstra* texts, in which their limited property rights and dependant religious identity precluded the possibility of their extensive/independent gift-giving.

The role and influence of courtesans/prostitutes is another vitally important aspect of the period under survey. This specifically pertains to early medieval Kashmir, where they played pivotal roles as dynasty makers/destroyers, power aspirants, court participants, and donors. Low origin, therefore, was no barrier to their exercise of power in the public domain. The activities of Jayamatī, Sāmbavatī, and Jayādevī, for instance, constitute a definite challenge to patriarchal values in their blatant use of sexual power to gain influence over royal and non-royal men. In fact, Jayādevī's influence over Lalitāpīḍa was used by her brothers to gain political control.

Additionally, their public presence was unequivocally stated in terms of their building activities as, for instance, the shrine built by Sāmbavatī who was a skillful mediator between political groups. I had also referred to the town built by the temple-dancer, Kamalā, in her name. Moreover, the participation of prostitutes at important gatherings, and their equation with prominent citizens argues a general acceptance of their role and status. Interestingly, while there is no evidence of powerful prostitutes in Kanauj or Bengal–Bihar, Kamalā, the temple-dancer from Bengal, was indirectly instrumental in the exiled Jayāpīḍa's resumption of power and eventually acquired great prominence in Kashmir by being a part of Jayāpīḍa's harem and building towns and temples in her name.

The agency of prostitutes is, however, best personified in the fictitious figure, Kaṅkālī, who changed names, locales, and professions in her bid to survive and who exemplifies the space accorded to intelligent, resourceful, and coldly logical women. Her consummate deception of and control over men is a reflection of gender relations in early medieval Kashmir where the power of women paralleled and often even superseded that of men.

Another notable feature of this period—that spans the histories of Kanauj and Bengal–Bihar—is the importance of matrilineal ties, exemplified in the support of Rāmapāla's maternal relatives in his regaining the throne from the rebel Kaivartas who enjoyed popular support. The financial, mental, and material support proffered to Rāmapāla by his maternal uncle, Mathaṇa of Aṅga, was the main factor that enabled the former to regain his kingdom and restore the Pāla rule. In fact, the marriages of Mathaṇa's daughter, Śaṅkaradevī, and his granddaughter, Kumaradevī, were engineered by Mathaṇa in Rāmapāla's interest to win over important allies. The assistance of Rāmapāla's maternal cousins in his protracted struggle against the Kaivartas, and Mathaṇa's aid in the subsequent consolidation of the kingdom, are equally significant. Incidentally, the close relationship between Harṣa of Kanauj and his uncle, Mādhavagupta, that enabled the latter to gain the throne of Magadha, is a factor of parallel weight.

Another important aspect of the period under survey pertains to the decisions taken by women like Rājyaśrī, Kāmandakī, Mahāśvetā and Kādambarī to abjure conventional social relations and lead lives of their choice. Although the latter three are fictional characters, the fact remains that such decisions directly contravene the Brahmanical norms and lawbooks according to which women, particularly of the upper castes, were not supposed to take any independent decisions regarding themselves. Social relations were constructed by powerful ritual values and, therefore, decisions to renounce them—fictional or otherwise—were doubly significant. A reappraisal of the choices available to women within the apparently rigid code governing their lives is warranted.

In each case, however, the underlying motives were varied. While Rājyaśrī was apparently impelled by grief in deciding to adopt an ascetic life, she postponed her decision in Harṣa's interests and accompanied him to Kanauj. Nevertheless, she continued to pursue an active interest in Buddhism and, quite plausibly, influenced Harṣa's religious beliefs. Mahāśvetā, on the other hand, is shown to deliberately flout social conventions and embrace an ascetic existence in anticipation of her lover's rebirth and in the teeth of parental opposition. Kādambarī's rejection of marriage, spurred by her friend's distress, is similarly notable.

The figure of the Buddhist mendicant, Kāmandakī, however, indirectly stresses the impact of the co-educational system on the lives of women. This is doubly significant in view of the fact that very little is otherwise known about women's access to education and the extent of the curriculum, contrasting, for instance, with the details available on the comprehensive training of prostitutes. While a few secondary sources agree that royal women had access to administrative training, the nature of this training and other aspects of female education are matters that have so far attracted little or no concern.

In these circumstances, Kāmandakī's ambition of fulfilling her male friends' vow of marrying their children off to each other, according lower priority to her life and religion, and subverting traditional notions of womanly weakness by manipulating all the male characters and ruthlessly effecting her plan is greatly significant. Saudāmanī, her friend, was similarly impelled towards an unconventional career choice by acquiring supernatural skills and a set of disciples. Their choices contrast with the conventional ministerial posts adopted by their fellow students, Bhūrivasu and Devarāta.

Another notable feature of early medieval north India pertains to certain deeply unconventional aspects of the literary sources of this period. The singular importance of Kalhaṇa's *Rājataraṅgiṇī* in its treatment of women as notable historical figures and its role in the reconstruction of the power of women in Kashmir has been repeatedly stressed. The ambiguity between the narrative and didactic sections that highlights this complex relationship of 'problem women' to power clearly distinguishes this text from others of its genre. Harṣa's 'sister plays' that feature the powerful chief queen, Vāsavadattā, and Bāṇa's works that are marked by an unorthodox view of social norms, are similarly significant. In fact, Bāṇa's fierce diatribe against the practice of *satī* and his unusual portrayal of women figures are particularly noteworthy. Of parallel significance are Bhavabhūti's plays that, on the one hand, rework traditional epics in a gender sensitive mode and, on the other, effectively integrate elements of women's education and agency.

So while certain sources may have clear patriarchal underpinnings (as, for instance, Rājaśekhara's *Karpūramañjarī*, which dilutes the chief queen's power), there are several others that are refreshingly sensitive to the role of women in society and are, therefore, invaluable in any gender reconstruction. Hence, while prescriptive sources regard women as potential threats to the social order, and recommend their protection and control, these can be juxtaposed with divergent sources that reveal the tension between prescription and practice.

The alarming indifference to gender issues, however, displayed by an overwhelming majority of historians of this period is an essential component of my study. As noted earlier, the trend of invisibilizing the role and presence of women is evident not just in works that provide a political/social/economic framework of the period or of the specific kingdoms under survey, but also in works that specifically purport to deal with issues of kingship or society.

Yet women were integral parts of the polity and society in early medieval north India and a refusal to acknowledge this could lead to distortions. Their role impinged on the very framework and socio-political structure of the period. Thus, for instance, Diddā's role or that of Vilāsadevī could be seen in the context of the formulation of claims to legitimacy and prestige in this period. Besides, if land grants held such a pivotal position in early medieval society, women who donated land were obvious participants in socio-economic processes.

Additionally, there were palpable variations in the power and authority of women *vis-à-vis* men and society as a whole. Women wielded both power—the ability to enforce their decisions,[3] and authority—the formal, legitimate right to influence people's decisions. A refusal to acknowledge this in the delineation of the polity and society could lead to further distortions. Explorations of female agency may, therefore, be viewed in relation to the patriarchal structure, its need for control over women, and the ability of women to subsume this edifice in certain regional contexts and situations. This necessitates a rethinking of the negotiation of female identities within a patriarchal set-up. Were patriarchal norms for women hegemonic in practice or was a certain amount of transgressive space allowed to them?

Additionally, it is important to acknowledge the linkages between gender and other social phenomena. For instance, the exercise of female influence was linked to status, contemporary power structures, donations and patronage, resources, identity, and so on. Links between contemporary kingdoms were also significant. Interestingly, despite the political, cultural, and commercial contacts between Kashmir, Kanauj, and Bengal–Bihar, the women in these kingdoms had varied roles and different modes of influence.

There are two major implications, therefore, for the period under survey. On the one hand, sweeping statements *cannot* be made to apply to early medieval north India as a whole without considering regional gendered variations in society and polity. On the other hand, one cannot assume a linear or progressive pattern in the status of women over this period. With the exception of Kashmir, where the assertion of female power seems to have been a fairly constant factor and where gender roles were relatively unstructured, the role and influence of women in Kanauj and Bengal–Bihar seem to have been expressed intermittently over this time-span. Hence, the question of women's agency—in its direct and indirect forms—is largely a contextual one.

The centrality of gender, however, in *any* reconstruction of the society and polity of early medieval north India is a fact that is underscored by this work. The apparent irrelevance of women to the political and social order needs to be questioned and analysed. In addition, the necessity of exploring the agency of different classes of women rather than treating them as one amorphous whole is also stressed. While the aim is not to denigrate alternative perspectives, this book has tried to underline that gender is, equally, a legitimate area for inquiry, research and historical integration.

NOTES

1. Joan Kelly's work provides a useful pointer to us. She takes the Renaissance as an illustrative case. Her contention is that while the developments of the age (roughly 1350–1530) widened the range of social and cultural expression, they affected women adversely, with the imposition of new restraints. There was, in fact, no renaissance for women—at least, not during those two hundred years. Hence, the pattern of relative loss of women's status is precisely in those periods of so-called progressive change (*Women, History and Theory*, Chicago, University of Chicago Press: 1984, pp. 19–50).
2. The inscriptions at Mathurā are particularly relevant as they document the involvement of some royal and mostly non-royal women in this activity, the latter comprising housewives, courtesans, female mendicants, and women belonging to families of dyers, dancers, ironmongers, cloak-makers and other varied professions. As Vijay Nath notes, more than one-third of the Mathurā donors were women, establishing their importance as a donor group in the post-Mauryan period: *Dāna: Gift System in Ancient India (c. 600 B.C.–c. A.D. 300): A Socio-economic Perspective*, Delhi, Munshiram Manoharlal: 1987, pp. 69–81. E. Hultzsch, *Corpus Inscriptionum Indicarum: Inscriptions of Aśoka*, vol. I, Varanasi: 1969, pp. 130–7, 158–9

and J.F. Fleet, *Corpus Inscriptionum Indicarum: Inscriptions of the Early Gupta Kings and Their Successors*, vol. III, Varanasi: 1970, pp. 260–4, 273–4 for information on women donors in the Mauryan and Gupta periods. Kalyani Das Bajpayee, *Early Inscriptions of Mathurā: A Study*, Calcutta, Punthi Pustak: 1980 on women donors prior to the seventh century AD.

3. In other words, the ability to 'get what one wants': Elise Boulding, *The Underside of History*, revd edn, Thousand Oaks, Sage Publications: 1992, vol. 1, p. 30.

Bibliography

Afonja, Simi, 'Women, Power and Authority in Traditional Yoruba Society', in *Visibility and Power: Essays on Women in Society and Development*, ed. Leela Dube, Eleanor Leacock and Shirley Ardener, Delhi, Oxford University Press: 1986, pp. 136–57.

Agrawal, Ashvini, 'Women in the Political Life of Kashmir (*c*. A.D. 650–1150)', in *Dimensions of Indian Womanhood*, ed. C.M. Agrawal, Almora, Shri Almora Book Depot: 1993, vol. I, pp. 85–94.

—— 'Economic Aspects of *Satī*', in *Women in Indian History: Social, Economic, Political and Cultural Perspectives*, ed. Kiran Pawar, Delhi, Vision and Venture: 1996, pp. 57–67.

Agrawal, C.M., ed., *Dimensions of Indian Womanhood*, Almora, Shri Almora Book Depot: 1993, vol. I.

Agrawal, J.N., *Inscriptions of Haryana, Himachal Pradesh, Punjab, Kashmir and Adjoining Hilly Tracts*, Delhi, ICHR/Agam Prakashan: 1999.

Agrawala, V.S., *The Deeds of Harsha*, Varanasi, Prithivi Prakashan: 1969.

Aktor, Mikael, 'Untouchables, Women and Territories: Rituals of Lordship in the *Parāśara Smṛti*', in *Invented Identities*, ed. Julia Leslie and Mary McGee, Delhi, Oxford University Press: 2000, pp. 133–56.

Ali, Daud, 'From *Nāyikā* to *Bhakta*: A Genealogy of Female Subjectivity in Early Medieval India', in *Invented Identities*, ed. Julia Leslie and Mary McGee, Delhi, Oxford University Press: 2000, pp. 157–80.

Allen, N.J. et al., ed., *Oxford University Papers on India*, Delhi, Oxford University Press: 1987, vol. I, pt 1.

Alphen, E.V., 'The Displacement of Male Sexuality: Reading From the Margins', in *Gender and Literature*, ed. Iqbal Kaur, Delhi, B.R. Publishing Corporation: 1992, pp. 131–48.

Altekar, A.S., *State and Government in Ancient India*, 3rd edn, Delhi, Motilal Banarsidass: 1958.

—— *The Position of Women in Hindu Civilization*, 2nd edn, Delhi, Motilal Banarsidass: 1959.

Archer, Leonie J., 'Notions of Community and the Exclusion of the Female', in *Women in Ancient Societies*, ed. Leonie J. Archer, Susan Fischler and Maria Wyke, London, Macmillan: 1994, pp. 53–69.

—— Susan Fischler and Maria Wyke, eds., *Women in Ancient Societies*, London, Macmillan: 1994.

Ardener, Shirley, 'The Representation of Women in Academic Models', in *Visibility and Power: Essays on Women in Society and Development*, ed. Leela Dube, Eleanor Leacock and Shirley Ardener, Delhi, Oxford University Press: 1986, pp. 3–14.

Arnold, David and Peter Robb, eds., *Institutions and Idealogies*, Richmond, Curzon Press: 1993.

Bae, Bak Kun, ed. and tr., *Nāgānanda of Harṣa*, Delhi, Motilal Banarsidass: 1992.

Bajpayee, Kalyani Das, *Early Inscriptions of Mathurā: A Study*, Calcutta, Punthi Pustak: 1980.

Bagchi, Jhunu, *The History and Culture of the Pālas of Bengal and Bihar (c. 750 A.D.–c. 1200 A.D.)*, Delhi, Abhinav Publications: 1993.

Bamzai, P.N.K., *Kashmir and Central Asia*, Delhi, Light & Life Publishers: 1980.

—— *Culture and Political History of Kashmir*, 1: *Ancient Kashmir*, Delhi, MD Publications: 1994.

Banerjea, J.N., *The Development of Hindu Iconography*, Calcutta, University of Calcutta: 1956.

Banerji, R.D., *The Pālas of Bengal*, Varanasi, Bhartiya Publishing House: 1973.

—— 'Naihāti Grant of Vallālasena', *Epigraphia Indica*, vol. IV, 1897, pp. 156–63.

—— 'Āmgachi Grant of Vigrahapāla III', *Epigraphia Indica*, vol. XV, 1920, pp. 293–301.

—— 'Barrackpur Grant of Vijayasena', *Epigraphia Indica*, vol. XV, 1920, pp. 278–86.

—— 'Bāngaṛh Grant of Mahipāla I', *Epigraphia Indica*, vol. XIV, 1918, pp. 324–30.

Banerji, S.C., *Cultural Heritage of Kashmir*, Calcutta, Sanskrit Pustak Bhandar: 1965.

Banerji, S.C. and A.K. Gupta, tr., *Bilhaṇa's Vikramāṅkadevacaritam*, Calcutta, Sambodhi Publications: 1965.

Barnett, L.D., 'Vappaghoṣavāṭa Grant of Jayanāga', *Epigraphia Indica*, vol. XVIII, 1926, pp. 60–4.

Basak, R., 'Tipperah Copper Plate Grant of Lokanātha', *Epigraphia Indica*, vol. XV, 1920, pp. 301–15.

—— 'Belāva Copper Plate of Bhojavarmadeva', *Epigraphia Indica*, vol. XII, 1914, pp. 37–43.

Basu, Aparna and Anup Taneja, ed., *Breaking Out of Invisibility: Women in Indian History*, Delhi, ICHR/Northern Book Centre: 2002.

Beal, Samuel, tr., *The Life of Hiuen-Tsiang by Shaman Hwui-Li*, Delhi, Academica Asiatica: 1973.

——tr., *Si-Yi-Ki: Buddhist Records of the Western World*, 2nd edn, Delhi, Munshiram Manoharlal: 1983.

Bhandarkar, D.R., 'The Buckala Inscription of Nāgabhaṭṭa', *Epigraphia Indica*, vol. IX, 1908, pp. 198–200.

Bhat, G.K., ed., *Bhavabhūti's Uttara-Rāmacarita*, Surat, The Popular Book Store: 1953.

—— 'The Detractors of Bhavabhūti', *Annals of the Bhandarkar Oriental Research Institute*, vol. LX, pts I-IV, 1979, pp. 151–7.

Bhattacharji, Sukumari, 'Prostitution in Ancient India', in *Women in Early Indian Societies*, ed. Kumkum Roy, Delhi, Manohar: 1999, pp. 196–228.

Bhattacharya, S. and Romila Thapar, eds., *Situating Indian History*, Delhi, Oxford University Press: 1986.

Bhattasali, N.K., 'Deulbāḍī Śarvvāṇī Image Inscription of Mahādevī Prabhāvatī, Queen of Devakhaḍga', *Epigraphia Indica*, vol. XVII, 1924, pp. 357–9.

—— 'Kedārpur Plate of Śrīcandradeva', *Epigraphia Indica*, vol. XVII, 1924, pp. 188–92.

—— 'The Rajibpur Sadāśiva-image Inscription of Gopāla III of Bengal', *The Indian Historical Quarterly*, vol. XVII, 1941, pp. 217–22.

—— 'Vajrayoginī Plate of Sāmalavarman', *Epigraphia Indica*, vol. XXX, 1958, pp. 259–63.

Bolon, Carol Radcliffe, 'Two Chalukya Queens and their Commemorative Temples: Eighth Century Pattadakal', in *Royal Patrons and Great Temple Art*, ed. Vidya Dehejia, Bombay, Marg Publications: 1988, pp. 61–76.

Borooah, A., *Bhavabhūti and his Place in Sanskrit Literature*, Assam, Publication Board: 1971.

Bose, Mandakranta, ed., *Faces of the Feminine in Ancient, Medieval, and Modern India*, Delhi, Oxford University Press: 2000.

—— 'Satī: The Event and the Ideology', in *Faces of the Feminine in Ancient, Medieval, and Modern India*, ed. Mandakranta Bose, Delhi, Oxford University Press: 2000, pp. 21–32.

Boulding, Elise, *The Underside of History*, revd edn, Thousand Oaks, Sage Publications: 1992, vol. I.

Bühler, George, 'Bānskherā Plate of Harṣa', *Epigraphia Indica*, vol. IV, 1897, pp. 208–11.

—— 'The Madhuban Copper Plate of Harṣa', *Epigraphia Indica*, vol. I, 1892, pp. 67–75.

Buitenen, J.A.B. van, tr., *The Mahābhārata: IV and V*, Chicago, University of Chicago Press: 1978.

Chakrabarti, Dilip K., *Colonial Indology: Sociopolitics of the Ancient Indian Past*, Delhi, Munshiram Manoharlal: 1997.

Chakrabarti, Kunal, 'Texts and Traditions: The Making of the Bengal *Purāṇas*', in *Tradition, Dissent and Ideology: Essays in Honour of Romila Thapar*, ed. R. Champakalakshmi and S. Gopal, Delhi, Oxford University Press: 1996, pp. 55–88.

—— 'Divine Family and World Maintenance: Gaṇeśa in the Bengal Purāṇas', in *From Myths to Markets: Essays on Gender*, ed. Kumkum Sangari and Uma Chakravarti, Delhi, Manohar: 1999, pp. 56–81.

—— 'Cult Region: The *Purāṇas* and the Making of the Cultural Territory of Bengal', *Studies in History*, vol. XVI, no. 1, 2000, pp. 1–16.

—— *Religious Process: The Purāṇas and the Making of a Regional Tradition*, Delhi, Oxford University Press: 2001.

Chakravarti, Uma, 'Conceptualising Brahmanical Patriarchy in Early India: Gender, Caste, Class and State', *Economic and Political Weekly*, vol. XXVIII, no. 14, 1993, pp. 579–85.

—— 'Gender, Caste and Labour: Idealogies and Material Structure of Widowhood', *Economic and Political Weekly*, vol. XXX, no. 36, 1995, pp. 2248–56.

—— 'Beyond the Altekarian Paradigm: Towards a New Understanding of Gender Relations in Early Indian History', in *Women in Early Indian Societies*, ed. Kumkum Roy, Delhi, Manohar: 1999, pp. 72–80.

—— *Everyday Lives, Everyday Histories: Beyond the Kings and Brahmanas of 'Ancient' India*, Delhi, Tulika Books: 2006.

Chakravarti, Uma and Kumkum Roy, 'In Search of Our Past: A Review of the Limitations and Possibilities of the Historiography of Women in Early India', *Economic and Political Weekly*, vol. 23, no. 18, 1988, pp. 2–10.

Chakraborty, Uma, *Kṣemendra—The Eleventh Century Kashmiri Poet*, Delhi, Sri Satguru Publications: 1991.

Champakalakshmi R. and S. Gopal, eds., *Tradition, Dissent and Ideology: Essays in Honour of Romila Thapar*, Delhi, Oxford University Press: 1996.

Chandra, Moti, *The World of Courtesans*, Delhi, Vikas Publishing House: 1973.

Chattopadhyaya, B.D., 'Currency in Early Bengal', *Journal of Indian History*, vol. LV, pt III, 1977, pp. 41–60.

—— 'Political Processes and Structure of Polity in Early Medieval India: Problems of Perspective', Presidential Address, *Indian History Congress Proceedings*, 44th Session, Burdwan, 1983, pp. 25–63.

—— 'Rājaśekhara, His Royal Household and its Religion: A Study of Some Aspects of the *Karpūramañjarī*', in *Religion and Society in Ancient India: Sudhakar Chattopadhyaya Commemoration Volume*, ed. Pranabananda Jash, Calcutta, Roy & Chowdhury: 1984, pp. 273–9.

—— 'Urban Centres in Early Medieval India: An Overview', in *Situating Indian History*, ed. S. Bhattacharya and Romila Thapar, Delhi, Oxford University Press: 1986, pp. 8–33.

—— *Aspects of Rural Settlements and Rural Society in Early Medieval India*, Calcutta, Centre for Studies in Social Sciences: 1990.

—— 'Historiography, History, and Religious Centres: Early Medieval North India, circa A.D. 700–1200', in *Gods, Guardians, and Lovers: Temple Sculptures from North India A.D. 700–1200*, ed. Vishakha N. Desai and Darielle Mason, New York, The Asia Society: 1993, pp. 33–47.

—— *The Making of Early Medieval India*, Delhi, Oxford University Press: 1994.

—— 'State and Economy in Northern India: 4th Century–12th Century', in *Recent Perspectives of Early Indian History*, ed. Romila Thapar, Bombay, Popular Prakashan: 1995, pp. 309–46.

—— *Representing the Other?: Sanskrit Sources and the Muslims (Eighth to Fourteenth Century)*, Delhi, Manohar: 1998.

—— 'General Editor's Preface', in *Women in Early Indian Societies*, ed. Kumkum Roy, Delhi, Manohar: 1999, pp. ix–x.

—— *Studying Early India: Archaeology, Texts, and Historical Issues*, Delhi, Permanent Black: 2003.

Chattopadhyaya, D., ed., *History and Society*, Calcutta, K.P. Bagchi & Company: 1978.

Choudhary, G.C., *Political History of Northern India (from Jain Sources—c. 650 A.D. to 1300 A.D.)*, Amritsar, Sohanlal Jaindharma Pracharak Samiti: 1954.

Coulson, Michael, tr., *Three Sanskrit Plays—'Śakuntalā' by Kālidāsa, 'Rākṣasa's Ring' by Viśākhadatta, 'Mālatī and Mādhava' by Bhavabhūti*, Harmondsworth, Penguin Books: 1981.

—— *A Critical Edition of the Mālatīmādhava*, New Delhi, Oxford University Press: 1989.

Cowell, E.B. and F.W. Thomas, tr., *The Harṣacarita of Bāṇa*, 2nd rpt., Delhi, Motilal Banarsidass: 1993.

Cunningham, A., *Coins of Medieval India: From the Seventh Century Down to the Muhammadan Conquests*, Varanasi, Oriental Books: 1967.

Dalal, Minakshi, *Conflict in Sanskrit Drama*, Bombay, Somaiya Publications: 1973.

Dandekar, R.N., ed., *The Age of the Guptas and Other Essays*, Delhi, Ajanta Publications: 1982.

—— 'The Svapna-Episode in the Svapnavāsavadattā', in *The Age of the Guptas and Other Essays*, ed. R.N. Dandekar, Delhi, Ajanta Publications: 1982, pp. 175–90.

Dani, A.H., 'Chandras of East Bengal', *Indian History Congress Proceedings*, pt I, 23rd Session, Aligarh, 1960, pp. 36–44.

Dasgupta, K.K., 'Last Days of the Maukharis', *The Indian Historical Quarterly*, vol. XXXVIII, 1962, pp. 242–6.

Dasgupta, Madhusraba, 'Usable Women: The Tales of Ambā and Mādhavī', in *Faces of the Feminine in Ancient, Medieval, and Modern India*, ed. Mandakranta Bose, Delhi, Oxford University Press: 2000, pp. 48–55.

Dasgupta, Manasi and Mandakranta Bose, 'The Goddess-Woman Nexus in Popular Religious Practice: The Cult of Manasā', in *Faces of the Feminine in Ancient, Medieval, and Modern India*, ed. Mandakranta Bose, Delhi, Oxford University Press: 2000, pp. 148–61.

Deambi, B.K. Kaul, *Corpus of Śāradā Inscriptions of Kashmir*, Delhi, Agam Kala Prakashan: 1982.

Dehejia, Vidya, ed., *Royal Patrons and Great Temple Art*, Bombay, Marg Publications: 1988.

Denton, Lynn Teskey, 'Varieties of Hindu Female Asceticism', in *Roles and Rituals for Hindu Women*, ed. Julia Leslie, London, Pinter Publishers: 1991, pp. 211–31.

Desai, Devangana, 'Art Under Feudalism in India (c. A.D. 500–1300)', in *The Feudal Order: State Society and Ideology in Early Medieval India*, ed. D.N. Jha, Delhi, Manohar: 2000, pp. 487–96.

Desai, Vishakha N. and Darielle Mason, eds., *Gods, Guardians, and Lovers: Temple Sculptures from North India A.D. 700–1200*, New York, The Asia Society: 1993.

Devahuti, D., *Harsha: A Political Study*, 2nd edn, Delhi, Oxford University Press: 1983.

Dhar, K.N., tr., *Śrīvara's Zaina Rājataraṅgiṇī*, Delhi, People's Publishing House: 1994.

Dhar, M.K., *Royal Life in Ancient India*, Delhi, Durga Publications: 1991.

Dhar, Somnath, *Kalhaṇa: The Poet Historian*, Delhi, Sahitya Akademi: 1978.

Dikshit, Ratnamayi, *Women in Sanskrit Dramas*, Delhi, Meherchand Lachhmandas: 1964.

Dishalkar, D.B., 'Barton Museum Bhāvnagar Inscription of Bhoja's Reign', *Epigraphia Indica*, vol. XIX, 1928, pp. 174–7.

Doniger, Wendy, *Splitting the Difference: Gender and Myth in Ancient Greece and India*, Chicago, University of Chicago Press: 1999.

Doniger, Wendy and Brian K. Smith, tr., *The Laws of Manu*, London/New York, Penguin Books: 1991.

Dube, Leela, 'Introduction', in *Visibility and Power: Essays on Women in Society and Development*, ed. Leela Dube, Eleanor Leacock and Shirley Ardener, Delhi, Oxford University Press: 1986, pp. xi–xliv.

—— 'On the Construction of Gender: Hindu Girls in Patrilineal India', *Economic and Political Weekly*, vol. 23, no. 18, 1988, pp. 11–19.

—— 'Gender Bias and Social Sciences', in *Women in Indian History: Social, Economic, Political and Cultural Perspectives*, ed. Kiran Pawar, Delhi, Vision & Venture: 1996, pp. 3–10.

Dube, Leela, Eleanor Leacock and Shirley Ardener, eds., *Visibility and Power: Essays on Women in Society and Development*, Delhi, Oxford University Press: 1986.

Dwivedi, R.C., 'Women in Classical Sanskrit Literature', in *Women Images*, ed. Pratibha Jain and Rajan Mahan, Jaipur, Rawat Publications: 1996, pp. 46–54.

Eisenstein, H., *Contemporary Feminist Thought*, England, Unwin Paperbacks: 1984.

Evans, Mary, ed., *The Woman Question*, London, Sage Publications: 1994.

Fischler, Susan, 'Social Stereotypes and Historical Analysis: The Case of the Imperial Women at Rome', in *Women in Ancient Societies*, ed. Leonie J. Archer, Susan Fischler and Maria Wyke, London, Macmillan: 1994, pp. 115–33.

Fleet, J.F., *Corpus Inscriptionum Indicarum: Inscriptions of the Early Gupta Kings and Their Successors*, vol. III, 3rd revd edn, Varanasi, 1970.

—— 'The Dighwa-Dubauli Plate of the Mahārāja Mahendrapāla I', *Indian Antiquary*, vol. XV, 1886, pp. 105–13.

—— 'The Bengal Asiatic Society's Plate of the Mahārāja Vināyakapāla', *Indian Antiquary*, vol. XV, 1886, pp. 138–41.

Gelblum, Tuvia, 'Classical Hindu Scriptures', in *Institutions and Idealogies*, ed. David Arnold and Peter Robb, Richmond, Curzon Press: 1993, pp. 35–44.

Ghosh, J.C., 'Notes on the Irda Copper Plate Grant of King Nayapāladeva', *Epigraphia Indica*, vol. XXII, 1938, pp. 43–7.

Ghoshal, U.N., 'The Position of the Brāhmaṇas in Ancient Bengal', *Annals of the Bhandarkar Oriental Research Institute*, vol. XLVI, pts I-IV, 1965, pp. 67–80.

—— 'The Dynastic Chronicles of Kashmir', *The Indian Historical Quarterly*, vol. XVIII, 1942, pp. 195–207.

Gilchrist, Roberta, *Gender and Material Culture: The Archaeology of Religious Women*, London and New York, Routledge: 1994.

Goldman, Robert P., 'Language, Gender and Power: The Sexual Politics of Language and Language Acquisition in Traditional India', in *Invented Identities*, ed. Julia Leslie and Mary McGee, Delhi, Oxford University Press: 2000, pp. 84–98.

Goldman, Sally J. Sutherland, 'Speaking Gender: *Vāc* and the Vedic Construction of the Feminine', in *Invented Identities*, ed. Julia Leslie and Mary McGee, Delhi, Oxford University Press: 2000, pp. 57–83.

Goyal, Shankar, *History and Historiography of The Age of Harsha*, Jodhpur, Kusumanjali Prakashan: 1992.

Goyal, S.R., *Harsha and Buddhism*, Meerut, Kusumanjali Prakashan: 1986.

Gulati, Saroj, *Women and Society: Northern India in the 11th and 12th Centuries*, Delhi, Chanakya Publications: 1985.

Gunrtoo, N.K., 'Introduction', in *Śrīvara's Zaina Rājataraṅgiṇī*, tr. K.N. Dhar, Delhi, People's Publishing House: 1994, pp. v-xxiii.

Gupta, Samjukta Gombrich, 'The Goddess, Women, and Their Rituals in Hinduism', in *Faces of the Feminine in Ancient, Medieval and Modern India*, ed. Mandakranta Bose, Delhi, Oxford University Press: 2000, pp. 87–106.

Gupta, Sanjukta, 'Women in the Śaiva/Śākta Ethos', in *Roles and Rituals for Hindu Women*, ed. Julia Leslie, London, Pinter Publishers: 1991, pp. 193–209.

Hackett, Rosalind I.J., 'Women and New Religious Movements in Africa', in *Religion and Gender*, ed. Ursula King, Oxford, Blackwell Publishers: 1995, pp. 257–90.

Hansen, Kathryn, 'The *Vīrāṅganā* in North Indian History: Myth and Popular Culture', *Economic and Political Weekly*, vol. 23, no. 18, 1988, pp. 25–33.

—— 'The *Vīrāṅganā* in North Indian History: Myth and Popular Culture', in *Ideas, Images and Real Lives: Women in Literature and History*, ed. Alice Thorner and M.K. Raj, Mumbai, Orient Longman: 2000, pp. 257–87.

Harshe, R.G., *Observations on the Life and Works of Bhavabhūti*, Delhi, Meherchand Lachhmandas: 1974.

Hultzsch, E., *Corpus Inscriptionum Indicarum: Inscriptions of Aśoka*, vol. I, new edn, Varanasi, 1969.

—— 'The First Inscription of the Vaillabhaṭṭasvāmin temple at Gwalior', *Epigraphia Indica*, vol. I, 1892, pp. 154–9.

Huntington, Susan L., *The 'Pāla-Sena' Schools of Sculpture*, Leiden, E.J. Brill: 1984.

Husain, Shahanara, 'Village Life in Early Medieval Bengal: A Study Based on the Subhāṣitaratnakoṣa', in *History and Society*, ed. D. Chattopadhyaya, Calcutta, K.P. Bagchi & Company: 1978, pp. 311–16.

Indra, *The Status of Women in Ancient India*, 2nd edn, Banaras, Motilal Banarsidass: 1955.

Jacobsh, Doris R., 'The Construction of Gender in History and Religion: The Sikh Case', in *Faces of the Feminine in Ancient, Medieval, and Modern India*, ed. Mandakranta Bose, Delhi, Oxford University Press: 2000, pp. 270–86.

Jain, Jasbir, 'Gender and Narrative Strategy', in *Gender and Literature*, ed. Iqbal Kaur, Delhi, B.R. Publishing Corporation: 1992, pp. 47–55.

—— 'Cinderella's Stepmother: An Analysis of a Counter-Image', in *Women Images*, ed. Pratibha Jain and Rajan Mahan, Jaipur, Rawat Publications: 1996, pp. 72–83.

Jain, Pratibha and Rajan Mahan, ed., *Women Images*, Jaipur, Rawat Publications: 1996.

Jaiswal, Suvira, 'Women in Early India: Problems and Perspectives', *Indian History Congress Proceedings*, 42nd Session, Bodhgaya, 1981, pp. 54–60.

—— 'Female Images in the Arthaśāstra of Kauṭilya', *Social Scientist*, vol. 29, nos. 3–4, 2001, pp. 51–9.

Jamison, Stephanie W., 'Giver or Given?: Some Marriages in Kālidāsa', in *Jewels of Authority: Women and Textual Tradition in Hindu India*, ed. Laurie L. Patton, Delhi, Oxford University Press: 2002, pp. 69–83.

Jash, Pranabananda, ed., *Religion and Society in Ancient India: Sudhakar Chattopadhyaya Commemoration Volume*, Calcutta, Roy & Chowdhury: 1984.

Jayaswal, K.P., *Hindu Polity*, 2 vols., Patna, Eastern Book Depot: 1988.

Jha, Bal Govind, ed. with Hindi tr., *Harṣa-Caritam of Bāṇabhaṭṭa*, Varanasi, Krishnadas Academy: 1994.

Jha, D.N., ed., *The Feudal Order: State Society and Ideology in Early Medieval India*, Delhi, Manohar: 2000.

Kale, M.R., ed. and tr., *Priyadarśikā of Śrī Harṣadeva*, rpt., Delhi, Motilal Banarsidass: 1977.

—— ed. and tr., *The Ratnāvalī of Śrī Harṣa-Deva*, 2nd rpt., Delhi, Motilal Banarsidass: 1995.

Kamerkar, Mani, 'History: Where are the Women?', in *Women's Studies in India*, ed. M.K. Raj, Bombay, Popular Prakashan: 1986, pp. 86–94.

Kane, P.V., *History of Dharmaśāstra*, Poona, Bhandarkar Oriental Research Institute: 1941, vol. II, part 2.

—— *History of Dharmaśāstra*, Poona, Bhandarkar Oriental Research Institute: 1946, vol. III.

—— *History of Dharmaśāstra*, Poona, Bhandarkar Oriental Research Institute: 1953, vol. IV.

Kapur, M.L., *Eminent Rulers of Ancient Kashmir*, Delhi, Oriental Publishers: 1975.

—— *The History and Culture of Kashmir*, 2nd revd edn, Delhi, Anmol Publications: 1992.

Kaul, G.K., *Kashmir (Through the Ages) (5000 B.C. to 1900 A.D.)*, Srinagar, Chronicle Publishing House: 1960.

Kaur, Iqbal, ed., *Gender and Literature*, Delhi, B.R. Publishing Corporation: 1992.

—— 'Introduction', in *Gender and Literature*, ed. Iqbal Kaur, Delhi, B.R. Publishing Corporation: 1992, pp. xi–xxi.

Keith, A.B., *A History of Sanskrit Literature*, London, Oxford University Press: 1920.

Kelly, Joan, *Women, History and Theory*, Chicago, University of Chicago Press: 1984.

Khan, J.A., 'Ideology of Motherhood in Ancient India', in *Women in Indian History: Social, Economic, Political and Cultural Perspectives*, ed. Kiran Pawar, Delhi, Vision & Venture: 1996, pp. 49–56.

Khanna, Madhu, 'The Goddess-Women Equation in Śākta Tantras', in *Faces of the Feminine in Ancient, Medieval, and Modern India*, ed. Mandakranta Bose, Delhi, Oxford University Press: 2000, pp. 109–23.

Kielhorn, F., 'Twenty-One Copper Plates of the Kings of Kanauj', *Epigraphia Indica*, vol. IV, 1897, pp. 97–129.

—— 'Khalimpur Plate of Dharmapāladeva', *Epigraphia Indica*, vol. IV, 1897, pp. 243–54.

—— 'Rajor Inscription of Mathanadeva', *Epigraphia Indica*, vol. III, 1897, pp. 263–7.

—— 'Pathari Pillar Inscription of Parabala', *Epigraphia Indica*, vol. IX, 1908, pp. 248–56.

—— 'Plate of Govindacandra and the Yuvarāja Mahārājaputra Āsphoṭacandra', *Epigraphia Indica*, vol. VIII, 1905, pp. 155–6.

—— 'Plate of Govindacandra and the Mahārājaputra Rājyapāla', *Epigraphia Indica*, vol. VIII, 1905, pp. 157–8.

—— 'Deopārā Stone Inscription of Vijayasena', *Epigraphia Indica*, vol. I, 1892, pp. 305–15.

—— 'Bādal Pillar Inscription of Nārāyaṇapāla', *Epigraphia Indica*, vol. II, 1984, pp. 160–7.

—— 'The Daulatapura Plate of Bhojadeva I of Mahodaya', *Epigraphia Indica*, vol. V, 1899, pp. 208–13.

—— 'Pāli Plates of Govindacandra and his Mother Rālhaṇadevī', *Epigraphia Indica*, vol. V, 1899, pp. 113–15.

—— 'Machhlishahr plate of Govindacandra', *Epigraphia Indica*, vol. V, 1899, pp. 115–16.

—— 'Three Copper Plate Inscriptions of Govindacandra of Kanauj', *Epigraphia Indica*, vol. V, 1899, pp. 112–16.

—— 'Bangāvan Plate of Govindacandra and his Queen Gosalladevī', *Epigraphia Indica*, vol. V, 1899, pp. 116–18.

—— 'Copper Plate Grant of Candradeva and Madanapāladeva', *Indian Antiquary*, vol. XVIII, 1889, pp. 9–14.

—— 'The Copper Plate Grant of Madanapāla and Govindacandra', *Indian Antiquary*, vol. XVIII, 1889, pp. 14–19.

King, Ursula, ed., *Religion and Gender*, Oxford, Blackwell Publishers: 1995.

Klapisch-Zuber, Christiane, 'Family Trees and the Construction of Kinship in Renaissance Italy', in *Gender, Kinship, Power*, ed. M.J. Maynes et al., Great Britain, Routledge: 1996, pp. 101–13.

Konow, Sten, 'The Sārnāth Inscription of Kumaradevī', *Epigraphia Indica*, vol. IX, 1908, pp. 319–28.

Kumari, Ved, *The Nīlamata Purāṇa*, Srinagar, J&K Academy of Art, Culture and Languages: 1968, vol. I.

—— tr., *The Nīlamata Purāṇa*, Srinagar, J&K Academy of Art, Culture and Languages: 1973, vol. II.

Leacock, Eleanor, 'Women, Power and Authority', in *Visibility and Power: Essays on Women in Society and Development*, ed. Leela Dube,

Eleanor Leacock and Shirley Ardener, Delhi, Oxford University Press: 1986, pp. 107–35.

Lerner, Gerda, *The Creation of Patriarchy*, New York, Oxford University Press: 1986.

Leslie, Julia, 'Strīsvabhāva: The Inherent Nature of Women', in *Oxford University Papers on India*, ed. N.J. Allen et al., Delhi, Oxford University Press: 1987, vol. I, pt 1, pp. 28–58.

—— *The Perfect Wife*, Delhi, Oxford University Press: 1989.

—— ed., *Roles and Rituals for Hindu Women*, London, Pinter Publishers: 1991.

—— 'Introduction', in *Roles and Rituals for Hindu Women*, ed. Julia Leslie, London, Pinter Publishers: 1991, pp. 1–13.

—— 'Śrī and Jyeṣṭhā: Ambivalent Role Models for Women', in *Roles and Rituals for Hindu Women*, ed. Julia Leslie, London, Pinter Publishers: 1991, pp. 107–27.

—— 'Suttee or *Satī*: Victim or Victor?', in *Roles and Rituals for Hindu Women*, ed. Julia Leslie, London, Pinter Publishers: 1991, pp. 175–91.

—— 'Suttee or *Satī*: Victim or Victor?', in *Institutions and Ideologies*, ed. David Arnold and Peter Robb, Richmond, Curzon Press: 1993, pp. 45–63.

Leslie, Julia, and Mary McGee, eds., *Invented Identities*, Delhi, Oxford University Press: 2000.

Lingat, Robert, *The Classical Law of India*, tr. J.D.M. Derrett, Delhi, Munshiram Manoharlal: 1973.

Loomba, Ania, *Gender, Race, Renaissance Drama*, Manchester, Manchester University Press: 1989.

Lyall, E., tr., 'Tārānātha's Account of the Magadha Kings', *Indian Antiquary*, vol. IV, 1875, pp. 361–7.

Madhavananda, Swami and R.C. Majumdar, eds., *Great Women of India*, Almora, Advaita Ashrama: 1953.

Majumdar, A.K., *Concise History of Ancient India*, Delhi, Munshiram Manoharlal: 1980, vol. 2.

Majumdar, N.G., 'Irda Copper Plate of the Kāmboja King Nayapāladeva', *Epigraphia Indica*, vol. XXII, 1938, pp. 150–9.

Majumdar, R.C., ed., *Classical Age*, Bombay, Bharatiya Vidya Bhawan: 1954.

—— 'Ideas of History in Sanskrit Literature', in *Historians of India, Pakistan and Ceylon*, ed. C.H. Philips, London, Oxford University Press: 1961, pp. 13–28.

—— ed., *The Vedic Age*, 4th edn, Bombay, Bharatiya Vidya Bhawan: 1965.

—— 'Sources of Indian History', in *The Vedic Age*, ed. R.C. Majumdar, 4th edn, Bombay, Bharatiya Vidya Bhawan: 1965, pp. 47–65.

—— ed., *The Age of Imperial Unity*, 4th edn, Bombay, Bharatiya Vidya Bhawan: 1968.

—— *History of Ancient Bengal*, Calcutta, G. Bharadwaj and Company: 1971.

—— 'Political History of South Bihar (550–750 A.D.)', in *Comprehensive History of Bihar*, ed. B.P. Sinha, Patna, Kashi Prasad Jayaswal Research Institute: 1974, vol. I, pt II, pp. 221–44.

—— *Ancient India*, 7th edn, Delhi, Motilal Banarsidass: 1974.

Maitreya, A.K., *The Fall of the Pāla Empire*, Darjeeling, University of North Bengal: 1987.

Mandal, B.C., tr., *Śrīkaṇṭhacarita: A Mahākāvya of Maṅkhaka*, Calcutta, Sanskrit Pustak Bhandar: 1991.

Mandal, Sushila, *History of Bengal: The Middle Age*, Calcutta, Prakash Mandir: 1970, pt I.

Mathur, Vina, *The Role and Position of Women in the Social, Cultural and Political Life of Kashmir: 7th Century-16th Century A.D.*, Jammu, Doron Publication: 1985.

Maynes, M.J. et al., ed., *Gender, Kinship, Power*, Great Britain, Routledge: 1996.

Mazumdar, B.P., 'Religion and Philosophy (500–1200 A.D.)', in *Comprehensive History of Bihar*, ed. B.P. Sinha, Patna, Kashi Prasad Jayaswal Research Institute: 1974, vol. I, pt II, pp. 403–501.

—— 'Role of the Ḍāmaras in Medieval Kashmir', in *Essays in Indian Art, Religion and Society*, ed. K.M. Shrimali, Delhi, Munshiram Manoharlal: 1987, pp. 27–36.

—— 'Merchants and Landed Aristocracy in the Feudal Economy of Northern India: Eighth to Twelfth Century', in *Land System and Rural Society in Early India*, ed. B.P. Sahu, Delhi, Manohar: 1997, pp. 142–50.

McGee, Mary, 'Introduction', in *Invented Identities*, ed. Julia Leslie and Mary McGee, Delhi, Oxford University Press: 2000, pp. 1–56.

Menski, Werner F., 'Marital Expectations as Dramatized in Hindu Marriage Rituals', in *Roles and Rituals for Hindu Women*, London, Pinter Publishers: 1991, pp. 47–67.

Mishra, S.M., *Yaśovarman of Kanauj*, Delhi, Abhinav Publications: 1977.

Mohan, Krishna, *Early Medieval History of Kashmir*, Delhi, Meherchand Lachhmandas: 1981.

Monier-Williams, M., *A Sanskrit-English Dictionary*, 12th rpt., Delhi, Motilal Banarsidass: 1995.

Morris, Pam, 'Literature and Feminism', in *Speaking of Gender*, ed. Elaine Showalter, London, Routledge: 1994, pp. 7–29.

Mukherjee, Meenakshi, 'Story, History and Her Story', *Studies in History*, vol. IX, no. 1, 1993, pp. 71–85.

Mukherjee, Prabhati, *Hindu Women*, revd edn, Calcutta, Orient Longman: 1994.

Mukherjee, S.N., ed., *India: History and Thought*, Calcutta, Subarnarekha: 1982.

Mukherji, R. and S.K. Maity, *Corpus of Bengal Inscriptions Bearing on History and Civilization of Bengal*, Calcutta, Firma K.L. Mukhopadhyay: 1967.

Mukund, Kanakalatha, 'Turmeric Land: Women's Property Rights in Tamil Society Since Early Medieval Times', in *Women in Early Indian Societies*, ed. Kumkum Roy, Delhi, Manohar: 1999, pp. 123–40.

Nath, Vijay, *Dāna: Gift System in Ancient India: A Socio-Economic Perspective*, Delhi, Munshiram Manoharlal: 1987.

—— '*Mahādāna*: The Dynamics of Gift-economy and the Feudal Milieu', in *The Feudal Order: State, Society and Ideology in Early Medieval India*, ed. D.N. Jha, Delhi, Manohar: 2000, pp. 411–40.

Niranjana, Seemanthini, 'On Gender and Difference: Towards a Re-Articulation', *Social Scientist*, vol. 22, nos. 7–8, 1994, pp. 28–41.

Niyogi, Puspa, *Brahmanic Settlements in Different Subdivisions of Ancient Bengal*, Calcutta, Indian Studies—Past and Present: 1967.

O'Connor, June, 'The Epistemological Significance of Feminist Research in Religion', in *Religion and Gender*, ed. Ursula King, Oxford, Blackwell Publishers: 1995, pp. 45–63.

Ojha, G.H., 'Partābgarh Inscription of King Mahendrapāla II', *Epigraphia Indica*, vol. XIV, 1918, pp. 176–88.

Orr, Leslie, 'Women's Wealth and Worship: Female Patronage of Hinduism, Jainism, and Buddhism in Medieval Tamilnadu', in *Faces of the Feminine in Ancient, Medieval, and Modern India*, ed. Mandakranta Bose, Delhi, Oxford University Press: 2000, pp. 124–47.

—— *Donors, Devotees, and Daughters of Gods: Temple Women in Medieval Tamilnadu*, New York, Oxford University Press: 2000.

Ortner, Sherry, 'Is Female to Male as Nature is to Culture?', *Feminist Studies*, I, 1992, pp. 5–31.

Pande, G.C., 'The Image of Woman in the Indian Tradition: Some Reflections', in *Women Images*, ed. Pratibha Jain and Rajan Mahan, Jaipur, Rawat Publications: 1996, pp. 39–45.

Pandit., R.S., tr., *Rājataraṅgiṇī*, Delhi, Sahitya Akademi: 1935.

Pateman, Carole, 'The Sexual Contract: The End of the Story?', in *The Woman Question*, ed. Mary Evans, London, Sage Publications: 1994, pp. 233–45.

Pathak, V.S., *Ancient Historians of India*, 2nd impression, Gorakhpur, Purva Samsthana: 1966.

Pati, Biswamoy, B.P. Sahu and T.K. Venkatasubramanian, eds., *Negotiating India's Past: Essays in Memory of Partha Sarathi Gupta*, Delhi, Tulika Books: 2003.

Patton, Laurie L., ed., *Jewels of Authority: Women and Textual Tradition in Hindu India*, Delhi, Oxford University Press: 2002.

Paul, Diana Y., *Women in Buddhism*, 2nd edn, California, University of California Press: 1985.

Paul, P.L., *The Early History of Bengal*, Calcutta, The Indian Research Institute: 1939, vol. I.

—— *The Early History of Bengal*, Calcutta, The Indian Research Institute: 1940, vol. II.

—— 'Relations of the Pālas and Senas of Bengal with the Other Provinces', *The Indian Historical Quarterly*, vol. XII, 1936, pp. 613–37.

—— 'Rāmapāla, the Last Great Pāla King', *The Indian Historical Quarterly*, vol. XIII, 1937, pp. 37–43.

Pawar, Kiran, ed., *Women in Indian History: Social, Economic, Political and Cultural Perspectives*, Delhi, Vision & Venture: 1996.

Philips, C.H., *Historians of India, Pakistan and Ceylon*, 2nd rpt., London, Oxford University Press: 1967.

Pires, Edward A., *The Maukharis*, rpt., Delhi, Ramanand Vidya Bhawan: 1982.

Prasad, Beni, *Theory of Government in Ancient India*, Allahabad, Central Book Depot: 1968.

—— *The State in Ancient India*, Allahabad, The Indian Press: 1974

Prasad, Beni, and R.C. Majumdar, 'Political Theory and Administrative System', in *The Age of Imperial Unity*, ed. R.C. Majumdar, 4th edn, Bombay, Bharatiya Vidya Bhawan: 1968, pp. 303–34.

Raj, M.K., ed., *Women's Studies in India*, Bombay, Popular Prakashan: 1986.

—— 'Permeable Boundaries', in *Ideas, Images and Real Lives: Women in Literature and History*, ed. Alice Thorner and M.K. Raj, Mumbai, Orient Longman: 2000, pp. 1–34.

Rajappa, Padmini, 'Bhavabhuti's Sita: A Woman of Substance', *The Times of India*, Delhi, 22 May 2001, p. 7.

Raman, K.V. et al., eds., *Śrīnidhīh: Perspectives in Indian Archaeology, Art and Culture* (K.R. Srinivasan Festschrift), Madras, New Era Publications: 1983.

Randle, H.N., 'India Office Plate of Lakṣmaṇasena', *Epigraphia Indica*, vol. XXVI, 1952, pp. 1–13.

Rangachari, Devika, 'Gender and the Historical Chronicle: A Study of Kalhaṇa's *Rājataraṅgiṇī*', unpub. M. Phil. dissertation, Department of History, University of Delhi, Delhi: 1997.

—— 'Kalhaṇa's *Rājataraṅgiṇī*: A Gender Perspective', *The Medieval History Journal*, vol. 5, no. I, 2002, pp. 37–75.

—— 'Coinage and Gender: Early Medieval Kashmir', in *Coins in India: Power and Communication*, ed. H.P. Ray, Mumbai, Marg Publications: 2006, pp. 46–55.

Rangarajan, L.N., ed. and tr., *Kauṭilya: The Arthaśāstra*, Delhi, Penguin Books: 1987.

Ray, S.C., 'Administrative System in Early Kaśmīra', *Annals of the Bhandarkar Oriental Research Institute*, 1957, vol. XXXVIII, pts III–IV, pp. 175–89.

—— *Early History and Culture of Kashmir*, 2nd revd edn, Delhi, Munshiram Manoharlal: 1970.

Ray, H.C., *The Dynastic History of Northern India*, 2nd edn, Delhi, Munshiram Manoharlal: 1973, vol. I.

Ray, Niharranjan, *History of the Bengali People (Ancient Period)*, tr. J.W. Hood, Calcutta, Orient Longman: 1994.

Ridding, C.M., tr., *Bāṇabhaṭṭa's Kādambarī*, Bombay, Jaico Publishing House: 1956.

Roy, Kumkum, 'The King's Household: Structure/Space in the Śāstric Tradition', *Economic and Political Weekly*, vol. 27, nos. 43 and 44, 1992, pp. 55–60.

—— 'Defining the Household: Some Aspects of Prescription and Practice in Early India', *Social Scientist*, vol. 22, nos. 1–2, 1994, pp. 3–18.

—— 'Where Women are Worshipped, there the Gods Rejoice', in *Women and the Hindu Right*, ed. Tanika Sarkar and Urvashi Butalia, New Delhi, Kali for Women: 1995, pp. 10–28.

—— ed., *Women in Early Indian Societies*, Delhi, Manohar: 1999.

—— 'Introduction', in *Women in Early Indian Societies*, ed. Kumkum Roy, Delhi, Manohar: 1999, pp. 1–45.

—— 'The King's Household: Structure and Space in the Śāstric Tradition', in *From Myths to Markets: Essays on Gender*, ed. Kumkum Sangari and Uma Chakravarti, New Delhi, Manohar: 1999, pp. 18–38.

—— 'Investigating Gendered Religious Traditions: A Review', in *Breaking Out of Invisibility: Women in Indian History*, ed. Aparna Basu and Anup Taneja, Delhi, ICHR/Northern Book Centre: 2002, pp. 13–23.

—— 'The Making of a *Maṇḍala*: Fuzzy Frontiers of Kalhaṇa's Kashmir', in *Negotiating India's Past: Essays in Memory of Partha Sarathi Gupta*, eds. Biswamoy Pati, B.P. Sahu and T.K. Venkatasubramanian, Delhi, Tulika Books: 2003, pp. 52–66.

Roychoudhuri, Bani, *The Political History of Bengal to the Rise of the Pāla Dynasty*, Calcutta, Sanskrit Pustak Bhandar: 1990.

Sahai, Bhagwant, *The Inscriptions of Bihar*, Delhi, Ramanand Vidya Bhawan: 1983.

Sahni, D.R., 'The Saheth-Maheth Plate of Govindacandra', *Epigraphia Indica*, vol. XI, 1912, pp. 20–6.

—— 'The Candrāvatī Plates of Candradeva', *Epigraphia Indica*, vol. XIV, 1918, pp. 192–209.

—— 'The Āhār Stone Inscription of Bhoja's Reign', *Epigraphia Indica*, vol. XIX, 1928, pp. 52–62.

—— 'The Don Buzurg Plates of Govindacandra', *Epigraphia Indica*, vol. XVIII, 1926, pp. 218–24.

—— 'Dewai Stone Inscription of the Shāhī King Bhīmadeva', *Epigraphia Indica*, vol. XXI, 1932, pp. 298–99.

Sahu, B.P., ed., *Land System and Rural Society in Early India*, Delhi, Manohar: 1997.

—— 'Introduction', in *Land System and Rural Society in Early India*, ed. B.P. Sahu, Delhi, Manohar: 1997, pp. 1–58.

Sangari, Kumkum, 'Consent and Agency: Aspects of Feminist Historiography', in *Women in Indian History: Social, Economic, Political and Cultural Perspectives*, ed. Kiran Pawar, Delhi, Vision & Venture: 1996, pp. 11–27.

—— *Politics of the Possible: Essays on Gender, History, Narrative and Colonial English*, Delhi, Tulika: 1999.

Sangari, Kumkum and Sudesh Vaid, eds., *Recasting Women: Essays in Colonial History*, rpt., Delhi, Kali for Women: 1993.

——and Sudesh Vaid, 'Recasting Women: An Introduction', in *Recasting Women: Essays in Colonial History*, ed. Kumkum Sangari and Sudesh Vaid, rpt., Delhi, Kali for Women: 1993, pp. 1–26.

Sangari, Kumkum and Uma Chakravarti, eds., *From Myths to Markets: Essays on Gender*, Delhi, Manohar: 1999.

—— 'Disparate Women: Transitory Contexts, Persistent Structures', in *From Myths to Markets: Essays on Gender*, Delhi, Manohar: 1999, pp. xi–xxx.

Sarkar, Tanika and Urvashi Butalia, eds., *Women and the Hindu Right*, Delhi, Kali for Women: 1995.

Sastri, Haraprasad, ed., *Rāmacarita: A Historical Record of the Pāl Dynasty by Sandhyākara Nandi*, Varanasi, Bharatiya Publishing House: 1973.

Sastri, Hirananda, 'Nālandā Copper Plate of Devapāladeva', *Epigraphia Indica*, vol. XVII, 1924, pp. 310–27.

—— 'Barah Copper-plate of Bhojadeva', *Epigraphia Indica*, vol. XIX, 1928, pp. 15–19.

—— 'Nālandā Stone Inscription of the Reign of Yaśovarmmadeva', *Epigraphia Indica*, vol. XX, 1933, pp. 37–46.

—— 'Nālandā Clay Seal of Harṣa', *Epigraphia Indica*, vol. XXI, 1932, pp. 74–7.

Sastri, K.N., 'Srinagar Inscription of Queen Diddā', *Epigraphia Indica*, vol. XXVII, 1956, pp. 153–5.

Sastri, S.M., 'Book Notice: The Sanskrit Poems of Mayūra and Bāṇa's *Caṇḍīśataka* by G.P. Quackenbos', *Indian Antiquary*, vol. XLVII, 1918, pp. 167–8.

Sen, B.C., 'Administration Under the Pālas and the Senas', *Indian Culture*, vol. VII, no. 2, 1940, pp. 203–19.

Sen, Nabaneeta Dev, 'Candrāvatī-Rāmāyaṇa: Feminizing the Rāma-Tale', in *Faces of the Feminine in Ancient, Medieval, and Modern India*, ed. Mandakranta Bose, Delhi, Oxford University Press: 2000, pp. 183–91.

Sengupta, Padmini, *The Story of Women of India*, Delhi, Indian Book Company: 1974.

Shah, K.K., 'Legal Rights of Women to Landed Wealth: A Case Study of Candella Queens', in *Women in Indian History: Social, Economic, Political and Cultural Perspectives*, ed. Kiran Pawar, Delhi, Vision & Venture: 1996, pp. 68–84.

Shah, Shalini, *The Making of Womanhood*, Delhi, Manohar: 1995.

—— 'In the Business of *Kāma*: Prostitution in Classical Sanskrit Literature from the Seventh to the Thirteenth Centuries', *The Medieval History Journal*, vol. 5, no.1, 2002, pp. 121–56.

—— 'Gender and Sexuality in Ancient Punjab: A Case Study of the Karṇa Parva in the *Mahābhārata*', in *Breaking Out of Invisibility: Women in Indian History*, ed. Aparna Basu and Anup Taneja, Delhi, ICHR/ Northern Book Centre: 2002, pp. 24–42.

Shali, S.L., *Kashmir: History and Archaeology Through the Ages*, Delhi, Indus Publishing Company: 1993.

Sharma, Baijnath, *Harṣa and his Times*, Varanasi, Sushma Prakashan: 1970.

Sharma, B.N., *Social Life in Northern India (A.D. 600–1000)*, Delhi, Munshiram Manoharlal: 1966.

Sharma, R.S., *Aspects of Political Ideas and Institutions*, 2nd edn, Delhi, Motilal Banarsidass: 1968.

—— 'Social and Economic Conditions (500–1200 A.D.)', in *Comprehensive History of Bihar*, ed. B.P. Sinha, Patna, Kashi Prasad Jayaswal Research Institute: 1974, vol. I, pt II, pp. 359–74.

—— *Perspectives in Social and Economic History of Early India*, Delhi, Munshiram Manoharlal: 1983.

—— 'Problems of Peasant Protest in Early Medieval India', in *Land System and Rural Society in Early India*, ed. B.P. Sahu, Delhi, Manohar: 1997, pp. 343–60.

—— 'The Feudal Mind', in *The Feudal Order: State, Society and Ideology in Early Medieval India*, ed. D.N. Jha, Delhi, Manohar: 2000, pp. 455–68.

—— *Early Medieval Indian Society: A Study in Feudalisation*, Kolkata, Orient Longman: 2001.

Sharma, Tripat, *Women in Ancient India*, Delhi, Ess Ess Publications: 1987.

Shastri, A.M., *India as Seen in the Kuṭṭanīmata of Dāmodaragupta*, Delhi, Motilal Banarsidass: 1975.

Showalter, Elaine, ed., *Speaking of Gender*, London, Routledge: 1994.

Shrimali, K.M., ed., *Essays in Indian Art, Religion and Society*, Delhi, Munshiram Manoharlal: 1987.

Shukla, N.S., *Cultural Trends in Kashmir and Kṣemendra*, Delhi, Nirman Prakashan: 1990.

Shukla, R.S., *India as Known to Haribhadra Suri*, Meerut, Kusumanjali Prakashan: 1989.

Shulman, David, ed., *Syllables of Sky: Studies in South Indian Civilization in Honour of Velcheru Narayana Rao*, Delhi, Oxford University Press: 1995.

Siegal, Lee, *Sacred and Profane Dimensions of Love in Indian Traditions as Exemplified in the Gītagovinda of Jayadeva*, Delhi, Oxford University Press: 1978.

Singh, Harihar, 'Women's Patronage to Temple Architecture', in *Women in Early Indian Societies*, ed. Kumkum Roy, Delhi, Manohar: 1999, pp. 286–98.

Singh, Pankaj K. and Jaidev, 'Decentering a Patriarchal Myth: Bhisham Sahni's *Mādhavī*', in *From Myths to Markets: Essays on Gender*, ed. Kumkum Sangari and Uma Chakravarti, Delhi, Manohar: 1999, pp. 3–17.

Singhi, N.K., 'Gender Theme: Issues and Perspectives', in *Women Images*, ed. Pratibha Jain and Rajan Mahan, Jaipur, Rawat Publications: 1996, pp. 55–71.

Sinha, B.P., *The Decline of the Kingdom of Magadha (c. 455–1000 A.D.)*, Patna, Motilal Banarsidass: 1954.

—— ed., *Comprehensive History of Bihar*, Patna, Kashi Prasad Jayaswal Research Institute: 1974, vol. I, part II.

—— 'Political History of South Bihar (750–1200 A.D.)', in *Comprehensive History of Bihar*, ed. B.P. Sinha, vol. I, pt II, Patna, Kashi Prasad Jayaswal Research Institute: 1974, pp. 245–80.

—— *Dynastic History of Magadha*, Delhi, Abhinav Publications: 1977.

Sircar, D.C., 'Great Women in North India: *c.* 400 B.C. to 1200 A.D.', in *Great Women of India*, ed. Swami Madhavananda and R.C. Majumdar, Almora, Advaita Ashrama: 1953, pp. 285–97.

—— 'Nimdīghi Inscription Mentioning Gopāla', *Epigraphia Indica*, vol. XXXV, 1962, pp. 228–33.

—— 'Gayā Inscription of the Time of Nārāyaṇapāla', *Epigraphia Indica*, vol. XXXV, 1962, pp. 225–28.

—— 'Ārmā Inscription of Madanapāla's Time', *Epigraphia Indica*, vol. XXXVI, 1964, pp. 42–4.

—— 'Nongaṛh Inscription of Madanapāla's Time', *Epigraphia Indica*, vol. XXXVI, 1964, pp. 41–2.

—— *Indian Epigraphy*, Delhi, Motilal Banarsidass: 1965.

—— *Studies in the Society and Administration of Ancient and Medieval India*, Calcutta, Firma K.L. Mukhopadhyay: 1967, vol. I.

—— *Studies in the Political and Administrative Systems in Ancient and Medieval India*, Delhi, Motilal Banarsidass: 1974.

—— *The Kānyakubja-Gauḍa Struggle*, Calcutta, The Asiatic Society: 1985.

—— 'Valgudar Inscription of Dharmapāla's Reign', *Epigraphia Indica*, vol. XXVIII, 1958, pp. 137–45.

—— 'Introduction', in A.K. Maitreya, *The Fall of the Pāla Empire*, Darjeeling, University of North Bengal: 1987, pp. i–xxiv.

—— 'Belwā Plate of Mahipāla I', *Epigraphia Indica*, vol. XXIX, 1957, pp. 1–9.

—— 'Bangāon plate of Vigrahapāla III', *Epigraphia Indica*, vol. XXIX, 1957, pp. 48–57.

—— 'Bhaturiya Inscription of Rājyapāla', *Epigraphia Indica*, vol. XXXIII, 1963, pp. 150–4.

—— 'Lai Inscription of Vikramadevī', *Epigraphia Indica*, vol. XXX, 1958, pp. 82–4.

—— 'Dhulla Plate of Śrīcandra', *Epigraphia Indica*, vol. XXXIII, 1963, pp. 134–40.

Smith, V.A., 'The Pāla Dynasty of Bengal', *Indian Antiquary*, vol. XXXVIII, 1909, pp. 233–48.

Spencer, George W., 'When Queens Bore Gifts: Women as Temple Donors in the Chola Period', in *Śrīnidhīh: Perspectives in Indian Archaeology, Art and Culture* (K.R. Srinivasan Festschrift), ed. K.V. Raman et al., Madras, New Era Publications: 1983, pp. 361–73.

Stearns, Peter N., *Gender in World History*, London and New York, Routledge: 2000.

Stein, M.A., tr., *Kalhaṇa's Rājataraṅgiṇī*, 3rd rpt., Delhi, Motilal Banarsidass: 1989, vols. I, II.

—— ed., *Kalhaṇa's Rājataraṅgiṇī*, rpt., Bombay, Motilal Banarsidass: 1988, vol. III.

Sufi, G.M.D., *Kashir: A History of Kashmir*, Delhi, Light & Life Publishers: 1974, vol. I.

Suru, N.G., ed. and tr., *Karpūramañjarī*, Poona, Ruparel College: 1960.

——ed. and tr., *Vākpatirāja's Gauḍavaho*, Delhi, Munshiram Manoharlal: 1975.

Sutherland, Sally J.M., 'Sītā and Draupadī: Aggressive Behaviour and Female Role-Models in the Sanskrit Epics', *Journal of the American Oriental Society*, 109.1, 1989, pp. 63–79.

—— ed., *Bridging Worlds: Studies on Women in South Asia*, Delhi, Oxford University Press: 1992.

—— 'The Bad Seed: Senior Wives and Elder Sons', in *Bridging Worlds: Studies on Women in South Asia*, ed. Sally J.M. Sutherland, Delhi, Oxford University Press: 1992, pp. 23–52.

—— 'Seduction, Counter-seduction and Sexual Role Models: Bedroom Politics and the Indian Epics', *Journal of Indian Philosophy*, vol. 19, 1992, pp. 53–61.

Talbot, Cynthia, 'Temples, Donors, and Gifts: Patterns of Patronage in Thirteenth-century South India', *Journal of Asian Studies*, 50, 1991, pp. 308–40.

—— 'Rudrama-devī, the Female King: Gender and Political Authority in Medieval India', in *Syllables of Sky: Studies in South Indian*

Civilization in Honour of Velcheru Narayana Rao, ed. David Shulman, Delhi, Oxford University Press: 1995, pp. 391–430.

Tarafdar, M.R., 'Trade and Society in Early Medieval Bengal', *Indian Historical Review*, vol. 4, no. 2, 1978, pp. 274–86.

Tawney, C.H., tr., *The Kathā Sarit Sāgara*, 3rd edn, Delhi, Munshiram Manoharlal: 1992, vols. I and II.

Thapar, Romila, 'Genealogy as a Source of Social History', *Indian Historical Review*, vol. II, no. 2, 1976, pp. 259–81.

—— *Ancient Indian Social History*, Delhi, Orient Longman: 1978.

—— 'The *Rāmāyaṇa*: Theme and Variation', in *India: History and Thought*, ed. S.N. Mukherjee, Calcutta, Subarnarekha: 1982, pp. 221–53.

—— 'Society and Historical Consciousness: The Itihāsa-Purāṇa Tradition', in *Situating Indian History*, ed. S. Bhattacharya and Romila Thapar, Delhi, Oxford University Press: 1986, pp. 353–83.

—— *Cultural Transaction and Early India: Tradition and Patronage*, Delhi, Oxford University Press: 1987.

—— ed., *Recent Perspectives of Early Indian History*, Bombay, Popular Prakashan: 1995.

—— *Śakuntalā—Texts, Readings, Histories*, Delhi, Kali for Women: 1999.

Thaplyal, K.K., *Inscriptions of the Maukharis, Later Guptas, Puṣpabhūtis and Yaśovarman of Kanauj*, Delhi, ICHR/Agam Prakashan: 1985.

Thorner, Alice and M.K. Raj, eds., *Ideas, Images and Real Lives: Women in Literature and History*, Mumbai, Orient Longman: 2000.

Trautmann, Thomas R., *Dravidian Kinship*, Cambridge, Cambridge University Press: 1981.

Tripathi, R.S., *History of Ancient India*, 3rd rpt., Delhi, Motilal Banarsidass: 1967.

—— *History of Kanauj to the Moslem Conquest*, rpt., Delhi, Motilal Banarsidass: 1989.

—— ed. and tr., *Samayamātṛkā of Mahākavi Kṣemendra*, Varanasi, Chowkhamba Vidyabhavan: 1967.

Tripathi, T.M., tr., *Kuṭṭanīmatam or Shambhali-matam by Dāmodaragupta*, Varanasi, Krishnadas Academy: 1991.

Uberoi, Patricia, 'Feminine Identity and National Ethos in Indian Calendar Art', in *Ideas, Images and Real Lives: Women in Literature and History*, ed. Alice Thorner and M.K. Raj, Mumbai, Orient Longman: 2000, pp. 322–46.

Vats, S. and Shakuntala Mudgal, eds., *Women and Society in Ancient India*, Faridabad, Om Publications: 1999.

Venis, A., 'The Benares Copper Plate Grant of Govindacandra of Kanauj', *Epigraphia Indica*, vol. II, 1894, pp. 358–61.

—— '(Kamauli) Copper Plate Grant of Vaidyadeva, King of Kāmarūpa', *Epigraphia Indica*, vol. II, 1894, pp. 347–58.

Verma, B.S., *Socio-Religious, Economic and Literary Condition of Bihar (from A.D.319–A.D.1000)*, Delhi, Munshiram Manoharlal: 1962.

—— 'Archaeological Excavation and Sites (320–1200 A.D.)', in *Comprehensive History of Bihar*, ed. B.P. Sinha, Patna, Kashi Prasad Jayaswal Research Institute: 1974, vol. I, pt II, pp. 530–60.

Vidyavinoda, P.B., 'Nidhānpur Copper Plates of Bhāskaravarman', *Epigraphia Indica*, vol. XII, 1914, pp. 65–9.

Vishnoi, Savita, *Economic Status of Women in Ancient India*, Meerut, Kusumanjali Prakashan: 1987.

Watters, T., *On Yuan Chwang's Travels in India*, 2nd edn, Delhi, Munshiram Manoharlal: 1973.

Wiesner, Merry E., *Women and Gender in Early Modern Europe*, Cambridge, Cambridge University Press: 1993.

Willis, Michael D., 'Religious and Royal Patronage in North India', in *Gods, Guardians, and Lovers: Temple Sculptures from North India A.D.700–1200*, ed. Vishakha N. Desai and Darielle Mason, New York, The Asia Society: 1993, pp. 49–65.

Winternitz, Maurice, *History of Indian Literature*, rpt., Delhi, Motilal Banarsidass: 1985, vol. III, pts I and II.

Women in India: A Bibliography, Delhi, Nehru Memorial Museum & Library: 2001.

Yadava, B.N.S., *Society and Culture in Northern India in the Twelfth Century*, Allahabad, Central Book Depot: 1973.

—— 'Problem of the Interaction Between Socio-Economic Classes in the Early Medieval Complex', *Indian Historical Review*, vol. III, no. 1, 1976, pp. 43–58.

Index